Rome Enters the Greek East

For Jeannie
Fortes Romani sunt tanquam caelus profundus—

Enn. *Ann.* 470

Rome Enters the Greek East

From Anarchy to Hierarchy in the Hellenistic Mediterranean, 230–170 BC

Arthur M. Eckstein

WILEY-BLACKWELL

A John Wiley & Sons, Ltd., Publication

This paperback edition first published 2012
© 2012 Arthur M. Eckstein

Edition history: Blackwell Publishing Ltd (hardback, 2008)

Blackwell Publishing was acquired by John Wiley & Sons in February 2007.
Blackwell's publishing program has been merged with Wiley's global Scientific,
Technical, and Medical business to form Wiley-Blackwell.

Registered Office
John Wiley & Sons Ltd, The Atrium, Southern Gate, Chichester, West Sussex, PO19
8SQ, United Kingdom

Editorial Offices
350 Main Street, Malden, MA 02148-5020, USA
9600 Garsington Road, Oxford, OX4 2DQ, UK
The Atrium, Southern Gate, Chichester, West Sussex, PO19 8SQ, UK

For details of our global editorial offices, for customer services, and for information
about how to apply for permission to reuse the copyright material in this book please
see our website at www.wiley.com/wiley-blackwell.

The right of Arthur M. Eckstein to be identified as the author of this work has been
asserted in accordance with the UK Copyright, Designs and Patents Act 1988.

Library of Congress Cataloging-in-Publication Data

Eckstein, Arthur M.
    Rome enters the Greek East : from anarchy to hierarchy in the Hellenistic
Mediterranean, 230–170 B.C. / Arthur M. Eckstein.
        p. cm.
    Includes bibliographical references and index.
    ISBN 978-1-4051-6072-8 (hardcover : alk. paper) ISBN 978-1-118-25536-0
(pbk. : alk. paper) 1. Greece—History—281–146 B.C. 2. Rome—Relations—
Greece. 3. Greece—Relations—Rome. I. Title. II. Title: From anarchy to
hierarchy in the Hellenistic Mediterranean, 230–170 B.C.
    DF238.E25 2008
    938 2.09—dc22

                                                            2007037809

A catalogue record for this book is available from the British Library.

Set in 10/12pt Plantin by Graphicraft Limited, Hong Kong

1 2012

Contents

Acknowledgments

This study of the early involvement of Rome in the Greek East has profited from the careful comments of several fellow scholars: Hans Beck, Craige Champion, Boris Dreyer, Erich Gruen, John Rich, and above all Andrew Erskine. My gratitude to them, of course, does not necessarily indicate their agreement with me. Conversations with the political scientists Richard Ned Lebow, Robert Jervis, and William Wohlforth have also been helpful to me – though, again, the same caveat holds. As usual, my wife Jeanne Rutenburg, herself a trained historian, has contributed many thoughtful and scholarly comments throughout the project, while making it a much less lonely task than it might have been.

Maps

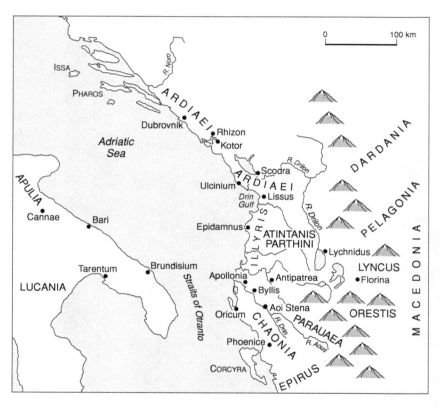

Map 1   The Adriatic and Illyria.

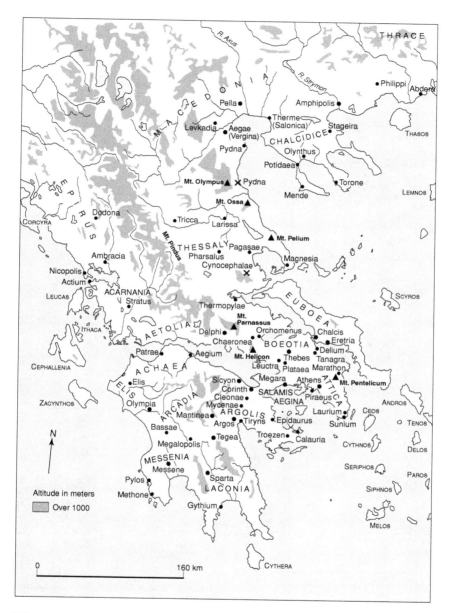

Map 2   European Greece.

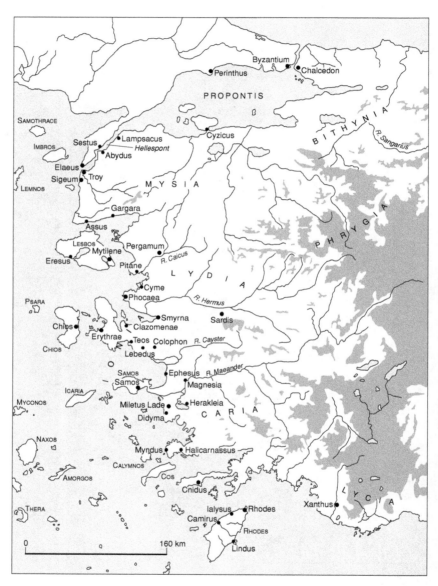

Map 3   The western coasts of Asia Minor.

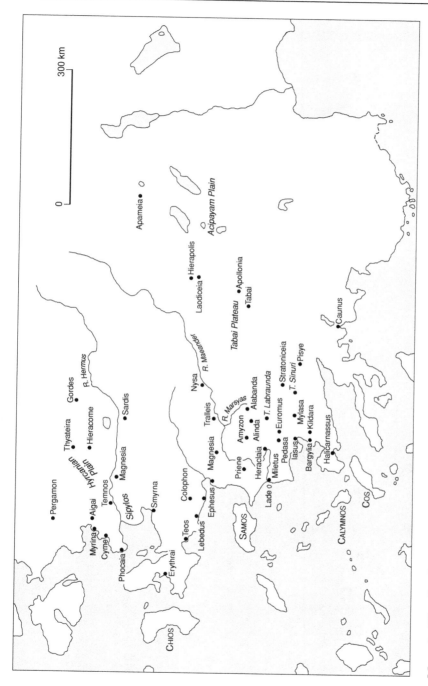

Map 4 The Southeast Aegean region.

PART I

ROME IN CONTACT WITH THE GREEK EAST, 230–205 BC

1

Roman Expansion and the Pressures of Anarchy

The purpose of this study is a reexamination of the early involvement of the Republic of Rome in the eastern Mediterranean, down to the replacement of the long-prevailing Hellenistic anarchy in the region by a hierarchy of states with Rome at the top. This was established by 188 BC, and brought a minimum of order to the Greek world in the subsequent period down to 171 BC – though not with total stability. The hierarchy was created by victories over Antigonid Macedon and then over the Seleucid Empire won by a coalition of Greek states at whose head stood not a great Greek power, but Rome.

In one sense, this subject is well-trodden ground. The ancient historical writer Polybius of Megalopolis, a near-contemporary of many of these events, showed the way in terms of both the geographical and the chronological scale of our study; and prominent modern scholars have been studying Roman imperial expansion into the Greek Mediterranean for over a century.[1] But Roman expansion in the East remains highly contentious territory. There are sharp clashes among modern scholars even over the historicity of certain major events, and always about the motives behind the actions of the states involved. There are especially sharp differences of analysis concerning the causes of Roman imperial expansion in the East (as well as, of course, Roman expansion in general), and the causes of Roman success.[2]

---

[1] See, e.g., Fustel de Coulanges 1893; Colin 1905; cf. Frank 1914; de Sanctis 1923.
[2] Amid the vast literature, see Colin 1905; Frank 1914; de Sanctis 1923; Holleaux 1935; Harris 1979: 195–7, 205–8, and 212–23; Gruen 1984: Ch. 11; Ferrary 1988: Part I; Derow 1989 and 2003.

Following this introductory chapter, the first part of the present study examines the extent of Roman geopolitical interest in the Greek East and the extent of Roman political gains in the region down to the period after the end of the first Roman war against Philip V of Macedon in 205. The second part of the study examines the crisis in the eastern Mediterranean that developed at the end of the third century BC. The intense scholarly debate begins here.

It was Maurice Holleaux who first proposed that Roman interest in the Greek world east of the Adriatic, and the extent of the Republic's concrete interests there, remained minimal down to 201/200 BC. Holleaux argued, further, that the situation was changed dramatically at that point because of the arrival at Rome of envoys from several Greek states, led by Rhodes and Ptolemaic Egypt, warning of the threat posed by the sharp rise in power of the expansionist monarchs Philip V of Macedon and Antiochus III (the Great) of the Seleucid Empire. It was the Greek envoys' news of a treaty of alliance between the kings to destroy the Ptolemaic kingdom altogether and gain its resources – an unusual if not unprecedented act in Hellenistic geopolitics – that compelled the Roman Senate to intervene for the first time with great force and large intentions in the East. Theodor Mommsen had already argued that it was the profound shift in the balance of power in the Greek East that led to the Roman intervention there in 200 BC; and Holleaux's thesis has in fact never been subjected to a detailed and thorough scholarly refutation.[3] Nevertheless, it has been steadily eroded over time to the point that many recent studies of this crucial period in Mediterranean history either downplay the importance of the Pact Between the Kings (for instance, Habicht, Badian, Errington, Harris), or fail to mention it altogether.[4]

Meanwhile, an entire school of scholars led by W. V. Harris has argued that Rome from the beginning was as voraciously imperialist and exceptionally aggressive in its ambitions in the eastern Mediterranean as in the West, and that therefore the only explanation needed for the Roman decision of winter 201/200 BC to intervene in the Greek East was the inherently brutal imperialism and ferocious bellicosity of

---

[3] Holleaux's major reconstruction of events was first published in 1921; page references here are to the 1935 edition. For Mommsen's view, see Mommsen 1903: 696–701, with the comments of Radista 1972: 564–5, and Eckstein 2006: 261.

[4] Downplaying the importance of the pact: see, e.g., Habicht 1957: 239 n. 106, and 240, cf. Habicht 1982: 146; Badian 1958a: 64 n. 3, cf. Badian 1964b: 135 n. 3; Errington 1971 and 1986; Harris 1979: 312 n. 2. Failure even to mention the pact as a factor in these crucial events: Ager 1991: 16–22 (in a study of Rhodian diplomacy in this period); Derow 2003: 58–9 (in a discussion of the origin of Roman intervention in the East in 201/200).

Roman society.[5] To be sure, Erich Gruen has attempted to restore the balance in analysis by emphasizing the powerful independent role which, he argues, the rival policies, expansive ambitions, mutual conflicts, and outright aggressions of the Greek states themselves played in the complex events that led to the rise of Roman power in the East, emphasizing as well the influence which Greek interstate practices had upon Roman approaches to the region.[6] But Gruen's attempt to bring the Greeks back in as a crucial factor in events has often been bypassed in recent scholarship in favor of the point of view promoted by Harris, which centers itself sternly on Roman action, Roman ambition, Roman expansion, Roman aggression – in short, on Roman imperialism.[7]

These are the main issues we will be tackling in the first two-thirds of the present study – which is a defense of the two fundamental elements in Holleaux's thesis. This defense is underpinned, however, not only by detailed scholarship in a traditional vein which underlines, as Gruen has done, the Greek impact upon complicated events, but also by the employment of modern international relations theory, which emphasizes the tremendous impact and pressures on the decision-making of all governmental elites caused, in what is essentially an anarchy, by the shifting distribution of power among states within an existing state-system (see below).

Let us look now in more detail at the controversy over early Roman involvement in the Greek East. Sharp disagreement exists, first, over the causes of Rome's two wars in Illyria, in 229/228 BC and in 219 BC. Sharp disagreement exists, second, over the nature and extent of the control Rome gained over Illyria as a consequence of these wars. Prominent scholars have recently argued that from 229/228 onward Rome had formally sworn treaties of alliance with the Greek polities and indigenous tribes in maritime Illyris, treaties that legally bound them to the Republic; thus the Romans intentionally created a powerful geopolitical stronghold from which further advances into Greece could be launched. Other scholars, however, deny that the results of these wars were nearly so politically and strategically far-reaching.[8] Third, major scholars argue that the impact – and perhaps even a goal – of the first Roman war

---

[5] See Harris 1979: Chs. 1–3 for the general theory, and 212–18 on the events of 201/200 BC. The influence of Harris' study has been widespread and profound: see, initially, North 1981; Rowland 1983; Rawson 1986; and in the long term, see the scholars listed below, n. 7.

[6] Gruen 1984.

[7] See, e.g., Mandell 1989 and 1991; Derow 1989, 1991, and 2003; Oakley 1993; Raaflaub 1996; Heftner 1997: 315–19; Habicht 1997: 185, cf. 194–5; Rosenstein 1999: 193–205; Campbell 2002: 167–9.

[8] See Derow 1991; Coppola 1993: 123–7; Habicht 1997: 189 – compared now with Eckstein, 1999; cf., Petzold 1971. Also important: Badian 1964a.

against Philip V of Macedon (214–205 BC) was the establishment of a large network of relationships with Greek states that set the stage for Rome soon thereafter becoming the major force in Greek politics. Yet the contrary has also recently been argued: that Greek ruling elites down to 205 viewed Rome's first war with Macedon as a war primarily fought among Greek polities in a Greek context, with Rome merely an ally of one side, and that this war left Rome with few political gains in Greece.[9]

On one reconstruction, Rome advanced purposefully into a powerful position among the Greek states well before the crisis that began to shake the eastern Mediterranean from 207 BC with the faltering and then the collapse of the Ptolemaic Empire. On the other reconstruction, however, the Romans merely acted energetically but sporadically from 230 BC to protect what they saw as their interests in the Greek East, but those interests were minimal, and Roman political aims and gains quite limited. As for the Illyrian polities, from 229 BC down to the outbreak of Rome's first war with Macedon in 214, and indeed well beyond it, they were linked to Rome solely by informal ties of friendship. Moreover, they were not very important places – and they were isolated by formidable mountains from the rest of the Greek world. Somewhat later, the first war between Rome and Macedon did confirm the Senate in a perception – originating in the invasion of Italy by Pyrrhus the king of Epirus in 280–275 BC – that significant threats to Roman security in Italy could suddenly emerge from the most powerful states of the East; and this probably led to a potential Roman desire to increase control over Greek affairs. But down to 205 BC this potential desire was not actualized; it was countered at Rome by a natural focus on Rome's terrible struggles in the West for survival, and consequently a lower level of concern about Greek affairs. Similarly, Rome was not yet an important factor in the decision-making of many Greek polities. This is the reconstruction of early Roman involvement in the Greek Mediterranean which will be supported in Chapters 2 and 3 – a view similar to that of Holleaux, but with new evidence and arguments.

This study also places the sudden emergence of deep Roman involvement in the Greek Mediterranean specifically within the framework of the crisis that convulsed the Greek world in the last decade of the third century BC. The origins and nature of this crisis will be our focus in the second part of the study (Chapters 4, 5, and 6). Detailed discussion is necessary because the thesis presented here is again close to that of Holleaux, and highly controversial: namely, that a profound crisis among the great Greek monarchies that began in Egypt ca. 207 and intensified

---

[9]   Compare Rich 1984 with Eckstein 2002. On the proper date for the formal outbreak of this war, traditionally but wrongly stated by scholars to be 211, see below, Chapter 3.

after 204 transformed the geopolitical situation in the East, and was the primary (though not the only) cause for the sudden expansion of Roman influence and power deep into the Greek world between 200 and 188. The faltering of the Ptolemies led first to the treaty of alliance between Antigonid Macedon and the Seleucid Empire to divide up the Ptolemaic realm, then to large-scale warfare in the Greek Mediterranean from the frontiers of Egypt all the way to the Hellespont (203/202–201 BC), then to a revolution in Greek diplomacy towards Rome (201/200 BC) – apparent in the desperate pleas by major Greek states for Roman help – and then to the decision of the Senate to initiate major diplomatic and military involvement in the eastern situation, an involvement that rapidly escalated because of unexpected events.

We approach this crisis by employing types of historical argument that are on the one hand traditional in ancient studies, but which are also set within a new and broad political-science framework. It is a theoretical framework unfamiliar to most modern historians of antiquity, a broad theoretical framework originating in modern international relations studies; and it helps explain the warlike conduct both of Rome and of the Greek states over *la longue durée*, while also helping to explain their specific conduct during the crisis of the eastern Mediterranean in the last decade of the third century. This theoretical framework is provided by the central school of thought in the modern study of international relations, a school of thought termed "Realism."

Realism focuses on the harsh and competitive nature of interactions among states under conditions of international anarchy.[10] It is a family of related yet sometimes competing theories both about individual state behavior and about the nature of interstate relations taken as a whole. These theories share certain pessimistic core hypotheses, and they all emphasize a profound connection between the behavior of individual states and the character of the international system of states in which polities are forced to exist. Realism is also in itself a work in progress: it is a research program, not a finished theoretical edifice.[11]

International-systems Realism accepts that the most important actors in international politics are "territorially organized entities": city-states or dynastic empires in antiquity; nation-states in the modern world.[12]

---

[10]   On the concept of international anarchy, see below.
[11]   On Realism as a family of related but competing theories, see, e.g., Wayman and Diehl 1994. As a research program: see Mastanduno and Kapstein 1999: 4.
[12]   On the centrality of "territorially organized entities," see Gilpin 1988: 304–5; cf. Mastanduno and Kapstein 1999: 7. This would mean that internal actors, whether they are social, political, or economic interest groups, are less important in interstate relations than the placement and interaction of territorially based power-entities within the interstate system.

But Realism posits equally that the character of the state-system within which any one state exists exercises a strong impact in itself upon the behavior of that state – for the pressures deriving from the system strongly encourage (though they do not determine) certain types of actions, while simultaneously they strongly discourage (though they do not forbid) other types of action. Bluntly, certain types of interstate systems – especially anarchic systems, such as the one that existed in the Hellenistic Mediterranean – encourage assertive and aggressive modes of conduct by all states, and simultaneously discourage passive and peaceable conduct. Within this generally system-focused approach, contemporary Realist analysis of interstate politics is based on three propositions.

First is the centrality of anarchy. The interstate world consists of a multiplicity of sovereign polities; in political-science terms anarchy is usually a multipolar system, in which different states may differ (often widely) in power but in which there is no predominant actor. And over this multiplicity of sovereign polities there is no regulating authority either, and little or no international law (and certainly no effective way of enforcing it). Each state thus determines its own interests independently, and acts accordingly and usually strongly to further those interests. Multipolar anarchy has been the prevailing structure of interstate life since the emergence of organized territorial entities.[13]

There are only two exits from anarchy. The first would be the establishment of true international law, through the voluntary agreement by all states that they will obey such law, and that such law will be enforced upon them by a strong enforcement mechanism of some kind. This development in international affairs is, of course, something that so far has never occurred. The second exit is through the emergence, more or less violently, of a stern hierarchy among states, in which one state exercises great power and control over others, enforcing a modicum of order to its own liking; in other words, the emergence of unipolarity, or hegemony, or empire. Yet unipolarity, hegemony, and empire are themselves relatively rare in the history of interstate relations, because of the ferocious persistence with which sovereign polities cling to their independence.

From anarchy as the prevalent structure of state-systems there derives a second proposition: the ruthless self-seeking to which an anarchic system leads all states – all states, one must emphasize, and not just a few "pathological" ones. This ruthless self-seeking occurs because in the absence of international law, states must provide for their own security; providing for security in an anarchic system takes power; and so power is sought most of all. Hence grim self-help and power-maximizing

[13]   On the characteristics of anarchy, see Waltz 1959 and 1979.

behavior become prevalent. Harsh behavior towards other states, tending towards expansion of power, originates both from greed and from fear, but primarily from fear and not from greed – that is, from the desire for self-preservation in a world of states made fiercely competitive by the overarching structure of anarchy.[14] In short: "States must meet the demands of the political eco-system or court annihilation."[15] Thus Rome certainly was in modern terms a ferociously aggressive and militarized state – but so were all large states in the Classical and then Hellenistic Mediterranean, so were all medium-sized states, and so were even most small states.[16] As Kenneth Waltz, the leading Realist theorist, puts it: in self-help systems, "competition produces a tendency toward sameness of the competitors."[17] Or, even more bluntly: "the units that survive [in an anarchy] come to look like one another."[18]

   The enduring prevalence of multipolar anarchy, combined with the ruthless self-help and power-maximizing behavior engaged in by all states simultaneously, leads to the third Realist principle: under anarchy, war, or the threat of war, is always present, and every state must be sternly prepared to defend its interests through organized military force. That is, "the state among states conducts its affairs in the brooding shadow of violence."[19] Nor does war occur primarily because of "miscommunication" among essentially well-meaning entities. It occurs primarily because of real conflicts of interest between bitterly competing, functionally similar, and highly militarized entities. Moreover, the nature of the state-system precludes easy and peaceful resolutions of such conflicts. Thus in an international anarchy – and again, anarchy has historically been the prevalent structure of state-systems – "war is normal."[20]

   A shocking statement. The idea is that under anarchic conditions – such as those existing in Mediterranean antiquity – wars are natural occurrences, and part of the normal conduct among states. Wars arise not

---

[14] See, e.g., Waltz 1988.
[15] Sterling 1974: 336; cf. Waltz 1979: 107 and 127 (emphatic). This is essentially what is called the "Offensive" Realist position. "Defensive" Realists argue that international anarchy in itself need not always lead to power-maximizing behavior on the part of states, but that only very harsh and demanding anarchic systems do so: see, e.g., Taliaferro 2000 and 2004: 17; cf. Wohlforth 2001 (employing early modern Russia and Eastern Europe as an example of a very harsh system). My argument is that the Hellenistic Mediterranean fits, precisely, the latter situation.
[16] See Eckstein 2006: Chs. 3–6.
[17] Waltz 1979: 118–28, at 127.
[18] Ibid.: 77; cf. Layne 1993: 11 and 15–16.
[19] Waltz 1979: 102. Modern political scientists call this the "sameness effect" (Layne 1993: 11 and n. 24).
[20] Waltz 1988: 620.

only out of the negative characteristics of the states themselves (e.g., intense militarism and a habit of aggressive diplomacy) – though such internal characteristics have traditionally been the focus of historians, and they are certainly important causal factors.[21] Rather, according to Realist theory, wars also arise – indeed, primarily arise – out of the structural defects of the international system itself, out of the system in which states exist, as a result primarily of the tensions, distrust, and clashes of objective interest which anarchic conditions promote and create.[22] Moreover, while the militaristic and aggressive internal cultures characteristic of states under anarchic conditions contribute importantly and synergistically to the prevalence of conflict and war in anarchic state-systems, these internal characteristics themselves derive in good part from the pressures of those systems – and emerge precisely because they are adaptive to those pressures.[23]

It is no accident that Realist paradigms of interstate behavior have their origins with thinkers (starting with Thucydides) whose life experience was formed by constant war and instability.[24] Conversely, times of peace and prosperity tend to bring forth criticisms of Realist assumptions about interstate life as too pessimistic, and so it was in the 1990s, when significant criticisms of the Realist paradigm as too pessimistic about interstate behavior appeared widely in the political-science literature. The argument was that although anarchy in a formal sense still prevailed in the post-Cold War world, its destructive pressures were being greatly alleviated by sophisticated diplomacy, rapid communications, and the existence of many independent international institutions of mediation.[25] In this period also, it was suggested by post-Modernists after "the linguistic

---

[21]   A classic example, focusing solely on Roman aggressiveness and militarism as the cause of Roman wars, is Harris 1979. Studies of modern states which take the same basic approach: Hobson 1902 (Victorian Britain); Williams 1962 (the United States); Fischer 1964 and 1969 (Wilhelmine Germany). This is rightly termed dangerously introverted historiography by Bayley 1988: 14–15.

[22]   Not even Waltz, the Realist scholar most focused on systems-level analysis, denies that the nature of the internal cultures of individual polities has an important and independent effect on international outcomes, including on the frequency of wars (i.e., it is an important "independent variable"): see Waltz 1959: 160; Waltz 1979: 102; Waltz 2000: 8. But it is not the central cause of warfare.

[23]   The fundamental study of this rather obvious point on the origins of militaristic and aggressive state cultures – a point that nevertheless still needs reassertion – is Gourevitch 1978; cf. Downing 1992 and now Jervis 2001: 287. Note Sterling's maxim: above, n. 15.

[24]   See most recently Schweller 1999: 30–1. Also Schmidt 1998: Ch. 1; Donnelly 2000: Ch. 1; cf. esp. Eckstein 2003.

[25]   This is called international relations Liberal Internationalism. Classic examples: Kegley 1993: 133–5 (Presidential Address to the International Studies Association), or the essays in Kegley, ed., 1995.

turn" struck historical studies that Realism was simply an artificial, dramatic, and destructive discourse, not related to anything real at all; rather, it was a self-fulfilling prophesy of conflict and war, for statesmen were trained in it, and then acted upon its assumptions. Thus if one changed this discourse to a more cooperative and communitarian one, international relations themselves would in turn become more cooperative, communitarian, and benign.[26] One must say, however, that the dismal events following September 11, 2001 have put a sharp brake on both types of criticism of Realism as too pessimistic.

But even if one accepts that not all interstate anarchies need be savage – and employment of the modern interstate system to demonstrate this is at best a debatable strategy –it is clearly the case that historically, some anarchic systems have been harsher and more cruel than others.[27] And it is equally clear that the state-systems that existed in Mediterranean antiquity were especially cruel anarchic systems. They fulfilled all the harshest expectations of the Realist paradigms of ferocious interstate interaction. International law was non-existent, and the few and informal customs of "proper" interstate behavior that stood in the stead of international law (such as not murdering ambassadors or not looting religious sanctuaries) had no means of enforcement. There existed a great multiplicity of fiercely independent and ferociously militaristic states, brutally contending with each other for survival, for scarce resources, for scarce security, and for power. It is no wonder, then, that the Realist paradigm originated in the reaction of ancient intellectuals (especially Thucydides) to this situation.[28] Realists in fact have always asserted that anarchy and its consequences are the great timeless factors in international relations.[29] Whether their paradigms are actually completely valid for modern interstate relations has become a subject of debate (see above); but their paradigms certainly appear to hold true for the more primitive conditions and more savage environment of Hellenistic antiquity. But two unique aspects of the exceptionally cruel interstate anarchy of the ancient Mediterranean need now to be underlined.

First, this was a world in which war was not only constant, but the states involved in constant warfare were, in general, extraordinarily

---

[26] This is called international relations Social Constructivism. Classic examples: Wendt 1992 and 1999; Vasquez 1999.
[27] See Wohlforth 2001 (on early modern Russia and Eastern Europe).
[28] On Thucydides and the founding of the Realist paradigm, see Eckstein 2003.
[29] Realist assertion of the universal applicability of Realist principles regarding anarchy and its consequences: see Waltz 1979: 66 and 126. Cf. also Doyle 1991: 175 ("the continuity of interstate anarchy"); Glaser 1997: 171; Elman and Elman 1997: 9 and n. 11, cf. 13–14; and Copeland 2000: Ch. 8 *passim* (esp. 233–4).

fragile. In the fifth and early fourth centuries BC, for instance, more than forty Greek city-states (*poleis*) were destroyed through warfare.[30] And unlike modern nation-states, even the strongest and most powerful of ancient states exhibit a large potential for collapse. To cite two examples: Carthage, in the western Mediterranean, went in just five years (245–240 BC) from being a great imperial power to being on the verge of destruction, the city itself almost captured by its own rebellious mercenary army; and the Ptolemaic regime, in the eastern Mediterranean, went in just seven years (207–200 BC) from being one of the three great imperial states in the Greek East to being on the verge of destruction, with a child on the throne, riots in the capital at Alexandria, a massive indigenous rebellion in Upper and Middle Egypt, and increasingly severe attacks upon it from outside Greek powers. Polybius, the greatest of the surviving Hellenistic historians, asserts (at 2.35) that even Rome might have disappeared under a tidal wave of barbarian (Celtic) invasions in the 230s and 220s BC. And the point is this: the inherent fragility of ancient states made the ferocity of their mutual competition a truly life-and-death struggle. As Thucydides (5.101) has the Athenians say to their victims the Melians, international relations is not a game played for honor, but a struggle for physical survival.[31]

Second, the primitive character of diplomatic interaction among ancient polities was itself an additional factor conducive to constant warfare. Ancient Mediterranean states employed ambassadors only on an ad hoc basis, usually during crises; no ancient state employed permanent ambassadors or permanent diplomatic missions to other states. Yet this is the type of constant diplomatic interaction and exchange of information which modern governments not only take for granted, but which helps ameliorate the tone and even the substance of modern interstate interactions. This is because permanent diplomatic representation allows modern governments to warn each other of possible conflicts of interest at an early stage, creating the possibility of modifying a policy at a point when no one is greatly committed to it. Moreover, such interactions in the modern world are usually couched in a specially tactful diplomatic language which has been developed over centuries, and which is employed by a corps of specially trained diplomatic professionals. But while such institutions are ameliorative of the competitive pressures and the tendency towards violence in modern anarchic state-systems,[32] the fact is that none of these ameliorative institutions existed in

---

[30] Detailed discussion in Eckstein 2006: 53–4 and n. 72.
[31] Fragility of ancient states: see detailed discussion in Eckstein 2006: Ch. 7.
[32] See, esp., Kegley 1993, and the essays in Baldwin, ed., 1993 and Kegley, ed., 1995.

Mediterranean antiquity. Ancient Mediterranean states sent out embassies to other states only as important issues arose, and employed diplomatic missions to deal with crises only at points where sharp interstate conflicts over objective state interests had already arisen: in other words, in situations that were inherently very difficult to resolve. In addition, there existed no trained corps of diplomatic professionals to deal with such crises; and even more importantly, the language of state interactions at the crisis stage was in antiquity usually brutal and blunt – resembling the language of bitter private quarrel.[33] Modern political scientists have expressed shock upon discovering all of this, and have emphasized how the primitive level of ancient diplomatic interaction, especially in an interstate crisis, was conducive to the outbreak of wars.[34] Some scholars have even described the ancient interstate situation as essentially "pre-diplomatic."[35]

Such a primitive level of interstate contact had a dangerous impact upon the interaction of states within what was already an anarchic and hence war-prone interstate structure. The limited institutional ability and even limited desire of ancient states to communicate continually with one another – what political scientists would call their low level of interdependence – in turn affected these states' very definition of what their interests were, and the perceived choices of action available to them to achieve those interests. When the governing elites of states are unsure of what the intentions of their neighbors are (because of lack of information), and inherently view them (correctly) as bitter competitors for scarce material and security resources, and have few contacts with them, they naturally tend towards assuming the worst about them. Ferocious competition, deep uncertainty, and mutual opacity among such states lead to a tendency for their governing elites to fear and hence to prepare to meet what the political scientists call "the worst-case scenario." And such widespread readiness among governing elites to accept the likelihood of a "worst-case scenario" was yet another factor conducive to a war-prone interstate atmosphere.[36] No wonder, then, that in Aristophanes' comic play *Peace* (421 BC), the hero arrives on Mt. Olympus to find that the gods themselves have departed in disgust,

---

[33] See the excellent discussion in Grant 1965: esp. 262–3.
[34] See Lebow 1991: 144–5; cf. Kauppi 1991: 119.
[35] Aron 1973: 15.
[36] On differing regimes of diplomatic process and their impact on the perceived choices available to states, see Keohane and Nye 1987: esp. 745–9. On the negative impact of "the uncertainty principle," mutual opacity, and the prevalence of "the worst-case scenario," see Morgenthau 1973: 208; van Evera 1998: 13–14. Kokaz 2001: 95, is far too optimistic on the peace-making efficacy of occasional "traveling ambassadors."

because not even they can get the Greeks to resolve the disputes that lead to constant war.[37]

Furthermore, the very fact that states tended to send out envoys to protest the conduct of other states only at the point where the clash of interests was obvious and sharp meant that such diplomatic interactions generally occurred at a point where stern considerations of status and prestige made compromise between governments extremely difficult.[38] To be sure, a state might sacrifice important interests when confronted by a greatly superior power – but this was action taken not for the sake of compromise and the preservation of international peace but rather for the sake of self-preservation. In that sense, crisis "diplomacy" between ancient states was simply an alternative means of pursuing the agenda of the more powerful. It might be a less violent means of interstate coercion, but coercion it was: the type of diplomacy that modern political scientists have termed "compellence diplomacy."[39]

The Republic of Rome habitually practiced such compellence diplomacy during its confrontations with other polities, and Rome has often been called to task (rightly) for doing so. But Rome has been called to task here as if this were a defect of aggressiveness characteristic of Roman diplomacy alone.[40] Yet Rome was not alone in this practice. On the contrary: it was the *common* method of crisis diplomacy among all ancient Mediterranean states; its prevalence can be traced back at least as far as the fifth century BC; and it was the usual conduct followed in crises between states throughout both the western and eastern Mediterranean throughout the entire Hellenistic period.[41]

Political scientists have underlined that such a habit of "compellence diplomacy" and "brinkmanship" among states can itself exercise its own independent negative impact upon interstate interactions in the modern

---

[37] Ar. *Peace*, 195–220; cf. Tritle 2007: 175 and 184. Tritle nevertheless is optimistic both about the possibility of interstate arbitration among the Greek polities, though he can cite no example where a powerful state submitted to it (175–7), and about the impact of the fourth-century Greek attempts to organize a "Common Peace" (*koine eirene*) among the city-states – though he knows that the latter was effective only when backed by the military might of a domineering hierarchical state such as Macedon (180–1). He is correct that Greek intellectuals were often appalled at the existing violence of the interstate situation (180–5); but the fact was that they could not stop it.
[38] See Lebow 1991: 144; Kauppi 1991: 119. Alonzo 2007 (esp. 215–16) is too confident about the ability of Greek prewar diplomacy to prevent the outbreak of conflict (and he does not cite any cases).
[39] On this type of diplomacy and its detrimental impact upon interstate relations, discussed in a modern context, see Ferrar 1981: esp. 194–200.
[40] See Veyne 1975: 819; Harris 1979: 217; Ferrary 1988: 48; Derow 2003: 59–60.
[41] Discussion in Eckstein 2006: Chs. 3, 4, and 5. Ferrar 1981 argues that such diplomacy is typical of states existing in an anarchic international system.

world, increasing the general atmosphere of anxiety and mutual suspicion; in social-science terms this is another independent variable conducive to interstate violence. It is fair to assume that the same was true in Mediterranean antiquity as well.[42] And there is another negative aspect to this phenomenon: compellence diplomacy rarely is, nor can it afford to be, a bluff; it is almost always backed by a true willingness to use violence to enforce demands.[43] That is: Rome, and the many states that interacted with Rome and competed bitterly with Rome for power and security, did not just seem tough; they *were* tough, and they were ready to fight. Hence crisis diplomacy in the ancient Mediterranean was, like war itself, often merely another facet of an interstate system founded on the brutal facts of power, another facet of almost unrestrained interstate competition and clashes of interest.[44]

In such a world it was obviously best to be as powerful as one could be – and hence to engage in power-maximizing behavior of the most ruthless kind. Rome did it. All ancient states – large, medium, and small – did it. This was the world in which Rome and its ferocious rivals had to live and operate.[45]

Let us be clear about this. The Roman Republic was a very heavily militarized and militaristic society, and its culture was obsessed with war. In our period, for instance, no candidate could run for even the lowest public office at Rome without having served ten campaigns in the army (Polyb. 3.19.4). This meant that the main life experience of young male aristocrats (those who would naturally be seeking to run for public office) was and had to be army service, and that the Senate (made up of all ex-public officials) thus consisted solely of men with long military experience. Similarly, in our period a stunning percentage of the Roman male populace as a whole served annually in the army: on average about 13 percent annually between 230 and 188 BC.[46] And, as we have said, Rome habitually engaged in assertive and aggressive diplomatic conduct – proclaiming Rome's alleged rights, complaining biiterly about the actions of others, and always seeking to gain new areas of influence. No one denies these aspects of Roman culture or Rome's internatonal behavior, or their importance to international outcomes.

---

[42]   On the negative impact of persistent "brinksmanship" upon the tone of modern interstate life, see Ferrar 1981: 194–200; Stevenson 1997a: 125–61, esp. 158.
[43]   See esp. Ferrar 1981: 194–5; so, too, Stevenson 1997a: esp. 134–5.
[44]   Cf. Strauss 1991: 203.
[45]   See Eckstein 2006: esp. Chs. 4, 5, and 6. On the mini-imperialisms of small ancient states, see Ma 2000.
[46]   See the chart in Hopkins 1978: 33. After 188 BC the crisis situation and the strain significantly lessen, so that the percentage of the male citizen population in the Roman army drops rapidly into single digits, a continuous phenomenon until ca. 110 BC (ibid.).

The analytical problem in terms of the causes of Rome's successful expansion is, however, that these characteristics were also the characteristics of all its rivals. At Rome there were ceremonies that celebrated the increase in state resources and power; the same was true at Athens, at Pergamum, in the Seleucid Empire – or at tiny Cos. At Rome the goddess Victory was worshipped – but the same was true at Tarentum, at Rhodes, and among the Hellenistic monarchies, which possessed "une véritable théologie de la victoire."[47] At Rome the primary pathway to power and influence for individuals in the state was through achievement in war. But the same was true in the Achaemenid Empire, at Classical Athens (and of course at Sparta); it was true at Carthage, among the great Hellenistic monarchies, among the Hellenistic federal leagues of city-states, and among Celtic tribes. At Rome, individual bravery in battle was greatly honored, in private and in public, and especially honored – for aristocrats – was victory in single combat. But the same was true of the Persians, the Achaean League, Epirus, Syracuse, Antigonid Macedon, the Seleucid realm, and Carthage. The Romans were stern and steadfast in war-making, grimly intent on prosecuting any war until victory was achieved, however long it took – but a stern steadfastness in war-making was also characteristic of Classical Athens, Corinth and Sparta, of Hellenistic Tarentum and Carthage, and even of Polybius' small city-state of Megalopolis. It is obviously important that the Roman Republic went to war with some rival polity almost every year; but, again, the same was true of the Achaean League in the third century BC, and of monarchs such as Seleucus II, Attalus I, Antiochus III, and Philip V: under the shadow of Alexander the Great, and under the pressures of the harsh environment, this was what it meant to be a king. It is therefore not surprising that in the 123 years between 323 BC (the death of Alexander) and 160 BC, there were only four years when one or the other of the great Hellenistic monarchies was not at war (i.e., when there was general peace in the Greek East), nor is it surprising that twelve of the first fourteen Seleucid kings died in battle or while on campaign. Again, the Romans each year celebrated religious ceremonies both in spring and autumn which appear to have had a direct connection to war; but the annual Macedonian religious ceremonies along these lines not only occurred at similar times, they were also much bloodier and more brutal. This fits with what Polybius indicated concerning the Macedonians: they – not the Romans – were the most ferocious of all soldiers he knew. The Romans were formidable (especially when defending their homeland of Italy from attack: 6.51.6–10), but

---

[47]   Lévêque 1968: 278.

the Macedonians enjoyed war as if it were a banquet (5.2.6), something he never comes close to saying about Romans. Polybius had seen both Macedonians and Romans in battle (see, e.g., 28.11).[48]

We may choose to view all the above Roman characteristics and customs, and the conduct connected to them, as "dark" and "pathological."[49] But despite the assumptions of many prominent modern historians of Rome, such pathology did not make the Romans exceptional within their environment. Within their environment, within the system of states in which Rome existed, the Romans were in fact quite similar in their pathologies to their neighbors and rivals, and their aggression had a rational basis, aiming at survival. If the Romans' militarism, bellicosity, and aggressive diplomacy appear extraordinarily pathological in modern terms, these characteristics are nevertheless only ordinarily pathological in their own world. This situation conforms, precisely, to Waltz's maxim concerning the tendency towards sameness among the competitors in harshly anarchic conditions.[50] And if the Romans' intense militarism, bellicosity, and aggressive diplomacy are in fact not extraordinary within their world, but are the common coin in which all their contemporaries and rivals dealt, then these characteristics simply cannot be (despite the opinion of many prominent modern scholars) the key explanation for the Romans' extraordinary success.[51]

In particular, modern scholars point an accusatory finger at the Roman senatorial aristocracy as the source of continual Roman war-making. Typical is the statement that "War was necessary to satisfy the material and ideological needs of the aristocracy." Perhaps created originally to deal with the real problem of violent neighbors that confronted Rome early in its history (though some scholars even doubt this, preferring to see the Romans as simply inveterately bellicose), the warrior aristocracy of Rome by our period, it is claimed, now headed a war machine that created the wars it required. In this way the aristocracy enriched itself through booty, while maintaining its social prestige through leadership

---

[48] On all this, see in detail and with extensive supporting evidence Eckstein 2006: Ch. 6. Note also Livy 32.17–18.1 (the evaluation of T. Quinctius Flamininus, after his defeat at Atrax, that the Macedonians were the better soldiers), and 45.30.7 (on the origins of exceptional Macedonian ferocity); both these passages are based on Polybian material: see Eckstein 1997: 181–2.

[49] The characteristics which sum up Roman culture in Harris 1979: see 53 ("pathological," with aggression having "dark and irrational roots"); cf. 50–1.

[50] See above, p. 9 and nn. 17 and 18.

[51] The thesis of Harris 1979: Chs. 1–3, and 5; cf. Harris 1984a and 1990; Rowland 1983; Cornell 1995; Rosenstein 1999; Derow 2003.

in war, hence enforcing the deference within Roman society which it felt was its due.[52]

Allegedly, the instrument for achieving these aristocratic goals was the Roman Senate, which "will have looked for war even when none was ready at hand."[53] The Senate was the central decision-making institution in foreign relations. It was a group of approximately 300 aristocratic ex-public officials, riddled (as far as we can tell) by faction and individual competition, while at the same time operating mostly by consensus, which meant that in the nature of things, serious decisions occurred only when problems were obvious to everyone. About half of the senators were men who would not advance beyond the lowest public office (the quaestorship) because of the limited number of available senior magistracies; this meant they would never command in war or gain much glory – which, in turn, meant that, however imbued such men might be with a warrior ethos from their early army experiences, they had little reason to vote for war simply out of their own personal ambition. Nor is it likely, given the intensely competitive atmosphere within the senatorial aristocracy, that many of them would vote for unnecessary wars simply to further the personal ambitions of someone else. On the contrary: plenty of evidence suggests that the social structure of the Senate often operated to restrain overwrought ambitions, that it did not act as a rubber stamp for those who wished triumphal parades, and that commanders (i.e., public officials) who were accused of having begun unnecessary wars found this to be a serious accusation indeed.[54] Moreover, the internal discourse at Rome emphasized that the only type of just wars – which were the only kind of wars approved by the gods – were defensive wars. This ideology is an odd one indeed for a state that is claimed to be an exceptional international predator. The ideology was of course subject to some manipulation, but there were limits.[55] Nor

[52]   See Harris 1979: 10–41; Raaflaub 1996 (the quote: 278). The "war machine": whether or not modern scholars of Rome have read the sociologist Joseph Schumpeter, it is his view of the origins of war and imperialism which they have adopted; see Schumpeter 1952: 25 (general statement), cf. 51–3 (on the Roman Republic). Schumpeter originally wrote this famous essay in Germany in the bitter aftermath of World War I, which he blamed on the European aristocracy's need for warfare in order to maintain its social position. Romans as inveterately bellicose, rather than responding to early challenges through the adaptation of militarism: see, e.g., Rowland 1983.
[53]   Oakley 1993: 16; this is also the entire tenor of Harris 1979: Ch. 5.
[54]   See the good discussion in Rich 1993; cf. already Sherwin-White 1980 (review of Harris); Sherwin-White 1984: 13–15 (on the social structure of the Senate); Wiseman 1985.
[55]   Hence, for instance, the successful prevention of war against Rhodes in 167 BC by M. Porcius Cato (consul 195); see the moralizing tone of his speech *For the Rhodians* (= Gell. 6.3) – the Rhodians have not injured Rome enough to deserve war – with Astin 1978: 273–81.

was it always easy to convince the *populus Romanus* to go to war (they were citizens and primarily farmers, not professional pirates) – as we will see when we discuss the Roman decision of 200 BC.

In a harsh anarchy such as the one in which Rome existed, in which war was always a threat, the focus of every government was on achieving self-preservation in the short term, and to plan for the long term would be pointless even if one had institutions capable of doing such planning.[56] The Romans did not have such institutions. The very structure of the Roman Senate militated against any long-term decision-making, and so the *Patres* stumbled along from crisis to crisis – just as every other ancient government did. None of these senators had staffs of experts to help him, and relatively few senators in our period had even been outside of Italy (and certainly not for long).[57] And decisions were made, one might almost say instinctively, on the basis of the governing elite's often bitter experience and perceptions of the outside world, of how the harsh anarchy of states within which Rome existed actually functioned, on what worked well for survival and power in a militarized environment, and what did not.[58]

The Romans were highly militaristic, bellicose, and assertive internationally, but so was every other state, and there is a better answer to the question of the origins of Rome's extraordinary success. It lies in cultural characteristics significantly different from Rome's stern militarism, bellicosity, and diplomatic aggressiveness – characteristics that allowed Rome to survive in its extraordinarily harsh environment, but that it shared with every other major ancient state. Rome's advantage, and the strong element of truth in the idea of Roman exceptionalism, lay elsewhere than in its bellicosity and aggression: it lay in the Romans' exceptional ability in Italy to assimilate or conciliate outsiders and foreigners, and in the exceptional Roman ability at alliance-management. Such alliance-management included occasional savage terrorism, and we should not doubt the ultimately military nature of Roman dominance in Italy. But unlike the Athenians, for instance, the Romans avoided imposing taxation or specific political regimes upon their allies, and they demonstrated

[56] Focus, in harsh anarchies, on self-preservation and survival above all: Waltz 1979: 91–2; cf. 107 and 127.
[57] On the inefficiency of the Roman Senate as a decision-making body see Astin 1968; Veyne 1975: 804–9; Eckstein 1987a: esp. xvi–xviii. On the senatorial lack of area experts in foreign affairs, see Gruen 1984: Ch. 6.
[58] On the impact of learned perceptions upon the interstate decision-making by governing elites – perceptions which themselves are in good part the result of the international environment – see Desch 1998: 144–5. Another way of saying this is that the Romans, through long experience, had become socialized to the harshness of their interstate world.

an extraordinary capacity to compromise with local elites and to provide those elites with a real stake in Roman success. The ability to conciliate outsiders went so far as the creation of the concept of Roman citizenship as purely a legal category, divorced from ethnicity or location or even language, to which local elites could aspire (again, something foreign to an exclusivist city-state such as Athens). Roman techniques of conciliation and the extension of citizenship brought all of Latium, with its large population, into the Roman state after ca. 340 BC, and in the third century BC these techniques (including the granting of citizenship) were being spread far beyond Latium. Even Hannibal's invasion of Italy, and his ability to inflict devastating military defeats upon the Romans on Italian soil, did not shake the heart of the Roman alliance-system – though no one knew that beforehand, and Hannibal had thought such victories would do so.[59] The solidity of the Roman alliance-system in Italy, based on the Roman capacity for deal-making (as well as, of course, on fear of Rome), was an extraordinary achievement. It eventually gave the Romans the advantage of possessing extraordinarily large *resources* which they could mobilize in the usual bitter competition for survival and power that characterized all states within the Hellenistic anarchy.[60]

Though wars between states are "normal" under anarchic conditions and require little explanation in themselves – and were certainly "normal" among these aggressive Hellenistic states – comparatively rare but hugely important historically are large-scale wars that simultaneously involve most of the polities within a state-system in one enormous struggle with one another. These cataclysms have, naturally, been intensively analyzed by modern political scientists, and Realists suggest that they often arise out of a particular structural cause within the state-system. Evidence indicates that within multipolar anarchic systems, dramatic shifts in the distribution of capabilities across the system often create these situations of special crisis. The sudden decline in the capabilities of one or more of the major actors in the system, and/or the dramatic growth in the capabilities of one or more of the other major units in the system, can be a dangerous moment for the system taken as a whole. In the terminology of political science, this is a "power-transition crisis." In such

[59] In the face of catastrophic Roman defeats in the early years of the Hannibalic War, about 40 percent of Rome's allies, mostly in southern Italy, went over to Hannibal (see Lazenby 1996: 44). It was a terrible blow; but this still meant that about 60 percent of Rome's allies stayed on the Roman side under very difficult circumstances (cf. Cornell 1996: 103).
[60] As Goldsworthy 2000: 70, says, the main targets of Roman imperialism were other imperialists. The basic Roman advantages in the harsh rivalry for power and security in the Hellenistic Mediterranean via the creation of a very large but also relatively well-integrated state were laid out long ago by Mommsen 1903: 412–30, esp. 428–30, cf. 451–2; cf. Strauss 1997; Eckstein 2006: Ch. 7; Rosenstein 2007.

situations, the distribution of status, territory, resources, and influence which have become traditional and habitual within the system develops an increasing disjuncture with the realities of power – and hence the system breaks down. The result of that breakdown tends to be large-scale war, the convulsion of the entire state-system – a phenomenon that political scientists call "hegemonic war." Hegemonic war, a struggle for leadership and control over the entire system, in turn creates – though only after massive violence – a new interstate structure that is now more in accord with the real balance of power and capabilities across the system.[61]

Obviously, "power-transition crises" are crucial moments in the life of international systems. The most famous such crisis is probably the decline of the Turkish and Austro-Hungarian Empires in the face of rising Serbian and (more broadly) Russian power in the early twentieth century, combined with the declining power of Wilhelmine Germany itself in relation to the rising power of Tsarist Russia. The resulting tensions led to the catastrophic World War I.[62] It is argued here that a similar power-transition crisis of profound proportions, occurring among the great Greek states of the eastern Mediterranean, occurring too within the heavily militarized and brutal anarchy that constituted the Hellenistic state-system as a whole, was similarly the catalyst for dramatic change. It led to the transformation of the system, through the sudden expansion of previously minimal Roman interest and intervention in the Greek East, and the emergence there instead of a Roman predominance that turned out to be permanent.

Throughout the third century, the state-system in the Greek Mediterranean had been a multipolar (fundamentally a tripolar) system, based on the predominance of three great states: Ptolemaic Egypt, the Seleucid Empire, and Antigonid Macedon. Each of these powerful monarchies had been founded by a marshal of Alexander the Great in the period of enormous chaos and violence in the East that followed his premature death. None of them was strong enough to conquer the other two (though the ambition was always there).[63] This multipolar (tripolar) state-system provided significant room for political and military maneuver by second-tier and even smaller states attempting to maintain their independence by playing off the three great powers against one another. But now one of these great powers that had traditionally been strong enough to provide a crucial balance within the triadic state-system of the Greek

---

[61] Hypotheses and evidence on "power-transition theory": Kugler and Lemke 1996: 3–35; Geller and Singer 1998: 72–5. On the structural link between the onset of power-transition crises and the onset of "hegemonic war," see Gilpin 1988.
[62] A useful analysis of World War I as primarily the result of a power-transition crisis within the European state-system: Stevenson 1997b: Ch. 5.
[63] See Ager 2003; Eckstein 2006: Ch. 4.

Mediterranean suddenly ceased being able to fulfill its accustomed systemic function. The weakening of Ptolemaic Egypt after ca. 207 BC and then its increasing collapse after 204 led to a dramatic redistribution of power across the Hellenistic state-system, and in fact the collapse of the Ptolemies destabilized the entire system. One result among several was a tremendous expansion in the power of the two other great states, Antigonid Macedon under its vigorous king, Philip V, and the empire of the Seleucids under its vigorous king, Antiochus III the Great. Another result was the unexpected appearance of no fewer than four embassies at Rome in winter 201/200 from Greek states, all pleading for Roman intervention and help in this crisis.

Political scientists stress that such power-transition crises are not only crises for the individual states directly involved but are also simultaneously *system*-level crises, affecting all states within the system simultaneously and synergistically, though each in a different way – which is one reason why such crises lead to fundamental changes in the shape of the system. And as we have already noted (above, p. 20), these fundamental shifts in power and capability within the system tend to be accompanied by great interstate violence – "hegemonic war." Thus the warfare that broke out on a large scale in the Greek East in 202, and which eventually involved the Romans by 200, was – however destructive – not an unusual development, given the collapse of Ptolemaic Egypt and the disruption of the state-system.

It is not that the emergence of a power-transition crisis makes large system-wide war inevitable. The Realist approach emphasizes the pressures exerted by the system, by the events of the power-transition crisis itself as the crisis unrolls, and even by the nature of the unit culture involved, but the approach is nevertheless not that deterministic (though it is sometimes accused of being so).[64] Thus careful and delicate diplomacy led to the power-transition crisis of 1989–91 coming to an end with the empire of the Soviet Union having disappeared, and the Soviet Union itself having disappeared, but without a war. Realists do argue, however, that the emergence of a power-transition crisis greatly increases the likelihood or probability of large system-wide war, because the issues involved are so important for all states within the system and for the system as a whole.

This probability increases with the harshness of the specific anarchic state-system under discussion – as well as with the lack of sophisticated instruments of diplomacy. But no one is denying here that human decision-making – the decisions of Greek, Macedonian, and Roman statesmen – played a crucial role in the profound transformation within the Hellenistic state-system that occurred between 207 and 188 BC. These

---

[64] Criticisms: see Levy 1988; Snyder 1991. Response: see, e.g., Waltz 2000: 24.

statesmen could have made different decisions, they could have chosen to act in ways significantly different from the ways they chose – ways, for instance, that were less militarily and diplomatically aggressive on behalf of the competing interests of their own polities. Thus Antiochus and Philip could have decided not to take voracious advantage of the sudden weakness of the Ptolemies; and the governing elites of the less powerful states could have decided to accommodate themselves to the suddenly expanding power of Macedon and/or the Seleucids, hoping to appease the appetite of the newly much more dominant powers (what the political scientists call "bandwagoning"), or even seeking to gain advantages from the new systemic configuration (what the political scientists call "jackel bandwagoning"), rather than calling in Rome to aid them in their military resistance. The Roman Senate, although faced with multiple Greek requests for help, could have decided not to intervene (indeed, the Roman assembly came close to deciding not to intervene, even though the Senate urged it – see below, Chapter 6). In any of these ways, the ancient Mediterranean world would have had a quite different history. There might have developed no major threat to the traditional balance of power if Philip and Antiochus had not decided to assault it; there might have emerged a bipolar system in the Greek East (dominated by Macedon and Syria) or even a unipolar structure in the Greek East (dominated by either Macedon or Syria) if the *Patres* in Rome had not decided to prevent it.

In history as it actually unfolded, however, it is significant that all these statesmen chose the types of policies and actions that, according to Realist theoreticians, *typically* happen among the fiercely independent states of anarchic systems when power-transition crises occur. Moreover, these decisions to a great extent derived from the pressures and the constraints which both the anarchic system in general and the inherent dynamics of such power-transition crises themselves imposed upon the human decision-makers, although we must also acknowledge as a very important causal factor the militaristic and independence-seeking internal cultures of the states involved.[65]

Modern students of political science have sometimes complained about the relatively small number of cases of power-transition crisis, resultant

---

[65]   On the increasingly stereotyped actions of decision-makers in a crisis as the crisis evolves over time and develops its own inner dynamic, see Wolfers 1962: 13–19; Lebow 1981: Ch. 5; Richardson 1994: 10–34. On the feeling among statesmen in such crises that alternative avenues of action are quickly closing off and that "there is no choice" (what is termed "cognitive closure" by the political scientists), see, e.g., Kauppi 1991: 115–16. Again, the militaristic and independence-seeking cultures we are discussing were themselves in great part the result of the pressures of the system, and of the often bitter experience of decision-making elites concerning the nature of those pressures: see above, p. 19.

hegemonic war, and major system-transformation with which they have had to work in laying out the fundamental factors that might lie behind such interstate phenomena.[66] The crisis that shook the eastern Mediterranean from ca. 207 onwards should be added to the list of those cases of power-transition crises which are discussed by political scientists. It has been missing from all such discussions because detailed know-ledge of interstate relations in the ancient world among political scientists, skimpy in any case, is most often limited to Thucydides, with a lesser emphasis on the conflicts between Rome and Carthage. Hellenistic history has received no attention, and has never been subjected to detailed analysis by political scientists. In a previous book I have sought to rectify this gap in general knowledge of the Hellenistic Mediterranean among political scientists, but that book was not focused – as this one is – on the detailed story of Roman relations with the Greek East; it dealt, rather, with the general problem of anarchic state-systems in Mediterranean antiquity.[67] My hope in this book is that political scientists as well as modern historians of antiquity will benefit from the theoret-ically informed reconstruction of the complicated evolution of Roman involvement in the Greek East which follows, and the detailed and theoretically informed reconstruction of the great transformaton in the state-system that convulsed the Mediterranean world at the end of the third century BC.

One must stress here that the large-scale interstate violence typical of power-transition crises did not begin in 200 BC with the Roman inter-vention in the East. In that sense, whereas modern international rela-tions theorists have been completely ignorant of the power-transition crisis that developed in the Hellenistic Mediterranean after 207, modern historians of antiquity have strongly tended to focus too narrowly on the Roman decision of winter 201/200.[68] All ancient states, even the most powerful ones, were fragile in a way in which modern nation-states are not: it was one of the factors contributing to the savage competition among them to gain resources, power, and influence.[69] The Ptolemaic state began to fall into serious trouble from ca. 207 BC with the emergence of an uncontrollable indigenous rebellion in Upper and Middle Egypt. The premature death of Ptolemy IV in 204 and the accession to the Ptolemaic throne of a child of 6 intensified the crisis. Large-scale interstate violence then began with the invasion of Ptolemaic territory in the Levant by King Antiochus III the Great in 202; this attack had been preceded (this

---

[66]   See Wohlforth 2000: 127 and 132.
[67]   Eckstein 2006.
[68]   Examples: Harris 1979: 212–18; Mandell 1989; Derow 2003: 58–60.
[69]   See above, pp. 11–12.

study will argue) by a treaty of alliance between Antiochus and Philip V of Macedon to destroy the Ptolemaic regime utterly; and as the large-scale war between Antiochus and the weakened Ptolemaic government continued, Philip V in 201 opened a major campaign of his own against Ptolemaic interests and holdings in the southeast Aegean. By summer 201 the eastern Mediterranean from Gaza to the Hellespont was already at war on a scale not seen in 100 years. This was the power-transition crisis, leading to hegemonic war, and thence to system transformation. Up to this point, the Republic of Rome was not involved.

There is no doubt that with the faltering and then the increasing collapse of the Ptolemaic state, a new and radically transformed inter-state system was about to emerge in the eastern Mediterranean. *Something* was going to replace the previous multipolar system based on a triad of great powers (Macedon, the Seleucid Empire, Ptolemaic Egypt). There is no doubt, either, that because the Ptolemaic regime had served the function, on the level of the system, of containing both the expansionist conduct of the Seleucid monarchy and to a lesser extent Antigonid Macedon, now that such containment had been greatly weakened the new system that was emerging would be characterized by the increased power of the most powerful states. Perhaps in the offing was a bipolar system in which Macedon and the Seleucids would confront each other across the entire realm of the Greek East; or perhaps the hegemony of one or the other of these two great states over the East would eventually have emerged (after yet another round of system-wide "hegemonic war"). What did emerge, however, was a surprise: the intervention of a large and powerful polity that had previously been mostly outside the orbit of the Hellenistic Greek system. This Roman intervention instigated a short but intense and violent period of hegemonic rivalry among Rome, Macedon, and the Seleucid monarchy (200–188 BC), a rivalry that ended with the emergence of Rome as the patron of what looked on the surface to be an artificially restored balance of power among the three great Greek states. As Waltz suggests, "Larger units existing in a contentious arena tend to take on systemwide tasks."[70]

The great Hellenistic historian Polybius described in extensive detail, especially in books 14–21 of his *Histories*, the process by which this sys-temic transformation at the end of the third century BC was accomplished. Polybius was a man widely experienced in political and military affairs, and an intellectually sophisticated observer and analyst of events.[71] Unfortunately, much of his work on the period of transformation has

---

[70] Waltz 2000: 34.
[71] Recent studies of Polybius (ca. 200–118 BC): Eckstein 1995; Champion 2004.

been lost, but enough survives to show that he approached the transformation in a theoretically informed manner of his own. He emphasized that the years between 204 and 200 BC witnessed the definitive emergence of a *symplokē*: a new "interconnectedness" between the eastern and western halves of the Mediterranean. This was an interconnectedness between events in the geographically separate regions of the Mediterranean basin that had previously not existed: events in the Greek East had previously not had an impact on the West, and vice versa. Polybius thought that the first steps towards this *symplokē* occurred in 217 BC, when Philip V of Macedon first turned towards the West and attempted imperial expansion at the expense of the Romans (whom he saw as weakened by the Hannibalic War), and that thereafter the two regional subsystems of states in the eastern and western Mediterranean gradually but increasingly became transformed through interaction into one single very large system. For Polybius the growth of the *symplokē* explained at a deep level the intervention of the great western power Rome in 200 BC into the power-transition crisis that previously had been limited to the Greek East; at the same time the Roman decision itself intensified the growth of the *symplokē*, until by the time Polybius was writing, ca. 150 BC, the *symplokē* was obvious to all.[72]

The final third of our study will cover the period of the great hegemonic wars between Rome, Macedon, and the Seleucid Empire, and the immediate consequences of those wars. The surprising result of the power-transition crisis in the East was that the Roman Republic managed by 188 BC to create what political scientists call a "unipolar" system in the Mediterranean. By the early 180s Rome as the leading state in a large coalition of primarily Greek allies had defeated both Antigonid Macedon and the Seleucid Empire, and had emerged as the sole remaining superpower. Yet both Macedon and the Seleucid Empire retained significant potential to challenge Roman preponderance if the right circumstances occurred, and meanwhile the Romans themselves – as, we will see, so often previously – withdrew completely back across the Adriatic to Italy once the crisis was over, leaving all Greek states with much independence. This suggests that even in the 180s, Roman strategic goals in the eastern Mediterranean remained highly limited in scope. Moreover, historically "unipolarity" tends strongly to exit backward into multipolarity rather than forward towards hegemony and

---

[72] On the *symplokē*, see esp. Walbank 1985: 313–24. This was not the only perspective Polybius brought to the crisis of 207/204–188 BC, however: he was a Hellenistic intellectual (and not a modern political scientist), so he also perceived at work in these events the power of the goddess Tyche (Fortune) as retributive justice against what he saw as the unjust behavior of Philip and Antiochus. Discussion of this aspect of Polybius' thought: below, Chapter 4.

empire.[73] Thus although a clear international hierarchy had now been established in the Mediterranean state-world, one that was gradually replacing the previously prevailing anarchy, this was not yet a stable situation. The future still remained to be written. But because "unipolarity" is an analytical category with its own specific characteristics, characteristics that have recently – for obvious reasons – been intensively studied by modern political scientists, here, too, a theoretical framework from political science will help us understand the unrolling of the historical process.

This book thus follows the example of Polybius in offering a theoretically informed narrative of world-historical events. As in my immediately previous book, this study is intended both for political scientists and for modern historians of antiquity – though in its detailed attention to the reconstruction of a relatively short but crucial and highly controversial period in ancient Mediterranean history, perhaps more for the latter now. In what follows, political scientists may be disconcerted by the extended and complex arguments sometimes necessary to establish even the basic narrative of events – to establish what, historically, actually occurred; but our information is so scanty that much effort must be devoted to this. Meanwhile, modern historians of antiquity may already be somewhat put off by the explicitness of the theoretical model into which rather traditional questions are being placed – and put off as well as by the unfamiliar terminology.

These are the problems inherent in attempting an interdisciplinary study combining two neighboring but differing scholarly disciplines: history and international relations. But not even the most traditional of historians engages in historical research and writing without some broad hypotheses in mind about how the world works.[74] The thesis I propose here concerning "how the world works," analyzing the events from ca. 230 BC down to ca. 170 BC primarily from an international systems and Realist perspective, is simply more explicit in its theoretical framework. And on the other side, no matter how attractively "logical" a theoretical framework such as Realism may appear to be for explaining international relations, that framework is worth only as much as the empirical evidence that supports it. It is therefore incumbent to establish first the historical facts involved in any case under discussion, for only then can analysis proceed. Thus for ancient historians I hope to use international relations theory to clarify and provide a new vocabulary for what occurred in the eastern Mediterranean in the crucial half-century under

---

[73] See esp. Layne 1993; Wilkinson 1999; discussion below, Chapter 8.
[74] See the comments of Carr 1952: Ch. 1; cf. Schroeder 1997: 65–8.

discussion, whereas for political scientists I hope this study will offer a new case study of systemic transformation for them to ponder and analyze.

We will proceed as follows. In the first section of the book, the involvement of Rome in areas east of the Adriatic before 200 BC will be traced in detail, the theme being the hesitant and minimal nature of Roman involvement in the region (Chapters 2–3). The second section of the book will deal with the power-transition crisis that shook the Hellenistic state-system after 207, originating in the increasing faltering of Ptolemaic Egypt (Chapters 4, 5, and 6). The third section of the book will deal with the period of hegemonic war and Roman intervention attendant upon the power-transition crisis (Chapters 7 and 8), and then describe and analyze the initial two decades of Roman unipolarity and Mediterranean interstate hierarchy in the period from the victory over Antiochus III to the reassertion of Roman power against Macedon after 172 BC. Once more, the theme will be Roman hesitation about large and continual entanglements in the East. The lack of intense Roman interest, and the ambiguities of unipolarity (as opposed to hegemony or empire), in turn allowed the Greek states in this period to retain a very significant sphere of independence – as both Greeks and Romans, looking back, understood (Chapter 9).

2

Rome and Illyria, ca. 230–217 BC

By the 230s BC, the Romans already had a long history of encounters with Greek city-states and Greek culture. But these encounters were of a special sort – their extensive and longstanding connections with the Greek states of southern Italy and Sicily; meanwhile, Roman connections with Greece proper remained minimal. Greek culture, transmitted via the Greek polities of southern Italy, had affected Rome from at least the sixth century onward, and increasingly so from the fourth century; meanwhile the Romans, in their geopolitical struggles with the great Greek city-states of Tarentum and Syracuse, had by the mid-third century asserted a tradition of hierarchy over these polities – a hierarchy established by success in war. Nevertheless, while the Greeks of the West naturally had firm links to the wider Greek world, they were also somewhat isolated from that wider world. So it is not surprising that the Romans' encounter with the Greeks of Italy and (later) Sicily remained Italy-centered, and did not lead to an immediate Roman involvement east of the Adriatic.[1] Indeed, the only lengthy Roman encounter with a Greek polity from across the Adriatic before ca. 230 was the invasion of Italy by Pyrrhus the king of Epirus, a relative of Alexander the Great,

---

[1] On Rome and the Greeks of the West, see in general Lomas 1993. Early Greek cultural impact: Cornell 1995: 86–97; the Greek impact in the fourth century: Wallace 1990. Roman military conflicts with the Italiote and Siceliote Greeks: Eckstein 2006: 149–67. On the isolation of the Greeks of the West, note that the historian Timaeus of Tauromenium (in Sicily) had to make a special plea for European Greek interest in their doings, ca. 280: see Momigliano 1977.

at the behest of the Greek city of Tarentum in 280–275 BC – an invasion which lasted years, and which Rome defeated only after sustaining massive losses. The experience of Pyrrhus will certainly not have given the Senate an optimistic view of the world east of Italy.[2]

That was the situation as it stood ca. 230 BC. This chapter argues that the Roman military expeditions to the northwest coast of Greece in 229 BC and again in 219 BC – the first Roman interventions in the Greek East – had consequences that were themselves minimal. The first war was fought to suppress serious piracy. Victory allowed Rome to rearrange the geopolitical situation in maritime Illyris to suit itself, but the result was merely the creation of informal friendships between Rome and a few scattered cities and tribes. The second war was fought, successfully, to suppress a dynast who was seeking to overturn these satisfactory if minimal Roman arrangements. It changed little. Beyond Illyria, there was little Roman involvement – even diplomatically – with the Greek states. Down to 217 BC Rome thus did not evince great interest in expanding its power and influence in the world east of the Adriatic. Such a reconstruction is controversial, however – and it will need to be argued in detail.

THE FIRST ILLYRIAN WAR

Official contacts between the Republic of Rome and the polities of the Greek East before ca. 230 were few and informal. Their known extent can be quickly summarized.

In 273 the Ptolemaic regime in Egypt sent an embassy to Rome that led to a Roman return delegation to Alexandria and the creation of a relationship of informal friendship – *amicitia* – between the two states. Such "friendship" was merely an expression of general goodwill, and carried no obligations.[3] The Romans may also have established such an informal *amicitia* with the island republic of Rhodes, off the southwest coast of Asia Minor, ca. 300 BC – but the historicity of this contact is uncertain.[4] In the 260s the city of Apollonia on the Greek side of the

---

[2] On Pyrrhus' war against Rome on behalf of Tarentum, see in detail Garoufalias 1979: Chs. 3–5. Impact on senatorial views of the powers that existed east of the Adriatic: see Siebert 1995: 237–8.

[3] On *amicitia* and its lack of obligations, see esp. Gruen 1984: 54–95. Ptolemaic relations with Rome from 273 – friendly but distant – are discussed in detail in Chapter 5, below.

[4] See the debate between Schmitt 1957 (who argues for historicity of this contact) and Holleaux 1935: 1–21 (who argues against). The inscription from Rhodes published by Kontorini 1983 appears to show that the Rhodians knew little in detail about Rome ca. 200 BC.

Adriatic evidently sent an embassy to Rome, for reasons unknown to us:
the envoys were maltreated by some young Roman aristocrats, who were
punished; that is all we know of the incident.[5] It is also possible that
sometime in the 240s or 230s Seleucus II initiated an informal *amicitia*
with Rome; but the historicity of this interchange has been challenged
as well, and in any case it clearly had no international repercussions.[6]
The Senate in the late 240s may also, at the request of the Acarnanian
League (in western Greece), have sought to mediate a war between the
Acarnanians and the Aetolian League – a mediation which the Aetolians
allegedly rejected with an insulting response; but the historicity of this
incident is very controversial and uncertain.[7] Similarly, there was a tradition that, from relatively early in the history of the Republic, the Senate
sent emissaries to ask questions of the oracle of Apollo at Delphi in
central Greece – but anything before the late third century is doubted
by most scholars who have examined those traditions closely.[8]

Rome at the founding of the Republic ca. 500 BC was already a major
city, by far the largest city in Latium – but as we have seen, evidence
is sparse for official Roman contacts east of the Adriatic during the first
250 years of Republican history. And these informal contacts have left
little trace in our evidence precisely because they had no practical consequences – and that is the case even with the two alleged contacts with
Greek states on the Adriatic coast. In sum, Errington is obviously correct
when he says that "*amicitia* with Rome could mean much or little, but
for the eastern Greeks before 229 it meant without exception little."[9]
Moreover, the original impulse for these contacts almost always comes
from the Greek side. Yet scholars have also established that knowledge

[5] On the embassy of Apollonia to Rome (reasons unknown) ca. 266, see Gruen
1984: 64 (with sources).
[6] The emperor Claudius discovered this long-forgotten *amicitia*: Suet. *Claud.* 25.3.
Many modern scholars doubt the incident because the Senate allegedly agreed to
friendship with Seleucus only if he lifted taxation from Ilium (Troy), the supposed
"mother-city" of Rome (ibid.) – an impossibly arrogant Roman response. But see
Gruen 1984: 64–5; Erskine 2003: 172–5.
[7] On whether Rome in the late 240s made a failed attempt at mediating between
the Acarnanians and the Aetolian League, being rejected with insults by the
Aetolians, contrast Gruen 1984 and Roy 2000 (doubting), with Corsten 1992 and
Dany 1999: 98–119 (affirming basic historicity). Our only source, Justin 28.1–2,
contains manifest chronological impossibilities, and given Rome's famously troubled
relationship with Aetolia after 196 BC (see below, Chapter 7), the possibility of anti-
Aetolian propaganda here is obvious.
[8] Doubts about Roman consultations of Delphi before the 220s: see Hoffmann 1934:
129–31; Fontenrose 1978: 65, 314, 334, 342–3; Gruen 1990: 9 and n. 18.
[9] Errington 1989a: 81; see in general his sensible discussion of early Roman contacts with the East at 81–5.

of and interest in the Romans by Greeks east of the Adriatic remained minimal down into the mid-third century.[10]

It is therefore striking that the first major Roman involvement in the East was a war. The war was fought on the Adriatic coast opposite Italy, against barbarian Illyrians, in 229. Polybius, the most sophisticated ancient writer on the rise of Rome, has put this war on the agenda for all modern scholars.[11] That is because he declares it marked an important step in the growth of Roman power and dominion (*dynasteia*) in the Greek East.[12]

Some scholars take Polybius here to mean that this war of 229 BC is important because it led to a major Roman political encroachment in Greece.[13] But Polybius' point is simpler: the war was important simply because it was the first Roman crossing of the Adriatic with a military force (2.2.1, explicit). The expedition in itself thus marked an important moment in the growth of that "geopolitical interconnectedness" (*symplokē*) between the separate eastern and western halves of the Mediterranean which is one of the two grand themes of Polybius' *Histories*.[14] Polybius' other grand theme is of course the rise of Roman power. But he placed even the *beginnings* of this East–West "interconnectedness" only in 217 (see 5.10.1). The First Illyrian War thus occurred more than a decade earlier, and for Polybius its importance lies in being a crucial event leading *towards* those beginnings.[15] Not surprisingly, then, no specific results in Illyria itself appear in Polybius' summations of the campaign (2.2.1 and 2.12.7).

This conclusion is important for our understanding of the postwar situation in Illyria. Differing visions of Roman expansion emerge depending on the intensity, formality, and geographical extent of postwar Roman control. The more stringent the control and the greater its geographical extent, the more one sees a large and intentional Roman encroachment into Greek affairs. The looser the control and the smaller its geographical extent, the more one sees a lack not of Roman power but of Roman interest. The latter position will be argued here.

The war itself was a response to violence on the Adriatic coast, unusual not in it character but in its scale. Northwest of Greece and Macedon

[10]   See Gruen 1984: Ch. 10.
[11]   On Polybius, see above, Chapter 1.
[12]   Polyb. 2.2.2; cf. 2.12.7, a somewhat different formulation.
[13]   Niese 1899: 281; Colin 1905: 24, 29, 49; Derow 2003: 51–3.
[14]   On *symplokē* at Polyb. 2.2.1, see Walbank 1957: 153. On *symplokē* as a central theme in Polybius' work, see Walbank 1985, and above, Chapter 1, p. 26.
[15]   See Walbank 1985: 314. Polybius evidently thinks of this war as a major event of what one might call the period of *epiplokē*, mere "contact" between East and West (see 2.12.7).

lived the Illyrian peoples. From their first contact with these non-Greek tribal societies, in the fifth century, Greek writers describe the Illyrians as turbulent and warlike. The excavated graves of Illyrian males are filled with weapons. Competition for scarce resources in the Illyrian coastal hills led to frequent intertribal wars, and to raiding and population movements towards the southeast. The rapid rise and fall of various tribes and warlords – no true states had time to evolve – made long-term Greek agreements with Illyrians difficult to construct.[16] And the Greeks joined in this militarized local anarchy (so typical of the ancient Mediterranean). Thus, as with the Greek city-states founded in southern Italy and in Sicily, the Greek *poleis* of maritime Illyris – Corcyra, Apollonia, Epidamnus – all proudly claimed to have conquered their lands from indigenous peoples by war.[17]

In the mid-third century the Illyrian tribal grouping called the Ardiaei, forced south by pressure from Celtic tribes in the Danube Valley, in turn conquered other Illyrian peoples along the Adriatic coast, gradually becoming the dominant Illyrian power. It was the continuing expansion of Ardiaean power southward in the late 230s that eventually aroused the attention of the Roman Senate.[18]

Polybius says that the Romans' concern was Ardiaean piracy. The Senate received increasing complaints about it from the merchants who plied the Straits of Otranto between Italy and Greece (2.8.2–3). The merchants operated primarily from the Latin *colonia* of Brundisium (Dio frg. 49.12), and some may have been Roman citizens, but many came from the Italiote Greek city-states that were now Rome's allies, and senatorial action on the allies' behalf would fortify Rome's position in southern Italy. In addition, Rome now had an important friend and ally in the Kingdom of Syracuse in Sicily, and Syracuse was heavily involved in the cross-Adriatic trade. The Senate later dedicated spoils from the Illyrian campaign in the great temple of Olympian Zeus at Syracuse (Livy 24.21.9), which suggests that Syracusan interests were involved in the war – and that King Hiero II had provided the Romans some sort of

---

[16] See Hammond 1966: 239–53, and esp. Dell 1970a: 116–17. On the poverty-stricken Illyrian country and the fierce competition for resources: Dell 1967a: 344–58. Militaristic character of male Illyrian graves: Wilkes 1992: 140–1.

[17] Wilkes 1992: 110–12. At Apollonia in the Hellenistic period indigenous people, in serf-like conditions, still worked the estates belonging to the Greek elite (ibid.: 127). On the similar violent colonial situaton in southern Italy and Sicily, see Eckstein 2006: Ch. 5.

[18] The struggle among the Illyrian tribes caused by increasing Celtic pressure from the north: Wilkes 1992: 137–49. Ardiaean conquests: Hammond 1966: 241–2.

help. Syracusan support and involvement, in turn, suggest how important the piracy issue really was.[19]

The growth of Illyrian piracy was only one element in a sudden and dramatic shift in the configuration of power along the Illyrian coast. Agron, the Ardiaean king, had gained control over many other Illyrian tribes (Polyb. 2.2.4); meanwhile the Kingdom of Epirus, which had previously provided a bulwark against Illyrian pressure towards the south, collapsed in 233/ 232 BC.[20] The new Epirote republic was weak; parts of the old kingdom broke away and became independent, including Acarnania in the south.[21] Agron soon took advantage of his own strength and Epirote weakness. This fit a pattern going back 150 years: whenever Greek states on the Illyrians' frontiers were beset with military and/or political weakness, the result was Illyrian expansion.[22] In this very period the Illyrian Dardani similarly sought to take advantage of Macedonian weakness, both in 229 (Justin 28.4.14) and again in 219 (Justin 29.1.10, cf. Polyb. 4.29.1).[23]

The severity of the Ardiaean challenge was shown by their victory in 231 over the army of the Aetolian League, at Medion in Acarnania (Polyb. 2.2.5–2.4.5). The Aetolians were besieging Medion in an attempt to take advantage themselves of the collapse of Epirus by forcing this city into the League, or else sacking it (Polyb. 2.2.6, 9, and 11). The Aetolians had already launched raids into both Epirus and Acarnania earlier in the 230s (Justin 28.2.14). This situation, too, was typical of the brutal conditions of the Hellenistic anarchy.[24]

The Illyrians followed up their victory over Aetolia in 231 by the capture of the Epirote capital of Phoenice in 230. These twin successes caused shock in Greece (Polyb. 2.6 and 2.9.8–9), leading to a military

---

[19]   On Italiote Greek interests and the First Illyrian War, see Gruen 1984: 69; and esp. Marasco 1986: 46–69; cf. Pohl 1993: 58–69. Marasco offers much archaeological evidence in support of Italiote involvement in the Adriatic trade, but thinks prominent Roman senators were also involved (69–71); there is no evidence, and the senatorial reluctance to intervene in the Illyrian problem (Polyb. 2.8.3 – see below) argues against it. On Syracusan involvement, see Eckstein 1980: 196 and n. 42; cf. Marasco 1986: 68.

[20]   On the date of the collapse of Epirus, see Dany 1999: 126–30.

[21]   Epirus as a crucial bulwark against the Illyrians: Dell 1970a: 118; Marasco 1986: 78–80. The break-off of Acarnania from Epirus in 232: Dany 1999: 130. The collapse of Epirus combined with the sudden expansion of the Ardiaei shows us the small state-system in northwest Greece undergoing its own power-transition crisis at this point (on the concept of "power-transition crisis" see above, Chapter 1) – with typically resultant chaos and war.

[22]   Historical precursors of Agron, going back to the 380s: Hammond 1966: 243 and 245–7; cf. Wilkes 1992: 120–4 and 146.

[23]   Cf. Wilkes 1992: 148–9.

[24]   For the politics, see Walbank 1957: 154.

response by both the Achaean League and the Aetolians, first on land
(230) and then by sea (229) – a military response not unlike the eventual Roman military response. If the Aetolians and the Achaeans had
been successful, then their power and influence in far northwest Greece
would have increased – just as Roman influence increased there as a
result of the eventual Roman success. Even as it was, the Aetolian League
made territorial gains (see below). The strong military response of the
Achaeans and the Aetolians to the Illyrian expansion, and the eventual
Aetolian territorial gains, put the Roman reaction and its consequences
into a wider systemic context – something which is necessary for good
analysis, though modern scholars have not usually done it, concentrat-
ing solely on Rome's action instead.

The united Aetolian and Achaean forces failed against the Illyrians,
however: there was a stand-off on land in 230, and an Illyrian victory
at sea in 229 (Polyb. 2.6 and 2.9.8–10.9). Worse, both Epirus and
Acarnania swore treaties of alliance with King Agron in 230 under which
they would cooperate with the Illyrians in war and resist both Achaea
and Aetolia (2.6.9–10, cf. 2.10.1). The Epirote government probably
also gave territorial concessions to Agron.[25] In 230 the Ardiaei also
launched powerful sea-borne raids as far as the southern Peloponnese
(2.5.1–2).[26] Then the next year, in 229, the Ardiaei flooded south again,
besieging Epidamnus and perhaps Apollonia, and capturing the great
island of Corcyra (Polyb. 2.10.7–11.9; App. *Illyr.* 7).[27]

Despite the Illyrian geopolitical expansion, there is little reason to doubt
Polybius' assertion that what worried the Senate in 230/229 was simply
Illyrian piracy, and not the problem of the rise of a powerful Ardiaean
state.[28] Senatorial concern about raiders in the Straits of Otranto is already
apparent in the foundation in 244 of the Latin colony at Brundisium.[29]
The Roman expedition to Illyria in 229 was very large (including 200

---

[25] Formal treaties: Walbank 1957: 158. Epirote concession of Atintania to Agron:
ibid., 156–7 (with sources). Importance of the Illyrian victories of 231–230: Dell
1967a. The Acarnanians fought on the Illyrian side against the Achaean–Aetolian
fleet in 229 (Polyb. 2.10.1).

[26] These raids were occurring regularly: Polyb. 2.5.1–2; cf. Plut. *Cleom.* 10.6 and
Paus. 4.35.5–7.

[27] Epigraphical evidence shows that Corcyra was engaged in anti-piracy activity
at this time: Marasco 1986: 79 and n. 247. The Ardiaean actions may have been
part of a general movement among the Illyrian peoples, for in early 229 the Illyrian
Dardani won a great victory over the Macedonian army and then invaded Macedon
proper: see Dell 1967b: 96 and n. 18.

[28] Despite Badian 1964a: 4–5; Errington 1972: 36; de Souza 1999: 79–80.

[29] Marasco 1986: 42–4 (convincing). Perhaps the Ardiaean situation also raised
concerns about the safety of the Roman colonies on the eastern coast of Italy, or
the sea route to them (so Derow 2003: 52–3) – but there is no evidence.

warships), but this need not indicate geopolitical concerns in the Senate about the Ardiaean state; Hammond argues that the scale of the forces was justified, given a campaign along 400 miles of difficult coast.[30] Moreover, we know that the Illyrian capture of Phoenice, while threatening to the Greeks in terms of Ardiaean overland expansion, was accompanied by an especially destructive attack by Ardiaean pirates on Italian merchants in the Straits (Polyb. 2.8.2). According to Polybius, it was the intensified merchants' complaints arising from this large attack that led the Senate finally to act (2.8.3). I see little reason to doubt this: Illyrian territorial gains southward along the Adriatic coast, by giving them new bases, would naturally make Illyrian piracy easier to conduct, and clearly it was already having a deleterious effect on the shipping lanes (Polyb. 2.8.2).[31] The sharply increased merchant complaints to the Senate about piracy should thus be seen as the primary cause of the Senate's decision to intervene with the Ardiaei. But if the Senate in 230/229 was responding primarily to concerns about increased Illyrian piracy in the Straits, this suggests that Roman goals in Illyria in 229 were always inherently limited.

A non-Polybian tradition does hold that Roman intervention was caused by pleas from the island state of Issa in the northern Adriatic, besieged by the Ardiaei, i.e., by complaints about Illyrian expansionism, not about Illyrian piracy.[32] But despite some scholars,[33] this tradition should not be accepted. It is a very pro-Roman account, with Rome depicted as coming to the aid of a civilized Greek city under siege by barbarians. Moreover, the sources agree that the focus of the war was in the southern Adriatic, not the north; Issa was a low priority for Rome, the last place reached (see Polyb. 2.11.2–12; App. *Ill.* 7). The Issa tradition probably arose because the Roman envoys sent to investigate conditions in Illyria in view of merchants' complaints found the Illyrians besieging Issa (Polyb. 2.8.5); hence came the idea that the war arose from complaints from Issa itself.[34]

In recent years, the most influential analysis of the expansion of Roman power has come from W. V. Harris, who argues that Rome's expansionist success was caused by its exceptionally intense bellicosity, brutality, and conscious imperialism.[35] In pursuing this theme of Rome as an exceptional predator among a significantly less aggressive community of Hellenistic polities, Harris argues that in 230/229 the Senate – ever on the watch

---

[30] Hammond 1968: 6.
[31] See Marasco 1986: 80.
[32] App. *Illyr.* 7; Dio frg. 12.49 = Zon. 8.19.
[33] Derow 1973: 118–34; cf. Errington 1989a: 87–8.
[34] See Gruen 1984: 361–2 (convincing).
[35] See Harris 1979: esp. Chs. 1–3, and 5. On the widespread influence of Harris' work, see Chapter 1, above, n. 5.

for new conquests – took the first chance it got to intervene in Illyria and to establish Roman power there.[36] But Polybius says the opposite – that the merchants' complaints about Illyrian piracy went for a long time unanswered by the *Patres* (2.8.3).[37] Moreover, that Rome, far from seeking any excuse for war, was reacting to disturbing developments on the Adriatic coast opposite Italy is shown by the *Greek* response to this situation, which was the same as the Roman response: an unprecedented military intervention in the region, including joint operations on land and sea by the Aetolian and Achaean Leagues. These two large Greek federal states were bitter rivals, and even when allied (as in the 230s) did not usually operate together militarily. The Greek response to the Ardiaean crisis of 231–229 was thus an exceptionally unified and energetic use of military force. Roman conduct regarding the Ardiaei should therefore not be seen as unique but rather as part of a broader and quite natural systemic response to the increasing success of Illyrian violence – which was, in turn, the result both of the energy of King Agron and (importantly) the collapse of Epirus.

The Senate acted only in response to serious complaints from victims of the greatly intensifying Illyrian expansion.[38] The governments of the Aetolian and Achaean Leagues did likewise – responding to pleas for help. Those appeals came first in 230 from the Epirote government (Polyb. 2.6.1), and then in 229 from Corcyra, Epidamnus, and Apollonia (2.9.8). The fact is that in the ancient Mediterranean, appeals by the weak to the strong were a general phenomenon of the anarchy, and were not limited to Rome, and forceful responses to those appeals were a general phenomenon of the anarchy, and were not limited to Rome.[39]

Indeed, one should underline that despite the embassy of Apollonia to Rome in the 260s, of which much has sometimes been made (above), the Apolloniates did not appeal to Rome when seriously threatened in 229, but – apparently still operating in a purely Greek political world – appealed instead to the Aetolians and the Achaeans for military help (Polyb. 2.9.8). The conduct of Apollonia thus appears to demonstrate both how insubstantial were those earliest contacts between Rome and the states east of the Adriatic, and how widespread outside the Roman context was the phenomenon of weaker states appealing to the strong.[40]

---

[36] Harris 1979: 197.

[37] Cf. Badian 1964a: 4–5; Marasco 1986: 94–6.

[38] This is true whether the complaining victims of Illyrian violence were Italian and Italiote merchants, or (less likely, see above) the Greek city-state of Issa.

[39] Discussion in Eckstein 2006: Chs. 3, 5, and 7.

[40] Similarly, Corcyra and Epidamnus, when threatened by the Ardiaei in 229, appealed to the Aetolian League and the Achaean League for aid – and were answered in the affirmative (though the help ultimately failed) – in a totally Greek context.

The anarchic nature of the Mediterranean environment itself fostered such appeals for help, for in a world without international law and/or the means to enforce it, those who could not defend themselves against violence by their own power had no option but to call upon the power of the more powerful for help. Such appeals were not always answered positively (previous complaints from the merchants about the Illyrians had led to no action by the Senate, and Saguntum in Spain would have a similar experience with the Senate in the late 220s).[41] But strong pressures existed on any powerful state to answer pleas for help positively: refusal to help might be seen as indicating geopolitical or military weakness – a dangerous step in an anarchy – as well as a sign to some other power that it could take one's place in a possibly significant region. Hence the pressures on a governing elite to run the political and military risks of answering a plea for help were stronger than the pressures pushing them towards running the geopolitical risks in not answering a plea for help. And those pressures to answer positively – like the pressures which drove the weak to ask for protection in the first place – were widespread, and derived in great part from the unforgiving nature of the anarchic system itself.[42]

The persistent pattern of appeals of the weak to great powers for protection was a type of conduct apparent already to Herodotus and Thucydides in the fifth century BC – and these writers already stressed its danger, for such pleas could lead to clashes among the larger powers themselves.[43] The Roman Senate, in responding to appeals arising from the greatly intensifying Illyrian attacks, was thus acting and taking risks within the logic of the anarchic system in which it existed; and both the Aetolian League and the Achaean League acted similarly, taking similar risks within a similar system.[44]

Nor would the Senate have gotten involved in Illyria in 230/229 *without* such urgent appeals for help (perhaps coupled with dire warnings). Illyria and its polities were little known to the *Patres* (though there had

[41]   On the appeals for help from Saguntum, originally rejected by the Senate: see Polyb. 3.15.1.
[42]   On the pressures generated by the anarchic system which pushed powerful states to respond to appeals for help from weaker states, see conveniently Eckstein 2000: 877–8.
[43]   The classic case is the positive response of the Athenians in 433 to the request for help from Corcyra when Corcyra was threatened by Corinth – a response which ultimately led to an Athenian conflict with Corinth and then to the Peloponnesian War (see Thuc. 1.24–55). The destabilizing impact of successful appeals from the weak to the strong upon the relations between great powers in the third-century BC western Mediterranean: see the comments of Hoyos 1998: 33–46 and 196–218.
[44]   On the functional similarity (sameness) of states as they operate under the pressures of anarchy, as adduced by Waltz ("the sameness effect"), see above, Chapter 1, at nn. 17–18 and 50.

been a brief contact with Apollonia); and in 230/229 Rome faced severe military problems within Italy itself. Roman fear of a massive Celtic attack from the Po Valley into central Italy had arisen in the mid-230s, because of new Celtic pressure on the Latin colony of Ariminum, which blocked the northern end of the traditional Celtic invasion route into the Roman heartland. These fears intensified in the early 220s. They are evident in the plan of 232 to distribute land near Ariminum to large numbers of Roman citizens, adding an additional bulwark against the northern threat; they are evident as well in the human sacrifices at Rome performed in 228 in order to protect the city from capture by the Celts. The Senate was correct to be worried: the massive Celtic invasion of central Italy finally came in 225, and though it was defeated at the great battle of Telamon in Etruria, Polybius stresses the seriousness of the danger which Rome and all Italy at that time had faced (2.35). Under these circumstances, there would have been little internal push ca. 230 for the Senate to get involved overseas in Illyria.[45]

No doubt the Senate responded to the pleas of the merchants knowing that war with the Ardiaei might ensue. But before one argues that this shows exceptional Roman belligerence,[46] remember that the Aetolian and Achaean Leagues answered Greek pleas for help against the Ardiaei by themselves sending a large army into Epirus in 230, and that in 229 – just as the Roman fleet was arriving – the Aetolians and Achaeans responded to new pleas by despatching a unified fleet of their own to maritime Illyris, whose purpose was to save Corcyra, and then to relieve Apollonia and Epidamnus much farther north (2.9.8–9). Once more, the pattern of action of the major states was the same.

Moreover, despite their military failures against the Illyrians in these years, the Aetolians apparently reaped a significant territorial reward from their military intervention in the northwest. Ambracia, an important city on the Adriatic coast and the capital of the kings of Epirus before the revolution of 233/232, was a member of the Aetolian League by the mid-220s, along with the region of Amphilochia immediately to its east.[47] Both Ambracia and Amphilochia were prosperous, and their acquisition extended the strategic boundaries of Aetolia to the Adriatic. Scholars

---

[45] On the growing Celtic crisis from the mid-230s, see Eckstein 1982; see esp. Polyb. 2.22.7–8 on the fears at Rome. On how the massive Celtic invasion of Italy led the Italian allies of Rome to feel that they were fighting on behalf of civilization itself, see Polyb. 2.23.12 with Williams 2001: 130, cf. 174.

[46] So Harris 1979: 196–7.

[47] Amphilochia a member of the Aetolian League by 223/222: *IG* ix².1.31, line 83. We only hear of Ambracia as a member of the League when Philip attacked it in 219 (Polyb. 4.61.1), but one can presume that it had joined at the same time as neighboring Amphilochia.

agree that they probably entered the League as a result of the Aetolian intervention in 231–229.[48] The acquisition of Ambracia and Amphilochia demonstrates the Aetolians' own expansionist impulse towards the northwest – already apparent in the siege of Medion in 232. That was the way the Hellenistic world worked: in an anarchy, every state wants increased power, for (at the least) it means increased control over a threatening environment.

The initial senatorial reaction to the new pleas of the merchants for help against the Ardiaei was not military, but diplomatic: an embassy was sent in 230 to Illyria to investigate the situation.[49] King Agron had meanwhile died, and his senior wife Teuta now ruled as regent for the infant Pinnes, Agron's son by another wife. The Roman envoys complained to Teuta about Ardiaean piracy and demanded that it end (Polyb. 2.8.6). This demand was not negotiable; the Illyrians had a chance to comply peaceably – but on pain of war if they did not. Roman diplomatic conduct here was harsh, and characteristically so.[50] But this does not mean that Rome was *exceptionally* harsh. We do not know if the Aetolians or Achaeans even bothered with diplomacy in 230 before taking the field against the Ardiaei. But if they did, the talks failed – which puts the Roman failure into perspective. That is: rather than being an example of exceptional diplomatic harshness, the Roman embassy to Teuta was typical. In fact, it was an example of the "compellence diplomacy" engaged in habitually by *all* major states in the ancient Mediterranean.[51]

Polybius blames both Teuta and the envoys for the angry tone and eventual failure of the talks (2.8.9–12). But this sort of angry scene was – again – all too typical of ancient diplomatic interactions.[52] The concessions that Teuta as regent of the Ardiaei could or would give Rome regarding Ardiaean piracy were limited, apparently because of the limited control that Ardiaean rulers exercised over private Ardiaean piratical enterprise; and these concessions were not enough for the Roman envoys. The clash of interests was real, and not readily resolvable under ancient diplomacy: the end of piratical behavior, demanded by the Romans, was not something the Ardiaean regime could or

---

[48]   Niese 1899: 267 and n. 6; Cabanes 1976: 201; most recently Scholten 2000: 151 and n. 81.
[49]   Polyb. 2. 8.3–13; App. *Ill.* 7; Dio frg. 19.45 = Zon. 8.19.
[50]   Emphasized esp. by Badian 1964a: 3–5.
[51]   On the habit of "compellence diplomacy" in the Hellenistic Mediterranean and its contribution to an overall atmosphere of distrust and coercion among states, see above, Chapter 1; cf. Eckstein 2006: Ch. 3.
[52]   See Eckstein 2006: Chs. 3, 4, and 5, for multiple examples. The basic discussion (focused on incidents among the Greeks): Grant 1965.

would promise (2.8.8–11).[53] Ancient sources allege that Teuta became so enraged by the Roman embassy that she had one of the Roman envoys murdered – though it is possible that the envoys' ship simply fell foul of the Illyrian piracy that Teuta declared she could not control (cf. Polyb. 2.8.8). In either case, the incident shows the turbulent situation in the Adriatic. The death of one of the Roman envoys now made war inevitable.[54]

The large Roman expedition against the Illyrians that followed, in summer 229, was a complete success from south to north. Demetrius of Pharos, Teuta's governor on recently conquered Corcyra, went over to the Romans; her forces were defeated in the field; the Greek cities on the Adriatic coast sided with Rome; so did important inland tribes. By spring 228 Teuta had sworn a peace treaty with Rome that broke her kingdom into pieces and forbade Illyrian piratical forays into the southern Adriatic.[55]

Soon after the victory, the Roman commander in Illyria sent envoys to both the Aetolians and the Achaeans, announcing the end of the Illyrian threat (Polyb. 2.12.4–6). After the peace treaty was sworn in 228, the Senate sent new envoys on the same mission, with Athens now included on the itinerary (2.12.8). Polybius says the Roman envoys were greeted warmly – for Rome had delivered the Greeks from their increasing fear of the Illyrians (2.12.6). Perhaps this story of the warm reception given the Roman envoys derives from a propagandistic account of the war and its aftermath by Q. Fabius Pictor, a senator and contemporary of these events who wrote a history in Greek depicting Rome as a civilized power.[56] Yet at 2.6.8 Polybius stresses the growing Greek fear of the Illyrians in a narrative of purely Greek events based on Greek sources, not Pictor. The fact was that the military endeavors by Greek states against the Ardiaei in 231, 230, and 229 had all failed. Thus if Polyb. 2.12.6 is not Polybius' personal judgment on why the Roman envoys were welcomed in Greece, but Fabius' judgment, one can still see why it was a judgment Polybius accepted. At Corinth (a member-state of the Achaean League) the senatorial envoys were even admitted as participants in the Isthmian Games: that is, they were accepted as honorary Greeks.[57]

---

[53] Cf. Marasco 1986: 83.
[54] The tradition: Polyb. 2.8.9–13; variants at App. *Ill.* 6; Dio frg. 19.45 = Zon. 8.19. See the sensible discussion of Gruen 1984: 360–1.
[55] For the details of the settlement, see below.
[56] On Pictor's ideology and intentions, see Dillery 2002; cf. the collection of texts and testimonia in Beck and Walter 2001: 55–136.
[57] Polyb. 2.12.8; cf. Zon. 8.19.

ROMAN RELATIONS ON THE ADRIATIC COAST AFTER THE FIRST ILLYRIAN WAR

The diplomatic missions of 229 and 228 bespeak a senatorial interest in affecting public opinion in European Greece, a perception of an advantage to Rome in gaining a good reputation among the Greek states as a protector against barbarian depredations. Yet the only official interaction with the Greek world which we know of during the next twelve years is the dedication of a large golden bowl at Delphi as a thanksgiving offering to Apollo for the Roman victory over the Celtic invaders of central Italy in the war of 225–222 – which would convey the same antibarbarian theme (Plut. *Marc.* 8.6). In addition, M. Claudius Marcellus ca. 221 made personal thanksgiving dedications at the temple of the Cabeiri on Samothrace and at the temple of Athena on Lindos on Rhodes – but this was not an act of the Roman state.[58] This apparent lack of Roman attention to the Greek world forms the context for discussion of Roman relations with those Greek states and inland tribes that had gone over to Rome in maritime Illyris in 229/228. The subject is controversial, yet crucial to our understanding of early Roman ambitions and interests across the Adriatic.

In 229/228 the Romans rearranged relations on the coast of Illyria to suit themselves – a classic imperialist action. They created relations with Greek towns and indigenous tribes, relations determined by Roman decision; and – again solely by Roman decision – they restricted the power of the Ardiaei. The Senate also established Demetrius of Pharos, a lieutenant of Teuta who had gone over to the Romans in 229, as an independent ruler: communities were simply handed over to him by Roman fiat (Polyb. 2.11.17; App. *Illyr.* 7).[59]

The situation of external hegemony over the polities of maritime Illyris would probably have been little different if the Aetolians and/or Achaeans, rather than the Romans, had been decisively victorious on the battlefield against the Ardiaei. The proof is that even despite military failure, the chaos of 231–229 led to the outright absorption of Ambracia and

---

[58] The senatorial dedication of the great golden bowl at Delphi after the defeat of the Celts in the mid-220s is the first historically certain Roman contact with Delphi: see Gruen 1990: 9 and n. 10. Marcellus' dedication on Samothrace and at Lindos: Plut. *Marc.* 30.4. The latter act need not be taken as indicating specially good official relations between Rome and Rhodes (see below, Chapter 3).

[59] No doubt the Senate decided on the Illyrian arrangements upon the advice of the consul Cn. Fulvius Centumalus, who had returned to Rome from Illyria, where his colleague remained on watch against the Ardiaei (cf. Polyb. 2.12.1).

Amphilochia into the Aetolian League.[60] But scholars early on asserted that the Senate in 228 went farther than informal hegemony, and established a formal Roman "protectorate" in and over Illyria. A map in the first edition of the *Cambridge Ancient History*, for instance, depicts "the protectorate" as a region 120 miles long, with formal frontiers extending 40 miles inland. Even when the hypothesis was dropped that Roman supervisory agents were present in the Illyrian polities,[61] this understanding of the postwar situation long held sway.[62]

Then Ernst Badian, in a famous study, attacked the idea of a formal "protectorate": the area of Roman influence was very limited, and there is no evidence anywhere of Roman ships or troops or administration. Badian proposed instead that the polities of maritime Illyris were linked to Rome after 229/228 by mere informal "friendship" (*amicitia*; Greek: *philia*). Yet he also argued that beneath this informal *amicitia* lurked an equally informal but binding relationship of *officium* ("duty") owed to Rome because of the *beneficia* ("favors") the Romans had performed for these polities in 229/228: ridding them of the Ardiaei and/or accepting them into Roman *fides* ("good faith"). Badian also held that the resulting interstate relationship was modeled on the Roman institution of *clientela*, whereby the weak within Roman society gave themselves into the informal protection of the powerful, and were thus protected – as long as they obeyed. Thus the Illyrian polities in 229/228, including what was left of the Ardiaean kingdom, all became literal client states of the Republic. And because of the severely hierarchical nature of the *clientela* relationship, the freedom of action of these polities in interstate politics henceforth became informally circumscribed by Rome's will. On such a view, "*amicitia* signified not so much collaboration as inferiority and subjection."[63]

Badian's hypothesis of "client states" in Illyria linked tightly to Rome by informal "obligation" was certainly a step forward from the idea of a formal postwar Roman "protectorate" in Illyria. It was also part of a larger vision of how Roman power was exercised in the East over the next 150 years: through the projection into the external world of the hierarchical Roman social institution of *clientela*. This hypothesis has been

---

[60]   See above, pp. 39–40.

[61]   This was alleged by Colin 1905: 26, but there is simply no evidence for it: see Larsen 1935: 198 n. 28.

[62]   Holleaux 1928: 836; a similar map in Walbank 1940: 19; cf. Larsen 1935: 199.

[63]   *Amicitia* in Illyria: Badian 1964a (originally 1952): 1–33. The *amicitia* established with Teuta in the name of Pinnes in 228: App. *Illyr.* 7 (explicit). The quote: Gruen 1984: 54.

very influential.[64] Nevertheless, the position taken in the present study is one of dissent.[65]

This is because the idea that Rome exercised informal power as patron over states that the Senate viewed as clients, which is alleged as the basis of Roman foreign relations for fully two centuries after ca. 265 BC, has left no convincing trace in our ancient evidence. The sole ancient reference to *patrocinium* and *clientela* in the context of Roman–Greek inter-state relations is Livy 37.54.17; and that passage cannot be pressed because it is just a clumsy translation of the original passage in Polybius (21.23) which has only ἐξουσία (Roman "authority").[66]

What we find in the sources instead are innumerable references to relationships of *amicitia* or *philia* – i.e., "friendship" – among states. Badian was well aware of this problem, and argued that *amiticia* or *philia* were mere euphemisms, politely covering the dependency which clientage imposed upon the weaker partner.[67] But this in turn requires significant evidence that foreign "friendship" was understood at Rome and by foreign states to be a euphemism for clientship; and there are hardly any such ancient statements – far fewer than one would expect if clientship was pervasive in the Roman treatment of foreign states.[68] Indeed, Cicero indicates that within Roman society such euphemism did not occur, and that, on the contrary, the creation of too unequal a relationship led Romans to apply the term *clientela* quickly and bluntly; hence Roman aristocrats were leery of accepting too many favors.[69] Moreover, our sources describe the relationships between Rome and its foreign "friends" using the emotive language typical of real friendships within Roman society, rather than the sternly legalistic language typical of *clientela*.[70] Thus it

---

[64]   For the crucial importance of *clientela* in Roman thinking about the external world in general, see Badian 1958a: esp. 41–2, 53–4, and 113, restated in Badian 1968: 14 and 93 n. 1, and again in Badian 1983: 408. Badian is followed by, e.g., Dahlheim 1968: 265–74 and Dahlheim 1977: 198–206; Errington 1972; Cimma 1976: 146–56; Edlund 1977; Briscoe 1981: esp. 382; Mandell 1989, cf. Wallace-Hadrill 1989a: 74–5. The issue will come up again, on a larger scale, in Chapters 7 and 9 below, but it is best to deal with it in detail here.

[65]   In this I follow Bleicken 1964; Gruen 1984: 158–200; Rich 1989; Burton 2003.

[66]   See Gruen 1984: 176–7, and now Burton 2003: 334 n. 7 and 356–7, decisive against, e.g., Briscoe 1981: 282 or Mandell 1989: 90. Four surviving inscriptions mention the personal patronage of individual Romans over foreign communities, but this is not the same as *clientela* of one state to another: see Badian 1958a: 156–7.

[67]   See Badian 1958a: 7 and 12–13.

[68]   See now Burton 2003: esp. 342 and n. 54. Note, for instance, that though Polybius well understands and records the Roman institution of hereditary patronage by a powerful Roman family for a foreign community (29.21.12: he calls it *prostasia*), he never speaks of a collective patronage of the Roman Republic over a foreign community: see Ferrary 1988: 118.

[69]   See Cic. *de Off.* 2.69, with the comments of Burton 2003: 342.

[70]   A point strongly made by Burton 2003: 354–6 (example: Syracuse), and 363 and 365 (example: Rhodes).

seems safer to take the ancient sources at their word: *amicitia* or *philia* means "friendship," and is not a euphemism or subterfuge for a far more hierarchical clientage which everyone understood bound the weaker partner to strict obedience.[71]

But if the Romans merely established in Illyria in 229/228 a series of informal friendships with various polities, how, then, was informal Roman hegemony exercised or enforced? In contrast to Badian's *clientela* relationship which informally but effectively restricted the actions of client states, Petzold argues that the polities of the region were free after 229/228 to conduct themselves much as they had done before – primarily on the basis of self-interest and *Machtpolitik*. That is, they were completely independent states, and behaved that way – though Roman power was now the most important factor in their political calculations.[72]

A wider-held scholarly opinion, however, now argues that Badian's view, rather than overstating the scope of Roman dominance in Illyria after 228 (as Petzold holds), actually understates it. Thus Ferrary, while accepting that the Adriatic polities were linked to Rome only by informal *amicitia*, argues from their apparent failure to speak for themselves in two important treaties that they simultaneously were officially regarded – by themselves, by the Romans, and by others – as subjects of Rome.[73] And Hammond, while emphasizing that the Adriatic *amici* were few and far between (see below), describes those few as under Rome's "direct control," the Greek coastal cities as "the zone of direct dependence on Rome," and Demetrius of Pharos' principality as the frontier zone "between Teuta and Rome." Indeed, Hammond considers the term "protectorate" to be itself merely a euphemism for the total subjugation of these places to Rome.[74]

Most striking in this respect has been the reconstruction of P. S. Derow. On the basis of a fragmentary inscription from the island of Hvar (ancient Pharos, off the Illyrian coast), which appears to refer briefly to the renewal of an "alliance" (συμμαχία) between Rome and Pharos, Derow proposes that a formal treaty of alliance between Rome and Pharos was sworn very early on, in 229/228 BC, and was then renewed in 219. He then argues that this alleged treaty of alliance was one of a series of formal treaties of alliance that Rome created right after the First Illyrian War with the Greek coastal cities of Illyria, and perhaps with some inland tribes as well. Such treaties would have formally forbade both parties to give aid (with specifics listed) to the enemies of the other party, while legally binding both parties to give aid to each other in case of war. But,

---

[71]   Cf. esp. Gruen 1984: 158–200; Burton 2003.
[72]   Petzold 1971: 214–15.
[73]   Ferrary 1988: 24–33, esp. 31–3.
[74]   Hammond 1968: 7–9, *passim*, and 1989: 23. So too Wilkes 1992: 162.

Derow asserts, one must not be misled by the language of mutual obligation; in reality all these polities were now required by treaty to support
Rome militarily in all future wars – and to support Rome diplomatically
between wars. That is, from 229/228 they were sworn permanently into
formal subjugation to Roman interests.[75]

Such an interpretation of the Pharos inscription would strongly support
W. V. Harris that Rome from the start of its cross-Adriatic relations was
aggressively expanding its power in the East. If already by 228 BC Rome
had concluded half a dozen or more formal treaties of alliance with
polities in Illyria, this would have created legal connections and concrete Roman interests east of the Adriatic at the earliest point when such
connections and interests could have been created. Derow's view of
the Pharos inscription has been influential, and Derow and those who
follow him are explicit that his thesis regarding the inscription supports
a general picture of an extraordinarily aggressive Rome, intent on
establishing from early on a real empire east of the Adriatic.[76]

This inscription, however, cannot bear the great political weight that
has been put on it. That is: though the Senate was assertive in Illyria
in 229/228, we should not, based on this inscription, accept a reconstruction of the postwar situation in which Roman control and concrete
interests existed on a permanent legal basis through sworn treaties.
I have dealt with this issue in detail elsewhere, and will simply summarize here.[77]

First, the date of the Pharos inscription is uncertain; it could have
been inscribed at any point from the late third century down into the
middle of the second century BC. But if the inscription is as late as 150
BC, it obviously would have no bearing on the earliest Roman involvement in Illyria.[78] Second, whatever its date, it is not clear that the inscription refers to a formal treaty of alliance. When the Senate and People
of Rome are first introduced on the inscription (Part A, lines 3–4), they
appear merely as "friends" of Pharos (φίλοι) – not formal allies. A reference to "alliance" does appear at lines 9–10 (συμμ[.......]), but the next
part of the text is lost, and this could be a reference not to a treaty of
alliance, but merely to informal "friendship and alliance": συμμαχία καὶ
φιλία, a translation of the Latin amicitia et societas. This latter phrase,

---

[75]   Derow 1991: 267–70, citing for the terms of such treaties the new inscription
recording the alliance between Rome and the Greek city of Maroneia in Thrace,
dated to the 160s BC.
[76]   See Derow 1991: 268–70; Coppola 1993: 105–27; Heftner 1997: 186, cf. 137;
Habicht 1997: 185, cf. 189 and 194.
[77]   See Eckstein 1999.
[78]   The problem was realized by Robert 1960: 539–40. Cf. also Eckstein 1999: 401–2.

though sometimes indicating a formal alliance, is most often merely a polite way of expressing informal friendship. In support of this interpretation is that we have no evidence of Roman treaties of alliance with any of the polities in Illyria even from much later periods under the Republic; for instance, Epidamnus, one of the cities that went over to Rome in 229 BC and a far more important place than Pharos, still possessed in the 40s BC merely informal *amicitia et societas* with Rome – not a treaty (Cic. *Fam.* 14.1.7).[79] Finally, the Pharos inscription indicates that the previous relationship between Pharos and Rome (whatever it was) now was being *renewed* (A, lines 3–10), and Derow suggests that this is an event of 219/218 BC – and hence that the original "treaty" dates to 229/228.[80] But the hypothesis of a *renewal* of a treaty of alliance between the Pharians and Rome in 219/218 BC is impossible. This is because at the alleged original time of the striking of this formal treaty, in 229/228, the Pharians were not an independent polity, and thus could not have sworn a treaty of alliance, or any sort of treaty, with anyone. The Pharians in 229/228 were the subjects of Demetrius of Pharos, who had sided with the Romans in the First Illyrian War and gained for himself a principality along the Illyrian coast. And Demetrius himself only had a relationship of informal *amicitia* with Rome (Dio frg. 53 = Zon. 8.19; cf. Polyb. 3.16.4). Pharos was Demetrius' chief possession: Polybius at 5.108.7 is perfectly explicit about that. Demetrius as an independent ruler might have sworn a treaty of alliance with Rome – though he did not; but the Pharians were not an independent entity in the 220s but Demetrius' subjects; they could not have done so.[81]

So the Pharians, historically, did not have a treaty of alliance with Rome – only *amicitia*. The friendship could have been established in any number of ways, depending on the date of the inscription (which, again, cannot be determined within a span of seventy years).[82] But with the idea eliminated that Pharos had a formal treaty of alliance with Rome dating from 229/228 BC, so too collapses the idea of widespread formal treaties of alliance in the 220s between Rome and the Illyrian polities.

---

[79] Diplomatic meaning of *amicitia et societas*: Eckstein 1999: 405–11. That this phrase (= συμμαχία καὶ φιλία) often meant something far vaguer than treaty relations was shown long ago by Sands 1908: 10–48 and 163–228. The example of Epidamnus: rightly stressed by Ferrary 1988: 30–1. The strategic importance of Epidamnus: Hammond 1968: 2 and 4.

[80] Derow 1991: esp. 265–6.

[81] Pharos as Demetrius' chief possession in 229–219, not an independent state: see Eckstein 1999: 411–15.

[82] Discussion of the possibilities: Eckstein 1999: 416. The fundamental study of the multiple ways by which *amicitia* could be established between Rome and a foreign polity remains Heuss 1933: 26–52 and 79–83.

Pharos cannot serve as an example of such a treaty, and there are no other possible examples in the evidence. We are left, rather, with the multiple references in our sources to Roman relationships of mere informal φιλία/amicitia along the Adriatic coast.

Ferrary accepts that the Adriatic polities had only informal amicitia with Rome. But as we have seen (above, p. 45), he still sees a postwar situation of formal and explicit Roman domination: as evidence, he points to the absence of these states from the treaty of alliance sworn by Rome and the Aetolian League against Macedon in 212/211 (Livy 26.24.12–13), as well as their absence from the treaty ending the war in 205 (29.12.14). This is indeed odd: other Greek states are listed; the origins of the war lay in Philip V's clash with Rome after 217 precisely over control of Illyria (see below, Chapter 3); and there was fighting near Apollonia right in 205 (Livy 29.12.6–7). Meanwhile, Pleuratus the king of the Ardiaei is attested as a swearer on the Roman side both in 212/211 and in 205 (24.40.12; 29.12.14). Ferrary suggests that Pleuratus' status was more independent than that of the Adriatic polities, and that by 212/211 if not well before, those states, though amici of Rome, had somehow formally come in dicio populi Romani – under Roman legal control. Hence they were deprived of the right to independent foreign relations, and this accounts for their absence from the treaties.[83]

If the polities of maritime Illyris came formally and early in dicio populi Romani, this would once again show – as with the thesis of Derow – an early aggressive Roman desire for continuous control over certain states in the East. But we should be wary of drawing far-reaching conclusions from the mysterious absence of the Adriatic polities from the accounts we possess of the treaties of 212/211 and 205. First, we do not have the complete texts of the treaties, but only summaries of the treaties from the literary historians. Second, the absence of free allies from agreements between major states is not unprecedented in Mediterranean antiquity. Thus Thucydides gives the direct text of a year-long truce sworn between Sparta and Athens in 424 BC – not a mere summary, as we have of the treaties of 212/211 and 205 – and it includes on the Spartan side envoys from Corinth, Megara, Epidaurus, and Sicyon, who swear to this truce (4.119). But it would be incorrect to conclude from the mysterious absence of (say) Tegea and Mantinea from this treaty, while other states are co-swearers, that by 424 these cities had fallen under direct Spartan rule. On the contrary: Tegea and Mantinea were independent members of the Peloponnesian League – so independent

---

[83]   Ferrary 1988: 32–3. Livy's account of the treaty of alliance does have a phrase referring to states in dicio (26.24.12), but it is not clear who is meant. See the opposing interpretations of Ferrary 1988: 32–3 vs. Petzold 1971: 215 n. 75.

that they were fighting their own local wars in the central Peloponnese at this time with the help of their own allies (Thuc. 4.134). Their absence from the truce of 424 reveals nothing. Or to take a Roman example: Philip V of Macedon fought on the Roman side against Antiochus III in 191–188 BC, yet he is absent from the summaries we possess of the peace treaty sworn between Rome and Antiochus in 188 – whereas Pergamum, another monarchy that fought on Rome's side, is such a swearer. But the absence of Macedon here tells us nothing about the legal status of Macedon in regard to Rome, and does not at all mean that Macedon, as opposed to Pergamum, had now fallen *in dicio populi Romani*. On the contrary: Macedon after 196 was an independent state possessing (it seems) informal friendship (*amicitia*) with Rome – while Philip in 191 had made an agreement with the Romans by which he entered the war against Antiochus on the Roman side, and under which he would gain territorially (Livy 39.23.10 – from Polybius).[84] In fact, it was not unusual in Mediterranean antiquity for envoys to be sent to allied states after the formal swearing of treaties of peace between the principals, to procure their separate swearing after the fact (see Thuc. 5.21–2; 5.77.8). The same process sometimes occurred with treaties of alliance (see Thuc. 5.47–8, where one already allied state, unmentioned in a new and broader treaty of alliance, is visited later by envoys of the principals to gain its separate adherence to the new treaty).

These cases weaken the large political conclusions Ferrary attempts to draw from the absence of the Illyriote polities from the versions we have of the treaties of 212/211 and 205. And here we should note another Illyriote absence. Polybius' account of this period provides his audience with four harshly anti-Roman speeches by Greek statesmen. The speakers accuse Rome of enslaving Greek states they had originally claimed to be helping against a third party, and they accuse Rome of intending to impose such a domination upon all of European Greece. The third and fourth speeches (set in 207 BC and then in 199 BC) are given before an audience of Aetolians – and the Aetolian League, as we have seen, had a strong interest in the political situation in maritime Illyris, and its elite would have been keenly aware of conditions there.[85] As proof of Roman perfidy, the speakers in these speeches list Greek cities that once were free but now are subjugated to Rome – an enslavement shown

---

[84]   On the nature of the informal *amicitia* between Rome and Macedon after 196, see Gruen 1973: 123–36. On the agreement of Philip to enter the war against Antiochus on the Roman side, see Walbank 1940: 207 and 227. Among Philip's other territorial gains was the great fortress-city of Demetrias in Magnesia, one of the traditional "Three Fetters of Greece": see Walbank 1940: 228–9.

[85]   The speeches: in 210 BC (Polyb. 9.32–9, esp. 38–9); 209 BC (10.25); 207 BC (11.4–6); and 199 BC (Livy 31.29.4–16; Polybian origin: see next note).

especially by Roman control over their foreign relations. The Greek cities listed are Messana, Lilybaeum, and Syracuse in Sicily, and Rhegium and Tarentum in Italy (Livy 31.29.8–10: from Polybius).[86] What is striking in this list, if Ferrary is correct, is the absence of the Greek cities of Illyria. Yet the Illyriote cities were on the Greek side of the Adriatic, much closer than the cities of Italy or Sicily – thus showing how near the danger of Roman domination had come; they were polities that the Romans had originally claimed to be aiding (against the Ardiaei), so that they fit the paradigm of Roman perfidy being asserted; and they occupied a region in which the Aetolians had a strong interest. It is hard to believe that if these cities had now fallen formally *in dicio populi Romani*, their fate would have been ignored: why mention distant Lilybaeum, at the far western tip of Sicily, when one could mention nearby Corcyra? If the Illyriote polities had been legally enslaved to the Romans for the previous twenty-five years, this would have been too vivid an example of Roman aggression to pass up in an Aetolian setting. Moreover, Polybius himself, essentially the composer of these speeches, was clearly very interested in Roman doings in Illyria, and, equally, it was his decision to put into the *Histories* these warnings of Rome's possible domination. That makes the absence of the Illyriotes here even more strange – if Ferrary is correct. So perhaps the answer is that the situation in maritime Illyris was actually not a striking example of Roman oppression of Greek cities and seizure of legal control over them.[87]

One may add that in the latter part of the Pharos inscription, the Pharians engage in important diplomacy with their mother-city Paros in order to replenish their population with new colonists, and Paros responds positively on this crucial matter, all without reference to Rome. The Pharians seek Parian aid on their own and there is no evidence of them asking Roman permission (see A, lines 9–22); moreover, the Parians treat the Pharian envoys as the envoys of a respected independent state (see A, lines 22–41, and B, lines 4–12). The inscription dates from 219 BC at the earliest – but it could be several decades later. The Pharians do not appear to be under any formal Roman *dicio* here.[88]

The war of 229/228 greatly increased Roman influence along the Adriatic coast – this is a given, and not disputed. If the Aetolians and

[86]   Livy here based on Polybian material: see Briscoe 1973: 115.
[87]   On these speeches as a political statement by Polybius, see Eckstein 1999: 415; Champion 2004: 56–7.
[88]   See Eckstein 1999: 417–18. This is so even though the inscription indicates that some sort of serious trouble had led the Pharians to perform *deditio* (absolute surrender) to Rome – after which the Romans had reconstituted the polity: A, lines 5–10. That would suggest that Rome would subsequently have very significant influence at Pharos; but formal *dicio*, removing Pharos from the interstate sphere, is another matter.

the Achaeans had defeated the Ardiaei in 230 or 229, then *their* power and influence in the region would have correspondingly increased as well. That is the way the Hellenistic world worked. But our conclusion is that the "friends" of the Romans in Illyria were at least legally completely free (see App. *Illyr.* 8) – and legally free states not sternly bound to Rome by the informal Roman institution of *clientela*. The Romans in fact were comfortable with the concept of friendship between unequals: it occurred all the time within Roman society.[89] And so the governments of the free *amici* of the Republic on the Illyrian coast understood that the Romans were far more powerful than they were, and as long as Rome stayed strong they would likely cooperate in whatever the Romans wished, and not only for reasons of *Machtpolitik* (though these were obviously important) but also for reasons of good faith (*fides*) and evolving friendship – when, that is, the Romans actually wished something from them (which, as we will see, was rare). Real if unequal friendships such as this were not an ineffective way for the Romans to manage their chaotic interstate environment.[90]

Did Rome in 229/228 establish a "protectorate" over these friends as a group? This early hypothesis still has its advocates.[91] The term "protectorate" dates from late nineteenth-century European colonialism, and its "imperialistic" connotations explain its attractiveness for modern scholars describing Roman relations in Illyria. But the term has a specific definition, which it would be unwise to ignore. Working from late nineteenth-century geopolitics, political scientists define a "protectorate" as a bordered political space that has lost both its sovereignty as a whole and its internal administration into the control of an imperial power.[92]

This description does not fit maritime Illyris. The Adriatic polities did not lose their legal sovereignty and were not *in dicio populi Romani* (see above). Under the peace of 228, Queen Teuta as regent for her

---

[89] See Burton 2003.
[90] Ibid.: 334 and 365. On the Roman concept of interstate *libertas* within a situation of hierarchy, see also Yoshimura 1984 (discussed below, Ch. 8). The Greeks, of course, understood from their own experience how such friendships between the more powerful and less powerful states worked: see Gruen 1984: 69–76; Ma 1999/2002: Chs. 3 and 4.
[91] See above, p. 45 and n. 74.
[92] Origins and meaning of the term "protectorate": see Abernethy 1986: 109; Taylor 1994: 151–62. Note that states under a protectorate so conceived, because they have lost their sovereignty, have "no international capacity at all": Lowes Dickenson 1926: 241; cf. Donnelly 2006: 149. In this sense, Ferrary 1988 – who thinks most Illyrian polities had no "international capacity" after 219 (see above, p. 45) – is essentially on the side of those who conceive of maritime Illyris as being a Roman protectorate. Of course, we have argued that Ferrary is incorrect on this point.

stepson Pinnes did swear that the Ardiaei would not sail south of the Lissus River for war. This shows the main Roman concern in the region – to protect Italian merchants in the Straits of Otranto from Ardiaean piracy. But, except for Issa, the Lissus was also north of the polities that in 229/228 had come into Roman *amicitia* and *fides*. Thus the Lissus boundary meant that these places were now under indirect Roman protection, for an Ardiaean attack on them would, by crossing the Lissus, be a violation of the peace of 228. The coastal principality which the Senate gave to Demetrius of Pharos provided an additional protection; his holdings, located between the remnants of the Ardiaean kingdom and the Lissus, created a new barrier to Ardiaean movement towards the south.[93]

Yet it should be stressed that the number of polities brought under this indirect protection was small. The ancient evidence allows us to enumerate only six: the cities of Apollonia and Epidamnus; the islands of Corcyra and Issa; the tribes of the Parthini and the Atintani.[94] And they formed no contiguous strip of territory. Corcyra was separated from Apollonia to its north by 100 miles of coast where other polities existed but were not Roman *amici*. Apollonia, in turn, was separated from Epidamnus to its north by 60 miles of bleak coastline where there were no polities; and behind this coastline the inland plain flooded and became impassable both in spring and autumn.[95] Meanwhile, the island of Issa to the north was separated from Epidamnus by fully 250 miles of mountainous coast under Ardiaean overlordship. This is is not a contained and controlled political space. It is not a distinctive region that can be called a "protectorate."

Moreover, there were polities that Rome might have brought into association in 229/228 or in 219, but did not. Oricum, 30 miles south of Apollonia, had a fine harbor important for the sea route between Italy and Greece, and would have served as a useful link between Apollonia and Corcyra. Polybius knew its strategic importance (see Livy 24.40.17 with Polyb. 8.1). But Oricum does not appear in Polybius' account either of 229/228 or of 219, and it is missing from the Adriatic polities linked to Rome in the text of the treaty of alliance between Hannibal and Philip V of Macedon in 215 (Polyb. 7.9.13). Oricum thus appears to have been completely independent in the period 230–215; its relations with Rome began only in 214, and then on its own initiative – asking for protection

---

[93]   The peace treaty: Polyb. 2.12.3, cf. 2.11.17; App. *Ill.* 7. The Ardiaei were also to pay a war indemnity (Polyb. 2.12.3). The geographical principles behind the peace of 228: see esp. Hammond 1968: 7–9.

[94]   See Badian 1964a: 7 and 23–4.

[95]   The uninviting nature of the coastline: Hammond 1968: 1–2; the often impassible coastal plain: ibid.: 1.

when attacked by Philip (Livy 24.40.2).[96] The city of Aulon, north of Oricum, was similar: it had a fair harbor, and would have formed a useful link between Oricum and Apollonia, but the Romans established no relations with it in 229/228 or in 219, leaving it, too, a "neutral."[97] Roman interest in the inland tribes was limited also. Many tribes sent envoys to the Romans as they advanced up the Adriatic coast in 229, but only the Parthini and Atintani were received into Roman *amicitia* (Polyb. 2.11.11). Both tribes dwelt quite close to the coast near Epidamnus.[98] Again, whereas Apollonia was a Roman *amicus*, no links were established with the Hellenized Illyrian city-states of Byllis and Amantia, 25 miles up the Aous River from Apollonia; yet these towns dominated their sector of the crucial overland route from the Adriatic southeast through the Pindus mountains into central Greece.[99] Nor did Rome establish connections with the Dassareti, who had been under Ardiaean domination before 229 and who controlled the strategic high passes eastwards over the Pindus Range into Macedon: the Dassareti, like the towns of the middle Aous, like Oricum and Aulon on the coast, were left alone, neutral and independent, both in 229/228 and in 219.[100]

Roman indifference to these strategically important places needs to be underlined. The Senate *could* have created a coherent, contiguous stretch of Roman-dominated seaboard below the Lissus, extending at strategic points far inland – but it did not. The extension of Roman control up the middle Aous and up to the Pindus passes would have been the best way both to protect the coast and to serve as a potential military springboard southeast into central Greece and/or eastward into Macedon. But the Romans were not interested.[101] This fits with the fact that for a decade after 229/228 we know of no Roman troops or ships in Illyria, nor even any Roman diplomatic interaction with any Adriatic polity. It all suggests that early Roman concerns in maritime Illyria were minimal.

[96]   Apollonia appealed for help against Philip in 214 on the basis of her loyalty to Rome (Livy 24.40.7); the appeal of Oricum was separate, and no relationship was asserted (24.40.2): see esp. Badian 1964a: 23–4; cf. Hammond 1968: 7. The importance of the harbor at Oricum (and the Romans' use of it after 214): Hammond 1968: 11.

[97]   See Hammond 1968: 9.

[98]   Location of the Atintani near Epidamnus: Hammond 1967: 600 (with evidence), cf. Hammond 1968: 7–8. Preferable to the location suggested by Cabanes 1976: 78–80: see Hammond 1989: 11–25.

[99]   Importance of the Aous route from the Adriatic to Central Greece: Eckstein 1976: 133. On Byllis and Amantia, see Hammond 1989: 16–17 and 19–20.

[100]   See Hammond 1967: 232–3, cf. Hammond 1968: 8.

[101]   The geography: Hammond 1968: 15–21; cf. Dell 1967b: 99, and Dell 1973: 306–9.

Petzold has proposed that there was no Roman "protectorate" in Illyria at all, merely a series of informal Roman friendships with a few disparate and geographically scattered polities. Powerful additional arguments can be offered in favor of that hypothesis.[102]

First, all our sources, led by Polybius, merely give a list of separate polities that came over to the Romans in 229; there is no constituted coherent entity here.[103] Second, the section of the treaty of alliance of 215 between Hannibal and Philip V dealing with Illyria makes no reference to an organized Roman area of power – and this treaty comes after the *second* Roman intervention, in 219. Instead we find, again, merely a list of seven named and geographically separate polities (Polyb. 7.9.13).[104] Yet terminology was available: for instance, in the Roman–Punic peace treaty of 241 as Polybius gives it, the term *eparchia* denotes the area of Roman control in Sicily (Polyb. 3.27.4) – and this is fifteen years before Sicily became a formal Roman province.[105] But in 215 not even Philip and Hannibal – enemies of Rome – thought of Rome as possessing an *eparchia*, an organized "protectorate" on the Adriatic. Only modern scholars do.

Perhaps we should term Illyria after 229 merely a Roman "sphere of influence."[106] This term, too, derives from late nineteenth-century European imperialism (first attested in 1869), and denotes a vaguer political situation than "protectorate." But again, we need to be clear on the definition: "a definite region within which a single external power exerts a predominant influence which limits the independence or freedom of action of states within it," and this influence "prevails . . . against the influence of other comparable powers over the region."[107]

Is this concept better than "protectorate" to describe the facts on the ground in maritime Illyris after 229/228 BC? The Romans understood that it was possible to have real *amicitia* between unequal partners, and so the prevalence of *amicitia* with foreign states need not have been an ineffective means of exercising strong influence when Rome wished.[108] The question is how often Rome wished to exercise it.

---

[102]   Petzold 1971: 206 and 220–1, followed only by Gruen 1984: :78 and 367–8. Contra: Ferrary 1988: 24–8; Hammond 1989 (the "Roman protectorate" as a distinct political entity with Romans in control); Adams 1993: 44 ("protectorate" with "direct dependents" such as Apollonia); Habicht 1997: 189 (the Roman "protectorate" an organized "bridgehead," intended for offensive operations against Macedon).

[103]   Polyb. 2.11; App. *Illyr.* 7–8; Dio frg. 49 = Zon. 8.19.

[104]   The seventh *amicus* – Dimallum – was the result of the war of 219 (see below).

[105]   On the term *eparchia*, see Whittaker 1978: 62–3.

[106]   So, e.g., Errington 1972: 40.

[107]   See Keal 1986: 124–5.

[108]   Despite, e.g., Gruen 1984: 75; see Yoshimura 1984; Burton 2003.

Evidence suggests that the Romans felt they could assert political authority over their *amici* in Illyria – when they wished to assert it. Thus at 3.16.3 Polybius accuses Demetrius of Pharos of having before 219 BC ravaged Adriatic polities which were "drawn up under the Romans" (ὑπὸ 'Ρωμαίους ταττομένας). And in the treaty between Hannibal and Philip V in 215 the Romans are even called "masters" (*kurioi*) of the seven Adriatic polities (Polyb. 7.9.13).

The assertion in the Macedonian–Punic treaty could simply be anti-Roman propaganda.[109] The assertion at Polyb. 3.16.3 is more serious, for it is Polybius' personal judgment of the situation. Yet his language actually cannot be pressed very far. We find the same terminology employed to describe Punic hegemony in western Sicily before 400 BC: the Sicilian cities are "drawn up under the Carthaginians" (ὑπὸ Καρχηδονίους ταττομένας: Diod. 15.15.1). But Punic hegemony in western Sicily in this period was quite loose, the towns having significant independence and there being no Punic administrative apparatus, though the towns depended on Punic military power for survival, and viewed Carthage as their champion against local threats from the Greeks (Diod. 13.43.3–4). And if Carthage was a champion which it was unwise to cross, the fact is that even as late as the 340s the Carthaginians had to "court" the support of these polities (Diod. 16.67.1). Perhaps something similar to this highly ambiguous arrangement existed in maritime Illyris.[110]

We would be on better ground if our sources referred to the Adriatic states as ὑπήκοοι – outright subjects of Rome. Appian does say that in 229/228 some Adriatic cities became subjects of Rome (ὑπήκοοι) – but then were freed (*Illyr.* 7–8). If so, he is referring to the formal ceremonies of absolute surrender (*deditio*) that must have occurred as the Romans advanced up the coast in 229. But according to our sources, the Illyriote cities came over voluntarily – to protect themselves from the Ardiaei.[111] Such voluntary *deditio* to Rome to escape from a third party usually turned out well for the community involved, and that is clearly what happened here: the Romans declared the surrendered polities free (ἐλευθέρας: *Illyr.* 8); thereafter, they had informal "friendship" (φιλία) with Rome.[112] The independent coinage of these cities continued unabated;

[109]   See Gruen 1984: 386 n. 46.
[110]   Discussion of the Sicilian situation and the terminology employed to describe it: Whittaker 1978: 67–8.
[111]   Corcyra (Polyb. 2.11.5 – emphatic); Epidamnus (2.11.10); Issa (2.11.11); Apollonia (2.11.8). Also: App. *Illyr.* 7 and Dio frg. 53 = Zon. 8.19.
[112]   Corcyra: Polyb. 2.11.6; Epidamnus: App. *Illyr.* 7; the Parthini and Atintani: Polyb. 2.11.8. The taking of Apollonia and Issa into "good faith" (πίστις) is equivalent: Polyb. 2.11.8 and 12, with Gruen 1984: 367–8 and n. 44. No formal treaties of alliance: see above. Voluntary *deditio* to Rome leading to informal *amicitia*: see Heuss 1933: 78–83.

and some cities continued for centuries to have dependent states of their own.[113]

It therefore appears that – despite Ferrary – Rome recognized the legal independence of the Adriatic polities. True, legal independence is not the same as the real thing; yet it is also not a small thing. Political scientists argue that a dominant state's granting or assuming the legal sovereignty of subordinate states, even while this "masks the realities of power," is also a significant protective device for the smaller states, for it hinders the most blatant forms of penetration and control.[114] Indeed, in the same passage where Polybius charges that Demetrius of Pharos committed aggression against states "drawn up under the Romans," he says that Demetrius in the late 220s thought Roman power was on the wane (3.16.2). Since pro-Demetrius factions arose in many Illyriote cities in this period (3.18.1), elements within their governing elites must have shared Demetrius' perception.[115]

How could such a fluid political situation occur? Political scientists argue that under conditions of international anarchy, authority, in order to *be* authority, must be asserted – and asserted often. And "control," in order to *be* control, must be asserted – and asserted often.[116] Hence D. B. Abernethy puts two factors first in a dominant–subordinate relationship between states: (1) consistent and broad interaction, (2) with historical depth. Without these interactions, sheer imbalance in power remains only a potential factor in relations.[117] This conception holds especially well for relations between strong states and weaker states in the Hellenistic Mediterranean – where power was unstable, fluid, and constantly contested.[118] Here we arrive at the key to the elusive nature of early Roman relations with her Illyrian *amici*. The Romans could easily have asserted formal control in Illyria after 228 – but they did not; they could easily have asserted informal but effective patron-type power in Illyria after 228 – but they did not. There was no Roman administration; there were no troops; there were no Roman ships; the Illyriote *amici* were not used as naval bases (why should they have been?); we

---

[113]   Coinage: Petzold 1971: 215–16; Gruen 1984: 368. The coastal dependencies of Issa: Polyb. 32.9; cf. Sherk 1969: nos. 24A–B (49 BC).

[114]   See Abernethy 1986: 110; Donnelly 2006: 162–3. This insight requires some modification of the emphasis on the power of informal clientship asserted by Badian (above, this chapter), which is paired with his dismissal of the efficacy of legalities (see Badian 1958a: 144–6).

[115]   This is discussed in detail below, p. 60.

[116]   See Mommsen 1986: 336; Taylor 1994; cf. Thornton 1965: Ch. 2.

[117]   Abernethy 1986: 105–7.

[118]   See Ma 1999/2002: Chs. 3 and 4.

do not even hear of diplomatic interchanges. The Romans seem completely absent.[119]

This absence of Rome from Illyria has a significant corollary. Political scientists stress a third factor in the creation and maintenance of dominant–subordinate relations between states: the decision-makers in the weaker state must *regularly* take into account in their decisions the possible responses of the more powerful state.[120] By the late 220s this was not always happening in Illyria with regard to Rome: see Polyb. 3.18.1. The impression of Roman power gained by the Adriatic polities in 229 must have been very strong; but the impression was not stable over time. These states had gone over to Rome partly in the hope that Rome would provide a continual balance of power against threats from the Ardiaei or Demetrius, but they were soon disappointed. From their perspective, the problem in maritime Illyris was not too much Roman control, but too little.[121] And because informal friendship is not a stable relationship, but is always evolving, there soon emerged pro-Demetrius factions in the Illyrian polities.[122]

The key element in a "sphere of influence" is that one power has predominant influence over the polities within a geographical area, and allows no significant competitors.[123] Under this definition, if Rome established a *de facto* sphere of influence in Illyria in 229/228, it did not last long. This is because Roman involvement with its string of scattered *amici* along the Adriatic coast disappeared, while by the middle or late 220s Demetrius of Pharos had reunified the Ardiaean kingdom under his leadership, and had thus become a competitor with Rome for influence with the Adriatic polities (Polyb. 3.18.1).[124]

These conclusions are important for the general thesis of this study. The Roman Republic was an aggressive state, diplomatically assertive, militaristic in culture, and always ready for war – as was true of every other major power within the Mediterranean anarchic system in which Rome existed, true of all second-tier powers, and true even of many small states.[125] Thus if Illyria had been important to Rome, there is no doubt that the Romans would have firmly sought to control it. But Illyria

[119]   See Badian 1964a: 7. The statement of Hammond 1989: 23, that from 228 BC "Rome controlled Corcyra as a naval base," is without ancient evidence.
[120]   Abernethy 1986: 107.
[121]   See Polyb. 2.11.5 with Petzold 1971: 215; Gruen 1984: 368 and n. 45.
[122]   On *amicitia* as unstable and always evolving, see Burton 2003: esp. 338–9. A good example in the Roman case is the evolution and then abrupt end of Rome's friendship with Syracuse: ibid.: 352–8; cf. Eckstein 1980.
[123]   Keal 1986: 125–6.
[124]   Detailed discussion of the rise of Demetrius' power: see below.
[125]   See Eckstein 2006: esp. Chs. 4–7. On the mini-imperialisms of even small Hellenistic states, see the startling essay by Ma 2000.

in the 220s was not – or not yet – important to Rome. Thus the Republic exercised only the loosest of hegemonies in Illyria. This is probably because the main Roman goal in the war of 229/228 had simply been the suppression of Ardiaean piracy; with that goal accomplished, the *Patres* were satisfied. The minimal number of relationships established in the region, their informal character, and the subsequent decade-long lack of direct Roman involvement all support the thesis that the Roman goal on the Adriatic coast in the 220s was not to "control" Illyria. In fact, to judge from the lack of diplomatic interactions, nothing in the entire Greek East was as yet important to the Senate.[126]

THE RISE OF DEMETRIUS OF PHAROS

The primary threat to the autonomy of the Adriatic Greek cities came in the 220s not from Rome but from the expanding power of Demetrius of Pharos. Under the peace of 228, Rome had granted Demetrius a realm situated between the Greek cities and what was left of the Ardiaean kingdom. But Demetrius then married Triteuta the mother of the Ardiaean heir-apparent Pinnes, and thus became regent for Pinnes (cf. Dio frg. 53 = Zon. 8.20). And by reuniting the territories of his own principality with that of the Ardiaei, he succeeded in recreating the powerful Ardiaean kingdom that Rome had abolished in 229/228.

Badian suggests that this development actually occurred via agreement with Rome, perhaps as part of the peace of 228 itself, and that Demetrius' policy was thereafter to strengthen his own power without alienating or threatening the Romans.[127] But the idea that Demetrius became regent via the treaty of 228 runs counter to our sources on the treaty: none mentions the removal of Teuta as regent (something hard to miss), while Polybius has the treaty being sworn with her, as regent (2.12.3). The conclusion must be that Rome intended in 228 that Teuta should be regent of a reduced Ardiaean kingdom, and that Demetrius should be ruler of a separate principality. The idea was to fragment Illyrian power.[128]

Demetrius, apparently, soon subverted this arrangement – but there was no Roman response. The Senate's concern in the mid-220s was focused elsewhere, on the terrible threat to central Italy posed by

---

[126]   Cf. Errington 1989a: 90; cf. Gruen 1984: 364 and 367–8.
[127]   Petzold 1971: 9 and n. 34, and 15.
[128]   Hammond 1968: 7 and n. 24; Petzold 1971: 206; Errington 1989a: 91. Criticism of Badian: Petzold 1971: 206 and n. 51. Dio frg. 53 = Zon. 8.20 appears to have Demetrius becoming regent *before* the treaty of 228. This cannot stand against Polybius' report that the treaty was sworn between Rome and Teuta.

the Gallic tribes of the Po Valley. This invasion finally came in 225, and the subsequent massive war lasted until 222. Polybius says that Demetrius' success in overthrowing Teuta, combined with the Celtic war in Italy, led him to discount both Roman interest in Illyria and Roman power in general (3.16.2). Demetrius was correct about the first point. Meanwhile, in 222 Demetrius led his Illyrians to fight for the Macedonians in their victorious war against Sparta in the far-off southern Peloponnese (2.65.4 and 66.5) – the victory at Sellasia that established a new Macedonian hegemony over much of Greece. Demetrius is alleged to have now seen Macedon, not Rome, as the rising power (Polyb. 3.16.4), and his relations with the Antigonid House were good (3.16.3). But Macedon at this point, like Rome, had little interest in maritime Illyris. The way to power in Illyria thus seemed open.[129]

Polybius' judgment was that Demetrius' conduct was aggressive, even reckless. And there is no reason to doubt that Demetrius took extraordinary chances to increase his power.[130] Among the Illyrians a ruler needed to lead in successful warfare in order to gain widespread loyalty, so once Demetrius was regent of the Ardiaei, he would have faced pressures in an aggressive direction no matter what his personality.[131] But Demetrius clearly did not need much of a push. Polybius of course had on hand a harsh Roman version of Demetrius' behavior here (via Fabius Pictor), but he did not use Fabius naively.[132] Moreover, he had accounts of Demetrius' later career in Greece, from contemporaries of those events, and with no Romans in the picture; they agreed with Roman sources in evaluating Demetrius as a very aggressive and even reckless person (3.19.9–11). Each of these sources has its biases (one of Polybius' main Greek sources was the Achaean Aratus of Sicyon, a rival of Demetrius as advisor to King Philip V). But it is hard to believe that the universally negative assessment of Demetrius had no basis in fact. Just the opposite: a historical reality must account for his universally negative depiction in Polybius' sources, sources which included men who knew Demetrius personally.[133]

Again, it may appear irrational to us that Demetrius doubted Roman power, but this does not mean the story is false. On the one hand,

---

[129] See Dell 1967b; Hammond, in Hammond and Walbank 1988: 354.
[130] Despite Badian 1964a: 12–16; Eisen 1966: 108–9; Errington 1972: 106–8, cf. Errington 1989a: 91–2.
[131] Dell 1970b: 30–8, and Dell 1970a: 116–17; cf. Petzold 1971: 212. See also below, p. 68.
[132] Polybius knew Fabius was prone to pro-Roman apologia (1.14), and approached him with care (3.8.1–9.8). See Meister 1975: 127–49.
[133] Discussion of Polybius' sources on Demetrius, both Greek and Roman: Eckstein 1994.

Demetrius was not alone in Illyria in doubting Roman power, as the rise of pro-Demetrius factions in numerous polities proves: unlike ourselves, the Adriatic states had little way of knowing that the Romans would remain dominant. And Demetrius' understanding of the rise of Macedonian power in European Greece in the 220s was accurate. On the other hand, we know that Demetrius lost the battle of Pharos in 219, and hence his empire, by incautious conduct (Polyb. 3.18.8–19.8), and that he lost the battle of Messene in the Peloponnese in 215, and hence his life, by incautious conduct (3.19.11). This is a consistent pattern of behavior. Indeed, without risk-taking Demetrius would never have become regent of the Ardiaei in the first place.[134]

Encouraged by the lack of Roman reaction to his unification of the Ardiaei, Demetrius began to extend his influence southwards (Polyb. 3.16.3). He created pro-Demetrian factions in the tribes south of the Lissus, especially the Parthini. This was a region where before 229 Ardiaean influence had been strong (App. *Illyr.* 7); now it was reasserted.[135] Polybius says many communities were involved, and that the pro-Demetrius factions were powerful enough in autumn 220/spring 219 to stage many coups d'état in Demetrius' favor (3.18.1).[136] Demetrius also gained direct control over the Atintani, east of Epidamnus (App. *Ill.* 8, placing this event in 225/222); they fought for him against Rome in 219 (ibid.).[137] In the late 220s Demetrius also seized the strategic town of Dimallum, 100 miles south of the Lissus in the hinterland of Apollonia; the Apolloniates did not have the capability or will to prevent it (Polyb. 3.18.1 and 3–4). The growth of the pro-Demetrius factions among the Parthini, the Atintanian decision to go over to Demetrius, and the lack of Apolloniate reaction to Demetrius' aggression at Dimallum all point to a changing perception in maritime Illyris concerning Ardiaean vs. Roman power – or rather, perhaps, Roman willingness to use power.[138]

THE SECOND ILLYRIAN WAR

Demetrius' aggressions in the late 220s were followed in 220 by a major piratical expedition (ninety warships) beyond the Lissus, led by Demetrius himself and by Scerdilaidas, another Illyrian dynast. They raided the

---

[134]   Consistent Polybian picture: Eckstein 1994: 50–5.
[135]   See Hammond 1968: 4.
[136]   The emergence of such powerful factions is unlikely to have been the work of merely a few weeks or months: see Badian 1964a: 15.
[137]   Hammond, 1968: 9 n. 37; cf. Hammond 1989: 14. The mid-220s date suggests that Demetrius' expansion had a long history without Roman response.
[138]   Cf. Petzold 1971: 214–15.

southern Peloponnese, and then Demetrius went on with fifty ships into the Aegean and the Cyclades – a region where Illyrians had never penetrated before. Polybius twice says that this raid was a complete breach of the terms of the treaty of 228 (3.16.3 and 4.16.6).

Some modern scholars disbelieve that Demetrius would have engaged in such reckless conduct. They argue that in this raid he was acting as ruler of his private empire based on Pharos, and not as regent of the Ardiaei, and thus did not break the treaty, or at any rate had no reason to think he was doing so; or perhaps Rome had not yet renewed the treaty of 228 with Demetrius as the ruler of the Ardiaei, so that technically he was not bound by it. Polybius' accusations about the treaty are thus merely reflections of Roman propaganda.[139] But when Demetrius launched his raid south of the Lissus he *was* regent of the Ardiaei. And his partner in the raid, Scerdilaidas, was the brother of King Agron.[140] To claim that the treaty of 228 did not apply although Demetrius was regent of the Ardiaei, his co-commander was a member of the Ardiaean royal family, and the raid involved almost 100 warships – this would reduce the treaty of 228 to a farce.[141] Nor is it convincing to argue that though the raid was bold, the dynasts – by not attacking the Illyriote friends of Rome and sailing straight to the Peloponnese – were trying not to provoke Rome.[142] The best way not to provoke Rome would have been to abide by the treaty of 228 and remain above the Lissus. Instead, a large Ardiaean war-fleet ravaged cities as far south as Pylos and as far east as the Cyclades.[143]

But with Rome remote and passive in the face of his earlier aggressions, Demetrius in 220 may not have been thinking about Rome at all, but solely about events in Greece. At the time of the raid, war had broken out between the Aetolian League and its allies against Philip V – the new king of Macedon – and his Hellenic Symmachy (including the Achaean League). This was a massive war for power in European Greece. The Aetolians were contemptuous of Philip because he was only

---

[139]   Badian 1964a: 14; Gruen 1984: 371; Coppola 1993: 50–1.

[140]   Scerdilaidas allied to but somewhat independent of Demetrius, with his own forces: Polyb. 4.16.9–10; this shows the complexity of Illyrian tribal politics. Brother of King Agron: Scerdilaidas' son Pleuratus (Livy 31.28.1) has the name of Agron's father (Polyb. 2.2.4), and royal blood is suggested by the fact that Scerdilaidas was the in-law of King Amynander of Athamania, a monarchy located between the Aetolian League and Epirus (Polyb. 4.16.9). See Hammond 1966: 243; Gruen 1984: 368 and n. 48, and 369.

[141]   See Petzold 1971: 212; Errington 1989a: 92; cf. Eckstein 1994: 57–8.

[142]   So Badian 1964a: 14; Gruen 1984: 370; Errington 1989a: 92.

[143]   Cf. Eckstein 1994: 58 n. 49. Derow 2003: 54, believes that Demetrius acted provocatively here because he knew he was next on the list of victims of Roman aggression. This is to put the cart before the horse.

17 years old and inexperienced; so they sought to destroy the dominating position in Greece that Philip's uncle and predecessor, Antigonus III, had won for Macedon in 224–222 in the war against Sparta, and to establish themselves instead as the dominant power. It was a typical action by a major state in the Hellenistic anarchy.[144]

On the way back from the Aegean raid, Demetrius fought on the Macedonian side; his fleet ravaged the coast of Aetolia (Polyb. 4.19.7–9). This fits his good relations with the Antigonids – but the raid on Aetolia was a mercenary transaction, paid for by Philip V (Polyb. 4.19.8). Meanwhile Scerdilaidas, back from pillaging the southern Peloponnese, took part in the war on the *Aetolian* side, raiding Philip's main ally Achaea: in part because Scerdilaidas' in-law, the king of Athamania, was an Aetolian ally, but in part – again – just for money (4.16.9–11). Demetrius and Scerdilaidas, then, were both involved in the war in Greece in 220 – and why should they not have been, given its importance, and the passivity of the Romans towards Illyria?

But in the spring of 219 the Senate decided to attack Demetrius. After a decade of indifference, Rome dispatched a large naval expedition, commanded by both consuls, to the Adriatic coast. Once more the question is why the Senate suddenly adopted an interventionist policy in Illyria.

Polybius' explanation focuses on Demetrius' delicts towards Rome, but adds a broader analysis of power relations in the western Mediterranean. He says that the Romans acted primarily because Demetrius was guilty of "ingratitude" and "recklessness" (3.16.4, cf. 16.1–2), and because he broke the treaty of 228 (3.16.3). But the *Patres* were also concerned both to secure Illyria in case of war with Carthage (3.16.1, cf. 16.4) and about the growth of the power of Macedon (3.16.4). The Romans believed they would have time to solve the Illyrian problem before war with Carthage burst upon them – but in this they were wrong (3.16.5). Some scholars see Carthage, then, as the key to events in Illyria.[145]

To Polybius, however, the actions of Demetrius – not war with Carthage – were central to the Roman intervention. Carthaginian power had indeed increased with the conquest of its large empire in eastern Spain between 237 and 220, and the Roman strategic position had simultaneously deteriorated because of the increased power of Carthage combined with serious restlessness among the powerful Celtic tribes in the Po Valley. Political scientists would say that such a shift in power towards parity in the western Mediterranean state-system between ca. 235 and 220 BC, i.e., away from the unchallengeable Roman preponderance

---

[144] On the origins of the Social War of 220–217 and the issues of power involved, see Scholten 2000: Ch. 5.
[145] See, e.g., Scullard 1980: 194.

of power that existed immediately after the First Punic War, made a new crisis more probable – though not certain.[146] Moreover, in 220 a Roman embassy to Hannibal, the new Punic commander in Spain, warning him not to attack Rome's *amicus* the city of Saguntum, had ended in failure, so relations between Rome and Carthage were strained.[147] But Polybius says that the Senate in summer 219 believed (wrongly) that war with Carthage was not imminent (3.16.5): so the Illyrian war was not an emergency operation taken to secure Rome's rear under a severe Punic threat.[148]

Many scholars take the link between Demetrius and Antigonid Macedon as the real clue to events. The thesis was laid out by Holleaux, and has been widely asserted recently. The idea is that behind Ardiaean expansion both in the 230s and then again in the 220s stood Macedon, and that Roman opposition to the Ardiaei in the late 230s and then to Demetrius in 219 was part of a larger geopolitical struggle: Rome's attempt to prevent the kings of Macedon from extending their influence and power to the Adriatic.[149]

The argument is as follows. The kings of Macedon had claims to influence in Illyria going back to Philip II, the father of Alexander the Great, in the mid-fourth century (see Isocr. *Phil.* 21). When the Ardiaei defeated the Aetolian main army at Medion in 231 (above), they were acting at the behest of King Demetrius II of Macedon (Polyb. 2.2.8). Conversely, when in 229 and 228 Roman envoys visited Greece to announce the success of the First Illyrian War (above, p. 41), they did not visit Macedon; perhaps they were making a political point. Polybius also says that Demetrius of Pharos, in undermining the peace of 228, "placed all his hopes" in Macedon (3.16.3). Demetrius and his Illyrians fought on the Macedonian side at Sellasia in 222, and (it is claimed) Polybius lists them among the Macedonian allies rather than among the mercenaries (2.65.4). Hence the Illyrians were at Sellasia because Demetrius was a formal ally of Antigonus III, or perhaps even because the Ardiaean state had become a formal member of Antigonus' Hellenic Symmachy, the new instrument of Macedonian power in Greece. The

---

[146]   Detailed discussion in Eckstein 2006: Ch. 5.
[147]   Ibid.; cf. Eckstein 1989.
[148]   See, e.g., Errington 1972: 106; Eckstein 1994: 49. Polybius' source for Roman thinking on the war of 219 was probably the contemporary Roman senator Fabius Pictor – whose biases, however, Polybius well knew (see above, n. 132).
[149]   See Holleaux 1935: 131–46; cf. LeBohec 1987: 203–8; Hammond, in Hammond and Walbank 1988: 353–4; Wilkes 1992: 162; Coppola 1993: 55–8, and 84; Champion 1997: 118; and Ampela 1998: 63, who sees the war against Demetrius of Pharos in 219 as Roman "aggression" against Macedon. Similar is Harris 1979: 138, who believes that from the beginning the ultimate "target" of Roman policy in Illyria was Macedon.

latter position is taken by Coppola, the latest scholar to study Demetrius' career in detail. Some scholars also suggest that in the great raid against the Peloponnese and the Cyclades in 220, Demetrius was doing Antigonid work.[150]

Antigonus III's reestablishment of Macedonian power in Greece in 224–222 reversed fifty years of relative Macedonian weakness, and might even have had an impact in far-away maritime Illyris. But despite recent assertions, it is untrue that Macedon had strong hereditary interests in that region: the kings of Macedon had never exercised any power there. What Isocrates says is that Philip II by energetic campaigning became "master of all the Illyrians *except* those who dwell along the coast" (*Phil.* 21), and soon Macedonian power declined even in the areas Philip had brought under his influence. A generation later, the Macedonian dynast Cassander attempted to extend his sway into maritime Illyris – and was sharply defeated. There follows nothing for a full century.[151] Antigonus III's victories in 224–222 led to the resurgence of Macedonian power in Greece, but this was unexpected, new, and unstable; Antigonus' death led the Aetolian League to launch a strong challenge to Macedon in 220. In the short term, all that the resurgence of Macedon and the resulting conflicts in Greece did was act like a magnet, drawing Illyrian warlords and their men southward in search of profit: Demetrius at Sellasia in 222; Demetrius as well as Scerdilaidas in Greece in 220.[152]

Thus the modern reconstruction of events in Illyria, in which Roman opposition to the expansion of Ardiaean piratical power southward was part of a larger struggle between Rome and Macedon, is – like the Roman "protectorate" in Illyria – a modern fantasy. It is a retrojection of the conflict between Rome and Macedon that developed after 217 back to a quite different period.[153] Polybius himself – for whom the eventual struggle between Rome and Macedon is a major theme – makes concern about Macedon only a minor factor in the senatorial decision of 219 (3.16.4). And we can see why, if we examine carefully Macedonian relations with the Ardiaei.

First, the Ardiaei attacked the Aetolians at Medion in 231 because Demetrius II of Macedon – unable to intervene himself because of other military pressures – paid King Agron to do it (Polyb. 2.2.8). Thus the Ardiaei were acting as Demetrius of Pharos would act later – as mercenaries fulfilling a task. The hiring of tribes of Illyrian warriors was a

[150]   Holleaux 1935: 141.
[151]   See convincingly Dell 1970a: 119–22; cf. Dell 1967b: 98–102; rightly accepted by Errington 1989a: 91.
[152]   Cf. Badian 1958a: 45.
[153]   Cf. Errington 1972: 106.

strategic tool of the Macedonian kings going back to the fifth century – although the Illyrians sometimes proved treacherous (Thuc. 4.124– 8). And the Antigonids used Illyrian mercenaries in large numbers long before 231, so there is nothing new about Medion.[154] Macedon did not help the Ardiaei in 229, during the First Illyrian War; in fact, in 229 they were under attack by other Illyrian tribes.[155] As for Demetrius fight- ing on the Macedonian side at Sellasia in 222, Polybius' description of Antigonus III's forces (2.65.2–5) is too ambiguous to support the idea that Demetrius fought as a personal ally of Antigonus, let alone that the Ardiaean state itself had now become a formal ally of Macedon: it is more probable that, as earlier in 231 and later in 220, the Ardiaei were being paid for their help.[156] Note, too, that during the great raid of 220, the forces of Demetrius and Scerdilaidas attacked the town of Pylos (Polyb. 4.16.7) – but Pylos belonged to the Achaean League, and the Achaean League was the premier member of Macedon's new Hellenic Symmachy. Achaean spokesmen later said that the Illyrians were work- ing for Aetolia, the opponent of Macedon, when they attacked Pylos (4.25.4, cf. 9.38.8). Perhaps – but in any case, Demetrius' and Scerdil- aidas' attack on Pylos puts paid to the idea that the Ardiaean monarchy was part of Macedon's alliance system.[157] Later in 220 Demetrius did help Macedon by raiding the coast of Aetolia (Polyb. 4.19.8–9), but this was done for money (4.19.8). His partner Scerdilaidas, as noted above, was meanwhile helping the Aetolians *against* Philip and the Hellenic Symmachy – again, mostly for the money (4.16.8, cf. 4.29.5–6).

Mercenary service on the scale that Demetrius offered did have polit- ical implications: Polybius says that Demetrius had friendly relations with Macedon because he had aided Antigonus III at Sellasia (3.16.3). But there is nothing of a formal alliance here, and if Demetrius hoped for Macedonian help in 219 on the basis of his service at Sellasia, he was mistaken – even though Philip V was nearby in Epirus in summer 219 with the main Macedonian army.[158] Coppola suggests that Philip's presence in Epirus in 219 had to do with the Roman expedition,[159] but

---

[154] See Dell 1967b: 95 and n. 12, and Dell 1970a: 117.
[155] See above.
[156] See Dell 1967b: 101 n. 31 (convincing).
[157] Pylos an Achaean possession: Polyb. 4.5.8, 4.25.4, and Livy 27.30.13, with Walbank 1957: 453; cf. Marasco 1980: 120. LeBohec 1987: 206–9, is thus forced to deny that the Illyrian attack occurred – unconvincing. Conversely, Coppola 1993: 80–1, argues that Pylos was not an Achaean possession – equally unconvincing: at the conference of the Hellenic Symmachy in summer 220 it is the Achaeans who complain of the Illyrian–Aetolian attack on Pylos, listed with attacks on Cleitor and Megalopolis, certainly members of the Achaean League (Polyb. 4.25.4).
[158] Gruen 1984: 369 and n. 49.
[159] Coppola 1993: 93–4, cf. 91.

the fact is that nothing came of it that helped Demetrius. Rather, Philip in summer 219 was focused on his war with Aetolia, intending to invade Aetolia from the west, and was detoured into Epirus by Epirote pleas to take a strategic fortress that blocked the head of the Ambracian Gulf (Polyb. 4.61.5, cf. 61.3); there is no mention of Demetrius' problem. Demetrius, however, was allowed to take refuge after 219 at Philip's court (3.19.8).[160]

In fact, the one Illyrian dynast who had a formal arrangement with Macedon in 219 was Scerdilaidas – and the Romans left him alone. Thinking that the Aetolians had cheated him of spoils from their joint attack on Philip's allies the Achaeans in summer 220, Scerdilaidas met with Philip in Illyria that autumn, agreeing to attack Aetolia with thirty ships each year in return for an annual monetary subsidy (Polyb. 4.29.6–7). But beyond the money, it appears that Scerdilaidas entered into the Hellenic Symmachy (μεθέζειν τῆς κοινῆς συμμαχίας: 29.7).[161] Yet in 219 the Romans did nothing against Scerdilaidas – so little was the threat of Macedonian influence of interest to them.[162] The loose Roman arrangements in Illyria after the victory of 219 (see below) also tend to show there was no Roman anxiety over Macedon.[163]

Thus it is most unlikely that in going to war against Demetrius in 219 the Senate was looking beyond Illyria into the larger issue of Macedonian preponderance in European Greece. The links between Demetrius and Macedon (such as they were) were irrelevant; Scerdilaidas, who actually did have a formal alliance with Macedon, was not touched; Roman involvement in the larger struggles for power in European Greece was non-existent, and Roman concern about them (or even knowledge of them) minimal. The hypothesis that Roman actions in Illyria are connected with anxieties about or competition with the Antigonids retrojects back into a different period the conflict between Rome and Macedon over Illyria that actually broke out only later, under far different conditions, during the crisis of the Hannibalic War (see below).[164]

Let us turn, then, to Demetrius' own actions. Despite Badian, Demetrius clearly could not increase his own power without subverting the treaty of 228, and thus offending Rome to the extent that the Senate

[160]   Gruen 1984: 371 and n. 64, thinks that Polybius' use of παραδόξως at 3.19.8 means that Demetrius' arrival at Philip's court was unexpected in a political sense, and thus limits Demetrius' links to Macedon even further. But all Polybius is saying at 3.19.8 is that Demetrius, hard-pressed by the Romans, unexpectedly *succeeded* in getting to Macedon: for the correct translation, see Chambers 1966: 106–7.
[161]   See esp. Coppola 1993: 85.
[162]   Emphasized by Gruen 1984: 373. Presumably Scerdilaidas for his part was careful in 219 not to help Demetrius.
[163]   Badian 1964a: 17; cf. Walbank 1957: 326–7. See below, pp. 70–1.
[164]   See, rightly, Errington 1972: 103.

cared about Illyria. Errington accepts that Demetrius' actions before 220 undermined the treaty of 228, but he stresses there was no Roman reaction at the time, that in 220 Demetrius sought to minimize the provocation of Rome in his great raid south of the Lissus by not attacking Rome's Illyriote friends (see above), and concludes that Demetrius in 219 simply fell foul of two consuls who had nothing to do that year. This parallels Harris' view that the key to Roman aggressiveness, including the war with Demetrius, was always internal, the Roman aristocracy being in constant need of a war to fight even if it had to manufacture one.[165] But this view is both excessively cynical towards Rome and not realistic enough about the harsh and violent world that the Romans continually faced in this period.[166] More persuasive is Errington's suggestion – somewhat contradictory to the first – that although no single action of Demetrius was sufficient to provoke a Roman expedition after 228, cumulatively and over time they built up suspicion and hostility towards Demetrius at Rome and thus prepared the way for the decision of 219.[167] Petzold's view is starker: once Demetrius succeeded in uniting his own principality with the kingdom of the Ardiaei, thereby disrupting the balance of small and unthreatening states that the Romans had created in maritime Illyris in 229/228, a confrontation between Demetrius and Rome was inevitable.[168]

In terms of power politics, Petzold may well be correct – but only if Illyria was important to the Senate. The problem is that Roman interest in Illyria after 228 was so small. This, and the Celtic crisis, is why there was no response to Demetrius' aggressive conduct. But Rome's lack of response in turn led Demetrius towards more aggressiveness. Not even the Roman war against the piratical Histri in the far northern Adriatic in 221 because of their attacks on Roman supply ships during the Celtic War deterred Demetrius from the great sea raid south the next year. Hence Coppola suggests, reasonably, that Demetrius was aware of provoking Rome when he crossed the Lissus in 220, but in view of previous Roman lack of response the raid seemed to him a way to solidify his rule over the divided and contentious Ardiaei, and not too dangerous.[169]

---

[165] Errington 1989a: 92–3; cf. Harris 1979: 195–7, and now Derow 2003: 54 (a variation).
[166] For detailed discussion, see Eckstein 2006: esp. Ch. 6.
[167] Errington 1989a: 91.
[168] Petzold 1971: 212.
[169] Coppola 1993: 93–4: a striking contrast with the cynical Derow 2003: 54, for whom Demetrius acted in 220 because he knew he was next on the list of innocent victims of Roman aggression (see above, n. 143). Coppola also thinks Demetrius hoped that if his action did cause trouble with Rome, he could depend on the support of Macedon (ibid., cf. 91). This is most unlikely: see above.

Dell goes farther, suggesting that political pressure to be found worthy of rule as an Ardiaean king forced Demetrius – though a Greek – into traditional sea-borne raiding: hence the accusation in Appian that Demetrius personally joined the Histri in piracy on Roman grain-shipping in the Celtic War (*Illyr.* 8).[170] Internal pressures could well have forced Demetrius to engage in sea-borne raiding, for an Illyrian ruler was above all a war-leader, and Demetrius as a usurper and a Greek might especially feel called upon to fulfill that role.[171] But it is hard to believe that even the rash Demetrius would have personally led attacks on Roman shipping;[172] so perhaps other Illyrian piracy against Roman ships in the Celtic War lies behind the accusation in Appian – for the Ardiaei were not easy to control (see Queen Teuta at Polyb. 2.8.8).[173] Gruen proposes that Demetrius' great sea raid of 220 led the Senate to believe that, like Agron and Teuta, Demetrius was becoming a threat to Italian merchants in the Straits of Otranto.[174] This makes sense; but Polybius, though he emphasizes the impact of the great sea raid of 220, is silent on senatorial concern about Ardiaean piracy against commerce.

Moreover, internal pressures to engage in piracy do not explain the steady expansion of Demetrius' power and influence mostly inland south of the Lissus. Demetrius thus had large-scale political ambitions, and attack on polities friendly to Rome is the main charge against him in Polyb. 3.16. The core of the problem is now clearer: a process was unrolling whereby Demetrius might soon displace Roman influence and be able to seize control over much of maritime Illyris for himself. Rome would then face not only a reunited Ardiaean monarchy but one which, led by a vigorous ruler, had again emerged as the dominant power on the coast, with strong forces both by land and by sea. Multiple dangers might follow, from intensified piracy in the Straits to a serious strategic problem in the East at a time when Roman relations with Carthage were worsening in the West.[175] In the aftermath of the Celtic War, the Senate's attention was somewhat focused on problems in the Adriatic anyway – as is suggested by the expedition against the piratical Histri in 221. Given this situation, one can see how, as Polybius explicitly says, the great raid of 220 triggered Roman intervention: it was simply the most spectacular example yet of Demetrius breaking the treaty of 228 (3.16.3 and 4.16.4).[176]

---

[170]   Dell 1970b: 30–8; cf. Coppola 1993: 91.
[171]   Cf. above, p. 59 and n. 111.
[172]   Despite Dell 1970b: 37.
[173]   Dell 1970b: 36–7.
[174]   Gruen 1984: 372, followed by Marasco 1986: 101–6. Cf. also Dell 1970b: 38.
[175]   See Hammond 1968: 11 n. 42; cf. Coppola 1993: 91–2.
[176]   Cf. Eckstein 1994: 58–9.

Thus the Senate in 219 decided to send large forces and both consuls against Demetrius. The size of the expedition is explained not because the consuls needed something to do, or because of fear of a response from Macedon. Rather, it parallels the successful Roman expedition in 229, combined with the recent difficult experience against the Histri, when the Roman expedition – though ultimately victorious – suffered heavy casualties in assaulting Histrian coastal fortresses.[177] As it happened, the senatorial decision to send large forces and both consuls to Illyria was a serious strategic mistake (as, conversely, Roman passivity in Illyria after 228 had also been a strategic mistake): when the Senate learned in summer 219 that Hannibal had attacked Saguntum in Spain in defiance of Roman demands to let the city alone, the *Patres* seem to have not known what to do.[178]

Roman wars were traditionally preceded by an embassy of complaint to the potential enemy, making demands about alleged delicts – on pain of war. This was the *rerum repetitio*, usually required by the gods for the initiation of a just war. The *rerum repetitio* is thus a classic example of what modern political scientists term "compellence diplomacy."[179] Even if we had no evidence that a *rerum repetitio* took place before the war of 219, we would thus assume a Roman embassy to Demetrius occurred – and that its complaints and demands were rejected. But a late source (Dio frg. 53 = Zon. 8.20) reports an embassy to Demetrius (though the story as we have it has some strange aspects); and the essence of the Roman complaint is that Demetrius had abused the friendship (*philia*) of Rome by attacking his neighbors. This is the same charge as in Polybius 3.16.1–4. Demetrius gives the usual ancient response to such "compellence": he rejects the complaints, and instead steps up his attacks (Dio frg. 53 = Zon. 8.20). Hannibal in Spain had behaved similarly when faced with Roman demands in 220.[180] If we take as a basic fact that Demetrius rejected a Roman *rerum repetitio* before the war started, the rejection gives us another clue to his mentality. To the Romans, of course, such *contumacia* in itself helped justify a military response.[181]

Demetrius' strategy was to hold in strength the fortresses of Dimallum near Apollonia in the south and Pharos itself, 300 miles up the coast

---

[177] See Oros. 4.13.16, with (rightly) Dell 1970b: 31.
[178] See, e.g., Rich 1996: 28–30.
[179] On the evolution of the *rerum repetitio*, see Walbank 1949; Wiedemann 1987.
[180] See Eckstein 1984: 65–6, and Eckstein 2006: Ch. 5.
[181] The Dio passage has errors of procedure (the embassy is sent by the consuls, who summon Demetrius to them), so great faith cannot be put in it – but something like this interaction is likely to have occurred. Badian 1964a: 16, has the Romans launching a surprise attack on an unoffending Demetrius – but then cannot explain why Demetrius was well prepared for the war (see below); cf. also Gruen 1984: 373.

(Polyb. 3.18.1). Perhaps he hoped that Roman forces would fail at sieges: the one Roman defeat in 229 had been the siege of the town of Nutria, and Demetrius – who was with the Roman army (2.11.6) – may have witnessed it.[182] But Demetrius' forces were defeated: the Romans took Dimallum in seven days, and later Demetrius' rashness lost him the decisive battle at Pharos. He ended up at the court of Philip V.[183]

The impact of this second Roman war in Illyria appears, however, to have been slight. Dimallum came into "friendship" with Rome (Polyb. 3.18.5 and 7.9.13), and so did Pharos, which from 219 was an independent state.[184] The consul L. Aemilius Paullus imposed conditions on the many polities – likely to have been from the Parthini – which surrendered to him after his victory at Dimallum (3.18.6–7).[185] The conditions Paullus imposed are unknown, but were probably not onerous: after all, Scerdilaidas, Demetrius' partner in the great raid of 220, was left alone, and the Senate continued *amicitia* with King Pinnes himself, who remained titular head of the Ardiaean kingdom (App. *Illyr.* 8). Most of the places given by Rome to Demetrius in 229/228 (except Pharos itself) must have remained under the control of the Ardiaean monarchy – which is why they are unmentioned in the list of polities under Roman overlordship in the treaty of alliance between Hannibal and Philip in 215 (Polyb. 7.9.13).[186]

The main outcome of the war, then – and hence its main goal – was the removal of Demetrius of Pharos from power, not the remaking or tightening of Roman arrangements on the Adriatic coast. And as we have seen, the evidence about Demetrius (Greek evidence as well as Roman) suggests that Roman worries about him were not unjustified.[187] Since this expedition of 219 was narrowly focused on removing Demetrius, there were no Roman embassies sent to the states of European Greece afterwards – unlike what occurred in 229/228. Evidently not even Epirus, just to the south, was contacted.[188] Nor did the Romans in 219 use the presence of their large military forces to extend their influence up the Aous Valley towards Greece, or up to the passes over the Pindus towards Macedon.[189] Whether this was intentional restraint or simply

---

[182]   Badian 1964a: 16.
[183]   For convenient summary of the fighting, see Eckstein 1994.
[184]   On relations between Pharos and Rome, see above, pp. 45–8.
[185]   See Walbank 1957: 330; these would be Parthinian towns such as Bargullum and Eugenium (Livy 29.12.3 and 13).
[186]   See Petzold 1971: 214 and 216; cf. Errington 1989a: 91.
[187]   See esp. Walbank 1957: 325; cf. Petzold 1971: 211–12 and Eckstein 1994.
[188]   Cf. Oost 1954: 22–3.
[189]   Cf. Hammond 1968: 15; Dell 1973: 306–7. Dimallum, taken into *amicitia*, lay some 30 miles inland – but in a far different watershed from the Aous route into Greece.

myopic Roman focus on Demetrius, the consequence was that in 219, as in 228, a large zone of independent highland communities remained between the region controlled by Macedon and the area of Roman influence on the coast. The Romans showed here a lack of concern not only for further expansion either towards Greece or towards Macedon, but also for protecting the coastal polities from the powerful pressure that Macedon potentially could exert upon them via Dassaretis. Macedon, in other words, was not yet on the Roman horizon.

But did the Roman intervention against Demetrius at least strengthen the Roman hold on their Adriatic *amici*, whose number grew from six to eight? The intervention was probably welcomed by the governments of the original six. The Corcyraeans greatly feared the Ardiaei, and from 229/228 looked to Rome as their protector against Illyrian attack (2.9.8 and 2.11.5). Apollonia had been directly threatened by Demetrius' seizure of Dimallum; Epidamnus was similarly threatened by Demetrius' domination of the Atintani and Parthini.[190] We do not know whether the original six gave Rome military help, but Apollonia must have been the port of disembarkation for the Roman troops attacking Dimallum. Presumably such an interaction strengthened Roman influence – yet in 214 the Apolloniates could not depend on automatic Roman help in case of attack (see Livy 24.40.2).

At the end of the summer the Romans departed. They had stayed in Illyria for a much shorter period than in 229/228. No military or naval forces were left behind; no administration was imposed; even the number of informal *amicitiae* was only slightly extended. As Badian says, "There was no desire to increase Roman commitments in the East or to multiply client states."[191] Hammond, by contrast, claims that in 219 Rome "asserted her full control" over the grouping of states which they had established in 229/228.[192] But as we saw above, to speak of a "grouping" of states established by Rome in 229/228 is itself to grant a sophistication to the Roman arrangements with six individual polities that arose from the first expedition which they do not deserve. Nor was there "full control" over the Adriatic states exercised by Rome during the previous decade – not because the government at Rome could not have imposed it, but because it was not interested in doing so.

The situation after 219 therefore remained much as it had been before. Pinnes the son of Agron remained the titular head of the Ardiaei, and an informal *amicus* of Rome. His kingdom, though divided by faction

---

[190]   We hear nothing of the island of Issa in 219, but given that it neighbored Pharos, the Issaeans probably felt threatened as well.
[191]   Badian 1964a: 17.
[192]   Hammond 1968: 12.

(see below), remained unified with Demetrius' old principality (except for Pharos, which became an independent state) – so it remained quite extensive. Along 400 miles of coast from Corcyra in the south to Issa in the north, there were a few widely scattered Greek polities possessing informal *amicitia* with Rome. The Parthini, Atintani, and the town of Dimallum were informal *amici* of Rome a bit farther inland. There was no Roman influence up the crucial Aous Valley, or in the high passes of Dassaretis; Scerdelaidas was left alone, despite his alliance with Macedon.[193] No doubt the Adriatic communities were impressed with the scale of the Roman forces and their quick success; there had been, as Gruen says, "a reassertion of authority."[194] But over the next five years, as the Hannibalic crisis rose up to engulf Italy, the Romans were once more too busy to exercise any "authority" over their scattering of friends in Illyria. One should remember that in Polybius' terms, in 219 we are still in the period just *before* even the beginning of the *symplokē*, the continual interconnectedness between the eastern and western halves of the Mediterranean.[195]

The Roman intervention against Demetrius directly benefited Scerdelaidas – Macedon's ally. There may have been tension between Demetrius and Scerdilaidas;[196] but in any case Demetrius' removal left him, as the brother of King Agron and with Pinnes very young, the dominant dynast among the Ardiaei. At first Scerdilaidas was Pinnes' major advisor, or perhaps he was regent; by late 217, however, Pinnes disappears; and Scerdilaidas is king.

In the summer of 218 Scerdiliadas with fifteen ships sailed south of the Lissus and the Straits of Otranto to aid Philip V in attacking the large island of Cephallenia (Polyb. 5.4.3). The Ardiaean warlord brought only half the ships his agreement with Philip required, because he had to deal with unrest against him among other dynasts in Illyria (ibid.). Philip's attack failed (5.4.13), but this was Scerdilaidas' second major breach of the treaty of 228 (similar to his actions in 220).[197] After what had happened in 219, how could Scerdilaidas have risked it? His behavior has led some scholars to suggest that the charges against Demetrius for having violated the Lissus treaty, central in all our sources

[193] See Badian 1964a: 17.
[194] Gruen 1984: 368.
[195] On the *symplokē*, see Chapter 1, and above, this chapter, p. 32.
[196] See Coppola 1993: 90. Scerdilaidas had been the chief general of his brother Agron (Polyb. 2.6.6), and may not have been happy to see the Greek Demetrius, the betrayer of Teuta in 229, as the regent for Agron's son Pinnes.
[197] See Holleaux 1928: 851–2.

on the war of 219, cannot be the real story.[198] But perhaps for Scerdilaidas the small size of the expedition (fifteen warships) mitigated the fact that it sailed beyond the Lissus. Much more importantly, though, is the fact that full-scale war between Carthage and Rome had broken out in spring 218: the Senate would have been riveted now by events everywhere but in Greece, and very unlikely to care about fighting between Greek states at Cephallenia. If there was a Roman response to Scerdilaidas' actions, it was minimal: an embassy to King Pinnes more than a year later (in late 217) reminded him to pay the war indemnity that the Ardiaei owed Rome (Livy 22.33.3). Still, it is striking that, as Hammond says, "the Roman settlement of 219 was treated with scant respect."[199] This must be because although the Romans had shown great power twice, they had not set up any system to stabilize their influence on the Adriatic coast – and now they were distracted by the terrible events in Italy. Thus the crisis of Rome in the early years of the Second Punic War left Scerdilaidas free to act. His perception of the opportunities in 218 turns out to be similar to Demetrius' perception of Roman weakness during the Celtic War of the 220s. It is an example of the savage nature of the Hellenistic anarchy.

But the next year, unhappy with his payments from King Philip, Scerdilaidas turned against Macedon. His ships attacked Antigonid naval forces off the island of Leucas (once again well south of the Lissus and the Straits of Otranto), and his army invaded Macedon itself overland through Dassaretis. This is a pattern of rash Illyrian behavior similar to that of Demetrius towards Rome. And Philip's response to Scerdilaidas' behavior was similar to Rome's response to Demetrius: a powerful military counter-attack; it drove Scerdilaidas' warriors out of Macedon, far to the northwest.[200] Once more we see how Roman actions look one way when viewed in isolation, but quite different when compared to the actions – the similar actions – of other major states in the Mediterranean anarchy. Roman conduct then seems part of a larger interstate pattern of the assertion of power by large powers in unruly situations. The difference is that because the Adriatic Sea separated Illyria from Italy, the Romans were less interested in the region than Philip now became.

---

[198]   Badian 1964a: 17.
[199]   Hammond 1968: 15.
[200]   See Polyb. 5.95.1 and 108.1–2. There is no evidence – and no reason to think – that Scerdilaidas here was acting somehow at Rome's behest, despite, e.g., Holleaux 1935: 165–6. Rather, this was a typical anarchic quarrel between Scerdilaidas and Philip: see, rightly, Badian 1952/1964a: 18; Gruen 1984: 374.

CONCLUSION

The two Roman wars in maritime Illyris hold interest for the history of Roman expansion because they are the first Roman military interventions east of the Adriatic. But this chapter has shown that the scale and character of Roman interest and involvement in the European Greek world (let alone the wider East) was minimal down to 217 BC. The Romans engaged in two wars against piratical Illyrian dynasts, in 229/228 and in 219. After their victory in 229/228, they made brief and friendly contact with the Aetolian League, the Achaean League, and Athens. But these contacts were not followed up, not even after the brief second war in the Adriatic in 219. Nor is there evidence that the major European Greek states took much notice of the Roman appearance on the northwest Adriatic coast – a region separated by massive mountains from central Greece. They continued to focus their energies, as always, on the ruthless struggle for power among themselves.

This chapter has also argued that in maritime Illyris itself the impact of the Roman interventions was smaller than most scholars have proposed. The coastal states must have been impressed with the size of Roman military interventions. And if formal treaties of alliance had been struck between Rome and these polities as a result, then one could say that the Senate in this period was interested in establishing dominance in Illyria – in establishing a powerful and organized hegemony, which might in the future act as a "bridgehead" into Greece. This reconstruction of the Adriatic situation after 229/228 has become widely influential. But we have shown that the alleged system of formal treaties of alliance with Rome created with the Adriatic states in 229/228 – or indeed, the existence of *any* Roman treaty of alliance in Illyris in this period – is simply not historical. The hypothesis is based on an implausible analysis of a fragmentary and undatable inscription from Pharos – an analysis that contradicts Polybius' evidence that Pharos could not have contracted any treaty with Rome in 229/228 because it was not in that period an independent state, but rather a subject of the warlord Demetrius of Pharos. Polybius, who was greatly interested in Demetrius and had good sources on his career, is not likely to have gotten this wrong. But with the elimination of the idea that Pharos in the 220s had a treaty of alliance with Rome, the reconstruction whereby Rome established multiple treaties of alliance in Illyria in 229/228 collapses, since Pharos was the only (alleged) example of such a treaty.

The hypothesis that a Roman "protectorate" on the Adriatic emerged from the interventions of 229/228 and 219 has also been shown to be unfounded. No ancient source speaks of it. We are merely told of six (later eight) polities coming to possess informal friendship with Rome as a result of the expeditions of 229 or 219. They were scattered widely along a coastline 400 miles long. Three of them were actually islands off the coast;[201] the territories of the others did not extend far into the interior. These Adriatic states might hope that Rome would protect them from the on-going and continual process of Ardiaean unification and expansion which was the major factor in the turmoil in maritime Illyris in this period – if, that is, Rome decided to respond to such a situation.[202] But if the Romans for their part assumed they could exercise their will over these *amici*, the fact is that between 229/228 and 219 they never did so – and the same was true between 218 and 214.

It may be too much even to speak of a Roman "sphere of influence" in Illyria, though that less institutionally coherent concept fits the situation better than does a "protectorate" or a system of treaties of alliance. The problem with the "sphere of influence" concept is that during the 220s the Romans allowed a strong *competitor* for influence in Illyria to emerge: Demetrius of Pharos, the new regent of the Ardiaei. Having united his personal domain with the remnants of the Ardiaean kingdom, Demetrius reconstituted Ardiaean power after its debacle in 229/228, and he gradually extended his power and influence into maritime Illyris – and indeed, both in 222 and 220 commanded Ardiaean forces in expeditions to the southern Peloponnese and beyond. And as the Ardiaei reemerged in the 220s as a major force confronting the weak and disunited polities of the Adriatic coast, conditions within many of these states gave rise to factions that favored cooperation with Demetrius.

The Republic of Rome reasserted its interest in and authority over maritime Illyris only in 219, in a campaign whose purpose was the removal of Demetrius. He had grown over-powerful, and proven himself untrustworhy by skirting and then overtly violating the peace treaty of 228 (especially in the great raid into the Aegean in 220). The Roman expedition of 219, like that of 229, shows that the Romans were (as always) prepared to take harsh steps to protect their security within the unending ferocious competition among ancient states for power. The war of 219 was also another demonstration that the Senate believed such security could best be established by applications of overwhelming military force. But the expedition of 219 had little impact beyond the removal of Demetrius. Roman forces were soon gone, there was no tightening

---

[201] Corcyra, Pharos, and Issa.
[202] See Petzold 1971: 214–15.

or restructuring of the loose connections Rome had formed with the "friendly" Adriatic states, and no diplomatic interaction at all with major states of Greece. It looks as if the Senate did not yet perceive maritime Illyris as a permanent strategic asset, or the Greek East in general as a permanent area of strategic involvement. Indeed, the Senate made a major error in not tightening its hold on Illyria in 219, and perhaps actually *creating* some sort of organized "protectorate" there – for it was not long before Philip V of Macedon began to turn his eyes towards the vulnerable polities of maritime Illyris.

3

Rome, the Greek States, and Macedon, 217–205 BC

This chapter examines Roman interactions with the Greek states and the Kingdom of Macedon during the crisis which confronted Rome during the Hannibalic War. The thesis is that, as with the early Roman interventions in Illyria (above, Chapter 2), Roman relations with the Greeks remained minimal in this period, as did Roman goals. The governments of most Greek states, meanwhile, did not yet see Rome as a major factor in Greek politics. Indeed, in their attempts between 209 and 206 to end the conflict which moderns (working from a Roman perspective) call the First Macedonian War but which Greeks at the time evidently called "the Aetolian War," the intent of the mediating Greek states – Ptolemaic Egypt, Rhodes, Athens, Chios – was primarily to create peace between the Aetolian League and Macedon. Rome was incidental to their efforts, or not considered at all. In fact, those efforts worked at cross-purposes to the Roman aim – which was to keep Philip V distracted from the Adriatic and Italy by means of a war in Greece. Greek mediation did facilitate the end of "the Aetolian War" in 206 – leaving Rome to fight on alone against Philip. The result was the compromise peace between Rome and Philip sworn at Phoenice in Epirus in 205.

This puts into startling perspective the sudden arrival at Rome from 202/201 BC of embassies from one Greek state after another, pleading for Roman help against Philip V and the Seleucid king Antiochus III. Three of these states, in attempting in 209–206 to mediate the "Aetolian War," had previously ignored and directly contravened Roman interests. Their embassies to Rome thus constituted a diplomatic revolution

– and an explanation is needed. The explanation is provided in Chapter 4.

THE ORIGINS OF THE FIRST MACEDONIAN WAR

War between Rome and Macedon was probably officially declared at Rome in 214 BC (see below). But major operations against Macedon, in conjunction with the Aetolian League which had now become Rome's ally, did not begin until autumn 211 BC. It is the latter date which scholars regularly and wrongly designate as the beginning of "the First Macedonian War." This odd scholarly situation reflects a central ambiguity: the Aetolians' war with Philip was not the same war as the Romans' war with him. This is true, too, for the rest of the Greeks. But one fact is not in doubt: Philip V was the aggressor in the war that emerged with Rome.

Coming to the Antigonid throne in 221 at the age of 17, Philip almost immediately faced a challenge from the Aetolian League to the new Macedonian hegemony in Greece established by his uncle and predecessor, the talented Antigonus III. The Aetolians were old opponents of Macedonian power, and because leaders in Aetolia thought Philip too young to be an effective ruler, Aetolian forces soon began aggression against Macedon's allies in the Peloponnese. This is another example of what even the rumor of weakness meant in Hellenistic power politics; we will see others.[1]

The Aetolian attacks led to the Social War of 220–217, fought on a large scale by the Aetolians and their allies against Philip V and the allies of Macedon (the Hellenic Symmachy). In this war Philip unexpectedly proved himself an outstanding military commander, and by 217 he held the advantage. But the tradition is that when in June 217 he heard of Hannibal's great victory over the Romans at Lake Trasimene in Etruria, Philip turned his thoughts from Greece to expansion in the West. This new policy was urged by Demetrius of Pharos, who had fled to Macedon after being expelled from his Illyrian dominions by Rome in 219 (see above, Chapter 2). Demetrius proposed that since Rome was being severely defeated, Philip should end the Social War, gain control of Illyria, and then launch an expedition against Italy (Polyb. 5.101.8). Even world

---

[1]   On how other states' perceptions of one's weakness attracted aggression in antiquity, see Eckstein 2006, esp. Chs. 3 and 4. The persistent conflict in Greece between the Aetolian League and Antigonid Macedon: see Scholten 2000: Chs. 2 and 4. The outbreak of war between the Aetolians and Philip V in 220: ibid.: 200–12.

dominion was possible – an idea that Philip found attractive. Demetrius had his own motives for advocating a western policy for Macedon (his hatred of Rome, and desire to regain his dominions in Illyria). It is in any case clear that just as the Aetolians in 220 sought to take advantage of Philip's perceived weakness, so Philip from 217 sought to take advantage of Roman weakness.[2]

At Naupactus in summer 217 Philip therefore arranged peace with Aetolia on the basis of the current military status quo. Polybius views Philip's decision to end the Social War and to expand Macedonian power towards the west as an event of world-historical importance. For the first time, policy decisions in the Greek Mediterranean are being based on what is happening in the West (the battle of Lake Trasimene). Philip's decision and its impact, in turn, now began the increasing development of "interconnectedness" (συμπλοκή) between the two previously separate halves of the Mediterranean world – one of the two great themes of Polybius' work (the other being the rise of Roman power). Before Philip's decision to turn towards the West the two parts of the Mediterranean world had existed as two separate systems of states, and events within one system had had little or no impact on the other. From the striking of the Peace of Naupactus, the situation changed.[3]

Polybius stresses the importance of the Peace of Naupactus by reporting a long speech by the Aetolian statesman Agelaus, urging peace but also predicting the possibility of *symplokē* (5.104.1–11).[4] Then Polybius appends his own comment: "This was the first point in time when the politics of Greece, Italy and Africa became an interconnected whole" (συνέπλεξε – 5.105.4):

> For Philip and the statesmen in Greece no longer made war and peace with each other based on events in Greece alone, but all eyes were turned to the events in Italy. Soon the same was true of the Aegean islanders and the people of Asia Minor. For those who had grievances against Philip, and some of the enemies of Attalus, no longer turned to the south and east, to Antiochus and Ptolemy, but to the west, some sending embassies to Carthage and others to Rome, and the Romans too began to send embassies to the Greeks, fearing the adventurous character of Philip and guarding lest he join in attacking them in their present critical situation. (5.105.4–8)

[2] World conquest: Polyb. 5.101.10, 102.1, 104.7, 108.5; 15.24.6; see esp. Walbank 2002a. Demetrius' motives: Polyb. 5.108.6.
[3] Hence, although Polybius gives prominence to the two previous military interventions undertaken by Rome in Illyria, he does not consider them to constitute even the beginning of the *symplokē*; they are, rather, examples of mere *epiplokē* (contact): see Polyb. 2.12.7 (see above, Chapter 2, at n. 15).
[4] On the historicity of Agelaus' speech in Polybius, see Champion 1997: 111–28.

The historian concludes: "I have now fulfilled my original promise, and have shown clearly how, when, and for what reasons the politics of Greece became interconnected with those of Italy and Africa" (συνεπλάκησαν: 5.105.4–9).

This passage is crucial to the entire structure of Polybius' *Histories* – yet many scholars view it as at best schematic, and perhaps even tendentious. Some find it hard to believe that Philip aimed at world conquest, in part because such an ambition violated what moderns term the "Hellenistic balance of power"; so this must actually be anti-Philip propaganda.[5] It is also unclear what "embassies" between Rome and the Greek states, or Carthage and the Greek states, Polybius means (5.105.7), for we know of hardly any.[6] The role of Demetrius of Pharos in urging Philip to end the Aetolian war and turn his attention towards Illyria and Italy sounds like court gossip, perhaps from Aratus of Sicyon, who was one of Demetrius' political enemies and one of Polybius' sources (and heroes). Aratus opposed the western policy (7.13.1); Polybius disapproves of it too, for it was a reckless scheme that ultimately led to the destruction of Macedon (5.102.1). Some scholars have also asserted that news of Roman defeats in Italy had nothing to do with Philip's ending the Social War, which, they argue, probably occurred because of a major invasion of Macedon by the Illyrian Ardiaei through the Pindus Range. The Ardiaei were led by Scerdilaidas, a former ally of Philip who had turned on him in a quarrel over payment for his support in the war with Aetolia (see above, Chapter 2). The pattern here in 217 would thus repeat Antigonus III's having to march north against a barbarian invasion of Macedon immediately after his great victory over Sparta in 222.[7] Nor should we accept that Philip had ambitions to invade Italy; he was only interested in asserting traditional Macedonian control in Illyria. All the rest is propaganda, or hindsight and abstract theorizing by Polybius.[8]

These criticisms of Polyb. 5.105 are, however, overblown. The evidence is conclusive that before 217 Macedon had never exercised control in maritime Illyris.[9] Philip's decision in 217 therefore meant the extension of focused Macedonian ambition in a new direction and into a new area; it was indeed a new departure. Nor can Scerdilaidas' invasion of Macedon have been the cause of the Peace of Naupactus. Before the peace conference he had violated his pact with Philip by capturing four Macedonian ships off western Greece (Polyb. 5.95.1–4), but this can

---

5 So esp. Klose 1982: 87–8.
6 So Walbank 1957: 629–30.
7 So Gruen 1984: 374.
8 So now Champion 1997: 118–19.
9 See above, Chapter 2, pp. 63–4.

hardly have caused Philip to make peace with Aetolia. Scerdilaidas did later launch a serious invasion of Macedon – but Philip learned of it only upon his return to Macedon *after* making peace (5.108.1). Something else, then, led Philip suddenly to end the Social War and turn to the West. Since it was not Scerdilaidas, what was it? Polybius' story of severe Roman defeat in Italy provides the answer. If Philip could seize bases in Illyria, it was not hard to conceive of further adventures: an invasion of Italy may sound reckless to moderns, but Philip's reputation was already that of a successful military gambler. The Romans, as we will see, took the threat seriously enough to engage in major military preparations to combat Philip's arrival.[10]

Similarly, while some scholars find Polybius' assertion that Philip aimed at universal rule hard to believe, the recent trend in the study of Hellenistic interstate relations has been to stress that there existed no Hellenistic consensual "balance of power" that might limit his ambitions. On the contrary: the Hellenistic world was one of savage competition, from the most powerful states down to the local wars between small places.[11] And Walbank has recently shown just how deeply the idea of universal rule was embedded in Antigonid royal ideology. The Antigonids viewed themselves as descended from Philip II and Alexander the Great (see esp. Plut. *Aem.* 12.5) – a falsehood, but one that demonstrates the scale of Antigonid ambitions. And of course they really *were* descended from Alexander's marshal Antigonus the One-Eyed and Antigonus' son Demetrius the Besieger, who had their own vast ambitions in Asia. Philip V's predecessor Antigonus III had tried to seize Caria, in southern Asia Minor, before turning successfully to the reestablishment of Macedonian hegemony in Greece. Nor is Polybius' assertion about Philip's ambition a one-time remark brought in at Naupactus; it recurs at crucial explanatory points later (see 15.20 and 15.24.1). Most importantly, we have the evidence of the contemporary poet Alcaeus of Messene, writing ca. 202–200 BC. He demonstrates that Philip's ambitions for universal rule were explicit and taken seriously in the late third century itself:

> Make higher, Zeus, the walls of Olympus: Philip can
> scale everything! Close the bronze gates of the Blessed
> Ones. Land and sea lie subdued beneath Philip's sceptre.
> All that remains is the road to Olympus. (*Anth. Pal.* 9.518)[12]

---

[10] On Philip as a gambler, see rightly Rich 1984: 129–30.

[11] See the detailed discussion of the trend in scholarship, and the evidence behind it, in Eckstein 2006: Ch. 4.

[12] The Antigonids' claim of descent from Philip and Alexander: see Walbank 2002a: 127–8. The implications of Antigonus III's campaign in Caria: ibid.: 130. The implication of Alcaeus' poem: 128.

It is unclear whether this poem is meant as praise of Philip or, on the contrary, is politically hostile – but for us the point is Philip's universal ambitions.[13] At the time of the Peace of Naupactus Philip was still only 21 – the age of Alexander when he came to the throne – and he was actually ahead of Alexander in accomplishment, having already established himself as a formidable military commander in his victories over the Aetolians. Polybius' claim that young Philip's fierce ambitions for new conquests played a crucial role at Naupactus (5.102.1 and 108.5) therefore has much to say for it. Though the extent of such conquests would have to depend on circumstances, Philip obviously intended them to be large.

What of the suspect "embassies" to which Polybius refers? The timescale is not clear, and need not be restricted to immediately after 217: Polybius is looking forward into an intensifying relationship between East and West. We know of no embassies between Carthage and the Greek states, except for the negotiations of 215 between Hannibal and Philip, and a coordinated strategy in the Adriatic between the Carthaginians and Macedon in 208.[14] We know of no embassies complaining to anyone in the West about Attalus I of Pergamum – but large sections of Polybius are lost, and we are not entitled to assume that the historian did not discuss something in a section now missing. We do know of Greek embassies complaining about Philip V; they are crucial events in 201–200 BC. And there were Roman embassies the other way: to Philip V demanding the return of Demetrius of Pharos, to King Pinnes the son of Agron, and then to Scerdilaidas, confirming the Ardiaean relationship with Rome (Livy 22.33.3 and 33.5: both in late 217),[15] and of course the series of negotiations with the Aetolian League, starting in 212, leading to the alliance of 211 (which fits Polybius' phrase about the Romans guarding against an attack from Philip while they were in difficulties because of Hannibal). Thus much of what Polybius says in 5.105 is confirmed in later details we possess, and nothing that Polybius says in 5.105 runs counter to known facts.

It is a matter of emphasis – and schematicism. Philip's first action in the West was to attack the Ardiaei and maritime Illyris (217 and 216); the war did not go well and need not have become a full-scale conflict with Rome. The treaty of alliance between Philip and Hannibal in 215, though a dramatic and unprecedented step in Macedonian diplomacy, focused on Punic recognition of Philip's control of maritime Illyris, and foresaw mutual aid against Rome only vaguely; and Philip never did invade

---

[13]   Ibid.: 128.
[14]   On these interactions, see below, this chapter, pp. 83–4 and 99–100.
[15]   Adams 1993: 42, wrongly has these embassies before Naupactus.

Italy. Yet this was followed in 211 by the equally unprecedented Roman alliance with the Aetolian League. To Polybius, writing seventy years later, these events did mark a great departure from the past; and Agelaus' speech at Naupactus contained a saying that was famous, and pointed in the same direction as Polybius: "the clouds that loom in the west" might eventually overwhelm the Greeks (5.104.10, cf. 104.2–3).[16] But part of Polybius' point is that in 217 we are still only at the first step of the development of interconnectedness (πρῶτον: 5.105.4). To many contemporaries the break with the past was not clear: not clear in 217–216, and (as we will see) not in 209–205 either.

In autumn 217 Philip drove Scerdilaidas from Macedon and seized much of Dassaretis as well as the Pindus passes (Polyb. 5.108.8). That winter the king had a fleet of 100 Illyrian-style light warships (*lembi*) built, and in summer 216 he sailed around the Peloponnese for Illyria. Such a fleet could deal with Scerdilaidas' naval forces, but was not capable of facing the Roman navy, with its numerous much heavier ships; Philip clearly did not think the Romans, deep in the Hannibalic crisis, would intervene (5.109.2).[17] Scerdilaidas, now king of the Ardiaei in place of Pinnes, appealed for help to Rome, and ten quinquiremes were dispatched from the Roman base at Lilybaeum in western Sicily (5.110.8). The Roman response to Scerdilaidas' pleas was minimal – not surprisingly, given Roman circumstances; and Illyrian *lembi* in 229 had defeated just such a small squadron of big ships, manned by Achaeans and Aetolians (Polyb. 2.10.1–6). Polybius thinks that in 216 this could have happened to the Romans as well (5.110.10) – and then they would have been too distracted by Hannibal to have prevented Philip's conquest of Illyris (ibid.). The impact of such a development on the Roman strategic position might have been quite serious. But instead of confronting the Roman squadron, Philip fled from the Adriatic when he received rumors that a Roman fleet was approaching. Eventually his fleet of *lembi* returned to Macedon (5.110.10–11). But significant Roman naval forces now took up positions at Brundisium and Tarentum (Livy 23.33.5).

Nevertheless, as Gruen says, "for the next five years the initiative stayed with Philip."[18] After Hannibal's great victory over Rome at Cannae (August 216), Philip sent envoys to Hannibal to conclude a formal alliance. Philip sought recognition of his (projected) conquest of Illyria

---

[16] The reference is to whoever wins the great war now convulsing the western Mediterranean, not merely Rome; for Hannibal, too, was well known to have modeled himself on Alexander the Great. On this, see now Hoyos 2003: 105.

[17] Cf. Badian 1964a: 19.

[18] Gruen 1984: 375.

from the victorious Hannibal – and perhaps he sought more. It was an act typical of the brutality of Hellenistic decision-makers, for Macedon and Rome so far had had almost nothing to do with each other (stressed by App. *Mac.* 1). But Philip "went with the camp of success" (Livy 23.33.4): Rome's weakness indicated there were advantages to be gained. King Hieronymus of Syracuse, the grandson and successor of Rome's friend Hiero II, made the same decision, at the same time, and for the same reasons: the Romans were losing the war with Carthage (see Polyb. 7.3). That was the way the Hellenistic anarchy worked.[19]

Philip was in the Peloponnese in 215, attempting to seize by treachery his erstwhile ally Messene.[20] He sent his courtier Xenophanes to Hannibal to negotiate the treaty of alliance. Xenophanes was captured in Italy by forces of the praetor M. Valerius Laevinus, but we are told that he talked his way out of Laevinus' hands by claiming he had come to Italy to negotiate an alliance between Philip and *Rome*. Laevinus was delighted, and sent him through the Roman lines – to Hannibal (Livy 23.33.6–8). The premise of this story is important: in 215 high Roman officials such as Laevinus still saw no fundamental clash of geopolitical interests between Rome and Macedon; nothing had happened since 230 in Illyria that made a Roman–Macedonian conflict seem inevitable or a Roman–Macedonian alliance seem ridiculous.[21] On the way back to Macedon from Hannibal, Xenophanes was captured again, this time with the treaty with Hannibal in his possession (Livy 23.38.7, cf. 34.9). It was thus that the Romans learned of the new threat that faced them.

The verbatim version of the treaty which we find in Polyb. 7.9 is evidently the text captured with Xenophanes (cf. 7.9.1); the Punicisms in Polybius' version attest to its authenticity.[22] The treaty is between Hannibal and Carthage, and Philip and the Hellenic Symmachy (7.9.5 and 7). This implies a meeting of the Symmachy Council which formally approved the alliance.[23] The treaty is concerned primarily with Illyria as Philip's share of the spoils after Hannibal's projected victory over Rome. The Illyrian communities under Roman overlordship are named (e.g., Corcyra, Apollonia, Epidamnus), and henceforth will belong to Philip; Demetrius of Pharos will get back his old dominions (7.9.13). Roman writers later exaggerated the terms of the treaty. Thus the Polybian treaty

---

[19]   On the details of Syracusan policy supporting Rome in 263–216 and the shift to Carthage under Hieronymus after Cannae, see Eckstein 1980b: 192–202.
[20]   Convenient detailed discussion, with sources: Walbank 1940: 72–4.
[21]   See App. *Mac.* 1 with Gruen 1984: 375 n. 92.
[22]   See Bickerman 1952 and Barré 1983; cf. Walbank 1967: 42–3; Errington 1989a: 96.
[23]   So esp. Hammond, in Hammond and Walbank 1988: 393–4.

envisions a postwar Italy in which a gravely weakened Rome still exists (7.9.12); in the Roman tradition Hannibal plans to annihilate it (Livy 23.33.11). In the Polybian text there is only a vague reference to mutual aid against Rome: "You [Philip] will be our ally in the war against Rome and give us such help as we request or upon which we mutually agree" (7.9.11); in Roman versions Philip is explicitly to invade Italy (in Livy 23.33.10, he is coming with 200 warships).[24]

Yet even in Polybius' sober account of the treaty an invasion of Italy by Philip is possible, and Polybius is explicit that the Romans feared Philip's daring and that he would attack them.[25] However innocuous the phrase in Polyb. 7.9.11 may look to modern scholars, it will have looked different to the Senate when the treaty was revealed in the desperate summer of 215.[26] Livy stresses the deep worry (*gravis cura*) of the *Patres* when they learned of the alliance: "for they saw how large a war with Macedon threatened, at a time when Rome could barely endure the one with Carthage" (33.38.5). The Roman tradition stresses the fear that Philip was coming to Italy (see App. *Mac.* 1; Zon. 9.4). And this is not pure propaganda, for the fear found expression in major government action: Rome's strong military reinforcement in the Adriatic region from autumn 215.[27] Upon learning of the treaty, the Senate ordered the fleet at Tarentum and Brundisium to be immediately doubled, from twenty-five to fifty-five ships, and that Brundisium (on the Adriatic coast) become the new base of operations for the reinforced fleet (Livy 23.38.8). P. Valerius Flaccus' orders were "not merely to defend the coast of Italy but to guard against the possibility of a war with Macedon" (23.38.9).[28] In the spring of 214 the command at Brundisium was taken over by M. Valerius Laevinus; his orders were "to protect the coasts of Brundisium and Calabria and to be vigilant against any movements of Philip" (Livy 24.10.4 and 40.1).[29] As Badian says, whatever Philip's actual plans were with Hannibal, "the Romans seemed to have every reason to fear his invading of Italy, and did fear it."[30]

---

[24] The Roman tradition on the alliance: Livy 23.33.10–34.1; App. *Mac.* 1.2; Eutrop. 3.12.3; Zon. 9.4.2 (from Cassius Dio). The differences between this tradition and Polybius: see Mantel 1995: 175–80.
[25] δεδιότες τὴν τοῦ Φιλίππου τόλμαν, καὶ προρώμενοι μὴ συνεπίθηται τοῖς ὅτε περιεστῶσιν αὐτοὺς καιροῖς (5.105.8).
[26] See the comments of Siebert 1995: 240.
[27] On the importance of the Roman military preparations in the Adriatic for our understanding of Roman worries after 215, see Siebert 1995: 239–41.
[28] *Non tueri modo Italiae oram sed explorare de Macedonico bello.*
[29] *Ad Brundisium orae maritimae, intentus adversus omnes motus Philippi, Macedonum regis . . . praesidentem classi Brundisio Calabriaequae circa litoribus.*
[30] Badian 1958a: 56 n. 4.

Philip followed the treaty with Hannibal by new attacks on maritime Illyris. In autumn 215 his forces may have attacked Corcyra (App. *Mac.* 1.2; Zon. 9.4).[31] In summer 214 he launched a major offensive: his army marched on maritime Illyris through Epirus (Plut. *Arat.* 51.1), while 120 *lembi* sailed around the Peloponnese again and up the Straits of Otranto. Philip besieged Apollonia and captured Oricum, 30 miles to the south. No Roman forces were stationed in Illyris; the Roman priority lay in protecting the coast of Italy. But the pleas for help from both Apollonia and Oricum reached M. Valerius Laevinus at Brundisium, and he decided to respond energetically; taking his fleet across the Adriatic, he drove the Macedonians from Oricum, and lifted the Macedonian siege of Apollonia by means of a surprise attack. Philip burned his fleet at the mouth of the Aous, and retreated overland to Macedon (Livy 24.40.3–16). Laevinus wintered his fleet at Oricum (Polyb. 8.1.6; Livy 24.40.17).

Philip may have thought the Romans would be too weak in 214 to respond to his attack on maritime Illyris. Indeed, Laevinus' intervention was a highly risky operation, coming at a point when the two best harbors on a difficult coast were already denied to the Roman fleet (Oricum in Philip's hands; Apollonia besieged by the Macedonians). But the reason given for Laevinus' crossing to Illyria is explicit: Oricum and Apollonia would be good bases for an attack upon Italy (Livy 24.40.5). A short time before, Laevinus had had to take swift action to prevent an attempt by Hannibal himself on the great port of Tarentum (Livy 24.20).[32] Some scholars see a connection between Hannibal's attempt on Tarentum and Philip's attack in Illyris;[33] but Laevinus, in any case, could afford no other interpretation. His energetic response was within the wide parameters of his orders from the Senate, for action to keep Philip away from Italy was already contemplated in his orders (Livy 23.38.5). The Senate accepted Laevinus' decision that his fleet should henceforth be based not at Brundisium but across the Adriatic in maritime Illyris. And our evidence suggests that sometime in 214 Rome formally declared war on Philip, on grounds of unprovoked attack (App. *Mac.* 1 and Livy 24.40.1).[34]

Though Apollonia was a military disaster for Philip, he did not give up his designs on Illyria. Polybius is admiring of Philip's stubbonness in adversity (see 16.28.3 and 7) – a typical ideological judgment of what

---

[31]   Historicity accepted by Hammond, in Hammond and Walbank 1988: 395 and n. 2.
[32]   See Siebert 1995: 241. Cf. also Zon. 9.4.
[33]   Gruen 1984: 376 n. 96.
[34]   See Hammond, in Hammond and Walbank 1988: 395.

was necessary in a harsh and anarchic world.[35] Blocked at sea in 214, Philip began attacking maritime Illyris by land from over the Pindus, and he made significant conquests in 213 and 212. The rest of Dassaretis fell to him, as did the Parthini and Atintani in the hinterland of Epidamnus, and Dimallum in the hinterland of Apollonia. There was no response from Rome – as there had been no Roman response when Demetrius of Pharos seized these communities in the 220s.[36] Laevinus remained on watch at Oricum, with his large fleet of fifty quinqiremes, but he was not given the land forces needed to defend Rome's inland *amici* from Philip's army; they may not have been available because of the Hannibalic crisis. The inland *amici*, left on their own, were unable or unwilling to put up a defense against Philip – just as they had been unwilling or unable to resist Demetrius.[37] By 212 Philip had reached the Adriatic coast again, seizing by a brilliant coup de main the port-town and fortress of Lissus (see Polyb. 8.13). The evidence from a coin-horde found at modern Scele, 30 miles northeast of Lissus, shows that the entire Scodra region – not just Lissus itself – came under Macedonian control; many polities were now striking coinage with Macedonian royal emblems. Thus the Ardiaean allies of Rome were driven from this whole part of the coast. And at Lissus the king once more began to build a fleet.[38]

Philip in control of a secure naval base in Illyria could (again) threaten Italy. Even in 212 this threat could not be discounted: the war with Hannibal was raging, and many polities in Sicily (including Syracuse in 214) and in southern Italy (including Tarentum in 213) had gone over to the Carthaginian side. Philip was famous for his military gambles, and we have a story that in 212 the Syracusans, under siege by Rome, asked him to intervene (Livy 25.23.8–9).[39] To modern scholars such a prospect seems (again) scarcely credible; but modern scholars do not have the heavy responsibilities or bitter experience of the Senate. With Lissus in Philip's hands, a threat to Italy could not be discounted.[40]

---

[35] Such stubbornness in war is wrongly attributed by some scholars to Rome alone, and broad implications about Rome's allegedly exceptional aggressiveness are then drawn: see, e.g., Gehrke 2002: 153–71.

[36] See above, Chapter 2, p. 60.

[37] Above, Chapter 2, pp. 60 and 72.

[38] On the extent of Philip's conquests by land in Illyria in 213–212, and numismatic evidence that Philip had begun to build a war-fleet at Lissus, see Hammond, in Hammond and Walbank 1988: 398–9 (convincing). The large extent of Philip's conquests around Lissus in the Ardiaean country, as demonstrated by the coinage: ibid.: 409–10; and cf. Livy 27.30.14, from Polybius (discussed below).

[39] On the grim situation facing Rome in southern Italy and Sicily in this period, see Lazenby 1996: 43–4. Philip's reputation as a gambler: Rich 1984: 129–30.

[40] The story of the Syracusan appeal to Philip is accepted by Rich 1984: 130.

The answer to the problem – which probably came from Laevinus, the commander on the spot – was to distract Philip by means of a war in Greece. Because of the severe pressures on Rome elsewhere, such a war was beyond Roman resources alone. Hence Laevinus entered into discussions at some point in 212 with the Aetolian League. The Aetolians were the obvious and the only choice for a Greek ally. They were traditional opponents of Macedon, had their own important interests in the Adriatic, and in 212 Aetolia was the only polity of weight in European Greece that was not on good terms with (or subordinated to) Philip, having lost the Social War of 220–217 against him. Indeed, it is a measure of Macedon's dominant position in European Greece in 212/211 that the other possible allies for Rome on the western coast of Greece – the Achaean League, Epirus, Acarnania – were all themselves members of Macedon's Hellenic Symmachy.[41] Laevinus' efforts to convince the Aetolians to take up arms against Philip as they had done before led to prolonged and difficult negotiations, for the Aetolians were hesitant about the alliance, given Roman weakness and Macedonian power. But new Roman victories in Italy and Sicily in the summer of 211 – the capture of Capua and Syracuse – convinced the Aetolians, and in early autumn the alliance was finally struck and joint Roman–Aetolian military operations began.[42]

We have accounts of the Roman–Aetolian treaty both in our literary sources and in an inscription found in 1962 recording most of it. The main terms were: the Romans and the Aetolians will go to war against Philip and his allies, the Aetolians providing most of the land forces and the Romans at least twenty-five quinqiremes; any cities taken in the war by Rome would belong to the Aetolian League, with the moveable booty going to the Romans; any cities taken jointly by Rome and Aetolia would go to the Aetolians, with the moveable booty being shared. Cities that came over voluntarily to Rome during Roman operations against them would (it seems) become *amici* of Rome, but could join the Aetolian League; cities that came over voluntarily during joint Roman–Aetolian operations could join the Aetolian League; the Romans promised to aid Aetolia in the conquest of Acarnania; peace with Philip could only be made by one partner if it also involved the other partner. Other states – Elis and Sparta in the Peloponnese (traditional enemies

---

[41] See Errington 1989a: 99.
[42] On the date of the agreement between Laevinus and the Aetolians – shown by the link in Livy between Roman successes in summer 211 and the final Aetolian decision (26.24.3) – see Badian 1958b: 197–203, and Rich 1984. Preliminary negotiations: Livy 26.24.1.

of Achaea), Attalus of Pergamum, Pleuratus and Scerdilaidas of the Ardiaei – could join the alliance on similar terms.[43]

What is striking in this treaty is, first, the Roman lack of interest in territorial gain. In fact, territorial expansion is foresworn – in contrast to the Aetolians, whose appetite for territorial gain is explicit throughout. This is a continuation of the lack of Roman interest in territorial dominion which we already saw in Illyria.[44] Second, the terms are far more advantageous to the Aetolian League than to Rome: the League is given numerous ways to expand its territory, whereas all Rome gets from the war is the possibility of booty (to finance continuing military operations).[45] But the primary Roman goal – and primary gain – was strategic: in the face of Philip's threatening advance (Polyb. 5.101.9– 102.1; 7.13.1), his diversion from the Adriatic to a war in European Greece was hugely in Rome's interest (Livy 26.24.16, explicit). That was the fundamental reason for the Aetolian treaty.

The primary Roman goal in the war was thus defensive – to keep Philip occupied in Greece. But it is likely that the Romans acted from a desire for revenge as well. Philip had struck at them when they had committed no hostile act against him, simply because they were vulnerable: he deserved a new war on his doorstep as a punishing response to his conduct, and to inflict harm upon him.[46] In a world of states obsessed with questions of status and the reputation for power, a phenomenon itself deriving from the pressures of the anarchic environment, the punishment of Philip by war would also help restore to Rome the status among other states, a status that Philip had injured, making it clear that Rome was a polity with which one did not trifle. In an anarchic interstate system, the restoring and preserving of such status was important in itself, for a reputation for strength and ferocious defense of one's interests helped deter others, and this in turn helped to preserve a state's real security.[47]

---

[43]   The terms of the Roman–Aetolian alliance: see Schmitt 1969: 258–66. Livy says there was a northern limit placed on Aetolian territorial gains, at Corcyra (26.24.11). The limit makes sense, given Roman interests in the southern Adriatic (so Gruen 1984: 378) – but interestingly, it is not on the inscription.
[44]   See the comments of Gruen 1984: 378; Errington 1989a: 100.
[45]   Ibid.
[46]   See Harris 1979: 213; Rich 1984: 129–31 and 149.
[47]   Establishment of status as a major concern of Roman foreign relations: Mattern 1999: Ch. 1; cf. Linderski 1995; Rosenstein 2007. Importance of maintaining reputation and status under a system of international anarchy: see Eckstein 2000: 876–9. Obsession with status as a result of anarchic conditions in general: see Anderson 1999, esp. Ch. 2: "Campaigning for Respect." Obsession with status probably also reflects the ethos of the aristocratic and slave-owning men who by and large made ancient diplomatic decisions: see Strauss 1986: 31–5.

The treaty with Aetolia and the war in Greece did lead to new Roman relationships in the East, with pro-Aetolian and/or anti-Macedonian Greek states: Elis, Messene, Sparta, Pergamum. These were simply a natural consequence of the events of the war – a war, to repeat, which was itself a Roman response to Philip's aggression.[48] And the intensity of these new relationships is uncertain. When the war ended in 205, the Romans withdrew back beyond the Adriatic, as they had done in 228 and again in 219; and it was not at Roman initiative that Rome reentered Greek geopolitics. It thus appears that from the Roman point of view, the war in Greece was merely an exigency of the larger struggle for survival in which Rome was engaged.[49] Rome's reversion to a lack of interest in Greek affairs in 205–200 makes it very unlikely that the alliances with Aetolia and other Greek states, or the war in which they were created, had as a conscious aim an increased Roman foothold in European Greece, let alone that it was seen at Rome as a stepping-stone to eventual full control of the region.[50] The Senate certainly wished to exert control in regions which it considered crucial – though Rome was less able to do so now, because of Hannibal. But Greece itself still evoked little interest among the *Patres*, so long as the threat from Philip was kept in check.

But while Philip was clearly the aggressor in the war between Rome and Macedon, it is equally clear that the Aetolians were the aggressors in their new war against Philip. The Aetolian League had sworn peace with Macedon six years previously, ending the Social War. There is no evidence that he had broken the peace, and though he was a threat to Rome, and waged war every year from 217 in the far northwest, in Greece proper since 217 there had been an unusual period of peace.[51] The Aetolian decision of autumn 211 thus seems the consequence of a pure calculation of strategic advantage: Aetolia was lured into a new war by the prospect of recovering with Roman backing the territories and status lost in 220–217, and seizing more, whereas Macedon after 217 was for the moment a satisfied power regarding Greece proper (and no wonder, given its dominating position). In other words, Philip began the war with Rome – but the Aetolians began war with him.[52]

According to Livy the Roman–Aetolian treaty of alliance was not formally sworn at Rome until perhaps summer 209 (*biennio post*: 26.24.14).

[48]   See, rightly, Errington 1989a: 99.
[49]   See, rightly, Holleaux 1935: 233.
[50]   *Pace* Rich 1984: 131, and 150–1; cf. also Hammond, in Hammond and Walbank 1988: 401.
[51]   On this, see esp. Hammond, in Hammond and Walbank 1988: 390.
[52]   The Aetolian strategic aims: see Polyb. 9.30.8–9, with Rich 1984: 145.

The reasons for the odd Roman delay in formalizing the Aetolian agreement escape us. Perhaps it was sheer Roman procedural clumsiness, and not hesitation over eastern policy.[53] Perhaps M. Valerius Laevinus had personally to defend the terms of the treaty (in which Rome got few concrete benefits) before the Senate, and this did not happen until after his consulship in 210, when he was busy in Sicily.[54] In either case, the long delay may have had significant diplomatic consequences, especially during the Greek mediation effort of spring 209 (see below).

To summarize. Philip V of Macedon was the aggressor in the war that began with Rome in 214 BC; he sought to take advantage of Rome's weakness following the terrible defeats Rome had suffered in Italy at the hands of Hannibal. Philip sought to gain control of Illyria – with perhaps more conquest at Roman expense to follow. It would depend on circumstances. But the Aetolian League was the aggressor in the war that began in Greece in 211, as the Aetolians sought to take advantage of Roman support to reopen – without provocation – the war with Macedon that had been ended by the Peace of Naupactus in 217. It was not Philip who violated the Peace of Naupactus, but Aetolia. In the actions of both Philip V and the Aetolian League we see the typical ruthlessness of Hellenistic states, in a fiercely competitive and anarchic environment. Rome was clearly ruthless, too – but this did not make the Republic exceptional in its policies, merely typical.

THE IMPLICATIONS OF GREEK MEDIATION DURING THE FIRST MACEDONIAN WAR

We turn now to a discussion of the attempts of various Greek states to mediate the new war in Greece that broke out in 211. This is done with the specific purpose of establishing the attitude of those states towards Rome in 209–205, and in particular, to what extent Rome and Roman interests were taken into account by them. We note immediately that according to our sources, the representatives of Macedon at the various peace conferences we will discuss consistently proclaimed that Macedon had not started the war that was being mediated. No one contradicted them (see below). This indicates *which* war – the war between Rome and Philip or the war between the Aetolians and Philip – was the focus of Greek mediation.

---

[53] So Badian 1958b: 206–8.
[54] So Errington 1989b.

Almost from the beginning of what modern scholars call the First Macedonian War, major Greek states sought to end it through diplomacy. Their efforts at mediation occurred each year between 209 and 206 BC, and brought peace between Macedon and Aetolia in 206. Mediation by other Greek states then helped bring peace between Macedon and Rome in 205.[55] Great uncertainty exists, however, over the goal of the mediators of 209–206. Did they focus primarily on the fighting between Macedon and Aetolia, i.e., to bring the Aetolians to peace with Macedon independently of Rome? Or did they always aim at a "comprehensive peace" in Greece that would include Rome? The first goal appears inimical to Roman interests, since it would have left the Romans alone to face Philip. The second goal, a "comprehensive peace," is more congruent with the Romans' strategic goal in the Greece in this period – which was to keep Philip from attacking them while they had their hands full with Hannibal. Either conclusion would tell us a great deal about the attitude(s) of these Greek mediating states towards Rome. In what follows, it will be argued that the prominent Greek mediating states of 209–206 focused their efforts on peace between Macedon and Aetolia, although this was inimical to Roman interests and counter to Roman wishes. Yet – to repeat – some of these very same states came to Rome a few years later, pleading for Roman intervention in the East against the aggressions of Philip and Antiochus. This is what I mean by a diplomatic revolution.

Maurice Holleaux was the first to argue that the Greek mediators of 209–206 primarily sought a peace between Macedon and Aetolia. The most forceful advocates that the mediators sought a "comprehensive peace" including Rome have been H. H. Schmitt and, more recently, J. W. Rich. Scholarly opinion remains deeply divided. The rest of this chapter is devoted to a reexamination of this important problem.[56]

What is striking about the peace negotiations of 209–206 as the sources present them is, first, how often the Romans are not present: these are

---

[55]   Kascéev 1997: 419–20, points out that the modern term "mediation" covers a wide range of different ancient diplomatic actions, from merely bringing the contending parties together for peace talks, all the way to active proposal of specific peace terms. Because of the sparseness of our evidence, we cannot often discern the exact nature of the interventions of the neutral states in 209–205. What is clear is that serious attempts at mediation were made in each year.

[56]   Holleaux 1935: 35–8 and 74–5; vs. Schmitt 1957: 17, 25–6, and esp. 193–211; and Rich 1984: 145–7. In support of Schmitt: in addition to Rich, see Ferro 1960: 7, n. 6; Will 1982: 90–1; Berthold 1984: 106 (without discussion); Hammond, in Hammond and Walbank 1988: 403 (without discussion); Warrior 1996: 44 and 99–100 (without discussion). In support of Holleaux: Walbank 1967: 229; Huss 1976: 129–31, and 167–8 (leaning); Lazenby 1978: 163 (without discussion); Habicht 1982: 135–6; Ager 1991: 16 (without discussion); and Eckstein 2002.

peace talks between Greek mediators on the one side and representatives of Macedon and Aetolia on the other. Second, as we have already noted, Greek contemporaries evidently called this war "the Aetolian War" – that is, Greeks perceived the main antagonists to be Macedon and Aetolia. To be sure, our only source for this is the Roman historical writer Livy, where the term appears several times – but Livy is explicit that for Greek events in this period he is relying upon Polybius, and has the utmost confidence in his work. This is what Polybius has contemporary Greeks calling the war.[57] Third, in the one case where Romans are attested as present at peace talks (207 BC), the Roman commander in Greece is shown attempting to subvert the negotiations entirely, although a "comprehensive peace" including Rome is what is under discussion.[58] This suggests that whether the Greek mediators sought a separate Macedonian–Aetolian peace or not, the issue for the Romans was that they did not want a mediation at all, no matter what its goals; Rome wanted the war against Philip to continue. These findings, in turn, show us how the policies of the Greek mediating states of 209–206 worked at cross-purposes to the objective Rome sought in Greece in this period. And the Greek mediators came to understand that they were indeed working at cross-purposes to Rome – as we see especially in the ferociously anti-Roman remarks of the Greek mediator in Polyb. 11.4–6. Nor does that text stand alone.

Let us proceed in succession through the attempts at mediation between 209 and 206, to see how far the mediating states acted contrary to Rome's interests.[59] One must say at the beginning that our sources on the diplomacy of 209–206 are of poor quality. Polybius covered these diplomatic efforts in detail, as is shown by the remaining fragments of his account at Polyb. 10.25 and 11.4–6. But most of Polybius' account is unfortunately lost. Livy preserves much information clearly based on Polybian material, but Livy's interest in Greek affairs is sporadic, and a two-year gap in his recording of Greek events is admitted at 29.12.1.[60]

[57]   The general statement on Polybius at Livy 33.10.10: *Polybii secuti sumus, non incertum auctorem eum omnium Romanarum rerum tum praecipue in Gracecia gestarum.* The "Aetolian War": Livy (P) 27.30.4 (*inter Philippum atque Aetolos bellum . . .*); 27.30.10 (*de Aetolico finiendo bello actum . . .*); 28.7.10 (*Aetolico bello . . .*) 28.7.14 (*de finiendo Aetolico bello ageretur . . .*). Polybian origin of this material: Schmitt 1957: 195. In the Roman perspective the war had a different name: *bellum Macedonicum* or *bellum adversus Philippum* (Livy 31.1.6 and 31.1.8: from Annalistic sources: see Warrior 1996: 26).
[58]   App. *Mac.* 3; see discussion below.
[59]   Much of what follows is based on Eckstein 2002.
[60]   On Livy, see Schmitt 1957: 193–4 and 198; Rich 1984: 136–9. On Appian, see below, pp. 105–6.

Later writers such as Appian give us what appears to be important information – but the historicity of that information requires explicit defense. Any reconstruction, especially of the events in 207 and 206 BC – where Polybius is mostly lost and which the Livian narrative barely touches – must therefore remain tentative.

The first attempt at mediation of the war by Greek non-belligerent states occurred in the spring of 209.[61] The Aetolian League and Rome had made significant gains in the war to this point: the capture of Anticyra in Phocis, and the large island of Aegina off Athens; the accession to the alliance of Elis, Messene, and Sparta; and the prospective large-scale military intervention on the allied side by Attalus I of Pergamum. But in spring 209 these gains were countered when Philip inflicted two severe defeats upon the Aetolians at Lamia in east-central Greece (Livy 27.30.1–2).[62] A unified embassy from Ptolemy IV, the Rhodian Republic, Athens, and Chios now came to Philip at Phalara, near the site of his victories (27.30.4). An inscription recording the death of a Chian ambassador at Alexandria in March 209 suggests that the mediation was organized by the court of the Ptolemies.[63] The envoys came, Livy says, "to bring an end to the war between Philip and the Aetolians."[64] Before seeing Philip the mediators evidently won Aetolian consent for the overture, since the Aetolians sent to Phalara a non-belligerent negotiator of their own, to join the peace talks: Amynander, king of Athamania.[65]

According to Livy, the four non-belligerent states were really acting from fear that Philip's war with Aetolia would lead to the growth of Macedonian power over European Greece (27.30.5). Presumably this analysis derives from Polybian material. Thus the primary goal of the Greek mediators was geopolitical: fearing another victory by Philip as in the Social War, they sought to limit the expansion of Macedonian power.[66] Disruption of commerce by the war may also have been a factor, since the Aetolians were famous privateers during wartime (see esp. Polyb. 4.3.1–3), and Rhodes, Chios, and the Ptolemies had important

---

[61]   Livy dates this mediation to 208, but the reference to the Nemean Games (27.30.9) shows that these events actually occurred the year before: see Schmitt 1957: 194.
[62]   Best detailed account of the early events of the war: Rich 1984: 131–4. Assessment of the situation after Philip's victories: Hammond, in Hammond and Walbank 1988: 403.
[63]   So Habicht 1982: 136–7 with n. 80.
[64]   *venerunt ad dirimendum inter Philippum atque Aetolos bellum* (Livy 27.30.4).
[65]   *adhibitus ab Aetolis . . . pacificator Amynander rex Athamanum* (Livy 27.30.4).
[66]   Primary goal geopolitical: see Habicht 1982: 137; Huss 1976: 129–31. Derivation of Livy 27.30 from Polybian material: Walbank 1940: 89–90.

commercial interests in the Aegean.[67] But note that from this economic perspective, a continuation of fighting just between Macedon and Rome would probably mean a war in the Adriatic and northwest Greece – an area of no interest to the Ptolemies, and much less important to the other commercially minded states.[68]

The discussions at Phalara between Philip, the mediators, and Amynander proved so promising that Philip agreed to a thirty days' truce, until direct negotiations with the Aetolians would begin at the city of Aegium in Macedon-allied Achaea (Livy 27.30.6, cf. 30.9). Who was included in this truce? Some scholars argue that nothing in 209 shows the mediating states intended to detach the Aetolians from Rome into a separate peace with Philip.[69] But Rome receives no mention in Livy's account of the Phalara mediation (27.30.4–6): we see only the inter-action of the mediators, the Aetolians' representative, and Philip, and the description of the private concerns of the mediators focuses totally on the problem of Philip's power and his conflict with Aetolia; Rome is absent. Indeed, there is no sign that the Romans even know about – let alone approve – the Phalara talks.[70]

These implications of Livy 27.30.4–6 are confirmed by the next item in Livy. After agreeing to the truce, Philip goes to Chalcis on Euboea, in order to prevent Attalus of Pergamum from landing there and seizing the fortress and the entire island; he continues to Achaea only after leav-ing a strong garrison on Euboea against a Pergamene attack (27.30.7–8). This shows that although there is a truce between Philip and the Aetolians as a result of the Phalara talks, Attalus is not expected to participate in it, nor (apparently) has he heard of it. Rather, Philip is concerned that Pergamene forces are about to attack key Macedonian strongpoints, and he initiates military steps (not diplomatic steps) to prevent these attacks. To be sure, Philip might not have known the exact whereabouts of Attalus and his fleet, but it would not have been hard for Philip or the Aetolians or especially the mediators to send heralds

---

[67] Aetolian privateering: Scholten 2000: Ch. 3. Ptolemaic motivation partly com-mercial: Manni 1949: 95. Economic motives even stronger for Rhodes and Chios: so Huss 1976: 130. In Polyb. 11.4.4–5, in a speech concerned primarily with geopolitical reasons for ending the war, its destructiveness upon innocent bystanders is stressed by a mediator who is probably a Rhodian (see below, pp. 107–8).

[68] See Huss 1976: 167, who notes that the Ptolemies – in contrast to their great desire to keep peace in Greece and the Aegean – had no interest or interests in the northwest.

[69] Schmitt 1957: 193–5; Rich 1984: 145.

[70] See esp. Holleaux 1935: 36 n. 4. Ampela 1998: 70, takes it as obvious that Rome was not intended to be included in the mediation of 209. But given the weight of scholarship on the other side of this issue, this position must be carefully defended.

to find Attalus and inform him of the truce. But neither Philip nor the Aetolians nor the neutrals are depicted in the month following Phalara as attempting this. Our information is of course fragmentary, but we do have a detailed account of Philip's actions (Livy 27.30.7–9) – and what we see are Philip's preparations against a major Attalid attack.

There is no reason to believe that Attalus was somehow in a different category from the Romans. The only difference in spring 209 was that – unlike the imminent military operations of Attalus – there was not even a rumor as yet among the Greeks as to when Roman military operations for 209 would begin (cf. Livy 27.30.11).

The Aegium conference took place a month later, and the assumptions behind it emerge clearly at Polyb. 10.25 – where we have an explicit attempt to split the Aetolians from Rome. This Polybian fragment is from a speech by an ambassador, and comes from the mediation efforts of 209.[71] The speaker says that at present the Aetolians and their allies are bearing the brunt of the fighting against Philip, while the Romans hang back like a heavy phalanx waiting for the light-armed forces to be exposed to danger first (10.25.1); such an analogy would have particular force in the aftermath of the recent Macedonian victories over the Aetolians at Lamia. The speaker then warns that if "the light-armed" are defeated, the phalanx (i.e., the Romans) will move off unharmed (25.5), but if "the light-armed" are victorious, not only will "the phalanx" move in to claim the main credit for the victory (cf. 25.2), but also the Romans will attempt to bring all of Greece under their control (25.5).

Since the speaker refers to Aetolian victory in the war as something "may the Gods forbid" (Polyb. 10.25.5), this speech most likely comes from a Macedonian, and not from an envoy of one of the mediating states.[72] Even if the speech is from a Macedonian, however, note that the speaker sharply differentiates the Aetolians and their allies from the Romans, points out the differing interests of the two sets of combatants, and seeks to create anger and fear concerning Rome among the former group. The tone of Polyb. 10.25 is thus consistent with Livy's account of the Phalara origins of the Aegium conference: this is primarily an effort to end the war between Macedon and Aetolia.

Another sentiment at Aegium hostile to the Romans appears at Livy 27.30.10: "they discussed the ending of the Aetolian war, so that neither the Romans nor Attalus would have reason to enter Greece."[73]

---

[71] See Walbank 1967: 229.

[72] See Holleaux 1935: 35 n. 4, and Walbank 1967: 228, against Schmitt 1957: 195, who suggests that the speech is by one of the mediators. If so, we would have Polybian accounts of *two* anti-Roman speeches by mediators during the war: here at 10.25 and later at 11.4–6 (see below). But openly praying against an Aetolian victory ("May the Gods forbid . . . ") would be impossibly tactless coming from a mediator.

[73] *de Aetolico finiendo bello actum, ne causa aut Romanis aut Attalo intrandi Graeciam esset.*

This is evidently a description of the general purpose of the peace conference, which should come from the mediators – and was perhaps their formal position.[74] At the Phalara talks the neutrals' private fear was the growing power of *Philip* (Livy 27.30.5), not of Rome and Pergamum, but there is no contradiction: the mediators' private fear of Philip could hardly have been stated in public either at Phalara or at Aegium in Philip's presence – while fear of Rome and Pergamum obviously *could* be stated in front of those states assembled for the Aegium talks.[75] Livy 27.30.10 is thus consistent with the entire public tone of the mediation of 209, which seems to be derogatory and excluding of the Romans and Attalus.

The Aegium conference collapsed when the Aetolians suddenly made a series of harsh territorial demands on Philip. Two of these demands would have helped restore Rome's position in Illyria: that Philip return Atintania to the Romans, and that he return the Ardiaei to the pro-Roman Illyrian dynasts Scerdilaidas and Pleuratus (Livy 27.30.13–14).[76] Livy then blames the collapse of the Aegium talks on the Aetolians' demands (27.30.11). This must reflect his source Polybius, who had little love for Aetolia, but there seems no reason to doubt this account.[77] As with the Phalara talks, the Romans were not present at Aegium, which explains why the sudden Aetolian demands outraged Philip: as Livy explicitly says, he viewed himself as the victor in the war and the Aetolian League as the defeated party (27.30.14).[78] Philip's attitude reveals the impact which he believed his victories had had on the military situation. It also reveals how much the focus at Aegium was on the Aetolians – for Philip had never beaten the Romans.

Rich argues that because the Aetolians' sudden demands at Aegium included one (or perhaps two) that would benefit Rome, the Romans' absence at Phalara and at Aegium means nothing: the Aetolian demands at Aegium show that Rome was always to be included in the peace.[79] But Livy says that the Aetolians' negotiating position hardened only when they heard that the Pergamene and Roman fleets had finally arrived in Greek waters (27.30.11), and that the new demands were never meant to be taken seriously (ibid.). Thus it appears that the Aetolians, at first demoralized by their defeats at Philip's hands, considered a separate peace with him – but when strong Roman and Pergamene reinforcements finally

---

[74]   Schmitt 1957: 195–6.

[75]   Ibid.

[76]   This latter demand demonstrates the enormous success of Philip's conquests in the Ardiaean country along the Adriatic coast in 212 (cf. above, p. 87 and n. 38).

[77]   On Polybius' generally negative attitude towards the Aetolians, see esp. Mendels 1984/1986: 63–73.

[78]   *enim vero indignatum ratus Philippus victos victori sibi ultro condiciones ferre.*

[79]   Rich 1984: 145.

arrived, they simply sought an excuse to break off the talks. This explains Philip's bitter remark at the end of the Aegium conference: he had always been for peace, the Aetolians for war (27.30.11).[80]

Ager has noted that the Aetolians had engaged in just such "zig-zagging" in diplomacy a few years before, during the Social War. In 218, momentarily demoralized by Philip's sacking of their capital at Thermum, they accepted a proposal from prominent Greek mediators (Rhodes and Chios, as in 209) for – precisely – a thirty days' truce, during which peace talks would begin (Polyb. 5.28.1). But when the Aetolians learned of political problems at Philip's court, they took heart, and suddenly backed off from the talks – and they backed off by making sudden new demands (5.29.1–3). This is the best explanation for the failure at Aegium as well: the Aetolians, having gained a month's respite from Philip and assured now of the arrival of the Roman and Pergamene reinforcements, subverted peace talks they felt they no longer needed, by making new and excessive demands (including a couple from which the Romans would benefit). But in that case, the Aetolians' demands at Aegium cannot count as strong evidence that the Romans were all along intended to be included in the peace of 209.[81]

To be sure, such a separate Macedonian–Aetolian peace was prohibited in the treaty of Roman–Aetolian alliance of autumn 211 (Livy 26.22.12). But the fact is that the Aetolians in 206 violated that very clause of the treaty, when – having again suffered heavy defeat at Macedonian hands – they *did* make a separate peace with Philip. So the Aetolians were not stopped by legalities. Similarly, the Punic–Macedonian treaty of alliance of 215 contained a clause forbidding a separate peace with Rome (Polyb. 7.9.12) – which did not prevent Philip in 205 from making a separate peace with Rome. In both cases one could make the argument from political-military necessity; but this simply reveals that in a world ruled by harsh power politics, such clauses in treaties were mere hopeful rhetoric. A striking example underlines this point: in Polybius' eye-witness account of the meeting in autumn 170 BC of the Achaean faction led by Archon and Lycortas (Polybius' father), to decide whether to back Rome in its new war against Macedon or to be neutral, a series

---

[80] *sed ut omnes socios testes haberet se pacis, illos [sc. Aetolos] belli causam quaesisse.* Such a statement only makes sense in the context of negotiations focused on Philip and the Aetolians, for Philip had been the obvious aggressor against Rome (from 217), whereas the Aetolians had been the aggressors against the king (from 211); see the first section of this chapter, above.

[81] On the Aetolian duplicity at Aegium, and the parallel from the Social War, see Ager 1991: 16. The Aetolian duplicity is also emphasized by Errington 1969: 56, and Hammond, in Hammond and Walbank 1988: 403 (both of whom, however, see the Aetolian demands at Aegium as having been formulated in a direct conspiracy with Rome to keep the war going).

of practical political considerations are brought forward on one side or the other – but one consideration that is *never* mentioned is that Achaea in 170 actually had a formal and sworn treaty of military alliance with Rome (Polyb. 28.6). That was immaterial.[82] And in 209, not only were the Aetolians uncertain about the scale of Roman military intervention in Greece that year (hence the relief they display at Livy 27.30.11), but their treaty of alliance with the Romans had not yet even been formally ratified at Rome – and this was after almost two years of waiting. That would be all the more reason for the Aetolians in 209, perhaps thinking themselves abandoned (as they did feel abandoned in 206), to feel free to leave the war after Philip's victories over them at Lamia.[83]

Schmitt, unlike Rich, accepts the trend of the Livian narrative and Polyb. 10.25 (above, p. 96) that the mediating states were negotiating with Philip and Aetolia in 209 for the purpose of a peace solely between Philip and the League. But he argues that such conduct should not be seen as counter to Roman interests. This is because a peace between Philip and Aetolia would soon have led to peace between Philip and Rome – as happened in 206–205.[84]

This argument is not convincing. A separate peace between Philip and Aetolia in 209 would have left the Romans alone in Greece to face Philip with the Hannibalic War still raging behind them from Italy to Spain. Given the strategic pressures, Rome might well have then made peace with Philip, yes, but most likely on disadvantageous terms – including Philip's retention of all his recent Illyrian conquests, including the port of Lissus. Such a settlement, occurring in an atmosphere of defeat and creating a permanent threat to Italy's Adriatic coast, would hardly have been in Rome's interest.[85] But in 209 to continue the war against Philip without Aetolia would not have been an attractive option either: it meant a war without major Greek help on land against a formidable and aggressive enemy. Consider simply the dilemma the Romans would have faced later in 209 itself, when a strong Carthaginian fleet appeared off Corcyra (Livy 27.15.8, cf. 30.16): what if Philip, now victorious and unopposed by Aetolia, had been free to march to the Adriatic coast at the same time? A strong Punic fleet appeared again off western Greece in 208,

---

[82]   See Eckstein 2002: 279 n. 34.

[83]   On the Roman delay in swearing the Aetolian alliance (Livy 26.24.14), see above, p. 91. On the absence of the Romans from the peace negotiations of 209, see already Eckstein 1988: 418 n. 22.

[84]   Schmitt 1957: 57, and 195–6.

[85]   Even in the separate peace between Rome and Philip in 205, when the balance of power was more in Rome's favor, the Romans conceded Atintania to Philip: Livy 29.12.13. Walbank 1940: 103, suggests that even in 205 Rome also conceded to Philip most of his Illyrian conquests of 213–212, including Dassaretis (though the fate of Lissus is unclear).

in a coordinated operation with Macedon (Livy 28.7.17–18, and 8.8), and that autumn Philip himself began to build a fleet of 100 warships (Livy 28.8.14).[86] In the actual circumstances of 209 and 208, with the Aetolians and their allies still heavily involved in the war, and Macedon weakened by a Dardanian invasion (see below), the Carthaginian naval threats to western Greece became mere raids – while Philip's ship-building program became delayed.[87] But the Punic naval expeditions to the Adriatic and Philip's ship-building would have looked dangerous indeed if Rome in 209 and 208 had had to fight in Greece on its own limited resources. The isolation of the Romans would have further worsened if, as happened historically, their ally Attalus of Pergamum had been driven from the war in 208 in defeat at Philip's hands (see below). It is thus very hard to see how the Greek mediators who sought a peace in 209 between Macedon and Aetolia – removing Aetolia from the war – were acting in Rome's interests.

The failure of the mediation effort of 209 did not dissuade the non-belligerent Greek states from making another effort a year later, in 208. The war by then seemed suddenly to have turned against Philip. A Dardanian invasion in autumn 209 gravely damaged Macedon, and Philip's northern frontier continued in 208 to be unsettled; yet in spring 208 many of Philip's allies both in central Greece and in the Peloponnese were also calling desperately on him for military help against the threats posed by Aetolian, Roman, and Pergamene forces and, in the Peloponnese, now from the forces of Sparta.[88] A new embassy from the non-belligerent states now appeared in Greece: the Ptolemies and Rhodes are explicitly mentioned, but (as in 209) others may have been involved.[89]

---

[86]   Even Petzold 1940: 49, who disbelieves most traditions about Macedonian–Carthaginian cooperation in 215–202, does not doubt these threatening Punic expeditions to western Greece. On the historicity of the expedition of 208 (Livy's information here clearly derives from Polybian material), see also Walbank 1940: 97 and n. 5; Hammond, in Hammond and Walbank 1988: 405.

[87]   Even so, by 201 Philip's war-fleet amounted to forty or fifty cataphracts, and some were very large ships: sources and discussion in Walbank 1940: 117 and n. 2, and Walbank 1967: 505. By 201 Philip also had about 150 light *lembi* (Polyb. 16.2.9).

[88]   On Philip's difficult strategic situation in spring 208, see Walbank 1940: 93–4. On the devastating Dardanian invasion, see Hammond, in Hammond and Walbank 1988: 403 (with sources).

[89]   Some scholars propose that Athens and Chios joined the mediators of 208: so Holleaux 1935: 119 n. 1; Walbank 1940: 94 n. 7. But Athens is missing from the list of persistent mediators in the neutral envoy's speech in Polyb. 11.4.1 (which falls in 207 – see below), which suggests that the Athenians did not continue their efforts after 209: see Habicht 1982: 136–7. Chios does appear at Polyb. 11.4.1, so perhaps the Chians did participate in 208 and Livy at 28.7.14 has abbreviated a longer list of mediators he found in Polybius: cf. Errington 1989a: 103.

The new embassy first approached the Aetolians, whom they found meeting with their Roman allies at Heraclea, west of Thermopylae (Livy 28.7.14). The mediators were then sent north to consult Philip (28.7.13). But the meeting with Philip was delayed, because Philip suddenly took the offensive against his multiple enemies – and he was spectacularly successful. He raided Heraclea and captured Thermopylae from the Aetolians, opening up central Greece to his army; he then defeated the Pergamenes near Opus, helping drive Attalus out of the war; then he conquered regions east of Thermopylae previously under Aetolian control (June–July 208).[90] By the time Philip met with the neutral envoys, at Elateia south of Thermopylae in July 208, he was flushed with victory. He gave the envoys a friendly but vague answer about ending the war, and sent them away (Livy 28.7.15). In fact, he was now more interested in advancing into the Peloponnese and striking a serious blow against Sparta, which he succeeded in doing (28.7.14–17). At this time, too, he was expecting substantial Carthaginian naval help for a new offensive in western Greece (28.7.17–18).

Did the mediators of 208 intend to include the Romans in their attempted peace? Schmitt and Rich are sure of this, because the mediators met at Heraclea with the assembled Aetolian magistrates, and Roman envoys were there (Polyb. 10.42.4).[91] Note that even if the Romans were to be included in the mediation of 208, this does not affect our findings about the mediation of 209. But in fact the evidence on 208 is quite ambiguous.

First, the envoys from the mediating states were clearly seeking a meeting with the *Aetolian* leadership as their initial step. As it happened, they found the Aetolian leaders gathered with envoys of P. Sulpicius Galba, the Roman commander in Greece, evidently discussing strategy for the war. But the presence of the Romans may have come as a surprise: Philip, for one, expected to find only the Aetolian magistrates when he raided Heraclea (Polyb. 10.42.4–5). That is, we should not think this a situation where the mediators intentionally invited the Romans to a preliminary conference on peace; rather, they dealt with the complex situation they faced when they arrived at Heraclea.[92]

Second, a story in Frontinus (*Strat.* 1.4.6) says that envoys from the Aetolians – without any Romans – went to discuss peace with Philip. The point of the story is that Philip tricked the Aetolian envoys into thinking he was interested in peace, so that he could then take the Aetolian

---

[90]   For a convenient summary of Philip's successes in this period, see Walbank 1940: 95–6.

[91]   Heraclea a meeting of the Aetolian magistrates and perhaps the Aetolian *Apocleti* or Inner Council: Walbank 1967: 257; cf. Schmitt 1957: 198.

[92]   See rightly Holleaux 1935: 36 n. 3 – admitted even by Schmitt 1957: 197.

position at Thermopylae by surprise.[93] This story in Frontinus, in which the Aetolians appear to be negotiating a peace on their own, tends to balance Livy's information that the Romans were present when the non-belligerent mediators met the Aetolian leaders at Heraclea. We must canvass the possibility that the events surrounding the mediation of 208 were more complicated than the passing references to it that we possess in Livy 28.7 – a narrative which itself shows some misunderstanding of Polybius' language.[94]

Finally, Livy's account of the meeting of the Greek mediators with Philip two months later displays characteristics that are odd if the underlying assumption is that the interlocutors are discussing a comprehensive peace including Rome. The subject of discussion is "the ending of the Aetolian war" (de finiendo Aetolico bello: 28.7.14). And that this means, precisely, the ending of the war between Macedon and Aetolia is supported by Philip's final remark to the mediators: he had not been the cause of this war (se neque causam eius belli fuisse: 28.7.15). A propagandistic statement, to be sure: but (as in 209) Philip's remarks would have been nonsensical if Rome was central to the peace under discussion, for everyone knew he had been the aggressor against Rome. Good propaganda requires at least some factual basis, and Philip's statement to the mediators is good propaganda only if Philip and the mediators were focused on his relations with Aetolia – for the Aetolians had started war against him, in 211 (see above).[95]

My point is not to prove that the mediation of 208 was intended solely to bring the war between Macedon and Aetolia to an end; it remains possible that the Romans were involved. My point is only that there is enough contrary evidence to make us cautious about assuming that the mediators of 208 were always focused on a "comprehensive peace."[96]

---

[93] Philippus . . . Graeciam petens, cum Thermopylas occupatas audiret et ad eum legati Aetolorum venissent acturi de pace, retentis eis ipse magnis itineribus ad angustias pertendit securisque custodibus et legatorum reditus exspectantibu inopinatus Thermopylas traiecit.

[94] Livy thinks that Polybius' reference to the Aetolians gathered at Heraclea (10.42.4) means a regular meeting of the biannual Panaetolian Assembly; but Polybius' language indicates merely a meeting of the Aetolian magistrates and the Apocleti: see Walbank 1967: 257. Rich 1984: 146, finds it "inconceivable" that the Aetolians in 208 might have found an opportunity to negotiate a peace with Philip on their own – but see Walbank 1940: 95 n. 1, who does not.

[95] The implication of de finiendo Aetolico bello is taken as obvious by Holleaux 1935: 36 n. 4. His position is strengthened by adding Philip's statement in the subsequent passage, 28.7.15 (se neque causam eius belli fuisse).

[96] If App. Mac. 3 is describing events of 208, this would be proof that the Romans had indeed been involved in the mediation of 208 (since there we have a speech of P. Sulpicius Galba): so argued by Ampela 1998: 70 n. 222. But App. Mac. 3 is obviously describing events of 207, not 208, as is proven by its parallel with Polyb. 11.4–6: see below, pp. 105–6.

The mediation effort of 208 failed to obtain even a serious discussion of peace terms by the belligerents. Philip especially seems to have been more intent on vigorously prosecuting the war than negotiating its end.[97] But in 207 important Greek non-belligerents tried yet again to bring about a negotiated peace, and this time matters proceeded much further.

Developments in the war made spring 207 a propitious time for a new initiative. The tide was continuing to run in Philip's favor – and the Aetolians were especially hard-pressed. The king's many victories in 208 had strengthened his and his army's already formidable military reputation: he could declare to his allies that no Greek forces now dared face him in battle (Livy 28.8.3, from Polybian material). Attalus of Pergamum, defeated by Philip at Opus, had been driven from the war, returning to Asia Minor to deal with an invasion of his kingdom by Philip's in-law Prusias I of Bithynia. This dealt the Aetolians a serious blow, depriving them of a major ally who was closer to them and more trusted by them than were the Romans.[98] The Roman naval campaign in the Aegean in 208, while destructive to Philip's allies, had little strategic impact, and then in spring 207 the Romans showed no sign of stirring from their bases in the Adriatic. Indeed, the legion sent to the Adriatic/ Greek theater with Laevinus' fleet in 214 was now withdrawn, perhaps to help deal with the impending crisis of the invasion of Italy by Hannibal's brother Hasdrubal. Thus Aetolia could not expect significant Roman help on land, only some naval raids.[99] Meanwhile, Philip's ally the Achaean League, under the energetic leadership of Philopoemen (one of Polybius' heroes), had produced a powerful new army. This shifted the balance of power in the Peloponnese against Aetolia's ally Sparta, which, instead of providing strategic aid to Aetolia, now faced its own severe problems.[100] Nowhere the Aetolians looked in spring 207 were their prospects promising.

Our information on the mediation effort of 207 consists of a brief and problematic account in Appian (*Mac.* 3), a vague reference in Dio (frg. 57.58, cf. Zon. 9.11), and a tantalizing fragment of Polybius (11.4–6).

[97] Cf. Errington 1989a: 103.
[98] On the close relationship between the Aetolians and the rulers of Pergamum, see McShane 1964: 100–2 and 106–7. Dating from before ca. 250, the relationship grew closer in the 220s (McShane 1964: 100–1). Attalus had even been elected one of the two Aetolian generals for 209 – a great honor (Livy 27.29.10 and 30.1).
[99] The withdrawal of the legion: Rich 1984: 153–5. Roman inaction in the Adriatic and Greece in spring–summer 207: Hammond, in Hammond and Walbank 1988: 406.
[100] On Philopoemen's reorganization and strengthening of the Achaean army, which led in 207 to the great Achaean victory over Sparta at Mantineia, see Errington 1969: 62–7.

The latter passage shows that Polybius covered this mediation in great detail.[101] But Polybius' main narrative is no longer extant, and Livy – whom one can normally depend upon in this period to give us at least Polybius' main points – chose not to cover the events of 207 and 206 in Greece. Livy's reason for ignoring Greek affairs is simple: the Romans had been inactive in Greece in these years (29.12.1).[102] This statement is repeated at 32.21.17 and at 36.11.11, which say that Rome had left the Aetolians alone to face Philip – and both these latter passages derive from Polybian material.[103]

The loss of both Polybius and Livy creates a problem in conceptualizing what occurred not only in the mediation of 207 but also in the entire period 207–205, which saw the end of the war between Macedon and Aetolia and then, a year later, the end of the war between Macedon and Rome. Because of the patchy nature of our sources, scholars have offered differing hypotheses on the sequence of events. The sequence followed here follows the scholarly consensus: that the Romans were militarily inactive both in 207 and in 206, which led the Aetolians – suffering severe invasion(s) of the Aetolian heartland by Philip in 206 – to abandon the war; the Roman expedition of 205, under P. Sempronius Tuditanus, then led to a compromise peace between Rome and Philip. Other scenarios propose that there was a large Roman expedition in 207, or that P. Sempronius Tuditanus' expedition actually arrived in 206 (not in 205); either scenario would show that Rome was prosecuting the war vigorously – which would be congruent with Rome having large geopolitical goals among the Greeks.[104] But such alternative scenarios fly in the face of most of our evidence (both Polybian and Annalistic), which indicates that after 208 Rome left the Aetolians on their own against Philip, and they fly as well in the face of the logic that must lie behind the Aetolian decision to seek a separate peace: why would the Aetolians have done so if the Romans were supporting them energetically with large expeditions in 207 or 206? The implication of the absence of Rome from the fighting in 207 and 206 supports our overall trend: that Roman goals in the war in Greece were strictly

[101]   On the dating of the fragment Polyb. 11.4.6 to summer 207 (certain): see below, and n. 103.
[102]   *neglectae eo biennio res in Graecia erant.* The obvious years are 207 and 206, since the Romans had been militarily active in 208 (see above).
[103]   Polybian derivation of Livy 32.21.27: Briscoe 1973: 1–2. Polybian derivation of Livy 36.11.11: Briscoe 1981: 1–2.
[104]   A large Roman expedition in 207: so Hammond, in Hammond and Walbank 1988: 406–7; large Roman political goals: ibid.: 401. A large Roman expedition in 206 (Sempronius Tuditanus): Rich 1984: 136–43; large Roman goals: ibid.: 131, cf. 150–1.

limited, primarily to keeping Philip distracted from the West while the Hannibalic crisis lasted. Hence the Romans devoted limited resources to it, for they were not yet much interested in Greek affairs per se.[105]

With Polybius and Livy absent, the late source Appian (*Mac.* 3) is our only narrative of the diplomacy of 207. And he must be used with caution. The early chapters of the *Macedonica* contain factual errors.[106] And there is a major error in *Mac.* 3 itself: the claim that a strong Roman army arrived in northwest Greece and carried out important operations with the Aetolians (the capture of the city of Ambracia) before the League concluded a separate peace with Philip. Perhaps this story reflects an actual action by P. Sempronius Tuditanus' actual expedition of 205 (the capture of the lesser-known town of Ambracus?).[107] But it is illogical that a major Roman army arrives in northwest Greece and the Aetolians go on to make a separate peace anyway. Since Livy's version of events is that the Aetolians made a separate peace because the Romans had abandoned them (29.12.1; 32.21.17; cf. 36.31.11) – a version which is based on Polybius, which is logical, and which Livy would not have put forth (since it reflects badly on Roman *fides*) unless he had strong evidence to believe it – it appears that if Appian's tale of major Roman help to Aetolia before the Aetolians' separate peace is not sheer confusion, then it derives from a Roman tradition whose intent is (precisely) to defend Rome from the charge of having abandoned Aetolia in 207–206. This does not raise our confidence in the general narrative of App. *Mac.* 3.[108]

Nevertheless, we should not dismiss Appian entirely, for part of his account of the mediation of 207 sounds very much like Polyb. 11.4–6 and provides a plausible historical context for that passage – as a whole range of scholars have pointed out.[109] According to App. *Mac.* 3, then, a delegation from non-belligerent states – Ptolemaic Egypt, Chios, Mytilene, and Amynander of Athamania – tried twice, at the Panaetolian

---

[105]   For detailed arguments against Rich, see Eckstein 2002: 18 n. 54. Note, e.g., that Livy 29.11.11 has Sempronius elected consul for 204 *in absentia* while in command of Greece. This places him in Greece in late 205 – but there is not enough campaigning in Livy 29.12 to fill up two seasons (206 and 205). For detailed arguments against Hammond, see Eckstein 2002: 18 n. 56. Hammond's thesis requires a large Roman expedition to Illyria which did not stay long and accomplished nothing – a very inefficient use of manpower in a crisis year that included Hasdrubal's invasion of Italy, and a very cumbersome way of dealing with the fact that clearly Rome sent no *permanent* help to its Greek allies in 207 or 206.

[106]   App. *Mac.* 4 has Philip conquering Chios during his Aegean campaign of 201 – which did not happen.

[107]   So Rich 1984: 143–4 (but wrongly dating these events to 206, see above).

[108]   Cf. Holleaux 1935: 245 and n. 2; Walbank 1940: 99 and n. 9; Rich 1984: 144.

[109]   See Holleaux 1935: 38 and n. 1; Schmitt 1957: 207–8; Rich 1984: 144.

Assemblies first of spring 207 and then of autumn 207, to bring about a negotiated peace. This time we are told directly that the aim of the mediators was at first a comprehensive peace including the Romans.[110] But Appian also says that P. Sulpicius Galba, the current Roman commander in Greece, sabotaged the peace effort: Galba claimed publicly that he did not have the legal power to commit Rome to peace, writing secretly to the Senate that it was to Rome's advantage that Aetolia should continue war against Philip.[111] The Senate then wrote to Greek allies, forbidding the peace. Then comes the tale of the large forces sent to help the Aetolians, and the joint Roman–Aetolian capture of "Ambracia" – all for naught, for the Roman forces immediately returned to Italy, and Philip recaptured Ambracia. At a second meeting concerning peace, the neutral envoys then spoke against Rome, questioning Roman motives and claiming that war between Aetolia and Philip was allowing Rome to form the habit of intervening in the affairs of the Greeks, to the detriment of Greek freedom. When Galba rose to reply, he was shouted down by the audience, so strong had anti-Roman feelings become. But the second meeting, too, failed to bring about a negotiated peace, and so the war continued for some time longer.[112]

Given the obvious problems in App. *Mac.* 3, it would be incautious to press the details. But it is striking that P. Sulpicius Galba in Appian opposes *any* mediated peace, since it is in Rome's interest that war should continue. That Rome is included in the mediation of 207, that the peace is intended as a "comprehensive peace," does not matter. Why a tradition of Galba's opposition to peace in general would have developed out of whole cloth is hard to see; and in fact we do not possess any ancient evidence of Roman encouragement for *any* of the mediators' several interventions. Moreover, Galba was the Roman commander in Greece in 209 and 208 as he was in 207, so perhaps he disliked the mediations of 209 and 208 as he did that of 207; perhaps he viewed the actions of the mediating states in 209 and 208 as contrary to Roman interest whether Rome was included in the peace effort or not (although more so in the latter case), as he did in 207. And in Appian, Galba's view of Rome's strategic interests in Greece is shared by the entire Senate – an indication of what his position on peace talks is likely to have been

---

[110] ἐπὶ διαλλαγῇ Ῥωμαίων καὶ Αἰτωλῶν καὶ Φιλίππου. Dio frg. 57.58 (cf. Zon. 9.11) reports that it was Philip, on the advice of envoys from Ptolemy IV, who took an important initiative in including the Romans in these negotiations.

[111] Galba's opinion: Ῥωμαίοις συμφέρει πολεμεῖν Αἰτωλοὺς Φιλίππῳ. Holleaux 1935: 36 n. 3, is thus correct about the clash of interests between Galba and the Greek mediators (despite Schmitt 1957: 209).

[112] App. *Mac.* 3 end–*Mac.* 4. Cf. Livy 36.31.11 (see below, pp. 110–11).

in 209 and 208. All this makes sense, and conforms to the Roman strategic need and primary goal of keeping Philip distracted in Greece, combined perhaps with the wish to punish Philip with war because of his treaty with Hannibal.[113]

The account in App. *Mac.* 3 also provides a plausible historical context for the important Polybian fragment 11.4–6. This is a speech by an envoy arguing for peace between the Aetolians and Philip, and it is extraordinaarily hostile to Rome. The speech belongs to Polybius' narrative of Greek events for 207, for it is preceded by the description of Hasdrubal's defeat at the Metaurus (11.1–3: June 207).[114] And the speaker of this very anti-Roman speech is an envoy from one of the mediating Greek states (clear from 11.4.1–2). The fragment as we have it does not give his name, but a gloss on one of the Polybian manuscripts identifies him as one Thrasycrates. There is a fair argument for identifying Thrasycrates as a Rhodian: Rhodes is singled out in the list of persistent mediators mentioned at the beginning of the speech, coming second after Ptolemy IV, and called formally ἡ τῶν Ῥοδίων πόλις, as compared to the simple ethnicity names given the other mediators.[115] Furthermore, the speaker comes from a state which has participated prominently in mediation efforts since the beginning (Polyb. 11.4.2), and he is from a state in the Aegean or Asia Minor, for he describes himself (11.4.6) as speaking on behalf of the Aegean islanders and the states in Asia Minor.[116]

That limits our choices even more obviously to Thrasycrates being a Rhodian. The reasoning is as follows. The Mytilenaean and Byzantine envoys (Polyb. 11.4.1) are from the Aegean, but we have no record of previous participation in the mediations (unless one takes 11.4.2–4 itself as referring to it). A Chian might fit, since there was Chian participation in the mediation of 209 (Livy 27.30.4), and perhaps in the mediation of 208 (but this is based only on Polyb. 11.4.2–4 itself).[117] But the Chians receive only a minor place in Thrasycrates' list of mediators. The Rhodians, on the other hand, are from the Aegean, are specially mentioned by Thrasycrates, and were prominent participants in the mediations both of 209 and 208; no other state fits so well.[118] As we will see, the probability that the anti-Roman Thrasycrates is a Rhodian peace

---

[113]   On Roman goals in the war, see discussion above, this chapter.
[114]   See Walbank 1967: 6 and 274.
[115]   See Schmitt 1957: 199; Walbank 1967: 275.
[116]   Lampela 1998: 70 n. 225, suggests that Thrasycrates was the Ptolemaic envoy; but Polyb. 11.4.6, quoted just above, proves this cannot be the case.
[117]   See above, this chapter, at p. 94.
[118]   Eckstein 2002: 288 and n. 66.

envoy has important implications as we consider the startling reversal of Rhodian policy towards Rome only a few years later.[119]

The anti-Roman tone of Thrasycrates' speech in Polyb. 11.4–6 is certainly not congruent with an attempt by the mediators to construct a "comprehensive peace" including the Romans (i.e., the "comprehensive peace" of Appian's first mediation of 207) – for the speech is tactless in the extreme if the point of the peace conference is to include Rome. But Thrasycrates' speech does fit very well with the anti-Roman tone of the speeches that Appian says the neutral ambassadors gave at the second mediation attempt, when it was known that Rome was opposed to any peace at all. It therefore seems reasonable to ascribe the speech in Polyb. 11.4–6, as many scholars do, to the second mediation of 207.[120]

Thrasycrates' speech is addressed specifically to the Aetolians (Polyb. 11.4.1). He speaks for all the mediating states (Ptolemy IV, Rhodes, Byzantium, Chios, Mytilene), saying that this is not the first or the second time that non-belligerents have made proposals to the Aetolians concerning peace – for they seek the Aetolians' ending of hostilities (11.4.1–2). They have sought this from the moment the war began, seeing the ruin it was bringing on the Aetolians and Macedonians, and the damage it might inflict upon Greek states as far away as Asia (4.2–6). The reference is clearly to the mediations of 209 and 208.[121] Thus Thrasycrates' opening statement suggests in itself, even if we had no other evidence (which of course we do), that the primary goal of the mediators was always the reconciliation of Aetolia and Macedon; that the neutrals have been trying to achieve this from the beginning is precisely Thrasycrates' point.

Thrasycrates then offers an extremely hostile depiction of Rome. The Aetolians, he says, are engaged in a war that is destructive, self-destructive, and dishonorable. They claim they are fighting for the freedom of the Greeks (against Philip), but in fact with regard to Rome they are fighting "for the enslavement and destruction of Greece" (11.5.1). The terms of the Aetolians' treaty of alliance with Rome are "disgraceful," turning over free Greeks "to the shameful violence and lawlessness of barbarians" (11.5.3 and 5.7).[122] And the war will result

---

[119]   Ibid.: 296–7.
[120]   So Schmitt 1957: 204–10; Ferro 1960: 7 n. 6 and 139–40; Lehmann 1967: 138; Rich 1984: 144–5.
[121]   Walbank 1967: 175.
[122]   This is a reference to the terms of the Roman–Aetolian alliance, whereby the Romans receive all the movable loot – including the enslavement of the free population – in any town in Greece they conquer, and share in the moveable loot in any town which the allies conquer together, the Aetolians in both cases receiving the town itself and its territory. See above, pp. 88–9.

in disaster to all Greeks, for once the Romans finish the war in Italy against Hannibal (as they soon will do), they will turn all their strength against Greece, on the pretext of helping the Aetolians against Philip, but really in order to subjugate Greece to themselves (11.6.1–2). The Aetolians should have foreseen all the negative consequences of their alliance with Rome from the beginning (6.5). But they certainly have no excuse now not to see the consequences – not after Roman atrocities such as those at Oreus and Aegina (6.6–8).[123]

Schmitt, defending the thesis that Roman–Rhodian friendship existed from ca. 306 BC – i.e., from 100 years before Thrasycrates' speech – minimizes the anti-Roman elements here, and their importance for understanding the attitude of Rhodes and the other mediators towards Rome.[124] This is not convincing. Polybius has no doubt reworked Thrasycrates' speech in his own vocabulary, but it still must reflect the tone of the original.[125] And the language Polybius has Thrasycrates employ is as violent as Polybian language gets: the shame ($\alpha i o \chi \acute{v} \nu \eta$) of associating with the Romans and their actions in Greece is constantly reiterated (11.4.8; 5.2; 5.7); the Romans are "barbarians," $\beta \acute{\alpha} \rho \beta \alpha \rho o \iota$, their actions $\beta \alpha \rho \beta \alpha \rho \iota \kappa \acute{o} \nu$ (5.6; 5.7); and the ascription of $\pi \alpha \rho \alpha \nu o \mu \acute{\iota} \alpha$ (lawlessness) to them (5.7) is especially damning, for Polybius uses this word only of the worst categories of people (criminals, Celts, the unruly mob).[126]

Berthold, too, minimizes the importance of Thrasycrates' speech, presenting it as just "unkind words."[127] But Holleaux is surely right to stress the wider implications of the speech's fiercely anti-Roman tone.[128] The Romans had already appeared previously as *barbaroi* in a Polybian speech set at a meeting in Sparta in 210 – along with the theme of the "deep shame" of Greeks allying themselves with these *barbaroi* (9.37.6, 38.5–6, and 39.1–5). This speech is given by an Acarnanian, i.e., by an envoy from a state allied with Rome's enemy Macedon, and the envoy

[123] Oreus on Euboea was plundered by Galba's forces in 208 (Livy 28.8.13), and Aegina was seized by Galba in 209. Galba's refusal to allow the ransoming of Aeginetan prisoners being sold into slavery became famous as a Roman atrocity – but in fact he soon relented (Polyb. 9.42.5–8). He eventually turned the island over to the Aetolians (as per the treaty of 211), who then sold it to Attalus of Pergamum: Polyb. 22.8.9–10, cf. 11.5.8.
[124] Schmitt 1957: 199–204; cf. also Berthold 1984: 106 and n. 12.
[125] See rightly Walbank 1967: 275, against Schmitt 1957: 202–3 (and note Schmitt 1957: 56, where Schmitt himself is much more willing to accept the basic historicity of the speech); in agreement: Champion 2000, esp. 434–5.
[126] Polybius' use of $\pi \alpha \rho \alpha \nu o \mu \acute{\iota} \alpha$ for the worst categories of people: Eckstein 1995: 122 and n. 15; 127 and n. 32; 137; 154; his use with the Romans: Champion 2000: 440–4.
[127] Berthold 1984: 106 and n. 12.
[128] Holleaux 1935: 37.

is seeking to prevent Sparta from allying with Rome; but that makes the reappearance of these same hostile motifs in the speech of a neutral ambassador during peace talks in 207 all the more remarkable. Rich admits that the vilification of the Romans in Thrasycrates' speech has significance for Rhodian policy, but he ascribes the hostile tone merely to the momentary bitterness of the neutral states over the Romans' sabotaging of the first mediation of 207; this, he argues, caused the neutrals to change their previous policy of urging a comprehensive peace including Rome, and to adopt a more hostile stance.[129] But if one accepts the import of part of Thrasycrates' Polybian speech (its virulently anti-Roman tone), then one should also accept the import of the rest – the assertion that the mediators had focused from the beginning on a reconciliation between Aetolia and Macedon (11.4.1–2). Perhaps this is propaganda constructed for the situation of autumn 207, when the rift between the Aetolians and Rome was widening over the issue of peace; but – again – the most effective propaganda has at least a partial factual basis. In fact, the statement of the mediator at Polyb. 11.4.1–2, as well as the tone of Polyb. 11.4–6 as a whole, fits with the anti-Roman tone that the neutral mediators had acquiesced in as far back as the peace talks of 209. This is important for understanding both the neutrals' policy towards the war in European Greece in these years and their general stance towards Rome.[130]

Polybius says that Thrasycrates' oration made an impact upon the Aetolians (11.6.9). Envoys from Philip then spoke: they said that if Aetolia wanted peace, Philip readily consented and the details could then be worked out; but if they did not want peace, then the Aetolians – not Philip – would be responsible for what then happened (11.6.9–10). The speech of the Macedonians in Polyb. 11.6 thus parallels the position which, we are told, Philip had maintained in all the previous negotiations: that this war was not of his making.[131] And note that the context of Polyb. 11.6 is *explicitly* negotiations for peace solely between Philip and the Aetolians – which is the only context where statements that the war was not of his making make sense.

The efforts of the Greek mediating states ultimately failed in 207. We do not know why: the Polybian fragment ends with the speech of the Macedonians; App. *Mac.* 3 is too summary; Dio/Zonaras is vague. Perhaps the mediators were unable to bridge a wide gap between the peace terms

---

[129] Rich 1984: 144 and 146.
[130] On the peace talks of 209, see Polyb. 10.25 (discussed above).
[131] See Livy (P) 27.30.11 (above, p. 97) and Livy (P) 28.7.15 (above, p. 102). The clear link between the Macedonians' statement in Polyb. 11.8.9–10 and similar statements at earlier peace talks by envoys of Macedon: Schmitt 1957: 201; Rich 1984: 145 and n. 188; Champion 2000: 432–5.

proposed by the Aetolians and those proposed by Philip. But Philip then led a major Macedonian invasion of Aetolia (Polyb. 11.7.2–3). And this invasion (or perhaps a second one, several months later) finally broke the will of the Aetolians to continue.[132] Sometime in 206 the Aetolians therefore came to a negotiated peace with Philip separate from Rome.[133] Roman policy obviously opposed this peace: in spring 205 the Romans finally dispatched a large force to northwest Greece under P. Sempronius Tuditanus, thus ending two years of neglect (Livy 29.12.1), in the expectation or hope that Aetolia was either still in the war or could be persuaded to rejoin it (29.12.2–6: explicit). Livy says that Sempronius was angry to learn that the Aetolians had made a separate peace with Philip – for this was a violation of their treaty of alliance with Rome (29.12.4).

The Romans had waited too long to send major reinforcements to northwest Greece. And we have a tradition that one of the mediators of 209, 208, and 207 in fact played a crucial role in bringing about the separate peace between Aetolia and Macedon in 206. That state was Rhodes, the state whose envoy had given the ferociously anti-Roman speech at the negotiations of autumn 207. Now, according to App. *Mac.* 4, the Rhodians were "promoters of the peace" of 206.[134] We are dependent, of course, on the questionable Appian here; but if Appian is correct, this would confirm our other evidence that the neutral states all along had focused primarily on ending the conflict between Aetolia and Macedon, with or without Rome. Now Rhodes – perhaps with the help of the others – had finally achieved it.[135]

Current scholarly consensus rightly puts the end of the fighting between Rome and Macedon in the next year, 205 BC. The reconstruction

---

[132] It is unclear whether the invasion of Aetolia in Polyb. 11.7.2–3 is the same as the one (different in detail) described retrospectively at Livy 36.31.11 (drawn from Polybian material), or whether there were two successive invasions by Philip. For alternate scenarios, see Schmitt 1957: 211 n. 1 (two invasions); Hammond, in Hammond and Walbank 1988: 405–6 (two invasions, different in date from Schmitt); Rich 1984: 147–8 (one invasion, autumn 207).

[133] Schmitt 1957: 211 n. 1, and Rich 1984: 148, place the peace in spring 206. Other scholars suggest it dates from the Panaetolian Assembly of autumn 206: this makes sense of Livy's remark that Tuditanus arrived in Illyria "when peace had just been made" (*vixdum pace facta* – 29.12.3, assuming this is the spring of 205): de Sanctis 1916: 430 n. 87, and 444; Holleaux 1935: 253 n. 4; Walbank 1967: 278; Hammond, in Hammond and Walbank 1988: 408–9; Errington 1989a: 101. Appian's employment of the term τέλος in *Mac.* 4 is an indication that the gap in time between the failure of the second attempt at peace in autumn 207 and the final Aetolian–Macedonian peace was substantial.

[134] διαλλακτήρων οἱ γεγονότων . . .

[135] Appian's report is accepted by Schmitt 1957: 206 n. 1. The Rhodian role in the Aetolian–Macedonian peace of 206 is missing from Berthold 1984: 106–7 (who also minimizes the anti-Roman implications of the Rhodian speech of 207: see above); nor is the question addressed by Wiemer 2002: 108–9, who inexplicably says that we have no word of Rhodian diplomatic activity between 207 and 201.

of events is thus that in spring 205 P. Sempronius Tuditanus arrived in northwest Greece, bringing a large Roman force to the Greek theater of operations for the first time in two years; after some fighting between Sempronius and Philip in maritime Illyris in summer 205, the neutral Epirotes – into whose territory the conflict was threatening to spread – took an initiative in offering to mediate a peace.[136] This led to successful peace talks in summer or autumn 205 between Sempronius and envoys from Macedon at the Epirote capital of Phoenice.[137]

Polybius described the Phoenice talks in detail – as he evidently described *all* the mediations of the war in detail. Thus we know the names of the three Epirote mediators, and even the order in which people spoke (Livy 29.12.12, from Polybian material). The talks went smoothly because both sides now thought peace was in their interest (29.12.7, 10, and 16): this was because Philip had given up hope in the Carthaginians (whom he now abandoned, contrary to the terms of his treaty with Hannibal), while the Romans – abandoned by the Aetolians – had no powerful allies left in Greece, and did not wish to devote large resources to fighting Philip.[138]

The terms of the peace involved only Illyria – which shows the narrowness of Roman concerns east of the Adriatic even in 205. Philip conceded some of his Illyrian conquests back to Rome: the Parthini near Epidamnus, and the town of Dimallum, near Apollonia. And Rome in turn conceded to Philip some of his conquests: the Atintani; part of Dassaretis; perhaps even Lissus. A compromise peace was thus concluded, soon formally ratified at Rome (Livy 29.12.13–16).[139]

[136] Rich 1984: 136–43, dates the campaign of Sempronius and peace with Macedon to summer 206; so too Kascéev 1997: 430. But the 206 date contradicts Livy 29.11.11 that the Romans neglected the war in Greece for two years (i.e., 207 and 206), and makes inexplicable Sempronius' presence with an army in Greece in late autumn 205 (when he was elected consul for 204 *in absentia*: Livy 29.11.10). See Eckstein 2002: 285 n. 54.

[137] Walbank 1940: 205, in contrast to Rich's suggested peace in 206 (see above, last note), suggests that peace talks at Phoenice went into spring 204, for Tuditanus was still commanding forces in Greece in late 205 (Livy 29.11.10). But the talks go quickly in Livy (29.12.12–13), and if a preliminary peace was concluded in summer or autumn 205, Sempronius and his forces would still have had to remain in Illyria until it was ratified at Rome (cf. Livy 29.12.16); and even after that, there would have been administrative work to do (e.g., diplomacy with the Parthini and other polities released from Macedonian control: cf. Livy 29.12.13). Thus there is no need to think that the peace talks themselves dragged on into 204.

[138] See Errington 1989a: 103–4. On Philip's violation of his treaty with Hannibal: Hammond, in Hammond and Walbank 1988: 409 (excused on grounds of circumstances).

[139] The peace terms of Phoenice: see Schmitt 1969: no. 543. Good discussions: Gruen 1984: 381; Errington 1989a: 104–5. On the fate of Lissus, see Hammond, in Hammond and Walbank 1988: 409–10 (though note the differing view of Gruen 1984: 381 n. 130).

If the terms of Phoenice meant that – for the moment – Philip was effectively acknowledging the legitimacy of Roman influence in the region (though see below), the peace of 205 equally meant Roman acknowledgment for the first time of the legitimacy of Macedonian influence in significant parts of Illyria, and those terms actually left Philip with the ability, as before, to threaten maritime Illyris from the land, via the passes of Dassaretis and the Atintani. This did not provide much protection for Rome's Illyrian friends.[140] Indeed, Polybius is explicit that Philip did seize certain areas in Illyria after Phoenice – areas that the Romans in 196 wanted back (Polyb. 18.1.14).[141] Perhaps the Macedonian absorption of these places was merely the result of frontier pressure and diplomatic inducements.[142] And the places – Lychnis and Parthus – were in any case inland and minor; the Romans in 196, having received them back from Philip, gave them to their ally the Ardiaean monarchy.[143] On the one hand, the situation suggests that whatever peace terms Philip swore at Phoenice had limited meaning for him; but on the other hand, the main strategic point of Phoenice was that Philip had now lost most of his interest in the Adriatic and was turning his attention eastwards (see next chapter).[144]

Livy gives a list of states appended to the peace treaty as supporters (*foederi adscripti*) of one side or the other. For Philip, these were Prusias king of Bithynia, the Achaeans, the Boeotians, the Thessalians, the Acarnanians, and the Epirotes; for Rome, these were the Ilians, Attalus of Pergamum, Pleuratus of the Ardiaei, Nabis of Sparta, the Eleans, the Messenians, and the Athenians. The list has produced significant scholarly controversy, especially about Ilium and Athens. Coming at either end of the list for Rome, they are deeply suspect, for neither the Ilians nor the Athenians had been involved as allies of Rome during the war, unlike the others in the list; the Athenians had actually worked against Rome (see above); and Appian (*Mac.* 4.1), based on a Greek source, emphasizes that Athens had no relationship with Rome prior to the Macedonian attack on the city in autumn 201. The *foederi adscripti* for Philip had, similarly, been his military allies.[145] The addition of the Epirotes

---

[140] A fact underlined by Badian 1958a: 61.
[141] Emphasized by Badian 1958a: 61–2 and 1964a: 22–3; Errington 1972: 131–43; Briscoe 1973: 55.
[142] So Badian 1958a: 61 and 1964a: 22–3.
[143] See Polyb. 18.47.12, cf. Livy 33.34.11, with Gruen 1984: 388–9.
[144] Gruen 1984: 388–9, convincingly shows, against Badian, that Philip's absorption of these Illyrian places after Phoenice cannot have been a cause of the war that later broke out between Rome and Macedon.
[145] Prusias had aided Philip against Pergamum (see above). On the Macedonian attack on Athens in late 201, see below, Chapter 5.

on Philip's side (despite the Epirote role in 205 as mediator!) complicates matters, for this appears to represent an additional diplomatic victory for Macedon; yet the nature of the subsequent Epirote relationship to Macedon is clear from the fact that the Epirotes would have joined Philip in 200 against Rome except for the arrival of a Roman army (Livy 32.12.1–2).[146] The appearance of Ilium and Athens on the Roman side of the list is therefore difficult to explain, and is most likely a Roman propaganda addition to an original authentic (Polybian) list. The Ilians were added because they gave additional luster to the Roman side of the list, since they were allegedly descended from ancient Troy (and the Romans made a similar claim); and the Athenians were added because Athenian complaints against Macedonian attacks in 200 were one of the causes of the second war between Rome and Philip, and hence the Athenians' appearance among the *foederi adscripti* at Phoenice in 205 gave a special justification for later Roman action (cf. Livy 31.6.1).[147]

No doubt the results of the war left both sides disappointed. Philip had failed to conquer Illyris completely, let alone go farther, and after autumn 211 enormous efforts on his part were required just to hold his own in Greece – where, however, his military reputation was now at its height. The Romans had seen Attalus of Pergamum forced from their coalition when he was defeated by Philip in Greece and his kingdom in Asia Minor invaded, and they were then abandoned by the battered Aetolians, in good part because of Roman unwillingness to commit large resources to the war. But it is doubtful that in 205 either side swore to the peace with the intention of renewing the struggle as soon as opportunity offered. With the failure of Hannibal, a western adventure for Philip was unattractive. Nor should we believe that Rome after 205 was looking for an eastern adventure – for an excuse to effect an "adjustment" in the peace in the East, as many scholars have argued.[148] Holleaux's arguments on this question still have great force.[149] The idea that the Roman Senate plotted long-range Machiavellian strategy misunderstands the way that Roman government (or any ancient government) lurched from crisis to crisis in a very dangerous world.[150] If the *Patres* had seen another clash with Philip as inevitable, why allow his army

---

[146]   Polybian origin of Livy's discussion of the pro-Macedonian Epirote attitude in 200: see Briscoe 1973: 2.

[147]   Good reasons for eliminating Ilium and Athens from the list of Roman *foederi adscripti* at Phoenice (despite Gruen 1990: 31–3): see esp. Dahlheim 1968: 209–21 (esp. 219 n. 99); Habicht 1982: 138–9; cf. Holleaux 1935: 54 n. 1, 56 n. 1, 259–60. The Roman tradition on the motives for the decision of 200 BC, as compared to Polybius' analysis: see below, Chapter 6.

[148]   So Balsdon 1954a: 32–3; Ferro 1960: 117–19; Harris 1979: 207–9; Rich 1984: 151; Errington 1989a: 106; and now strongly reasserted by Derow 2003: 58.

[149]   Holleaux 1935: 286–97; cf. Walbank 1940: 105; Gruen 1984: 381 and n. 131.

[150]   See Astin 1968, and Eckstein 1987a: esp. xix–xxi and 319–24.

and his treasury time to recover, why allow him time to build his war-fleet into a major instrument of power – all of which occurred after 205? The Roman People, though exhausted by the Hannibalic War, might have put up with a continuing if limited conflict with Philip, leading to a better outcome; but once peace had actually been established in 205 the *Patres* ran the risk of opposition to initiating a brand-new war with him – again, as historically occurred. The evidence indicates, rather, that Rome was never committed to a full war-effort in Greece, in part from lack of resources but also – under the terrible pressure of Hannibal – from lack of ambition. Rome's primary goal in Greece was always simply to prevent Philip's involvement in Italy; Laevinus in 210 told the Senate that the alliance with Aetolia allowed the legion in the Adriatic to be withdrawn, for the fleet would now be enough to keep Philip from Italy (Livy 26.28.1–2). The Phoenice talks, in their own way, achieved this goal; and so, in spring 204, the Romans – as in 229/228 and 219 – withdrew all their forces from east of the Adriatic.[151]

For the theme of this chapter, what is also striking about the successful mediation at Phoenice in 205 is who was *not* there: the mediating states of 209–206. No envoys of the Ptolemies, or Rhodes, or any of the other Aegean Greek polities, previously so persistent in the efforts for peace in 209–206, helped to reconcile Rome and Macedon in 205. This is yet more evidence that the Greek states that had been so anxious to bring peace between Macedon and Aetolia had less concern about relations between Macedon and Rome; evidently they did not view the continuation of war in northwest Greece as a matter requiring their attention.

The one previous mediator present at Phoenice in 205 was Amynander the king of Athamania (Livy 29.12.12), and his presence proves the point about the others – for his polity, unlike the others, was geographically proximate to the fighting, and he was concerned – as the Epirotes were – to keep the Roman–Macedonian war from spreading into his territory. During the war, Amynander's stance had fluctuated greatly: a pro-Aetolian mediator in 209 (Livy 27.30.4), perhaps a mediator in 207 (so App. *Mac.* 3), he then allowed Philip to launch a major invasion of Aetolia via his mountain kingdom in exchange for gaining the island of Zacynthus from Macedon (Livy 36.31.11); now he reappeared as a mediator. The sequence shows a typically ruthless Hellenistic ruler at work. But the other mediators of 209–206, coming as they did from the eastern Mediterranean, had always had a different focus of concern.[152]

---

[151]   See Holleaux 1935: 286–97; cf. Walbank 1940: 105.
[152]   Huss 1976: 167 and n. 67, correctly notes the absence of the Ptolemies from the Phoenice negotiations – and ascribes it, precisely, to lack of Ptolemaic interest in events in northwest Greece.

The absence of the Greek mediators of 209, 208, 207, and 206 from Phoenice in 205 is of a piece with the Rhodians helping to create a separate peace between Macedonia and Aetolia in 206. The interests of the mediating states did not run parallel to the interests of Rome, and these states pursued their own interests energetically even when they ran counter to those of Rome.

CONCLUSION

Polybius proclaimed that the first steps towards *symplokē*, the "inter-connectedness" between the eastern and western halves of the Mediter-ranean, were taken in summer 217 with Philip V's peace with Aetolia and his turn to expansion towards the west. But neither the development of the *symplokē* nor the understanding that it was occurring were instan-taneous. The Greek mediators in the First Macedonian War still acted in 209–206 as if they were dealing with an almost purely Greek political situation. Their efforts were focused on ending war between Macedon and the Aetolians. If Rome was present, it was only peripheral.[153]

The mediating states of 209–206 were willing for Rome to be included in a peace in Greece if that were part of the package bringing the war between Macedon and Aetolia to an end. But it does not look as if such a "comprehensive" peace was envisioned by the mediators in 209; such a peace may have been envisioned in 208, but this is uncert-ain; it was definitely envisioned during the first mediation of 207, but not in the second mediation. Nor is it the case, as Schmitt asserts, that the prominent non-belligerent mediators reveal no "direkt antirömische Politik."[154] The scathing denunciation of Roman motives and conduct by the Rhodian mediator Thrasycrates in Polyb. 11.4–6 belies this, the second mediation of 207 occurred against explicit Roman wishes, and even Schmitt admits that the mediators' eventual success in helping create the separate Macedonian–Aetolian peace of 206 put Rome in a difficult strategic position, with wars being waged simultaneously against Carthage and Macedon, and with no allies in Greece.[155] Moreover, the main issue is not even whether the mediators included the Romans in their efforts for peace, since it appears from App. *Mac.* 3 that the Roman Senate desired above all a continuation of war between Aetolia and Macedon – i.e., it was opposed to mediation *in toto*. In the only media-tion where we have evidence of direct Roman inclusion – in 207 – the

---

[153]   See Holleaux 1935: 36–8.
[154]   Schmitt 1957: 25.
[155]   Ibid.: 26.

Romans (we are told) attempted to sabotage the entire effort, first in secret and then openly, in order to keep the war going. And this led to the famous scene where the speech of a Roman general, P. Sulpicius Galba, was shouted down by the angry Greeks.[156]

If we had the complete text of Polybius for these years, the clash of interests beween Rome and the mediating states would probably be even clearer. Polybius stressed this conflict: why else would he have chosen to report in such detail the hostile oration of Thrasycrates (11.4–6)? And that speech was only one of an entire series of speeches in this section of the *Histories* in which Roman motives and goals were castigated and the fears of some Greeks concerning Roman intervention in Greek affairs underscored for the audience. The series began with Agelaus' speech at Naupactus in 217 (Polyb. 5.104: "the cloud in the west"), continued with the anti-Roman speech of Lyciscus of Acarnania at Sparta in 210 (Polyb. 9.37.4–39.5), the anti-Roman orator at the mediation of 209 (Polyb. 10.25), and culminated in Thrasycrates' violently hostile speech in 11.4–6. To include these speeches in the *Histories* was not merely an artistic decision on Polybius' part (though it was that), nor was it simply the reporting of important speeches that had actually been made (though it was that too); it was, above all, a political analysis, voluntary and Polybius' choice, written from a time fifty years onward when all these warnings appeared to have come true. But this means that Polybius depicted the relations between Rome and the Greek states which sought to mediate the war in Greece in 209–206 as distant or non-existent; and sometimes their interests clashed. When that happened, the Ptolemies, the Rhodians, and the others implemented their own desires, excluded the Romans when necessary, and harshly criticized them.[157]

And yet within five years of the peace between Aetolia and Macedon which Rhodes (and others?) helped engineer in 206 against Roman interests and expressed Roman wishes, envoys from many of these same mediators of 209–206 (including Rhodes) appeared before the Senate, pleading for Roman military intervention in the Greek East. We can now see just what a revolution in Mediterranean diplomacy the arrival at Rome of these envoys was – how suddenly and sharply the policy of these Greek states had changed. Moreover, the Senate, having previously accepted a compromise peace with Philip in 205 in order to be free of Greek affairs, answered these Greek appeals positively (even when faced with

---

[156] See above, pp. 106–7.
[157] On Polybius' political choice in including these speeches, see Champion 2000, and 2004: 193–202.

the deep reluctance of the Roman People), thus precipitating the Second Macedonian War.[158]

Some excruciatingly important, indeed revolutionary, geopolitical development must lie behind this sudden revolution in Mediterranean diplomacy. The most obvious development was the discovery by the Ptolemies and the Rhodians of "the Pact Between the Kings" – the secret treaty of alliance between Philip V and Antiochus III to destroy the entire Ptolemaic Empire, struck ca. 203/202 BC (so Polyb. 3.2.8 and 15.20: emphatic). This threatened to destroy the existing Hellenistic state-system, the de facto balance of power among the three great monarchies. If we had the complete text of Polybius' *Histories*, we would see how, in Polybius' thought, the Pact led directly to the second great stage in the development of the *symplokē* – the Roman intervention in the East in 200 BC. But the historicity of the pact between Philip and Antiochus, and the relationship of the pact to the Roman decision of 200, have often been strongly questioned. The historicity of the alliance between Philip and Antiochus thus becomes our next topic, with analysis of the Mediterranean-wide impact of the pact – that is, its disruption of the Mediterranean state-system – to follow thereafter.

---

[158] Note by contrast Warrior 1996: 44 and 99–100, who asserts without discussion that Rhodes and Athens had always worked for reconciliation between Philip and Rome (i.e., during the First Macedonian War), leading to a further assertion (again without discussion) that the embassies of these states to Rome in winter 201/200 were simply a natural outgrowth of previous relations (ibid.). This is a complete misreading of the situation.

PART II

THE POWER-TRANSITION CRISIS IN THE GREEK MEDITERRANEAN, 207–200 BC

4

The Pact Between the Kings and the Crisis in the Eastern Mediterranean State-System, 207–200 BC

INTRODUCTION: ROME AND THE GREEKS, 205–200 BC

The thesis of this study so far has been that Roman interest in the Greek world east of the Adriatic, and Roman concrete interests there, were minimal down to 200 BC. The Senate did perceive the Greek East as a region where threats could emerge against Italy. The invasion of Italy by King Pyrrhus of Epirus in 280–275, at the behest of the Greek city of Tarentum, had been a bitter experience for Rome: Pyrrhus had done much damage, caused significant defections from the Roman alliances in Italy, and caused enormous Roman casualties. The *Patres'* sensitivity to a renewal of such a threat is shown by the sharp Roman military re-action – even in the depths of the crisis of the Hannibalic War – to the decision of Philip V of Macedon in 217 to turn his expansionism towards the west (a decision provoked, in turn, by Philip's perception of grow-ing Roman weakness under the hammer-blows inflicted upon Rome by Hannibal and Carthage).[1] But Rome had many security concerns else-where than in Greece, and more important ones (Celtic northern Italy, for one); and the events of this first war against Philip V (214–205 BC) had not left the Romans with many ties in the Greek world.[2]

---

[1] On Pyrrhus' invasion of Italy, see conveniently Eckstein 2006: Ch. 5. On Philip's aggressions as the cause of the First Macedonian War, see above, Chapter 3.
[2] On the correct date for the beginning of the first Roman war with Macedon (as opposed to 211 BC, which is only the date of the entrance of the Aetolians into the war), see above, Chapter 3, p. 86.

After the Peace of Phoenice ended the war with Macedon in 205 BC, the Roman position east of the Adriatic returned to what it had been in 228 or 219: it consisted solely of an informal Roman sphere of influence among the polities along the Illyrian coast in far northwest Greece. The events of the war had also led in a natural manner to informal ties of friendship (*amicitia*) with states in the Peloponnese that fought beside Rome and the Aetolians against Philip (i.e., Elis, Messene, and Sparta), as well as informal friendship with the Kingdom of Pergamum in western Asia Minor.

Relations between Rome and Pergamum were especially good after the war for a religious reason. Beyond the joint effort against Philip (from which, however, King Attalus was forced to withdraw in defeat in 208),[3] Attalus provided Rome crucial help in 205 in obtaining the favor of the goddess the Great Mother of Pessinus. In that year the *Patres* received reports of disturbing omens, which led them to order a consultation of the Sibylline Books (a set of prophesies in the hands of Roman priests); there emerged a prophesy that Hannibal could only be driven from Italy when the Great Mother of Asia Minor was brought there (Livy 29.10.4– 8). It may seem odd that the Senate would discover a prophesy requiring that help come to Italy from so far away geographically, but the East as a religious world was not unknown to the Romans, especially from the 220s.[4] Yet there remained in Roman culture in this period something of a reluctance to consult foreign deities (Val. Max. 1.3.2),[5] and it is noticeable that the senatorial envoys sent east as a result of the omens of 205 went first to consult the cult-center of Apollo at Delphi (with which Roman relations were themselves relatively new), to get Apollo's approval for their task in Asia Minor, about which they were unsure (Livy 29.11.5–6).[6]

We do not know if Polybius covered the incident with the Great Mother, since the relevant parts of the *Histories* are lost. But if he did, the Achaean historian would no doubt have depicted it as part of the developing (but not yet fully developed) *symplokē* between the two halves of the Mediterranean. The senatorial embassy went on to Pergamum, where it sought help in obtaining the black meteorite image of the Great Mother of Pessinus. And Attalus helped the embassy obtain this object, which was brought back to Rome with enormous ceremony.[7] Gruen sees this

---

[3]   See above, Chapter 3.
[4]   See above, Chapter 2, at nn. 8 and 58. The Sibylline Books (of unknown origin) were themselves written in Greek.
[5]   See the comments of Hoffmann 1934: 131.
[6]   Roman relations with Delphi probably only began in the mid-220s: see above, Chapter 2, at n. 8.
[7]   Sources are multiple, and are conveniently collected at Broughton 1951: 304.

interaction as a stroke of Roman international diplomacy that looked towards future involvement in the Greek world: by 205 it was clear that Hannibal would be defeated, and the Senate took action with Pergamum in order to solidify diplomatic relations with a relatively power-ful potential ally in the Greek East – a region to which Rome would soon be turning its attention.[8] But Burton's interpretation of the Great Mother incident is more convincing: Livy is explicit that religious anxiety in Rome at the appearance of the omens, not strategic confidence, led to the embassy to Pergamum to gain the favor of the Great Mother in the form of the black stone (29.10.4). There need be no implication of long-term Roman ambitions in the eastern Mediterranean here: Attalus was simply the ruler of the friendly state nearest to Pessinus, from which the Sibylline Books demanded the object be obtained if Hannibal were to be driven from Italy.[9] And it was Italy here, as always, that was the center of the *Patres*' concern.[10] There were no further interactions with Pergamum for five years – and then the new interaction was initiated by Pergamum, not Rome.[11]

Indeed, over the next five years the Romans did nothing whatsoever to enhance any relationships in the East. As Livy explicitly says, Rome as yet had no permanent allies there (29.11.1). The four new and infor-mal friendships that emerged out of the First Macedonian War (Elis, Messene, Sparta, Pergamum) were balanced by the bad blood that now existed between Rome and the Aetolian League, since both the Romans and the Aetolians felt that the other side had abandoned them in the last years of the war.[12] And to the governments of Elis, Messene, and Sparta, it was the Aetolian League and the Achaean League that were important in their foreign relations – not Rome. Meanwhile, the Peace of 205 was followed by complete Roman military withdrawal back to Italy.

To be sure, there was a tradition found in the Roman Annalists, and recorded by Livy, that there were Roman envoys in European Greece from 203 onwards, observing with suspicion the doings of Philip V, eventu-ally warning the Senate that he was a greater and stronger Pyrrhus; and three Roman warships were stationed off the coast of Illyria as well (Livy 30.26.2–4).[13] But there is a strong argument for rejecting this informa-tion, since the same Livian passage also gives us the obviously false tale

---

[8]   Gruen 1990: 5–33.
[9]   See Burton 1996.
[10] On the Italy-centered nature of Roman strategic concern, see Eckstein 1987a.
[11] This was the desperate Pergamene embassy to Rome in winter 201/200 BC, plead-ing – along with embassies from other Greek states – for Roman intervention against Philip V; see below, Chapters 5 and 6.
[12] See above, Chapter 3.
[13] For this Annalistic tradition, cf. also Justin 30.3.2; Zon. 9.15.

that Philip supplied troops to Hannibal in Africa for the climactic battle with Rome at Zama in 202, and clearly the latter is part of the propaganda justification for the eventual second war with the king (30.26.4, cf. 30.33.5). Moreover, even if one were to accept Livy 30.26.3–4 here (which one should probably not do), these Roman actions hardly amount to much.[14] There was thus no reason to expect that Roman armies and fleets would soon reappear in the Greek East. Yet that is what occurred. The question is why.

THE CRISIS OF PTOLEMAIC EGYPT
AND THE POWER-TRANSITION
CRISIS IN THE EAST

We now come to the next hypothesis that is central to our study. It is that a really exising and severe crisis in the balance of power in the state-system of the Greek Mediterranean at the end of the third century – and not an internally generated and exceptionally predatory Roman imperialism – was the crucial cause behind the Roman decision in 200 to intervene for the first time with great force in the Greek East.

After ca. 207 BC, the faltering and then increasing collapse of Ptolemaic Egypt – a development which Rome had literally nothing to do with – plunged the Hellenistic state-system into its worst geopolitical crisis in eighty years. The crisis of the Ptolemies contained three major elements. First, from ca. 207 Egypt was wracked by a massive rebellion of the indigenous population against Ptolemaic rule. The rebellion centered in Upper Egypt, in the Thebaid, and lasted for fully twenty years. It spread north into Middle Egypt, and even parts of the Nile Delta were continuously in turmoil.[15] In 205 the priests of Amon in Thebes proclaimed an indigenous pharaoh – Haronnophris, one of the rebel generals – following the traditional Egyptian religious ritual; after Haronnophris' death, the priests appointed a second indigenous pharaoh with full ritual, Chaonophris. Meanwhile, in the indigenous-controlled area, Greek

---

[14]   Accepting the Roman Annalistic tradition in Livy: Balsdon 1954; Warrior 1996, esp. 101–3. Against: de Sanctis 1923: 121 n. 55; Holleaux 1928: 156 n. 1; Petzold 1940: 44–7; Broughton 1951: 322 n. 3; Gruen 1984: 222 n. 86, and 383. The Livian tradition even has these Roman envoys in Greece organizing Greek military resistance to Macedonian aggression in 202: see 30.42.1–10, which would be a more serious action if it were at all believable.

[15]   After September 207, documents in the name of the Ptolemaic kings disappear from the Thebaid (see Veïsse 2004: 18–19), and by 206 the rebellion was in full swing both in Upper Egypt and as far north as the Delta: ibid.: 22–5 (with sources). Geographical extent of the rebellion: ibid.: 7–20 (with sources). Rebellion began on a small scale ca. 216.

administrators were slaughtered.[16] The authority of the indigenous regime was somewhat spotty even in Upper Egypt, and the Ptolemies evidently retained a few places under their control; but even in areas in Middle Egypt and the Delta where the indigenous regime was not able to establish itself, the result was not peaceful Ptolemaic administration, but constant violent raiding and counter-raiding.[17] Moreover, the government of the indigenous pharaohs was soon wealthy enough to hire large numbers of Nubian and Ethiopian mercenaries to supplement their Egyptian soldiers.[18] This situation worsened greatly after the premature death of Ptolemy IV in 204, and the accession to the Ptolemaic throne of a child who was only 5. The widespread chaos in the countryside was now matched by a second major element: chaos in the Ptolemaic government and in the capital of Alexandria itself. A series of unpopular caretaker governments, ruling in the name of the child Ptolemy V, followed one another in Alexandria in quick succession, replaced via coups, murders, and riots. Soon a third major aspect of the crisis emerged: the death of Ptolemy IV and the instability in Alexandria unfortunately coincided with the return of the Seleucid monarch Antiochus III in triumph from his great conquests in Iran and Afghanistan – and by the summer of 202, the faltering Ptolemaic Empire was coming under increasingly strong external attack from foreign Greek powers.[19]

But because Ptolemaic Egypt performed the important system-wide task of balancing the power of the Seleucids (and to a lesser extent the power of Antigonid Macedon), the crisis of the Ptolemies also soon became a crisis of the Hellenistic state-system as a whole. As noted in Chapter 1, political scientists term such a system-wide crisis caused by the decline or collapse of one of the great states previously essential to the maintenance of the balance of power in a state-system – and/or the sudden rise of another great state – a "power-transition crisis." Such power-transition crises lead inevitably to fundamental transformations in the character of the state-system, as the number of great powers within the system increases or decreases, sometimes radically. Usually these transformations in the configuration of the state-system (though not always) are accompanied by, and indeed are achieved through, large-scale interstate violence.[20]

---

[16]   On the two pharaohs: Clarysse 1978; Veïsse 2004: 83–99. On the fate of the Greeks: Veïsse 2004: 129 (with sources).
[17]   See Veïsse 2004: 18.
[18]   Ibid.: 85–6.
[19]   More details below, pp. 141–4.
[20]   Evidence and importance of power-transition crises in international relations, Geller and Singer 1998: 72–5; Organski and Kugler 1980; Gilpin 1988; Lemke and Kugler 1996: 3–33. See above, Chapter 1, pp. 20–1. Massive violence: see below.

That is what occurred in the Greek Mediterranean between 207 and 188 BC. For eighty years the Hellenistic state-system had been founded on a fragile balance of power among the three great powers of Ptolemaic Egypt, the Seleucid Empire, and Antigonid Macedon.[21] But after ca. 207 BC the Ptolemaic regime began to falter, and after 204 it headed into collapse. The question was what structure would replace the previous triadic balance of power – for that the triadic balance of power *would* be replaced was now clear.

Political scientists have shown that such power-transition crises are dangerous and usually violent moments in international relations. Drastic changes in the distribution of real power across a system of states often lead to what political scientists call "hegemonic war" – massive violence that brings into being a new interstate structure, one more in keeping with the new distribution of real power among the states involved. To be sure, hegemonic war is not inevitable, and does not *have* to happen as a result of a power-transition crisis; the nature and quality of human decision-making in such a crisis matter enormously.[22] But the collapse of Ptolemaic Egypt did in fact cause hegemonic war within the Hellenistic state-system to occur. That a profound military-political crisis in the Greek Mediterranean was resulting from the collapse of Egyptian power became clear after winter 203/202, when increasingly severe attacks on weakened Egypt began to come from the Seleucid monarchy of Syria, and soon from the Seleucids and Macedon together.

The trend of modern scholarship concerning the Mediterranean crisis at the end of the third century has been, however, to focus on the military aggressiveness of Rome, which is viewed as an exceptional and predatory aggressiveness supposedly caused by deep militaristic pathologies within Roman society.[23] This approach is too simplistic: it ignores the fact that other states in the Mediterranean system were as militaristic and aggressive as Rome was, and that they were central actors in the unrolling of these events.

The Roman Republic was certainly a profoundly militaristic and diplomatically aggressive state.[24] But of what major state or even second-tier state in the Hellenistic Mediterranean could this not be said? The pervasiveness of bellicose attitudes and aggressive conduct among ancient

---

[21]   On the triadic balance of power and its inherent fragility even in the mid-third century, see Ager 2003.

[22]   Thus careful diplomacy by all sides in 1989–91 prevented large-scale war from occurring as a result of the collapse of the Soviet empire in eastern Europe, and then the collapse of the Soviet Union itself – a classic power-transition crisis.

[23]   Among a large literature, see, e.g., Harris 1979: Ch. 5 (on the crisis of 207–200 BC: 212–18), and recently Derow 2003: 58–60.

[24]   See above, Chapter 1, pp. 15–19.

Mediterranean polities indicates that Roman behavior was not exceptional for the period, and suggests, further, that Roman behavior was not primarily the result of something exceptionally "dark and irrational" within Roman society itself.[25] Rather, such bellicose attitudes and aggressive conduct were primarily (though not solely) derived from the unforgiving pressures of the anarchic environment in which all these ancient states existed. It is precisely because militarism, bellicosity, and aggressiveness were adaptive responses to the pressures deriving from the anarchic state-systems of which they were all units that most states in the ancient Mediterranean had developed in a similar militaristic and aggressive fashion. Strikingly, this includes states both east and west (Carthage, Rome, Macedon, Aetolia, Pergamum, the Seleucids), states of every size (large, medium, and small), and states of every political description (democracies, republics, federal leagues, and monarchies).[26] Polities needed to develop these characteristics – "pathological" as some of them seem now to us – or else they would not have survived. The Hellenistic Mediterranean is thus a classic example of what the political scientist Kenneth Waltz has called the regression of all states towards functional similarity under anarchy. Moreover, the simultaneous existence of all these militaristic societies within a state-system that lacked international law created a situation that itself was highly conducive to almost continual war – if only because war was the most direct way for objective clashes of interest between states to be resolved.[27]

Such a "systems" approach gives agency in history not merely to individual states but to the anarchic structure and harsh characteristics of the state-system as a whole. It allows us to lift our eyes from the individual "unit" within the system (in this case, primarily Rome), to examine the broader political field within which that unit exists. Such an approach also stresses the tragic nature of interstate politics in the multipolar structure of Hellenistic militarized anarchy, and does not find a single "evil" or "pathological" state as the sole actor responsible for major events, and especially not for broad systemic transformation.[28]

Finally, such a "system-level" perspective helps us understand the specific characteristics and dangers of the type of crisis that engulfed

---

[25]   The image of "dark and irrational" bellicose Rome: Harris 1979: 53, cf. 51.

[26]   Discussion in detail in Eckstein 2006: Chs. 3–6.

[27]   "Regression towards functional similarity" under anarchic conditions: see, e.g., Waltz 1979: 96–7. "War is normal" under such systems: Waltz 1988: 620.

[28]   Detailed discussion of this approach: Eckstein 2006: esp. Chs. 2 (general principles), 4 (the Hellenistic anarchy), and 6 (Rome within the Hellenistic anarchy). For summary discussion of Rome as ferocious but unexceptional within its ferocious interstate world, see above, Chapter 1. On "evil" vs. "tragedy" in Realist theory, see Spirtas 1996; cf. Copeland 2000: 165–8.

the eastern Mediterranean after ca. 207 BC. Without at all denying or downplaying the diplomatic and military aggressiveness of Rome, we no longer need view Rome in isolation, or view its decisions as unique. We can compare Roman decisions and actions to those of the other states involved in the crisis, both the powerful and the less powerful. We can compare Roman, Antigonid, Seleucid, Ptolemaic, Attalid, Rhodian, and Athenian actions as the crisis unfolded – while recognizing that it unfolded under the synergistic impact of all these multiple actions together. And we can even compare those decisions and actions to those taken by other states in similar power-transition crises throughout history: for instance, in the famous crisis in the European state-system caused by the decline in the relative power of the Austro-Hungarian Empire in 1903–14, which led to World War I; or in the systemic crisis caused by the inability of the traditional European powers France and Britain to contain the expansion of Germany or Japan either before or during World War II, which led to the subsequent and rather unexpected emergence of both the United States and the Soviet Union as the new international hegemons.[29]

The crisis in the Greek East from ca. 207 BC could have resulted in the previous tripolar balance of power among the great states being replaced by an emergent bipolar structure, with the monarchies based in Macedon and Syria as the two poles of Greek geopolitics. Or it could even have resulted – no doubt after more system-wide war – in one of these two monarchies emerging as the true system hegemon, the sole surviving superpower. As it happened, however, the crisis resulted in Rome emerging as sole surviving superpower, as the unipolar power in what had become a Mediterranean-wide state-system. But Roman goals east of the Adriatic remained limited even after the victory over Antiochus III in 188 BC, and the Senate had no need or desire to replace the new informal hierarchy of states established by 188 with direct Roman rule – nor could it easily have done so in terms of its available military manpower. The first steps in direct Roman rule in the East did not occur, in fact, until half a century later.[30]

But such a reinterpretation of the central importance of the crisis in the Hellenistic East after 207 BC requires evidence that not only did such a crisis happen, but that it was of extraordinary intensity – a true

---

[29] For a system-level analysis of the events leading to World War I, see Stevenson 1997a: esp. Ch. 5. For a system-level analysis of the crises of 1939–41, see Schweller 1998.

[30] On the Roman manpower problem and hence limited Roman aims in the eastern Mediterranean, see Sherwin-White 1984: 9–10, modified somewhat now by Rosenstein 2004.

"power-transition crisis," rather than a mere excuse for Roman aggression. And if it can be shown that there existed a pact between Philip V of Macedon and Antiochus III the Seleucid monarch from winter 203/202 BC to divide up the entire weakening empire of the Ptolemies, including Egypt itself, this would be decisive evidence in favor of a true system-wide crisis coming forth in the East.[31] The problem with such a reconstruction of events, however, is the problem addressed in this chapter: that the character, terms, and even existence of the treaty of alliance between Philip and Antiochus are among the most contentious questions in Hellenistic history. This chapter argues that the pact did exist, and that it contained the most far-reaching and dangerous terms.

THE SCHOLARLY CONTROVERSY OVER THE PACT BETWEEN THE KINGS

The disagreements about "the Pact Between the Kings" started in antiquity. Six sources provide evidence on the secret agreement. They are led by Polybius – a sophisticated researcher and writer who (even in the fragmented condition of his work) tells us much about the pact and emphasizes its political importance. Most of the other sources are second-rate and late: they disagree with each other and with Polybius on the details of the pact; and occasionally the pact is reported as a mere rumor.[32]

Among modern commentators, the broadest claims for the importance of the pact come from Holleaux: he argues that the terms of the secret agreement between the kings were extremely far-reaching, and that news of it caused the Romans to enter a new war against Philip V of Macedon, thus bringing Roman power permanently into the Greek world.[33] Yet important studies have challenged the very existence of the pact. Thus Magie argues that Polybius was fooled here by the propaganda of his mostly Rhodian sources; and Errington proposes that behind Polybius' assertions (and ultimately all assertions) about the pact is a misunderstood local agreement between Philip V and Zeuxis, the Seleucid commander in Asia Minor, regarding not wide aggression against

---

[31] For the date of the pact as Polybius understood it, see the discussion in Schmitt 1964: 226–9, esp. 229.

[32] Polyb. 3.2.8, 15.20, 16.1.8–9, and 24.6, cf. 14.1a.4–5; Livy 31.14.5; App. *Mac.* 4 (somewhat confused); Justin 30.2.8, cf. Pomp. Trog. *Prol.* 30; Hieron. *In Dan.* 11.13 (= Porphyry, *FGH* 260 F 45); and John Antioch. frg. 54 (*FGH* IV: 558; confused). Rumor: App. *Mac.* 4, cf. Justin 30.2.8.

[33] Holleaux 1935: 306–22; cf. McDonald and Walbank 1937; Walbank 1940: 127–8; Stier 1952: 101–4; Albert 1980: 104–6; Chamoux 2002: 114.

the Ptolemies but local aggression against Pergamum and Rhodes.[34] Strong doubts about the existence of the pact have also come from Habicht, Badian, Harris, and Warrior.[35] The corollary of this position is suspicion of the idea that (false) news of the (alleged) pact – which by its very nature could only be a rumor – would have had great political impact, especially in far-away Rome. Hence the pact cannot have been the fundamental reason why the Senate decided in the winter of 201/200 to intervene in the Greek East.[36] Occasionally now, in important studies of this period, the pact is not even mentioned.[37]

Despite the attacks on the historicity of the pact, the modern scholarly supporters of the existence of *some* sort of agreement between Philip and Antiochus are probably currently in the majority – as they always have been. Yet even among the supporters of the pact there is wide variation of opinion about its actual terms: these range from acceptance of the full Polybian model involving the total dismemberment of the Ptolemaic domains including Egypt itself, all the way to recent assertions that the pact merely mandated each king's non-interference in the independent actions of the other monarch in (respectively) western Asia Minor and the Levant. The latter sort of reconstruction would make the existence of the pact a much less important factor in the Roman decision of 200 BC.[38]

The evidentiary situation is complicated by new epigraphical discoveries which show that arguments about Seleucid administrative practices that have been employed to deny Errington's thesis about Zeuxis are insecurely based.[39] But other new epigraphical evidence seems to concern an actual incident of the working of the pact during the campaigning season of 201.[40] Meanwhile, some scholars maintain that the pact existed

---

[34]   Magie 1939: 32–44; Errington 1971: 336–54, strongly reiterated in Errington 1986: 5 n. 16.
[35]   Habicht 1957: 239 n. 106, and 240, cf. Habicht 1982: 146; Badian 1958a: 64 n. 3, cf. Badian 1964b: 135 n. 3; Harris 1979: 312 n. 2; Warrior 1996: 16–17. Cf. also de Regibus 1951: 99, and de Regibus 1952: 97–100; Rawlings 1976: 18–19, cf. 23 n. 26.
[36]   Balsdon 1954: 37; Badian 1958a: 64; Errington 1971: 347–54; Rawlings 1976: 18–19, cf. 23 n. 26; Warrior 1996: 17 and n. 16; earlier: Magie 1939.
[37]   See Ager 1991: 16–22; Derow 2003: 58–9; commented on above, Chapter 1, n. 4.
[38]   Full acceptance of the Polybian model: Schmitt 1964: 226–36, 242, cf. Schmitt 1969: 228–91. Coordinated dismemberment of Ptolemaic domains outside Egypt: Albert 1980: 105 and n. 486; Scullard 1980: 246 and n. 2; Walbank, in Hammond and Walbank 1988: 343; Green 1990: 304. Mere non-interference in each other's aggressions: Briscoe 1973: 37–9; Berthold 1976: 100–1, cf. Berthold 1984: 110–11; Klose 1982: 64–8; Will 1982: 116; Gruen 1984: 387; Buraselis 1996: 154 n. 19; Lampela 1998: 76; Ma 1999/2002: 74–6; and Wiemer 2001b: 84.
[39]   See below, pp. 169–72.
[40]   See below, pp. 177–8.

but, whatever its terms, it had little military or diplomatic importance, not just with the Romans but even in the eastern Mediterranean itself – a position that manages simultaneously to accept and reject our source traditions.[41] Such a "compromise" position has even been adopted by Errington himself – who asserts in the new edition of *The Cambridge Ancient History* that even if the pact *did* exist, it was (again) aimed primarily at Pergamum and Rhodes, not primarily at the Ptolemies.[42]

The present chapter offers new (and newly necessary) arguments in favor of the proposition that we are on safest ground if we adhere as closely as we can to what Polybius appears to tell us about the pact, unless there is overwhelming evidence against it – which, I think, is in no case true. That is: the version of the pact found in Polybius did exist, it had the decisive impact on Mediterranean politics which Polybius says it did, and it had that impact precisely because states knew it existed as Polybius described it.

The crisis in the eastern Mediterranean at the close of the third century has now become the focus of this study. What is proposed is that with the outbreak of major indigenous rebellion in Upper and Middle Egypt in 207 and then the premature death of Ptolemy IV in 204 and his replacement by a child, events which resulted in the collapse of Ptolemaic power, the Hellenistic state-system began to undergo a major power-transition crisis. This system-wide crisis led to the world-historical events of the last years of the third century. But equally involved in the discussion is our evaluation of Polybius as a historian. Polybius asserts strongly that the pact between Philip and Antiochus to divide up Egypt was a primary cause of the destruction of the Macedonian monarchies and the rise of the hegemony of Rome over the Greek East. On one level, a secular level, he depicts these events in a manner compatible with modern international-systems analysis.[43] But if Polybius is wrong about the very existence of the pact between Philip and Antiochus, or if he has grossly exaggerated its scope, then we must revise our assessment of Polybius as a historical thinker radically downward. Thus the Pact Between the Kings confronts us with a crucial issue not only of the actual historical evolution of the Hellenistic world, but also of Polybian historiography.[44]

---

[41] Cf. Berthold 1976: 101–2, and Berthold 1984: 120–1; Gruen 1984: 387–8.
[42] See Errington 1989a: 254.
[43] Polybius also has a moral and even a quasi-religious point to make about the pact and its impact: see below.
[44] Cf. the comments of Schmitt 1964: 242–3. Polybius as an ancestor of modern international-relations theory precisely in his analysis of the crisis at the end of the third century: see Eckstein 2006: Ch. 4.

POLYBIUS' HYPOTHESIS

Polybius obviously considered the Pact Between the Kings an important event – but just how important it is within the fundamental structure of his *Histories* has often been missed. The agreement between Philip and Antiochus makes its first appearance in Polybius' general explanation of the scheme of his work, after the two introductory volumes, at the beginning of Book 3. In this "table of contents" (3.2–5) Polybius instructs his audience as to the major themes and events he will cover – and here the pact actually receives more space than the end of the Hannibalic War itself.[45] Moreover, it is described with an emotion unusual within Polybius' dry listing of events in the "table of contents":

> I shall tell . . . how, upon Ptolemy [IV] passing from life, Antiochus and Philip – conspiring together to dismember the domain of his successor who was only a child – began to engage in evil acts, Philip setting off to lay hands on Egypt [?], and the regions around Caria and Samos, while Antiochus attacked the regions around Coele Syria and Phoenicia. (3.2.8)[46]

Within the "table of contents" appear many historical figures with controversial reputations: Hannibal (3.2.1); Perseus of Macedon (3.5.2); Antiochus IV of Syria (ibid.); Prusias II of Bithynia (ibid.). Polybius describes some of these men as having acted out of hope, or fear (3.2.2; 3.3.5). But no one else in the "table of contents" is described like Philip and Antiochus, as having acted evilly (κακοπραγμονεῖν . . .) – except for savage Celts (παρανομία: 3.3.5).[47] Polybius' moral condemnaton of the two kings therefore stands out strikingly from the rest of the "table of contents" in 3.2–5 – and thus alerts the audience to how important the subject of the two kings' pact against young Ptolemy will be.

The second Polybian reference to the pact has not often been discussed by scholars but has its own significance. At the beginning of Book 14, Polybius states why he is now about to change his method of literary-historical presentation. Every Olympiad-period of four years contains important events, he says, but the up-coming Olympiad (the 144th: 204–201 BC) has special historical importance (14.1a.2). He then

---

[45] Compare the length of Polyb. 3.2.8 with 3.3.1.

[46] The manuscripts at 3.2.8 all have "Egypt" (τοῖς κατ᾽ Αἰγύπτον), but this reading has often been rejected. For discussion, see below, pp. 139–41.

[47] Total lawlessness (παρανομία) is in fact typical of barbarian conduct in Polybius: see 5.111.7 and 21.49.4, with Eckstein 1995: 122. It is thus significant that Polybius also ascribes *paranomia* to Philip and Antiochus – in a later discussion of the pact (15.20.6).

stresses the two major developments in this Olympiad. The first is the Roman victory in the Hannibalic War: who would not wish to have detailed knowledge of that (ibid.)? And the second:

> Besides this, the policies and character of the kings (τὰς προαιρέσεις τῶν βασιλέων) became perfectly clear during these years. For everything that was only a matter of gossip about them before, now became completely known to everyone, even to those who were uninterested in world affairs. (14.1a.4)[48]

As Walbank says, this is a reference to the pact between Philip and Antiochus: the point is the pact – which is explicitly not gossip – and the great impression it made when it became known.[49] Precisely because of the special importance of these two developments, Polybius continues (i.e., the end of the Hannibalic War and the revelation of the policies and character of the kings), he has decided, instead of dealing with the events of each two years within a single volume as before, to restrict himself now to dealing only with the events of *one* year per volume (14.1a.5).[50] Thus Polybius considers the Roman victory over Hannibal and the behavior of the kings to be of such historical significance that he has decided to proceed much more slowly in his presentation of events. The proclamation in 14.1a of this major change is intended to attract the attention of his audience.[51]

In fact, Polybius departed even further in Book 14 from his usual method of presentation. Previously he had surveyed the world, describing events region by region in each volume of the work; but except for Scipio's victory at the battle of Zama, Book 14 is almost totally focused on the events in one region: Egypt. We have unfortunately lost most of that account, but a gloss on the Polybian manuscript indicates that the Egyptian material was enormous in length, running to forty-eight manuscript sheets. The importance of the crisis in Ptolemaic power would thus have been underlined for the audience far more clearly in the complete version of the *Histories* than appears in the remnant of Book 14 that has survived for us.[52]

---

[48] For τὰς προαιρέσεις τῶν βασιλέων at 14.1a.4 as denoting both policy and character, see Walbank 1967: 424.
[49] Ibid.; cf. also Pédech 1964: 110 n. 56.
[50] On the previous system of two years per volume, see, e.g., Polyb. 9.1.1 (explicit).
[51] Walbank 1967: 424 and 471. Yet Polyb. 14.1a is missing from the list of ancient references to the pact in Magie 1939: 32–4; Schmitt 1964: 237–9 ("Die Quellen"), cf. Schmitt 1969: 288–9; Errington 1971: 338–42 ("The Evidence"); Will 1982: 116; Gruen 1984: 387 n. 164. Except for the brief remark by Pédech 1964, only Walbank has pointed out the relevance of the passage for our topic.
[52] See Walbank 1985: 319 and n. 58.

Polybius' account of the secret agreement between Philip and Antiochus cannot therefore be dismissed as a mere uncomfortable aberration within Polybius' on-going historical narrative. On the contrary: Polybius' belief in the historicity and importance of the pact has helped structure his entire *Histories* in a fundamental way. Polybius consistently and confidently proclaims this (3.2.8; 14.1a.4–5).

The third appearance of the pact in the extant *Histories* is at 15.20, a famous passage that is central to the debate over the existence and geopolitical importance of the agreement. Yet even here the full intellectual implications have often been missed. Those implications concern something even more important than the structure of the *Histories* – namely, Polybius' structure of historical causation itself.

In 15.20 Polybius castigates Philip and Antiochus for their agreement to divide up the Ptolemaic domains; we now learn that it was a formal treaty (συνθῆκαι: 15.20.4).[53] Polybius launches a cascade of moralizing invective against it. As long as Ptolemy IV was alive, the two kings offered him help of which he had no need.[54] But when Ptolemy IV died and left only an infant on the throne, whose regime it was the natural duty of the kings to protect, they instead encouraged each other to tear apart the orphan's dominion, and to destroy him (15.20.2). Nor did the two kings even bother with any pretext for this shameful deed (αἰσχύνη), as even tyrants do (20.3). Rather, they acted as beasts do (θηριωδῶς) – simply devouring the weak (ibid.). The treaty was "the very image of impiety towards the Gods, cruelty towards men, and boundless greed" (20.4). But, Polybius continues, he who finds fault in Tyche (Fortune) for her arbitrary conduct of human affairs will now be reconciled to her when he learns how afterwards she made the two kings pay for their crime:

> For even while they were still breaking their pledged faith with one another, and destroying the kingdom of the child, Tyche alerted the Romans, and very justly visited upon the kings the very evils which they had planned in their total lawlessness to bring upon others. (20.6)[55]

Polybius then explains that Philip and then Antiochus were almost immediately defeated by the Romans, and were thus not only prevented from lusting after the property of others (as before) but were forced to

---

[53]   Cf. Schmitt 1969: 289–90.

[54]   This is evidently a reference to the indigenous rebellion which began ca. 216, becoming widespread in Upper and Middle Egypt in ca. 207/206. See above.

[55]   For ἐπιστήσασα Ῥωμαίους as meaning "alerting the Romans" to Philip and Antiochus, see Eckstein 2005, and Chapter 5, below. The correct translation of this phrase has important implications concerning Polybius' view of the impact that news of the treaty had at Rome.

pay war-indemnities to Rome and to obey Roman orders (15.20.8).[56] And then, during the reigns of the two kings' successors, Tyche brought total destruction to one of these dynasties (the Antigonids), and calamities nearly as bad to the other (20.9).

For Polybius, then, the power of Tyche to create even the most formidable of world-historical events is shown by the fate of the kings who made the criminal pact. Moreover, the punishment Tyche inflicts on Philip and Antiochus leads directly to the rise of Roman power over the Greek world, for the Romans, alerted to the situation, then act as Tyche's avenging punishment on the immoral conduct of the kings. Polybius thus links the evil treaty between Philip and Antiochus morally to the existence of Roman hegemony over the Greeks. The audience is told this with much emphasis.[57]

Polybius reiterates this theme fourteen volumes later. In discussing how Rome's intervention prevented the conquest of Alexandria and Egypt by Antiochus IV, the son of Antiochus III, and led instead to Antiochus' diplomatic humiliation (168 BC), Polybius comments that "Tyche had so arranged things" that the destruction of the Antigonid monarchy in Macedon simultaneously saved the Ptolemies and Egypt, for Antiochus would never have obeyed the Roman demand to withdraw from Egypt if he had not known of the defeat of King Perseus and Macedon by Rome (29.27.11–12).[58]

Such passages have aspects that make modern scholars uncomfortable. They prefer Polybius the political scientist, who sets out a careful and secular causal schema for events, distinguishing true cause ($\alpha i \tau i \alpha$) from public pretext ($\pi \rho \acute{o} \phi \alpha \sigma \iota s$) from $\alpha \rho \chi \eta$ (the beginning of action) – all occuring on the purely human plane and involving purely human motivations and conduct.[59] Polybius indeed repeatedly says that he is delineating crucial aspects of causation of events at the human level for his audience.[60] He also emphasizes human institutions as causative. Thus the question he asks at the start of his work is a strictly secular one: "How and under what political structure and mode of life did the Romans succeed in bringing almost the entire world under their domination in less than 53 years?" (1.1.5).[61] This question is answered in the analysis

---

[56]   On the meaning of $\phi \acute{o} \rho o s$ at 15.20.7 (normally "tribute" but here war-indemnity), see Walbank 1967: 474.
[57]   See Walbank 2002b: 251.
[58]   For the close conceptual linkage between Polyb. 15.20 and Polyb. 29.27, see Walbank 1967: 474; and cf. Walbank 1979: 406.
[59]   On this scheme of human causation in Polybius, see esp. Pédech 1964: 80–8; cf. Eckstein 1989: 1–4.
[60]   See Derow 1994: 84–90.
[61]   See Walbank 1972: 130–1; Derow 1994: 89.

of the virtues of Roman political structure and culture given in Book 6, and it is a purely secular analysis.[62] At the secular level, too, Polybius presents his readers with an analysis in which Philip V and Antiochus III, focused on the opportunity offered them in the Greek East by the collapse of Ptolemaic power, wrongly ignore the emerging Mediterranean-wide interconnectedness (symplokē) – the symplokē that then leads to the Roman intervention from the West to stop the kings.[63]

Nevertheless, Polybius was not a modern intellectual but a Hellenistic one, and partook deeply in the Hellenistic interest in the power of Fortune.[64] Polybius thus believed in the power of Tyche to affect the greatest of events – he says so repeatedly. Depending on the specific incident, Polybius conceived Tyche as acting in an arbitrary way, or as acting as retributive justice, or as part of the plan of Providence. But whichever version of Tyche Polybius employs, this is a crucial aspect of his thought and cannot be ignored.[65]

Especially concerning the rise of Rome, Polybius does not restrict himself to a secular vision, or to political-science type questions (though this is what modern scholars find most comfortable and even illuminating). Rather, at 1.4.1–2 Polybius also emphatically states that the most remarkable aspect of the period covered in his *Histories* is that Tyche appears to have guided almost all the affairs of the world in one direction, towards the rise of Rome; and it is the duty of the historian "to show his audience the operations by which she accomplished her purpose." And this, he says, he has striven to do (1.4.4).

Thus in his thinking about causation, including the causes of the rise of Roman power, Polybius operated on a "double track" – on both a secular and a metaphysical level.[66] And in Book 15 he is explicit: Roman victory in the Second Macedonian War and then in the Syrian War was Tyche's revenge for the evil Pact Between the Kings (15.20.5–8).[67] This, in turn, is part of "a supernatural pattern which interprets the ruin of

---

[62]   The best discussion of Book 6 remains Walbank 1972: Ch. 5. Polybius asks a similar institutional question, in similar language, about the successful expansion of the Achaean League to the conquest of the entire Peloponnese (2.38.1, parallel to 1.1.5), and provides a similarly institutional answer (2.38.8–9).

[63]   See Walbank 1985 on the working of this concept in Polybius' *Histories*; and cf. Eckstein 2006: Ch. 4, for the connection of *symplokē* to ideas about the evolution of regional subsystems into larger, connected systems in modern international-systems theory.

[64]   On the important place of Tyche in the thought of Hellenistic intellectuals: see Green 1990: 400–2.

[65]   As does, for instance, Derow 1994: 89–90, who denies Tyche as a serious Polybian explanation of events "except once" – at 36.17 (a passage he finds depressing).

[66]   See now Walbank 2002b: 251–2 and 255.

[67]   See Walbank 2002b: 251.

Macedon and the rise of Rome as the work of a divine power exacting retribution for moral delinquency."[68] Indeed, in 23.10–11, eight volumes later, Tyche is still shown avenging herself directly on an elderly Philip because of his earlier crimes.[69] And just as Polybius in 23.10–11 depicts Philip's tragic execution of his own son Demetrius as part of Tyche's revenge upon him, so Polybius evidently depicted Antiochus III as having murdered *his* son (Livy 35.15.4–5, drawing on Polybian material) – thus reinforcing the parallels between the fate of the two kings.[70] As we have seen (above, p. 135), the world-historical result of the revenge of Tyche upon the Antigonids and Seleucids for their immorality is still being given a prominent explanatory place as late as Book 27: it is why Antiochus IV is prevented by Rome from conquering Egypt in 168 BC.

Polybius, then, intended his statement in 15.20 to be taken with deep seriousness. The passage is not a lapse into rhetorical excess, nor an aberration within his on-going "realistic" narrative. Rather, it exemplifies an entire theory of historical causation, and describes one of the most important operations by which Tyche accomplished her purpose in the world. Polybius thus not only assigned historical and political import- ance to the Pact Between the Kings, he assigned it even a metaphysical importance.[71]

Two more passages need mention. First, only a few chapters after Polybius' first and emphatic reference to the pact (3.2.8), he asserts the special importance that correct knowledge of treaties will have for his audience – including for active statesmen (3.21.8–10). This assertion then leads to Polybius' attack on the historian Philinus of Agrigentum for having made a *non-existent treaty* (between Rome and Carthage) the centerpiece of his historical work (3.26). Thus in reporting on the treaty between Philip and Antiochus, Polybius was dealing with a topic (treaties) where he himself had underlined to his audience the import- ance of getting the facts correctly – and had bitterly criticized historians who did not.[72] Secondly, in 16.20 – in the context of the war in the Aegean in 201 provoked by Philip's aggression against the Ptolemies – Polybius challenges his audience to prove anything he is reporting as intentionally untrue, and to criticize him harshly if such is the case (16.20.8–9). This is part of Polybius' claim to be *especially* authoritative

---

[68] Ibid.: 252.
[69] See Walbank 1938: 55–68.
[70] See discussion in Walbank 1938: 62–8, and Walbank 2002b: 251.
[71] See Polyb. 3.2.8; 14.1a.4–5; cf. 27.29.11–13.
[72] On the unlikelihood that Polybius was wrong about the non-existence of "the Philinus Treaty," see Badian 1979: 167–9; cf. Hoyos 1985.

about the events in the period covered in the 144th Olympiad (16.14.4) – i.e., in the years 204–201 BC. Polybius' assertion of special authoritativeness for this period comes with a claim that he has access to an exceptionally wide variety of sources on this period – all of which he says he used carefully and critically (16.14–20 passim, cf. esp. 16.14.1–2). Among the two most important events included in that Olympiad, and hence included in Polybius' special claim to authoritativeness, is the Pact Between the Kings.[73]

If we had the complete text of the *Histories* instead of our fragments, the treaty between the kings would probably stand out even more strikingly than it now does. Polybius must have given a detailed account of the terms of the treaty in a passage that has disappeared: probably it immediately preceded 15.20, for the latter is merely Polybius' moralizing *commentary* on those treaty terms.[74] And Polybius may well have discussed the secret treaty again during his detailed discussion of Philip's diplomacy with Egypt ca. 204–202 (an account now lost, but referred to at 15.23.13). This is because Philip carried on his negotiations to become father-in-law of Ptolemy V and protector of Egypt simultaneously with his negotiations with Antiochus for the joint destruction of Ptolemy V and Egypt – an extraordinary act of duplicity.[75]

Thus the treaty between Philip and Antiochus is the central element in the most crucial part of Polybius' narrative of the rise of Rome to world power. The treaty is given enormous causal importance, both at the secular and the metaphysical level, and was even basic to the literary structure of the *Histories*. In a society much given to ridicule – and in a work where he had severely criticized those who made non-existent treaties a central element in their historical work (3.26) – it is unlikely that Polybius would have dared to make the pact so important unless he believed he had excellent evidence that it existed, and existed along the lines he reported. We do not have to make Polybius a paragon of historical thought here – we only have to make him minimally competent.[76]

Given these considerations, the consequences for our opinion of Polybius as a historian are devastating if he is wrong about the pact – either about its existence or about the far-reaching nature of its terms. And by his persistent pronouncements, it is Polybius himself who has consciously raised the stakes so high. The treaty between the kings is thus a central issue not merely in the course of ancient Mediterranean history but in Polybian studies. Is there enough evidence to overturn him?

---

[73]   See further below, pp. 174–6.
[74]   See Schmitt 1964: 237; Pédech 1964: 110.
[75]   See Walbank 1967: 486. On these negotiations, see below, pp. 143–4.
[76]   See the comments, in a different context, of Badian 1979: 167–9.

PHILIP AND THE PACT:
EGYPT OR THE AEGEAN?

The major problem with the pact for modern scholars has been Polybius' statement implying that the treaty included the conquest of Egypt (3.2.8) – an attack attributed to Philip alone. Early editors of Polybius found this so unlikely that they emended τοῖς κατ' Αἴγυπτον at 3.2.8 to τοῖς κατ' Αἴγαιον (that is, Ptolemaic holdings in the Aegean islands). The emendation is widely accepted.[77] It has the advantage of restricting the treaty to Philip's known aggressions in 202–200, which were all in the Aegean region. Moreover, a free hand for Philip in the Aegean seems a reasonable trade-off for allowing Antiochus to advance in the Levant (3.2.8) – while we thus avoid the question of just how the Ptolemaic homeland of Egypt was going to be divided up between the two kings.[78] In addition, scholars have persuasively argued that Polybius at 3.2.8 is describing the kings' actual actions after 203/202, not merely their plans (ἤρξαντο . . . ἐπιβάλλειν); but since neither Antiochus nor Philip ever actually attacked Egypt itself – as Polybius well knew (see 16.10) – something here seems to be wrong.[79]

If this emendation is correct, then Polybius never referred to terms in the pact that foresaw the destruction of Ptolemaic rule in Egypt itself. This would make the alliance between Philip and Antiochus, though a serious international event, not a world-shattering one. But though the arguments in favor of the emendation to τοῖς κατ' Αἴγαιον have some force, the emendation must nevertheless be rejected. The fact is that Polybius at 3.2.8 is referring to Egypt.

First, the manuscripts are unanimous in reading τοῖς κατ' Αἴγυπτον – and with 3.2.8 we are dealing with nine manuscripts, deriving from at least three separate medieval traditions. It would need especially strong arguments to overturn such a widespread and unanimous text.[80] Further, as both Holleaux and Walbank have said, the proposed emendation

---

[77]   On the emendation, see esp. Pédech 1954: 391–3. Accepting the emendation: Magie 1939: 32–3; Errington 1971: 339–40; Huss 1976: 218–19 and n. 303; Albert 1980: 105 n. 486.

[78]   Cf. Errington 1971: 339–40.

[79]   Ibid. On this meaning of Polyb. 3.8.2, see also Schmitt 1964: 252–3; Huss 1976: 219 n. 303.

[80]   The three separate major traditions are the mss. *Vaticanus gr.* 124 ("A"); *Monacensis gr.* 157 ("C"); and *Urbinas gr.* 102 ("F"). With their various subtraditions, there are a total of nine mss. involved. Note, for instance, *Vaticanus gr.* 1005 ("Z"), descended from a tradition common with "C" – which omits καὶ Καρίαν at 3.2.8, but still has κατ' Αἴγυπτον. Discussion of the manuscripts of Book 3: Foucault 1972: 228.

– τοῖς κατ' Αἴγαιον – is simply not good Polybian Greek for the islands of the Aegean. But both Holleaux and Walbank made this assertion about τοῖς κατ' Αἴγαιον only briefly and in passing, without supporting arguments – and hence scholarship has ignored them here.[81] That is unfortunate. The term Αἴγαιον is in fact extraordinarily rare in Polybius: other than the passage in dispute (3.2.8), it appears just once in the entire extant text of the *Histories* – and there (at 16.34.1) it means literally the sea itself, not the Aegean island-states. Polybius' actual term for the Aegean island-states is abundantly attested: never τὰ κατ' Αἴγαιον, but always αἱ νῆσοι (the islands).[82] Particularly instructive is 5.34.7, where the Ptolemaic dominion in the Aegean (Philip's alleged target if the emendation is correct) is called τοῖς κατὰ . . . ταῖς νήσοις, and 21.42.4, where aggression against the Aegean states (by Antiochus III) is aggression τοῖς ἐπὶ ταῖς νήσοις. Many other examples could be cited. Holleaux and Walbank are correct.

But this is only the beginning of the problems for the supporters of the emendation. Pédech has pointed out that in 16.10 Polybius expects Philip to sail for Alexandria in Egypt after his naval victory over Rhodes in summer 201 – and chastises him for failing to do so. The Greek historian even launches here into a moralizing disquisition on how those who have great ambitions and have striven hard towards them often do not take the great opportunity when it is finally offered to them. This passage clearly shows that Polybius *did* think an attack on Egypt itself was part of Philip's plans in this period, and assumes that his audience has been fully informed of this fact and fully understands it – for otherwise his comments about Philip make no sense.[83] Moreover, Polybius' phrase here is that after his victory over the Rhodians, Philip was now able "to *complete* his sailing to Alexandria" (τελεῖν τὸν εἰς τὴν Ἀλεξάνδρειαν πλοῦν). As Schmitt says, the appearance of the verb τελεῖν here suggests that in Polybius' conception, *all* of Philip's actions in his warfare in the southern Aegean in 201 were actually a unified operation that had as its final goal a sudden descent on Alexandria. This would tie the

---

[81] Holleaux 1938: 70 n. 1, and Holleaux 1952a: 163 n. 3; Walbank 1967: 472. Ignored: Holleaux and Walbank here are missing from all the discussions in n. 46 above.

[82] For αἱ νῆσοι as the Polybian phrase for the Aegean island-states, see also 4.16.8, 19.7, and 19.8; 16.26.10; 27.3.1. The phrase also appears in inscriptions: see *Syll.*[3] 390 and 455. For the inhabitants of the Aegean island-states, Polybius' phrase is οἱ νησιῶται: 5.105.6; 6.49.10; 11.4.6. For the southern region of the Aegean, Polybius sometimes employs the phrase αἱ Κυκλάδες, or αἱ Κυκλάδες νῆσοι: see 4.16.8; 18.54.8; cf. 3.16.3. Again, he never employs οἱ κατ' Αἴγαιον.

[83] See Pédech 1954: 393; cf. McDonald and Walbank 1937: 182–3: but they assert that Polybius must be exaggerating the pact, and hence they still opt for Αἴγαιον at 3.8.2. Walbank has since changed his mind about 3.2.8 (see above).

evidence in 16.10 even more closely to the (unemended) meaning of Polybius' statement at 3.2.8.[84] In sum: 16.10 very powerfully supports the idea that the manuscripts at 3.2.8 are indeed correct.[85]

Again, Polybius twice says that Philip and Antiochus aimed at the total destruction of the child Ptolemy and his rule (3.2.8; 15.20.2). On its face, this means more than depriving him of his overseas provinces. Similarly, when Polybius says that Tyche wreaked upon the kings and their descendants the fate they had prepared for Ptolemy (15.20.6–8), he means in Philip's case the total destruction of his dynasty, and in Antiochus' case calamities that verged on it (20.8) – not the loss of some outer provinces. Moreover, of the six separate sources on the kings' pact, five indicate that Egypt itself was a main target; only one very late source seems to indicate that the kings' objectives were more limited. This demonstrates what the thrust of the ancient tradition was.[86]

The arguments in favor of accepting the unanimous manuscript reading τοῖς κατ᾽ Αἰγύπτον at Polyb. 3.2.8 are therefore extraordinarily strong. But this means we cannot escape the proposition that Polybius believed, and told his audience, that Philip and Antiochos envisioned an attack upon Egypt itself. Some scholars, however, cannot accept that the ambitions of the two kings extended so far – to the total disruption of the balance of power in the Greek world.[87] And it is especially difficult to believe that Antiochus would have allowed Philip the lead in the assault on Egypt proper (which is what Polyb. 3.2.8 says), with consequent access to its vast resources: what would have been left to him?[88] Now that what Polybius said about the place of Egypt in the kings' pact is clear, we thus face the problem of whether what he said is *a priori* impossible.

It is not. To begin with, there clearly was a widespread perception in these years that the Ptolemaic regime had become gravely weak. This

---

[84]   Schmitt 1964: 253.

[85]   Pédech 1954 (392–3) disposes of an emendation of 3.2.8 proposed by Holleaux: κατὰ Κίον (see Holleaux 1935: 70 n. 1, and Holleaux 1952a: 162 n. 3). This emendation is not acceptable because the city of Cius was not an important place (unlike Samos or Caria, referred to in 3.2.8), and because Philip's conquest of it had nothing to do with his plotting against the Ptolemies (the city had no ties to them) – the subject of 3.2.8. Nor is κατὰ Κίον paleographically close to κατ᾽ Αἰγύπτον, which makes it hard to see how the "corruption" could have occurred.

[86]   Sources: the Polybian passages; Livy 31.14.5; App. *Mac.* 4; Justin 30.2.8, cf. Pomp. Trog. *Prol.* 30; John Antioch. frg. 54. Only Jerome seems to have something different here: *ut proximas civitates regno suo singuli de regno Ptolemaei ungerent* (*in Dan.* 11.13). See Schmitt 1964: 251, and Schmitt 1969: 290.

[87]   See, e.g., Braunert 1964: 94–5; Klose 1982: 80–6.

[88]   Similarly, in Appian's version of the pact, Egypt itself is to go to Antiochus, with Philip getting Cyrene (*Mac.* 4) – yet scholars find it hard to believe that Philip would have allowed such a vast increase in *Antiochus'* power: Holleaux 1928: 150. App. *Mac.* 4 has several confusions: see Badian 1964b: 113.

explains the attempt of Cleomenes of Sparta, as early as 220, to stage
a coup d'état against the lethargic government of Ptolemy IV. According
to Polybius and Plutarch (and they were working here from separate
traditions), Cleomenes was not only personally contemptuous of Ptolemy
IV as a ruler, but sensed that the regime in general had only weak support: it was dependent upon fickle acceptance by foreign mercenaries
and the Alexandrian populace.[89] Cleomenes' coup failed – but as early
as 210 Antiochus III himself perceived the Ptolemaic regime to be so
fragile that he intended an invasion of Egypt proper (Polyb. 5.62.4–
5).[90] Three years later a grave new weakness of the Ptolemies appeared,
one to which we have already referred: a massive indigenous rebellion
broke out, centered in Upper Egypt but extending as far north as the
Nile Delta. It was apparently led by the Egyptian troops whom Ptolemy
IV had been forced to recruit to defend the Ptolemaic regime a decade
previously from the campaign by Antiochus III in 217 that ended at the
great battle of Raphia (Polyb. 5.107.1–3, criticizing this decision). By
207/206 the rebellion had taken intractable root in the Thebaid (Upper
Egypt), and soon the priests of Amon in Thebes, following the full traditional ritual, crowned Haronnophris, one of the rebel generals, as the
true pharaoh; later he would be succeeded as pharaoh by a second rebel
leader, Chaonophris. Fighting now spread as far north as Lycopolis
(Middle Egypt), and the government at Alexandria was unable to put
down the rebellion completely even in the nearby Delta, let alone
farther up the Nile Valley.[91]

   With the sudden death of Ptolemy IV and the accession of the 5-year-
old child Ptolemy V to the throne (autumn 204), the situation for the
regime gravely worsened.[92] The caretaker governments for the child
were unstable and riddled with factionalism; in Alexandria, chaos and
rioting often reigned.[93] In summer or autumn 202 Ptolemy V's chief
minister Tlepolemus could be accused of plotting to turn the throne
over to Antiochus III (Polyb. 15.25.34–5) – or to seize it himself
(15.26.5–7). This shows how shaky the Ptolemaic regime was. In
197/196 – at a time when the government still had not gained control
over Middle and Upper Egypt – there was yet another attempted coup

[89]   See Polyb. 5.36.3–9; Plut. *Cleom.* 33. The different traditions on Cleomenes'
coup: Walbank 1957: 565–7. On the dangerous powers of the mercenaries at
Alexandria in this period, see esp. Griffith 1935a: 126–8.
[90]   Antiochus' plan was abortive, but it already shows the scale of his ambitions.
Discussion: Tarn 1928: 729; Ager 1991: 14.
[91]   For detailed discussion of the rebellion, see Veïsse 2004; cf. Pestman 1956 and
1995; Clarysse 1978; McGing 1997. See also above, this chapter.
[92]   On the date of Ptolemy IV's death, see Walbank 1936: 20–34.
[93]   Alexandrian chaos and rioting: Polyb. 15.24a–36; cf. now Mittag 2003: 168–72.

d'état in Alexandria, this time by the Aetolian mercenary general Scopas. Polybius says that Scopas' mercenary forces were sufficient to carry out the coup and depose Ptolemy V (18.53.4): it was mostly Scopas' own sloth and indecision that allowed Ptolemy (still only 13 years old at this point) to survive the crisis (18.52.1–6). Here in Book 18, as in Books 3 and 15, the fact that Ptolemy V was "still a child" constituted a terrible weakness – and a great temptation to others (18.53.4).[94] We have already seen that Polybius thought Philip planned a sudden descent on Alexandria in 201 (above) – but Philip was not alone. Shortly after the failure of Scopas' coup, Antiochus III heard a rumor that Ptolemy V was dead, and Antiochus himself sailed to take Alexandria (autumn 196). Livy (working from Polybian material) says that the Seleucid king intended to rule the entire country: *suam fore Aegyptum . . . censebat* (33.41.3).[95] The rumor of Ptolemy's death turned out to be false, and so Antiochus turned back when his fleet was halfway to Alexandria. But nothing demonstrates more clearly how Egypt was "in play" in this period. The obvious weakness of the Ptolemaic regime made it an obvious target. And, despite some scholars who adhere to an older and idealized view of Hellenistic geopolitics, important studies have demonstrated conclusively that the conduct of Hellenistic kings was not likely to be restrained by any concept of maintaining a general balance of power, let alone any concept of a consensual community of polities that limited the aggressive expansion of their dynastic states.[96]

Philip's special interest in Egyptian affairs in the period just before the alleged pact with Antiochus is itself well attested. He was negotiating with the Alexandrian government at that time for the marriage of one of his daughters to Ptolemy V. The negotiations probably began while Ptolemy IV was still alive.[97] But Philopator's premature death and the accession of the child now led the managers of the Ptolemaic regime to pursue the marriage tie to Macedon with the utmost urgency (autumn 204 or spring 203), and these negotiations included a plea for Philip's direct military help in case of attack from Antiochus (Polyb. 15.25.13) – which shows how the threat from the Seleucid king already loomed large among Egyptian concerns at this point.[98] Philip, himself one of the great generals of the age, would have been a formidable

---

[94]   On Scopas' attempted coup, see Walbank 1967: 642, with 46.
[95]   Cf. App. *Syr.* 4. Polybian derivation of Livy 33.41: see Briscoe 1973: 320–1 and 325–6.
[96]   For full discussion of the grim evidence, see Eckstein 2006: Ch. 4. Note especially the studies of Lévêque 1968; Austin 1986; Ager 2003.
[97]   The negotiations: Polyb. 15.25.13; 16.22.16. For their date of inception, see Holleaux 1935: 78–9; cf. Huss 1976: 128–9.
[98]   See Huss 1976: 84.

father-in-law to Ptolemy V under any circumstances, but this was all the more so if Ptolemy's regime wanted Macedonian military intervention. It is easy to see how these negotiations would have impressed Philip with Alexandrian weakness – and with the vision of himself as protector of Egypt.[99]

It was in this period of Philip's interest in Egypt that the indigenous rebellion against the Ptolemies in Upper and Middle Egypt reached ever more dangerous proportions with the formal religious proclamation of an indigenous pharaoh (above). Meanwhile, savage riots in Alexandria brought down the government of Ptolemy's prime minister Agathocles (Polyb. 15.24a–36: summer or autumn 202), showing how unstable was Egypt's capital. Philip, who had agents and spies everywhere (Polyb. 13.5.7, cf. 5.101.6), must have known the nature of the multiple crises now besetting the Ptolemies. And it is possible that after spring 203 one of the foreign mercenary commanders at Alexandria was Dicaearchus – who had been one of Philip's secret agents in the Aegean the previous year (see Polyb. 18.54.11).[100]

In other words: conditions for a landing in Egypt in 201 by Philip probably appeared propitious. The new caretaker government for Ptolemy V that replaced the murdered Agathocles in summer or autumn 202, headed by Tlepolemus, owed its shaky power to massive rioting against the previous regime, and soon proved to be faction-ridden, lethargic, and unpopular; it was unlikely to prove a rallying point of loyalty.[101] With the government at Alexandria itself offering Philip a way to be the military protector of Ptolemy (Polyb. 15.25.13), there is no reason to doubt Polybius that Philip now conceived a special interest in Egypt – nor can the idea that he sought to establish Macedonian domination there be dismissed as *a priori* outlandish. Rather, this fits with what Polybius repeatedly says about the huge scope of Philip's ambition – nothing less than to establish his rule over the entire Mediterranean world (ἡ τῶν ὅλων δυναστεία). The ancient evidence for the large scope of Philip's ambitions has been discussed in Chapter 3, above.[102] When Alcaeus of

---

[99]   The Ptolemaic government can have been under no illusions about Philip – but clearly it feared Antiochus III more. Their actions demonstrate again the validity in antiquity of the thesis of Walt 1987, that states under pressure align with the *least* dangerous great power.

[100]   Was Dicaearchus recruited for mercenary service in Egypt by his friend Scopas, during Scopas' recruiting drive in Greece in winter 204/203 (cf. Polyb. 26.6)? This would explain Dicaearchus' absence from Philip's military endeavors after 204, despite his great success as a naval commander (cf. 18.54.7–11, with Walbank 1940: 110). Dicaearchus' friendship with Scopas: Polyb. 18.54.6–7. Scopas' later attempted coup d'état against young Ptolemy: above.

[101]   For this aspect of the Egyptian crisis of 202–201 see esp. Will 1982: 105–12.

[102]   See esp. Polyb. 5.102.1, 104.1, 108.5, 15.24.1.

Messene wrote ca. 202–200 that, in view of Philip's enormous military achievements on land and sea, "all that remains is to conquer Olympus," he could have added: or perhaps Alexandria.[103]

Polybius indicates that Antiochus III had similar ambitions for unlimited, world-wide rule (11.39.14–16). It used to be fashionable, as with Polybius' statements about Philip, to pass this off as an exaggeration; but Polybius' assertions about Antiochus' reputation for capacity for world-wide rule have been confirmed by an important inscription from the Greek city of Teos, dated to ca. 204/203, which welcomes his rule west of the Taurus.[104] Additional evidence now comes from a cuneiform text showing that on a date equivalent to April 6, 205 BC, Antiochus, returning from his enormous reconquests of the eastern Seleucid dominions as far as the Indus, partook formally in the Royal New Year Festival at Babylon, taking up the Cloak of Nebuchadnezzar – a ritual that had implications of world-wide rule.[105] Moreover, it was precisely in the years 204–202, following his return from his Alexander-like eastern conquests, that Antiochus – in imitation of Alexander – now took the title of *Megas*: "The Great."[106]

The huge extent of Antiochus' general ambitions is therefore clear, and those ambitions provide support for the notion that by 203/202, Egypt itself was a target. As we have seen, that was true of Antiochus' intent both earlier, in 210, and later, in 196. There is no reason why the situation should have been different in 203/202–200 – when, if anything, Egypt was even weaker and more vulnerable than in either 210 or 196. But here we arrive at the real crux concerning the place of Egypt in the Pact Between the Kings. Polyb. 3.2.8 states that Philip began attacking Egypt, but all Antiochus did was begin to attack Coele Syria and Phoenicia; and it seems inconceivable – *a priori* – that Antiochus would have conceded to Philip the attack on Egypt. That would have given Philip too much power, while depriving Antiochus himself of potentially vast resources.[107]

Any answer to this question must be speculative, since we lack information concerning the exact terms of the pact. Polybius' Books 15

[103] On the political implications of Alcaeus' poem (*Anth. Pal.* 9.518), see above, Chapter 3, with Walbank 2002a: 128.
[104] Doubts about Polyb. 11.39.14–16: see, e.g., Schmitt 1964: 90. The Teos inscription: see Herrmann 1965: 113–16; Rawlings 1976: 2–3; Ma 1999/2002: 71–3. Cf. Walbank 1967: 316 and 638–9.
[105] On this new cuneiform text, see Sherwin-White and Kuhrt 1993: 130–1 and 199–200.
[106] This is shown by inscriptions from his vassal-cities Teos and Amyzon: discussion in Ma 1999/2002: 272–6.
[107] See Schmitt 1964: 253; Errington 1971: 346; cf., in general, McDonald and Walbank 1937: 183.

and 16 exist only as small and discontinuous fragments, and among the passages lost is, unfortunately, his description of the specific terms of the treaty (see above); the evidence from the other sources is brief, vague, and/or suspect. The limitations on what we can say here are obvious.

There do remain possible hints in the surviving Polybian material. As Schmitt notes, the wording of Polyb. 15.20.2 is that the kings "urged each other on . . . to get rid entirely of the orphan."[108] A mutuality of effort against Ptolemy V is implied here, and the verb Polybius employs for that mutual effort – ἐπανελέσθαι – has in general an extremely harsh meaning: to murder someone (most often), to destroy him (literally), or (at a minimum) to overturn a political regime. Schmitt assumes the totalizing meaning of ἐπανελέσθαι at 15.20.2 as obvious, without discussion.[109] Examination of general Polybian usage shows that Schmitt's interpretation is correct.[110] Nor do we have to rely on mere general usage here. As Mauersberger points out in regard to ἐπανελέσθαι 15.20.2, in the very next sentence, at 15.20.3, Polybius equates the mutual action undertaken by Philip and Antiochus against Ptolemy V with literal destruction, ἀπώλεια: in a savage world the weak are eaten, swallowed whole, by larger and more powerful animals. Hence Mauersberger translates ἐπανελέσθαι at 15.20.2 as "umbringen, beseitigen."[111]

In 15.20 Polybius is therefore saying that Egypt was going to be swallowed whole, as a mutual project of the two kings. We do not have the details of their agreement as it appeared in Polybius; that passage is lost. But a mutual project of "swallowing Ptolemy completely" (15.20.2) implies an understanding of what the benefits to each king were going to be. Polyb. 15.20.2 thus implies that the agreement foresaw a point (depending, presumably, on the development of circumstances at Alexandria as Egyptian holdings came under ever more severe attack) where the child Ptolemy V would be overthrown, the dynasty would hence come to an end, and some sort of sharing out of the resources of Egypt would then occur between Philip and Antiochus. But the idea was that the ultimate benefits would (somehow) be mutual: ἀλλήλους,

---

[108]   παρακαλέσαντες ἀλλήλους . . . ἐπανελέσθαι τὸν ἀπολελειμμένον.

[109]   Schmitt 1964: 251.

[110]   See Mauersberger 1961: cols. 861–2, vv. ἐπαναιρέω, ἐπαναίρεσις, where we find literal murder (twenty-one cases), literal destruction (five cases), and overthrow of regime (two cases: 9.33.6; 21.11.10) – the latter would still make our point. Only once, at 1.10.8, might ἐπανελέσθαι mean something less literally annihilating: "to crush utterly" in the sense of "to bring under total domination" (equivalent to δεσπόζειν: ibid.). But that is clearly not the meaning at 15.20.2 (see immediately below).

[111]   Mauersberger 1961: col. 861.

διασπωμένων δὲ τὴν τοῦ παιδὸς ἀρχήν (15.20.7).[112] That such was Polybius' understanding of the nature of the pact is confirmed by Livy 31.14.5, which derives from Polybian material, and informs the audience that according to the treaty, the wealth of Egypt, which both kings coveted (ambo . . .), would soon be divided between them (divisae . . .).[113]

Yet at Polyb. 3.2.8, in the "table of contents," Philip attacks Egypt by himself while Antiochus is busy in the Levant. Since we should probably take 3.2.8 not as a depiction of the actual terms of the agreement but as a description of the kings' actual actions subsequent to the pact,[114] this passage need not be seen as contradicting the idea implicit throughout Polyb. 15.20 – that a sharing in the removal of Ptolemy V was somehow envisioned in the agreement.

Yet if Antiochus had not allowed Egypt to him, how was it politically possible for Philip "to begin attacking Egypt" (3.2.8) – i.e., to work himself into a position in the southern Aegean to make a sudden descent from those Aegean bases, alone, on Alexandria – as Polybius implies in 16.10 was Philip's plan all along?[115] Schmitt stresses here Polybius' statement at 15.20.6 that the kings, because of their savage and uncontrolled greed, soon betrayed each other (παρασπονδούντων μὲν ἀλλήλους), a betrayal that occurred "when they were tearing apart the child's dominions" (ibid.). On the basis of this statement Schmitt proposes that in Polybius' conception, Philip's projected descent on Alexandria in 201 was not part of the pact with Antiochus, but rather was a betrayal of it.[116]

Such a betrayal of a treaty-partner and ally would certainly be consistent with Polybius' vision of Philip in this period. Though only fragments of the relevant volumes of the Histories survive, these show how strongly Polybius emphasized from Book 7 onwards that ever since Philip's "change of character for the worse" ca. 217/215 BC, treachery to friends and allies had been a hallmark of the king's personality and policies.

The phenomenon first occurred, Polybius says (amid a cascade of negative moralizing), with Philip's impulse in 215 to seize the citadel of his treaty-ally Messene (7.11–14) – a "treachery" (7.12.8) later carried through, despite the wise counsel of Aratus of Sicyon, who is one

---

[112]   Errington 1971: 347, unaccountably claims that Polybius in 15.20 does not assert that the kings intended to destroy the Ptolemies.
[113]   The Polybian derivation of Livy 31.14.5 is clear, for Livy at this point in his narrative has just shifted the scene from Rome to Greek affairs; see Briscoe 1973: 94.
[114]   See Schmitt 1964: 252–3; Errington 1971: 340; Huss 1976: 219 n. 303; and above, at n. 75.
[115]   On the phrase τελεῖν τὸν εἰς τὴν Ἀλεξάνδρειαν πλοῦν at 16.10.1, see above.
[116]   Schmitt 1964: 253. For Polybius' probable conception of how Antiochus betrayed Philip, see below.

of Polybius' heroes.[117] Moreover, Polybius says, Aratus paid for his effort to make Philip act honorably: the king had him poisoned (8.12.2).[118] At Argos in 210, a city that was his ally, Philip spent his time raping citizen women (10.26, with another cascade of negative moralizing). And, acting for his own strategic interests, Philip later betrayed the Argives to their hereditary enemy Sparta (Livy 32.28, based on Polybian material).[119] Philip made a secret pact to help the Cretans in their war against Rhodes ca. 205 – although he was officially at peace with Rhodes; Polybius twice calls this policy "evil" ($\kappa\alpha\kappa\sigma\pi\rho\alpha\gamma\mu\sigma\sigma\acute\nu\eta$: 13.3.1, 5.1). Philip also sent a secret agent to burn the Rhodians' dockyards (13.4–5, with more moralizing), and secretly gave the mercenary commander Dicaearchus a war-fleet to pillage peaceful Aegean shipping ("an act of treachery": 18.54.8).[120] In 202 Philip forced the strategic cities of Lysimacheia and Chalcedon on the Hellespont to withdraw from their alliances with Aetolia, and took them over – even though, Polybius stresses, he had just sworn a treaty of peace with Aetolia (15.23.8–9). During this campaign Philip gained control of the city of Cius peacefully; but he then looted it and sold its entire population into slavery – "an act of vicious treachery" (15.23.4), which was also a betrayal of his in-law Prusias, to whom he had promised Cius as a living entity (15.23.10).[121] Then, after agreeing to the surrender of Thasos on generous terms, Philip betrayed the city when it opened its gates, selling the entire population into slavery (Polyb. 15.24.1–3). At Cius and Thasos, Polybius emphasizes, Philip acted for immediate, tempting advantage (money for his treasury from the mass sale of slaves: 15.23.1), without considering the long-term negative political impact of such treacherous behavior (24.4). Finally, there are Philip's negotiations to become the father-in-law and protector of Ptolemy V – undertaken, Polybius says, while Philip was also in negotiations with Antiochus to destroy the Ptolemaic dynasty utterly (see above).

Thus Polybius' narrative from 217/215 down to 200, through eight volumes of the *Histories*, stressed Philip's habitual treachery towards friends and allies; and the historicity of these incidents is not doubted. Hence there is nothing *a priori* implausible about Philip being prepared to betray Antiochus, too, if the opportunity to seize Alexandria for himself came up. It may seem to us short-sighted, but so were his actions at Thasos and Cius (as Polybius underlines at 15.24.5–6); and Philip always found military gambles tempting.[122] The seizure of Alexandria would have hugely

---

[117]   For discussion, see Walbank 1940: 77–8.
[118]   On this tradition, see Walbank 1933: 156–7.
[119]   Detailed discussion: Eckstein 1987b: 213–33.
[120]   On Philip and Dicaearchus, see Walbank 1940: 110 (cf. above, p. 144).
[121]   Discussion: Walbank 1940: 115.
[122]   See esp. Rich 1984: 129–30.

strengthened his prestige with the Greeks (and perhaps even decisively shifted in his favor the balance of power in his relationship with Antiochus). The "betrayal" thesis, first proposed by Schmitt, thus fits well both with the immediate strategic situation of Philip ca. 201 and with Polybius' depiction of Philip's personality and policies.

There is a second, if less likely possibility. Historians assume that Antiochus would never give up Egypt to Philip because this would have allowed Philip access to enormous resources. But in the circumstances of Egypt in 201, the resources were not that large. Alexandria itself was in chaos (Polyb. 15.24a–36); access to the resource-producing countryside was gravely limited by the huge indigenous rebellion.[123] In such conditions, and given that Philip's envoys to Antiochus could argue that Ptolemy V's government was offering to make Philip the military protector of Egypt anyway – i.e., that Philip might find a way to gain power in Egypt even if his negotiations with Antiochus fell through (cf. Polyb. 15.25.13) – perhaps Antiochus actually allowed Philip "Egypt" in the pact.[124] In return Antiochus would be guaranteed the rich provinces of Coele Syria and Judaea without Philip's opposition – and the Ptolemaic government, distracted by Philip's attack, could not itself have defended them. Moreover, it might have seemed questionable to Antiochus whether Philip could gain control over Alexandria, let alone control over the countryside, or having gained it, hold on to it when he was so far from his bases in the Aegean and Macedon. And failure on Philip's part could well lead to the arrival of Antiochus himself – marching easily overland with his main army from nearby Judaea – as the true Greek ruler of Egypt.[125]

Nevertheless, for Antiochus to cede "Egypt" officially to Philip – even an "Egypt" that now meant little more than turbulent Alexandria and its environs – would have been dangerous. Philip's resources were very slender for dealing with the Egyptian situation, his strategic position even if he seized Alexandria successfully would have been perilous; but Philip saw himself as a new Alexander: Alexander's resources had been slender too – and Philip's military skill was famous. This makes it hard to believe that Antiochus would have gambled that Philip would fail, and so it is better not to assume that in Polybius' conception of the pact, Philip was officially allotted Egypt. More likely, the pact contained a (vaguely phrased) reference to the "sharing" of Egypt between the two monarchs – this appears to be the implication both of Polyb. 15.20.2

[123] See Clarysse 1978: 243–53.
[124] On the advantage Philip would have had in the negotiations with Antiochus because of the marriage-offer he already possessed from Ptolemy V, see – with due caution – Dreyer 2003: 138.
[125] On Philip's difficulties even if he successfully seized Alexandria, see de Sanctis 1923: 10–11.

and Livy 31.14.5. – but the details were never specified and would depend on the situation as it developed. If we cannot be sure between these two alternative scenarios, this only reveals how much crucial information about Mediterranean high politics in this period has been lost.

Still, the above discussion has established the following: Polybius reported that Egypt itself was a main target of Philip and Antiochus; that the aim of the Pact Between the Kings was the total destruction of the Ptolemies; and that there are no reasons *a priori* to think that this account of the treaty between Philip and Antiochus is impossible or nonsensical – or even, given the ruthless nature of Hellenistic politics, particularly improbable. After all, a coalition of kings headed by Seleucus I, Cassander, and Ptolemy I had worked to destroy utterly the large realm of Antigonus the One-Eyed and his son Demetrius the Besieger (ancestors of Philip V) in 301 BC, dividing the territory of the defeated monarchs among themselves; and when the regime of Demetrius I the Besieger in Macedon itself had later weakened in the 280s, King Lysimachus from Thrace and King Pyrrhus from Epirus had simultaneously invaded from two directions, dividing Macedon between themselves.[126] Indeed, it tells us a great deal about the anarchic and ruthless nature of the Hellenistic state-system in which Polybius lived that the historian expected his readers to believe without any difficulty his report about the alliance between Philip and Antiochus.[127]

To have established that there are no *a priori* reasons for thinking Polybius' account of the pact impossible or nonsensical does not automatically mean, however, that the story Polybius tells us is secure. Report of an important event might be plausible in itself, but still might be wrong. And scholars have produced a series of arguments to suggest that Polybius' account of the pact is not *a priori* but *de facto* wrong. It is to these arguments that we now must turn.

PHILIP'S CAMPAIGN AGAINST THE PTOLEMIES, 201–200

One crucial argument brought forward against the existence of the pact has been that from what we can tell from our evidence, Philip did not

---

[126] On the geopolitical background and the divisions of the spoils after the battle of Ipsus, see conveniently Will 1989: 57–61. On the destruction of Demetrius in 288, see conveniently Walbank, in Hammond and Walbank 1988: 227–38. There were negotiations before the double invasion of 288 was launched (Plut. *Demetr.* 44.1; *Pyrrh.* 11.1), but the agreement on the division of Macedon was always uneasy (Plut. *Pyrrh.* 12.2–3), and only lasted three years, after which Lysimachus attacked Pyrrhus' position and threw him completely out of the country.
[127] See the comments of Austin 1986: 437.

focus his aggressions in the Aegean in 202–200 on the possessions of the Ptolemies. Some scholars even suggest that Philip on purpose avoided attacking them. If so, it would be hard to accept that Philip's actions in 202–200 were founded on an anti-Ptolemaic pact with Antiochus – let alone that Philip all along was intending to attack Egypt itself. The thesis that Philip did not attack Ptolemaic possessions in the Aegean in 202–200 was first argued by Holleaux – who believed in the existence and great political importance of the pact, but who suggested that the Romans were more concerned with Antiochus' aggressions against Egypt than with any aggressions against Egypt by Philip.[128] But Holleaux's arguments have then been taken up and expanded by other scholars who greatly minimize the importance of the pact, or who deny its existence altogether.[129]

New evidence suggests, however, that such an assessment of Philip's depredations in the Aegean in 202–200 is incorrect. We know that in 200 Philip captured the economically important region of Aenus and Maroneia in Thrace from the Ptolemies (Livy 31.16.4–6).[130] The doubts have centered on Philip's campaign the previous year, in the southeast Aegean in 201. Discussion of that campaign is difficult because our evidence is fragmentary, and because the campaign ultimately failed, so that its final goals remain elusive.[131] By bringing together the current scattered studies of the situation in the Aegean ca. 201, however, we can show that, just as in 200, a whole series of important Ptolemaic holdings were indeed seized by Philip – or that he attempted to seize them. Such a conclusion greatly changes our understanding of the crucial campaign of 201, and hence of the relationship of Philip's conduct in 201 to the (alleged) anti-Ptolemaic pact with Antiochus.

It is best to proceed *seriatim* through the evidence concerning individual victims of Philip's attacks during the Aegean campaign of 201.

(1) *Samos.* This was the greatest of the prizes seized by Philip in 201. It was the main Ptolemaic naval base in the Aegean, and the fleet stationed there was large (Polyb. 5.35.11); when Philip seized Samos, he gained more Ptolemaic warships than he could find crews to man them (16.2.9). The strategic impact of Philip's action may have been very wide: it not only gravely weakened the remnants of Ptolemaic hegemony in

---

[128]   Holleaux 1935: 290 n. 1, and 117–18.

[129]   See Magie 1939: 37–40; McDonald and Walbank 1937: 185; Errington 1971: 341–2 and 348; Berthold 1976: 101 and n. 22; Rawlings 1976: 23 n. 26; Klose 1982: 66; cf. Briscoe 1973: 39 (a variation). The lack of Philip's aggressions against Ptolemaic holdings in the southern Aegean (as the situation was understood in 1964) made even Schmitt uneasy: Schmitt 1964: 258.

[130]   Economic importance of Aenus and Maronea: Rostovtzeff 1941: 111, 744, 764. Polybian derivation of the material in Livy 31.16: Briscoe 1973: 94 and 101.

[131]   Cf. the comments of Wörrle 1988: 442 n. 74.

the Aegean by cutting islands and coastal cities off from the Ptolemaic naval forces that had been the basis of that hegemony, but even as far away as Syria the notable Ptolemaic weakness at sea during Antiochus III's advance down the Levantine coast in 201 may have been caused in part by the loss of the Samian fleet to Philip.[132]

Those scholars who deny the existence or the importance of the pact argue that Samos voluntarily came over to Philip because he was a friend of Egypt, and that he soon withdrew from the island – the implication being that he was not interested in keeping this strategically valuable possession, and perhaps even freed it to go back to the Ptolemies.[133] This reconstruction cannot be accepted. Polybius' account of how Philip came into possession of Samos is lost, but the nature of the Polybian tradition is clear: Philip seized Samos by force. Thus Appian says that Philip "captured" the island (*Mac.* 4); and Livy, on the basis of Polybian material, reports the bitter complaints of the Samians against Philip's occupation, which was characterized by "foul and inhuman crimes" (31.31.4).[134]

Neither passage is strong in itself: as we have noted, App. *Mac.* 4 has confusions (it wrongly has Philip also capturing Chios), and Livy's information is from a speech by a Roman ambassador, and hence is inherently biased. But it would be unwise to dismiss this consistent tradition, and to argue instead (on no evidentiary basis) that Philip's rule on the island was a friendly one – as does Magie.[135] This is because a contemporary Samian inscription honors the physician Diodorus son of Dioscurides for his heroic role in the successful and bloody rebellion that threw out the Macedonian garrison from the island.[136] Both Walbank and Berthold argue that the rebellion the inscription describes was locally inspired, and hence has no import for Philip's relations with

---

[132]   See Holleaux 1952b: 233.
[133]   Magie 1939: 38 and 41; Berthold 1976: 101 n. 22. Magie 1939: 38, Errington 1971: 341, and now Ampela 1998: 76 n. 5 and 87 n. 56 all argue that Philip only seized Samos because of its strategic location, which split Pergamum off from Rhodes – i.e., he would have avoided attacking it otherwise. McDonald and Walbank 1937: 185 and 199, Walbank 1940: 117, Hammond, in Hammond and Walbank 1988: 414–15, and now Lampela 1998: 87 and n. 56 agree with Magie that even *after* the seizure of Samos and its fleet, Philip remained on good terms with Egypt (!).
[134]   *nefanda atque inhumana scelera.* From Polybian material: see Briscoe 1973: 1–2, and 129.
[135]   Magie 1939: 38–9 and n. 30.
[136]   Detailed discussion of the inscription, first published in 1926: Habicht 1957: 233–41. Magie 1939: 39 n. 30, tries to disconnect the events of the inscription from Philip's occupation, but has not been followed: see Austin 1981: 117–18; Shipley 1987: 192–4; Ma, Derow, and Meadows 1995: 78.

the Ptolemies or his alleged aggressive ambitions towards them.[137] But this thesis is belied by the happy proclamation on the inscription (line 27) of the return of Samos to Ptolemaic hegemony following the successful conclusion of the fighting. The Samian rebellion against Philip thus had significant international implications – and so, we may be assured, did Philip's original seizure of the island.[138]

A likely scenario for Philip's seizure of Samos is suggested by Will: in 201 Philip's fleet descended on the unsuspecting Samians and the Ptolemaic garrison and fleet, who assumed that Philip still had friendly relations with the Ptolemies, and perhaps even saw him as a protector. Philip then secured the Ptolemaic fleet and the island by a coup de main.[139] If this is what stood in the original Polybian narrative, it would of course have been another example of Philip's habitually treacherous behavior. In any case, it is quite clear that Philip's seizure of Samos was not viewed by anyone at the time as a friendly act. Only modern scholars do so.

(2) *Miletus*. This important city opened its gates to Philip in fear following his naval victory over Rhodes at Lade in 201, and voted public honors to Philip and his admiral Heracleides (Polyb. 16.15.6). But Philip treated Miletus harshly, depriving it of the territory and town of Myus north of the city and giving Myus instead to Magnesia-on-the-Meander, one of his local allies (16.24.9).[140] The Milesians bitterly resented the loss of Myus, and later fought a war with Magnesia to regain it.[141]

Philip's hostile domination of Miletus is thus not in question. What is in question is the relationship of Miletus to the Ptolemies. The city came under Ptolemaic influence after the mid-third century – no doubt because of the powerful Ptolemaic naval presence on nearby Samos – and became a formal ally of Alexandria.[142] But Magie asserts that by 201 Miletus was an independent state, so that Philip's seizure of the city, and his harsh treatment of it, tells us nothing about his conduct

---

[137]   Walbank 1940: 117–18; Berthold 1976: 101 n. 22.
[138]   See, rightly, Schmitt 1964: 257–8; Briscoe 1973: 37 n. 5; Wörrle 1988: 442.
[139]   Will 1982: 127. Earlier: Walbank 1940: 117, who nevertheless holds that this did not disrupt Philip's friendly relations with Alexandria (!). Cf. also Hammond, in Hammond and Walbank 1988: 414–15. Variations: McDonald and Walbank 1937: 185 and 199; Errington 1971: 341.
[140]   Discussion: Huss 1976: 200–1; Ma 1999/2002: 79–80. Philip's good relations with the Magnesians: Dusanic 1983: 11–48.
[141]   Mastrocinque 1979: 166, unaccountably argues that Philip's relations with Miletus were friendly. The later Milesian war with Magnesia to regain Myus: *SIG*[3] 588. Errington 1989b makes a good case for dating this war to the late 180s. If so, then Myus remained under Magnesian conrol for almost twenty years.
[142]   For discussion, see Huss 1976: 200; Sherwin-White 1978: 96 and n. 70.

or attitude towards the Ptolemies. This hypothesis has been accepted by some scholars.[143]

There is no direct evidence. But Holleaux adduced strong indirect evidence that Miletus at the end of the third century was still closely tied to the Ptolemies, based on the diplomatic status of the small town of Amyzon, inland east of Miletus. An inscription from Amyzon records the Seleucid conquest of the town in spring 203, and appears to show that the primary relationship of Amyzon before 203 had been an alliance with Ptolemaic Egypt.[144] We must say "appears to show," because although Ptolemy IV is prominently mentioned on the inscription, there is a lacuna right at the point where the nature of the relationship between Amyzon and the Ptolemies is stated. But what is clear is that Ptolemy IV is made responsible for establishing the original rights of Amyzon towards a hegemonic power – rights now confirmed and to continue under the Seleucids (lines 4–5). The most obvious reconstruction is that these rights of Amyzon, established by Ptolemy IV, had to do with Amyzon's relationship with Ptolemy himself. This in turn indicates the existence of an alliance between Amyzon and the Ptolemies before 203. But an alliance of Amyzon with the Ptolemies makes no geopolitical sense unless the maritime cities to the west of Amyzon (that is, Miletus and Heracleia-by-Latmus) were in a similar diplomatic-military relationship to Alexandria: for how else could Amyzon, otherwise cut off from the sea and thus cut off from Ptolemaic power, have hoped to benefit from a Ptolemaic alliance?[145]

Holleaux's argument has been accepted by many scholars.[146] But recently it has been challenged by Ma, Derow, and Meadows. They propose that when Zeuxis, Antiochus III's viceroy in Asia Minor, took Amyzon in 203, Seleucid rule replaced not a Ptolemaic alliance but rule by the local warlord Olympichus of Alinda (a vassal of Philip V), who had conquered Amyzon from the Ptolemies perhaps three decades previously. If this reconstruction is correct, then the inscription reveals nothing about the extent of Ptolemaic influence in Amyzon at the end of the third century, nor along the Milesian coast; instead, the inscription might suggest hostile relations between Antiochus and Philip.[147]

[143] Magie 1939: 38 n. 29; cf. Errington 1971: 31 and 348; Berthold 1976: 101 n. 22; Klose 1982: 66.
[144] Welles 1934: no. 38.
[145] Holleaux 1952b: 329 – an addendum from 1952 to a series of articles on Philip's campaign published in the 1920s. See L. Robert, in Holleaux 1952b: 211 n. 1.
[146] See Pédech 1964: 117 and n. 86; Günther 1971: 92; Huss 1976: 220–1; Walbank 1982: 231 – who now bluntly calls Miletus and Myus "Ptolemaic cities"; Errington 1990: 197.
[147] Ma, Derow, and Meadows 1995: 76–80.

Serious doubts are possible, however, about this interpretation of the inscription. There is no mention of Olympichus of Alinda anywhere on the inscription. It is especially important that there is no room for Olympichus in the crucial lines 4–5, which discuss the guaranteed maintenance by the Seleucids of the previous relations between Amyzon and the hegemonic power there, a relationship explicitly said to have been established by Ptolemy IV; that is, there is no room for a reconstruction such as: "and those things approved of by Ptolemy in his [letter?, alliance? and maintained by Olympichus . . .”]. This is far too long for the lacuna on the stone. Only Ptolemy's grant of rights to the town is mentioned, and there is room only for Ptolemy's name. This suggests *prima facie* that the Seleucid general Zeuxis seized Amyzon from the Ptolemies, not from Olympichus, and that this inscription is an agreement whereby the previous rights of the town under the Ptolemies would be maintained under the Seleucids. Such aggression by Zeuxis would conform to the pattern of Seleucid expansion in western Asia Minor at Ptolemaic expense which new inscriptions increasingly reveal at the end of the third century.[148] And while Amyzon is fairly close to Alinda, and was strategically located on the route west from Alinda towards the coast, and might thus have been a tempting target for Olympichus, he did not always get his way with his smaller neighbors, for they sometimes found powerful means of diplomatic protection.[149] All in all, there seems little reason to alter Holleaux's understanding of this inscription – or the implications Holleaux adduced from it about the persistence and extent of the Ptolemaic diplomatic system that existed westward of Amyzon along the Milesian coast in 203.

Yet acceptance of Holleaux's thesis about Amyzon affects our understanding of Philip's conduct in the southeast Aegean in 201. It means that, as most scholars now accept, Miletus probably was in some sense a Ptolemaic city in 201. It means that Philip's seizure of Ptolemaic Samos can thus no longer be viewed as an exceptional act by Philip, somehow to be explained away. This is because we now have *two* major Ptolemaic holdings conquered by Philip in the campaign of 201. Polybius recorded both cases (see 16.2.9 and 15.6); and so perhaps it becomes clearer why he believed in the anti-Ptolemaic pact.[150]

---

[148]   See the example of Bargylia, discussed below. The failure of Olympichus to appear anywhere on the inscription would be especially odd if he had been in control of Amyzon for thirty years, as implied by Ma, Derow, and Meadows 1995: 77–8.
[149]   See now Meadows 1996: esp. 257–65, for a discussion of how Olympichus' threat to the town of Iasus was thwarted ca. 215 BC.
[150]   Note also that inscriptional evidence shows that Miletus in the late third century was a friend and ally of Cos (see Sherwin-White 1978: 130 n. 254) – whose Ptolemaic alliance is discussed below.

(3) and (4) *Bargylia and Theangela*. A newly published important inscription, a Rhodian decree found at Bargylia on the Carian coast and dating from ca. 195–185 BC, has now revealed that during the campaign of 201 Philip V seized Theangela in the hinterland of Bargylia and then gave it over to the forces of Antiochus III "at the time that King Antiochus was warring against the current King Ptolemy [V], and the soldiers of King Antiochus had occupied [—]a and Thodasa" (lines 10–12). The incident here could only have happened in late 201, when Philip's army, having raided Pergamum, moved south into Caria. The implication of the Bargylia inscription is that just as Thodasa and the other (unnamed) town in the Bargylian hinterland were part of the Ptolemaic hegemonic system along the Carian coast in 201, and hence fell to Seleucid forces, so too Theangela was Ptolemaic, and fell to Philip. Furthermore: if all these places in the hinterland of Bargylia were Ptolemaic in 201, then it stands to reason that their metropole Bargylia must have been Ptolemaic as well. And we know that Philip seized Bargylia itself in autumn 201 (Polyb. 16.24.1).[151]

We have now established that there were at least four Ptolemaic victims of Philip V's campaign in the southeast Aegean in 201. Three of them (Samos, Miletus, and Bargylia) were important places. The idea that Philip was not attacking Ptolemaic holdings in the southeast Aegean in 201 can thus be put to rest. The evidence is clear that he was. And where there are four Ptolemaic victims of Philip, perhaps there are more.

(5) and (6) *Cos and Calymnus*. Cos was the birthplace of Ptolemy II, was eulogized by famous court poets at Alexandria because of this, and had strong sentimental ties with the Ptolemaic dynasty.[152] Inscriptions indicate that Cos was clearly part of the Ptolemaic sphere of influence in the southeast Aegean into the late third century, and followed Ptolemaic policy especially when Egyptian interests were involved; it was likely a legally autonomous ally of Alexandria, but not a dependency.[153] Ptolemaic rulers expended much wealth in beautifying its capital city; relations with Alexandria were always excellent; even well after our period, we find an official inscription celebrating a Coan pageant in honor of

---

[151] Initial publication of the inscription: Blümel 2000: 94–6. On the political implications of the inscription: see the important study by Dreyer 2003. Cf. also Wiemer 2001a: 12–13, and below. Writing before the publication of the new inscription, Ma 1999/2002: 77, hypothesized that Philip might have conquered Theangela but given it to Ptolemaic Halicarnassus; we now know that he gave the town to Antiochus III instead.

[152] On the poetry of Callimachus and Theocritus in praise of Cos, see Sherwin-White 1978: 97–8.

[153] The situation of Cos within the Ptolemaic sphere of influence: Welles 1934: 129–30 (an independent ally); Huss 1976: 228; Sherwin-White 1978: 90, 93–7, and 118–19 (extended discussion of the evidence, in agreement with Welles).

(apparently) Ptolemy VI. Throughout the third century the presence of the great Ptolemaic naval base at Samos may have facilitated the friendly relationship, but even with the decline in importance of Ptolemaic naval power in the southeast Aegean from the mid-190s, relations between the governments of Cos and Alexandria remained warm.[154]

Cos certainly also had good relations with other states besides the Ptolemies in this period, and especially with Rhodes. Hence the Coans shortly after 220 facilitated an arrangement by which Rhodes provided large-scale financial help (technically a loan) to the city of Sinope on the coast of the Black Sea.[155] More significant is that Cos evidently participated with Rhodes in the First Cretan War, a war against Cretan pirates, ca. 205–204; a Coan naval squadron fought a successful battle with the pirates.[156] We can therefore perceive that as Rhodian power grew after ca. 220, Rhodes became a new and important factor in the foreign relations of the Coan government. Scholars have stressed that since Rhodes itself had excellent relations with Alexandria, the friendship of Cos with the Ptolemies did not fundamentally alter with the rise of Rhodian naval power.[157] Nevertheless, the question is whether Rhodes had now replaced Alexandria as the primary focus of Coan allegiance. This is especially the case because Cos also sided with Rhodes against Philip V in 201: a Coan inscription appears to refer to this anti-Macedonian alliance, and we know from Polybius that following Philip's victory over the Rhodians at Lade, the Rhodian fleet briefly employed the harbor at Cos.[158]

But the diplomatic situation as it actually existed ca. 201 is completely cleared up by an inscription involving the Coan relationship with nearby Calymnus. Calymnus was a close associate of Cos, and had joined in *homopoliteia* (i.e., absorption) with Cos sometime around 205, in which

---

[154] Close relations between Cos and the Ptolemies into the second century: Huss 1976: 228; cf. Sherwin-White 1978: 118–19. The Coan pageant in honor (it seems) of Ptolemy VI: *SIG*³ 1028, with Huss 1976: 228.

[155] Inscriptional evidence for Coan help with the Rhodian loan: see Sherwin-White 1978: 118; Berthold 1984: 93–4 and n. 38. Sinope was threatened by Mithridates II of Pontus: Polyb. 4.56.1–57.1.

[156] Inscriptional evidence and discussion in Sherwin-White 1978: 119–20; Baker 1991: 13.

[157] Sherwin-White 1978: 118–19; Baker 1991: 13.

[158] See Polyb. 16.15.4, with Walbank 1967: 519. The "allies" (σύμμαχοι) of Cos in the crisis of 201 are referred to in an inscription concerning a special monetary subscription from Coan citizens to support defense expenditures, and although no specific allied state is named in the inscription, it is plausible (esp. in view of Polyb. 16.15.4) that the leading ally was Rhodes: discussion in Sherwin-White 1978: 120–1. Rhodes, not the Ptolemies, as the primary leader of Coan foreign relations after ca. 220: so Baker 1991: esp. 12–17.

Calymnus became part of the Coan state as a deme of Cos.[159] The inscription under review celebrates the reinstitution of this *homopoliteia* ca. 200 BC, after a break in it, and Sherwin-White plausibly suggests that the break was caused by the occupation of Calymnus by Macedonian forces after Philip's victory at Lade.[160] The inscription gives the oath of Coan citizenship which, upon reinstitution of the *homopoliteia*, the Calymnians were to swear: they were to uphold the Coan democracy, oppose any attempts to set up an oligarchy or a tyranny, be just judges and impartial citizens, not allow any diminution of Coan territory but on the contrary strive as far as possible to leave the territory of Cos larger than before, and (lines 18–19): "I will abide by the friendship and alliance with King Ptolemy and the agreements that have been ratified by the *damos* and the other allies." In other words, one of the conditions of the Calymnian *homopoliteia* with Cos was that the Calymnians would preserve the Coans' formal alliance with Alexandria.[161]

To be sure, other allies of Cos are mentioned briefly in the citizenship oath – but they are not even named; not even Rhodes is named, so that we do not even know if Rhodes is being numbered among these allies. The centerpiece of the foreign relations part of the oath, placed first and foremost, is the friendship and formal alliance with the Ptolemies. It is this relationship above all that the Calymnians, as Coans, swear to preserve; in 200 BC it is still this alliance which is the lodestar of Coan foreign relations. Indeed, the celebratory tone of this inscription, and its emphasis on restoration (*apokatastasis*) to a previously satisfactory status quo after disruption, recalls the restoration of the Ptolemaic alliance (again the term is *apokatastasis*) celebrated on the inscription from Samos after the overthrow of Macedonian occupation (discussed above).[162]

Several inscriptions indicate severe attacks upon Cos and Calymnus at the end of the third century: their countrysides were ravaged, Calymnus evidently lost completely from Coan control, and an attempt made to establish a permanent hostile fortress on the southern coast of Cos itself.

---

[159]   See Holleaux 1952b: 276 and n. 5, and Sherwin-White 1978: 125 and n. 231 (with evidence). The term *homopoliteia* means more than "mutual citizenship": Sherwin-White 1978: 125 n. 233. Indeed, the commander of a Coan squadron that fought against Cretan pirates in 205–204 was a Calymnian: ibid.: 125 and n. 230.
[160]   Ibid.: 126–8.
[161]   Text of the *homopoliteia* of Cos and Calymnus: Schmitt 1969: 285–7. Lines 18–19: ἐμμενῶ δὲ καὶ τᾶι ποτὶ Βασιλῆ Πτολεμαῖον φιλίαι καὶ συμμαχίαι. Commentary: Herrmann 1965: 36–7; Sherwin-White 1978: 126–30. Note the oath to increase the power of Cos as much as possible and not let it diminish – a typical product of the harsh pressures of the anarchic Hellenistic environment; see Eckstein 2006: 192.
[162]   The parallel is noted by Sherwin-White 1978: 127–8. Ptolemaic Egypt still the primary Coan external relationship in this period, with the transition to Rhodian leadership occurring only in the 190s: ibid.: 130.

These inscriptions are fragmentary and unfortunately do not reveal who the enemy was. But the scale of the threat is so large, and the danger so great, that scholars are unanimous in accepting that the culprit was Philip V, and that these attacks occurred during his summer campaign in the Aegean in 201.[163]

Thus if we unite all the evidence, it indicates that we now have not four Ptolemaic victims of Philip in 201, but six (i.e., Cos and Calymnus). Four of those six, including Cos, are significant places. In terms of the historicity of the alleged pact between Philip and Antiochus and its focus against the Ptolemies, this is important information to possess.

(7) *Heracleia-by-Latmus.* This important city had a long history of friendship with the Ptolemies, and by the same reasoning as that concerning Miletus (namely, the Ptolemaic hegemony down to ca. 203 over Amyzon, inland east of both Heracleia and Miletus: see above), Holleaux concluded that Heracleia was still within the Ptolemaic sphere of influence in 203, and perhaps a formal ally of Alexandria. This hypothesis has been widely accepted.[164] And in 1988 Wörrle brought forth good arguments that Heracleia-by-Latmus – like Miletus – fell into the control of Philip V at the end of the third century.[165]

The clue is a slim one – so often the case, given the loss of so much of our information about the period. A fragmentary inscription from Heracleia, the letter-forms of which are late third or early second century, published by Segre in 1952, honors two brothers for showing good will towards the Heracleiotes after their appointment as political overseers (ἐπιστάται) of Heracleia by an unknown king.[166] The king is not likely to have been a Ptolemy, for the Ptolemaic regime did not employ the title ἐπιστάται for its local governors overseas.[167] And the two men are not likely to have been agents of the king of Pergamum, since in

---

[163]   The attacks on Cos and Calymnus: *SIG*³ 568 and 569, and cf. Schmitt 1969: no. 545, with Sherwin-White 1978: 126–30. Philip the culprit: so Holleaux 1952b: 276; in agreement: Walbank 1940: 118 and n. 6, and 120 and n. 3; Briscoe 1973: 37 and n. 8; Sherwin-White 1978: 126–30; Baker 1991: 25; Ma 1999/2002: 79. We do not know the relative chronology of events between Philip's attacks on Cos and Calymnus and Philip's naval victory over Rhodes at the battle of Lade – i.e., which preceded the other.

[164]   Holleaux 1952b: 329; Huss 1976: 201; Wörrle 1988: 433–6. On Amyzon, see above.

[165]   Wörrle 1988: 433–6.

[166]   Segre 1944/1945 (1952): 25–6 (no. 23).

[167]   There are only two cases where the term ἐπιστάτης is used of a Ptolemaic official overseas; both are special commands in the 260s connected with naval operations during the Chromonidean War (*OGIS* 44: Thera; *IG* XII: 5, 161: Keos). Hence the regular title of the Ptolemaic commander on Thera was τεταγμένος ἐπὶ Θέρας (*OGIS* 102, 110, 735). Discussion: Wörrle 1988: 436 and nn. 2–43, cf. Bagnall 1976: 124–7.

this period Attalid power did not extend anywhere near this far south.[168] By contrast, the regime of Philip V regularly used the term ἐπιστάται for local governors, and in fact Philip was using this term for his local governors precisely in the newly conquered parts of nearby Caria in the period beginning in 201.[169]

The only alternative to Philip in control at Heracleia is Antiochus III, after he came to dominate this part of western Asia Minor in 197/196; like Philip, the Seleucids regularly employed the title *epistates* for a local governor. This is the solution favored both by Segre and by J. and L. Robert; Segre wishes to date the inscription to ca. 191.[170] But Wörrle points out that a difficulty has emerged for this thesis: an inscription from Heracleia (first published in 1988) deals with the creation of friendly relations between Heracleia and Antiochus III in the mid-190s BC, and shows that in the mid-190s the official dating by *stephanophoroi* at Heracleia was different from the official dating by *stephanophoroi* employed on the inscription honoring the two brothers. This means that the inscription honoring the two brothers cannot date from the mid-190s or later; rather, it must be earlier.[171] Since the letter-forms are late third or early second century, the inscription thus must date from just *before* the mid-190s. Hence the king for whom the brothers ruled cannot be Antiochus, since Antiochus did not become dominant at Heracleia until the mid-190s, as the second inscription shows. So the king for whom the brothers ruled cannot be Ptolemy, Attalus I, *or* Antiochus. That leaves only Philip. The implication is that since Heracleia was probably still Ptolemaic ca. 203 (see above), the new regime of Antigonid ἐπιστάται must derive directly from Philip's campaign of 201. That is: another result of the campaign of 201 was that Heracleia-by-Latmus, like its

---

[168] The unlikelihood that the two overseers of Heracleia are Attalid: see Segre 1944/1945 (1952): 25–6 – reinforced now by an inscription showing Antiochus III in 204/203 successfully engaged in anti-Attalid operations at Teos, far to the north of Heracleia. Thus Attalid power was even more geographically restricted towards the south in this period than previously thought: see Herrmann 1965: 29–159.

[169] Philip's regular use of the title ἐπιστάται to denote local governors: see Bengtson 1944: 324–67. Philip's use of this title for his administrators on the Carian coast: *Inscr. Stratonikeia* I: 4 (spring 198 BC), with the comments of Wörrle 1988: 436 n. 44.

[170] Segre 1944/1945 (1952): 25–6; J. and L. Robert 1983: 187–8. Seleucid use of the title ἐπιστάτης to denote a local governor: see now Sherwin-White and Kuhrt 1993: 165 (numerous examples).

[171] Both official chronologies are dated from the stephanophorate of a Demetrius; but in the inscription honoring the two brothers this is Demetrius son of Apollonius, whereas the new inscription shows that official chronology by the mid-190s was dated from the stephanophorate of Demetrius son of Demetrius. See Wörrle 1988: 434 and n. 33.

neighbor Miletus, fell from Ptolemaic hegemony into the power of Philip. This is Wörrle's conclusion.[172]

Perhaps Heracleia-by-Latmus, like Miletus, made a quick and peaceful submission to Philip following his naval victory over Rhodes at Lade (cf. Polyb. 16.15.6). But on the inscription published in 1988, the Heracleiotes in their talks with the envoy of Antiochus to establish friendly relations with the Seleucids refer to the calamitous condition of their countryside caused by recent war (Inscr. No. 2, lines 12–14). Which war is unclear, but the only known fighting in the region right before the mid-190s was Philip's large-scale campaign of 201. This makes it likely that it was an invasion of Heracleiote territory by Philip after Lade, with resulting ravaging of the countryside, that eventually forced the surrender of Heracleia to him – as Wörrle and now Ma indeed conclude.[173] In addition, the presence of the two Antigonid *epistatai* in command of the city is an indication in itself that (as at Samos) a garrison was imposed on Heracleia – with all the tensions that would involve with the indigenous population.[174] It may also be that, as with Miletus, Philip punished Heracleia by awarding some of her territory to his ally Magnesia-on-the-Meander. This would explain the reference on the new inscription to land problems (No. 2, lines 12–14), explain as well the presence of Heracleia as an ally of Miletus in her later war against Magnesia (*SIG*[3] 588, line 59ff.) – and explain, too, why the Heracleiotes in the mid-190s were pleading for help from the representative of Antiochus III in order to regain lost Heracleiote territory (Inscr. No. 3, lines 9–10).[175]

We now have a list of seven polities that were certainly or probably under some sort of Ptolemaic hegemony in 201 – Samos, Miletus, Theangela, Bargylia, Cos, Calymnus, and Heracleia-by-Latmus – and which were certainly or probably attacked and/or occupied by Philip during his campaign in the southern Aegean in 201. In a word, the argument against the historicity of the anti-Ptolemaic Pact Between the Kings on grounds that Philip in his campaign in the southeast Aegean in 201 did not attack Ptolemaic holdings – and even consciously avoided them – has collapsed.[176]

To this list one might consider adding three other possible cases, though they are more speculative. We know that Philip attacked both Cnidus and Chios unsuccessfully in 201, but did conquer the smaller island-state

---

[172] Wörrle 1988: 436; in agreement: Ma 1999/2002: 77 and n. 93.
[173] Ibid.: 443; Ma 1999/2002: 80. The text of the inscription: ibid.: 423.
[174] Wörrle 1988: 442; cf. Ma 1999/2002: 80.
[175] Wörrle 1988: 442 and 444 (cf. 446 and n. 100).
[176] Oddly, Wörrle asserts that the new inscriptions from Heracleia have no bearing on this question. (ibid.: 441 n. 71). I hope to have shown this is not the case.

of Paros, devastating it.[177] It is often assumed that these were all independent and neutral polities in 201, so Philip's attacks on them tell us nothing about his intentions towards the Ptolemies.[178] That may be the case, but direct evidence is once again lacking; and there is indirect evidence to suggest we should be a bit careful about our assumptions.

Thus Cnidus, attacked by Philip, had a history of friendly relations with the Ptolemies, including in the late third century. The Cnideans had been on good terms with Ptolemy IV, as is shown by the statue honoring Sosibius, Ptolemy IV's prime minister, that they erected in their city (*OGIS* 79). Cnidus also had friendly relations with Ptolemaic Bargylia (*Inscr. Iasos* 606), and it is attested at the end of the third century as a friend and ally (φίλος καὶ σύμμαχος) of Ptolemaic Cos.[179] Huss therefore has significant support in his suggestion that Cnidus at the end of the third century was (somehow) within the Ptolemaic sphere of influence, and Sherwin-White posits that the close association between Cnidus and Cos reflects a strong Ptolemaic affiliation.[180]

Chios and Paros are more speculative, but intriguing. Chios was attacked unsuccessfully by Philip in 201. Inscriptions honoring the Ptolemies appear regularly at Chios throughout the third century; the Chians were consistent allies of the Ptolemies in their efforts to end wars between the Aetolians and King Philip both in 217 BC (the Social War) and again in 209 and 207 (the First Macedonian War); moreover, inscriptional evidence suggests that this diplomatic cooperation was coordinated by the court at Alexandria. Chios, then, had a close friendship with the Ptolemies, which is attested as being in strong working order in the last decade of the third century.[181] Paros, conquered by Philip in 201 and embittered against him, also had a long history of good relations with the Ptolemies, perhaps because it was not far from the major Ptolemaic base at Samos. Paros was unusual in having a cult to Arsinoe, the sister and queen of Ptolemy II, for only in polities where Ptolemaic influence was especially strong does this cult appear; and an honorific inscription

---

[177]   Philip's unsuccessful attack on Cnidus is recorded in a marginal note in one of the mss. of Polyb. Book 16: *Urbinas gr.* 102 ("F"), at 16.11.1. Philip's attack on Chios: App. *Mac.* 4.1 (inaccurate); Plut. *Mor.* 245C; cf. Polyb. 16.2.1–3 (name of city not mentioned but see Ma 1999/2002: 76). Philip's conquest of Paros: Livy 31.15.8 and 31.31.4 (based on Polybian material: Briscoe 1973: 94 and 97, and 129).

[178]   See Holleaux 1921: 91 and 317–18 with n. 2; Magie 1939: 40–1 with n. 36; cf. Errington 1971: 341 and 348.

[179]   Sherwin-White 1978: 130 n. 254 for the unpublished inscriptional evidence.

[180]   See Huss 1976: 195; Sherwin-White 1978: 130. By contrast, Ma 1999/2002: 77, declares with no discussion that Cnidus was an independent neutral.

[181]   Chios and the Ptolemies: Huss 1976: 222 and n. 325. On their diplomatic coordination with the Ptolemies, see above, Chapter 3, pp. 94–5.

published in 1965 suggests that relations between the Parians and Ptolemy IV were much closer than Magie, for one, had originally thought.[182]

Except in the case of Cos and Calymnus, which we know were official allies of the Ptolemies, the fragmentary condition of our literary and epigraphical evidence prevents us from saying with security whether any of the above states was an independent friend of the Ptolemies, a legal ally of the Ptolemies, or some sort of dependency of the Ptolemies. Nor can we always be certain of the nature and extent of Philip's aggressions against every one of these polities. Nevertheless, a definite pattern in Philip's campaign in Caria and the southern Aegean in 201 has emerged from the above discussion. We can now say that a successful attack by Philip on Cos and Calymnus, or on Cnidus or even Chios, would have been major blows against the Ptolemaic diplomatic system that existed in the southern Aegean region in 201, that Philip probably tried it, that Philip's brutal conquest of Paros may have been another such blow (though this is speculative), and that if – as seems likely now – Heracleia-by-Latmus submitted to him in 201, that was yet another major blow. The linchpin of the system had been the Ptolemaic naval base at Samos, with its powerful fleet, which Philip had seized; the fall of the large Ptolemaic city of Miletus to him had surely been important too; and the Ptolemaic city of Bargylia and the Ptolemaic towns in the hinterland of Bargylia had fallen to him soon thereafter.

To be sure, Philip in the southeast Aegean in 201 did not limit his attacks solely to dependencies of the Ptolemies. For instance, inscriptional evidence indicates he devastated and occupied the island of Nisyros, southeast of Cos, which was in this period either a neutral state or under Rhodian hegemony, and Philip's fleet probably conducted similar raids against Rhodian dependencies in the nearby islands.[183] Nor did Philip attack *every* Ptolemaic holding in the southern Aegean or on the Asia Minor coast. Important Ptolemaic cities such as Halicarnassus and Caunus were passed by – a fact stressed by Magie to suggest that Philip's relations with the Ptolemies during 201 were not (despite Polybius) openly hostile.[184] But Philip's forces had failed in assaults on Cos, Cnidus, and Chios (see above); and the king did not attempt a direct assault on the city of Pergamum when his forces devastated the surrounding countryside, but no scholar doubts that Philip was at war in summer 201 with the

---

[182]   Paros and the Ptolemies: Huss 1976: 251 and n. 391; cf. Sherwin-White 1978: 100 (who emphasizes the implications of the Arsinoe cult).
[183]   Philip's attack on Nisyros and the probable status of the island: see Sherwin-White 1978: 124 and 127; Baker 1991: 25–6. Probable attacks on other Rhodian dependencies: see Holleaux 1952b: 278.
[184]   See Magie 1939: 38.

Attalids (Polyb. 16.1.1–6). Moreover, by the time Philip's army reached Caria overland after the raid on Pergamum, it was in poor condition (Polyb. 16.24.4–9), and thus hardly in a state to conduct a serious siege. Hence there is no justification for the idea that Philip's decision not to attack Halicarnassus or Caunus indicates a pacific policy towards the Ptolemies. He did not attack these places because he could not attack them.

After a strikingly successful beginning in summer 201, Philip's campaign in the southeastern Aegean and Caria in fact ended up as a stalemate. He had won a naval victory over the Rhodians at Lade – the victory after which, Polybius believes, he should have sailed for Alexandria (16.10) – but soon afterwards Attalus I of Pergamum joined the war against him. Since Pergamum and Rhodes were bitter rivals, Philip cannot have expected this.[185] A second naval battle, off Chios and against the combined Rhodian and Pergamene fleets, ended in a draw. Philip then landed his army and marched on Pergamum itself, whose suburbs he devastated. Attalus did not dare come out from his fortifications to meet Philip in battle, but rather than attempt a siege of Pergamum itself on top of its formidable mountain, Philip turned south overland into Lydia and Caria. Though his conquests continued (as we see in the new Bargylia inscription), his army ran into severe logistical problems, and almost starved. The king was eventually blockaded in Bargylia by the combined Rhodian and Pergamene fleets (autumn). But he escaped in spring 200, and took his forces back from the southeast Aegean to European Greece. Nevertheless, though his southern adventure was (for the moment) at an end, Philip in spring and summer 200 pursued a successful campaign of conquest in the northern Aegean – Polybius praises his energy (Polyb. 16.28.3–9) – and his main targets, though not his only ones, were once again Ptolemaic.[186]

Philip's successful attacks on the economically important Ptolemaic cities of Aenus and Maroneia in Thrace in 200 have already been noted. But these cities were not alone. We must add a whole list of other Ptolemaic polities he now seized: Cypsela, Doriscon, and Serrheum in Thrace; Elaeus, Alopeconnessus, Callipolis, Madytus, and Sestus in the Hellespont.[187] Most of these places were not important; one (Sestus) was quite important. It has sometimes been doubted whether Sestus was actually a Ptolemaic possession in 200, but Polybius stresses that the Ptolemies controlled the important cities of the Hellespont coast

---

[185]   For the bitterness of the rivalry, see below, Chapter 5.
[186]   For the course of the fighting see conveniently Walbank 1940: 121–37.
[187]   Philip's conquests: see Livy 31.36.3–6a (Polybian derivation: Briscoe 1973: 94 and 101). That all or most of these towns were Ptolemaic holdings is shown by Polyb. 5.34.8; for discussion, see Huss 1976: 211–13.

(5.34.8), and we have a contemporary Sestian inscription honoring Ptolemy IV, his queen, and his son (*OGIS* 88) – the political implication is obvious.[188] In explaining Philip's attacks, the argument is sometimes made that there was no reason anymore for Philip in 200 to try to keep the friendship of Alexandria; this, allegedly, accounts for Philip's "change" to making overt attacks on a whole series of Ptolemaic possessions. Thus, according to Briscoe, "Philip's attack on the Thracian towns is his first full-scale assault on Ptolemaic possessions."[189] As if maintaining the friendship of Alexandria was possible after the seizure of the main Ptolemaic naval base in the Aegean and a good part of the Ptolemaic fleet! On the contrary: what we see in 200 is merely the same pattern and policy we saw in 201. The king took from the weakened Ptolemies whatever he could.

The conclusion from the above discussion is that Polybius' assertion concerning an anti-Ptolemaic treaty of alliance between Philip and Antiochus cannot be disproved by appeal to Philip's actions in the Aegean in 201–200 any more than the pact can be disproved on *a priori* grounds. Our information, though scanty, is consistent with the idea that starting in spring 201 Philip launched a powerful attack on the Ptolemaic military-diplomatic system in the southern Aegean (which he in turn apparently saw as the gateway to Alexandria itself: cf. Polyb. 16.10), followed by attacks in 200 on many Ptolemaic targets in the northern Aegean and the Hellespont. And it is striking that the more information we come to possess through the discovery of new inscriptions, the more Polybius' depiction of the events of this period is confirmed.

But scholars have not only sought to undermine Polybius' account of the anti-Ptolemaic pact by arguing – incorrectly – that Philip V never attacked Ptolemaic holdings in the southeast Aegean in 201; they have also proposed that Philip's campaign in Caria in autumn 201 was actually aimed at securing the region against Antiochus III himself, and that in this campaign Philip attacked cities belonging to the Seleucid monarch. The cities are Stratoniceia, Alabanda, and possibly Mylasa, all in inland Caria.[190]

That Stratoniceia came into Philip's control at this time is shown by contemporary inscriptions, and is referred to in Livy (based on Polybian

[188] See Huss 1976: 210–11, against Holleaux 1952b: 317 n. 3.
[189] Briscoe 1973: 100; variations: Magie 1939: 37; Walbank 1940: 133; Errington 1971: 351; Klose 1982: 66 n. 174.
[190] Philip's Carian campaign of autumn 201 aimed primarily against Antiochus: see Ma, Derow, and Meadows 1995: 71ff.; Buraselis 1996: 154 n. 19; cf. Ma 1999/2002: 78–9. Philip's alleged attacks on Seleucid holdings: Magie 1939: 41; Errington 1971: 342 n. 16 and 349.

material).[191] We do not know how Stratoniceia fell to Philip; it could have been through negotiated surrender, but violence is certainly possible.[192] The argument of some scholars is that Stratoniceia was a Seleucid foundation (cf. Strabo 14.1.25) – and thus close to Antiochus III's heart. Similarly, we know that Philip's forces, desperate for food in autumn 201, ravaged the lands of Alabanda (Polyb. 16.24.6), and an inscription shows that Antiochus from ca. 204 had friendly ties with Alabanda (*OGIS* 234). And Mylasa, which Philip unsuccessfully attacked in autumn 201 (Polyb. 16.24.7), may also have been a Seleucid holding. The argument is that if these places with their close connections to Antiochus III were attacked by Philip in autumn 201, then Philip could not simultaneously have been a partner in a pact of strategic cooperation with Antiochus.[193]

None of these cases, however, turns out to be strong evidence against the existence of the pact. Antiochus III's propaganda in the latter part of his reign certainly stresses his desire to regain the patrimony of the Seleucids in western Asia Minor (as well as Europe) – and Stratoniceia might seem a prime candidate. But when Philip attacked it in 201, the city was controlled by the Rhodians, not the Seleucids (cf. Livy 33.18.20 and 22, based on Polybian material), and this had been the case for more than forty years. It was from Rhodes – with whom he was at war – that Philip took Stratoniceia in 201; and so in 197 the Rhodians tried to recapture it (Livy 33.18.20–2: they failed).[194] Moreover, we know from events subsequent to the Rhodian failure at Stratoniceia in 197 exactly what Antiochus' attitude was towards the city: the king himself soon helped the Rhodians to regain it, as a gesture of goodwill (Polyb. 30.31.6, cf. Livy 33.18.22, from Polybian material).[195] Thus whatever ancestral ties existed, Antiochus' interest in Stratoniceia in this period was minimal; its capture by Philip in autumn 201 was of immediate concern only to the Rhodians – who had long controlled it.

In contrast to Stratoniceia, the ties of Alabanda to Antiochus are clear, but here the situation is complicated in a different way – for Philip's

---

[191]   Thus Philip V and his local commander are being honored at Stratoniceia in spring 198 BC: *Inscr. Strat.* I: 3 and 4; cf. Magie 1939: 41 n. 41. Stratoniceia was still in Philip's hands a year later: Livy 33.18.19ff.; Polybian origin of the Livy passage: cf. Briscoe 1973: 2 and 280.

[192]   Magie 1939: 41 (opting for the latter; there is no evidence).

[193]   On Stratoniceia and Alabanda, see Magie 1939: 40–1; cf. Errington 1971: 342 n. 16, and 349; Briscoe 1973: 38 and n. 5. On Mylasa, see Holleaux 1952b: 262; cf. Briscoe 1973: 38 n. 5.

[194]   Polybian derivation of Livy 33.18: Briscoe 1973: 280; Rawlings 1976: 10–11. On Rhodian control of Stratoniceia (dating from the 240s), see McShane 1964: 97 and n. 14.

[195]   Discussion: Rawlings 1976: 10–11.

official relations with the city were friendly (cf. Polyb. 16.24.6). To be sure, with his army starving during the autumn of 201, Philip took what he had to from the Alabanda hinterland (16.24.4 and 8); but he acted similarly towards Magnesia-on-the-Meander, a city with whom he had excellent ties (cf. 16.24.8–9) – and later, he sought to repay the damages (24.9). The pillaging of the Alabandan countryside by Philip's desperate soldiers should therefore not be viewed as a blow intentionally aimed at the interests of Antiochus.

Mylasa, unsuccessfully attacked by Philip in autumn 201, is the weakest case here. Olympichus of Alinda, who controlled Mylasa for an unknown length of time in the late third century, had once served as a mercenary commander for King Seleucus II, and that is the only link between Mylasa and the Seleucids – a tenuous link indeed. Inscriptions show that Olympichus from ca. 227 BC was close to Macedon and the Antigonids, and from 221 close to Philip, far closer than he was to the Seleucids.[196] Yet we also know that from 209/208 Mylasa had mutual citizenship (*isopoliteia*) with Ptolemaic Miletus (*Inscr. Milet.* I: 146). Perhaps the town was in fact independent.[197] The *isopoliteia* between Mylasa and Ptolemaic Miletus might even lead one to speculate that Mylasa was somehow within the Ptolemaic sphere of influence, and thus list Mylasa as another one of Philip's Ptolemaic victims.

And our newest epigraphical information in fact destroys the thesis that Philip's warfare in Caria in late 201 was aimed not so much at the Ptolemies as at securing a Macedonian domain there against the ambitions of Antiochus. The newly discovered inscription from Bargylia, to which we have already referred, reveals an action of Philip that points in exactly the opposite direction. The Bargylia inscription shows that in 201 Philip, having conquered Ptolemaic Theangela in Caria, actually handed over the town to the forces of Antiochus that were conducting their own offensive against Ptolemaic holdings in the region (lines 10–13). That is: with the discovery of the Bargylia inscription, we now have direct evidence that Philip in autumn 201 was engaged in overt military cooperation with the Seleucids, even to the point of turning over cities to them.[198]

In sum, the evidence does not support the hypothesis that any of the three alleged "Seleucid" victims of Philip in Caria in late 201 were in the Seleucid sphere of influence – let alone under direct Seleucid control – when Philip attacked them. Philip's attacks on these places thus

---

[196] See Holleaux 1952a: 156–62; Berthold 1984: 111 and n. 24; Meadows 1996: 257–65.
[197] So Walbank 1967: 531.
[198] See above, p. 156, with Wiemer 2001a: 12–13 and Dreyer 2003.

cannot be employed to challenge the historicity of the pact with Antiochus. And meanwhile the new Bargylia inscription shows that Philip in Caria in 201, far from being concerned to create an Antigonid domain in opposition to the forces of Antiochus III that were advancing through the region, was cooperating militarily with those Seleucid forces and even turning over captured towns to them. So this argument, too, against the existence of the Pact Between the Kings has now collapsed.

PHILIP V, ANTIOCHUS III, AND ZEUXIS

One final piece of evidence in the controversy over the pact needs discussion. Polybius says that when Philip's army suffered from want of supplies as he marched south into Lydia in late summer 201 following his raid on Pergamum, Philip called upon Zeuxis to supply his forces with grain, as well as to cooperate with him in the other ways "as stipulated in the treaty" (16.1.8).[199] Zeuxis in this passage is referred to without explanation to the audience, so Polybius must have introduced him earlier. He is a man well known to us now from recently discovered inscriptions – in fact the most important Seleucid commander in Asia Minor.[200] The obvious conclusion is that "the treaty" of Polyb. 16.1.8 (τὰς συνθήκας . . .) – a formal treaty, previously discussed (otherwise it would be introduced to the audience here), according to which Antiochus' commander Zeuxis was required to provide Philip and his army with substantial if indirect military support if called upon – is in fact the Pact Between the Kings. And when Polybius reports that although Zeuxis promised to give Philip the help the treaty stipulated (κατὰ τὰς συνθήκας: 16.1.9), he did not intend to keep his word (ibid.), this sounds much like Polybius' remark in 15.20.6 that Philip and Antiochus, after agreeing to the treaty, and while they were tearing apart the child's kingdom, immediately began to betray each other as well.[201] Later, when Philip's army was on the verge of starvation in Caria, Polybius says that Zeuxis did provide Philip with supplies (16.24.6). Indeed, Polybius indicates that Zeuxis' help in Caria was an important factor – though not the only one – in allowing Philip's army to survive (ibid.).[202]

---

[199] διεπέμπετο [sc. Φίλιππος] πρὸς Ζεῦξιν, παρακαλῶν αὐτὸν σῖτον χορηγῆσαι καὶ τὰ λοιπὰ συμπράττειν κατὰ τὰς συνθήκας.

[200] On the precise political status and power of Zeuxis, see below.

[201] The connection is briefly noted by Briscoe 1973: 38 and n. 4.

[202] See Hammond, in Hammond and Walbank 1988: 416. Because of the large gaps in Polyb. 16, we cannot know how Polybius explained Zeuxis' decision finally to fulfill his promises to Philip.

The implication of Polyb. 16.1.8–9 and 24.6 is that Polybius not only commented on the Pact Between the Kings in analyses separate from his on-going narrative, but that he actually integrated the *working* of the treaty into the on-going narrative itself – reporting its impact on the local level.

The evidence of Polyb. 16.1 and 16.24 is thus disturbing for scholars who deny the existence of the pact. And it should be disturbing also for those who propose that although the treaty did exist, it was merely an agreement of non-interference in each other's aggressions[203] – for Polyb. 16.1 shows that significant military cooperation, outright *support* for each other's aggressive projects, is directly mandated in the treaty.[204] Indeed, the only way to escape the implications of Polyb. 16.1 and 16.24 has been to extend the accusation of Polybius' incompetence as a historian from his general analytical comments on one of the most important periods in his *Histories* to include now his actual historical narrative.

Magie led the way here. Since he believed that the treaty between Philip and Antiochus was the product of Polybius' imagination or that of his sources, Magie suspected the historical correctness of Philip's request to Zeuxis for help "according to the treaty." In other words, the incident in Polyb. 16.1 never happened.[205] Magie's thesis required him also to doubt the historical correctness of Polyb. 16.24, where Zeuxis does provide some supplies to Philip: this incident also never happened.[206] This is certainly one way to deal with inconvenient evidence; but – not surprisingly – no one has been willing to follow Magie along this line of argument.

A much more serious challenge has come from Errington. He admits that the interactions between Philip and Zeuxis happened, that there was a formal agreement at the heart of those interactions, and that Polybius believed this formal agreement was the pact between Philip and Antiochus.[207] But Errington then argues that Polybius, or perhaps his source, is wrong on this last point: rather, an ad hoc local agreement between Philip and Zeuxis, perhaps involving Philip's promise not to attack Seleucid Lydia in exchange for a promise of Zeuxis' indirect support against their mutual enemies Pergamum and Rhodes, has somehow become confused with the alleged pact between Philip and

---

[203] See the list of scholars in n. 38, above.
[204] The parallel with Philip's handing over Theangela in Caria to the Seleucid armies later in 201 (see above, pp. 156 and 167) is clear.
[205] Magie 1939: 39.
[206] Ibid.
[207] Errington 1971: 351–2.

Antiochus.[208] Indeed, perhaps this local treaty between Philip and Zeuxis, combined with knowledge of the simultaneous and hence seemingly coordinated aggressions of Philip and Antiochus in this period, is itself the *origin* of the entire mistaken story of the treaty between the kings.[209] Thus Polyb. 16.1 and 16.24 are either irrelevant to the existence and nature of the pact (for in reality the treaty – συνθῆκαι – in Book 16 was merely a local sworn agreement with Zeuxis aimed at Pergamum and Rhodes), or else the evidence in Polyb. 16.1 and 16.24 actually works against a broad-based "secret treaty" ever having existed.

Errington's thesis has often been rejected, yet only – again – on the basis of an *a priori* argument: that it is inconceivable that Antiochus would have allowed a mere local "satrap" such as Zeuxis to determine independently such important policy as the Seleucid reaction to the military presence of Philip in Asia Minor. This response to Errington was originally put forward by Berthold, and has won the approval of prominent scholars.[210] But new epigraphical discoveries have shown that this response is no longer a valid one.

In 1986 Errington himself published a new inscription found at Euromus in Caria (a town inland of Miletus, near Amyzon), which records the striking of a treaty of friendship and military alliance between Euromus and Zeuxis.[211] Euromus had gone over to Philip V in 201 (indeed, the town was now calling itself Philippi), but Zeuxis in turn was bringing it under Seleucid protection and hegemony. The date of the interaction given on the inscription equates to August/September 197 – i.e., this event came in the aftermath of Philip's disastrous defeat by the Romans at Cynoscephalae.[212] The inscription shows that the negotiations were conducted entirely between the Euromians on one side and Zeuxis alone on the other; Antiochus was never involved. Yet the establishment of a military alliance between Euromus and the Seleucids had wide geopolitical implications, for it brought Seleucid hegemonial ambitions in Caria into conflict with the similar ambitions of Rhodes. The Rhodians in this period had taken a stance as the champion of the smaller Carian states against Philip – and in autumn 198 had presented themselves publicly in peace negotiations alongside the Romans as the champions of the freedom of Euromus specifically.[213] Furthermore, since the policy of Rome

---

[208]   Ibid.: 352; strongly reiterated in Errington 1986: 5 n. 16.
[209]   Errington 1971: 352.
[210]   See Berthold 1976: 100–1, and Berthold 1984: 110 n. 23; cf. Gruen 1984: 387 n. 163; Walbank 1994/2002b: 251 n. 6.
[211]   Errington 1986: 1–7.
[212]   Ibid.: 2; cf. 4.
[213]   See Polyb. 18.2.3, with Errington 1986: 4–5 and n. 16; cf. Rawlings 1976: esp. 5–13.

at this point was to support the Rhodians' position that the Carian states should be "free," Zeuxis' actions in taking Euromus under Seleucid hegemony posed potential complications with Rome as well.[214] Yet the power on Zeuxis' part to make important diplomatic decisions on his own makes sense, for the Euromus inscription also establishes what Bengtson suspected fifty years ago and what J. and L. Robert suggested in 1983: that Zeuxis was no mere "satrap."[215] On the contrary: his title on the Euromus inscription shows that Zeuxis was viceroy over all Asia Minor for Antiochus, with explicit power to act everywhere in the king's name.[216]

Moreover, Zeuxis' personal importance as demonstrated at Euromus has been demonstrated again by another Euromian inscription published in 1993, which refers to "the alliance with the Great King Antiochus negotiated with Zeuxis"; the inscription also shows that the military alliance which Zeuxis negotiated made specific stated requirements upon the Euromians.[217] Similarly, new inscriptions from Heracleia-by-Latmus show that the Heracleiotes in the mid-190s also negotiated an alliance with the Seleucids directly with Zeuxis, who acted independently and with Antiochus not directly involved. It is further clear that Zeuxis' actions at Heracleia again ran athwart the Rhodians' policy of "freedom" for the Carian cities, and this time involved a polity far more important than Euromus. Moreover, Zeuxis' freedom of diplomatic decision-making is revealed by the fact that the terms of the alliance he negotiated with the Heracleiotes were different and tougher than the terms he negotiated with the Euromians.[218] Given this new epigraphical information, scholars now also suggest that Zeuxis was personally responsible for negotiating the terms under which Amyzon came under Seleucid hegemony in 203. This would fit the pattern.[219]

The conclusion must be that Errington's thesis concerning Zeuxis and Philip in 201 cannot be dismissed by an *a priori* appeal to supposed Seleucid administrative procedures. Zeuxis was no mere "satrap" but a

---

[214] Errington 1986: 4–5 and n. 16.
[215] Bengtson 1944: 110–11; J. and L. Robert 1983: 187–8.
[216] From the Euromus inscription, it appears that Zeuxis' title was ὁ ἀπολελειμμένος ὑπὸ τοῦ Βασιλέως Ἀντιόχου ἐπὶ τῶν ἐπιτάδε τοῦ Ταύρου πραγμάτων (lines 4–5).
[217] See Errington 1993: 24–7 (no. 5, lines 7–8).
[218] Zeuxis as the independent negotiator at Heracleia: Wörrle 1988: 445–8. Wörrle is cautious on the possible negative impact of Zeuxis' diplomacy at Heracleia for Seleucid relations with Rhodes (447). But given their own large ambitions in Caria, the Rhodians could not have been pleased with Zeuxis' actions; on Rhodian–Seleucid rivalry in Caria: Rawlings 1976: 5–13; Errington 1986: 5 n. 16.
[219] See Ma, Derow, and Meadows 1995: 73–4.

viceroy accustomed to making wide-ranging decisions on his own judgment, for the benefit of Seleucid interests as he perceived them. That
is: even under so formidable a ruler as Antiochus III, Seleucid administration in Asia Minor was quite decentralized. Errington was correct
about this all along. And thus he ends his discussion of the implications
of the first Euromus alliance-inscription for the problem of Zeuxis' relationship to Philip and the problem of Polybius' alleged Pact Between
the Kings with the declaration: "Ich bleibe bei meiner Meinung zum
'Geheimabkommen.'" That is: Polybius' "Pact Between the Kings" is
a mistake for a local pact between Philip and Zeuxis – perhaps based
on a Rhodian lie, or an exaggeration of the local pact.[220]

Yet the new Euromian and Heracleiote inscriptions only show that
it would have been politically possible from King Antiochus' side for
Zeuxis to strike a local agreement with King Philip in 201. They do not
demonstrate that Zeuxis did so. And new arguments can be brought
forward – and now must be brought forward – to show that Polybius
could not have mistaken such a local pact between Zeuxis and Philip
aimed at Pergamum and Rhodes for a treaty between Philip and
Antiochus aimed at the Ptolemies.

First, we noted above that Zeuxis in Polyb. 16.1 appears without
an introduction. This means he has been discussed previously. This underlines an important fact: while *we* must make do with the small fragments
of Books 15 and 16, Polybius had the complete text in front of him.
Now, in Polyb. 16.1.8–9 "the treaty" on which Philip bases his request
to Zeuxis (ἀι συνθῆκαι, twice) is also – like Zeuxis – referred to without any introduction. This means that this treaty, too, had already been
discussed previously. In our current fragmentary version of Book 16,
we might confuse "the treaty" of 16.1.8–9, if it was a local agreement
between Philip and Zeuxis, for the treaty between the kings. But if Polybius
here actually *was* thinking of a local pact struck between Philip and Zeuxis
in Asia in 201, he could not have confused it with the treaty between
Philip and Antiochus (concluded long before Philip even arrived in Asia),
for he would already have described the striking of the local συνθῆκαι
between Philip and Zeuxis in a passage which has now been lost to
us but which he had available. In other words, Polybius *must* have
known which συνθῆκαι he was referring to without further explanation
in 16.1.8–9 (even if we ourselves might be uncertain, because of the
fragmented nature of our text).

But not even Errington proposes that at 16.1.8–9 Polybius thought
he was referring to anything other than the Pact Between the Kings.

---

[220]   Errington 1986: 5 n. 16. This thesis is accepted by Warrior 1996: 16 n. 15.

This is because the συνθῆκαι of Polyb. 16.1.8–9 bear a striking resemblance to the συνθῆκαι between Philip and Antiochus in 15.20. And since this treaty between Philip and Antiochus *had* previously been discussed by Polybius in Book 15 and with great emphasis, it makes sense that Polybius in 16.1 should refer to these συνθῆκαι – on the basis of which Philip asked for Zeuxis' military help – without thinking at all that he had to explain or introduce the treaty to his audience.

Moreover, it is hard to see when in Polybius' narrative of 201 this hypothetical "local treaty" between Philip and Zeuxis would have been made. Whatever treaty is being discussed in Polyb. 16.1, it was struck well before the events described there. But Philip's actions did not impinge on Zeuxis' area of responsibility until Philip was about to enter Seleucid Lydia following his attack on Pergamum (cf. Polyb. 16.1.6–7). Yet the attack on Pergamum was itself a response to Attalus' decision to come to the aid of Rhodes after Philip's naval victory at Lade; and this decision was a surprise to Philip.[221] Polybius indicates that until this turn of events, Philip's intention was conquest in the southeastern Aegean – and ultimately in the direction of Alexandria (cf. 16.10). Need for Zeuxis' local aid would hardly have been in Philip's mind at that point. Yet, again, the συνθῆκαι referred to in Polyb. 16.1 had clearly been struck well before Philip encountered Zeuxis on the Lydian frontier.

Errington is not truly on safe ground even in terms of Hellenistic royal administration. While the new inscriptions from Euromus and Heraclea show that Zeuxis had the power to conclude treaties of alliance independently of Antiochus, these are treaties with cities and towns – not with a king. It is quite inconceivable that a great monarch such as Philip V of Macedon would have deigned to enter into negotiations for the creation of a formal, sworn treaty between himself and a mere subordinate administrator of another king, even as high an administrator as Zeuxis; no king would allow such a diminishing of his own status. No parallels for treaties between a king and a subordinate administrator of another monarch exist. Kings negotiated formal treaties with kings – for obvious reasons of maintaining prestige; none would place himself on a level equal to that of another monarch's subordinate. But we must stress again that Polybius in 16.1.8–9 is explicit about a formal treaty which Zeuxis is being called upon to fulfill (συνθῆκαι, twice) – so this is precisely what Errington has proposed. It seems most unlikely.

On a wide variety of grounds, we thus can exclude the possibility that Polybius, in the course of assembling and writing up his information

---

[221]   See Walbank 1940: 118–19, on how these military-diplomatic events of 201 developed.

about the events in Asia Minor in 201, personally became confused between a local "treaty" between Philip and Zeuxis and what he believed was a local impact of the treaty between Philip and Antiochus. "The treaty" is referred to without introduction in Polyb. 16.1, so it had been discussed for his readers previously, and Polybius, with the full text of the *Histories* in front of him, would have known exactly which treaty he meant. Moreover, it is very difficult to see Philip negotiating formal συνθῆκαι with Zeuxis, since that would have been beneath his status as a monarch. And it is equally difficult to see when, given Philip's intentions early in the campaign of 201 (and it would have had to be early in the campaign because, again, "the treaty" appears in 16.1 without introduction), the king would have thought such a "local treaty" with Zeuxis was necessary. And meanwhile, of course, we know that the Pact Between the Kings *had* recently been discussed in detail by Polybius, and its geopolitical importance strongly emphasized (in Book 15) – so here is one treaty that would have needed no introduction in 16.1.

This still leaves us with the possibility that not Polybius but rather Polybius' sources (oral or written) somehow did make this confusion – or perhaps deception – and that Polybius has simply followed them. The Rhodians are the obvious candidates to have perpetrated an exaggeration of a local (informal) agreement between Philip and Zeuxis into a wide-reaching and formal treaty between Philip and Antiochus threatening to the entire balance of power in the East; this is because the Rhodians were very anxious in 201 to involve Rome in their war against Philip, and such an exaggeration would have suited their propagandistic purposes at Rome – for they needed something to frighten the Romans into intervening against Philip.[222] It is clear that Polybius often drew in his *Histories* upon Rhodian material,[223] and Errington suggests that the Rhodian historians Zeno and Antisthenes were the specific culprits who misled Polybius here. Bluntly: Antisthenes and Zeno repeated the distortions originating with the Rhodian envoys to Rome in 201, and Polybius, deceived by the two Rhodian historians, has innocently but fatally repeated the Rhodian distortion by which an informal local agreement between Philip and Zeuxis became the Pact Between the Kings.[224]

But as is well known, Polybius was a skeptical (even sour) writer who did not use his sources uncritically.[225] And for this particular period in

[222] This is the position taken by Magie 1939: 42–4; cf. Errington 1971: 352–4; Berthold 1976: 100–7, and Berthold 1984: 120–5. Wiemer 2001b: 84.
[223] See now Wiemer 2001b; convenient summary at 11–18.
[224] Errington 1971: 352; cf. the variation of Habicht 1957: 240 n. 11; Wiemer 2001b: 85.
[225] See esp. Meister 1975. Polybius devotes an entire volume (Book 12) to attacks on other history-writers, especially Timaeus: see Sacks 1980.

Asia Minor he explicitly says that he has many sources – i.e., not just a couple – and that he has approached all these sources with care and a critical eye (16.14.2). At the least, this passage shows that Polybius had numerous ways to check on what the Rhodians Antisthenes and Zeno reported.[226]

Nor is there the slightest doubt that Polybius would have done so, that he would have checked on what Antisthenes and Zeno said – for he also specifically tells us that he does not think Antisthenes and Zeno were worthwhile as historians (16.14.3), that he employed them only with great care (14.10), and he warns his audience to do the same (ibid.). In fact, Polybius then devotes a long section of Book 16 to a severe criticism of Antisthenes and Zeno: their inaccuracy, their careless methodology, their obvious biases (16.14–20). For Schmitt, such Polybian remarks are enough in themselves to remove the possibility that Polybius was grossly misled by the two Rhodian historians.[227] In view of firm assertions to the contrary by many scholars since Schmitt, however, the problem needs to be revisited.

Polybius says that he found two major faults with Antisthenes and Zeno as historians. First, they were patriotically biased: they were guilty of distorting inconclusive Rhodian military operations, and even Rhodian military defeats, into Rhodian victories (16.14.5). Second, and even more crucial for us, is a criticism that has not previously been stressed in scholarly discussion. Polybius three separate times warns his audience that Antisthenes and Zeno exaggerated the scale of the events they were discussing.[228] Polybius declares that these exaggerations were committed either in the service of Rhodian patriotic propaganda and/or because of Antisthenes' and Zeno's sheer love of drama.[229] But exaggeration in the service of Rhodian patriotic propaganda, or for the sake of sheer over-dramatization, is precisely the delict that Errington accuses the Rhodian writers of having foisted on Polybius regarding the Pact Between the Kings, as the Rhodian embassy to Rome in autumn 201 had already done: exaggeration of a local and limited agreement between Philip and Zeuxis into a formal, wide-ranging, and very threatening treaty between Philip and Antiochus. But since Polybius turns out to be particularly sensitive to the faults of exaggeration and over-dramatization

---

[226]   A point stressed by Dreyer 2003: 136.
[227]   Schmitt 1964: 242.
[228]   Polyb. 16.14.3 (exaggeration of the scale of the battle of Lade, as well as turning it into a Rhodian victory); 16.17.5–7 (exaggeration of the length of the underground section of the Alpheus River near Megalopolis – with a sarcastic comment); 16.19.8–11 (exaggeration of the number of members of the family of Antiochus III at the battle of Panium in 200 BC, and exaggeration of their activities).
[229]   Patriotism and drama: 16.14.5; drama alone: 16.17.5–7 and 19.8–11.

in Antisthenes and Zeno, since he was well aware that the Rhodian historians tended towards exaggeration both for Rhodian propagandistic purposes and out of sheer love of drama (16.14.5), since he says he had numerous other sources for this period (16.14.2), and since he proclaimed a specific expertise on treaties (3.21.8–10), and believed and proclaimed that some treaties he found in historians were in fact falsehoods (3.26: the famous "Treaty of Philinus"), the likelihood that Polybius would have fallen for such a Rhodian trick of exaggeration – and more, would have been so naive as to make the Rhodian trick the centerpiece of his *Histories* – must be viewed as very remote.[230]

Two additional factors need mention. First, it is clear that among the many sources Polybius had available for the events in western Asia Minor at the end of the third century (16.14.2) were sources especially knowledgeable about the Macedonian side of these events. Hence Polybius knows that Philip secretly sent spies into Italy in 204/203, to assess the strategic situation there (13.5.7); and he even knows the names of the spies (Damocles and Python), and their individual personalities (ibid.). This sort of information most likely came (in oral or written form) from high Macedonian informants.[231] But the more information of this sort that Polybius possessed from the Macedonian side, the less probable it is that he would have been misled by mendacious Rhodian propaganda into believing that a mere local and informal agreement between Philip and Zeuxis was in actuality a formal treaty of alliance between Philip and Antiochus threatening the entire balance of power throughout the East. Such a mistake (or, bluntly, a lie) fit Rhodian propaganda very well (see above), but it would hardly fit Macedonian propaganda, since it made both Philip and Antiochus into ruthless aggressors – as we see from Polybius' bitter comments in 15.20. Polybius is in fact explicit that he had several Macedonian propagandistic versions of Philip's career available to him (8.8.5–9). That is: he had on hand several panegyric histories of Philip, written by the king's "court historians" (8.8.5–9, cf. also 3.32.8). As a critical researcher, Polybius naturally evinces distrust of these Macedonian court historians, on grounds of their pro-Macedonian bias (8.8.5). Nevertheless, these sources must have provided him with the Macedonian propaganda position on all major issues, including the major issues surrounding the origins of the Second Macedonian War – an event, after all, that was crucial to Philip's career

---

[230] For Polybius' criticism of Philinus of Agrigentum for having made a non-existent treaty the foundation of his work on the First Punic War, see above, this chapter.

[231] For Macedonians knowledgeable about the Antigonid court as prominent among Polybius' sources (oral and written), see Pédech 1964: 361–2.

and the entire history of the Antigonid dynasty. Thus Polybius was never dependent purely on a Rhodian version of events (see 16.14.2). And he would especially not have been dependent purely on Rhodian sources on this vitally important topic.[232]

This brings us to our second point. Although six sources on the alleged treaty between the kings are still extant (in itself a testimony to how widespread discussion of the treaty was in antiquity), none of them indicates that either Philip or Antiochus ever denied that the pact existed; the ancient tradition differs in many details but is uniform on this. Polybius, we have just seen, had available the Macedonian propaganda version of Philip's career, yet he never indicates that there was any controversy over the existence of the pact. Two rather late sources – Appian and Justin – do report the pact as merely a "rumor"; but this makes the kings' failure to deny the "rumor" – a rumor which had such potentially and then actually damaging political impact on their fortunes – all the more striking.[233]

Here the newly published inscription from Bargylia once more comes into play. The inscription is actually a Rhodian public document, as is shown by its dialect.[234] The inscription thus demonstrates that the Rhodian government *knew* that Philip in Caria in 201 was actively cooperating with Antiochus against the Ptolemies. Philip's actions included cooperation with Seleucid military attacks on Ptolemaic holdings: hence on the inscription we see Seleucid military forces seizing Ptolemaic holdings in Caria (including Thodasa and another town whose name is only partly preserved), while Philip gives over to them the Ptolemaic town of Theangela, in the hinterland of Bargylia, which he himself has just captured (lines 10–13). The Bargylia inscription thus puts paid to Magie's argument that the cooperation between Philip and the Seleucids recorded in Polybius 16.1 and 16.24 was a fiction.[235] And the Bargylia inscription puts paid as well to the thesis that the Pact Between the Kings merely mandated non-interference with each king's aggressions – for it shows military cooperation between Antigonid and Seleucid forces against the Ptolemies, at least after the event.[236] And note that the Theangela incident occurs in the very same period – autumn 201, when Philip was campaigning in Caria – when, according to Polybius, Zeuxis was

---

[232]   Polybius in 8.8.5–9 (cf. 3.32.8) may be referring to the historians Strato (cf. Diog. Laert. 5.61) and Poseidonius (cf. Plut. *Aem. Paul.* 19): see Walbank 1967: 361.
[233]   See, rightly, Schmitt 1964: 243; Albert 1980: 105 n. 485.
[234]   See Blumel 2000: 94–6; Wiemer 2002: 1.
[235]   Wiemer 2001a: 12; cf. Dreyer 2003: 124.
[236]   Wiemer 2001a: 12; cf. Wiemer 2001b: 74–85, esp. 83; and, more forcefully, Dreyer 2003.

giving logistical support to Philip's army (16.24.6). Moreover, the agreement that lay behind the events on the Bargylia inscription was clearly between King Philip and King Antiochus, not between King Philip and Zeuxis – for it is to (the government of) King Antiochus, not to Zeuxis (who is absent from this inscription) that King Philip gives over Theangela (lines 12–13).[237] The Bargylia inscription thus also – and most importantly – puts paid to the idea that the Rhodians exaggerated some local agreement between Philip and Zeuxis into the wide-ranging treaty of military-political cooperation between Philip and Antiochus.[238]

Finally, the initiator of the war between Antiochus and Ptolemy on the Bargylia inscription is clearly Antiochus, not Ptolemy (lines 10–11). This is presented as an objective fact: he is the aggressor.[239] Since the inscription dates from the mid-190s, i.e., from a time when relations between Rhodes and Antiochus III had actually become relatively friendly, it is striking that Antiochus' conduct as an aggressor is nevertheless depicted here in the same fashion as it was depicted by the Rhodian envoys at Rome in 201.[240] In other words, the Rhodians (and the Pergamenes and the Egyptians) at Rome in autumn 201, in making the accusation of an agreement contracted between the Philip and Antiochus for large-scale aggression against the Ptolemies, were not dealing in mere propaganda, let alone lies. Or rather, as we have said before in this study, the most effective propaganda is usually the truth.[241]

CONCLUSION

It now appears that there are no good reasons – either *a priori* reasons of logic or Hellenistic geopolitics, or because of historical facts concerning the fighting in 201–200 or the actions of Philip V or the Seleucids (as

[237]   Wiemer 2001a: 12; Wiemer 2002: 83; cf. Dreyer 2003: 128. Contrast the prominence given Zeuxis on the Seleucid alliance inscriptions with the cities of Euromus and Heracleia: above.
[238]   See esp. Dreyer 2003: 124.
[239]   σ]υστάντος δὲ πολέμου βασιλεῖ Ἀντιόχοι ποτὶ βασιλῆ Π[τολ]εμ[αῖ]ον . . .
[240]   Wiemer 2001a: 13, is incorrect to hypothesize from the simple and objective statement in lines 10–11 of the Bargylia inscription that the Rhodians in 201 did not see the war as a Seleucid pillaging of helpless Ptolemy V; true, moralizing rhetoric is missing from the inscription, but the fundamental Rhodian perception of Antiochus as the aggressor in the new war is the same. See rather the conclusion of Dreyer 2003: 123. On Rhodian hostility towards Antiochus still in 197 – and their eventual working out of a *modus vivendi* – see Chapter 5, below.
[241]   The Rhodians were backed in their accusations by envoys from Pergamum: App. *Mac.* 4.1, cf. Livy 31.1.2. Justin 30.2.8 reports that a Ptolemaic embassy brought word of the pact to Rome. Discussion of this issue is best left for Chapter 6, below.

far as we can adduce them) – to conclude that Polybius' account of a treaty concluded between Philip V and Antiochus III aimed at dismembering Egypt and its empire was a falsehood. That is: such a treaty of alliance existed. Moreover, it is clear both from the diplomatic-military interactions between Philip and the Seleucid viceroy Zeuxis in Asia Minor in 201 as recorded by Polybius, and from the new inscription from Bargylia, that this treaty went far beyond each king's non-interference in the other's aggressive projects – which is a thesis some scholars have accepted as a kind of compromise with the true skeptics on the existence of the treaty. Rather, the Pact Between the Kings foresaw the overt support by one side of the aggressive projects of the other side – and that support occurred. It is also clear that Philip did indeed attack important Ptolemaic holdings in the southeast Aegean in 201, and several major places fell into his hands: Samos and its fleet (crucial to the maintenance of the entire Ptolemaic system in the region); Miletus; Bargylia (and Theangela); Heracleia-by-Latmus. Other polities that were within the Ptolemaic system of sphere of interest in the southern Aegean in 201 did not fall to Philip only because his attacks on them failed: Cos (and Calymnus), and Cnidus. Meanwhile, Philip in 201 never attacked any Seleucid dependencies in western Asia Minor – the kind of conduct that might suggest the Pact Between the Kings did not exist.

Finally, there seems no reason to doubt Polybius' explicit statement in 16.10 that the goal of Philip's campaign in the southeast Aegean in 201 was ultimately a descent on Alexandria itself by sea. This indicates the extent to which the Pact Between the Kings meant the overturning of the triadic balance of power between the Antigonid, Seleucid, and Ptolemaic regimes that had been the basis of the state-system in the eastern Mediterranean for the previous eighty years. And as Philip launched his anti-Ptolemaic campaign in the Aegean, Antiochus from bases in Syria launched a powerful offensive into the Ptolemaic Levant: Coele Syria, Phoenicia, Judaea. Our information is fragmentary, but it appears that Antiochus opened the war in 202, and that a very large-scale offensive carried him as far south as Gaza by 201; a Ptolemaic counter-offensive followed in 200, but Antiochus then completely crushed the Ptolemaic army at the battle of Panium, in northern Judaea. It may have been at this point that Antiochus, who was already calling himself, in imitation of Alexander, Antiochus *Megas*, "Antiochus the Great," now also took the title of "Great King" – that is, the successor both of Alexander and of Achaemenid Persia.[242]

---

[242] See Ma 1999/2002: 276. On the events of the Fifth Syrian War, see Holleaux 1957: 317–31; Grainger 1991: 99–105.

The scale of warfare in the Aegean and the Ptolemaic Levant that burst on the world from 202 onward lends credence to what Polybius says in 15.20: that the treaty between Philip and Antiochus was enormous in scope and ambition, initiated by monarchs who possessed unlimited expansionist ambitions. This means that Polybius placed a real crisis in the international system of the eastern Mediterranean at the center of his history of the rise of Rome to hegemony over the Greek world. Indeed, it is striking and important, both for our understanding of these events and for our evaluation of Polybius as a historian, that as more information about this crucial period has become available to us from inscriptions discovered during the past twenty-five years, the more Polybius' view of the crisis seems solidly supported.

Thus in political-science terminology it was a real and profound power-transition crisis – not a fantasy, nor propaganda concocted by the Rhodian government – which confronted the Greek states of the eastern Mediterranean by summer 201. We now turn to the Greek reaction to that situation, and then to the Roman reaction. The Greek reaction to the crisis formed a crucial part of the background to the eventual Roman decision to intervene in the East; and in Polybius' view, this latter decision marked the decisive step towards the full development of "interconnectedness" (symplokē) between the western and eastern Mediterranean. And the actual actions now taken by Rhodes, by Pergamum, by the Ptolemies, and by Athens will serve to emphasize once more that the picture of systemic crisis in the eastern Mediterranean depicted by Polybius was historically correct: for polities that are themselves limited in military and political power do not take the dangerous actions in the real world now to be discussed if they are confronted by mere ghosts.

5

Reaction: Diplomatic Revolution in the Mediterranean, 203/202–200 BC

INTRODUCTION

The aim of the previous chapter was to establish that Polybius' pact between Philip V and Antiochus III did exist, that it was an agreement that foresaw wide-ranging military cooperation between the two powerful monarchs, and that it was aggressively focused against the gravely weakened empire of the Ptolemies. The tripolar balance of power existing in the Greek Mediterranean had always been unstable, and had always been only *de facto*; there had never developed any recognized limits on conduct or ambition on the part of any of the three great monarchical states, each of which instead maintained the largest possible geographical claims and ambitions, both in general and upon each of the others.[1] The faltering of Ptolemaic power after 207, and then its accelerating collapse, severely disrupted what was always an unstable tripolar system, precipitating what political scientists call a power-transition crisis in the Greek East.

Such crises occur when a major polity within an anarchic state-system suddenly weakens, either relatively or absolutely; Ptolemaic Egypt suddenly weakened both relatively and absolutely. Such crises are rarely resolved

---

[1] It is still sometimes thought that there was a conscious recognition among the great Hellenistic Greek states of the value of a general balance of power among them which limited their expansionist efforts: see, e.g., Braunert 1964; Klose 1982; Bederman 2001: 43 and n. 63. This view has rightly come under increasing attack; the breakthrough studies here are Lévêque 1968 and Austin 1986. On Hellenistic interstate instability, see now Ager 2003, and Eckstein 2006: Ch. 4.

without enormous violence, what political scientists call "hegemonic wars." That is what occurred in the eastern Mediterranean in this period. The large-scale interstate violence leads to the emergence of a new structure of authority, privilege, status, and power within the state-system, a structure more in line with the new redistribution of actual power among the states within the system. The strains caused by a deep power-transition crisis, and those caused by subequent large-scale hegemonic war, were what all the polities in the state-system in the Greek Mediterranean began to undergo after 207. And by 188 a new and radically different interstate structure in the East had emerged out of the massive violence.[2]

One major expression of the crisis caused by the growing collapse of the Ptolemies, and one central consequence of it, was the striking of the treaty between Philip V and Antiochus III in winter 203/202 to divide up the Ptolemaic Empire between them.[3] The Pact Between the Kings signified that with the collapse of the power of the Ptolemaic regime, the geopolitical situation in the Greek East was never going to return to the old tripolar balance of power (Antigonids, Seleucids, Ptolemies) that had prevailed for the previous half century. That was gone, and some other structure was now going to replace it. Moreover, the large-scale violence that soon occurred as the old system collapsed was most likely to benefit the most powerful states within the state-system, for they had the greatest military resources, and hence the greatest ability to enforce their will – and thus to take advantage of the chaos. Any new interstate structure was therefore likely to be based on the increased domination of the most powerful states, over both the state-system as a whole and over the less powerful states within it. Perhaps a bipolar Greek world would emerge, divided between the domination of Antigonid Macedon and that of the Seleucid Empire; or perhaps, after a second round of hegemonic war, one of these two great states would actually develop into the unipolar power, or (more strongly) the sole system hegemon. But neither of these likely outcomes occurred. Out of the chaos caused by the collapse of the old order in the Greek East the Republic of Rome, intervening from what had previously been the far western periphery of the Greek state-system, emerged instead as the preponderant Mediterranean state.

---

[2]   On power-transition crises within interstate systems, and the resulting likelihood (though not certainty) of hegemonic war, see, e.g., Gilpin 1988: 591–613; Waltz 1988: 615–28. On the events after 207 BC in the Greek East as a typical example of such a power-transition crisis, see Eckstein 2006: Chs. 4 and 7, as well as above, Chapters 1 and 4.
[3]   On the date of the striking of the agreement, see above, Chapter 4, p. 129 and n. 31.

The present chapter outlines how the less powerful Greek polities played a crucial role in this unexpected development. The relative political independence of the second-tier states within the Hellenistic state-system – the Rhodian Republic, the Kingdom of Pergamum, the Aetolian League, the Achaean League, Athens – had been facilitated by the tripolar balance of power. The existence of three rivalrous great monarchies had allowed the second-tier states significant room for political and diplomatic maneuver among the major powers, and hence opportunity to carve out their own independent spaces. But, conversely, the collapse of the Ptolemaic regime threatened the relative independence which the old tripolar balance of power had facilitated, for it was likely to lead to the greatly increased power of the two most powerful dynastic realms. This was the threat the medium-sized Greek states increasingly faced after ca. 204 (when the premature death of Ptolemy IV brought a child to the already weakening Ptolemaic throne). And though the power of Rome eventually came to constitute the ultimate threat to the independence of these states – as modern historians now see, and as Polybius himself, writing ca. 150 BC, already well saw – the main threat for these states by 201 BC was the immediate threat, and that threat was Greek. It came from the suddenly and enormously expanding military and political power of Philip and Antiochus, not from Rome. The second-tier states acted as best they could in the chaos at the end of the third century to defuse this immediate and profound threat, and it should be stressed that they were successful; if they did not take the long view, it was because they could not afford to do so.

Much evidence shows that news of the threatening Pact Between the Kings had a profound political impact throughout the eastern Mediterranean, and led directly to important actions taken by the medium-sized states. The clearest example is that of the Republic of Rhodes. It can be demonstrated that the Rhodians based radical changes in their foreign relations, both in 201 and later, on the assumption that the pact between Antiochus and Philip existed, and that it not only threatened the Ptolemies with destruction, but indirectly formed an enormous threat to Rhodian independence as well. It will also be argued below that knowledge of the pact – as far-reaching a treaty as Polybius claimed it to be – had a similar radical impact on the policies of Pergamum, of Athens, of Ptolemaic Egypt (naturally enough), and finally upon Rome itself.

But to understand why the diplomatic revolution in the Mediterranean which we are about to describe occurred, one should also understand that while the Pact Between the Kings played a decisive immediate role, the transformation in Mediterranean geopolitics derives ultimately not from the pact itself but rather from the fundamental power-transition crisis caused by the collapse of Egypt. The treaty between Philip and

Antiochus was simply one important consequence of that collapse. The decision of the less-powerful states to appeal for help to Rome in the face of the threat from Philip and Antiochus – a threat that could no longer by balanced by Egypt – was another consequence of the Ptolemaic collapse. And the Roman decision to respond to the pleas of the Greek states and to intervene in the eastern situation was, at least in good part, yet a third consequence of that collapse.

This is not to minimize the impact of individual human decision at any point in the unrolling of events. Power-transition crises do not make large-scale hegemonic war inevitable, merely more probable: skillful diplomacy, for instance, prevented just such a potentially cataclysmic outcome as the Soviet Union collapsed in 1989–91. But in the Hellenistic Mediterranean, delicate and skillful diplomacy is exactly what one could not expect. We are dealing in all directions with heavily militaristic cultures, dominated by proud aristocrats, and with mechanisms for interstate diplomacy that were primitive or even counter-productive for peace – for instance, the widespread habit of compellence diplomacy conducted in public.[4] Meanwhile, the harsh nature of Mediterranean anarchy itself created an unforgiving interstate environment that encouraged certain kinds of decisions and militated against other (more peaceable) ones. Such a perspective seeks to situate human decisions, important as they are, within an overarching anarchic structure that made its own grim demands on state behavior, within a systemic crisis which contained its own unrolling dyamic, and within an inevitable on-going structural transformation that no one could escape. We proceed by examining the governmental actions of each important weaker state in turn.

RHODES

First, then – Rhodes. The Rhodians were leaders in spreading the story of the treaty of alliance between Antiochus and Philip (Livy 31.2.1, cf. App. *Mac.* 4). But the government of the Republic of Rhodes did not merely talk in this period but *acted*, and not just diplomatically but also militarily, upon the assumption that there was a pact between Philip and Antiochus and that the pact severely threatened Rhodian interests. The strongest evidence that the Rhodian government knew for a fact that an agreement between Philip and Antiochus existed comes now from the newly published inscription from Bargylia, a Rhodian document that refers to military cooperation between Philip and Antiochus in 201 in

---

[4]   The impact of compellence diplomacy is discussed above, Chapters 1 and 2.

aggression against the holdings of the Ptolemies.[5] The most direct evidence that the Rhodians viewed the agreement as so detrimental to their interests that they were prepared to respond not only diplomatically (as at Rome in 201/200) but also militarily comes from events four years later, in spring 197. These later events, in turn, spread light on the decision of the Rhodian government to confront Philip V militarily in the southeast Aegean in the summer of 201.

Polybius' narrative of the eastern Aegean in the spring of 197 was evidently quite full; but as usual, we have only a few fragments. One of those fragments, however, records an ultimatum that Rhodes sent to Antiochus III: as the Great King was preparing to expand westward along the southern coast of Asia Minor, Rhodian envoys officially told him that Rhodes would prevent him from sailing further west than the Chelidonian Promontory (18.41a.1; cf. Livy 33.20.2–3). The Rhodians by this decision threatened to abandon an existing official relationship of friendship with Antiochus (Livy 33.20.7, cf. Polyb. 18.41a.1), and to enter instead into a state of war with the Great King. Why did the Rhodians take this decision? From 201 they were already at war with one major king, Philip V, and in spring 197 they had naval forces stationed in the Aegean against Macedon while they engaged in major land operations – including set-piece battles – against Macedonian garrisons in Caria.[6] Now the Rhodian Republic was also threatening a naval war with the conqueror of Asia.[7]

Polybius comments that the Rhodians acted "not out of any long-standing enmity [towards Antiochus], but suspecting that, by giving support to Philip, he would become an impediment to the freedom of the Greeks" (18.41a.1).[8] The alleged desire of the Rhodians to protect "the freedom of the Greeks" sounds like Rhodian propaganda, as does the effusive praise of the Rhodians' courage in confronting Antiochus in the parallel passage in Livy 33.20, which clearly comes from Polybian material. So ultimately all this must derive from a Rhodian or pro-Rhodian source that Polybius accepted.[9] But the main point for us seems unquestionable: in spring 197 the Rhodian government assumed that Antiochus

---

[5]   See above, Chapter 4, esp. pp. 177–8.
[6]   These garrisons were the result of Philip's relatively successful campaign of 201: see above, Chapter 4.
[7]   On the extensive Rhodian land operations against Philip's forces in Asia Minor in spring 197 see Rawlings 1976: 10, with sources. Rhodian naval operations in the Aegean in 198 and early 197: see Berthold 1984: 137, with sources.
[8]   In Livy this Polybian statement becomes part of the actual ultimatum from the Rhodian envoys to Antiochus: see Livy 33.20.2–3 with Walbank 1967: 603.
[9]   See Rawlings 1976: 10 and n. 18; Wiemer 2001b: 107–11. On the alleged Rhodian policy of "the freedom of the Greeks," see below.

was coming west in order to bring aid to Philip (Polyb. 18.41a.1; cf. Livy 33.19.11). That would be a very dangerous development if true, for the war that Rome and its Greek allies were fighting against Philip in European Greece had not yet reached a decisive point. Livy 33.19.11, which is based on Polybian material, explicitly accepts the Rhodian evaluation of Antiochus' intentions,[10] and the analysis of the strategic situation in the Mediterranean in spring 197 from Spain to Syria at Livy 33.19.7 similarly envisions the two kings now coming together and uniting their military forces.[11]

But why would Antiochus be coming west to the aid of Philip? The obvious answer is that we are dealing here with suspicions in the Rhodian government created by Rhodian knowledge of the anti-Ptolemaic pact of alliance between the two kings. This is confirmed by the description in Livy (based on Polybius) of how Antiochus intended to expand along the coast: he would proceed by conquering the cities that belonged to the Ptolemies (33.19.11) – which is what occurred (ibid.).[12] This understanding of the origins of Rhodian action in spring 197 is confirmed by Livy's statement at 31.14.9 (again, drawing on Polybius) that Philip in 200 had been heartened in his war against Rhodes and Pergamum by the strategic prospects which his pact with Antiochus opened for him.[13] It is possible that Seleucid forces had in fact already invaded Pergamene territory in 198, and done significant damage.[14]

We need not accept these Rhodian suspicions of Antiochus coming west to aid Philip as the whole truth behind Antiochus' advance in spring 197. But it is significant that Polybius (and Livy) found the Rhodian suspicions reasonable.[15] It is even more significant that Rhodian fear

---

[10]   *Philippum – necdum enim debellatum erat – exercitu navibusque adiuturus.* Polybian derivation: Briscoe 1973: 2; cf. Rawlings 1976: 5–6. It is unclear whether this is Livy's opinion (based on suspicions recorded by Polybius) or Polybius' own judgment: see Walbank 1967: 603.

[11]   *In unum ambo simul contulissent vires.* Again, we do not know whether this is Livy's judgment or that of Polybius: see Briscoe 1973: 284. The theme of alliance between Philip and Antiochus in 197, with Antiochus coming west to help Philip, appears also in the retrospective speech of Antiochus' minister Menippus to the Aetolians in 192 (Livy 35.32.8–9; from Polybian material: Briscoe 1981: 2, cf. 195).

[12]   Detailed discussion of Antiochus' military advance along the southern coast of Asia Minor in spring 197: Grainger 2002: 35–47.

[13]   *Sed animos ei faciebat praeter ferociam insitam foedus inctum cum Antiocho, Syriae rege . . .* Polybian derivation: Briscoe 1973: 94.

[14]   On Antiochus' campaign against Pergamum in 198 (found only in a desperate Pergamene report to Rome at Livy 32.8.9–16), see Schmitt 1964: 269–76; cf. Rawlings 1976: 4. Doubts about the historicity of this attack, as mere Pergamene propaganda: see Ma 1999/2002: 279–81; Grainger 2002: 31–5. Sincerity of the belief both in Rhodes and perhaps even in Rome that Antiochus was coming west to cooperate with Philip: see Briscoe 1973: 286.

[15]   See Walbank 1967: 603; Rawlings 1976: 6.

of cooperation between Antiochus and Philip was so strong in spring 197 that the government took the decision to confront Antiochus diplomatically, attempting to block his advance towards the west (Polyb. 18.41a.1; cf. Livy 33.20.2–3). This is not mere propaganda; it is very serious government action. But most significant of all is that the Rhodians also began preparations to battle Antiochus at sea off the Chelidonian Cape, with the goal of preventing him from linking up with Philip. They decided to do this despite the formidable fleet the Great King had assembled – 100 large decked warships (cataphracts), plus 200 lighter vessels (Livy 33.19.9) – and despite the strain already imposed on Rhodian resources by the on-going fighting on land against the forces of Philip in Caria.[16] Hence the Rhodian government in spring 197 seems to have withdrawn the warships it had operated in European Greek waters against Philip in 198, in order to concentrate all its naval forces off Rhodes for the projected confrontation with Antiochus near Cape Chelidonae – an even more impressive demonstration of Rhodian governmental seriousness.[17] Even more clearly than the decision to send an embassy to Antiochus warning him not to advance further west, the decision taken by the Rhodian government to prepare for a large-scale war with Antiochus (Livy 33.20.11: explicit) cannot be mere self-serving propaganda intended to exaggerate the pact between Antiochus and Philip – the sort of propaganda which scholars have accused the Rhodians of retailing to gullible states during these years, especially at Rome.[18] On the contrary: these decisions constituted the most dangerous of official policies, namely war with a great power. That is: in spring 197 the Rhodians were preparing to risk their navy, and perhaps much more, to prevent what they feared was a link-up between Antiochus and Philip.

Conversely, the crisis between Rhodes and King Antiochus immediately eased when news arrived at Rhodes that the Romans and their Greek allies had won a smashing victory over Philip at the battle of Cynoscephalae, and that the war in Greece was essentially at an end (June 197). The Rhodian government, thus freed from its fear of dangerous collaboration between Philip and Antiochus, now reversed its policy, and decided to allow Antiochus to enter the Aegean unopposed. Livy (drawing again upon Polybian material) is explicit about what occurred: "with the fear of Philip dispelled by the receipt of this news [of Cynoscephalae], the Rhodians abandoned their intention of going

---

[16]   Discussion of the large size of Antiochus' naval forces as he came west: Briscoe 1973: 285; Grainger 2002: 36–7. His land forces were also very large: Livy (P) 33.20.9, with Briscoe 1973: 285 and Grainger 2002: 37.
[17]   See the reconstruction of Rhodian movements in Berthold 1984: 137–40.
[18]   So esp. Magie 1939: 32–44; cf. Berthold 1976: 104–5.

to confront Antiochus with their fleet" (33.20.10).[19] Recent epigraphical discoveries have shown that Antiochus' subsequent advance worked at cross-purposes to Rhodian interests in Caria: the Seleucids soon gained control of cities such as Euromus and Heracleia-by-Latmus, whose independence had previously been guaranteed in public declarations by the Rhodians.[20] And Rhodes, for its part, now acted to seize control of several nearby Ptolemaic dependencies – polities left unprotected by the helpless Alexandrian government. This was apparently part of the Rhodians' arrangement with Antiochus. It was, of course, a typical example of the geopolitical ruthlessness of Hellenistic states.[21]

The main development to see, however, is that once the threat of Seleucid military unification with Philip's forces was removed by Philip's defeat at Cynoscephalae, the Rhodians soon arrived at a political *modus vivendi* with Antiochus (Livy 33.20.10, from Polybian material). This Seleucid–Rhodian diplomatic arrangement is another concrete fact, and it lasted from 197 throughout most of the 190s. It suggests that the Rhodian Republic was prepared to accept, if it had to, a significant increase in Seleucid power and influence in western Asia Minor – primarily at Ptolemaic expense but even somewhat at the expense of Rhodes (though by compensation Rhodian power and influence expanded over other – previously Ptolemaic – areas, and Antiochus even provided help in the Rhodian reconquest of Stratoniceia from Philip's forces).[22] The hard fact of this Rhodian–Seleucid *modus vivendi* after Cynoscephalae confirms, in turn, that Polybius was correct that what drove the Rhodians to contemplate war against Antiochus in the spring of 197 was not the Great King's arrival in southwest Asia Minor per se, but his perceived deadly coordination with Philip, who had already achieved much in western Asia Minor and was not yet defeated at Cynoscephalae. The Rhodians

---

[19] *hunc nuntio accepto Rhodii dempto metu a Philippo omiserunt consilium obviam eundi classe Antiocho*; Polybian derivation: see Briscoe 1973: 286.
[20] Rhodian championship of the freedom of Euromus: Polyb. 18.2.3; its new military alliance with the Seleucids, dated to August/September 197: Errington 1986. Heracleia-by Latmus, well within the Rhodian sphere of influence, brought into Seleucid hegemony in this period: Wörrle 1988.
[21] The Ptolemaic polities involved were Caunus, Myndus, Halicarnassus, and the island of Samos. Antiochus also turned over the inland city of Stratoniceia to Rhodes, after the Rhodians failed to retake this Rhodian holding by siege from Philip's forces, which had seized it. Best discussion of these developments: Rawlings 1976: 9–13. These actions allow us to look somewhat askance at Rhodian proclamations of "the freedom of the Greeks" (ibid.).
[22] Discussion of the *modus vivendi*: Rawlings 1976 (who wrote without the inscriptional evidence we now have of Seleucid hegemony at Euromus and Heracleia after 197 – a Seleucid expansion which makes the arrangement between Antiochus and the Rhodians even more striking). Rhodian–Seleucid cooperation at Stratoniceia: Polyb. 30.31.6, cf. Livy 33.18.22, and above, Chapter 4, p. 166.

must have feared that such a combination and collaboration would put Rhodes in an untenable and perhaps fatal strategic situation, trapped in a pincer between the two expanding monarchical hegemonies. They were prepared to go very far to prevent such a development – and this is why the disaster to Philip at Cynoscephalae changed everything.[23]

The point here is not merely historiographical, i.e., to offer yet more Polybian-derived evidence for the historicity of the Pact Between the Kings – though it is that. The point is also historical: to show the radical impact of the treaty on actual Rhodian governmental *actions*, actions whose historicity is not in dispute. The Rhodians based their dangerous naval confrontation with Antiochus III in spring 197 on the assumption that the alliance between Philip and Antiochus existed, that it was in working order, and that it constituted a profound threat to the Rhodian state.

We do not know how the Rhodian government originally obtained its knowledge of the pact. Perhaps when the Rhodians learned in 202 of Philip V's depredations in the Hellespont, or in early 201 when they learned that Philip was preparing for a campaign in the southeastern Aegean, Rhodian envoys went to the court of Antiochus III to seek his help (they can hardly have gone for real help to the Ptolemies, their more traditional ally, whose weakness at this point was clear) – and they were then shocked by the response they received from Antiochus.[24] In any case, the agreement between the kings was certainly clear to the Rhodians by the summer of 201, when the Rhodian government saw Philip and the forces of Antiochus cooperating militarily against holdings of the Ptolemies in southwest Asia Minor – as the Bargylia inscription now reveals.[25] And the Rhodian actions later in spring 197 – dangerous actions – show that the Rhodian government at that time still believed in the threat posed by the Pact Between the Kings.

These are crucial findings about Rhodian policy – for though prominent scholars accuse our information on the Pact Between the Kings of being merely deceptive Rhodian propaganda,[26] no second-tier state would have made preparations for a war against the conqueror of all Asia on the basis merely of its own consciously deceptive propaganda. Nor is it likely that the Rhodians somehow managed to deceive *themselves* about the nature of the crisis now occurring in the eastern

---

[23]   No doubt the presence of large Roman forces deployed in European Greece against Philip in 197 made the Rhodian decision to concentrate their navy against Antiochus that spring much easier: see Berthold 1984: 141. One need only imagine how desperate the situation would have looked to the Rhodian government that spring *without* the intervention and presence of the Romans.

[24]   This is the suggestion of Berthold 1976: 102–3.

[25]   See above, n. 4.

[26]   Discussion in Chapter 4, above. See, e.g., Magie 1939: 32–44.

Mediterranean.[27] The fact is that no second-tier state would have run the terrible risks the Rhodians were getting ready to run in the spring of 197 unless its government possessed absolutely secure information about the nature and scale of the threat it faced – in this case (in other words), secure intelligence about the pact.

If in 197 the Rhodians threatened war against Antiochus III, four years earlier their actions had been similarly radical: Rhodes had actually gone to war against Philip V when his forces appeared in the southeastern Aegean. As is well known, the Rhodians for the previous 100 years had generally sought to be independent non-belligerents among the struggles of the three great monarchies, although they strove simultaneously to do their part to prevent any of the great states from establishing a preponderance of power.[28] The Rhodian Republic, as a polity existing in the militarized Hellenistic anarchy, was of course prepared to go to war both locally and in the wider Aegean to defend its own interests or to extend its power and influence. Thus in 220 Rhodes was simultaneously organizing war against the city-state of Byzantium in the Hellespont, coming to the military defense of the city-state of Knossos on Crete against its rivals, *and* pursuing Demetrius of Pharos' large force of Illyrian pirates across the eastern Aegean – a wide geographical spread of activity indeed. Again, after 204 Rhodes was involved in large military operations against the Cretan bases of Aegean pirates (the so-called First Cretan War).[29] But even operations such as the First Cretan War were far different in scale and danger from a war against Macedon. In the previous century Rhodian neutrality towards the great Hellenistic powers had been broken only once: in ca. 260 the Rhodians went to war against Ptolemaic Egypt, evidently because Ptolemy II's naval strength (over 300 warships – larger than the war-fleet of either Rome or Carthage in the First or Second Punic War) had threatened to dominate the entire eastern Mediterranean. But Rhodes in ca. 260 had been joining a large anti-Ptolemaic alliance, including Antigonid Macedon.[30] In 201 the Rhodian motive in going to war was presumably also to prevent the dominance of the Aegean by a single powerful state: in this case, the Antigonids. But the war against Philip occurred in far more dangerous

[27] Implied by Errington 1971: 351–2.
[28] On this general Rhodian stance, see Schmitt 1957: 54–5; Berthold 1984: 57–8, cf. 91; Ager 1991: 10.
[29] Rhodes and Byzantium in 220: Polyb. 4.47–52; Rhodes and Knossos: Polyb. 4.53.1–2 and 55.1–2; Rhodes and Demetrius of Pharos: Polyb. 4.16.6–8 and 19.8. Discussion: Berthold 1984: 94–9. The First Cretan War: see Brulé 1978: 29–56.
[30] Discussion: Berthold 1984: 89–92. Rhodian motivation: ibid.: 91. The only known Rhodian action was the defeat of a Ptolemaic naval squadron off Ephesus (Polyaen. 5.18).

circumstances. It was a Rhodian war against one of the two strongest Greek powers, ruled by one of the greatest generals of the age, undertaken originally without the help of any other Greek state.

We need to clarify when the Rhodians made this decision for war. Modern scholars often state that when the Rhodians learned in 202 of the fate of the city of Cius – destroyed by Philip, and its population enslaved, despite Philip's previous promises to the Cians as well as pleas for mercy from envoys of Rhodes and other states – the Rhodians declared war on him.[31] This modern construct is based on Polybius' statement that when the Rhodians learned that Philip had destroyed Cius and enslaved its population, "they from that day viewed Philip as their enemy, and made their preparations with that in mind" (Polyb. 15.23.6). But we should not view this passage as recording an official declaration of war. The Rhodian envoy at the peace negotiations with Philip at Nicaea in autumn 198 never even mentions Cius as an issue: it is Philip's conquests of 201 and 200 that are the focus (Polyb. 18. 3.11–12).

What Polybius says at 15.23.6 is merely that the atrocity at Cius caused the Rhodians to hate Philip (so also 15.22.5) and to take preparations against him – not that they declared war on him.[32] The historian is talking about sentiments; similarly, he says that the atrocity against Cius despite Rhodian pleas for mercy revealed Philip's hostile sentiments towards Rhodes (15.23.2).[33] And Polybius' next sentence equates the Rhodians' hatred of Philip caused by Cius with the hatred that the Aetolians now felt towards Philip, also caused by the destruction of Cius (15.23.7–8); but the Aetolians did not declare war on Philip until three years later, in summer 199, and this despite several attempts by other states to involve them in the war.[34] Thus Wiemer in his recent study must be correct that the Rhodian decision for war came only when, on top of everything else (including the shocking revelation of the pact with Antiochus), Philip appeared as a conquerer in the southeast Aegean in spring 201.[35] To go to war against Philip was a radical act by the Rhodians, and the atrocity at Cius in 202, though it created anti-Philip feeling, was not the issue that provoked such a radical act; the decision only came with Philip's menacing advance into the southeast Aegean the next spring. The Rhodian decision for war against Philip in spring 201 thus

[31]   See Polyb. 15.22.1–23.8, with Berthold 1976: 97 and Berthold 1984: 112; Errington 1989: 252; Ager 1991: 20.

[32]   ὁ δὲ τῶν Ῥοδίων δῆμος ἀπὸ ταύτης τῆς ἡμέρας ὡς περὶ πολεμίου διελάμβανε τοῦ Φιλίππου καὶ πρὸς τοῦτον τὸν δκοπὸν ἐποίετο τὰς παρασκευάς. See the careful translations of this passage in Holleaux 1935: 292 n. 5, and in Petzold 1940: 32.

[33]   See Walbank 1967: 477.

[34]   Discussion below, p. 214.

[35]   Wiemer 2001b: 69–74.

seems similar to their decision for war against the advancing Antiochus in spring 197. And yet this Rhodian decision of 201 was unlike previous Rhodian responses to the appearance of Antigonid forces in the southeast Aegean. That is another concrete fact – to which we now turn.

The radical nature of the Rhodian decision to go to war with Philip V in 201 is underlined by the very different interactions of the Rhodians with Antigonus III Doson, Philip's predecessor and uncle, in a similar situation a generation earlier. In 227 BC Antigonus III arrived with a fleet and an army in the southeastern Aegean, and campaigned successfully on the Carian coast north of Rhodes, winning over significant cities – as Philip V did in 201.[36] Antigonus had engaged in a major ship-building program for the purpose of asserting Macedonian power in the Aegean and off the coast of Asia Minor; and he was the grandson of Demetrius the Besieger, a monarch who had famously besieged Rhodes itself in 305–304.[37] Yet what is striking, as Walbank remarks, is the Rhodian reaction: there was none.[38] Indeed, our sources are explicit that relations between Antigonus Doson and the Rhodians at this time were good. Thus Antigonus is prominent among those who provided aid to Rhodes after the great earthquake of 228 there (Polyb. 5.89.6–7). Even more strikingly, this Antigonid aid to Rhodes after the great earthquake was military: timber and pitch to help rebuild the Rhodian fleet. This means that Macedon was actually providing crucial military aid for the Rhodian fleet the year before the king himself appeared with large naval and land forces in the southeast Aegean and Caria. From this we may conclude that no confrontation with Rhodes was foreseen over this – and of course there was none.[39]

Nor is there any indication of an escalating clash of interests between Rhodes and the Antigonids in the next decades. Philip V and the Rhodians did back different cities among the quarreling polities on Crete in 220, a contest which Philip eventually seems to have won.[40] But in the Social War of 220–217, and again and even more importantly in the First Macedonian War of 214–205, the Rhodians acted as mediators

---

[36] Antigonus won over Mylasa, Euromus, Iasus, and towns around the Bay of Bargylia, and there was some sort of interference at Samos; sources and discussion: Walbank, in Hammond and Walbank 1988: 343. According to Trogus, *Prol.* 28, Antigonus "conquered Caria" (*Cariam subegit*) – an exaggeration, but suggestive of the scale of the campaign.

[37] See the comments of Walbank, in Hammond and Walbank 1988: 343. The famous "Colossus of Rhodes," the great statue of the sun-god Helios at the entrance to the city's harbor, was built from the captured seige-machines of Demetrius' failed attack on the city.

[38] Walbank, in Hammond and Walbank 1988: 343.

[39] Ibid.: 345; cf. Walbank 1957: 620.

[40] Berthold 1984: 102–3.

attempting to bring about a compromise peace between Macedon and its enemies. These actions were no doubt undertaken primarily in the interests of Rhodes itself, to help end the disruption of Rhodian trade into Greece, especially in grain (which Rhodes dominated), and to help prevent the rise of one dominating power in the Aegean, namely Philip (see Livy 27.30.9–10).[41] But in the mediations especially during the First Macedonian War, the Rhodian actions were also definitely in Philip's interests as well, for the Rhodians were involved in persistent (and eventually successful) attempts to split the anti-Macedonian alliance of 212/211 in two by separating the Aetolian League from its ally Rome. Polybius credits the Rhodian diplomat Thrasycrates with an extraordinarily harsh anti-Roman speech to the Aetolian Assembly during the mediation of 207, in which Thrasycrates calls the Romans barbarians with whom it was shameful for a Greek state to be allied, and warns of Roman ambitions in Greece (Polyb. 11.4.1–6.8). And it appears that the Rhodians were then instrumental in 206 in bringing about a peace between Macedon and Aetolia, separate from Rome, advantageous to Macedon, and contrary to Rome's interests and stated policies (App. Mac. 4.1).[42]

The contrast is very sharp between the *modus vivendi* of Rhodes and Antigonus III Doson along the Carian coast in 228–227, the quite good relations between Rhodes and Philip V himself right down through 206, and the sudden Rhodian war against Philip V in 201. It is as sharp as the difference between the Rhodian confrontation with Antiochus III in spring 197 and the *modus vivendi* reached with Antiochus' expansion once Philip had been defeated at Cynoscephalae. Engaging in war was, of course, not unusual for the Rhodians (see above), and after 204 they were involved in major operations on Crete. But the war against Philip in 201 was a profound departure from the long-term Rhodian policy of avoiding war with a first-rank power – especially when (as was the case at first in 201) no allies were immediately available. An explanation for this volte-face is needed.

No doubt the aggressive conduct of Philip in the Aegean from 204 was increasingly disturbing. We are even told that one of Philip's agents attempted in 204 to burn the Rhodian fleet – an act that might well have provoked war; but Polybius implies that this plot was only discovered long after the event, and the incident had no impact upon Rhodian

---

[41]   The Livian assessment here is based on Polybian material: see above, Chapter 3, pp. 94–5.

[42]   Persistent Rhodian attempts at mediation in the Social War: see Berthold 1984: 103–4; Ager 1991: 15. Persistent Rhodian attempts at mediation in the First Macedonian War: see above, Chapter 3.

policy towards Macedon at the time.[43] The huge build-up of Philip's war-fleet after 204 was no doubt also an act which could be viewed as provocative at Rhodes – but by spring 201 Philip's war-fleet was so much larger than the Rhodian fleet that perhaps Philip's fleet had actually become a factor leading the Rhodians to *avoid* war with the king if possible.[44] The ruthlessness of Philip's actions against the cities he conquered in the Hellespont during 202 made him enormously unpopular at Rhodes (Polyb. 15.24), and his conquests came in a region that was economically crucial for the Rhodian grain trade from the Black Sea. Yet the potential threat here was still not enough for the Rhodians in 202 to risk a war with Macedon, and they did not respond militarily.[45] Then in 201 Philip's fleet and army arrived in the southeast Aegean and engaged in large military operations – yet his aggressions were aimed primarily against Ptolemaic holdings, not at Rhodes.[46] Are Philip's actions along the Carian coast enough in themselves to account for the Rhodians going to war against him, a response that involved such enormous dangers to the Rhodian state? Philip's uncle Antigonus III's similar actions in the same region a generation earlier had not provoked such a response. And Philip later repeatedly claimed, with some reason, that he had not started the war with Rhodes, but that the Rhodians had attacked him.[47]

The best explanation for the radical Rhodian action of summer 201 is therefore similar to the explanation adduced for the radical Rhodian action of spring 197. The Rhodian government would of course have been concerned in 201 about the unpopular and ruthless Philip's large operations in the southeast Aegean, but it had secure additional information that tipped the scales towards war. The additional factor, we suggest, was Rhodian knowledge of the Pact Between the Kings – which Rhodian envoys would soon be emphasizing at Rome (App. *Mac.* 4.2) – and Rhodian awareness of the threatening geopolitical implications of the pact for Rhodes itself as well as for all the less powerful Greek states. This is why the Rhodians resolved in 201 on the unusual and dangerous course of war to prevent the expansion of Philip V into the southeast Aegean and thus closer to Antiochus, just as four years later in spring

---

[43]   See Polyb. 13.3–5, with Walbank 1940: 111.

[44]   The regular Rhodian war-fleet in the late third century numbered around thirty cataphracts: see Walbank 1967: 505, with sources. By summer 201 Philip's fleet had fifty-three cataphracts (including Ptolemaic ships seized at Samos), and some of these were of extraordinary size: ibid., with sources.

[45]   See above, p. 190.

[46]   Detailed discussion of Philip's campaigns in 201 and 200: see above, Chapter 4.

[47]   See Polyb. 16.34.4 (Philip to M. Aemilius Lepidus at Abydus in 200); 18.6.2 (Philip to T. Quinctius Flamininus at the Nicaea peace conference of 198). Philip technically correct: see Walbank 1967: 544 and 557.

197 they were prepared for the unusual and dangerous course of war against Antiochus to block his expansion westward in the direction of Philip.

PERGAMUM AND RHODES

Radical change in policy in response to the events of 201 is not limited to Rhodes. Attalus I, the king of Pergamum, soon joined the Rhodians in military resistance to Philip. The Pergamene alliance with Rhodes in 201 was itself a reversal of thirty years of Attalid policy, for since the emergence of Pergamum as a power on the west coast of Asia Minor in the 230s, the relationship between Pergamum and Rhodes had been one of tension and rivalry. Hence Attalus is strikingly absent from the long list of kings and states – some as far away as Sicily – who provided aid to Rhodes after the great earthquake of 228 (Polyb. 5.89).[48] Hence, too, we find Pergamum supporting Byzantium against Rhodes in the war of 220 (Polyb. 4.47–52).[49] The destruction in 213 of the Seleucid pretender Achaeus, previously active in western Asia Minor, removed a main obstacle to Pergamene expansion in this period, and this change in the balance of power in Attalus' favor led in turn to increased tensions between the Pergamene monarchy and Rhodes.[50] After 213 Attalus also engaged in a vigorous naval building program, indicating large ambitions in the Aegean; soon his war-fleet, like that of Macedon, outnumbered the Rhodian fleet – surely an unwelcome development at Rhodes. Attalus' ambitions for an empire in the Aegean are clear from his participation as an ally of Rome and the Aetolian League against Philip V in the First Macedonian War; he intervened militarily in European Greece for the first time, gained control of the great island of Aegina off the coast of Athens (probably in 209), and in 208 engaged in significant operations against the island of Euboea and on the Greek coast north of Thermopylae. Meanwhile, Rhodes was again working at cross-purposes to Pergamum, seeking to end the war in Greece via a compromise peace between Philip V and the Aetolian League. A remark from 209, clearly deriving from Polybian material, gives as one motive

[48]   See Starr 1938: 65 and n. 9, who also notes on the list of helpers of Rhodes the presence of Prusias I of Bithynia – who was Attalus' inveterate enemy; so too McShane 1964: 96–7 and 117; Berthold 1984: 92–3. Antigonid Macedon, another enemy of Pergamum, is also on the list of helpers of Rhodes (above, p. 192) – and Prusias soon contracted a marriage alliance with the Antigonids.
[49]   Discussion: Berthold 1984: 94–6.
[50]   See Berthold 1984: 105; Ager 1991: 17.

of the Rhodians and the other Greek mediators of the war a suspicion of Attalid ambitions in the Aegean and European Greece (Livy 27.30.10). It was a suspicion backed by hard facts.[51]

It would thus have taken an extraordinary geopolitical development to cause the Attalid government to reverse its long history of tension and hostility with Rhodes and to become instead the Rhodians' chief military ally in 201 in a war against Philip. Relations between Pergamum and Macedon were certainly poor, but undertaking a war against Philip in the conditions of 201, with only Rhodes as an ally, was a far more dangerous proposition for Pergamum than its previous participation in the much larger anti-Macedonian alliance of ca. 210, which included both Rome and Aetolia – and from which Pergamum had nevertheless emerged quite battered.[52] And the immediate consequences of the decision to go to war against Philip show the risks involved: Attalus I was almost killed in the fighting at the naval battle of Chios, and Philip launched a devastating invasion of Pergamene territory right up to the walls of the capital itself – an invasion that Attalus was helpless to prevent (see Polyb. 16.1–2).

What motivated this Pergamene reversal towards Rhodes and the decision to go to war against Macedon, with all its dangers? After all, like Rhodes, Attalus I had not reacted to or resisted the similar expedition of Philip's uncle Antigonus III Doson to the southeast Aegean in 227. Some scholars suggest that Attalus was motivated by Philip's aggressions in the nearby Hellespont region in 202, and/or by the threat of a renewed Macedonian hegemony in Caria south of Pergamum in 201, and/or by the fact that Philip V had Prusias I of Bithynia – Attalus' inveterate enemy – as his son-in-law.[53] But none of these motives is attested in our (admittedly skimpy) sources; and they are not probable in themselves. Philip's kinship and alliance with Attalus' enemy Prusias I of Bithynia was of long standing; there was no reason why in 201 it should have become the occasion of a new war. Indeed, the Rhodians themselves

---

[51]   Attalid ambitions: see Holleaux 1935: 204–7; Starr 1938: 65–6; McShane 1964: 110; Berthold, 1984: 105–6 and n. 10. After 210 the Pergamene war-fleet numbered thirty-five cataphracts to the Rhodian thirty: Livy 28.5.1 with McShane 1964: 109 and n. 57; Polyb. 162.9–10 with Walbank 1967: 505. Aegina was bought from the Aetolian League, which had gained the island, in accordance with the treaty of 211, as a result of its conquest by P. Sulpicius Galba: Polyb. 11.5.8 and 22.8.9–10 with McShane 1964: 107 and n. 50. Later, in the 190s, the Attalids claimed all of Euboea as their share of spoils from Philip: see Polyb. 18.47.10–11 and Livy 33.34.10, with McShane 1964: 130–1. The Romans allowed them only the island of Andros (Livy 31.45.7–8).

[52]   On Attalus I's military setbacks against Macedon and withdrawal from the war in 208, see above, Chapter 3.

[53]   So Hansen 1971: 46–50; McShane 1964: 120; Berthold 1976: 97 n. 4.

had a long-standing friendship or alliance with Prusias; it was an aspect of the traditional Rhodian–Pergamene hostility, and the struggle for power on the Asia Minor coast.[54] As for Philip's attacks in the Hellespont in 202, none was aimed at possessions of Attalus. Though they did contravene the interests of Attalus' friend the Aetolian League, it is not surprising that they brought forth no Attalid attempt to defend the cities under attack. And in 201 Philip's aggressions were far off in the southeast Aegean (and, we have argued, aimed ultimately towards Alexandria), not in the nearby Hellespont. Philip's large naval expedition may have threatened the interests of Rhodes, but Pergamene interests in the southeast Aegean were minimal – which is perhaps why the Macedonian expedition to Caria in 227 under Antigonus III had not led to a confrontation. Moreover, since ca. 204 there were regions subordinate to the Seleucids standing directly between Pergamum and the southeast Aegean, lessening even further any Pergamene interest further south. Philip at the peace conference at Nicaea in 198 later argued that he had been attacked by Attalus without cause (Polyb. 18.6.2); since none of his actions in 202 or 201 was directly aimed at Pergamum, one can see why he made that claim.[55]

Political scientists who have studied the processes by which balances of power are created by smaller states in their attempt to resist a rising system hegemon have argued that only in moments of perceived extreme danger to the entire multipolar system do the intense local or regional rivalries of these states, on which they normally focus and which militate against alliance-making against a larger but somewhat distant power, get put aside. As Wohlforth puts it: "the systemic imperative may need to reach extremes in order to overwhelm local considerations."[56] In this respect it is striking that only one motive appears in our (skimpy) sources for the Attalid volte-face of 201, one motive that led to the momentary burying of the intense and long-standing regional rivalry between Pergamum and Rhodes in order to create the unusual united front against Philip V – and that motive has to do with what we may indeed call "an extreme systemic imperative." Both Justin and Appian indicate that the Rhodians were leaders at Rome in emphasizing to the Senate the Pact Between the Kings (Justin 30.3.5; App. *Mac.* 4.2), and

[54] McShane 1964: 120. The Rhodians and Prusias had in fact been formal military allies against Pergamum during the war over Byzantium in 220 (see Berthold 1984: 95).
[55] See Walbank 1967: 544.
[56] Wohlforth 2002: 102. The "myopia" caused by regional rivalries is one of Wohlforth's lists of difficulties that hinder the attempts of smaller states to balance against a rising system hegemon.

three sources indicate the close connection between this Rhodian embassy and a parallel embassy from Pergamum (Livy 31.2.1; Justin 30.3.5; App. *Mac.* 4.2). Hence the strong probability is that when the Rhodian envoys at Rome in late 201 warned the Roman Senate about the pact, the Pergamene envoys with them at Rome were in strong support.[57]

This is, admittedly, only indirect evidence of Pergamene motivation, and in the absence of direct evidence about the motives behind Attalus' decision we can only speculate. But given the implications of Livy, Appian, and Justin, it seems probable that the Rhodian revelation to Attalus of the scale and nature of the pact between Philip and Antiochus was what led to Attalus' decision for war against Philip – with the Rhodians as allies – while Philip still could be resisted. The Pact Between the Kings constituted a threat to the entire Hellenistic state-system, and the appearance of Philip's large forces in the southeast Aegean, and his seizure of the great Ptolemaic naval base at Samos, constituted convincing evidence – along with the concurrent Seleucid offensive against Ptolemaic towns in western Asia Minor (e.g., in the hinterland of Bargylia) – of the pact in devastating operation.[58] The Rhodian–Pergamene military alliance, an unprecedented reversal in the policies of these two states towards each other stretching back decades, can thus be seen as an additional concrete expression of the diplomatic revolution that was taking place in the Greek Mediterranean in 201 as knowledge of the far-reaching and threatening nature of the pact spread.[59]

RHODES AND ROME

Another volte-face, equally as startling, also occurred in that summer of 201. The nature of Rhodian relations with Rome earlier in the third century is a topic that has been hotly debated.[60] But what is abundantly clear is that Rhodian policies in the decade before 201 had worked at

[57] So Briscoe 1973: 43; Gera 1998: 62 n. 9.

[58] So already Walbank 1940: 126 (who did not have the benefit of knowing of the inscription, only published in 2000, which now reveals cooperation between Philip and Seleucid forces in the Bay of Bargylia).

[59] Cf. Polybius' programmatic statement in 14.1a that "the revelation of the policies and character of the kings" was one of the main dynamics of the 144th Olympiad, 204–201 BC (discussed above, Chapter 4).

[60] There was a tradition that Rhodes had a long-standing relationship of informal *amicitia* with the Roman Republic: for sources and discussion, see Schmitt 1957: 1–49 (accepting this tradition), vs. Holleaux 1935: 30–46 (who denies authenticity). Konterini 1983 has shown, on the basis of a recently discovered inscription dealing with Rhodian diplomacy with Aetolia ca. 200, that detailed Rhodian knowledge of Rome at that point was in fact minimal (see esp. 31–2).

cross-purposes to Rome, and that the Rhodian government had especially been against Roman intervention in Greek affairs. Rhodian participation in the Greek efforts at mediation in the First Macedonian War had been persistent in 209–206, and had been against Roman interests as the Senate saw them, for the *Patres* were opposed to any mediation of the war in Greece: they wished instead for Philip V to remain distracted by this war so that any ambitions he might have about invading Italy were moot. In addition, as we have argued in this study, a good case can be made that the mediation efforts of 209–206 had been directed primarily at establishing peace between the Aetolian League and Philip, independently of Rome if necessary. The sharp clash between Roman purposes and Rhodian interests culminated in autumn 207 in the bitterly anti-Roman speech by the Rhodian diplomat Thrasycrates at the peace talks in Aetolia (Polyb. 11.4–6). And the Rhodians evidently followed up Thrasycrates by helping mediate the eventual separate peace struck between Philip and Aetolia in 206 (App. *Mac.* 4.1) – an Aetolian decision that the Romans angrily viewed as an Aetolian betrayal of their alliance.[61]

Thus the Rhodian Republic in the decade before 201 had followed a policy opposed to the purposes of Rome in Greece, opposed Roman involvement in Greek affairs in general, and in the end – in Thrasycrates' speech to the Aetolians in 207 – displayed itself publicly as overtly hostile to Rome. The Rhodians then worked successfully to bring about a separate Macedonian–Aetolian peace in 206 – a peace that Rome vehemently opposed, and one that injured Rome strategically. Yet suddenly, in summer 201, we find the Rhodians sending ambassadors to Rome and pleading for large-scale Roman intervention in the Greek Mediterranean. The Rhodians made this plea for this Roman intervention although, as Thrasycrates' speech makes clear, they were well aware of the military power of Rome, and that this power might in itself upset the balance of power that had previously existed in the Greek East – the multipolar system that the Rhodians had sought through many vicissitudes to preserve, for it allowed significant freedom of action to the second-tier polities.

Berthold, for one, has denied that the Rhodian action in calling for Roman intervention was a serious reversal of Rhodian policy.[62] But this is simply not the case. In view of the harsh Rhodian words about Roman intentions and behavior in the East expressed publicly in 207, followed by the Rhodian mediation of the peace between Macedon and Aetolia

---

[61] Detailed discussion on the events of 207 and 206: see above, Chapter 3.
[62] See Berthold 1984: 123–4.

in 206, it is clear that the Rhodian action of 201 in sending to Rome to ask for diplomatic and military intervention does indeed constitute a radical change in attitude and policy.[63]

One can now posit that the fundamental problem facing the Rhodian government in 201 was that – whatever threat Roman power ultimately constituted to the Greek states – the tripolar system in the East which the Rhodians had always sought to preserve faced a far more immediate threat from Philip and Antiochus. Indeed, the old balance of power had *already* been destroyed. It had fallen apart, first, because of the increasing collapse of Ptolemaic Egypt, and second, because the collapse of Egypt had led to the alliance between Philip and Antiochus to divide up the weakened Ptolemaic Empire and thus to increase their own power vastly. By the summer of 201 both Philip and Antiochus were engaged in massive military offensives. It was this unprecedented and desperate geopolitical situation that led Rhodes to form a military alliance with King Attalus I of Pergamum – an unprecedented act for Rhodian policy, as it was for Attalid policy. Second, and somewhat later, the situation led the Rhodians to reverse completely their previous stance of opposition to any large Roman intervention in Greek affairs, and instead to send an embassy to Rome to plead for just such intervention.

We can even hazard a guess as to the specific circumstances that forced that Rhodian decision to send an embassy to Rome: for the initial stage of the war against Philip did not go well, leading to Philip's victory over the Rhodian fleet off Lade near Miletus (mid-summer 201). G. T. Griffith long ago made the attractive suggestion that it was the Rhodian defeat at Lade, a defeat that appeared to establish Philip's naval dominance throughout the southeast Aegean, that caused the Rhodian government in desperation to dispatch envoys to Italy for help.[64] The new information from the Rhodian inscription from Bargylia adds a new element to our understanding of Rhodian calculations: for the inscription, which depicts Philip turning over a conquered Ptolemaic town to the advancing army of Antiochus, shows that the Rhodians knew in summer 201 just how closely Philip and Antiochus III were now cooperating.[65]

It is true that the Pergamene–Rhodian war effort against Philip went better later on, and that even though Philip devastated the Pergamene hinterland, by winter 201/200 he was blockaded in Bargylia by the

---

[63] See (e.g.) Schmitt 1957: 60–3.
[64] Griffith 1935b.
[65] See above, Chapter 4. Since Attalus had good relations with the Romans, having been their ally in the First Macedonian War and then having been of vital help to them in procuring the Great Mother of Pessinus for transport to Italy in 205 in order to fulfill an oracle of victory over Hannibal (see above, Chapters 3 and 4), perhaps it was Attalus who encouraged the appeal to Rome.

combined Pergamene and Rhodian fleets; and then in the spring of 200 Philip left the southeast Aegean entirely and went far to the north, to the Hellespont. But unified Rhodian–Pergamene efforts in the summer of 200 to rescue the strategic town of Abydus on the Asian side of the Gallipoli Straits, besieged by a resurgent Philip, were totally ineffectual – and Philip intended to use Abydus, which he eventually captured, as a base for new land operations against Pergamum (Polyb. 16. 29.2).[66] Similarly, unified Rhodian–Pergamene attempts to protect Athens against Macedonian attack in spring 200 (the Athenians having now entered the war: see below) were a failure.[67] Indeed, the severe pressures upon Rhodes caused by the war with Philip are apparent from the fact that when, despite the eventual Roman decision to intervene (see below, Chapter 6), Roman military help still had not arrived in the Aegean by the summer of 200, the Rhodian government seriously considered an Achaean offer to mediate the war against Macedon (Polyb. 16.35.2).[68]

EGYPT AND ROME

The government of the Ptolemies also entered upon a radical change of policy towards Rome in 201. The relationship between the Ptolemaic monarchy and the Roman Republic had been through most of the third century vaguely friendly but distant. To be sure, in 273 Ptolemy II had initiated a diplomatic friendship by sending an embassy to the Roman Senate; this led to a Roman return embassy to Alexandria, and to the conclusion of what was probably informal *amicitia* between Rome and the Ptolemaic state.[69] The interaction was not unique: Ptolemy also initiated a similar relationship of friendship (*philia*) with Carthage in this period – and perhaps in the very same year (cf. App. *Mac.* 1).[70]

---

[66]   Ineffectual Rhodian–Pergamene help to Abydus: Polyb. 16.30.7, 31.3, 34.1, and Livy 31.16.6–8; cf. Wiemer 2002: 220. Few will follow the baroque thesis of Golan 1985 that Rhodes purposely allowed Abydus to fall to Philip in order to create another piece of useful atrocity propaganda against the Macedonian king.
[67]   See Wiemer 2002: 220.
[68]   See Burton 2003: 358. Wiemer 2002: 218, cf. 208 n. 7, dismisses this Achaean effort too quickly.
[69]   Eutrop. 2.15; Dio frg. 41 = Zon. 8.6; Dion. Hal. 20.14.1–2; Val. Max. 4.3.9; Justin 18.2.9; cf. Gruen 1984: 62–3.
[70]   Discussion: Lampela 1998: 39. But Lampela (33–7) is unconvincing that the Ptolemies and Rome contracted a formal treaty of friendship in 273: note App. *Sic.* 1, where the Ptolemaic government pleads a relationship of friendship (φιλία) with Rome – the same relationship it has with Carthage – as the reason for refusing Carthage a loan during the First Punic War. An argument based on an actual treaty would have been much stronger.

Whatever this "friendship" struck up with Rome in 273, the two states remained merely on each other's distant horizon in subsequent decades. There is no evidence that the *amicitia* encompassed trade agreements; in the third century there does not appear to have been much commerce between Rome and Egypt.[71] The government of Ptolemy III was neutral during the First Punic War (see App. *Sic.* 1). The Senate probably sent an embassy to Alexandria in 241 announcing the successful conclusion of the great war; in Roman tradition, this event – anticipating much later developments – became a (most improbable) offer of aid to Egypt against the threat of the Seleucids.[72] The Egyptian stance of neutrality towards the western powers continued in the Second Punic War. In 215 Ptolemy IV gave sanctuary to the Campanian noble Decius Magius, who opposed Hannibal's harsh rule in Capua, when Magius escaped from Punic captivity; but Magius was not a pro-Roman and he refused to fight on the side of Rome against an independent Capua (Livy 23.10.3–13). When an anti-Roman government under King Hieronymus took power at Syracuse after the death of Rome's friend Hiero II, Ptolemy IV maintained the traditional Ptolemaic ties of friendship with the government of Syracuse – although the Ptolemaic court also accepted exiles who opposed Hieronymus.[73] In 211 or 210 the Roman Senate sent an embassy to Alexandria to buy a large amount of Egyptian grain, because of a severe shortage of grain at Rome caused by the war in Italy (Polyb. 9.11a). This embassy is probably the one that in Livy renews *amicitia* with the Ptolemaic regime (27.4.10). But the nature of this "friendship" is clear from the fact that the Romans sought to buy the grain: they were not asking Ptolemy IV to give it to them as a gift, nor did Ptolemy offer to do so. While it is likely that Ptolemy agreed to this business deal, not even that is certain. In sum: down to ca. 210 the relationship between Rome and Alexandria remained friendly and correct but hardly close.[74]

---

[71]   See Peremens and van't Dack 1972: 667; Gruen 1984: 674–6; admitted even by Lampela 1998: 48, despite a strenuous effort to prove the opposite.
[72]   See Eutrop. 3.1, with Gruen 1984: 676; Lampela 1998: 52–5, after noting the historical improbability of Roman military aid to Alexandria against the Seleucid Empire in 241, and acknowledging that Eutropius also has the Seleucid king wrong, is inclined to believe the offer was made because the Senate knew it would not be accepted. This seems too baroque.
[73]   Hieronymus, the new king of Syracuse, sent an embassy to announce his accession and maintain the Egyptian connection which Syracuse had long had: Polyb. 7.2.2. But Hieronymus' uncle, who broke with the new king's anti-Roman policies, also found refuge in Alexandria: see Livy 24.26.1 and 26.6, with Huss 1976: 173–5.
[74]   See Walbank 1967: 137. Doubts that Ptolemy agreed to sell the grain: Heinen 1972: 640. But Livy 31.9 suggests (though does not prove) the opposite. Lampela 1998: 61 and 62, unaccountably sees this grain deal as war-time "humanitarian aid" to Rome on the part of Ptolemy IV.

That the Ptolemaic government in this period pursued its own traditional interests, in which Rome was barely present, is also shown – as with Rhodes – by the persistent Ptolemaic efforts to bring peace between Philip V and the Aetolian League during the First Macedonian War. Envoys from Egypt, in collaboration with Rhodes and other smaller states, led serious peace-making efforts in 209, 208, and 207; and there is evidence that the mediation was organized at Alexandria from the beginning.[75] In Chapter 3 above, and again in this chapter in examining the volte-face in the Rhodian stance towards Rome in 201, we have already underlined how much those peace efforts ran directly counter to Roman purposes in Greece, since the Senate wanted the war against Philip in Greece to continue – while we have also suggested that the Greek mediating states focused in any case primarily on bringing about a peace between Macedon and Aetolia, separate from Rome.

It appears that in 209–207 both Rhodes and the Ptolemaic government still saw the war in European Greece as fundamentally a war among Greeks. They were interested in restoring good conditions for commerce in Greece and the Aegean; beyond that, the main issue was maintaining a reasonable balance of power among the Greek states of Europe. At first Rome and its interests thus appeared to the mediators as peripheral to what contemporary Greeks called "the Aetolian War." But the Ptolemaic envoys also partook in the mediation effort at the Panaetolian Assembly in autumn 207 that witnessed the violent anti-Roman speech by their Rhodian colleague Thrasycrates. Moreover, our evidence is that far from anyone objecting, Thrasycrates' speech won wide Greek support.[76] Thus, whereas down to 210 Roman–Ptolemaic relations had been friendly but distant, Roman and Ptolemaic interests actually clashed during the attempted mediations of the war in Greece between 209 and 207. This is admitted even by Lampela, who in general seeks to emphasize the solidity of the Ptolemaic–Roman relationship before 200: "Ptolemy IV's policy towards Rome was friendly, but not particularly so at that time." Exactly my point.[77] And it is in this context of friendly Ptolemaic relations with Macedon (and much more distant relations with Rome) that we find the Alexandrian government in 204–203

---

[75] See Habicht 1982: 136–7 with n. 80, on the basis of *ISE* no. 33 (cf. above, Chapter 3, pp. 94–5).

[76] See Polyb. 11.6.9; cf. App. *Mac.* 3.2.

[77] Lampela 1998: 71 n. 233. On the purposes of the Greek mediators, see above, Chapter 3. Meadows 1995: 55–6, who like Lampela 1998 sees a long history of sincere Roman–Ptolemaic friendship throughout the third century, makes no mention of the Egyptian role in the mediations of 209–207.

seeking Philip V himself as the father-in-law of the new child-king Ptolemy V and protector of his regime.[78]

The Ptolemaic turn to Rome for help in 201 thus represents almost as sharp a volte-face towards Roman intervention in the East as that of the Rhodians themselves. What caused it? In the years before 201 the government of Ptolemy V, already beset by a massive indigenous rebellion in Upper and Middle Egypt, and with a child on the throne, was engaged in a desperate effort to find a protector against the threat from the outside posed by the Seleucids. Among the first actions of the new government when 5-year-old Ptolemy V officially took the throne in winter 204/203 was the dispatch of three embassies, two of which sought to ameliorate the external threat facing Egypt (Polyb. 15.25.13–15). One embassy urged Antiochus III to maintain his current friendship (*philia*) with the Ptolemies, and not to break the peace treaty between the two states that dated from after the Egyptian victory at the battle of Raphia in 217. A second embassy (as we have just noted) entered into negotiations with Philip V to arrange a marriage-alliance whereby Philip would become the father-in-law of Ptolemy – and the protector of Egypt. The latter was clearly the main hope of the Alexandrian government for protection. A third embassy was dispatched to Rome; it proceeded slowly, and visited various European Greek states first. This occurred when Ptolemaic envoys were hiring mercenaries in Greece to aid Egypt against a potential aggressive war from Antiochus (Polyb. 15.25.16). But while Rome was the final destination of this third embassy, its purpose at Rome is not stated (cf. 15.25.15). Probably its task was simply to announce the accession of Ptolemy V; it is certainly difficult to imagine that this embassy – at a time when Rome was still heavily engaged in the Hannibalic War – would have been seeking Roman aid against the Seleucid threat.[79] It is not even clear that this embassy ever reached Rome.[80]

The problem for Alexandria, of course, was that at the same time that its envoys were negotiating with Philip to become the father-in-law of Ptolemy V and protector of Egypt, Philip was engaged in secret diplomacy with Antiochus to divide up the empire of the Ptolemies, including Egypt itself.[81] The subsequent shocking revelation of the

---

[78] Discussion above, Chapter 4, pp. 143–4.
[79] See Walbank 1967: 485; Gruen 1984: 679; and Meadows 1995: 53 and n. 47, vs. Holleaux 1935: 50 and 71–2. Ptolemy of Megalopolis, who headed the third embassy, evidently said that it was sent primarily because of Alexandrian internal politics, in an effort by the Ptolemaic prime minister Agathocles to send his rivals away from Egypt (see Polyb. 15.25.15 with Walbank 1967: 438 and 480).
[80] Cf. Meadows 1995: 53 and n. 47.
[81] Detailed discussion above, Chapter 4, pp. 143–4 and 148.

Pact Between the Kings (cf. Polyb. 14.1a) was what must have led the Alexandrian government to seek help now in the only place left where decisive help could be found: Rome (autumn 201). That is the story we find in Justin's epitome of the first-century BC historian Pompeius Trogus. In Justin, an Egyptian embassy is sent to Rome because of know-ledge at Alexandria of the pact between Philip and Antiochus, the purpose of which is to divide Egypt and its possessions among the two kings; the embassy announces the pact to the Senate and asks for protection. In Justin this embassy is so desperate for Roman protection that it also asks for a Roman *tutor regis*, a special personal protector, for young Ptolemy V (30.2.8).[82] The Egyptians find themselves supported at Rome by embassies from Rhodes and from Attalus of Pergamum (30.3.5). The Roman response in Justin is to send out an embassy whose purpose is to demand that both Philip and Antiochus refrain from attacking Egypt (30.3.3).[83] The purpose of this Roman embassy in Justin clearly equates to the purpose of the Roman embassy sent to the East in spring 200 as described by Polybius (16.27.5): to warn Philip away from attacking the Greeks, and to bring about an accommodation between Antiochus and Ptolemy.[84]

The account of the Egyptian embassy to Rome in Justin 30.2–3 has sometimes been doubted; in other words, no Ptolemaic embassy with a message about the alleged pact ever appeared before the Senate.[85] It is true that Justin/Pompeius Trogus is the only source which mentions the Ptolemaic warning and plea to the Senate, while in Appian the Senate receives a warning about the pact from the Rhodians and the Pergamenes, and the Ptolemies are not mentioned. Doubts have been increased by Justin's further story that the Alexandrian government also asked Rome for a *tutor regis*, especially because the alleged "personal protector" in this tradition is the young M. Aemilius Lepidus.[86] In fact, we will see that a fair case can be made for accepting even some version of this latter information.[87] And although little survives of Pompeius Trogus, we know that ancient opinion ranked Trogus as a fine historian on the level of Sallust, Livy, and Tacitus. That is, while Justin is only an epitomator, he is deriving his material from a first-rate and responsible historical writer.[88] And here one may note two indisputable facts: at

[82]   *legatos Alexandrini ad romanos misere, orantes ut tutelam pupili susciperent tuerenturque regnum Aegypti, quod iam Philippum et Antiochum facta inter se pactione divisisse dicebant.*
[83]   *Mittuntur itaque legati, qui Philippo et Antiocho denuntient, regno Aegypti abstineant.*
[84]   Cf. Meadows 1995: 49–50.
[85]   See, e.g., Gruen 1984: 677.
[86]   See, e.g., Briscoe 1973: 57; Huss 1976: 169.
[87]   See below.
[88]   See Richter 1987: 148–9.

Abydus in summer 200, a Roman envoy demanded the end of Philip's aggressions against Ptolemaic holdings on pain of war (Polyb. 16.34.3–4), while that autumn this same envoy, along with his two colleagues, successfully turned Antiochus III away from an invasion of Egypt proper – despite the crushing victory which the Great King had just won over the Ptolemaic army at Panium in Judaea.[89] Hence the actions and concerns of the embassy sent by the Senate to the Greek East in 200 make it clear that by spring 200 the *Patres* perceived there were simultaneous aggressions from both Philip *and* Antiochus taking place against Ptolemaic Egypt, and had come to think of those aggressions as somehow linked together into a single problem – to be handled by an embassy conveying a similar message to both monarchs. It is logical to assume that this analysis did not originate with the Senate itself, but rather that the *Patres* were responding, as Justin indicates, to disturbing information about Philip and Antiochus brought before it by a desperate government at Alexandria, increasingly the victim of both kings.[90]

ATHENS

In late 201 BC the Athenian government also took a radical decision: it, too, asked the Roman Republic for military intervention against Philip V. For thirty years, since the Athenians' successful rebellion from Macedon in 229, the Athenian government had followed a policy of neutrality towards the great Greek monarchies (see Polyb. 5.106.6–7: explicit). But neutrality has its nuances, the Athenians were especially friendly with Ptolemaic Egypt, and they had been involved in the attempt to mediate peace between Macedon and the Aetolian League in 209 (Livy 27.30.9–10) – a mediation probably organized from Alexandria and at cross-purposes with Rome, as we have seen.[91] The precipitating cause of serious new trouble between Athens and Macedon was, Polybius evidently said, a minor event: the profanation of the Mysteries of Eleusis by two Acarnanians – men from a state that was an ally of Macedon – and the subsequent execution of these men at Athens. The date for the profanation is secure: mid-September 201 (the religious celebrations took place at the autumnal equinox); the executions followed soon thereafter.

[89] On the Roman role in preventing a Seleucid invasion of Egypt after Panion, see conveniently Eckstein 2006: Ch. 7, and in more detail below, Chapter 6.
[90] On the Egyptian embassy at Rome in 200, see also Livy 31.9.1–4.
[91] Detailed discussion: above, Chapter 3. The special Athenian friendship with Egypt in the late third century: see Polyb. 5.106.7–8; Habicht 1992.

The government of the Acarnanian Confederation then complained to Philip (then in Caria), or to Philip's government in Macedon, and this in turn led to an invasion of Attica by Acarnanian troops aided by Macedonian forces (probably in November 201).[92]

At some point between the spring of 201 and the spring of 200, the Athenian Assembly took another anti-Macedonian action: it voted to eliminate the two Athenian tribes that honored the Antigonid dynasty (the tribes *Antigonis* and *Demetrias*). These two tribes had been added to the traditional Athenian ten tribes more than a century earlier, in 307–306, following the liberation of Athens from the Macedonian dynast Cassander by Antigonus I and his son Demetrius I, to honor the liberators of the city. In 224 or 223, following the Athenians' successful rebellion against Macedon, a tribe honoring the Ptolemies had been added (*Ptolemais*), which brought the total of Athenian tribes to thirteen; this special new honor given the Ptolemies indicates that beneath official neutrality there was (as Polybius says) a pro-Ptolemaic tilt to the new government.[93] Still, the tribal names honoring the Antigonids had not been dropped: they had survived the Athenian rebellion of 289/288 against Demetrius I, survived the Chremonidean War of the 260s between Athens and Macedon, even survived the successful Athenian rebellion against Macedonian rule in 229. Yet an inscription indicates that sometime in 201/200 the two "Macedonian" tribes were now eliminated, and thus there were for a time only eleven tribes at Athens. But the number was raised to twelve in the spring of 200 when a new tribe was voted into existence: *Attalis*, in honor of King Attalus of Pergamum – a man who was an enemy of Philip and who at this time was at war with Philip. The honor given Attalus in fact occurred in connection with the Athenian declaration of war against Philip.[94]

If the Athenian tribes honoring the Antigonid dynasty were dropped following the Acarnanian–Macedonian raid on Attica ca. November 201 – as most scholars argue – this still seems an Athenian action as radical (or even more radical) than the execution of the Acarnanians after the Mysteries, because the honorific "Macedonian" tribes at Athens

---

[92]   The narrative of these events is in Livy 31.14.6–10, derived from Polybian material (cf. Briscoe 1973: 95). There is no need to push the Acarnanian invasion into spring 200, despite Warrior 1996 (whose chronology ends up with an improbably compressed sequence of events in spring 200). See rather Ferguson 1932: 141 n. 1; Habicht 1982: 44–5.

[93]   See Polyb. 5.106.7, with Habicht 1992: 74–7. This helps explain Athenian participation with the Ptolemies in the attempted mediation between Aetolia and Philip in 209 (Livy 27.30.4; see above, Chapter 3).

[94]   On the date and circumstances of the creation of the tribe *Attalis*, see Ferguson 1932: 141, n. 1.

had survived much greater and more direct conflicts with Macedon.[95] But it is possible (though less likely) that the vote to eliminate the "Macedonian" tribes actually preceded the Acarnanian attack of ca. November 201, for the reorganization of the territory of Attica and of the Athenian population from thirteen tribes down into eleven tribes was a complex political process involving multiple decisions concerning how to redistribute the ca. 140 Athenian demes (neighborhoods) within the new tribal system, yet we know that although the eleven-tribe organization did not last long, this process was in fact completed; an inscription of spring 200 records the completed system in operation. Such a reorganization will have taken a significant amount of time – certainly several months.[96]

In any case, it is clear that the violent reaction of the Athenians to the alleged profanation of the Mysteries by the two Acarnanians in September 201 did not come out of nowhere, but was likely an expression of preexisting anger at Philip and those states allied with him: it was part of a pattern that included the enormous insult of eliminating the "Macedonian" tribes.[97] To judge from Livy 31.14.6 and 9, both of which passages are drawn from Polybian material, Polybius chastised the Athenians for beginning a conflict with Macedon over such a passing incident as the profanation of the Mysteries by the two Acarnanians.[98] But this does not mean that Polybius thought the profanation of the Mysteries was the real cause of events; he may simply have been criticizing the Athenians for employing here an unjustifiable excuse (*prophasis*) for a radical action behind which lurked deeper and truer and more justifiable concerns.[99]

Perhaps the source of Athenian anger – as was true of other Greek states – had to do with Philip's savage behavior in the Hellespont in 202: the destruction of the city of Cius and the enslavement of its population, followed by the enslavement of the population of Thasos

---

[95]   The radical nature of the Athenian action in eliminating the tribes: McDonald and Walbank 1937: 191. The dropping of the "Macedonian" tribes as a reaction to the Acarnanian attack: so Ferguson 1932: 140, and 141 n. 1; Habicht 1982: 145–6. Best discussion of the inscription showing eleven tribes: Pritchett 1954: esp. 163–4.

[96]   Months, not weeks, required for such a reorganization: Habicht 1982: 147.

[97]   McDonald and Walbank 1937: 190–2.

[98]   Polybius evidently saw the execution of the two Acarnanians as disgraceful (*foede*: Livy 31.14.6), and the stated cause of the conflict insufficient (*haudquaquam digna causa*: 14.9). The criticism is emphasized by Habicht 1982: 143–4.

[99]   The parallel would be Polybius' criticism of Hannibal for beginning war with Rome over Roman interference at Saguntum, a situation where he had a weak case, when that was not the real reason for his hostility – which had to do with the Roman seizure of Sardinia seventeen years before, a situation where Carthage had a strong case: see Polyb. 3.15 and 3.30.3–4 with Eckstein 1989.

as well, contrary to pledged promises from the king. Polybius is clear that these actions made Philip widely unpopular.[100] But one other event should be noted: in the summer of 201, well *before* the alleged profanation of the Mysteries by men belonging to a state allied to Macedon, a new Athenian tribal cycle began, and the tribe chosen (and chosen out of order) to be first tribe in the rotation – the place of special honor – was the Athenian tribe of *Ptolemais*, the tribe created in 224 or 223 to honor the Ptolemies.[101] In the situation of summer 201, this unusual choice is not likely to be an accident; the special honoring of the Ptolemies, when combined with the escalating anger against men associated with Philip a month or two later, and then the elimination of the "Macedonian" tribes shortly after that, suggests that the Athenian anger at Philip in summer/autumn 201 had somehow to do with his actions against the Ptolemies. This was recognized long ago.[102] Perhaps Philip's assaults in the spring and summer of 201 on the Ptolemaic possessions in the southeast Aegean upset the Athenians. But of course there is another (or a contributing) possibility: that the Athenians had learned of the Pact Between the Kings (from the Rhodians, or from Attalus?) – that is, they had learned of Philip's and Antiochus' intended destruction of Athens' friend the Ptolemies and of the entire Hellenistic balance of power that had allowed Athens to follow an independent course ever since 229.[103]

According to Livy, there were three separate embassies from Athens that came to the Romans seeking military aid against Philip. To judge from its place in the Livian text, the first came to Rome in late 201; probably it complained of the raid on Attica launched by Philip and the Acarnanians.[104] There was a second embassy at the beginning of the consular year 200 (*Atheniensium nova legatio*: Livy 31.5.6), announcing how Athens was under severe threat from Philip. A third embassy headed to Rome in autumn 200 to complain about the actual siege of Athens now begun by Philip's army; the Athenian envoys encountered Roman forces as they were landing in Illyria (Livy 31.14.3, cf. 22.4). Pausanias saw an inscription at Athens honoring Cephisodorus, the head of an embassy seeking help from the Romans (1.36.6), and in the 1930s just such an inscription was discovered and published.[105] Some scholars wish

---

[100]   See Polyb. 15.22–4, discussed above in relation to Rhodes.
[101]   The special honoring of *Ptolemais* in summer 201: Ferguson 1932: 141, 143.
[102]   See, rightly, McDonald and Walbank 1937: 191.
[103]   Suggested by McDonald and Walbank 1937: 191. Cf. Polybius' general statement at 14.1a on the dismay caused by the spread of this knowledge among the Greeks.
[104]   Livy 31.1.9–2.1; cf. also App. *Mac.* 4. The raid: Livy 31.14.6–10. Date of this attack: see above, n. 92.
[105]   Meritt 1936: 419–28.

to combine into one embassy Livy's first and second Athenian embassies, which appear in Rome closely together in time and with similar complaints about Philip; this is possible, though it requires significant confusion on Livy's part.[106] One of these embassies to Rome in winter 201/200 (if there was more than one) was probably headed by Cephisodorus. The Athenians themselves did not declare war officially on Philip until the spring of 200,[107] but there is no reason to doubt the tone the Athenians at Rome employed to describe Philip's conduct. If the Athenians were motivated to punish Philip's allies the Acarnanians at the Eleusinia of September 201 because of bitterness at the news of Philip's aggressions in the Aegean (perhaps including news of the pact) – as is suggested by the vote earlier in the summer of 201 to honor the Ptolemies by specially placing *Ptolemais* first in the new tribal cycle – then it is clear how strongly the Athenians would have supported the reports about Philip and Antiochus given to the Senate at that time by the Rhodians, Pergamenes, and Ptolemies.

The Athenian action in sending an embassy to Rome to seek help against Philip represents – as with so many other Greek states – a sharp change in attitude towards Rome. Previous relations between Athens and Rome had probably been correct and friendly but distant. Senatorial envoys had visited Athens in 228 to announce the Roman victory against the Ardiaei and the end of the piratical threat in the southern Adriatic (Polyb. 2.12.8, cf. Zon. 8.19). The visit might have constituted the creation of a relation of informal *amicitia* – or perhaps not, and in any case there is no attested connection between Athens and Rome for the next twenty years. But in 209 Athens was one of the polities that sought to mediate between the Aetolian League and Philip V (Livy 27.30.4, from Polybius); as we have noted, this mediation was probably co-ordinated by Alexandria, and paid little attention to Roman interests.[108]

Yet the Athenians are listed as *adscripti* on the Roman side at the peace sworn between Philip and Rome at Phoenice in Epirus in 205 (Livy 29.12.14). This is odd, since no Athenian action in support of Rome during the war is known – whereas (as we have just seen) the Athenians had engaged in mediation in 209 that was contrary to Roman interests. But while the Athenians appear in the list of *adscripti* on the Roman side, they appear at the very end, almost as an appendix; hence it has long been suspected that they are a false addition to the list, added by Roman Annalists who later emphasized the role of the Athenian pleas against Philip in bringing on the second war with Macedon. The goal of the false addition would be to justify the Roman response to

---

[106]   Gruen 1984: 386 n. 157; Warrior 1996: 40–1.
[107]   Sources and discussion in Habicht 1982.
[108]   Discussion: above, Chapter 3, pp. 94–100.

Athenian pleas in 201/200. Holleaux's point here remains strong: if the Athenians were publicly and officially friends and protégés of Rome from 205 onwards, it is unlikely that Philip or his offiicials – anxious above all to avoid another war with Rome (as Polyb. 16.24.2–3 makes clear) – would have authorized the attacks on Athens that began ca. November 201.[109] Nor if Athens had been an *adscriptus* on the Roman side to the Peace of Phoenice could Philip in late summer 200, after himself besieging Athens and ravaging the Attic countryside, have nevertheless warned the Romans against doing anything that might violate the Peace (Polyb. 16.24.5–7).[110]

Thus the Athenian decision to approach Rome for help – like the similar decisions of the Rhodians and the Ptolemies – represented another aspect of the diplomatic revolution that shook the Greek Mediterranean after 203/202. It was a volte-face caused by the cascading sequence of events incumbent first upon the increasing collapse of Egypt, and then the revelation to the Greeks of the Pact Between the Kings.

AN AETOLIAN APPEAL?

Did the Aetolian League send an embassy of appeal to Rome in this period as well – an embassy that was bluntly rejected by the Senate on grounds that the Aetolians had proven themselves unreliable allies during the First Macedonian War? This is the ancient tradition; it would mean that the Roman Senate in this period received a total of five separate complaints against Philip, or Philip and Antiochus, from five different Greek states.[111] The date of the Aetolian embassy is, however, uncertain, and the historicity of the embassy has been doubted – most famously by Badian.[112]

The issue is difficult, but a good case can be made that the Aetolian embassy of complaint is historical, and a fair, if speculative, case can be made that it occurred in autumn 202. If so, the embassy had no direct relationship to the revelation of the existence of the pact between Philip and Antiochus, which only became known at Rome a year later, in autumn 201; rather, it dealt with separate, earlier aggressions on the part of Philip – aggressions which the *Patres* chose to ignore. Perhaps the Aetolian plea

---

[109]   Holleaux 1935: 266. On the *foederi adscripti* to the Peace of 205, see above, Chapter 3, pp. 113–14.

[110]   Gruen 1984: 441 n. 15.

[111]   That is: Rhodes; Pergamum; the Ptolemaic government; Athens; and the Aetolian League.

[112]   Badian 1958b: 208–11; earlier: Passarini 1931: 266. Following Badian: Ferrary 1988: 51 and n. 26. Most recent discussion: Warrior 1996: 84 n. 16, who is neutral on historicity.

added somewhat to the general atmosphere of suspicion of Philip at Rome (cf. Livy 31.1.9). But the rejection of the Aetolians by the Senate would also show that down through autumn 202 the stance of the *Patres* towards intervention in the Greek East remained what it had always been: reluctant. This, in turn, would be further proof that some unusual eastern development caused the sudden and radical shift in senatorial attitude in late 201.[113] Such a conclusion depends, however, both on the historicity and the date of the Aetolian embassy.

An Aetolian embassy to Rome complaining about Philip's aggressions appears in both Livy and Appian. Livy 31.29–31 depicts a debate at the Panaetolian Assembly of spring 199: Roman envoys have come to urge the Aetolians to join the war now being waged against Philip by Pergamum, Rhodes, Athens, and Rome; Athenian and Macedonian envoys are also present at this assembly, the former to support Rome, the latter to urge the Aetolians to stay out of the war. In the ensuing debate the Macedonian envoy remarks on the arrogance and fickleness of the Romans, noting that the Senate had recently insultingly rejected Aetolian requests for aid concerning Philip's violation of peace (31.29.4).[114] Scholars are agreed that the Livian depiction of this spring 199 assembly is based on Polybian material – as is the case with most of Livy's narrative of events in the East in this period (33.10.10, explicit).[115] Meanwhile, Appian – clearly based on a Greek source as well – has an Aetolian embassy of complaint against Philip coming to the Senate in this period, and being rejected (*Mac.* 4). As Badian admits, the onus is thus on those who would deny the historicity of the Aetolian embassy.[116]

There are no overwhelming arguments for denying the historicity of the embassy. Regarding the statement by the Macedonian envoy in Livy 31.29.4 about the previous Roman rejection of the Aetolians, one would have to argue that this is a false insertion into the Polybian narrative by a Roman Annalist – and there are no good grounds for why inserting this particular story would be conducive to the *maiestas populi Romani* (the type of propagandistic historical writing for which the Annalists are well known). To be sure, in his own speech in Livy 31.31 the Roman envoy L. Furius Purpurio makes no response to the

[113] Cf. Holleaux 1935: 293–7.
[114] " 'An imitar,' inquit unus ex legatis, 'Romanorum licentiam, an levitatem dicam, mavultis?' Qui eum legatis vestris Romae responderi ita iussissent, 'Quid ad nos venitis, Aetoli, sine quorum auctoritate pacem cum Philippo fecistis?' " The reference is to Philip's violations of the peace treaty he had concluded with Aetolia in 206, separate from Rome.
[115] See Badian 1958b: 210; cf. Walbank 1967: 530–1; Briscoe 1973: 130.
[116] Badian 1958b: 210.

Macedonian remark. But, despite Badian, this does not mean that the Macedonian remark is a later insertion.[117] Furius' speech is simply focused on refuting the main thrust of the speech of the Macedonian, which puts forth serious accusations of Roman oppression of Greeks and other Roman allies in Italy and Sicily as a warning to the Aetolians about what Roman policy in Greece might become. Moreover, these accusations about Roman oppression of former allies could be combatted, more or less (see 31.31.6–16), but regarding the previous Roman rejection of the Aetolian embassy – and hence the alleged Roman hypocrisy in now urging the Aetolians to join the war against Philip – there was no reponse that Furius could make without making the situation worse, for any response would involve rehearsing again the conflicted history of Roman–Aetolian relations. Not every accusation requires a specific answer; so perhaps in Polybius the Roman envoy Furius simply took the path of diplomatic reticence on this point. To conclude that Livy 31.29.4 is a false Annalistic insertion into generally Polybian material simply because of the absence of a Roman response to the accusation at 31.29.4 is thus a long leap.

A second argument is that App. *Mac.* 4, including its information about the Aetolian embassy and its blunt rejection, cannot be trusted. The passage contains at least two major errors: that Philip V captured Chios in his Aegean campaign of 201, and that the Ptolemaic ruler at the time of the crisis was Ptolemy (IV) Philopator when it was Ptolemy (V) Epiphanes. Moreover, while Livy 31.29 provides no date for the Roman rejection of the Aetolian appeal, Appian appears to place the Roman rejection of the Aetolian appeal *after* the arrival of the Rhodian and Pergamene embassies complaining about Philip, i.e., in late 201 or early 200. If that is where Appian places the Aetolian embassy, the chronology is impossible to accept.[118] The reason is the widespread ancient tradition (including in Appian) that the embassies from Rhodes and Pergamum were crucial in deciding the Senate to push for a powerful military intervention in the East.[119] But if the Senate had already decided on a major Roman intervention against Philip before the arrival of the Aetolians, it would make no sense that the *Patres* would then alienate the Aetolians by insultingly rejecting their appeal for aid against Philip: on the contrary, the Aetolians at that point would have been offering themselves as a welcome addition to the anti-Philip alliance.

---

[117] Badian 1958b: 210 and n. 3.

[118] Despite Meloni 1955: 45–9; Ferro 1960: 46–7; Derow 1979: 7–8; Meadows 1995: 51–2.

[119] Livy 31.2.1–2; Justin 30.2.3–4; App. *Mac.* 4; cf. Polyb. 16.24.4 (and 15.20.6 – on which, see below, Chapter 6).

The strategic and military value of Aetolia is precisely why the Romans, once they had indeed decided on the new war (winter 201/200), now made persistent diplomatic efforts to get the Aetolians to join them. Our literary sources record a Roman overture to Aetolia first in the spring of 200, i.e., not long after the point when Appian appears to place the Roman rejection of the Aetolian plea for help; and we have seen that the Romans made a second effort in the spring of 199.[120] In addition, a recently discovered inscription from Rhodes appears to indicate a third, previously unknown Roman effort, this time employing the Rhodians as intermediaries to try to persuade Aetolia to join the war.[121] All these efforts failed – but they illustrate how much the Roman government in 200–199 appreciated the value of Aetolian military help, and how eager the Romans were to get it. This makes it very unlikely that an Aetolian initiative coming in winter 201/200, after the appeals of the other Greek states, would have been rebuffed. Further, Gruen points out that a passage in Livy which is based on Polybian material shows that in summer 201, before any effort was made by Rhodes and Pergamum to gain support at Rome, Attalus sought to get the Aetolians as allies of Pergamum and Rhodes against Philip but was rejected (31.46.4); and the Aetolians rejected a similar Rhodian–Pergamene request again in summer 200 (31.15.9–10). No one doubts the historicity of these passages.[122] But the Aetolian rejection of the offered alliance of Rhodes and Pergamum against Philip in summer 201 (Livy 31.46.4) makes no sense if it occurred at the same time that the Aetolians, fearing Philip, sent to Rome asking for help against him: on the contrary, the Aetolians at that point would have been glad of the Rhodian–Pergamene offer (and negotiations regarding alliance would have ensued). Conversely, Aetolian caution after an insulting Roman rebuff would explain why the Aetolians *were* unwilling to involve themselves against Philip in summer 201.[123] If the Aetolian embassy to Rome is historical, it thus must precede summer 201.[124]

[120] See Polyb. 16.27.4 (spring 200); Livy 31.29–31 (spring 199); cf. Holleaux 1935: 293 n. 1.
[121] See Konterini 1983: esp. 31–2; followed by Ager 1991: 22.
[122] Perhaps Konterini's inscription should be linked to this second Rhodian–Pergamene effort.
[123] See rightly Gruen 1984: 396 n. 14; earlier: Holleaux 1935: 293–7; Griffith 1935: 5–6. Polyb. 16.24.4, which shows Philip in summer 201 fearing both the Aetolians and embassies to Rome, is too vague in phraseology to argue that he specifically feared an Aetolian embassy to Rome, for the reference might well be to an Aetolian military attack: see Walbank 1967: 530.
[124] The hypothesis of Holleaux 1935: 293 n. 1; followed by Walbank 1940: 36; Oost 1954: 41; cf. Gruen 1984: 396 and n. 14 (with new arguments).

This means, however, that we are forced to rearrange the narrative of Appian in order to make it "fit" both with what our other ancient evidence suggests and with a modern reconstruction. This is clearly dangerous methodology.[125] Two factors mitigate the situation. First, we cannot be certain that Appian's text actually places the Aetolian embassy in 201. App. *Mac.* 4 looks very much like a summary of Polybius' Book 16, and Polybius says that his organization of events sometimes required him to lump together events of two years into one discussion (cf. 15.24a).[126] Second, there is an obvious point when the Aetolians might have gone to Rome to protest Philip's violation of peace. We know that Philip in the summer of 202 attacked cities in the Hellespont that were members of the Aetolian League: Lysimacheia, Cius, and Chalcedon. Polybius says these actions were violations by Philip of his peace treaty of 206 with Aetolia (15.24.7–10). Thus from Polybius we have specific Macedonian actions which equate in nature to the Aetolian complaints at Rome in Appian, and the Polybian date for them is summer 202.[127] And Livy (31.1.9) even lists the Aetolian complaints about Philip's violation of the peace of 206 as one of the reasons for the Roman decision of 201–200.[128] This is obviously false as a motive for the Roman intervention of 200 in the East, since Rome had angrily opposed that separate peace. It is, however, another indication of the tradition that the Aetolians had complained to Rome about this, for what else but the Aetolian complaint could be the origin of this idea?[129]

There is one more piece of evidence to bring into play – powerful evidence that has previously received no attention in this context. Plautus' comic play *Stichus* was produced at Rome in the autumn of 200. The play is in part a bitter commentary on the economic plight of ordinary Romans displaced by the violence of the long war against Hannibal; they often cannot even find enough to eat (cf. 167–70). At one point the protagonist Gelasimus hopes to salve his hunger by eating at the home of his patron Epignomus, who has recently returned from the East a wealthy man. But Gelasimus is denied a place at Epignomus' table, denied even the lowest place at the table which he begs for, because Epignomus is entertaining nine envoys from the Greek city of Ambracia (494–504). Plautus' satirical political point seems to be that powerful people in Rome in this period are paying more attention to the problems of Greeks than to the plight of ordinary Romans displaced by the

---

[125] The critique of Holleaux by Badian 1958b: 208–9, and Derow 1979: 7–8.
[126] Cf. Dorey 1960: 9 and n. 1.
[127] See Griffith 1935: 5–6.
[128] *Infensos Philippo . . . ob infidam adversus Aetolos aliosque regionis eiusdem socios pacem.*
[129] Cf. Briscoe 1973: 52–3.

Hannibalic War, a sentiment that in itself indicates the reluctance of the Roman populace at this point about any new involvement in the East. Nor is it likely to be coincidental that this play was staged as part of the Plebeian Games of autumn 200 held by the aedile Cn. Baebius – whereas the Senate's eventual proposal to intervene in the East against Philip (spring 200) was publicly and at first successfully opposed by the aedile's relative Q. Baebius, tribune of the plebs in 200, on grounds that the Roman People had been burdened with too many wars (Livy 31.6.4). Indeed, the *comitia centuriata*, at Baebius' urging, at first overwhelmingly voted down the senatorial proposal for war with Philip (Livy 31.6).[130] But beyond the general confirmation of the political situation which *Stichus* offers, most interesting is the specific origin of the nine greedy Greek envoys in the play; they are said to be from Ambracia (*Stich.* 494) – and Ambracia was a major city of the Aetolian League.[131] At least *prima facie*, this looks to be quite contemporary evidence that an embassy from the Aetolian League had indeed recently come to Rome with its problems: this event was familiar enough to the Roman audience in 200 to be the subject of a bitter joke in the *Stichus*.

All in all, a powerful case can be made for the historicity of the Aetolian embassy to Rome to complain about Philip. And a fair case, though speculative, can be made for placing this embassy in the autumn of 202 – as Holleaux saw long ago. This finding has two important implications. First, if Holleaux is correct, then the senatorial rejection of the Aetolian embassy shows that as of the autumn of 202, the *Patres* were reluctant to reengage with events occurring east of the Adriatic.[132] Second, the incident shows that the Aetolian complaints – concerning Philip V's aggressions against polities that were adherents of the Aetolians in the Hellespont region – were not enough to change this senatorial reluctance.[133] Yet within a year this situation would be radically transformed, with the Senate itself strongly urging and pressuring a reluctant Roman People to declare war against Philip V of Macedon, while also sending out an embassy to Antiochus III concerning that king's advance on Egypt. Assuming the historicity of the Aetolian embassy and that it belongs in autumn 202 – though admittedly, these are large assumptions – it is thus possible for us to perceive that a radical transformation in senatorial attitude occurred sometime between autumn 202 and winter 201/200.[134]

---

[130]   Discussion in detail below, Chapter 6.
[131]   On Ambracia as a major city of the Aetolian League since ca. 230, see Scholten 2000: 150–1.
[132]   Griffith 1935b: 5.
[133]   Ibid.
[134]   Holleaux 1935: 293 n. 1.

Whatever transformed the attitude of the Senate occurred within that year-long interval. And it must have involved issues larger than merely new aggressions by Philip V – for on the above reconstruction the Aetolians had complained to Rome about the new aggressions of Philip in 202 to no avail. There is an obvious answer here – that the *Patres* were affected by the stream of embassies from Greek states arriving in Rome during the autumn of 201 (at least four such embassies), complaining not merely about individual acts of aggression by Philip and by Antiochus, but placing those incidents within a larger and more threatening picture: the picture that emerges from the geopolitical consequences of the Pact Between the Kings.

THE DIPLOMATIC REVOLUTION

It seems likely that without Roman intervention, Philip V and Antiochus III would have reworked the Greek Mediterranean to suit themselves. Only three Greek states sought to oppose them: the Ptolemaic regime, the Republic of Rhodes, and the Kingdom of Pergamum. But the increasing weakness of the Ptolemaic regime was the cause of the geopolitical crisis in the East in the first place; and Pergamum and Rhodes were only second-rank powers, and old rivals brought together into fragile alliance only because of the severity of the threat posed by Philip and Antiochus. Together, Pergamum and Rhodes with great difficulty and initial set-backs were able to hold Philip to a standstill in 201. But they could not have withstood the unified power of the kings, and given the newness and fragility of the Pergamene–Rhodian alliance, one or the other (or both) of these states might well soon have sought an accommodation with the new hegemons of the East. An effort by Attalus of Pergamum in the summer of 201 to gain Greek strength for the anti-Macedonian coalition by attracting the Aetolian League into the war was a failure (Livy 31.46.3–4: from Polybius).[135] Thus in the summer of 201 there was only one alternative to a looming negative future, only one way for the weaker states to save their independence, only one power left to which Egypt, Rhodes, and Pergamum could appeal for desperately needed relief from the combined expansionist aggression of Philip and Antiochus. That power was Rome.[136]

[135] See above, p. 214.
[136] Even if the Aetolian appeal to Rome in 202 is historical (see above), the League by 201 was maintaining neutrality. And the Aetolians' rejection of the attempt of their old friend Attalus to involve them in the struggle against Philip (Livy 31.46.4) indicates both the power of Macedon and the terrible nature of the Pergamene–Rhodian strategic dilemma as long as their horizon was limited to the Greek Mediterranean.

In going to Rome, the governing elites in Alexandria, Pergamum, Rhodes, and Athens (and the Aetolians earlier, if their plea is historical) must have known that the price for Roman intervention in terms of an eventual Roman patronage over a Hellenistic balance of power artificially restored by Roman military power – or even in terms of outright Roman hegemony over Greek affairs – might well be high. That these governments chose to ask Rome for help in the crisis does not mean that Rome had an especially good reputation with them. In fact, the evidence indicates that Rome did not have an especially good reputation with them – certainly because of the brutality of Roman war-making in Greece between 211 and 205, and perhaps in part because of the Roman abandonment of Aetolia after 207.[137] Rather, the conduct of the Greek states seems a classic example of what the political scientist Stephen Walt sees as an inherent dynamic in the creation of alliances between weaker states and stronger ones under conditions of anarchy: weaker states when faced with a crisis turn to the *least*-threatening great power for protection; but least threatening does not mean unthreatening. The choices weaker states face in an anarchy are inherently bleak.[138]

In other words, the Greek governments in 201 faced problems more immediate than the looming power of Rome – for Rome was geographically far away and her power was a problem for the long-term future. In the moment, Roman power was in fact needed, as the weaker Greek governments struggled to deal somehow with the far more pressing problems that Philip and Antiochus would soon emerge through warfare as the all-powerful arbiters of interstate life in the Greek East, or, worse, that either Philip *or* Antiochus (after yet more war) would eventually emerge as the sole and overpowering hegemon over the Greek state-system. In the face of such threats, the possible consequences of Roman intervention were a cost that the governing elites in these states were evidently prepared to pay.

In attempting to deal with the fundamental shift in geopolitics that was occurring in the East, and the immediate and severe threat they confronted from Philip and Antiochus, the Greek governments were engaged in an instinctive "balancing" against the suddenly expanding power of the kings. It is more problematic whether they were consciously seeking such a balance. There is little evidence of explicit Greek theorizing either by political thinkers or by statesmen concerning the "balance of power" – which suggests that no doctrine was being consciously

---

[137]   On the poor Roman reputation among the Greeks ca. 200, see Badian 1970.
[138]   Walt 1984: esp. Chs. 1 and 2.

applied.[139] Indeed, important studies now posit that even in the eighteenth century in Europe, the "classical age" of balancing behavior among nation-states, governmental policy did not often aim consciously at maintaining a balance, but at simply defending the polity; so, under the pressures of interstate anarchy, balancing is often simply the geopolitical outcome of state behavior.[140] This puts into a larger context the conduct of the Greek states in 201 in seeking to defend themselves against the expanding power of the kings: the Greeks' conduct amounted to balancing, but it was the natural and instinctive working out of habits of self-defense within a multipolar anarchic system. Weaker states had been seeking the protection of stronger states against dangerous local threats for centuries in the Greek world – and, for that matter, in the western Mediterranean as well.[141] As Waltz puts it: "We find states forming balances of power whether or not they wish to."[142] This is because balancing is above all a *process*, "an international process which, when operative, tends to create roughly equal distributions of power between opposing states or coalitions of states."[143]

Yet it is reasonable to ask why these states, instead of turning to Rome for help, did not seek to make an accommodation with the rising power of the kings (i.e., adopt a stance of appeasement), or even decide to join with the monarchs to reap their own share of spoils from the faltering Ptolemies. In political-science typology, this type of conduct is called "bandwagoning" behavior.[144] We have been emphasizing the general and rather predictable workings of an anarchic state-system when viewed at the system level, but one answer here may lie, by contrast, in the impact of specific Greek cultural ideals. Instinctive balancing was clearly habitual among Greek states, and the entire history of Greek interstate relations is in one sense a history of wars of adjustment of the balance of power – wars of balancing *process*.[145] Many factors – including the

---

[139]   On "instinctive" balancing by the less powerful Greek states in 201–200: see Schmitt 1974: 83–4. The relative absence of explicit "balancing" in Greco-Roman geopolitical thought: see Wight 1977: 24.
[140]   On this point, see Claude 1962 (fundamental); cf., e.g., Jervis 1997 and now Jervis 2001: 287. The explicit goal of "balance" as not even a prevalent state goal in the eighteenth century, the alleged classic period of such conduct: see now Sofka 2001.
[141]   See Eckstein 2006: Chs. 3–5. This is "empire by invitation": Lundestad 1986 and Lundestad 1990: Ch. 1.
[142]   Waltz 1979: 125.
[143]   This is the definition of Lake 2001: 62.
[144]   On the temptations of "bandwagoning" and "jackel bandwagoning" vs. "balancing" in the modern interstate system, see Labs 1992; Kaufman 1992; Schweller 1994; and Schweller 1998.
[145]   See Eckstein 2006: Ch. 3.

prevalence of multipolarity in itself – have been suggested as conducive to such balancing conduct; but one factor in Greek conduct may have to do with the prevalence of "honor" as a social ideal among the slave-owning elites who were primarily responsible for determining policy in most Greek states, and the fact that the dominant social metaphor among those elites was the metaphor of "slave vs. free." Such cultural ideals militated against both appeasement and "bandwagoning," since such conduct might be seen as in itself dishonorable and/or "slavish," therefore ignoble, and hence to be avoided. In other words, cultural factors may have led Greek states more than modern states into following the pattern of alliance-formation in the face of threat suggested by Walt.[146]

This, of course, is a bit speculative. What is a fact, and a striking fact, is the revolution between 206 and 201 in the attitude of these Greek polities towards Roman intervention. Where previously all these states except Pergamum had worked at cross-purposes to Roman involvement in Greek affairs, now suddenly all four (Rhodes, Pergamum, Athens, and Egypt) were pleading for it. Some fundamental geopolitical development had brought about this radical transformation. We have proposed that this development was the revelation to the governing elites of these states of the Pact Between the Kings (cf. Polyb. 14.1a). And this, as will now become clear, is what Polybius himself believed and indeed explicitly stated – though the nature of his narrative has not been sufficiently appreciated by modern scholarship because that narrative only exists in the form of discontinuous fragments.

THE GREEK EMBASSIES AT ROME: POLYBIUS' VIEW

Prominent modern scholars have argued that "Polybius makes no suggestion at all that the pact was directly responsible for Roman intervention in the East in 200 and later," and that "we can be sure beyond reasonable doubt that Polybius did not make Roman knowledge of the 'pact' a cause of the war."[147] Alternatively, scholars have argued that we simply cannot know what Polybius said on the causes of the Second Macedonian War, because the fragmentary character of his surviving text on this period does not allow us to have an opinion.[148] If this were the case, it would leave us in great doubt as to what occurred in Rome in winter 201/200. But in fact, the scholars who argue that Polybius did

---

[146] See the comments of Strauss 1986 and 1991.
[147] Balsdon 1954: 37 (the first quote); Errington 1971: 354 (the second quote).
[148] So Derow 1979: 10.

not place Roman knowledge of the Pact Between the Kings at the center of the Roman decision to intervene in the East, or that we simply cannot know what Polybius said on this subject, are not correct.

We have indeed totally lost Polybius' account of the Roman decision of winter 201/200, which must have been a highly detailed discussion. We must therefore make do with clues from the surviving fragments of what he wrote elsewhere in the *Histories*. Nevertheless, enough evidence exists to indicate strongly that the Pact Between the Kings played a large role not only in Polybius' general analysis of the onrolling crisis, but specifically in the reasons he gave for the Roman decision of winter 201/200 to intervene in the eastern Mediterranean.[149]

The crucial statement is found in Polyb. 15.20. This is a passage we have discussed before – a heavily moralizing, negative commentary on the nature of the Pact Between the Kings.[150] Philip and Antiochus are described as men without morality, as impious savages and rapacious beasts, taking advantage of the weakness of Ptolemy V, who was only a child (15.20.2–4). But, Polybius continues, those who find fault with Fortune (Tyche) for her conduct of human affairs will now be reconciled with her when they learn how she soon made the two kings pay the due penalty for their evil conduct (20.5–6):

> For even while they were still breaking their pledged faith with one another and destroying the kingdom of the child, Tyche alerted the Romans (ἐπιτστήσασα ʿΡωμαίους), and very justly visited upon the kings the very evils which they had planned in their total lawlessness to bring upon others.

In the short run, Polybius continues, the Romans defeated Philip and Antiochus in war, so that the kings were not only prevented from lusting unjustly after the possessions of others (i.e., the Ptolemies), but were forced to submit to Rome (20.7). And in the long run, he says, the Antigonids were brought to utter destruction and the Seleucids to a condition approaching it – while the situation of the Ptolemaic House revived (20.8).

For our purposes, the key phrase in this passage is at 15.20.6: ἐπιστήσασα ʿΡωμαίους [ἡ Τύχη]. The proper translation of 15.20.6 is central to our argument. And although for a long time the passage was not well understood, a recent detailed study of Polybius' use of language, and especially his use of the verb ἐφίστημι, has established that Polybius

---

[149]   What follows is a summary of Eckstein 2005, where the argument is presented in greater detail.
[150]   See above, Chapter 4, pp. 134–5.

in commenting on the pact is saying that "Fortune alerted the Romans" to the bad conduct of the two kings against Egypt.[151] The alternative and long dominant reading has been that Polybius in 15.20 is merely saying that as a matter of fact Fortune "raised up the Romans" to punish the kings for their bad conduct – which would tell us something about the process that occurred in the eastern Mediterranean between 200 and 188 BC, but nothing about what occurred in Rome itself in winter 201/200.[152] The recent detailed word-study of 15.20.5–6, however, has shown that this meaning would be absolutely unprecedented in Polybian usage, whereas by contrast, ἐφίστημι is employed by Polybius dozens of times in the extant text to mean "to alert someone"; moreover, this usually has the consequence that the person who is alerted changes his conduct.[153] This phenomenon within Polybian language usage, and its importance for the proper understanding of 15.20.6, was noted long ago by Passarini and then by Walbank, but their remarks were only brief and made only in passing. Because neither great scholar provided a detailed argument, their correction of the long-standing translation of 15.20.6 has been ignored – wrongly. But we now know that Passarini and Walbank were exactly correct in their understanding of the meaning of 15.20.6.[154]

Having established this fact, having established the proper translation of Polyb. 15.20.5–6, we then have to ask how Fortune accomplished her goal – how it was that Fortune alerted the Romans to the bad conduct of the kings, to (in fact) the pact. And the answer is both obvious and provides us with a previously unsuspected clue concerning how Polybius depicted the events at Rome in winter 201/200. For who could Tyche have employed to "alert the Romans" to the evil actions of the

---

[151]   See Eckstein 2005.

[152]   Almost every translator of Polybius 15.20 since Casaubon and Schweighauser has translated 15.20.6 in that fashion. Casaubon 1609: 986, on 15.20; Schweighauser 1789–95: on 15.20; Schweighauser 1822: s.v. ἐφίστημι: *opponere*. See Strachan-Davidson 1888: 398 n. 6: "Fortune set the Romans on them"; Shuckburgh 1889: 153: "Fortune brought the Romans upon them"; Paton 1925: 509: "Fortune raised up against them the Romans"; Roussel 1970: 781: "Fortune a dressé contre eux les Romains"; Scott-Kilvert 1979: 483: "Fortune brought the Romans upon them"; Mari 2003: 205: "essa chiamo in causa i Romani." The only exception is Weil 1995 at 15.20: "Quand la Fortune attira l'attention des Romains . . ." But Weil gives no reason in support of this (correct) translation.

[153]   See, e.g., Polyb. 2.61.11; 5.85.12; 23.11.4; 27.9.6; 30.6.1; 38.8.4; many other passages could be cited. Hence both Mauersberger and Collatz, Gutlaf, and Helms, in the modern lexicons of Polybian language, agree that ἐφίστημι in Polybius most often means *Augnen offnen; aufmerksam machen; bekannt machen*: Mauersberger 1961: s.v. ἐφίστημι, coll. 1060–2; Collatz, Gutlaf, and Helms 2003, s.v. Yet they make a unique exception at 15.20.6.

[154]   Passarini 1936: 182 n. 1, and Walbank 1967: 474. Supported in detail now by Eckstein 2005.

kings, to the kings' evil pact against the child Ptolemy V, except the multiple Greek embassies that appeared before the Senate at that time? Indeed, a surviving fragment of Polybius already shows Philip in autumn 201 worried about the impact that these multiple Greek embassies might soon have at Rome (16.24.1–3). Thus, if the above translation of Polyb. 15.20.6 is correct – that Fortune "alerted the Romans" to the Pact Between the Kings – then we have strong evidence that Polybius both highlighted the role in the Roman decision of winter 201/200 played by the embassies from the several Greek states we have been discussing, and held that the focus of these embassies' message was on the threat posed by the pact.

In Polybius' view, then, the pact is what Tyche made the Romans attend to, and Tyche employed the several Greek embassies to do this. Moreover, in Polybius' conception, once the Senate had been alerted to the pact by the Greek embassies, the response of the Romans (as so often with Polybian use of ἐφίστημι and those who have been alerted) was to change their conduct. That is, the Senate decided that it was necessary to intervene in the Greek East again, and possibly on a large scale. Hence Polybius goes on to state in 15.20 that Tyche, having alerted the Romans, then employed the Romans to punish the kings for their savagery towards the child-ruler Ptolemy V – by using the Romans to visit upon the dynasties of Philip and Antiochus the dismal fate they had planned together, in their pact, to inflict upon the helpless Ptolemies (15.20.7–9).

When its language is correctly understood, Polyb. 15.20.5–6 therefore shows that for the Achaean historian, a key element in the crucial message brought to Rome by the Greek envoys in autumn 201 was to draw the Romans' attention specifically to the pact between Philip and Antiochus (which is the overall subject of 15.20); and the result of this new knowledge was a sharp turn in senatorial attitude towards intervention in the East. Polybius, in other words, foregrounded the Pact Between the Kings in his discussion of Roman decision-making in winter 201/200. This is important information for us to have as we consider the crisis of 203/202–200.

We can now see as well that Tyche's punishment of Philip and Antiochus for the crime – the pact – against the child Ptolemy V is in fact the key incident upon which Polybius' entire conception of the fall of Macedonian power is built. On the subject of the fall of Macedonian power he was clearly impressed by the prediction of Demetrius of Phalerum, in the latter's essay *Peri Tyches* of ca. 300 BC, that Tyche in the future would contrive to bring down Macedonian power unexpectedly, just as Tyche in Demetrius' time had unexpectly brought down the power of Persia. This was a prediction which Polybius thought "godlike" – for it had come true in his own generation; he is emphatic about this in 29.21, a dramatic passage near the point where he originally intended to end the *Histories*. Indeed, Tyche appears as the patroness behind the rise of Roman power as early as Polyb. 1.4.1–5.[155]

Nevertheless, Polybius' analysis of events at Rome in winter 201/200 must have contained more than discussion of Tyche – and more than the Greek embassies. For Polybius was well aware of the question of the Romans' own motives. We know that he thought Rome was in general an aggressive and expansionist polity, and that the Roman victory in the Hannibalic War had led to a Roman ambition to control the entire Mediterranean world (Polyb. 3.2.6). Elsewhere he conceived of this Roman ambition as having emerged even earlier, after the First Punic War.[156] Not that Polybius thought Rome's ambition was unique: it is important to realize that he thought Carthage, Philip V, and Antiochus III all possessed similar world-wide ambitions in this period.[157] Further, he thought that somehow the Roman war with Philip that began in 200 had its origins in the Hannibalic War itself, and emerged naturally from it (3.32.6). Perhaps he was thinking that the Senate, once presented with new evidence of the scale of Philip's ambitions, was prepared to take new revenge on Philip for what it saw as Philip's aggression against Rome after Cannae.[158] Yet none of this should be taken to mean that Polybius thought Roman intervention in the affairs of the Greek East was somehow inevitable once the victory over Carthage had been won. Something else had to happen to bring about that development.

In other words, Polybius' analysis of what occurred at Rome in winter 201/200 was quite complex. He liked to emphasize the power of large underlying factors, and large historical patterns: in the arrival of the Greek embassies at Rome in late 201 he clearly saw the workings of Tyche as retributive justice (see above), but he also saw this as the working out at the secular level of the *symplokē* – the new "geopolitical interconnectedness" between events in the eastern and western Mediterranean which he thought began to be operative from ca. 217, and which was

---

[155]   On Polybius' view of Tyche and the prediction of Demetrius of Phalerum, see Walbank 1979: 393–5. On the placement of Polybius' reference to Demetrius' prediction near the original projected end of his *Histories*, see Walbank 2002b: 251–2. Demetrius' prediction about the fall of Macedonian power as something "more than human": see Polyb. 29.21.7.

[156]   See 1.3.6 and 1.63.9; cf. 15.9.2 and 10.2, where the ambition is implied as already existing before Scipio's decisive victory over Hannibal at Zama in 202.

[157]   See 15.9.2 and 4–5 (on Carthage); on Polybius' (correct) conception of the world-conquering ambitions of Philip and Antiochus, see above, Chapter 4.

[158]   For different interpretations of what Polybius meant by his statement concerning the "organic" connection between the Hannibalic War and the war against Philip, see Pédech 1969: xviii; Walbank 1972: 162 and n. 46.

one of the two major themes of his work.[159] Here in winter 201/200 was the first case where aggression in the Greek East, in a struggle purely between Greek states in a Greek context, called forth a large and enduring military-diplomatic reaction from the West. Here was the first case where the two Mediterranean sub-regions, whose interactions had been growing in number and intensity since 217, now became a single large system. In part this growth was natural; in part the events of winter 201/200 were the result of the voluntary actions of the less powerful Greek states in going to Rome for help against the kings, and the voluntary decision of the Senate to answer their plea for help; in part it was all the result of Tyche. Note that in this sense, the problem for Philip and Antiochus was that they did not correctly conceive the arena in which they were operating; assuming that their arena of concern was the Greek Mediterranean alone – the traditional area, after all, of Greek warfare – they did not see how the growth of the Mediterranean-wide *symplokē* made far more difficult their plans for decisive expansion.[160]

But Polybius also left significant room for what he calls at 3.32.7 "the many and varied intermediate causes" of major events.[161] This is because he was interested not merely in underlying causes and large historical patterns but also (as he often proclaims) in the question of why humans make the kinds of specific decisions they make.[162] So Polybius accepted underlying factors in the Mediterranean geopolitical situation as it existed in 201–200 in bringing Roman intervention in the on-going crisis and wars in the Greek East, factors including Roman aggressiveness on the one hand and Tyche's punishment of Philip and Antiochus for their own ruthlessness on the other, but as far as the actual outbreak of the Second Macedonian War as well as the growth and achievement of the *symplokē* are concerned, Polybius probably also thought of the arrival of the Greek embassies at Rome as both a contingent event and a necessary catalyst. For in the actual historical circumstances of winter 201/200, it was the arrival of the Greeks and their message that moved the Senate actually to act to intervene in the East.[163] Such a reconstruction of what Polybius said occurred in Rome with the arrival of the Greek

[159]   On the place of the *symplokē* in Polybius' thought on the rise of Rome, see Chapters 2 and 3 above.
[160]   See briefly Eckstein 2006: Ch. 3, end.
[161]   See the discussion in Walbank 1972: 162–6.
[162]   See the programmatic discussion in 3.6–10, with Pédech 1964: 80–8, and Eckstein 1989: 1–3.
[163]   On the analytical distinction between fundamental factors that favor war and system change in an anarchic interstate environment, vs. the occurrence of specific catalysts – contingent events – that are necessary for the actual decisions that lead to the outbreak of particular system-changing wars, see Lebow 2001: 591–616 (fundamental).

embassies would fit perfectly with Polybius' view that historical causes (*aitiai*) are always those factors which – one way or another – bring about human perceptions and human decisions.[164]

While we perhaps still do not know all the causal factors Polybius depicted in his account of the crucial Roman decision of winter 201/200, we can now say that at least we know two factors which he depicted as crucial to the Roman decision: the arrival of the Greek embassies, and the news of the pact. This conclusion depends upon our translation of Polyb. 15.20.6 being correct – but the case for its being correct is very strong. And if it is correct, then the Greek historian saw as a central event in Mediterranean history that Tyche, employing the multiple Greek embassies of winter 201/200, alerted the Romans to the dangers of the Pact Between the Kings. Indeed, if our interpretation of Polyb. 15.20.6 is correct, then Polybius himself is the likely ultimate source of all the traditions among the Greek historical writers that the arrival of the Greek embassies at Rome in late 201, with their complaints against the kings, led to the Roman decision.

CONCLUSION

Of course, Polybius' conception of the events of winter 201/200 at Rome may not be complete in terms of all the factors involved in the Roman decision (especially regarding possible rivalries within Roman aristocratic politics at the time).[165] His conception of events may, indeed, have been excessively theoretical, especially in its emphasis on the first decisive working of the *symplokē*. Yet Polybius was an experienced politician and general who knew how ancient internal politics worked and how ancient interstate politics worked; he was a sophisticated intellectual who had access to multiple sources on the crucial events of the years 204–200 BC – a point he strongly underlines (16.14.2); and he did not employ those sources uncritically – another point he underlines and, indeed, demonstrates in detail (at 16.14–20). This means that Polybius' conception of events must be given very significant weight, and what we can now discern of his version of the events at Rome in winter 201/200 should have an important bearing on our own understanding of what actually occurred. In other words: we can now say with fair confidence that the arrival of the Greek embassies and specifically their warnings about the pact must have played a significant role in the Roman decision to intervene in the geopolitical crisis and wars going on in the East.

---

[164]   See Polyb. 3.6.7, with the scholarship cited in n. 143 above.
[165]   See below, Chapter 6, for discussion of that factor.

It is an important discovery that Polybius evidently gave prominence in his narrative of the world-historical decision made at Rome in winter 201/200 to what modern political scientists would call "the power-transition crisis" then engulfing the Greek Mediterranean. This was a power-transition crisis that had already brought on (again, to use modern international-system terminology) a system-transforming "hegemonic war" – with fighting under either Antiochus III or Philip V raging by summer 201 from the frontiers of Egypt at Gaza into Asia Minor and the Aegean.[166] The faltering and then increasing collapse of Ptolemaic power after ca. 207, the failure of power in a state that had been one of the three great pillars of the *de facto* triadic balance of power regulating geopolitics in the eastern Mediterranean ever since ca. 280, precipitated a whole series of disruptive developments. These disruptive developments changed the structure of the interstate system in the Greek world, sharply redistributing the capabilities and power among states across the system in favor of Macedon and the Seleucid Empire.

It is important to see that this disruption eventually reached right across the entire Mediterranean world. First came the faltering and collapse of Egypt; then the striking of the Pact Between the Kings; then the large-scale military aggressions of Philip and Antiochus at Ptolemaic expense consequent to the pact; then the desperate military and diplomatic reactions to this Antigonid and Seleucid military expansion on the part of Rhodes, Pergamum, Athens, and the Ptolemaic regime; and then came the final link in the chain: the reaction to all this at Rome once the Greek envoys arrived with news of what was occurring in the East, and pleading for help.

Mommsen understood the evolution of the crisis in just this way: he concluded that Rome in 201/200 responded primarily to the precipitous shift in the balance of power among the great Greek states caused by the faltering and collapse of the Ptolemies – which was the crucial development.[167] One can also employ the terminology of the political scientist Thomas Christensen in an illuminating fashion here: after 207 and especially after 203/202 the sudden weakness of "the most vulnerable significant actor" in the Hellenistic state-system – Ptolemaic Egypt – tempted the radical expansion of its traditional rivals (Macedon and Syria), in turn sending destabilizing shocks and ripples throughout the system, shocks and ripples that eventually reached all the way to Rome.[168]

---

[166]   On this terminology, see above, this chapter, p. 182.
[167]   Mommsen 1903: 696–701; cf. Raditsa 1972: 564–5.
[168]   Christensen 1993: 329–30. Needless to say, Christensen does not have Hellenistic history in mind when he emphasizes the importance for the stability of a state-system of "the most vulnerable significant actor" in the system; but this makes Christensen's paradigm all the more interesting.

The crisis attendant upon the Pact Between the Kings caused a revolution in the stance of the weaker Greek states towards Roman intervention in Greek interstate politics. Rhodes, Athens, and the Ptolemies, in their attempts at mediation during the First Macedonian War, had as late as 206 worked at sharp cross-purposes to Roman goals east of the Adriatic. In 207 the Rhodians in particular had made vehemently hostile statements in public against Rome as a polity and against its intervention in Greek affairs, and envoys of the Ptolemies had stood by while the Rhodians mounted their vituperative public attack; in 206 the Rhodians had then helped arrange the separate peace between Macedon and Rome's ally the Aetolian League which so angered the Romans.[169] Yet now it was the Rhodians and the Ptolemies who were leading the procession of Greek states going to Rome to urge Roman intervention in the Greek world. The very presence of envoys from the Rhodian and the Ptolemaic governments, appearing before the Senate, thus demonstrates not only the cataclysmic impact of the Pact Between the Kings upon the Greek state-system. At the level of international-relations theory, this is a case where fundamental changes in the structure of the state-system (i.e., a transformation in the distribution of power across the system) led quite logically – as Realist theory posits it would do – to radical changes in the behavior and policies of the individual states within the system.[170]

This latter formulation is important for demonstrating the importance of system-level analysis. But it is not the whole story of what occurred in the East between 203/202 and late 201. Nor is it the whole story of what occurred at Rome in the winter of 201/200 – as we will see when we turn in detail to the Roman decision, in the next chapter below. It is not the case that changes in the structure of the international system, in themselves, must produce certain violent consequences – though they tend strongly to do so. The internal characteristics of states also count, in terms of their will and ability to resist or not to resist the momentum created by the structural changes. This is because the specific reactions of states (i.e., their governing elites) to systemic crisis derive not only from the pressures, constraints, and temptations imposed by the system upon all units within it, but also from the internal characteristics of those units (the states) themselves. Even the staunchest of system-level

---

[169] The Rhodians' public attack on Rome and Roman policies at the famous scene at the peace conference at the Panaetolia of autumn 207: see above, Chapter 3. Rhodian role later in arranging the separate peace between Macedon and Aetolia, and Roman anger over this development: see App. *Mac.* 4 with discussion above, Chapter 3.

[170] For this formulation, cf. Friedberg 1988: 4.

theorists admits the role of unit culture and unit-level analysis for our understanding of the reactions of states to systemic crisis.[171] Thus among the Hellenistic states, i.e., their governing elites, at the end of the third century BC, the Greek polities as well as Rome, one must include as explanatory factors of their conduct their ferocious desires for independence, their focus on honor and their fear of appearing weak or submissive, their prevailing militarism and reliance upon violence in interstate politics, and the prevailing perception of cruel interstate competition which characterized all their internal cultures.

These prevailing militaristic, bellicose, and diplomatically aggressive internal cultures (themselves the product of the pressures upon them of the ferocious anarchy in which all these states were forced to live) constitute one primary reason leading the weaker Greek states instinctively to seek to balance against the rapidly expanding power of Philip and Antiochus by going to Rome, rather than attempting policies of appeasement towards the kings, or to "bandwagon" with the monarchs by joining their expansionist project as allies on the best terms they could get. And, as we will see, it was a similarly harsh and militaristic internal culture, a culture imbued with a pessimistic view of the external world, that played an important role in leading the Romans, when confronted with the message from the Greek embassies of 201/200, to intervene forcefully (and eventually with military force) in the crisis. But the many modern scholars who foreground the hypothesis of exceptional Roman aggressiveness and bellicosity as the key to understanding the events of 201/200, i.e., who foreground the *Primat der Innenpolitik*, have adopted too simplistic an approach. The system-level pressures upon the Greek states and the causal force of the internal cultural characteristics of those states were themselves central to the revolutionary interstate transformation that occurred in the Mediterranean at the end of the third century. And without denying in the least that the Roman Republic was indeed an aggressive and bellicose polity, as was the case with all major and even second-rank Hellenistic states, we can now perceive in at least a preliminary fashion the powerful external and systemic forces at work both in the crisis of 203/202–201 and at Rome in winter 201/200 – i.e., the *Primat der Aussenpolitik* in the Roman decision. It is to the Roman decision that we now turn.

---

[171]   See, e.g., Waltz 1979: 76–7 and 122. The fundamental study of the problem of simultaneously employing different levels of analysis in the study of international relations (i.e., systemic-level and unit-level analysis) is Singer 1961.

6

Diplomatic Revolution in the Mediterranean, II: The Roman Decision to Intervene, 201/200 BC[1]

THE CONTROVERSY

Envoys from four Greek states – Egypt, Rhodes, Pergamum, and Athens – arrived in Rome in the autumn of 201, pleading for Roman intervention against Philip V of Macedon and Antiochus III of Syria, and warning of severe consequences should the power of the two kings be allowed to expand unimpeded. The Senate and People of Rome decided to answer the pleas for help and the warnings from the Greek envoys, and to intervene strongly in the affairs of the Greek Mediterranean. The Roman decision was to send out a diplomatic mission first, in an attempt to control the kings' actions; this decision occurred in the spring of 200. But major military intervention was clearly envisaged at least against Philip if the diplomatic mission should fail. The departure from Rome of the designated commander in Greece, P. Sulpicus Galba, was in fact long delayed, in part for religious reasons and perhaps in part because of difficulties in conducting the levy for soldiers. But Roman military preparations continued throughout the summer of 200, and in the autumn a large Roman army, supported by a strong naval force, landed in Illyria, with the intention of attacking Macedon.

The amount of information we possess on the Roman decision of spring 200 allows us to adopt what may be called a "layered" approach in our analysis. This is an approach that combines the insights of international

[1] Much of the discussion here partly summarizes (but also significantly extends) the discussion in Eckstein 2006: Ch. 7.

systems theory concerning the process of increasingly violent redistribution of power and capabilities occurring in the Greek East (which we have emphasized) and the systemic pressures that pushed the Romans themselves to intervene in that process, with discussion of important aspects of Rome's own internal ("unit") culture that were conducive to this aggressive world-historical decision. Room even exists in such a "layered" analysis for discussion of the impact of specific individuals. And there is no contradiction in seeking to combine the insights available at all these levels of analysis into one complex picture.[2]

The question before us is why the Romans answered the Greek pleas for help. The fundamental answer given by many modern scholars is that the Roman Republic in the third century BC was a war machine dependent on continual warfare to maintain its internal social, political, and economic stability. This Roman "war machine" was made up of three basic elements: (1) the warlike and warmongering Roman aristocracy, imbued with a warrior culture and dependent upon continuous warfare against external enemies (real, exaggerated, or even fabricated) in order to maintain its wealth, prestige, and influence as the leaders of Roman society; (2) the needy Roman populace, eager to enrich their difficult lives with booty and/or with land taken from others; and (3) the Roman alliances with the other polities of Italy – an alliance-system that was inherently prone to war because the basis of the system was war-making. All this was combined with a generally hostile, suspicious, and aggressive Roman attitude towards the outside world. From this perspective – the perspective of the *Primat der Innenpolitik*, emphasizing the structures within Roman economy, society, and culture that were conducive to bellicosity and expansion – the decision of 200 is unsurprising. It was inherent in the bellicose and aggressive character of the Roman state and society, and the decision of 200 is merely the expression of that Roman bellicosity and aggressiveness in that particular year. In such a view, the events we have described in such detail as they were unrolling in the eastern Mediterranean merely provided an opportunity, or even merely an excuse or pretext, for the continuing pathological exercise of Roman militarism, expansionism, and aggression.

This view did not always dominate modern scholarly reconstructions of the Roman decision of 200.[3] But, as discussed in Chapter 1, this view dominates now. The way was led by W. V. Harris, whose study of Roman militarism fundamentally changed the manner in which we view the Republic. His conclusion was that Rome in general was the exception

---

[2] On the "layered approach," see Lebow 1991 and Johnson Bagby 1994.
[3] See esp. Mommsen 1903: 696–701; and in general the historiographical overview in Raditsa 1972.

among Hellenistic states in being dark, irrational, and pathological in its culture, a predator of exceptional power and savagery. This view has recently been reiterated in important work by Peter Derow.[4]

Rome in the Middle Republic certainly was a culture that was heavily militaristic, the Republic was certainly guided by a senatorial aristocracy imbued with a warrior ethos, and the *populus* was certainly habituated to war and to service in the army. These factors made a substantial contribution (as what political scientists call independent variables) to the frequency of Roman wars.[5] But the Roman Republic would not have survived long in its violent and anarchic environment if it had not developed these internal characteristics.[6] Moreover, it has been argued in this study that however militaristic, bellicose, or aggressive Rome was, this did not make it exceptional or exceptionally pathological among the states existing within its environment; the Romans faced a world in which the harsh pressures of the anarchic environment had led to the "functional similarity" of all states. The imperialism of Antigonid Macedon under Philip V and the Seleucid realm under Antiochus the Great demonstrate this point in a quite obvious manner among the great Greek states; Carthage – though outside the range of our study – was another major imperialist state; and Rhodes and Pergamum, though second-tier states, were equally aggressive and militaristic (though they had fewer resources). To understand the world-historical events that occurred at the end of the third century BC one must avoid an introverted historiography that looks at Rome alone. Rather, one must lift one's eyes from Rome to examine the entire geopolitical picture.[7]

The main issue before us is therefore whether the arrival of the Greek embassies at Rome in autumn 201 merely provided a convenient excuse for the on-going exercise of general and long-term Roman bellicosity and aggression towards the entire outside world – the current scholarly *communis opinio* – or whether the information from the Greek envoys acted instead as a crucial catalyst that turned Roman attention towards a truly dangerous situation in the Greek Mediterranean, truly reshaping previous senatorial thought about the East and making the Senate far

---

[4]   See Harris 1979: Chs. 1–3 and 5; cf. North 1981; Mandell 1989; Derow 1989, and 2003: 58–60; Ampela 1998: 74 and 77; and cf. already Veyne 1975: 838–9; "Pathological": Harris 1979: 53, cf. 50–1.

[5]   On the bellicosity of Roman internal culture, fundamental is Harris 1979: Chs. 1–3.

[6]   Cf. Sterling 1974: 336: "States must meet the demands of the political ecosystem or court annihilation."

[7]   On functional similarity of all states under anarchy, see Waltz 1979: 97. On Philip and Antiochus, see Chapters 4 and 5 above. On Rhodes and Pergamum, see Chap. 5 above, and Eckstein 2006: Ch. 4. On Carthage, see Ameling 1993. The dangers of "introverted historiography" focusing on one state when seeking to explain imperial outcomes: Bayley 1988: 14–15.

more willing than before to consider the high-risk option of war, because the Greeks made the Senate believe there were greater ultimate risks in a policy of inaction. This would be a reconstruction of the decision of 200 based on the *Primat der Aussenpolitik*.[8]

THE GREEK EMBASSIES TO ROME: PRETEXT OR CATALYST?

If one examines the situation facing Rome in the winter of 201/200, a reconstruction in which the coming of the Greek envoys merely provided an excuse for a self-confident Roman expansion in the East does not seem very plausible. To be sure, Rome in spring 201 had finally achieved victory over Hannibal and Carthage, bringing the Second Punic War to a satisfactory conclusion. But the struggle had lasted eighteen years, and – after catastrophic defeats in the early years, followed by a long period of bloody stalemate – the victory had come at enormous cost. The war in fact had left the Roman state and its populace exhausted. The general scale of Livy's census figures suggest that since the 220s Rome had lost almost half its male citizen population available for army service; as the epitomator of Livy sadly says, the low number of citizens in the census of 209 reveals "how many men the unfavorable outcome of so many battles had carried off from the Roman People."[9] Hannibal supposedly boasted that during his long invasion of Italy he destroyed 400 Italian towns and killed 300,000 Italians (App. *Pun.* 134); if one defines "town" broadly, and includes civilian populations among the casualties, these figures may not be far off.[10] The Romans, themselves retaliating against polities in Italy that went over to Hannibal, had of course contributed to the widespread destruction. Thus neither the allies who had remained loyal to Rome, nor those who had defected to Carthage and had then suffered savage punishment at Roman hands, could have been eager for a major new war. It is clear that significant portions of Roman Italy had been devastated by the Hannibalic War; in 200 BC much good farmland was for sale (Livy 31.13.6).[11] It is thus

---

[8] On the distinction in general between pretexts and true catalysts, see Lebow 2001: esp. 614.

[9] Livy *Per.* 20 places the number of adult male Roman citizens as about 270,000 before the outbreak of the Second Punic War. By 209 that number had sunk to 137,000 (*Per.* 27). The quote: *Per.* 27. The numbers had substantially recovered by 201: 219,000, according to *Per.* 29, but this is still well below the figures twenty years previously. The precise numbers cannot be trusted, but the trend is clear enough.

[10] See Cornell 1996: 103 and n. 22.

[11] Ibid.: 103–11; cf. also Hopkins 1978: 1–56.

not surprising that the protagonist of Plautus' comic play *Stichus* – produced at Rome in the autumn of 200, only months after the Roman decision to intervene in the East – is an impoverished and bitter small farmer, dispossessed by the war, and angry at the Greeks for taking up his patron's attention.[12]

In addition, there was serious new trouble brewing on the Celtic frontier in northern Italy. After a period of relative peace since 216, Celts launched large-scale raids against Roman territory in the summer of 201, and the Boii then administered a severe defeat to Roman forces under the consul P. Aelius Paetus. The defeat of a consul was shocking – and many men in the Senate may even have feared that another Gallic invasion of central Italy was looming.[13] The *Patres*' concern over Celtic unrest in the Po Valley was justified. Encouraged by the great victory of the Boii in 201 over Paetus, in the summer of 200 a confederation of Celtic peoples attacked the two large Roman colonies in the central Po Valley; one of these, Placentia, was overrun and destroyed, while the other, Cremona, came under serious siege. This was a serious crisis.[14]

Modern scholars, as we have noted, often assert that the two consuls each year were eager for warfare in order to gain personal glory, and that this was a crucial mechanism behind Roman expansion.[15] But in return we have argued against this being a central factor in the general making of policy, because ambitious consular commanders were balanced in the Senate by the majority of senators who themselves had *not* achieved tremendous glory in their own magistracies, and thus had no burning desire to see others achieve victories and *gloria* – especially if no real threat existed. The Senate was therefore not a mere machine for creating triumphal parades, but a far more cautious institution.[16] In any case, it is quite clear from the Celtic threat in 201–200 that a war in the Greek East was not necessary in order for the new consuls of 200 to achieve whatever glory they wished. The new Celtic danger in the north, signaled in summer 201 by serious raids and then the severe defeat of the consul Paetus, a danger arising from Rome's most traditional enemies – enemies who were only separated from Roman central Italy by the

---

[12]   The *Stichus* as a neglected source on the situation in Rome ca. 200 BC, see above, Chapter 5.
[13]   Paetus' defeat in 201 by the Boii: Livy 31.2.7–10 with Eckstein 1987a: 54–5. Senatorial fears of a new Celtic invasion of central Italy (previous invasions had come in 225 and – with half of Hannibal's army being Celts – in 217): Zon. 9.16 with Eckstein 1987a: 63–8 and 282–3.
[14]   Detailed discussion of the opening of the great Celtic War of 201–191: Eckstein 1987a: 56–8.
[15]   See, e.g., Harris 1979: 10–40.
[16]   See above, Chapter 1. On the careful granting of triumphs, see Rich 1993: 49–53, and Eckstein 2006: Ch. 6.

Apennine Mountains and thus constituted a direct threat to the Roman heartland – would have served perfectly well as a consular theater of military action. The consuls of 200 did not need a Roman war in the East.

Finally, it appears that the recruiting of an army in spring and summer 200 for the war in Greece put a severe strain on available Roman military manpower. The *populus Romanus* was reluctant to authorize such an intervention in the East precisely because they were exhausted by the Hannibalic War (Livy 31.6.3–6).[17] Even after war against Philip was reluctantly voted by the Assembly (see below), a special dispensation was voted which exempted from the new draft all veterans who had served with P. Cornelius Scipio Africanus (Livy 31.8.6). Even so, there was a mutiny in 199 among embittered long-serving veterans in the eastern army (32.3.2–7). Buraselis thus makes a fair argument that while the late departure of the consul P. Sulpicius Galba for the East (he only arrived in Illyria in the autumn of 200) was in good part caused by his duty to fulfill serious religious obligations that had emerged in Italy (see below, p. 250), it was also caused in part by the sheer difficulty he faced in holding the conscription.[18]

One crucial structural change in the western Mediterranean state-system did facilitate Roman intervention in the East: the disappearance of Carthage as a major competitive power with Rome. The end of the Hannibalic War left Carthage with no overseas possessions, no army, and a risible fleet.[19] The new balance of power in the western Mediterranean left Rome more free to exercise the option of projecting power into the Greek East than it would have been had the Republic still been encumbered in the West with Carthage as a significant and worrisome challenger.[20] Yet the Roman freedom of action arising from the great victory over Carthage and absence of Punic power seems more than balanced in 201 and 200 by Roman exhaustion – and the renewed threat from the Celts.

All these pressures within Italy worked against a major Roman intervention in the East. Still, if Rome had been long and deeply involved in the geopolitics of the Greek world before 201–200 BC, then the Roman decision to intervene in the power-transition crisis and hegemonic warfare

---

[17] *Id cum fessi diuturnitate et gravetate belli sua sponte homines taedio periculorum laborumque fecerant . . .*
[18] Buraselis 1996: 155 n. 21.
[19] On the terms of the Peace of 201, see Schmitt 1969: no. 548.
[20] Similarly, the disappearance of the USSR as a major competitor whose constant counter-weight had "disciplined" American foreign policy meant that in the 1990s the US government had much more freedom of action in interventions overseas (which it indeed exercised), without having to increase the existing size of its armed forces: see the comments of Waltz 2000: 18.

engulfing the Greek Mediterranean in 201–200 might still appear a natural development – a natural consequence of the increase in Roman power, combined with long-term Roman interest and accumulated concrete interests in the East.[21] But Chapters 2 and 3 of this study have sought to show that before 201–200, Roman interest and involvement in Greek geopolitics, and concrete interests in the East, were minimal. A summary follows of what we have established on that score.

The Roman military interventions in Illyria in 229/228 and 219 had both been against the piratical conduct of the Illyrian Ardiaei (first under Queen Teuta, then under Demetrius of Pharos), and had resulted only in a scattering of informal friendly states along the Adriatic coast directly across from Italy – an area far removed in any case from central Greece. The First Macedonian War (214–205) was at heart a defensive Roman response to Philip V's powerful aggressions in Illyria and his alliance with Hannibal, aggressions initiated because the king believed Rome was already beaten in the Second Punic War. The conflict did lead to increased Roman contacts among the Greek states as the Romans sought allies against the power of Macedon – because Rome itself, so hard-pressed by Carthage elsewhere, could commit only limited resources to counter Philip's expansion. The Romans established relations with the Aetolian League, Sparta, and Messene, and across the Aegean with the Kingdom of Pergamum. But the course of the First Macedonian War shows that Roman interest east of the Adriatic was limited to keeping Philip V so embroiled in Greece that he could not contemplate an invasion of Italy in conjunction with his ally Hannibal. The war ended in a compromise peace with Philip in 205, and mutual concessions in Illyria; it also ended badly in terms of Roman relations with the Aetolians, since the minimal Roman war effort, and the Aetolians' subsequent separate peace with Philip in 206, led each side to believe it had been betrayed by the other. This was the sum total of relations between Rome and the Greek East ca. 200 BC.

But these findings from Part I of our study only deepen the apparent paradox of the Roman decision of spring 200 to intervene in onrolling eastern events which, on the surface, had little to do with Rome. The decision was not a natural development caused by an ever-intensifying Roman involvement across the Adriatic. The Senate in 201–200 BC did have bitter experience of the aggressive ambitions of powerful Hellenistic monarchs: first through the invasion of Italy by King Pyrrhus of Epirus in 280–275, which did great damage, and then in Philip V's recent attempts to seize Illyria and (the Senate feared) probably a

---

[21]   So, e.g., Harris 1979: 212–18; Derow 2003.

great deal more. So it seems reasonable that the Senate in 201/200 understood how serious security threats might arise from the powerful monarchies in the East – a concern intensified by the conduct of Philip V. But in autumn 201 the Roman decision-making elite was not looking for a war in the Greek Mediterranean. This is not because the Senate was averse to actions aimed at increasing Roman power and influence – including in the East. On the contrary: desire to increase Roman power, influence, and control over its international environment was the general stance taken by the *Patres*. It constituted what Paul Veyne has called "the imperialism of routine."[22] This "imperialism of routine" was in fact a stance common to all major Hellenistic states – and common to Hellenistic medium-sized states as well, and common even with many small states.[23] Rather, Rome was indifferent at first to the major events unrolling in the Greek East because (1) the Republic was exhausted by the long and terrible war just concluded with Carthage, while (2) Roman involvement and interests in the eastern Mediterranean were up to this point minimal. Indeed, we know that the *Patres* were still so uninformed in these years about the geography of European Greece that the Senate needed a basic geography lesson on this subject in winter 198/197 BC – and this was in the third year of the new war against Philip.[24]

Thus even though the *Patres* understood that serious threats to the security of Rome and Italy could, under certain circumstances, arise from the powerful monarchies east of the Adriatic, it is clear that without a specific catalyst to set off these fears, Rome would not have acted in the Greek Mediterranean immediately after the Second Punic War. One must add that given the disorganized nature of the Roman Senate, an institution of about 300 men divided into many groups, factions, families, and personalities in constant and fluid interaction with each other, it was natural that the Senate tended to avoid thinking about long-range and subtle problems. This included the problems in the East caused by the collapse of Ptolemaic Egypt. As a group, the *Patres* could be quite efficient when confronted with a specific crisis. But the Senate as an institution tended just to "muddle through," in 201–200 BC it had much on its mind, and it contained very few men with extensive experience in the Greek world.[25]

---

[22]   Veyne 1975: 794.
[23]   See above, Chapter 1.
[24]   See Polyb. 18.11.2–12, Livy 32.37.1–5, cf. App. *Mac.* 8, with Eckstein 1987a: 284. Contrast Harris 1979: 217, who depicts Rome's "intrusion" into Greek affairs in 200 as simply the next and inevitable imperialist step, after victory over Carthage, in the implacable Roman advance.
[25]   On all this, see in more detail Chapter 1, above.

So a catalyst was required in order to bring the crisis in the East to the *Patres'* attention, and to cause the (surprising) decision for action there. It is clear that the catalyst (on this reconstruction, a *necessary* catalyst) was the arrival before the Senate of embassies from at least four Greek states, warning of the conduct and dangers posed by Philip and Antiochus. The political scientist Richard Ned Lebow has defined a diplomatic catalyst as information or an event that (1) significantly reshapes the thinking of an important decision-making elite about external affairs so that (2) the costs and risks of inaction suddenly appear more dangerous than do the costs and risks of acting forcefully.[26] In Lebow's terminology, therefore, the four Greek embassies of autumn 201 acted as such a catalyst, because (1) the information the envoys brought with them significantly reshaped the thinking of the Roman decision-making elite about eastern events, so that (2) it led the Senate to the perception that the costs and risks of Roman inaction in the East were more dangerous than the costs and risks of acting forcefully there.

We have already established the nature of that information. Close examination of Polyb. 15.20.5–6 in Chapter 5 above has shown that Polybius evidently depicted the Greek envoys of autumn 201 as warning the Senate that Philip V and Antiochus III, each already a militarily very formidable and aggressive monarch, had made a pact to destroy the Ptolemaic state; if the project succeeded, it would enormously increase the power of the two kings. As we have also seen in Chapter 4 above, Polybius told his audience that both Philip and Antiochus desired world-wide rule – and it is likely that the Greek envoys were not shy about making a similar declaration. Our analysis of Polyb. 15.20.5–6 strongly reinforces the statements we find in other, later sources that both the Ptolemaic government (Justin 30.2.8–3.5) and the government of Rhodes (App. *Mac.* 4) warned the Senate about the Pact Between the Kings and its implications. Since both Livy and Justin link the embassy from Pergamum that arrived at Rome in autumn 201 directly with the embassy from Rhodes (Livy 31.2.1; Justin 30.3.5), we can in turn assume that the envoys from Attalus I strongly seconded this information.[27] We have also demonstrated in detail in Chapters 4 and 5 above that despite some scholars, there is no convincing evidence that the Greek envoys were inventing or even exaggerating the terms of the Pact Between the Kings. That is, the envoys were presenting the *Patres* with a real crisis, one that had already forced each of their governments to take extraordinary actions (the military alliance struck between Pergamum and

---

[26]   On the function of "catalysts" in the development of international crises, see Lebow 2001: esp. 614.

[27]   Cf. Briscoe 1973: 43; Gera 1998: 62 n. 9; cf. above, Chapter 5, pp. 197–8.

Rhodes against Philip; the elimination of the "Macedonian" tribes at Athens; the Rhodian, Athenian, and Ptolemaic governmental decisions to appeal to Rome). This was the real crisis – i.e., the power-transition crisis – into which the pact between Philip and Antiochus, followed by their aggressions against the tottering Ptolemaic regime, had plunged the Greek East.[28]

Beyond the general geopolitical crisis that was convulsing the East, one specific argument that the Rhodian and Pergamene envoys may have used before the Senate was to warn the *Patres* that Antiochus III's formidable navy (100 quinquiremes), might soon be joined by Philip V's own large and newly built navy. Philip's navy now contained over fifty quinquiremes, counting captured Ptolemaic vessels – and in summer 201 this navy had just shown itself to be a highly effective force off the coast of Asia Minor.[29] As G. T. Griffith pointed out long ago, the Greek envoys, in order to arrive at Rome in the autumn, would have been dispatched while the fierce naval fighting between Philip on the one side, and Pergamum and Rhodes on the other, was at its height. Whatever had happened afterward in the southeast Aegean, this was the situation the envoys would have reported at Rome.[30] Such a report would have had an impact upon the *Patres*, who well understood that sea-power had been vital a decade previously in preventing Philip from attacking coastal Illyria – or from coming to Italy. Now Roman control of the seas immediately east of Italy was potentially at risk.[31]

The envoys from Alexandria, meanwhile, warning also of the pact (Justin 30.2.8–3.5), could point to Philip's seizure of the great Ptolemaic naval base at Samos, occurring in tandem with Antiochus' overland invasion of Ptolemaic Coele Syria and Judaea, to demonstrate the scale of combined aggression that the Ptolemaic regime faced.[32] And as Grainger has recently suggested, the envoys could point as well to the danger if the potential resources of Egypt were added to the substantial resources already possessed by Philip and/or Antiochus. At Raphia in 217, the combined armies of Antiochus and Ptolemy IV had totaled 150,000 men; at Panium in 200, the combined armies of Antiochus and Ptolemy V had perhaps totaled 120,000 men. These were forces trained, ready for

---

[28] Scholars who argue that the Greek governments exaggerated or even invented the pact, in order to seek safety for their own polities: Magie 1939: 42–4; Errington 1971: esp. 352–4, cf. Errington 1986: 5 and n. 16. See above, Chapter 4.
[29] On the size of Antiochus' navy ca. 197 BC, see above, Chapter 5; on the size of Philip's navy after his seizure of Samos in early summer 201, see above, Chapter 4.
[30] Griffith 1935: 6–9.
[31] See Griffith 1935: 8–9 and 12–13.
[32] So Gera 1998: 62–3.

battle, and actually in the field; and they were twice the size of the huge Roman army at Cannae. The union of (say) Antiochus with the resources of Egypt might eventually create military resources triple those that had been available to Hannibal and Carthage; the union of Philip with the resources of Egypt might eventually mean military resources perhaps double those which Carthage and Hannibal had enjoyed. This can hardly have been a comforting prospect at Rome. The real crisis in the East had widespread negative implications even for the West.[33]

Some scholars argue that the alarm evidently caused in the Senate by the news of the Pact Between the Kings occurred because the Romans did not understand the limited goals of wars among the Greek states. This is an old view of the nature of the Hellenistic balance of power, which sees the Greek Mediterranean as essentially a consensual community of states which recognized each other's legitimate existence and hence were limited in their expansionist ambitions; and it is a view still sometimes repeated.[34] But much recent work has emphasized instead the ruthless nature of Hellenistic geopolitics and the instability of the balance of power among all the Greek states – all of them in actuality ferocious competitors with each other for security and power. The latter position is the one taken here.[35] By 201 BC the Senate, of course, had long experience of the ruthlessness of power-politics among states in the Mediterranean anarchy, both in Italy itself and in the western Mediterranean in general – a ruthlessness which Rome of course shared, and in which it participated.[36] And while most Roman senators in 201 probably had no detailed knowledge of the Greek world, one may still suggest that they had a general impression: that the great states of the East were as ruthless as Rome itself and its neighbors in the West. The *Patres* knew enough – from the earlier Roman experience of Pyrrhus as well as from the direct experience of Philip V himself – to be wary of certain developments there.

One other important factor in the eventual decision of the Senate to intervene in the eastern crisis needs to be underlined: the terrible experience of Hannibal's invasion of Italy. The Carthaginian general had inflicted devastating – almost fatal – damage upon Rome and, importantly, he had struck at the Republic from bases of operation seemingly impossibly far away (in Punic Spain). After the experience of Hannibal, one can

---

[33] See Grainger 2002: 28.
[34] See Griffith 1935: 6; Braunert 1964: 95; Veyne 1975: 823 and 837–8, cf. also 795 and 800; Klose 1982: 80–6; cf. in general Bederman 2001: 43 and n. 63.
[35] See Lévêque 1968; Austin 1986; Ager 2003; Eckstein 2006: Ch. 4; and above, Chapter 1.
[36] See in detail Eckstein 2006: Ch. 5.

see why *any* warning of a looming threat from great powers overseas was more likely to be taken seriously by the Senate. Indeed, Livy is explicit about the direct link in many people's minds between what was now seen as dangerous Roman indecisiveness in the years before the Hannibalic War over the issue of the town of Saguntum, the memory of Hannibal's subsequent devastating invasion of Italy, and the decision in 201/200 to act decisively in the East (31.7.2–3: see below).[37]

In sum, we must give crucial weight in the Roman decision of 200 to a contingent and unexpected event: the arrival at Rome in autumn 201 of a series of embassies from important Greek states. There were at least four such embassies, all warning the Senate about the conduct and intentions of Philip and/or Antiochus, and all pleading for Roman intervention and help. It was an extraordinary event. And without this extraordinary event – without this contingent catalyst – there would simply have been no Roman decision to intervene in the crisis in the Greek East in 200: *sine qua, non.*

THEORETICAL PERSPECTIVES

Modern international relations theory has helped us in this study to understand the general Roman situation by emphasizing the pressures to aggressive action that drive all states that exist within an anarchic, competitive, and heavily militarized state-system. Theory can also help us to understand not just the effect of the four Greek embassies upon the Senate, but also why the eventual Roman response to intervene occurred. In modern political-science terms, what the Greek envoys presented was a classic "worst-case scenario" about the security threat posed by the Pact Between the Kings. And the *Patres* responded the way that governing elites in anarchic state-systems usually respond when facing the prospect of a worst-case scenario.

We briefly discussed the concept of the "worst-case scenario" above in Chapter 1; at this point more detail is required.[38] Political scientists argue that a major problem in interstate relations is that no state (i.e., no governing elite) can accurately know the capabilities of the other states

---

[37]   See, e.g., Siebert 1995: 242, on the relationship between the Hannibalic experience and the feelings behind the Roman decision of winter 201/200. This is not to say that Roman conduct in the origins of the Second Punic War was itself innocent; on the contrary, Roman diplomacy was, up to a point, highly aggressive: see, e.g., Rich 1996. But this does not change the memory of having left Saguntum in the lurch, or the trauma inflicted by Hannibal.

[38]   See Chapter 1, above, pp. 13–14.

with which it is competing in the system. In fact, it is by no means easy to know its own power-capabilities accurately, and hence, and crucially, it cannot know with certainty the relationship of its own power-capabilities to the power-capabilities of other states. Ignorance may not be total, but information on the capabilities of other states is usually uncertain, sporadic, and difficult to interpret, and meanwhile, in a state-system that is a militarized anarchy, distrust of the motives and intentions of other states is strong (and, one may add, rightly so). Thus even in the modern world, with all the many sources of intelligence available to governing elites, states are to a significant extent opaque to one another. Political scientists call this condition of mutual opacity "the uncertainty principle." The most troubling aspect of this situation is that the true power-capabilities of states in relation to the power-capabilities of other states within the system can only become fully known in one way: through the cruel test of war.[39]

Now the opacity of states – "the uncertainty principle" – was far more intense and pervasive in the Hellenistic Mediterranean than in the modern world, because ancient states possessed far fewer instruments of intelligence-gathering than do modern states. One starts from the fundamental fact that no ancient state ever had a permanent embassy stationed in another state – a condition of lack of mutual communication that shocks modern political scientists.[40] Among many other deleterious effects, this lack of permanent embassies stationed abroad meant that information about foreign polities came to ancient decision-making elites in a far more haphazard and undependable manner than is true for modern states. The occasional chance presence of merchants in foreign ports, or other informal sources, was simply no substitute for regular intelligence-gathering run by a permanent embassy.[41]

Given "the uncertainty principle," even modern states in an anarchic state-system are thus always preparing themselves to counteract not merely known dangers but also unknown dangers, to prepare not just for any anticipated threat but also for any greater than anticipated threat – i.e.,

[39] The importance of opacity and "the uncertainty principle": Morgenthau 1973: 208. Actual power-capabilities and comparative power-capabilities of states unknown – even to themselves – until tested in war: see Levy 1983: 24; Blainey 1988: 114; Thompson 1988: 41; Wohlforth 1994–5: 104–5, 123, and 127; Jervis 2001: 281–2 and n. 2.

[40] See Chapter 1, above. Discussion of the widespread negative impact of this diplomatic primitiveness: see Eckstein 2006: esp. Chs. 3–5 and 7.

[41] Indeed, information sent to an ancient government by these informal sources was sometimes inaccurate and/or self-serving. See the behavior of the provocative "friends" of Athens at Mytilene in 427 BC (Ar. *Pol.* 1304a), or the use which Ap. Claudius Caudex made of Punic merchants at Rhegium in 264 BC, who unwittingly misled the Carthaginian admiral across in Sicily as to Roman intentions (Zon. 8.9).

to face "the worst-case scenario." They do this because they must. The manifold pressures originating in the harsh international environment push all states in this direction, and to do otherwise is – or is felt to be – irresponsible governance.[42] This was obviously true also of Republican Rome, with its suspicious stance towards the outside world – and if that stance was similar to that of all other major Hellenistic states, this only serves to demonstrate once more the general harshness of the Hellenistic state-system for all involved. The long and bitter struggle of Rome to attain power and security in the cruelly competitive environment first of central Italy and then of the wider western Mediterranean made such a suspicious attitude towards the outside world all too natural. In other words, both correct caution and the bitter impact of Roman history predisposed the *Patres* towards believing in "the worst-case scenario."[43]

The situation at Rome in the winter of 201/200 is a striking example of just this sort of attitude. When the Greek ambassadors presented the threatening prospect of Philip and Antiochus to the Senate, they were presenting a "worst-case scenario." The actions of Philip and Antiochus were an immediate and severe threat to the independence of the polities of the Greek envoys, but the threat the kings posed to Rome was only indirect and long term; nevertheless, the Greek ambassadors presented the Senate with the darkest possible implications of the situation. This does not mean they were consciously exaggerating, let alone lying. On the contrary, their own internal cultures, "socialized" to the harsh nature of the militarized anarchy in which their states existed, were themselves imbued with "worst-case scenario" thinking. Nor were the envoys even mistaken. We have argued in this study that the Pact Between the Kings was real, as was the system-wide threat the pact posed and the system-wide crisis it greatly helped provoke once the Ptolemaic regime began to falter and collapse. Naturally, these facts must have helped make the warnings of the Greeks at Rome more believable. And once the *Patres* had been presented with the threatening prospect laid out by the Greek envoys, the pressures on senators from many directions not to ignore

---

[42] See Jervis 1976: 58–113; Taylor 1978: 130; Waltz 1988: 619; Sheehan 1996: 8; Glaser 1997: 184.

[43] On the deleterious impact of the mutual "opacity" of states under anarchy see Morgenthau 1973: 208. The relationship of the opacity of states and the uncertainty principle to governmental thinking concerning "the worst-case scenario:" ibid., and van Evera 1998: 13–14. On the harsh lessons taught Roman decision-makers by the long struggle to survive and prevail in Italy and then the western Mediterranean, see Eckstein 2006: Ch. 5. Of course, when all governmental elites in a state-system are socialized to such thinking, the result can be a self-fulfilling prophecy: see Jervis 2001: 283.

this "worst-case scenario" – pressures deriving from system reality as well as from Roman internal culture and from recent bitter memory as well – would have been very strong.

In short, from the perspective of "worse-case scenario" theory the decision of the Senate in winter 201/200 was a quite natural response. The *Patres* could not know the actual extent of the threat to Rome posed by the hugely expanding power of Philip and Antiochus; they could not know the actual extent or the limits of the power possessed by the kings; they could not even know the power of the Roman State in relation to the threat the kings posed. But many senators must have come to feel that to ignore the problem presented to them by the Greek envoys, and to let the problem grow, was highly dangerous. Experience of the harsh interstate world in which Rome had long participated – and especially the impact of Hannibal's invasion – had "socialized" the *Patres* precisely in that direction.[44]

It is equally important in terms of our analysis to understand that the arrival of the Greek embassies before the Senate, and the crucial role they played as the catalyst for the Roman decision to intervene in the East, was at the same time a *typical* event of ancient Mediterranean politics. That is: in ancient state-systems, weaker states under severe local pressure often called upon a more powerful state for help. This was because in the harsh anarchy of the ancient Mediterranean, survival and protection required power, including most importantly military power; and if a weaker state could not protect itself by means of its own power, then it needed to gain the power of someone else.

This phenomenon is already depicted as a commonplace in our earliest historians of interstate life, Herodotus and Thucydides, writing in the fifth century BC: the Ionian states call upon Sparta and Athens for help against Persia in 499; the states of European Greece call upon Gelo of Syracuse for help against Persia in 480; Corcyra in the 430s calls upon Athens for protection when threatened by Corinth; Potidaea calls upon Corinth when confronted by Athens; Corinth calls upon Sparta when confronted by Athens. In fact, in Thucydides' view (1.3.2 and 1.9.2), pleas from weaker states to strong states for protection were an interstate phenomenon that had existed since the formation of organized

---

[44]   A classic case of the impact of this type of "worst-case scenario" thinking is the growth in the mid-1890s of British fear that Britain would soon confront a military coalition consisting of France, Russia, *and* Germany (or, alternatively, France, Russia, and the United States); however bizarre this concern appears to us now, it led to a real and ferocious naval building program, at enormous expense. See Friedberg 1988: 157–65.

states themselves.[45] And the phenomenon was as common in the western Mediterranean as it was in Greece: Punic states in Sicily called upon Carthage for protection against the Greeks; Teanum Sidicinum called upon Capua for protection against the Samnites; Capua called upon Rome for protection against the Samnites; Tarentum called upon King Pyrrhus of Epirus for protection against Rome; the Mamertines called upon Carthage and Rome for protection against Syracuse; the Torboletae called upon Hannibal for protection against Saguntum; Saguntum called upon Rome for protection from Hannibal.[46] In other words: when Rhodes, Pergamum, Egypt, and Athens called upon Rome for protection against Philip and/or Antiochus, this was, from one perspective, a typical inter-action of the anarchic Hellenistic system, part of the way of life of ancient Mediterranean states – though from another perspective, the arrival of the embassies must have been totally unexpected at Rome, for rarely had Greek states gone so far away to find a strong state to help them, and never before to Rome. This in itself, of course, shows the desper-ation of the Rhodian, Pergamene, Ptolemaic, and Athenian governments in summer 201.[47]

Moreover, throughout Mediterranean antiquity decision-makers in the more powerful states tended to answer such pleas from weaker states in the affirmative. To be sure, the Roman Senate did not always answer every plea for help positively: for instance, in 240 it rejected a plea for protection against the Carthaginians from the city of Tunis in North Africa, on grounds that the city belonged to the Carthaginians, with whom Rome was now at peace (see Polyb. 1.83.11).[48] But Rome often did respond in the affirmative to such calls for protection – as one can see from the list of examples above. Some scholars have depicted this trend at Rome to answer pleas for protection from smaller states as if it were a uniquely aggressive Roman trait.[49] But Rome was no different here than any other great Classical or Hellenistic state. Polybius, for one, thought that positive responses to pleas for help were natural for any powerful entity, and ascribes this common practice of powerful states

---

[45]   Recent discussions include Crane 1992 and Eckstein 2006: Ch. 3.
[46]   Recent discussion in Eckstein 2006: Ch. 5.
[47]   The only parallel in terms of distance is when the Greek states of Europe went to Gelo of Syracuse, to plead for military help against the looming and greatly feared Persian invasion of European Greece in 480 (see Hdt. 7. 145 and 157–63). The parallel is instructive in terms of the Greek perception of the intensity of the crisis in 201/200.
[48]   Note the formal Roman requirement that a polity offering *deditio*, absolute surrender into Roman power, not be under the legal jurisdiction of another state: see Livy 1.38.3, with the comments of Eckstein 1995.
[49]   See Harris 1979: 189 and 217.

both to a natural expression of their *megalopsychia* (greatness of spirit) and to the desire to publicly display it – i.e., the issue is partly one of honor and prestige (24.10.11). The list of incidents above in which Rome was not involved supports Polybius' point about the phenomenon being widespread.

Modern political scientists, like Polybius, see the acceptance of weaker polities into the protection of the stronger as a widespread and natural phenomenon, a direct consequence of the interstate anarchy, and they emphasize the systemic pressures that favor it. First, in an interstate anarchy and in the absence of effective international law, threatened polities can only turn to the strong; and second, powerful states tend to respond affirmatively to calls for protection from weaker polities since this increases their own power, resources, and prestige – and/or such a response serves to prevent the accretion of power, resources, and prestige to other large states with which the powerful states are competing.[50]

In accepting the pleas for help from weaker states threatened by powerful neighbors, powerful states in antiquity accepted the risk that such local conflicts might turn into larger conflicts with those other large states.[51] Yet this risk was evidently preferable in general to the risk of appearing weak or hesitant in the interstate arena, or the risk involved in abandoning significant (or even possibly significant) regions and their resources to another great power.[52] Conversely, the governing elite of a weaker state facing a severe local threat was well aware that when it asked a stronger state for protection, it was running the risk of paying a high price for that protection – that it was possibly engaging in what modern political scientists call "empire by invitation." But under the harsh pressures of a militarized anarchy, and in the absence of international law, weaker states were sometimes forced to make these difficult choices.[53]

---

[50]   On the reasons for the behavior of the weaker state, see Walt 1984: esp. Chs. 1 and 2. On the reasons for the behavior of the strong, see Glaser 1992 and 1997.
[51]   On the occasionally negative impact on relations between competing great states of what he views as a natural process of interstate life throughout antiquity, see Hoyos 1998: Chs. 3, 12, and 16.
[52]   On the Roman willingness to accept into their protection states which were at high risk – conduct that can appear to us highly provocative on the Romans' part – and a defense of such willingness on grounds of the grim *Realpolitik* that ruled antiquity, see esp. Raaflaub 1996: 292.
[53]   On "empire by invitation," see Lundestad 1986, and 1990: Ch. 1. The example Lundestad employs here is the initiatory role played by European states in the 1940s, states directly threatened by the Soviet Union (unlike the US, which was not), in the creation of NATO. In the case of the Greek appeal to Gelo in 480, it turned out that his stated price for help was actually too high (Hdt. 7.161–2).

THE ROMAN DECISION

The highly unusual situation whereby embassies from at least four important Greek states all arrived in Rome at about the same time in autumn 201 to ask for protection against the same aggressive and expansionist monarchies would certainly have made rejection of the Greek pleas and warnings difficult for the Senate. Nevertheless, the *Patres* had free will: they could have decided to ignore the multiple pleas from the Greeks, and to ignore their warnings, especially since the Greek embassies were asking for Roman protection against powers that were known to be very formidable, but that were distant and not yet directly threatening Rome. Nothing was foreordained. So there is truth in the assertion of de Sanctis and other scholars that the Roman decision of winter 201/200 to accept the pleas of the Greek states for intervention in the East was an act of will, growing in some sense from the Romans' desire to dominate their environment.[54] The stance of the Senate was traditionally that Roman power and influence should always be increased if they could be; this is what Veyne has called "the imperialism of routine," and to some extent it is on display here.[55]

It is also certainly the case that by the third century the Roman State had adopted a habit of command towards the entire outside world.[56] Some scholars see this habit of command as an indication of exceptional Roman aggressiveness and bellicosity.[57] But while we should admit the negative impact which this Roman habit could have on Roman interactions with other polities, the analytical problem here is a familiar one: the desire to dominate, to exert as much control over one's environment as possible, and the habit of command – like the engagement in almost constant warfare – does not differentiate the Roman Republic from any other Classical or Hellenistic state. And this is the case despite the widely varying sizes of those polities (large, medium, small) and their widely varying internal structures (monarchies, oligarchies, democracies, federal leagues).[58] The desire to dominate, the habit of command, and the tendency to respond positively to pleas for help from weaker states can all be seen as arising from a militaristic and aggressive unit culture.[59]

---

[54] De Sanctis 1923: 21–31; in similar highly moralizing vein: Harris 1979: 212–18; Mandell 1989.
[55] Veyne 1975: 794.
[56] On the Roman "habit of command," see Derow 1979. On the Roman will to be "free," without having to consider others, see Veyne 1975: 794–6.
[57] See Derow 1979, 1991, and 2003; Harris 1979; Mandell 1989.
[58] See, e.g., Forde 1986: 442; or Eckstein 2006: Ch. 4.
[59] See, e.g., Harris 1979, or Rosenstein 1999: 193–205.

But while these are important factors (what the political scientists call independent variables) in the situation, they are not the entire story. Equally, and simultaneously, such bellicose and diplomatically assertive conduct was a natural response to the dangers and pressures of the anarchic interstate environment – which is why those responses were so similar and widespread, and why states of such varying size and such varying internal structures all engaged in such similar conduct. What this means in the context of the Mediterranean crisis of 201–200 is that by responding to the Greek pleas and warnings, Rome was simply participating in the destabilization of the Mediterranean state-system caused ultimately by the collapse of the Ptolemies, a destabilization participated in by many other states simultaneously, and all for similar motives. The Romans were, in fact, rather late in the game in contributing their own part to this system-destabilization.

All these considerations of system-derived and internal pressures behind the Roman decision would make sense to any modern political scientist. But Rome was also a highly religious ancient culture, the Roman elite as well as the populace desired the support and protection of the gods – and here a special factor in the decision of winter 201/200 comes into play.[60]

The Kingdom of Pergamum, as we have seen, was one of the states pleading for Roman intervention (Livy 31.2.1; App. *Mac.* 4). As we have also seen, Attalus I of Pergamum had been an ally of Rome and the Aetolian League in the First Macedonian War, until defeat on the battlefield by Philip V in 208 and a simultaneous invasion of Pergamum by Philip's in-law Prusias of Bithynia had driven him from Greece.[61] But Attalus' relationship with Rome remained good, and he appears as an *adscriptus* on the Roman side at the Peace of Phoenice in 205 (Livy 29.12.14). These considerations alone would have given greater weight to the Pergamene pleas for help in autumn 201 than those coming from the other Greek states, with which Rome's relations up to this point had been distant, if not cool.[62] But there would also have been a very special reason for senatorial attentiveness to the envoys of Attalus. As we have further seen, in 205 the Senate had received a prophesy that

---

[60]   On Roman religiosity, see below, and pp. 255–6 (with sources, and modern scholarship).

[61]   See above, Chapter 3.

[62]   Again, the Ptolemies, Rhodians, and Athenians had recently all worked at cross-purposes to Rome in attempting to bring the First Macedonian War to a mediated conclusion – and the Rhodians had expressed violent hostility in public towards both Roman policy and Rome itself (see above, Chapter 3). On the question of Athens as an *adscriptus* on the Roman side to the Peace of Phoenice (probably a fabrication by Roman historical writers), see above, Chapter 3.

Hannibal would not be driven from Italy until the goddess called the Great Mother was brought from Asia Minor to be worshipped at Rome. The Senate sent an embassy to Attalus, seeking help in procuring the Great Mother of Pessinus in central Anatolia; Pergamum was the friend of Rome nearest to Pessinus. The Pessinus temple was not in territory that Attalus controlled, but he persuaded the priests there to give the Romans the Black Stone, a central cult-object of the Great Mother. The Black Stone was then conveyed to Rome with great fanfare – including miracles that allegedly took place as the ship bearing the Black Stone came up the Tiber.[63]

The special effort done for Rome in 205 by the Pergamene king would no doubt have made the declarations of his envoys to the Senate four years later even weightier. And the religious aspect here should not be minimized: Roman gratitude for the coming of the Great Mother would have been intensified because Hannibal by autumn 203 had indeed left Italy, as the oracle had predicted – recalled by the Punic Senate to defend Carthage from the invasion of Africa launched by P. Cornelius Scipio. Senators well understood that military events at the secular level had relieved Italy of Hannibal after fifteen terrifying years; but there were probably also many who were impressed with the apparent connection between the coming of the Great Mother and the departure of Hannibal. Our sources stress that the Romans of the late third century were a deeply religious people, and this was especially the case in crises (see, e.g., Polyb. 3.112.9 – emphatic). And Polybius is explicit that even in his own somewhat later period (ca. 150 BC) most senatorial aristocrats were pious believers (6.56.12–15: a passage that has too often been ignored).[64] Polybius' continuator Poseidonius underlined the traditional intensity of Roman religious feeling, still prevalent in his own time – that is, a century after the events under discussion here (Ath. 6.274A). Indeed, even after the Roman declaration of "conditional" declaration of war against Philip in spring 200, the departure of the consul P. Sulpicius Galba for Greece was long delayed in good part because of the perceived religious necessity to investigate a major sacrilege at the Temple of Persephone at Locri (Livy 31.13.1) – and an entire campaigning season was thereby lost. Here, too, a connection existed between the supernatural and secular planes: for senators will have known that a similar looting of the Temple of Persephone by King Pyrrhus of Epirus in 275 was followed by a severe storm which inflicted great damage on

---

[63] On this important incident, see above, Chapter 4, pp. 122–3, and Burton 1996.
[64] But on Polyb. 6.56.12–15, see rightly Morgan 1990: 14–15, in contrast with the Roman cynicism about religion alleged by Harris 1979: 166–75. On the depth of Roman religiosity, see also Lind 1972: 250–2 (with sources).

Pyrrhus' fleet as he was crossing back home from Italy to Greece. The Romans did not want this to happen to them.[65]

In sum, there were probably many men in the Senate in winter 201/200 who sincerely felt that King Attalus had done Rome a great favor with the Great Mother, and that Rome owed him a real debt.[66] And we can be more exact. One of the envoys the Senate sent out in 205 to obtain the Great Mother was Ser. Sulpicius Galba; he was a close relative (probably the brother) of P. Sulpicius Galba, one of the two men elected consuls for 200 – and P. Sulpicius Galba was the most vigorous proponent of intervention in the East.[67] It is also likely that P. Sulpicius Galba led the attempt in 196 to reward Attalus for his participation in the eventual war against Philip by giving Pergamum the important Macedonian-held cities of Oreus and Eretria on the island of Euboea. But this significant extension of Pergamene power across the Aegean was blocked by the Roman commander T. Quinctius Flamininus, who wished these cities left free of all foreign control.[68] Thus the circle around Ser. and P. Sulpicius Galba would have been prominent among those senators predisposed to give heavy weight to the pleas and warnings from King Attalus. And beyond the goodwill accrued by Pergamum for its actions since 210, and the Roman debt owed Pergamum because of the Great Mother, the Pergamene envoys will of course have argued that intervention in the Aegean was also in Rome's ultimate best interest, given the broad geopolitical threat posed by the Pact Between the Kings.[69]

[65] The incident with Pyrrhus: Livy 29.18.6; cf. Warrior 1996: 69–70. Problems in the conscription of an army for Greece probably also account for the long delay in Galba's departure for Greece: see above, p. 235 and n. 19.
[66] Linderski 1993 points out how important the Romans believed maintaining proper relations with the gods was to the safety of the state.
[67] On Ser. Sulpicius Galba see Broughton 1951: 304, with sources. McShane 1964: 121 n. 100 notes that Attalid interests receive special emphasis in Roman diplomatic confrontations with Philip in spring and summer 200 (see Polyb. 16.25.4; Livy 31.16.2).
[68] Polybius 18.47.19 and Livy 33.34.10 both say that turning over the Euboean cities to Pergamum was the majority opinon of the senatorial Commission of Ten – of whom P. Galba was the most senior figure, and a person of pronounced opinions. On the dispute between Flamininus and the Ten over this, see esp. Walsh 1996: 357 and n. 53. On Flamininus' policy of "Freedom of the Greeks," see Chapter 7, below.
[69] Again, it is crucial here to understand that the warning about the pact would have been central to the Pergamene plea as Polybius conceived events (cf. 15.20.5–6, with discussion in Chapter 5, above). I suggest as a parallel here the warning that the Megalopolitan envoys in Polybius are depicted as giving to Antigonus Doson when asking for help in 225 against Cleomenes of Sparta: concerning the threat posed by Cleomenes ultimately to Macedon, "they implored him to look to the future," for Antigonus has the choice of facing Cleomenes in the Peloponnese, backed by the Achaean League, or of facing him later as he invades Thessaly, now backed with many Greek allies including the subordinated Achaeans

This raises the issue of Livy's understanding of the causes of the new war that eventually broke out between Rome and Macedon. It is clear that he had two differing versions of the Roman decision of winter 201/200. The Polybian version (we have argued) emphasized the Pact Between the Kings, and this theme is prominent whenever Livy seems to be depending on Polybian material (as in 31.14.4–5), But Livy's account of the Roman decision of 200 BC is based far more on the Roman historical tradition, the Annalistic tradition. The Annalists placed emphasis on Philip's attacks against Greek states that were friends of Rome as the fundamental reason for the Roman decision (*ob iniurias armaque illata sociis populi Romani . . .* – 31.6.1) – a version of events that underlined Roman protection of friendly states, and hence appealed to the traditional Roman morality of *fides*. This is something different from the pact.

In depicting the decision of spring 200 BC, Livy has perhaps combined these two traditions to produce his own synthesis.[70] But Livy's divergence from Polybius' suggested emphasis on the pact should not be exaggerated. Nor was the Roman Annalistic tradition untrue *per se*. Rome's friend Pergamum, after all, was indeed at war with Macedon, and in the late summer of 201 – when Attalus dispatched his envoys to Rome – the Attalid kingdom was not doing well; not only had Philip mounted a serious naval challenge to the combined fleets of both Pergamum and Rhodes, but he had launched an invasion of Pergamum right up to the walls of the capital, which Attalus had been unable to prevent and which had done great damage.[71] The other Greek states under attack had previously not had close relations with Rome (a fact we have stressed in Chapters 3 and 5, above); but it would not be surprising if they, too, pleaded their own specific cases of victimization along with the broader geopolitical issues. The Roman tradition stressed the former aspect of the interaction – the Romans in the role of protectors of victims of aggression.[72] But even the Annalistic tradition acknowledged the latter aspect, that geopolitical considerations had played a role in

(2.49.6). Gruen 1984: 101–2, followed by Warrior 1996: 43, suggests that the Greek envoys were only asking for Roman mediation of the conflicts with Philip and Antiochus. That is not the ancient tradition, nor is it consonant with later Roman actions (see below).

[70] Cf. Warrior 1996.

[71] On the course of the fighting in the Aegean in 201, see above, Chapter 4. Livy also retails some obvious Roman propaganda about the Senate now taking revenge for Philip having sent Macedonian troops to help Hannibal in Africa in 202: 30.33.5 and 31.1.1. This is the kind of story that gave the Annalists a bad name, and few scholars accept it: see Walbank 1967: 456; Briscoe 1973: 55. Warrior 1996: 103, tries to save other Annalistic traditions to which this story is connected, concerning the presence of a few Roman figures in Greece in 203: on which, see above, Chapter 4.

[72] Cf. Briscoe 1973: 55–6 and 95–6; cf. Warrior 1996: 43–5.

the Roman decision: the Annalists stressed the growing power of Philip, and the fear this inspired at Rome (Livy 31.3.4–6, and all of 31.7). Nor can we even say that the connection between Philip and Antiochus was absent from the Annalists, for the envoys dispatched in the spring of 200 to give Rome's ultimatum to Philip were also given the task – according to Livy – of remonstrating with Antiochus about his attacks on Egypt (Livy 31.2.3–4 with 33.39.1). This is different from Polybius, but not that much different.[73]

In fact, where Polybius differs most sharply from Livy and the Annalistic tradition is not in his emphasis on the grave geopolitical concerns at Rome in 200 but in his emphasis on the Roman ambition after the Hannibalic War to extend control over the entire world (see esp. 3.6.2). This factor is missing from the Roman Annalists and from Livy. Is this conscious deception? But Roman internal discourse in this period emphasized "defensive" war (in whatever sense) – not Rome's right to imperial aggression.[74] And for understanding Polybius' point of view, it is important that to him the Romans were not exceptional in their large expansionist aims: their great ambitions did not differ from the great ambitions of Philip and Antiochus – or, for that matter, those of Carthage.[75] To Polybius, that was the way of the world.[76]

What is certain is that after hearing the envoys from the Greeks, the Senate passed a resolution (*senatus auctoritas*) proposing to the *comitia centuriata* (the Army Assembly, i.e., the assembly of the Roman People responsible for declaring peace and war) that an ultimatum be sent to Philip that he cease his attacks against Greek states, failing which there would be war with Rome. This amounted to a proposal that a "conditional" declaration of war against Macedon be declared by the Roman People. In addition, the Senate proposed that diplomatic pressure also be put on Antiochus III, seeking to prevent him from making an attack on Egypt proper.[77]

---

[73] Conversely, Polybius' depiction of events must have had the Greek envoys not only emphasizing the broad geopolitical issues but also asking for help because of the individual "aggressions" to which each state had been subjected: that would be rhetorically effective.

[74] Such an internal discourse may be naïve, but it is not likely to be consciously hypocritical: see discussion in Eckstein 2006: Ch. 6. The best contemporary example is Cato the Elder's defense of the Rhodians from a proposed declaration of war against them in 167; he argued successfully that they had not injured Rome enough to warrant such a step: see Astin 1978: 273–81.

[75] Polybius' emphasis on the same will to power in Philip and Antiochus as he perceived in the Romans: see above, Chapter 4. His conception of Punic ambitions: 5.104.3 and 15.9.5–6 (highly rhetorical).

[76] See esp. his comments at 5.67.12–68.1 and 5.106.4–5.

[77] On the development of the Roman custom of "conditional" declarations of war, replacing declarations of war by fetial priests at the frontier of the enemy state, for

Since in winter 201/200 neither Philip nor Antiochus represented a direct threat to Rome, the senatorial resolution envisions what modern international relations theorists call preventive war.[78] But preventive wars are often politically controversial, precisely because a direct threat is lacking. And so when the senatorial resolution came before the Roman People, the *comitia centuriata* rejected the senatorial resolution and voted overwhelmingly against declaring war on Philip (Livy 31.6.3). Livy says that the Assembly was urged to reject the senatorial war-motion especially by the tribune Q. Baebius, who accused the Senate of "sowing the seeds of war upon war" without considering the needs of an exhausted populace who wished to enjoy peace after the long struggle with Carthage (31.6.4).

The reasoning of the Senate in favor of preventive war, and the bitter experience of interstate life that lay behind it, seem apparent in a speech which Livy attributes to P. Sulpicius Galba, one of the two consuls of 200. The context of the speech is an informal public meeting (*contio*) following the initial overwhelming rejection of war by the People. Galba is seeking to convince the *populus* to vote again, this time in favor of war:

> It seems to me, citizens, that you do not understand the question before you. The question is not whether you will have peace or war – for Philip will not leave that matter open for your decision, seeing that he is preparing a mighty war on land and sea. Rather, the question is whether you are to send your legions across to Macedonia, or meet the enemy here in Italy. What a difference that makes, if you never knew it before, you found out during the recent war with Carthage. . . . So let Macedonia, not Italy, have war; let it be the enemy's farms and cities that are laid waste, not ours!
>
> We have already learned from experience. . . . Go to vote, then, with the blessings of the Gods, and ratify what the Senate has proposed. (31.7.2–3 and 13–14)

The emphasis here is on a looming threat in the East, and not, for instance, on the individual aggressions of Philip against Rome's Greek friends – and not at all, let it be said, on the prospect of glory, loot,

---

the distance from the city of Rome to potential enemies had increased, see Walbank 1949: 15–19. The basic principle of *rerum repetitio* and *iustum bellum* – that bad behavior on the other side was the main issue and that such delicts had to be rectified if war with Rome were to be avoided – of course did not change. The embassy to Antiochus is discussed in detail below, Chapter 7.

[78] A "preventive war" is a war undertaken to deal with a possible long-term threat (i.e., to attack first when there is no immediacy of being attacked, though there is a long-term problem); this is in contrast to a "preemptive war," which is a war undertaken to deal with an immediate threat (to attack first when one is clearly about to be attacked). See Evans and Newnham 1998: 448–50.

and imperial power. But insofar as Galba does mention Philip's aggressions against the Greeks (as at 31.7.6–7), he draws a lesson from the fate of Saguntum in Spain in 219: because the Romans did not militarily aid those under attack by Hannibal far away, they soon faced the invasion of Italy itself.[79]

Did the real P. Sulpicius Galba actually say something like this at a decisive public meeting that preceded the second Army Assembly-meeting, the meeting that eventually did reluctantly vote in favor of "conditional" war with Philip and the entering into forceful diplomacy with Antiochus? If he did, it would be important for our understanding of the mood in Rome (and especially among the *Patres*) in the winter of 201/200. That is, it was a mood of concern about developments in the East, not a mood of triumphant imperialism.

Livy was of course writing 200 years later, and studies of the Latin of Galba's speech as we have it in 31.7 demonstrate that the speech is, in its rhetorical construction as well as in its wording, essentially a composition by Livy himself.[80] Moreover, to judge from Cicero's silence about Galba in his history of Roman public speaking in the *Brutus*, no published speeches of P. Sulpicius Galba existed in the 40s BC. So Livy was probably not working from any original Galban text.[81] But we need not follow Harris in asserting that the speech therefore "has no claim whatsoever to authenticity"; i.e., that it is invented out of whole cloth.[82] Livy employs speeches only rarely in his narrative of the post-legendary period, but where the sources of these "historical" speeches can be checked (for instance, back to approximately parallel passages in Polybius), the essence of the speeches as presented by Livy reflects what was in his sources.[83] And we are concerned here merely with the basic theme of Galba's speech, not with its Latin style or detailed rhetorical construction. Quillin has pointed out that the main point of the speech is quite simple enough to have been remembered: Rome must fight Philip either in Macedon now or in Italy later, Rome must go to war with Philip now

---

[79] *Patiamur expugnandis Athenis, sicut Sagunto expugnando Hannibalem passi summus, segnitiam nostram imperiri regem. Non quinto inde mense, quem ad modum ab Sagunto Hannibal, sed quinto inde die ab Corintho solverit naves, in Italiam perveniet.* On the ideological power of this passage about Saguntum, see Merton 1965: 11–12. On the theme of future but real geopolitical threats, note Polyb. 2.49.6, the Megalopolitan warning to Antigonus Doson concerning the ambitions of Cleomenes III of Sparta (discussed above, n. 69).
[80] The fundamental study remains Ullmann 1929: 135.
[81] See Quillin 2004: 775 and n. 15.
[82] Harris 1979: 214; cf. Harris 1984b: 190. So also, e.g., Dahlheim 1968: 242–4.
[83] See Walsh 1963: 219–44; Luce 1977: 161–71. On Livy's accurate reflection of what appears in Polybian speeches specifically, see Pédech 1964: 277; Briscoe 1973: 18.

or wait until he becomes a second Hannibal. Thus the idea that some-one (for instance, Cato the Elder) heard the speech and transmitted its simple and clear thrust so that it became part of Roman tradition is not difficult to imagine.[84] One may add that no scholar expresses doubt over Livy's account in the previous chapter of Book 31 that the tribune Q. Baebius gave an anti-war speech before the People during the contro-versy over whether to declare war on Philip, a speech in which he used the memorable phrase that the Senate was "sowing the seeds of war upon war" (Livy 31.6.4: see above). The fundamentals of political debate, when the issues are as simple as this, are easily remembered.

Moreover, the main theme of Galba's speech as we have it in Livy – that the terrible trauma so recently suffered compels Rome now to expand greatly its sphere of concern, influence, and power, in order to ensure that Rome never suffers such a trauma again – turns out to be, accord-ing to modern scholars of international relations, the *typical* response of a powerful polity that yet has come to realize how vulnerable it is to a sudden and devastating attack. This combination of a sense of power and a sense of vulnerability is a major source of expansive action. That Galba's speech is typical of a great state's response to the traumatic experi-ence of vulnerability as underlined by modern political scientists does not of course prove the historicity of Galba's speech. But the pattern is suggestive.[85]

In terms of following a "layered" approach in analyzing the Roman decision of 200, we arrive at this point at the personal motives of the consul P. Sulpicius Galba. The augural lottery had allotted him the com-mand against Macedon, should it come to war (Livy 31.6.1). Since Galba had already commanded in Greece during the First Macedonian War (in 210–207), scholars have sometimes found it highly suspect that the lottery result gave Macedonia to him again; it seems too militarily convenient.[86] But recent studies have reasserted the honesty of the annual

[84]   Cf. Briscoe 1973: 20–2, and Quillin 2004: 776. Thus in a speech reported both by Cato (frg. 86 Peter) and later Livy (22.51.2), Livy imposes his own Latin style, but the essential content remains the same as in Cato: see Badian 1966: 17 and Quillin 2004: 776.
[85]   See Copeland 2000: Ch. 6, on how the American experience of Pearl Harbor led to military preparations to deal with the possibility of a hostile Soviet Union even while the USSR was still an American ally. Note especially the emotion and the rea-soning in the memorandum of Vice-Admiral Russell Willson, from August 1945 (Copeland 2000: 164): it could have come from Galba's speech. Then, too, there is the new US strategic doctrine published in 2002 – in good part a response to the devastating terrorist attacks on New York and Washington in 2001; note the tradi-tion into which the new strategic doctrine is put by Gaddis 2005.
[86]   See McDonald and Walbank 1937: 207; Scullard 1973: 93; Briscoe 1973: 69–70, cf. 45.

lottery for *provinciae*: the lottery procedure was overseen by a board of priests (the augurs), and was hedged about with ceremony and religious feeling; the lottery-pitcher itself was one of the main symbols of the augural priests; and an innocent child picked from the augural lottery-pitcher the differently colored wooden balls that determined which official got which *provincia*. Hence the probability is strong that the augural lottery of *provinciae* for 200 BC was honest. P. Sulpicius Galba may thus have felt, if anything, that the gods had given him a special responsibility in this year for defending Rome from a severe threat.[87]

Numerous scholars have also proposed that the ambition of Galba and his supporters to win the glory of a military victory over Philip – a victory which, given Philip's reputation as a conqueror, would be as great as the victory just won by Scipio Africanus over Hannibal – played a role in their advocacy of the eastern war.[88] Ambition for *gloria* is always likely to be present in a Roman aristocrat, and a great victory over Macedon would have hugely enhanced the influence of Galba and his circle of supporters (whoever they were) both in the Senate and before the *populus Romanus*. Nevertheless, one should be cautious about positing that mere personal or factional ambition is the key for our reconstruction of political events at Rome in 200. Such a reconstruction is actually founded on our knowledge that Rome was going to win the Macedonian war. Yet although *we* know the Romans are going to win, the Romans did not know. The armies of Rome suffered ninety major defeats on the battlefield under the Republic; dozens of army commanders were killed in battle in the fourth and third centuries alone. It is well for us to remember the ferocity and difficulty of the world in which the Romans lived.[89] Moreover, P. Sulpicius Galba had not done very well in his military command against Philip V in Greece in 210–207 – and such an experience of the difficulty of dealing with Philip might have led Galba to conclude that victory was in fact uncertain and would be difficult to achieve, and the Macedonians very formidable opponents. Indeed, one could argue that Galba's experience of Philip's formidable army and formidable generalship in 210–207 makes more understandable the fears of Philip which we find attributed to Galba in his speech to the people in Livy 31.7. And the hard fact is that Galba's eventual campaign against Philip in 199 was not a success: he exhausted his army

---

[87]   Religious honesty of the lot: Eckstein 1976: 122–5, and now the thorough study by Stewart 1998: Ch. 1.

[88]   So Dorey 1959; Briscoe 1973: 45–6; Harris 1979: 217–18 (Sulpicius and his supporters felt "entitled to the opportunities of war"); Will 1982: 142–3; Errington 1989b: 255–6; Hamilton 1993: 559–67; Ampela 1998: 77.

[89]   Roman defeats: see Rosenstein 1990, esp. the startling list in the Appendix.

by attempting an invasion of Macedon from the west which ultimately had to be abandoned, and later that winter there was a serious mutiny among his troops.[90]

Despite the passage of a senatorial resolution in favor of war, it is also clear that at least some senators strongly opposed the war, and were prepared to oppose it in public and before the *populus*. The obvious example is the tribune Q. Baebius' strenuous and initially successful opposition to the senatorial war motion, which led to its rejection by the Army Assembly (Livy 31.6.3–4). But Baebius came from an important senatorial family. Tradition held that Q. Baebius Tamphilus, a relative of this tribune (perhaps his father), was a member of an alleged senatorial embassy that warned Hannibal in 219 to desist from his siege of Saguntum – but perhaps this Q. Baebius was instead a member of the (certainly historical) Roman embassy of 220 that warned Hannibal not to attack Saguntum in the first place; in any case, in 218 he was a member of the senatorial embassy that delivered the Roman war-ultimatum to Carthage – which demonstrates his political prominence.[91] Another relative of Q. Baebius the tribune of 200 (perhaps his brother) was Cn. Baebius Tamphilus, who was aedile of the plebeians in 200. Hence we have two close relatives (perhaps brothers) in office at the same time – which shows the political influence of the family. Moreover, Cn. Baebius the aedile was responsible in autumn 200 for the production of Plautus' comic play *Stichus* – the play in which, as we have seen, envoys from Greece are castigated for taking up "room at the dinner table" that rightfully belongs to Roman farmers impoverished and made desperate by the Hannibalic War. The political point of this scene in a play produced by Cn. Baebius the aedile is thus precisely the same as the political point made by Q. Baebius the tribune.[92] Cn. Baebius the aedile went on to win election in autumn 200 immediately from the aedileship to be one of the praetors for 199 – which again suggests the power of his family as well as (again) the popularity of his political position. Cn. Baebius was then badly defeated in summer 199 by the Insubrian Gauls in the great war that had broken out in the Po Valley in summer 200, with

[90]   Convenient discussion of this campaign in Walbank 1940: 144–7, with the judgment that at the end of 199, Philip "could regard the year's record as a qualified success" (147) ; so, too, Errington 1972: 143; Eckstein 1976: 126–7, and 1987a: 271–2. Mutiny: Livy 32.3.2–7 (see this chapter, above).

[91]   Q. Baebius Tamphilus in 219 and on the embassy to Carthage in spring 218: see Broughton 1951: 237 and 239 (with sources). Perhaps on the embassy of 220 to Hannibal in Spain, not the (alleged) embassy of 219: see Briscoe 1973: 71.

[92]   Plaut. *Stich.* lines 494–504, cf. lines 167–70, discussed above, Chapter 5 . Cn. Baebius put on Plautus' play as part of the Plebeian Games of autumn 200 (cf. Livy 31.50.3).

the loss of almost 7,000 Roman soldiers (Livy 32.7.5–7); but his career was only delayed, not destroyed: he was eventually elected consul for 182 (though against severe opposition). His brother M. Baebius was then elected consul for 181 – in elections overseen by Cn. Baebius himself.[93]

The Baebii, then, were a powerful family, and so when we find Q. Baebius as tribune in 200 successfully opposing before the People the war-motion of the Senate, we should not think of him as a lone or eccentric figure. He convinced the vast majority of the *populus* that his position was correct – and meanwhile his relative Cn. Baebius the aedile had the same critical position concerning the new war. Moreover, no tribune attempted to veto Baebius' speech against the senatorial motion. This all suggests that, though it was not the majority opinion among the *Patres*, there were prominent and influential men who thought the intervention in the East was unnecessary and/or unwise, or that Rome was too exhausted to take on this new burden. Given the lack of deep and continuous senatorial interest in the East and the lack of major concrete Roman interests there which we have sought to elucidate in this study, the existence of significant senatorial opposition in winter 201/200 to undertaking a potentially large-scale and costly (and merely preventive) war in the Greek world is, in fact, not surprising.

We cannot know who else among the *Patres* agreed with the Baebii on this issue. It is sometimes suggested that P. Cornelius Scipio Africanus himself – the recent conqueror of Hannibal – opposed the new war. In 200 BC he would have been the single most important and influential senator in Rome. Scipio's alleged opposition to the proposed intervention in the East is based partly on the fact that one of the compromises about the new war made in 200 was that none of Scipio's veterans would be subject to the draft for it, although they could volunteer if they wished (Livy 31.8.6). This measure to protect Scipio's veterans looks a bit like a response to the tribune Q. Baebius' complaint in Livy 31.6.4 that "the seeds of war upon war" were being sown by the Senate despite an exhausted populace. And since a certain L. Baebius was one of Scipio's officers in Africa (Livy 30.25.2), some scholars posit that the Baebii were traditionally Scipio's lieutenants and henchmen. If so, then the hand of Scipio lies behind Q. Baebius and the initial rejection of the war-motion by the Army Assembly.[94]

---

[93]   On Cn. Baebius Tamphilus and his brother M. Baebius, see Broughton 1951: 324 and 326 n. 3. Cn. Baebius' defeat as praetor, and subsequent political career: Rosenstein 1990: 24–5 (with sources). Cn. Baebius' holding of the elections for 181: Livy 40.17.8.
[94]   So Dorey 1959: 293–4; Scullard 1973: 42 and 87; Briscoe 1973: 70–1; Hamilton 1993.

The personal links between Africanus and the Baebii are tenuous, however – restricted to Livy's brief reference to one minor officer serving with Scipio in Africa, a man who never appears again. And it is significant that we have no actual information on Africanus' position on the proposed eastern intervention. Given his great prominence in 200 and the intense interest he evoked in the Roman historical tradition, if Scipio in the Senate had openly opposed the eastern war – let alone, as major scholars argue, if he were the center of active and effective opposition to it – we would surely have heard about it.[95] Moreover, when we do finally get a statement from Scipio concerning the Roman stance in the East – and it only comes in winter 195/194 – he states in the Senate that the *Patres* were making a great mistake in withdrawing the Roman army in Greece back to Italy when there remained a serious threat in the East from Antiochus III (Livy 34.43.1–5). The *Patres* rejected Scipio's advice (ibid.), and perhaps he acted here partly from a desire to have the Greek command himself, since he had been elected one of the consuls for 194 (though Livy does not even hint at such a motive). Livy's foregrounding of Scipio's opposition to Roman withdrawal from the East in winter 195/194 is exactly the kind of story we would expect to find in the Roman tradition if Scipio had strongly opposed intervention in the East in 200 – he was a very important man. But what we find, rather, is that the conqueror of Hannibal was strongly in favor of maintaining a *forward* policy in the East in 195/194 – and the appearance of that later sentiment is yet another reason why we should be wary of assuming that in 200 Scipio was opposed to intervention against the great Greek monarchs.[96]

Yet to demonstrate that senatorial opinion was divided over the East in 200, it is enough to show that the intervention was strongly opposed by the Baebii. They were a powerful and influential family, and need not have been anyone's henchmen or lieutenants to have had an impact. Indeed, the highly unusual rejection of the senatorial war-motion by the *comitia centuriata* was something very unlikely to have occurred in the first place without the existence of significant opposition to the war among the Roman decision-making elite.

The original stance of the Army Assembly against war was eventually changed by persuasion coming from a powerful group within the Senate. Livy has the Senate itself, after the first rejection of the senatorial

---

[95] See the comments of Rich 1976: 80 n. 66, and Quillin 2004: 775.

[96] Scipio's opposition to Roman withdrawal from the East, and the decision of the Senate to ignore his advice and order the withdrawal of the troops, is discussed below, Chapter 7. Scipio in 194 ended up fighting as consul against the Celts in the Po Valley – not very successfully (see Broughton 1951: 343).

resolution, issuing a formal warning that postponement of the war would be harmful to the State (31.6.6).[97] And Galba's speech before the *populus* at the informal *contio* before the second Assembly-meeting (31.7) was, as we have seen, a proclamation that preventive war was necessary: better to strike Philip now in Greece than to wait for him to invade Italy. In Galba's speech as we have it in Livy (unlikely to be fictional in basic content – see above), the emphasis is on self-defense. And the theme of the speech as we have it fits with the tone of the formal warning of the Senate after the People's first rejection of the resolution (Livy 31.6.6). Nevertheless, the war in the East was controversial with the *populus*, and it remained so; there were public complaints by the tribunes in winter 198/197 about senatorial management of the war, and the Army Assembly voted for peace in 196 despite the pleas of the then-consul M. Claudius Marcellus (son of one of the great Roman heroes of the Hannibalic War) that the war continue until Philip had been truly destroyed. The reluctance of the Roman People to undertake serious involvement east of the Adriatic could hardly be clearer.[98]

Since the Senate officially advised for "conditional war" in the East, and pushed hard to get its proposal finally through the Army Assembly, and since the People in the end officially voted for it, one cannot say that the Romans were drawn into major intervention in the Greek Mediterranean against their will. Whatever the impact of the envoys from the four beleaguered Greek states, the final decision was the result of the Roman governing machinery alone. Thus the Senate made a conscious decision in winter 201/200 to assert Roman power in the Greek world, as it had done in 229 and 219 against the Illyrians, and as it had done from 216 in response to Philip V. Furthermore, the Senate decided that this intervention would be on a far larger scale than any previous one. The *populus Romanus* in spring 200 eventually – reluctantly – agreed.

Was this step taken lightly, almost without thinking, because it was simply part of the annual "war machine" that constituted Roman society? So some scholars have argued.[99] But not only do we have abundant evidence that the Greek envoys presented the Senate with an ultimately very threatening situation in the eastern Mediterranean (see above), but the seriousness with which the majority of the *Patres* viewed the strategic

---

[97]   *Ediceret castigaretque segnitiam populi atque edoceret quanto damno decorique dilatio ea belli futura esset.*

[98]   Tribunician criticism of senatorial management of the war (winter 198/197): Livy 32.38.3–8. Marcellus' failed attempt to keep the war going (spring 196): Livy 33.25.4–7.

[99]   So, e.g., Harris 1979: 212–18; Derow 2003.

danger that had emerged in the East is shown by the fact that any Roman war there was going to be so expensive that the Roman Treasury would not be able to pay off the public debts incurred to private citizens during the Hannibalic War. The repayment of these State debts to individuals had previously been in the works (Livy 31.13.4–9). The debts had originated in a financial crisis caused in 210 in good part by the need to man and equip the large naval forces necessary to fight the *first* war against Philip in Greece (see Livy 26.35.10). Thus the prospect of a second war with Philip was going to delay the repayment of debt incurred in good part by the first war.[100] And the crucial fact here is this: the majority of the private creditors who would now be forced to wait for the repayment of their money were themselves senators (Livy 26.36: explicit).[101]

Not surprisingly, the Senate's decision upset those to whom the Roman State owed money (Livy 31.13.2–4). Their complaints were mollified by a second senatorial decision, to offer *ager publicus* (public land) near Rome to these creditors at a minimal rent (31.13.5–9). But this financial compromise meant that in addition to the heavy new expenses that the Treasury would inevitably incur from a new war in Greece (expenses that necessitated the delay in the repayment of the public debt in the first place), there would be a further loss of state revenue because this *ager publicus* near Rome could ordinarily have been let out at a higher rent. Nor should one imagine that this was a particularly satisfactory deal for the creditors. We know they did not find it so, because four years later, in 196, they protested again about the money the State still owed them from 210 and which had still not been repaid (Livy 33.42).[102] The conclusion is clear from the evidence of the new financial burden on the Treasury caused by the senatorial decision to intervene in the East in 200: decision-making elites do not make decisions that impose such heavy costs on the State, and which especially impose such *personal* financial burdens on many of the decision-makers themselves, unless they are sincerely motivated by serious security concerns.[103]

---

[100] Buraselis 1996: 158, asserts that the financial crisis of 210 had only to do with manning and equipping a fleet for Sicily, but this is simply wrong: Livy in discussing the financial crisis emphasizes as its cause the war with Philip far more than the Sicilian situation (*aut Siciliam obtineri aut Italia Philippum aceri posse at tuta Italiae litera esse . . .* – 26.35.10).

[101] Noted by Buraselis 1996: 158–9.

[102] Discussion of the financial dispute in 196: see Buraselis 1996: 171.

[103] The administration of the cumbersome loan settlement may have become an added problem – along with the religious issues and the difficulties in army recruitment – accounting for the late departure of the consuls of 200 for their *provinciae*: see Buraselis 1996: 149 n. 2.

Buraselis has recently proposed a different interpretation of the financial issue facing the Senate in the winter of 201/200: that the Senate voted to intervene in the East partly *in order* that the large costs of the new war might cause the Treasury to delay the heavy expense of having to pay back the public debt.[104] This seems implausible. If maintaining the financial solvency of the Treasury had been the primary senatorial goal in 200, then *delaying* intervention in the East – not proceeding with it – would obviously have been the best policy, for even with (or especially with) a Celtic rising in the Po Valley a likelihood, such a delay in the East would have meant significantly less strain on the Treasury. Moreover, a delay in intervention would have allowed the paying back, without harm to the Treasury, of the special private debt – the majority of which debt (to repeat) was owed to many among the *Patres* themselves (Livy 26.36); it was the prospect of war in the East that stopped the payment (31.13.4–9: explicit). Yet even though in winter 201/200 a delay in intervening in the East would have been financially beneficial to the State as well as financially beneficial to many individual senators, the fact is that the majority of the Senate nevertheless voted for the intervention in the East, with all the financial costs (including personal financial costs) that such a course involved.[105] The implications of the financing problem revealed by Livy 31.13 are therefore clear in terms of our appreciation of the real gravity with which the Senate perceived the situation in the eastern Mediterranean in winter 201/200. These implications were pointed out long ago by G. T. Griffith, and he should still be followed.[106]

The seriousness with which the *Patres* viewed the security situation is also demonstrated by the military steps they ordered in the winter of 201/200. It appears that in late autumn 201, even before the first actual vote in the Army Assembly (which, of course, failed), the Senate ordered a large war-fleet, previously stationed off the African coast as part of the final military effort against Carthage, north into the Adriatic. We are told that the task of this fleet was to watch against Macedonian action, and the Senate appointed as its commander M. Valerius Laevinus, one

---

[104] Buraselis 1996: esp. 173–4.

[105] Of course, the outbreak of large-scale fighting in the Po Valley in summer 200, which began with massive Celtic attacks on Placentia and Cremona, might eventually have served to undermine such a projected "peace dividend" in any case. But we are discussing how the financial situation would have looked to the *Patres* in the winter of 201/200.

[106] See Griffith 1935: 1. Coarelli 1977: 4 and 12–13, suggests that the financial strain at Rome at this time caused the censors of 199 (Scipio Africanus and P. Aelius Paetus, cos. 201) to refrain from any public building – something these prominent men cannot have liked.

of the Roman commanders-in-chief in the First Macedonian War, and consul in 210 (Livy 31.3.2–4).[107] The fact that the ex-consul Laevinus, a notoriously touchy man, was willing to take this command even though it came only with the much lower rank of pro-praetor shows the gravity with which important senatorial figures were viewing the situation: it parallels similar instances of "patriotic self-sacrifice" in taking lower offices than one deserved which we see during the crisis years of the Hannibalic War.[108] Meanwhile, although the demobilization of the large Roman armies of the Hannibalic War continued – as the worn-out *populus* demanded – a new legion of allied troops was sent specially to guard Bruttium (Livy 31.8.11), and plans were made to establish colonies of Scipionic veterans in Apulia (Livy 31.4.3). Siebert has suggested that the legion of allies was sent to Bruttium primarily to guard against bandits, and thus should not be seen as part of any defensive Roman war preparations against Macedon.[109] But the allied force sent to Bruttium is specifically presented by Livy as part of the preparations for war (31.8.7), and so when its task is described as the guarding of the Bruttian region (*quibus praesidiis . . .*), this must mean (despite Siebert) not the hunting down of robbers but rather the protection of the region from external attack. Hence Livy pairs its task with that of the legion of allies that was sent at this time to guard the northern frontier against the Gallic threat (ibid.). Bruttium and Apulia both faced towards Greece and the East – and their loyalty to Rome was suspect, for these regions had sided with Hannibal. Thus one should see the senatorial action here in connection with the dispatch of Laevinus' fleet to the Adriatic as part of the series of moves made by the *Patres* to shore up the defenses of the Italian peninsula in the face of what was perceived as a possibly very serious threat from the East.

There is yet more evidence of the gravity with which the Senate had now come to view the situation, and with specific regard to the threat posed by the kings in *combination*: the embassy the *Patres* sent out to the eastern Mediterranean in spring 200 not only carried a stern ultimatum to Philip demanding changes in conduct from him on pain of war, but the Roman envoys had a second major assignment as well – to attempt to mediate the on-going war between Antiochus and the

---

[107] Laevinus had been Roman commander in the Adriatic from late 215 until spring 210, and had been the architect of the alliance with Aetolia (212/211): on his earlier command, see Broughton 1951: 255, 260, 265, 269, and 275 (with sources); on his command in winter 201/200, see Broughton 1951: 321 and 322 n. 3.

[108] Parallel case: Cn. Servilius Geminus the consul of 217 merely a subordinate commander at Cannae in 216. The dispatch of this fleet into the Adriatic has sometimes been doubted as an Annalistic invention, but see Briscoe 1973: 60.

[109] Siebert 1995: 243.

Ptolemaic regime. The latter task deserves underlining since this is apparently the first time Rome ever attempted to mediate a war between two major Greek states. Thus it marked a significant new departure in Roman international behavior – as significant a departure in Roman diplomacy as the very large preparations now set in train against Philip V in Greece marked a significant departure in the Roman military stance towards Greece. Such a departure appears yet again to demonstrate that the Senate took the information from the Greek embassies very seriously, information which – as we can again now see – did indeed concern *both* Philip and Antiochus simultaneously.[110]

These measures taken by the Senate were all very serious ones. No doubt there were internal factors that helped pushed Rome towards a major war in the East in 200, including the prevailing Roman culture of militarism, the Romans' instinctive "habit of command" aimed at other states, perhaps even factional rivalries within the senatorial aristocracy and jealousy of Scipio Africanus.[111] The serious and concrete defensive steps now taken by the *Patres* suggest, however, that we are dealing primarily with a feeling among most of the Senate that Rome "had no choice" – as Galba tells the populace – but to respond forcefully to the situation revealed by the Greek envoys. In political-science terminology, the Greek envoys took the *Patres* to "cognitive closure" on the nature of the threat Rome faced from the East, and the probable need for war.[112] In part this tendency towards "cognitive closure" about external threats was the result of the long-term socialization of the *Patres* into the unforgiving and harsh interstate system in which Rome existed, and the long experience of the Senate as to how that system worked; this experience left them with a bias towards pessimism, towards believing "the worst-case scenario" – and, of course, with a readiness to take up the sword. Indeed, recent work by political scientists has stressed that a bias towards pessimistic analysis of strategic situations is a common phenomenon among decision-making elites in states that exist within especially fierce

---

[110]   That is: the Roman embassy to Antiochus in 200 reinforces Polybius' evident story of the diplomatic impact at Rome of the news of the Pact Between the Kings. The embassy to Antiochus as the first Roman attempt to mediate between major Greek states: see Gruen 1984: 111–12 (with sources). Rome may have earlier failed ca. 247 BC in an attempt to mediate between Acarnania and the Aetolian League, but the incident is of uncertain historicity, nor was this a major war: see above, Chapter 2.
[111]   The latter factor is stressed as the key one by Dorey 1959; cf. Scullard 1973 or Hamilton 1993; but there is no evidence.
[112]   On the dangers of "cognitive closure" in a crisis, and the feeling of "having no choice" – widespread among states in conflict throughout antiquity – see, e.g., Kauppi 1991: 114–16, and Eckstein 2006: Ch. 2, with multiple examples in Eckstein 2006: Chs. 4–5.

and competitive state-systems, as the Romans did.[113] The Roman decisions of winter 201/200 thus support Waltz's maxim that while all states in a competitive anarchy greatly desire to expand their power, "in crucial situations, the ultimate concern of states is not for power but for security."[114]

CONCLUSION

Modern international-systems theorists have done important work on the role of perception in interstate relations in general and its role in crises within state-systems in particular.[115] Perceptions and threat assessment form a crucial link between the structural changes that may occur at the system level (that is, the real changes in the real distribution of power across the state-system), the internal unit cultures of the individual states existing within that system (in the Hellenistic Mediterranean, these internal cultures were usually heavily militaristic), and the resultant conduct of individual states. Or to put it more simply, threat assessment plays the part of an often-invisible transmission belt connecting the reality of objective change to the eventual state behavior which responds to that change.[116] Thus, even acknowledging that the objective characteristics of a harsh anarchic system and the pressures generated by those characteristics are important factors encouraging state action in certain directions (usually aggressive) and discouraging state action in other directions (usually peaceable), there is still the question of how statesmen grasp the situation they are in – grasp it from a position *inside* the system.[117] Because statesmen's perspectives, for instance, from inside the changing systemic structure of a power-transition crisis, can be skewed or distorted, and because the information they possess regarding ongoing change external to their own polity is always incomplete and sometimes inaccurate, in one sense statesmen are reduced to making guesses about the threats their states face. International-relations scholars emphasize that as a result, mistakes by statesmen in understanding the actual situation in the state-system are common. And yet because significant action in the real interstate world flows from those "guesses,"

---

[113] See Wohlforth 2001: 229–30 (early modern Russia); cf. Brooks 1997: 454.
[114] Waltz 1988: 616. The pessimism here learned over time about the severity of the external threats which Rome faced would of course only have been intensified (as we have stressed) by the recent trauma of Hannibal's invasion.
[115] See, e.g., Friedberg 1988; Wohlforth 1993; Richardson 1994: Ch. 12; Mastny 1996.
[116] Friedberg 1988: 13.
[117] Ibid.: 8.

the guesses – right or wrong – "have become historical facts."[118] They produce large effects in world politics.[119]

The Roman perception of the situation that had developed in the Greek East was crucial to the world-historical events that occurred at Rome in winter 201/200. The *Patres* were guessing about the situation in the East – and their guesses, and the results of their guesses, became vitally important historical facts.

Not all forms of guessing in interstate relations, however, are equally imprecise.[120] Our discussion has sought to show that there was a sudden and serious new assessment within the Senate concerning the gravity of the new threats to Rome in winter 201/200 BC, and that this assessment derived primarily and most importantly from information provided by envoys from the four Greek states who appeared before the *Patres* in autumn 201, pleading for help against Philip and/or Antiochus. To scholars interested in the decisive impact of governmental-elite perception upon the course of interstate relations in general, and upon the course of systemic power-transition crises in particular, we need go no farther than this point to have presented them with a new and significant case study. Indeed, to scholars who emphasize the causal impact of perception, it does not matter very much whether the Greek envoys were right or wrong in the pessimistic assessment of the eastern situation that they gave the Roman Senate; what counts is the crucial impact this information had within the Senate, the role this information (whether correct or incorrect) played in bringing about the *Patres*' decision for major Roman intervention in the eastern Mediterranean.[121] We have argued above

---

[118] Gulick 1967: 28; cf. Morgenthau 1973: 154 (the "hunches" that governmental elites must employ to determine action). In antiquity this general problem was exacerbated by the lack of systematic information that polities had about one another: see above, Chapter 1, and this chapter, p. 242.

[119] See now Jervis 2001: 282. In this study we have noted several such mistaken governmental hunches: those of Queen Teuta in 230, of Demetrius of Pharos in ca. 225–219, of Philip V in 217–216 as well as the governmental elite of Syracuse in 214, all of whom mistakenly overestimated their own power within the current interstate system while underestimating the potential power of Rome; in the case of Philip and Syracuse, they also overestimated the power of Carthage within the system. For their part, the Roman Senate had not thought that Syracuse, long a staunch ally of Rome, would join Hannibal's alliance; see Eckstein 1987a: Ch. 5. Another example of Roman shock at the action of a foreign state is the defection of Capua to Hannibal in winter 216/215: see von Ungern-Sternberg 1976.

[120] Friedberg 1988: 11.

[121] On the role of information, perception, and threat-assessment "guessing" as decisive in determining the development of crises, see Friedberg 1988: 7–20. On the role of contingent events, such as the arrival of the Greek envoys in Rome in autumn 201, acting as catalysts to bring into reality what were otherwise only potential situations, see Lebow 2001.

that once Polybius is correctly understood, it is clear that he regarded the information the Greek envoys brought to Rome in winter 201/200 as crucial to the Roman decision, and that amid all the Greek complaints and information presented at Rome, Polybius foregrounded their information about the Pact Between the Kings. That is: in his view the pact was central to what the Greek envoys told the Senate, central to the *Patres'* new threat assessment, and central to the decisive actions the Senate then took to deal with the perceived threat.[122]

If we turn now to the question of the usefulness of structural realist theory as a method for understanding the fundamental course of interstate crises, however – as opposed to perception theory – in fact it matters very much whether what the Greek envoys said in the Senate in autumn 201 was objectively true. Indeed, it matters very much whether the very presence of the ambassadors from the four Greek states in Rome – a diplomatic revolution in Mediterranean interstate politics (as we have emphasized in Chapter 5, above) – was itself the result of a profound and objective transformation in the structure of the state-system in the Hellenistic East, a radical change in the distribution of power across the Greek state-system, or merely an exercise in self-interested and distorted Greek propaganda.

We have argued in this study that the Greek ambassadors told the Senate the truth. The structure of the state-system in the Hellenistic East, based upon the triadic balance of power that had existed for eighty years between Antigonid Macedon, the Seleucid Empire, and the Ptolemaic regime, began to undergo very dramatic change ca. 207. The faltering of the Ptolemaic regime – the massive indigenous rebellion in Middle and Upper Egypt, then the premature death of Ptolemy IV in 204 and his succession by a child – led to a sudden, unexpected, and profound redistribution of power across the Hellenistic system. The collapse of the Ptolemies led to a decisive expansion in the power of both Philip V and Antiochus III, expressed most brutally and directly in their alliance to divide up the entire Ptolemaic realm (winter 203/202), followed by their large-scale aggressive warfare against Ptolemaic holdings (see Chapter 4, above). The expansion of the kings in turned triggered desperate military resistance from some of the second-tier states – and eventually triggered an appeal for help to Rome (see Chapter 5, above). When the Roman Senate, on the basis of the disturbing information provide by the Greeks, then pushed the Army Assembly into a conditional declaration of war, the thesis of this study is that the Roman Republic,

---

[122]   On the correct interpretation of the crucial passage Polyb. 15.20.6, which in turn gives us crucial information on how Polybius viewed the process of decision-making at Rome in winter 201/200, see above, Chapter 5.

like Philip, Antiochus, and the second-tier Greek states, was ultimately responding to the same really-occurring systemic crisis – the crisis ultimately caused by the Ptolemaic collapse.[123]

All these states, including Rome but not just Rome alone, responded in essentially the same way to the crisis – aggressively. Strictly speaking, this need not have happened; the governing elites in all these states possessed freedom of will. Philip and Antiochus could have decided not to take advantage of Ptolemaic weakness (indeed, Polybius in 15.20 says it was their moral duty not to take advantage of the child Ptolemy V). The weaker Greek states could have decided to appease the newly emerging hegemons of the system – Macedon and Syria – or even to bandwagon with them in hopes of joining in the spoils deriving from the Ptolemaic collapse, rather than resisting the kings' expansion militarily and then seeking help from a power on the periphery of the traditional Hellenistic system. Or as Polybius, with his emphasis on the emergence of the Mediterranean *symplokē* (interconnectedness), would put it: the Greek states need not have intentionally sought to "enlarge" the traditional Greek state-system by bringing in Rome as part of their struggle to find a balance to Philip and Antiochus and to remain independent. But they did, and thus they played a crucial role in the emergence of a single Mediterranean state-system out of what had previously been two regional subsystems (eastern and western Mediterranean). Finally, the Roman Senate could have decided not to intervene in the onrolling crisis in the Greek East despite the multiple Greek pleas for help. Rome, after all, was exhausted from the Hannibalic War, faced serious military problems from the Celts in northern Italy, and the decision to intervene caused political division as well as serious financial problems for the state. Thus, the pressures from the anarchic character and the changing structure of the interstate system (in this case, the pressures from the dramatically changing distribution of power across the Hellenistic system after 207 and especially after 204) shaped and shoved the decision-making, but did not determine the actions of states.[124]

Nevertheless, the crisis of the Hellenistic state-system, combined with the heavily militarized internal cultures of all the polities within the system – characteristics in turn deriving in good part from the pressures of the harsh state-system in which they existed, and their governing elites' bitter experience of that system – and combined too with the ferocious desire to maintain independence (the weaker states) and/or to exert increased control over one's environment (the stronger states), all of this

---

[123]   This, as we have said, was the view of Mommsen 1903: 696–701.
[124]   This is to paraphrase the general rule of Waltz 2000: 24 (in a modern context, of course).

combined synergistically to produce the outcome that occurred. The power-transition crisis that began ca. 207 need not have turned out that way. But neither is it surprising, from a systems-analytical perspective, that it did turn out that way.

Even so, it was a close-run decision at Rome whether or not to intervene in the crisis in the Greek East. There was a strong senatorial majority in favor of intervention, but there also appears to have been significant senatorial opposition to it, on the grounds that the threat in the East was not immediate and the populace was exhausted by the Hannibalic War; and so, in the initial meeting of the Army Assembly the proposal from the Senate for conditional war against Philip V was defeated, and indeed overwhelmingly defeated. This was because the voters in the Assembly were both exhausted from the Hannibalic War and unconvinced that the threat in the East was so severe as to require a preventive war. We find these sentiments reflected in the behavior of Q. and Cn. Baebius, scions of a powerful senatorial family: Q. Baebius the tribune helped engineer the initial rejection by the Army Assembly of the *senatus auctoritas* favoring intervention, while Cn. Baebius the aedile later in 200 put on a play indicating the dissatisfaction of economically hard-pressed ordinary Romans with having to help the Greeks. But in the end the *Patres* managed to convince the *populus Romanus*, worn out though the Roman People were by the terrible struggle with Carthage, and (presumably) worried too about new threats on the Celtic frontier, to accept a probable new and major war in the East. It appears from the tradition concerning the speech which the consul P. Sulpicius Galba made at the informal *contio* before the second Assembly that the main argument employed by the Senate majority was that such a preventive war against Philip was the best way to safeguard Roman security from the threat now posed by the emerging Hellenistic hegemons in the East. The transformation of the Greek interstate system that was now occurring, a transformation in favor of the increased power of the more powerful states, was ultimately threatening to Rome, and to prevent this threatening transformation was also beyond the military power of the second-tier states within the system, such as Rhodes and Pergamum. Yet the new eastern war always remained controversial at Rome, from beginning to end, and the *populus Romanus* voted for peace in 196 against the wishes of the current consul, M. Claudius Marcellus. Nevertheless, the Roman decision of winter 201/200 to intervene in the Greek East – although it was in fact a near-run decision – confirms yet another of Kenneth Waltz's maxims: "larger units existing in a contentious arena tend to take on systemwide tasks."[125]

[125] Ibid.: 34.

Polybius, indeed, thought that the Greek envoys to Rome in the winter of 201/200 did even more than act as the catalysts who brought about Roman intervention in the chaos in the East caused by the power-transition crisis that began with the collapse of Egypt. To Polybius the Greek envoys of 201/200 were, in addition, crucial agents in the growing *symplokē* – the "interconnecting" of the previously separate eastern and western Mediterranean state-systems into one single Mediterranean-wide system. This transformation of the two regional subsystems into one grand Mediterranean state-system was (as we have seen) one of the two fundamental geopolitical themes of Polybius' *Histories* – the other being the rise of Roman power. Once more, the process which Polybius describes here (in his own terminology, of course), and which so impresses him in its importance, is not at all foreign to modern political-science analysis of the evolution of state-systems. Thus the eminent political scientist Raymond Aron refers to circumstances which lead to "the enlargement of the diplomatic field"; Robert Gilpin writes that "with the aging of an international system and the expansion of states, the distance between states decreases, thereby causing them increasingly to come into conflict with one another," and "the once-empty space around the centers of power in the system" now disappears; and Barry Buzan puts it this way: it sometimes happens that "increased interaction capacity" between states leads "regional subsystems of states" to change into a single system.[126] Polybius could not have said it better, and for him this process was (at least at the secular level) both a very real process and the most profound cause of the events at Rome in winter 201/200.[127]

We, too, turn now to focus on how the single Mediterranean-wide system of states came into its initial shape. And once more, the employment of modern political-science concepts will help our analysis both of the hegemonic wars of 200–188 BC which the Roman decision of 201/200 helped bring about, and of the crucial first stages of what became universal Roman predominance.

[126]   Aron 1973: 87–8; Gilpin 1981: 200–1; Buzan 1993: 66–80.
[127]   Polybius of course also adduced a moral/religious meaning to the Roman decision, based on his negative moral evaluation of the conduct of Philip and Antiochus against Egypt, in which Tyche (Fortune) as retributive Justice played a central role: see above, Chapter 4. On Polybius' "two-track" analysis here (secular/metaphysical), see Walbank 1994/2002b.

PART III

FROM HEGEMONIC WAR TO HIERARCHY, 200–170 BC

7

Hegemonic War, I: Rome and Macedon, 200–196 BC

INTRODUCTION

Within the eastern regional state-system of the Hellenistic Mediterranean, a system-wide hegemonic war had emerged by 202 BC in response to the power-transition crisis caused by the faltering and then the collapse of the Ptolemaic regime based in Egypt. Such hegemonic war is a typical phenomenon of anarchic state-systems as they undergo a crisis when a major pillar of the state-system is challenged or begins to fail.[1] At the end of the third century BC, the collapse of Egypt thus led to a system-wide war to determine the new leadership and new structure of the regional system in the eastern Mediterranean. This war was already under way by the summer of 202, with large-scale fighting from Gaza all the way to the northern Aegean.[2] The governments of the less powerful Greek polities had existed in relatively satisfactory conditions under the *de facto* tripolar balance of power that had characterized the old system (dominated by the Antigonids, the Seleucids, and the Ptolemies); they were now determined to resist the bid for system-wide hegemony launched by Philip V of Macedon and Antiochus III of Syria in the wake of Ptolemaic collapse – a bid sealed

---

[1] On the concept of "hegemonic war" caused by a power-transition crisis within an anarchic state-system, see Gilpin 1988 (cf. above, Chapters 1 and 5).

[2] On the crisis within the Hellenistic state-system after ca. 207 and esp. after ca. 204, see above, Chapters 4 and 5.

in "the Pact Between the Kings" between Philip and Antiochus (winter 203/202), which aimed at the total destruction of the weakened Ptolemaic Empire.[3]

The governments of the less powerful states came to believe, however, that their own efforts would be insufficient to block Philip and Antiochus, and that the consequences of this failure would be disastrous for their cherished independence. These governing elites were likely correct: the power-transition crisis that began ca. 207 and accelerated after ca. 204 favored a great accumulation of power in the Greek state-system by those regimes that already possessed the power to take advantage of the weakened Ptolemies. The tripolar structure in the Greek Mediterranean was collapsing in violence, and it would not be resurrected; a different structure was going to replace it. In the summer of 201 it was not yet clear what that structure would look like: a bipolar structure focused on the Antigonid and Seleucid monarchies (their power swollen by the wealth and territory seized from the destroyed Ptolemies) appeared likely, though even the emergence of Philip V's Macedon or Antiochus III's empire as the sole system-wide hegemon was not out of the question.

Under these desperate circumstances the solution found by the governing elites of the weaker states was to seek a balance against the kings by expanding the boundaries of the state-system itself. And so envoys from at least four Greek governments appeared at Rome in the autumn of 201, seeking to draw the great military power of the western Mediterranean, which hitherto had played only a peripheral role in Hellenistic politics (see above, Chapters 2–3), directly into the hegemonic warfare now convulsing the Greek East. These Greek embassies formed the catalyst for a broadening of the hegemonic war in the eastern Mediterranean into a war involving the entire Mediterranean.

A half-century later, the historian Polybius of Megalopolis could see the results. The Hellenistic power-transition crisis at the end of the third century had indeed profoundly transformed the ancient world. It had led to two unexpected outcomes. First, the envoys from the Greek states had precipitated major Roman intervention in the eastern crisis, and following two wars, first a war between Macedon and a coalition now led by Rome, and soon afterwards between the Seleucid monarchy and a coalition led by Rome, the result had been the emergence of Rome as the guarantor of an artificially revived triadic balance of power in the Greek East. This artificially revived triadic balance of power – the

---

[3] On the historicity of the Pact Between the Kings, see above, Chapter 4.

weakened Antigonids, the weakened Seleucids, the somewhat restored Ptolemies[4] – remained unstable, as one can see from the attempt of Antiochus IV to conquer Egypt in 169–168 BC, a conquest that would have been successful except for yet another Roman intervention. Second, the series of Greek embassies to Rome in winter 201/200 BC had been the catalyst also for the permanent enlargement of the Hellenistic regional diplomatic field into one large Mediterranean-wide system. The embassies precipitated the increasing integration of what had previously been two separate regional subsystems of states (eastern and western Mediterranean) into one large system. And it was a system with Rome as the predominant power from Spain to Syria. In short, this was Polybius' *symplokē*: the new Mediterranean-wide "interconnectedness."[5]

The *symplokē* came into full existence with the arrival of the Greek embassies at Rome in autumn 201. In this chapter and the next, we examine the period of savage hegemonic rivalry and system-wide wars that led to the establishment of Roman military and political predominance in the eastern Mediterranean. The period of hegemonic rivalry and system-wide hegemonic war began in earnest in 202 BC, with the attacks on the empire of the Ptolemies by Philip V and Antiochus III. It came to an end only with the acknowledgment of Roman military superiority and political hierarchy in the Treaty of Apamea in 188 between Rome and Antiochus III.

The Treaty of Apamea sealed the emergence of a new systemic structure in the Mediterranean. This new systemic structure was brought into being through massive violence. But one should realize that this was not unusual; according to modern scholars of international relations, massive violence is what usually occurs when a power-transition crisis shatters an entire anarchic system of states. And what emerged in 188 was not merely a single Mediterranean state-system where previously there had been two regional subsystems, but a system of "unipolarity," with Rome established as the sole remaining superpower from Spain to Syria. It was now possible that the anarchy that had always reigned throughout the Mediterranean world of states would be replaced by a stable hierarchy: a Roman hegemony or even empire. But the possibility that this development might occur did not mean that it was inevitable that it would occur. Nothing was certain as yet.

---

[4]   See Polyb. 15.20.6–8 (explicit).
[5]   On Polybius' concept of *symplokē*, see discussions above, pp. 26, 32, 79–83, 180, 270.

CONFRONTATION WITH PHILIP:
THE SECOND MACEDONIAN WAR

In the spring of 200 the Roman Senate dispatched three envoys to European Greece with an ultimatum to Philip, and with a further mandate to remonstrate with Antiochus about his aggressions against Egypt.[6] The Roman envoys were C. Claudius Nero, consul in 207 (and victor at the decisive battle of Metaurus against Hasdrubal the brother of Hannibal); P. Sempronius Tuditanus, consul in 204 (who had negotiated the Peace of Phoenice which had ended the First Macedonian War); and a younger man, M. Aemilius Lepidus. It was a distinguished group, from the highest Roman nobility, and in P. Sempronius Tuditanus it included one of the very few senior figures in the Senate who ca. 200 BC had diplomatic experience in the Greek East.[7]

The envoys first visited several states along the western coast of Greece, to round up support for the possible war looming between Rome and Macedon: the Epirotes, the Athamanians, and the Aetolians; they even visited the Achaeans, who were formal allies of Philip (Polyb. 16.27.4).[8] The envoys' task is not surprising, since the previous Roman interventions in Greece had always included significant diplomacy, and the Roman experience among the Greek states since 214 had been that allies against Macedon were available and useful. The polities on Polybius' list were all ones with which Rome was familiar from the first war against Philip; but diplomatic efforts with the western Greek polities were unsuccessful. The envoys then proceeded onward to Athens.[9]

The Roman stance towards Philip is made clear by the envoys' later public ultimatums to the Macedonians. The first ultimatum was given to Philip's general Nicanor as he was approaching Athens to attack the city (late spring 200), and a second and final ultimatum was given to Philip personally (late summer 200) as he was besieging the city of Abydus on the Asian side of the Dardenelles – a place crucial for grain supplies to Athens, which Philip also intended to use as a base of operations for

---

[6]   For this latter part of the task of the envoys, see Polyb. 16.27.5 and 34.2; Justin 30.3.3–4 and 31.1–2; App. *Mac.* 4; cf. Livy 31.2.3–4 (Annalistic). Detailed discussion below, this chapter.

[7]   Sources on the embassy: see Broughton 1951: 321.

[8]   Tuditanus would have personally known the men in the government of Epirus, as well as Amynander of Athamania, because of their participation with him in the peace negotiations at Phoenice in 205, as well as Philip V himself (see above, Chapter 3).

[9]   Polyb. 16.27 presents the envoys' earlier travels to the western Greek states in a retrospective from the later situation at Athens; see Walbank 1967: 528.

a new attack on Pergamum (cf. Polyb.16.29.2). The Romans' ultimatum demanded that Philip stop making war on the Greeks – and that he pay compensation to Pergamum and Rhodes for his aggressions, as well as put a stop to his attacks on the Ptolemies (Polyb. 16.34.3). The envoys' ultimatum was backed by a senatorial decree, presumably the decree that led to the "conditional war" vote in the Army Assembly in the spring of 200. Its demands about the Ptolemies therefore refer not to Philip's seizing of numerous Ptolemaic towns in Thrace in the summer of 200, which occurred after the passage of the decree, but specifically to the impact of his campaign in the Aegean in 201.[10] The declarations of the senatorial envoys publicly presented the Romans, for the first time, as major protectors of the Greeks against Macedonian imperialism.[11]

This Roman embassy, as we have noted, also had a task with Antiochus III – to provide diplomatic assistance to the Ptolemaic regime against the Seleucid monarch.[12] Rome was clearly not prepared to make war on both these great kings simultaneously, however; and presumably the Senate chose Philip because he was nearest, because of his previous bad relations with Rome, and because of the specific complaints that had been made against him especially by Pergamum. But the envoys' instructions concerning Antiochus demonstrate that the Roman government was seeking to deal in *some* way with both Philip and Antiochus simultaneously in spring and summer 200 – and this shows once more, if only indirectly, the importance of the Pact Between the Kings in the depiction of the situation in the East by the Greek envoys at Rome in winter 201/200.

The ultimatum to Philip at Abydus was delivered personally by M. Aemilius Lepidus. It was certainly yet another example of ancient compellence diplomacy in a crisis between states; and as usual, it failed. To Philip, as to most Hellenistic monarchs, imperial expansion was his life's work, the proof of his status and greatness; he was hardly likely to accede to the Roman demands to stop. Philip himself was in fact far more habituated to issuing ultimatums than receiving them.[13] Indeed, the city of Abydus which Philip was besieging when he received the Roman demands had recently refused just such a Macedonian ultimatum (Livy 32.17.4); the Abydenes preferred to stand a siege rather than submit

---

[10]   Despite Gera 1998: 65–6.
[11]   Cf. Ferrary 1988: 46–7.
[12]   Above, p. 276 and (for the sources) n. 6.
[13]   Recent examples of Philip's own habit of compellence diplomacy, right from summer 200: Livy 31.16.4–5 (seven Greek cities in Thrace and the Thracian Chersonese).

to the king, and eventually they even preferred to commit suicide en masse rather than submit – and they win Polybius' praises for it. Such was the world in which Philip – and the Romans – lived.[14] And so Philip, too, like the Abydenes, refused to submit to the demands of others. He rejected the Roman ultimatum with a proud statement implying that events in the eastern Mediterranean were none of Rome's business – and so, by the autumn of 200, Macedon and Rome were engaged in what moderns call the Second Macedonian War.

The first eighteen months of the war with Macedon did not go very well for the Romans. To be sure, they pursued a strategy of offense against Philip, as P. Sulpicius Galba the consul of 200 had indicated to the Army Assembly was the safest course;[15] and a strong army under Galba was landed in Maritime Illyris in autumn 200. Little occurred that autumn aside from Roman raiding along the routes into the Pindus Mountains towards Macedon, and naval raids against Philip's allies in the Aegean. These incidents served to confirm Galba's reputation among the Greeks for brutality – a reputation earned as Roman commander in Greece in 210–207.[16]

Nevertheless, Galba – in the traditional Roman manner – also engaged in diplomacy, seeking to gain allies for Rome for the next summer's campaign. In the winter of 200/199 and again in the spring of 199 he made serious attempts to bring the Aetolian League into the war against Macedon – but was unsuccessful.[17] Galba did, however, win over King Amynander of Athamania, Pleuratus the ruler of the Ardiaei (the son of the long-term Roman *amicus* Scerdilaidas), and Bato, a Dardanian chieftain.[18] It may even be that based on these allies Galba

---

[14] Polybius' praise of the Abydenes, including for committing mass suicide rather than surrender: 16.30–1 and 16.34.11–12 (cf. Livy 31.17–18), with the comments of Eckstein 1995: 52–4.

[15] See above, Chapter 6.

[16] On Galba's reputation, see Paus. 7.8.2. The Aegean fighting in autumn 200 saw Roman naval forces destroy Chalcis, Andros, Acanthus, and Oreus, while Galba's own troops destroyed Antipatreia at the foot of the Pindus; for details, see Eckstein 1976: 126. This was traditional Roman war-making, the purpose of which was to gain the quick submission of strategic areas (ibid.: 135). Philip V followed the same practice, and for the same reason: hence the fates of Aenus and Maronea in Thrace during Philip's offensive there in the summer of 200 (Livy 31.16.4).

[17] Livy 31.28.3 and 31.29–33; Attalus I of Pergamum had also made an unsuccessful attempt to bring the Aetolians in against Philip in summer 201, and another unsuccessful attempt in spring 200 (see Livy 30.46.3–4 and 31.15.9–10, both passages based on Polybian material: cf. Briscoe 1973: 1). An inscription from Rhodes seems to reflect yet another effort with Aetolia, by Rome and Rhodes in 200: see Konterini 1983: esp. 31–2. The Attalid efforts and the Rhodian effort with Aetolia are discussed above, Chapter 5.

[18] Livy 31.28.2 – autumn 200.

hoped for the campaign for 199 to launch a triple invasion of Macedon, so large and from so many directions that Philip would be overwhelmed: the Dardani and Ardiaei from the northwest, the Roman main army from the west, and Amynander and if possible the Aetolians from the southwest.[19] If this was the plan, it miscarried: the Aetolians, as we have seen, remained neutral in spring 199; the raids of the Adriatic tribes were ineffective; and most importantly, Galba's own attempt to break through the Pindus Range with the main Roman army and bring Philip to battle in western Macedon accomplished little against Philip's skillful generalship. By the autumn Galba was back where he had started, on the Adriatic coast. The morale of Galba's army was in fact shaken by the difficulties of the mountain campaign and its lack of success, and in winter 199/198 P. Villius, the new Roman commander in the war, faced a serious mutiny among his troops (Livy 32.3.2, attributing the mutiny to problems originating under Galba).[20] Meanwhile, the Aetolian League finally did enter the war against Macedon in summer 199, under the mistaken impression that Galba's invasion of Macedon was succeeding (Livy 31.40.7–10); but when the Aetolians invaded Thessaly on their own – an operation not coordinated by Galba – Philip severely defeated them (Livy 31.41.7–42.9). All in all, Philip had every reason to believe that in 199 he had more than held his own.[21]

In the spring of 198 a third Roman commander took charge of the war: the consul T. Quinctius Flamininus. The orthodox scholarly position on Flamininus remains that he represents a new and more sophisticated approach in Roman dealings with the Greeks. Not only did Flamininus already have command experience among the Greeks of southern Italy, but he was fluent in Greek (both in speaking and writing), and some scholars argue that he was chosen for the eastern command in 198 precisely because of these special qualities; in short, he was "an Eastern expert."[22] But aside from Plutarch's portrayal of Flamininus as "the first Roman philhellene," in an artificial parallel with the Achaean general Philopoemen whom Plutarch depicted as "the last of the Greeks,"[23] there is little ancient evidence to support this view of Flamininus. Indeed, Flamininus' election to the consulship for 198 was

---

[19] So Walbank 1940: 141; cf. Eckstein 1976: 126–7.
[20] On the details of Galba's mountain campaign of 199, see Hammond 1966: 39ff., esp. 45.
[21] See the comments of Walbank 1940: 147; Errington 1972: 143.
[22] See Badian 1970: 35–8 and Badian 1971: 110; cf. Briscoe 1972: 42; Armstrong and Walsh 1986; Walsh 1996.
[23] See esp. Plut. *Comp. Flam.* and *Phil.*

controversial precisely because he seemed so unqualified for this high post and had so little previous command or political experience: he was under 30 and had not even held the praetorship yet. And not even Plutarch ascribes his election to any special knowledge of the Greeks.[24] Flamininus did, however, have powerful friends (cf. Polyb. 18.11.2). Once elected consul, Flamininus was assigned the war against Macedon – but this was not a senatorial decision to put a "Greek expert" into the field. On the contrary: Flamininus and his consular colleague Sex. Aelius Paetus, who was equally inexperienced in high command, explicitly rejected an arranged distribution of their respective provinces, and submitted themselves instead to the traditional lottery for provinces run by the augural priests (Livy 32.8.1 and 8.4). Flamininus' command was simply the result of the luck of the augural lottery.[25]

Given this background, it is not surprising that Flamininus' behavior as commander in Greece in 198 was quite similar to that of Galba. His arrival did not mean a fundamental shift away from a military solution, or the inauguration of a special diplomatic offensive. On the contrary: just like Galba, Flamininus focused on a traditional military offensive, attempting a decisive invasion of Macedon with the main Roman army. The only difference was that he shifted the direction somewhat, coming at Macedon from the southwest through Thessaly rather than from the west, directly through the Pindus Range, where Galba had been foiled. This military solution was clearly what Flamininus in 198 preferred, and if he had succeeded, the postwar political situation in Greece would have looked far different from the one that actually emerged – for neither the Achaean League nor Thebes and Boeotia would have ended the war on the Roman side, and thus there would have been no "grand coalition" of free Greek states led by Rome against Philip, a development that had its own major impact on the final settlement. But Flamininus' military

---

[24]   The controversy over Flamininus' lack of qualification for high office: see Livy 32.7.8–10 with Eckstein 1976: 123–4. Plut. *Flam.* 1.4–2.1 indicates that Flamininus won election because of his previous service on a commission settling Roman veterans in southern Italy in 200–199 (cf. also Livy 31.4.1–3 and 49.5–6). True, he had before that commanded the Roman garrison at Tarentum (Plut. *Flam.* 1.4) – an important Greek city – but the Romans had besieged and utterly sacked it after its defection to Hannibal, leaving it devastated and depopulated when Flamininus was there.

[25]   The honesty of the augural lottery for *provinciae* has sometimes been questioned, but recent research has stressed its honesty: see the discussion in Chapter 6, above, in connection with P. Sulpicius Galba receiving the command against Macedon in 200. Since Flamininus and Paetus in spring 198 overtly rejected an arranged distribution of provinces, this makes it even more unlikely that the lottery was then "managed" in favor of "the Greek specialist" Flamininus.

plans – again like those of Galba – failed, and his army suffered a significant defeat at Atrax in Thessaly. According to Livy (based on Polybian material), the defeat at Atrax made Flamininus wonder whether his Roman forces were even capable of facing the Macedonian phalanx in a set-piece battle (32.18.1). King Philip himself evidently drew an even stronger conclusion about Macedonian military superiority from the victory at Atrax (Livy 33.4.1).[26]

Flamininus in spring 198 did make a special effort to spare neutral Epirus from plundering as his troops marched through the country on their way into Thessaly; and in the autumn he gained a major diplomatic victory when his brother Lucius got the Achaean League to desert its long-term alliance with Macedon and join the war on the side of Rome. But while Flamininus' sparing of Epirus may have been an effort to effect Greek public opinon (so Plut. *Flam.* 5.1), it may equally have been simply the result of the Epirotes not opposing the Roman advance (so Livy 32.14.6 – derived from Polybian material).[27] And the Achaeans certainly did not change sides because they were impressed by the philhellenism of any Roman. On the contrary: the Achaean volte-face in autumn 198 occurred because of dissatisfaction with Philip's own high-handed behavior towards Achaea and his recent atrocities committed in Thessaly (see below), but especially because of fear that Philip could not protect Achaea from Rome – fear that was provoked by very unsubtle Roman threats.[28]

Those Roman threats, decisive in the Achaean decision, were backed by grim reality: Flamininus and his brother Lucius had shown through-out 198 that, like Galba before them, they were not averse to pillaging and/or destroying Greek cities for strategic and even terroristic purposes (Phaloria, Eretria, Carystus, Daulis, Elateia).[29] Flamininus may have been personally charming to certain envoys from Greek states (emphasized by Plut. *Flam.* 5.4–6); but the fact is that by the autumn of 198 he and his brother were as unpopular among the Greeks because of their brutalities as Galba had been (Paus. 7.8.1; cf. App. *Mac.* 7). But to

[26]   Both these Livian passages are based on Polybian material (see Briscoe 1973: 1).
[27]   Cf. Briscoe 1973: 1.
[28]   See the analysis of the decisive speech of the Achaean *strategos* Aristaenus during the crisis (Livy 32.21, from Polybian material) in Eckstein 1976: 138–41. Having to deal not only with Rome but with a possible simultaneous war initiated against Achaea by King Nabis of Sparta was another factor in the Achaean decision: Livy 32.21.27.
[29]   Phaloria: Livy 32.15.2–3; Eretria: Livy 32.16.15–17; Carystus: Livy 32.17.1 with Eckstein 1976: 135 n. 51; Elateia: Livy 32.24.6–7 with the implications of the inscription *ISE* no. 55, on the restoration of the Elateians to their city ca. 191.

catch the full flavor of the war in Greece in 198 it is important to note that Philip himself had destroyed numerous Greek towns in Thessaly, in an attempt through a scorched earth policy to impede the Romans' advance northwestwards towards Macedon.[30] In sum: Flamininus does not represent a departure in Roman conduct towards the Greeks. What we see instead in 198 is the brutality of the struggle for power now occurring between Rome and Macedon, a struggle in which smaller Greek polities were being victimized by one side or the other.

The decisive year was 197. Flamininus brought Philip to battle at Cynoscephalae in central Thessaly. The battle was a near-run thing, and at first Philip seemed about to win an even greater victory than at Atrax the previous year. But the king committed his main forces to a disorganized and imprudent attack when he believed that Flamininus' army was already on the run (Philip was always an impetuous gambler); the Macedonians instead got themselves surrounded and were severely defeated, with large losses to the infantry phalanx. One of the enormous advantages the Romans possessed in the ferocious struggle for power and security in the Hellenistic Mediterranean was that their resources were large (especially in comparison to their competitors); this in turn was the result of their careful organization of Italy – the construction of a political accommodation with the many and varied Italian peoples that nevertheless left Rome dominant. Thus Rome had been able to accept the frustrations and outright defeats of 200, 199, and 198, though not without tension.[31] But – and perhaps this was a surprise to many – Philip's resources turned out to be more limited and fragile. After Cynoscephalae he could not replace his decimated army, and therefore he sued for peace.[32]

[30]   These included the towns of Phacium, Peiresia, Euhydrium, Eretria-in-Thessaly, Palaepharsalus: see Livy 32.15.1, 15.4, 15.9 (cf. Livy 39.25.8, with Walbank 1940: 153).

[31]   Detailed discussion of this general Roman advantage and its origins, perceived early on by Mommsen: see Eckstein 2006: Ch. 7 (and above, Chapter 6). Continued tension over the eastern expedition: see the harsh criticism of the management of the war by the tribunes Q. Fulvius and L. Oppius Salinator in spring 197: Livy 32.28.3–8.

[32]   That Philip's resources turned out to be limited does not mean that people in Rome thought this was so in 200: Philip had fought Rome to a draw in the previous war, which had lasted nine years (214–205). This is the principle of "mutual opacity" concerning the relative power-capabilities of states, which ultimately can be tested only in war: discussion in Chapters 1 and 6, above. Greek thinkers certainly did not think Philip fragile, as the poem of Alcaeus from ca. 200 depicting Philip storming Mt. Olympus shows (discussion above, Chapter 4). On the unexpectedly cataclysmic nature of the battle of Cynoscephalae for Macedon, see Eckstein 1995: 183–92 (with sources).

"THE FREEDOM OF THE GREEKS"

After Cynoscephalae a preliminary peace agreement was negotiated between Philip and his Greek allies, and Flamininus and his Greek allies, and the peace was formally established in spring 196. The main influence behind its character was Flamininus. Though his political experience with the Greeks before his consulship had been limited (see above), and his conduct of the war had been typical in its Roman brutality as well as in the Roman search for allies, Flamininus in 197 and 196 evolved a sophisticated view of what postwar arrangements in Greece should look like. He made his view prevail in a general way with the Senate in the winter of 197/196, and then in detail with the commission of ten senators sent out to Greece in 196 to oversee the peace.[33] Polybius evidently attributed the increasing sophistication in Flamininus' thinking – summed up in the phrase "the Freedom of the Greeks" – to the beneficent political influence exercised over him from autumn 198 by the Achaean statesman Aristaenus of Dyme, who in 198 had engineered the Achaean accession to the anti-Macedonian alliance.[34]

The Greeks had reason to be concerned about Roman intentions now that Macedon had been decisively defeated. The governments of the states that had pleaded for Roman aid against Philip and/or Antiochus in the winter of 201/200 had understood there would be a price to pay for Roman protection; their calculation had been that Philip and/or Antiochus constituted a far worse and more direct threat to their independence than Rome did.[35] Even in Livy (who is drawing on Polybian material), the speech of the Athenian envoys to the Aetolians in spring 199, delivered as part of Galba's attempt to bring the Aetolians into the war, is anti-Macedonian rather than offering a positive image of Rome.[36] The speech in Livy delivered by the Achaean statesman Aristaenus to the Achaean Assembly a year and a half later, in autumn 198, to persuade the Achaeans to change sides (again based on Polybian material) has as its themes

---

[33] The Commission included the two previous commanders in Greece during the war – the stern P. Sulpicius Galba (cos. II 200) and P. Villius Tappulus (cos. 199) – as well as three other ex-consuls. Flamininus' influence over the Commission sometimes took much persuasion: see Eckstein 1987a: 298–300.

[34] Detailed discussion in Eckstein 1990.

[35] See above, Chapter 5. Thus the governments of Rhodes, Pergamum, Athens, and the Ptolemies had turned to Rome because it was "the least-threatening great power" they faced – which did not mean they thought of Rome as unthreatening. On the principle involved in such alliance-formations under anarchic conditions, see Walt 1984: Chs. 1 and 2.

[36] Livy 31.30 with Heidemann 1966: 20 and 30–3. Polybian derivation: Briscoe 1973: 129.

dislike of Philip's tyrannical behavior, combined with his inability to protect his allies, combined with fear of Roman brutality – though we do find a brief positive hope of *libertas* coming from the Romans.[37] In the spring of 197, Aristaenus apparently employed similar arguments primarily of grim *Machtpolitik* to convince the Thebans and Boeotians to desert Philip (Livy 33.2.4).[38] The fact was that the Romans already exercised stern control over Italy and Sicily, regions with numerous Greek polities – and Macedonian propaganda during the Second Macedonian War emphasized the threat to all Greeks posed by prospective Roman domination (as one can see from the Macedonian speech at the conference with the Aetolians in spring 199). This was a repetition of the propaganda against Rome of Philip and even of some of the non-belligerent mediating states during the First Macedonian War.[39] The general brutality of Roman war-making in Greece, including under Flamininus – the sacking of Greek towns and cities – will not have increased Greek confidence in Roman intentions; Greek feelings of hostility towards Flamininus have left their mark in both Pausanias (7.8.2) and Appian (*Mac.* 7).

And indeed, there were some bad signs. Flamininus ordered that as part of the spoils of the war a famous statue of "Jupiter the Ruler" be taken from its traditional site in Macedon and brought instead to Rome, where it received worship on the Capitol; the symbolism in the transfer of this great cult-image of dominating power was obvious.[40] Nor did Flamininus appear averse to high-handed action against Greek politicians he perceived as anti-Roman, including, it seems, acquiescence in winter 197/196 in the murder of Bracchyles, a prominent leader in Boeotia.[41] Flamininus even allowed the issuing of gold coinage on

---

[37] See Livy 32.21.36; derivation from Polybian material: see Eckstein 1990: 53–8. Polybius evidently left out of his version of the speech a promise from L. Flamininus to return to the Achaeans the major city of Corinth if they sided with Rome; Corinth had been under Macedonian control since the 220s (Plut. *Flam.* 10.2; cf. Polybius himself at 18.45.12). Perhaps Polybius did not believe the promise was important, given the grim strategic situation the Achaeans faced in autumn 198 – though perhaps he left Corinth out of Aristaenus' speech in order to defend Achaea from later Aetolian accusations of pure territorial greed (see below, pp. 288–9 and n. 61).
[38] From Polybian material: cf. Briscoe 1973: 248.
[39] On Macedonian propaganda and anti-Roman fears expressed even by envoys of neutral mediating states during the First Macedonian War, see above, Chapter 3. Macedonian propaganda in 200 and 199: see Ferrary 1988: 45 (with sources).
[40] See Cic. *Verr.* 2.4.129 with the comments of Gruen 1992: 104–5.
[41] On this incident – initiated by the Aetolians, not Flamininus – see Polyb. 18.43. Livy 33.27–8, though drawing on Polybius, suppresses Flamininus' indirect role in the murder. Derow 2003: 61, sees the murder as a typical act of Roman imperialism; Badian 1958a: 75, stresses, however, that Flamininus did not (could not) simply order the murder. See, by contrast, Philip V's murder of the anti-Macedonian politician Chariteles in Achaea: Livy 32.21.23.

which his own portrait appears to echo that of the portrayal of Greek monarchs.[42]

Yet on the other hand was the singular fact that by 197 Rome had come to stand at the head of a grand anti-Macedonian coalition of free Greek states: not just the original combination of Pergamum, Rhodes, and Athens, but also the Aetolian League, the Achaean League, the Kingdom of Athamania, and Thebes and the Boeotian League.[43] The politics of the peace settlement turned out to reflect this large network of alliances that had evolved during the course of the war: everywhere the Romans looked in European Greece by 197/196 there were only "friendly" Greek states, and this was a good geopolitical situation to occupy – and to preserve. We should stress as well, however, that the settlement reflected a continued lack of Roman interest in permanent involvement in Greek politics. Once the threat posed by the military resources and will to power of Philip V was gone – and thus the Pact Between the Kings crippled by the defeat of Macedon – that seemed accomplishment enough, and the peace settlement led to a complete Roman military and diplomatic withdrawal back to Italy. Thus the Romans pursued, though now on a larger scale, the same type of "smash and leave" policy towards situations east of the Adriatic which – as we have seen – they had pursued earlier in the two Illyrian Wars and the First Macedonian War.[44]

Theoretically, Flamininus in 196 could have proposed to the senatorial commission that Rome simply transform European Greece into a permanent Roman *provincia*, to be ruled directly by a magistrate or promagistrate sent out periodically from Italy, and garrisoned by Roman troops. This would have paralleled the recent decision by the Senate (in spring 197) to establish two permanent *provinciae* in eastern Spain in view of the continuing instability there, and the point would have been to establish complete Roman control. But it is clear that such a step regarding Greece never occurred at this time to any Roman.[45]

Again, the large ad hoc coalition of Greek states that Rome ended up leading against Macedon during the Second Macedonian War could

[42] Gruen 1984: 167, suggests that this coinage was actually issued at Greek initiative, but the absence of Greek mint-marks and the name "T. Quincti" in Latin script and in proper Roman grammatical form shows that the proconsul himself issued it: see Ferrary 1988: 92 n. 155.
[43] Boeotia and the anti-Macedonian alliance: Livy 33.1–2; Plut. *Flam.* 6; Zon. 9.16. By spring 197, the only major Greek state still allied with Macedon was Sparta; this was in part because Philip had bought King Nabis' loyalty by turning over to him the city of Argos. Discussion in Eckstein 1987b.
[44] On "smash and leave," see above, Chapters 2 and 3; and below, pp. 301–2.
[45] The Roman decision of spring 197 to create two permanent *provinciae* in eastern Spain: see Richardson 1986: 64–78.

have provided the Romans with a structure for an institutionalized if indirect hegemony in the Aegean, with Rome as the head of a large permanent league of Greek polities.[46] Such a system would have paralleled the mid-fourth-century League of Corinth of Philip II and Alexander the Great; and the contemporary Hellenic Symmachy of Antigonus III and Philip V himself was an even more obvious model, since it had existed as in instrument of Macedonian hegemony right up to Cynoscephalae.[47] Indeed, Ferrary argues that Flamininus experimented in this direction in the three years after Cynoscephalae, employing the Hellenic Symmachy of the Antigonids as an institutional model for a permanent Rome-headed alliance of Greek states.[48] But the only possible historical support for the hypothesis of Roman experimentation in permanent alliance is the war that Rome and some of her Greek friends fought against Nabis of Sparta in 195, and all one sees in 195 is a natural process whereby Flamininus calls a conference of such Greek states as might wish to join with Rome and the Achaean League in this war in the Peloponnese. The result was merely an ad hoc coalition of the willing, with major elements of the anti-Philip alliance – namely, Pergamum, Rhodes, and Aetolia – missing.[49] Moreover, the procedures of allied consultation which Flamininus followed, both before the war and during its various stages, were far more democratic than Macedon's Hellenic Symmachy. And afterwards, of course, the Romans left Greece entirely. This is not a Roman version of the Hellenic Symmachy.[50]

In fact, despite the efforts of recent scholars, Larsen was correct long ago: "Though Flamininus must have known of this organization [sc. the Hellenic Symmachy], and though he called meetings of his Greek associates, he did not organize Rome's free friends in Greece in a permanent League."[51] It is clear that no formal institutions ever

[46]   Walsh 1996: 350, emphasizes the smooth working of the coalition, including co-ordinated diplomacy at Rome in winter 198/197 and winter 197/196.
[47]   Cf. Ferrary 1988: 83–91. On the institutions of the Hellenic Symmachy headed by Macedon in 224–197, see Aymard 1938: 54–7.
[48]   Ferrary 1988: 88–91; cf. already Mastrocinque 1983: 103 (without extensive argument).
[49]   On the other hand, Philip V (who viewed Nabis as a traitor to his own cause) contributed troops: discussion by Hammond, in Hammond and Walbank 1988: 448.
[50]   Thus whereas Philip V twice decided on truces during Symmachy wars because as formal hegemon of the Symmachy he did not need to consult anyone, Flamininus consistently consulted with the Greek principes (Livy 34.26.4–8), and declared himself ready to follow the vote of the states at war against Nabis on questions of war or peace (Livy 34.24.6 and 34.34.2). Ferrary 1988: 90, himself acknowledges this latter difference.
[51]   Larsen 1935: 205. So, too, de Sanctis 1923: 105; Aymard 1938: 279 n. 18; Gruen 1984: 147.

emerged for exercising a Roman hegemony over Greece via a permanent league of Greek states headed by Rome. Indeed, as Ferrary himself finally admits, a formal Hellenic Symmachy headed by Rome, with its own set rules and consultative procedures, would have been even harder for the Senate to accept than for the Greeks themselves, since such a free-standing and self-functioning alliance was foreign to Roman tradition.[52] So it is perfectly natural that we do not hear of such an idea ever being discussed by Flamininus and the senatorial commission that came out to Greece in 196 to work with him on the final shape of the peace settlement – and we have much evidence on those deliberations.[53]

Ferrary goes on to argue, however, that although no formally constituted league of Greek states modeled on the Hellenic Symmachy but headed by Rome was established in 196–194, Flamininus did leave behind in 194 "une sorte de symmachie informelle," so that in case of future need a Roman magistrate and military commander could unite – probably at Corinth – the equivalent of a Panhellenic Council (*Synedrion*) to coordinate military action headed by Rome.[54] But there is no evidence for this "informal structure," and Ferrary himself admits that when Antiochus III invaded Greece just two years later, in 192 (see below), no such alleged "structure-in-waiting" was ever activated. In fact, there is simply no reason to believe in its existence.[55]

In sum, although the Roman victory in the Second Macedonian War did increase the *de facto* weight of Roman political power among the Greeks of Europe and the Aegean, as was only natural, the peace of 196 did not give any formal or institutional expression to this power: no Roman *provincia*, no Roman-dominated and permanent league of states, not even an informal and merely potential league-in-waiting left in place for emergencies. In fact, the Romans in these years did not even swear any formal treaty of alliance with any *individual* Greek state.[56]

[52]   Ferrary 1988: 93. Rome traditionally dealt one by one with individual allied states, in a situation where Rome because of its geopolitical weight was naturally the only "center."
[53]   On the deliberations of Flamininus and the senatorial commission, see Eckstein 1987a: 295–300 (with sources).
[54]   Ferrary 1988: 93–4.
[55]   Ibid.: 94–5. Ferrary suggests that this failure in the crisis of 192 to bring the "structure-in-waiting" into actuality via a grand coalition meeting at Corinth was, for Flamininus, a bitter disappointment (95). One can only reply: not if Flamininus never envisaged such a thing in the first place.
[56]   It has sometimes been argued that Philip V now became a treaty-bound ally of Rome, but Gruen 1973 convincingly argues that in fact he never did. The Achaean League eventually received a treaty of alliance, but not until (at the earliest) 192 or 191 BC, as a Roman reaction to the looming threat of Antiochus the Great; see Badian 1952: 76–80.

What Flamininus and the Commission of Ten did impose was a situation in which no Greek state would be a predominant power within the region. First, they allowed Philip V to remain as ruler of Macedon – and of a Macedon which, though dramatically reduced in territory and military power, was still a stable and potentially strong polity.[57] This decision, already presaged in Flamininus' moderate attitude towards Philip after Cynoscephalae in 197, aroused the ferocious opposition of the Aetolian League, the traditional rival of Macedon in central Greece. The Aetolians – who claimed with some justice to have played a major role at Cynoscephalae – preferred that the Antigonid regime be destroyed, a measure that would have made the Aetolians the predominant power in central and even northern Greece; but it was the Romans' decision that counted. The proconsul and the senatorial commission did free enormous swathes of territory from Macedonian control: the Thessalians (who had been under Macedonian control for 150 years), the Perrhaebians, the Dolopians, the Magnesians and Orestae, Thasos and the cities along the Thracian coast, Philip's conquests from his campaigns in Asia Minor in 201 and 200, as well as the great Macedonian military bases of Demetrias, Chalcis, and Corinth, and the secondary bases at Oreus and Eretria. Most of these places, large and small, now became independent states. Nor was this a cynical policy of "divide and conquer," for Flamininus and the Ten allowed or even encouraged the freed states to band together into regional leagues: Perrhaebia, Euboea, Boeotia, Magnesia, Thessaly.[58]

Flamininus and the Commission also gave certain polities into the hands either of the Aetolian League or the Achaean League, as rewards for Aetolian or Achaean support in the war.[59] The Aetolian government believed, however, that for their efforts with Rome against Macedon going back to 211 they deserved a far greater increase in towns, territory, and power than Flamininus and the Commission awarded them.[60] The Aetolians were particularly angered because although Flamininus denied them the larger territorial accessions they desired, he simultaneously gave the Achaean League the major city of Corinth, one of the great

---

[57]   See Polybius' comments on Philip's postwar strengthening of the kingdom (25.10).
[58]   See, rightly, Ferrary 1988: 105.
[59]   For sources, see conveniently Gruen 1984: 146–7.
[60]   The Aetolians gained Phocis and Locris in central Greece; these areas had once been part of the League, but Phocis defected ca. 225 and Locris had been conquered by Philip in 208: Walbank 1967: 617–18, with sources. The Aetolians deeply desired Phthiotic Achaea farther east, which had been theirs ca. 229, and the Commission might well have agreed to this, but the Aetolians were blocked by Flamininus: see Walsh 1993, with sources.

Macedonian military strongholds. Corinth had been taken from the Achaean League by Philip V's predecessor Antigonus III in the 220s; regaining the city satisfied a great Achaean ambition, and made the League the greatest power in southern Greece.[61] Yet – to repeat – most of the polities freed from Macedonian control were to remain independent.[62]

The details of the peace settlement, along with the general principle of interstate "freedom" that would henceforth be backed by Rome, were proclaimed by Flamininus' herald to an assembled Greek audience at the Isthmian Games near Corinth in June/July 196. Together, these elements constitute what scholars call "the Isthmian Declaration." The general principle was that the states and peoples of Greece would be free: free not only of Macedonian hegemony and control, but totally free; free from all foreign garrisons, free from all taxes imposed by any foreign great state, and free to live under their own ancestral laws – free (in a word) not just from Macedon but from Rome. And the seal on this promise of freedom for the Greeks was the promise that the Roman army in Greece would soon be returning to Italy. No Roman soldier would be left east of the Adriatic; nor would any Roman political over-seers – nor even any Roman diplomats – be left in its wake.[63]

The general meaning of Flamininus' doctrine of "the Freedom of the Greeks" seems clear enough. The concept as employed among the great Hellenistic Greek states went back to the Successors of Alexander. And while the Successors founded powerful territorial monarchies, it would be wrong to see the Hellenistic idea of proclaimed "freedom" for smaller states as mere cynicism, for the monarchies faced strategic concerns that were so numerous, and projection of power overland was so slow and expensive, that kings were willing to come to a *modus vivendi* with smaller states in return for their support.[64] In the 190s BC the most

---

[61] Hence the Aetolian remarks in 195 that the Achaeans were merely mercenaries who had deserted Philip to go the highest bidder: Livy 34.23.6 (based on Polybian material: see Briscoe 1981: 85).

[62] Flamininus' relations with the Aetolians were poor, having begun to deteriorate with a typical ancient dispute over who deserved more honor and credit for the Cynoscephalae victory: see Eckstein 1987a: 287–9 (with sources). Impact upon the territorial settlement: Walsh 1996: 353. By contrast, Flamininus' relations with the Achaeans were good, especially because of the Achaean leader Aristaenus of Dyme: see Eckstein 1990, and below.

[63] On the Isthmian Declaration and preceding events, see Polyb. 18.44–8; Livy 33.30–5; Plut. *Flam.* 10ff.; App. *Mac.* 9.3ff.; Justin 30.4.117ff.; Val. Max. 4.8.5; Zon. 9.16. The Greek states were to be ἐλευθέρους, ἀφρουρήτους, ἀφορολογήτους, νόμοις χρωμένους τοῖς πατρίοις (Polyb. 18.46.5).

[64] See esp. Gruen 1984: Ch. 4 and Ma 1999/2002: Chs. 3 and 4, both of whom emphasize a complex, fluid, and interactive relationship between free *polis* and Hellenistic king.

extensive Greek employer of the concept of "freedom" was Antiochus III as he advanced westward through Asia Minor. With Antiochus, too, the employment of "freedom" was not without meaning, for precisely the geopolitical reasons outlined above.[65] And political scientists have emphasized that the recognition of legal independence and self-government puts subtle but real limits on the conduct of a great power in relation to a weaker one.[66]

The Romans themselves, however, only came slowly to the concept (or slogan) of "Freedom of the Greeks." Proclamations of "freedom" are absent from Roman propaganda about the expeditions to Illyria (where the main idea is protection from barbarians), and equally so during the First Macedonian War.[67] The ultimatum which the Roman envoys at Athens in the spring of 200 gave Philip's general Nicanor merely demanded an end of Philip's wars against the Greeks and the payment of an indemnity to Pergamum; there was nothing about Greek "freedom."[68] The ultimatum which M. Aemilius Lepidus personally gave to Philip at Abydus that summer was similar. It did contain a new senatorial demand that Philip withdraw from certain Ptolemaic possessions, but the intention was to give those places back into the control of the Ptolemaic government after the Macedonian withdrawal, not to set them free.[69] In spring 198 and then again in autumn 198, Flamininus at conferences with Philip demanded that Philip withdraw from specified Greek territories in return for peace – but he gave no indication of the fate of those territories after the Macedonian withdrawal. Such demands for an enemy's withdrawal from territory were traditional Roman military-diplomatic practice, and do not indicate anything new; the only "freedom" here is a demand that this territory be free of the power of Philip.[70]

In the Polybian tradition it is the speech of Aristaenus of Dyme to the Achaeans in autumn 198, advocating that they change sides to Rome, followed somewhat more strongly by the speech of the Greek envoys to the Senate at Rome in the winter of 198/197, which give us the first hints at the concept of Greek "freedom" in the sense of the Greeks living in general enjoyment of freedom from all outside powers; but these

[65]   See Ma 1999/2002: Chs. 3 and 4 for detailed discussion.
[66]   See Abernethy 1986 (esp. 110), and Donnelly 2006 (discussed above, Chapter 2).
[67]   Rightly emphasized by Gruen 1984: 144.
[68]   See Eckstein 1990: 47; Walsh 1996: 345.
[69]   Polyb. 16.34, cf. Livy 31.18. Petzold 1940: 37, wrongly saw the essentials of the Isthmian declaration here; compare Badian 1958a: 67 with n. 4.
[70]   See Heidemann 1966: 105 n. 2; Seager 1981: 109–10; Eckstein 1990: 48. Diod. 28.11 has Flamininus at the Aous Conference in spring 198 giving the full Isthmian program of freedom as the Roman demand on Philip, but this is obviously a retrojection back two years: see Walsh 1996: 347–8.

are only hints.[71] The first explicit statement envisioning a complete Roman as well as Macedonian withdrawal from Greece after the war only comes in Roman statements in discussions with the Greek allies in the summer of 197, following the victory at Cynoscephalae.[72] But Roman policy remained uncertain: the Commission of Ten came out to Greece in 196 bearing a *senatus consultum* that proclaimed all Greeks *except* the former subjects of Philip were "to be free and to enjoy their own laws."[73] This is the first official Roman pronouncement where "the Freedom of the Greeks" has positive content: many Greeks were to be free and enjoy their own laws. This represents a departure, has strong elements of Greek tradition, and probably reflects ideas brought to Rome by lieutenants of Flamininus in the winter of 197/196.[74] Still, "freedom" in the *senatus consultum* applies only to some Greek states: others, the subjects of Philip, are to be turned over to the Romans, and put *in dicionis populi Romani* with no indication of their ultimate fate.

Indeed, there was strong sentiment within the Commission of Ten in spring 196 that because of Antiochus III's continuing advance through western Asia Minor towards Europe, and his enormous army and fleet, the most strategically important of Philip's possessions should either be occupied by Roman troops into the foreseeable future or (in the case of Oreus and Eretria) turned over to Pergamum.[75] But Flamininus not only convinced the *decem legati* to enunciate the full series of rights of "freedom" announced at the Isthmia (i.e., freedom from foreign taxes and garrisons, and the right to live under one's own laws), but also persuaded them to limit the exceptions to this principle solely to the former great Macedonian bases at Demetrias, Chalcis, and the Acrocorinth (the so-called "Three Fetters of Greece," because of their strategic locations and powerful fortifications). These three places were indeed to be held by Roman troops, but only temporarily – until the situation with Antiochus III was clarified.[76] And even though Romans

---

[71] The brief hint in Aristaenus' speech: Livy 32.21.36, emphasized by Eckstein 1990: 54–8. The Greek envoys at Rome: Polyb. 18.11.7, cf. 11.4 and 11.11, emphasized by Ferrary 1988: 68 with n. 34, and Walsh 1996: 352.

[72] See Polyb. 18.36.4 (χωρισθέντων Ῥωμαίων ἐκ τῆς Ἑλλάδος), with Eckstein 1990: 49. The idea comes from King Amynander of Athamania, but it is clear he is speaking for Flamininus: see Sacks 1975: 102–3.

[73] Polyb. 18.44.2, cf. Livy 33.30.2.

[74] See Eckstein 1987a: 293 and 197; Eckstein 1990: 50.

[75] On this latter point, see Polyb. 18.47.10 and Livy 33.34.10.

[76] Greek envoys to Rome in winter 198/197 had themselves stressed to the Senate the strategic importance of the "Three Fetters" (Polyb. 18.11), so it is no surprise that the Commission of Ten was reluctant to let them go. Flamininus got the fate of Oreus and Eretria referred to the Senate – who set them free (including free from Attalus). Discussion and sources: Walsh 1996: 357 and n. 53.

temporarily occupied the Acrocorinth, the Achaean League received back the city of Corinth itself. In this way, and thanks to Flamininus' persuasion of the Commission, what had previously been wartime propaganda now became actual Roman policy.[77]

In one aspect the Isthmian Declaration was quite traditional – its promise of ultimate complete Roman withdrawal from Greece. This was a pattern set in the previous Roman wars on the Illyrian coast and then in the first war with Macedon: once the immediate geopolitical problem east of the Adriatic was dealt with, the Romans all went back home to Italy. This traditional Roman way of dealing with large problems across the Adriatic must have made the Roman decision for complete withdrawal once Philip had been defeated seem natural, if only because any other policy would have been a sharp break from the past. And yet this withdrawal of Roman troops would have enormous strategic consequences.[78]

Nevertheless, some scholars see the proclamation of "the Freedom of the Greeks" as a sham, as – precisely – a new and sinister departure from previous Roman practice, indeed as a proclamation of Roman rule over the entire Greek world. This is the cynical view of W. V. Harris.[79] Ferrary, as we have seen, views the Isthmian Declaration as part of a process whereby the Romans established themselves as hegemons over an informal and "potential" alliance-system of technically free polities, a system not that dissimilar, he holds, to the previous hegemonial structure in Greece overseen by Macedon.[80] Or as another scholar puts it, " 'The Freedom of the Hellenes' means Roman domination."[81] Was that the case? It is to this crucial question that we now turn.

The argument is that because the Senate, the Commission of Ten, and the proconsul Flamininus granted all Greek states "freedom" in the Isthmian Declaration, they were really asserting that the victor had the right to determine not merely the status of defeated Macedon, but also the status of non-belligerents and even of Rome's allies, "thus making the Greek states subject to Roman hegemony."[82] The fine words of the Isthmian Declaration thus provided "a veneer of legality" for Roman

---

[77] For Flamininus' persuasion of the Commission of Ten, see Eckstein 1987a: 297–9, with sources; cf. Walsh 1996: 363.
[78] On the Roman withdrawals from the Illyrian coast in 228 and 219, and again in 205, see above, Chapters 2 and 3.
[79] Harris 1979: 142.
[80] Ferrary 1988: 86 and 93 – a thesis discussed above, pp. 286–7.
[81] Mandell 1989: 94, cf. 90–1 (an assertion of "Rome's suzerainty" over Greece) and 93; the same implication in Derow 2003: 61.
[82] Mandell 1989: 90; Derow 2003: 62.

rule over Greece.[83] That is, the Declaration was at bottom an *order*, an order to all Greeks – the defeated enemy, the allies, the non-belligerents all alike. And it was an order not only to Greek states in Europe but even to a substantial number of polities in Asia (especially to those polities Philip had conquered in Asia Minor in 202–200).[84] The *senatus consultum* of spring 196 even included an order to King Prusias I of Bithynia to set free the city of Cius (in the Hellespont region), though Prusias had received the city as a gift from his in-law Philip V after Philip had seized and sacked it, and even though Prusias was a sovereign king. The Roman attitude is thus one of arrogance.[85] Equally important is that Flamininus in the winter of 195/194 took a strong hand in the *internal* political ordering of numerous Greek polities that had previously been under Macedonian control. This occurred on Euboea and in Thessaly, where Flamininus made decisions to weaken the factions, previously dominant, that had supported Philip, and to penalize their members, while supporting his own adherents, thus establishing his own idea of pro-Roman political stability. Such direct Roman interference in the internal affairs of Greek states made a mockery of the claim at the Isthmia that Rome was providing the Greek states a guarantee of internal freedom from foreign interference.[86]

There are thus clear reasons why some modern scholars assert – as the contemporary Aetolians themselves soon began to assert (Polyb. 18.45.6, cf. Livy 34.49.6) – that at the Isthmia the Greeks, instead of being liberated, had simply exchanged one master, Macedon, for another, Rome. "Some believed them," as Derow remarks approvingly.[87] And it is true that in 196 the representatives of the Roman Republic determined and commanded both the general shape of Greek politics and the fate of many individual Greek polities. It is also true, and striking, that in 195/194 – a year and more after the Isthmian Declaration – we find Flamininus

---

[83] Mandell 1989: 90.

[84] See esp. Derow 2003: 61–2. Hence the Isthmian Declaration proclaims that Philip's conquests in Asia from the campaigns of 202–200 were to be free, and Euromus, Pedas, Bargylia, Iasus, Abydus, and Perinthus are mentioned by name (Polyb. 18.44.4).

[85] Cius given to Prusias by Philip: Polyb. 15.21. The Roman order that Cius be freed: Polyb. 18.44.6.

[86] Flamininus' interventions: Livy 34.48.2; a specific example confirmed by inscription: Chyretiae in Thessaly: *SIG*³ 594, with Armstrong and Walsh 1986. Mandell 1989: 90, sees Flamininus' conduct here as a savage *fulfillment* of the real meaning of the Isthmian Declaration.

[87] Derow 2003: 61. Ferrary 1988: 81, is incorrect to state that the Aetolians' accusation about the mere change of masters refers to Chalcis, Demetrias, and Corinth alone.

himself personally establishing to his own taste the internal orders of many Greek states formerly under Macedonian control.[88]

I think that what should be stressed here, however, is not Roman "domination" but ambiguity. First, while the Isthmian Declaration was primarily the result of Roman decisions, it would be simplistic to believe there was no Greek contribution to it. The rights proclaimed at the Isthmia were typically Greek; we know that the Greek envoys to the Senate in winter 197/196 were urging that the settlement after the war go precisely in this direction;[89] and it is likely that in this matter Flamininus acted with the advice of Greeks he trusted, especially the Achaean statesman Aristaenus of Dyme.[90] As for the Roman demand that Prusias I free the city of Cius, on the one hand this fits with the general Isthmian principle of restoring to freedom those cities in Asia that had been conquered by Philip, and on the other hand the destruction of Cius had enraged the Rhodians, who had pleaded with Philip to spare it (Polyb. 15.20–4), so it is likely that the Romans' action regarding Cius actually came at the urging of their allies the Rhodians. Indeed, it is well to remember that the grand coalition of Greek states headed by Rome that had emerged by 197 was a living alliance where the allies had relationships with each other quite separately from Rome,[91] and where opinions were forthrightly expressed both to each other and to the Romans.[92] From this perspective of a multiplicity of actors, it would also be simplistic to think that as the governments of the smaller Greek states looked towards the postwar period they were only concerned about the power of Rome: part of the relief felt by some Greeks when the content of the Isthmian Declaration was announced at Corinth in 196 may have been because the Romans had decided not to enhance greatly the power of the Aetolian League.[93]

Finally, Flamininus' official interventions in the internal politics of the Euboean and Thessalian cities were classic imperialist acts, bald assertions of Roman political superiority and dominance, and a bad omen

---

[88]   He also personally established the frontiers of others, as at Chyretiae, where the frontiers established by Flamininus were still in force fifty years later: see *SIG*[3] 674, with Eckstein 1987a: 321 and n. 178.

[89]   Polyb. 18.11.4, 7, and 11; cf. above, pp. 290–1.

[90]   At least that is how Polybius portrayed the situation: see Eckstein 1990.

[91]   Hence the splendid Achaean honors voted to Attalus of Pergamum in 197 because of his large gifts of grain; the honors included a portrait in gold and an annual cult-festival in his honor (Polyb. 18.17).

[92]   As is clear from our accounts of the Tempe Conference in summer 197 (Polyb. 18.36–7; Livy 33.12; App. *Mac.* 9.1), or the conference held before the war against Nabis of Sparta in spring 195 (Livy 34.27.6), and during the siege of Sparta (Livy 34.33.9–34.9). See, in general, Burton 2003.

[93]   Cf. Ferrary 1988: 82.

for the future.[94] We should also remember, however, that Flamininus did not intervene like this in the internal affairs of most Greek states. The former Macedonian possessions on Euboea and in Thessaly appear, rather, a special case – places where Flamininus was concerned to complete the destruction of Antigonid power by removing the local agents of Macedon who had been put in place by orders of Philip.[95]

The universal tradition in our sources is that Flamininus' announcement of the general principle and the territorial details of the postwar settlement in fact produced enormous enthusiasm in the crowd at the Isthmia.[96] Were the Greeks naïve here, or perhaps pathetically trying to curry favor with their conquerors? But Polybius, even from his perspective of fifty years later, when Roman–Greek relations had taken a tragic turn, agrees with the positive assessment of the Isthmian Declaration of most contemporaries except the Aetolians: "For it was a wonderful thing that the Romans had incurred every expense and peril for the sake of the liberty of the Hellenes" (Polyb. 18.46.14).[97] This statement parallels Polybius' judgment that Rome's ally Attalus I of Pergamum died in 197 "while engaged in the most noble enterprise of fighting for the cause of Greek freedom" (18.41.9, cf. 21.20.5). Such statements would make no sense if Polybius thought the result of the Second Macedonian War had simply been that the Greeks exchanged Macedonian masters for Roman ones. Indeed, the family of Polybius and the circle of men around whom he grew up in his native Megalopolis in Arcadia were personal enemies of Aristaenus of Dyme, the most famous Achaean advocate of the link to Rome, so that the historian was making a sharp break with both local and family tradition in his positive judgment on these events.[98] Nor can the reason for the positive assessment be that Polybius was a sycophant

---

[94] Flamininus earlier had also acquiesced in the murder of the Boeotian leader Bracchyles by the Aetolians (above, p. 284). He could be ruthless (as we know from his brutal war-making in 198). But the Bracchyles affair was a secret affair, unofficial – and Aetolian inspired.
[95] Flamininus presented his actions as liberation, as is implied in the first lines of the inscription from Chyretiae in Thessaly (above, n. 86) – nor should we be totally cynical about this.
[96] Sources on the joyful Isthmian scene: see above, n. 63. According to Polybius, even the vaguer and limited decree of the Senate in spring 196 was received with widespread satisfaction: 18.45.1.
[97] An assessment which Livy, naturally enough, echoes: 33.33.5. So, too, Plut. *Flam.* 11.4.
[98] Megalopolis was one of the cities in the Achaean League with close ties to Macedon (in part because the Antigonid kings had rebuilt the city after its destruction by Sparta in 223), and the Megalopolitans in 198 opposed Aristaenus' policy of leaving Macedon and siding with Rome; moreover, Polybius' father Lycortas was a personal enemy of Aristaenus. For Polybius' defense of Aristaenus, see 18.11–13. On all this, see Eckstein 1987b.

of the Romans, for Polybius in his *Histories* does not hesitate to criticize the Roman government on numerous occasions when he believes
it has acted ruthlessly or in a duplicitous manner on the international
scene.[99] Moreover, Polybius raises serious questions at the general level
about the moral and political character of Roman hegemony in the East
as it developed later, after ca. 180 BC (cf. 3.3.4; 24.8–11). But this means
that – by contrast – Polybius' positive assessment of the Roman proclamation of Greek freedom in the mid-190s, and its practical impact, should
be taken seriously.[100]

Polybius' assessment is supported, of course, by the numerous
official honors created for Flamininus or the Romans that sprang up
among the Greek states after 196, honors that were unusual in scale,
and expressed a general satisfaction with the peace settlement.[101] The
theme of freedom (*eleutheria*) found widespread official expression in these
honors: for instance, in the creation of the annual *Eleutheria* Games at
Larissa in Thessaly, where the new Thessalian Confederation (itself
a creation of Flamininus and the Commission) met to worship Zeus
Eleutherios (*Syll.*[3] 613) – or in the Achaean ransoming of the surviving Romans whom Hannibal had sold into slavery in Greece after
Cannae two decades earlier: freedom for freedom (Plut. *Flam.* 13.6).
This emphasis on *eleutheria* parallels Flamininus' own extraordinary
dedication at Delphi of the shield which he carried at Cynoscephalae,
with an inscribed poem emphasizing how he, the descendant of Aeneas,
brought *eleutheria* to the Greeks (Plut. *Flam.* 12.6).[102]

On a cynical analysis, the official acts by Greek states might seem
evidence merely of sycophancy towards Roman power.[103] But it is very
hard to see how Flamininus would dare to challenge the most famous
oracle in the Mediterranean world by being a hypocrite and liar to Apollo
of Delphi. If anything, Flamininus' dedication of the shield is a promise
to Apollo that he will keep his word.[104] And some scholars argue in favor
of accepting Flamininus' sincerity here not merely because he thought

---

[99]   See Polybius' criticism of Roman policy at 3.30.4 towards Carthage in the Sardinia
crisis of 238/237 BC, or towards the Ptolemies in the 160s (31.10); towards
Pergamum in the 160s (30.1–3), or towards the disputes between Carthage and
Numidia (31.2), or towards the Seleucids (32.1.2, cf. 33.18), or towards his personal friend Demetrius I of Syria (31.2 and 11).
[100]   Detailed discussion in Eckstein 1995: Ch. 1 and (esp.) Ch. 7.
[101]   See the list in Walbank 1967: 613–14.
[102]   On the honors to Flamininus see Walbank 1967: 613–14.
[103]   So Mandell 1989: 91.
[104]   It may be that the shield dedication was written by Greeks and reflects Greek
perceptions (cf. Erskine 2003: 42) – which would be interesting in itself. But
Flamininus no doubt oversaw the general sentiment.

the Isthmian policy would bring geopolitical advantages to Rome in terms of public opinion (see below), but also because as bringer of a real freedom to the Greeks he gained so much honor among them. This was the sort of ambition for fame that moved ancient men greatly.[105]

Impressive support for the positive judgment of Polybius comes from the contemporary verses of Alcaeus of Messene, who ca. 196–193 BC penned a poem contrasting Flamininus with Antiochus III: Antiochus was coming to European Greece like a new Xerxes, to invade and enslave it; but Flamininus had freed Greece from its enslavement (*Anth. Pal.* 16.5 = Plut. *Flam.* 12.5–6). This appears to be a sincere sentiment.[106] Similarly, a contemporary inscription shows the government of the city of Lampsacus in western Asia Minor seeking Roman guarantees of δημοκρατία and αὐτονομία, in preference to any promises being offered by King Antiochus.[107] There is thus good evidence to suggest that the Romans' declaration of "Greek Freedom" at the Isthmia was not viewed by most contemporary Greeks as a sham – just the opposite. Of course, the propaganda of the angry Aetolians pointed to the continued Roman occupation of Demetrias, Chalcis, and the Acrocorinth, "the Three Fetters of Greece," as evidence of Rome's hypocrisy and oppressive intentions – but that argument fell away when the Romans evacuated the three fortresses in spring 194 and Flamininus and his entire army returned home across the Adriatic to Italy, leaving European Greece empty of any official Roman presence.[108]

None of this means, however, that the Senate or the Commission of Ten or Flamininus himself intended the Greek states now to be free to go their own way in geopolitics, without considering Roman interest. The Greeks had gained freedom and self-government; that was true of many individual polities as well as European Greece as a whole, liberated from Macedonian domination; but in the Hellenistic world these meaningful freedoms nevertheless did not exclude having an informal attachment to a stronger power.[109] The Isthmian Declaration of 196 and the Roman evacuation of 194 did not mean that European Greece was

[105] See Ferrary 1988: 105–12; Walsh 1996: 345 and 362–3.
[106] See Gruen 1984: 147 n. 88, and even the more cynical Ferrary 1988: 86. We do not know whether the poem is responding to Aetolian anti-Roman propaganda (so Walbank 1943: 9), or to the threatening approach of Antiochus' military forces several years later (so Kuijper 1972: 254–5).
[107] *Syll.*³ 590, lines 33–4. At this time the Rhodians, too – if one believes Livy – were calling the Romans "the liberators of Greece" (*Romanis liberantibus Graeciam*: 33.20.3). This was quite a contrast to their suspicions during the First Macedonian War (cf. above, Chapter 3).
[108] Cf. Ferrary 1988: 96–9.
[109] Cf. Gruen 1984: 147; Ferrary 1988: 99–104.

now to be a neutral zone between the two remaining superpowers.[110] Nor did the Senate intend that henceforth Rome would simply be one important factor, even the preponderant one, in a Greek equilibrium, along with the Antigonids and the Seleucids. Rather, both Macedon and the Seleucids were to be excluded from European Greece.[111] In short, the Roman goal in European Greece was henceforth to prevent any *other* great power from dominating it; and thus it is clear that the Senate viewed Greece as an informal Roman "sphere of interest" in the classic definition evolved by modern political scientists: a region where a single great power has no serious competitors for influence.[112]

The problem emerging out of the Second Macedonian War, however, was that the arrangements the Romans chose to leave behind them in Greece to enforce the exclusion of other powers were of the most informal kind, not backed by any institutional or military presence. Badian underlines these points, but goes on to argue that to shore up the Roman position in Greece the Senate depended after the Roman withdrawal on the (allegedly) strict though informal obligations of interstate *clientela* – which the Romans had won for themselves through their "favors" to the Greeks.[113] As we saw in our discussion of the earlier situation between Rome and the Illyrian polities after 229/228 BC, however, the evidence that the Romans employed the moral obligations of patron–client relationship in interstate relations as a means of exercising control over weaker states is strikingly slim. Thus despite Badian, all the Romans appear to have left behind them when they withdrew from Greece in spring 194 were free *amici*.[114] As Larson says, "Rome naturally expected her friends to be friendly." But that turned out not to be enough to prevent a new crisis.[115]

---

[110]   Despite Stier 1952: 162, or Scullard 1973: 100.

[111]   See, rightly, Ferrary: 100. The Isthmian Declaration made this clear as far as Macedon, and Roman diplomacy would soon assert this position in regard to the Great King.

[112]   To repeat from Chapter 2 above, a "sphere of interest" is a region which a great power does not administer or directly control but where the great power does not allow any competition for influence from any outside great power. The classic example has been the United States' relationship with Latin America: see Triska, ed., 1986. The essays in Triska stress the difference between this sort of relationship and the contemporary relationship of the Soviet Union to Eastern Europe – which was buttressed by the formal Warsaw Pact treaty of alliance and permanent organization. I am arguing that this is exactly what Rome did *not* create in Greece by the Isthmian Declaration.

[113]   Badian 1958a: 74–5; see also, e.g., Errington 1972: 151–5; Mandell 1989: 91.

[114]   Against Badian in general see Gruen 1984: Ch. 4, and now Burton 2003. Detailed discussion of the inadequacy of the thesis of informal *clientela* as an alleged instrument of Roman foreign relations: above, Chapter 2.

[115]   Larsen 1935: 195.

Here we arrive at the heart of the political weakness of the Isthmian Declaration: the Romans were still in the midst of a ferocious hegemonic rivalry, this time with the Seleucid Empire. This hegemonic struggle, one should recall, was a byproduct of the power-transition crisis in the state structure of the eastern Mediterranean (and now in the Mediterranean as a whole) originally caused by the collapse of the Ptolemies. As it turned out, this power-transition crisis was in 194 still unresolved; the defeat of Macedon left a final contest now between Rome and the Seleucid Empire.[116] But our discussion of the Isthmian Declaration shows it to have been mostly a way of propagandizing general Roman magnanimity while evading any direct or entangling Roman commitments in Greece.[117] The Senate, the Ten, and Flamininus had created only a most informal attachment between the Greek states and Rome – and political scientists emphasize that such informal attachments, by virtue of being so informal, can only achieve reality through being continually *in action* between the powerful state and the weaker one. But the main Roman action was complete withdrawal.[118] Thus if a main purpose of the Isthmian Declaration was to evade direct Roman commitments in Greece, to avoid continuous entanglements now that Philip had been dealt with – i.e., the traditional Roman stance of "smash and leave" – then this was certainly not a prudent decision either in terms of the relations the Senate wished with the Greeks, or in terms of the ambitions of Antiochus III. That is: even in 196–194 most men in the Senate did not realize that they would soon be facing another crisis in Greece.[119]

Flamininus seems to have thought that Roman withdrawal would be the best way to foster Greek support for Rome in case of any forward move by Antiochus, for the withdrawal would demonstrate both his own good faith and Roman *fides* in general.[120] Flamininus turned out to be wrong about the practical impact of Greek goodwill – as Scipio Africanus warned the Senate in the spring of 194.[121] Whatever claims

[116] See briefly, from a political-science perspective, Liska 1978: 10, and in more detail Eckstein 2006: Ch. 7.

[117] Gruen 1984: 146.

[118] On the dynamics of non-institutionalized, informal relations between dominant and subordinate states, see Abernethy 1986, cf. Mommsen 1986, discussed above, Chapter 2, in relation to Rome and the polities of Illyria.

[119] With the looming confrontation with Antiochus, we see yet another aspect of Polybius' *symplokē* (the interconnectedness of events in East and West) – in this case, the impact that the Roman withdrawal from Italy would have on Antiochus in his bases in Asia Minor. In that sense the Senate failed to understand the workings of *symplokē*, as many contemporaries also did (see above, Chapter 3), although the process was strongly apparent to Polybius, writing from the perspective of ca. 150 BC.

[120] Cf. Eckstein 1987a: 311–15.

[121] Ibid.: 313–15. On Scipio's opinion, see also above, Chapter 6, p. 259; and below, p. 301.

the Romans later asserted in their diplomacy with Antiochus, the reality was the evacuation of Roman armed forces; the reality was the withdrawal of Roman power; and this was decisive in terms of the hegemonic rivalry between Rome and Antiochus from the spring of 194 onwards. This was because Antiochus himself interpreted the Isthmian Declaration not as the Aetolians did (and as some cynical modern scholars do), but precisely as most contemporary Greeks did: as an indication of Roman lack of interest in maintaining control over Greece.

The ambiguity of the situation in terms of Roman–Greek relations is clear from the speech which Livy – drawing on Polybian material – has Flamininus give to the Greek leaders assembled at Corinth in the spring of 194 as the Roman army was departing.[122] Flamininus tells the Greek leaders to trust in the words and deeds of the Romans, whose relationship in regard to the Greek states he describes as "friends" (*amici*: Livy 34.49.7; cf. *amicitia* at 34.48.3). No doubt this was not a friendship of equals, since it had begun with an enormous "benefaction" from the Roman side, a benefaction that Flamininus repeatedly stresses; and everyone understood this. But neither are the Greeks called *clientes* of Rome, nor is Rome described as their *patronus*. The Romans had not employed the language of *clientela* with the polities of Illyria a generation earlier – where instead, as here, we find an emphasis on trust, good faith, and friendship; they did not employ it now with the European Greek states; and there is no reason to believe they were secretly thinking it.[123] Flamininus' language of friendship, his *concept* of Roman–Greek relations, is polite; and perhaps, from the point of view of the ultimate geopolitical interests of Rome in Greece, it was too polite.

Flamininus then tells the Greek leaders that Rome expects them to use their freedom in a responsible and moderate manner and to make the Senate always believe that the gift of liberty, won for the Greeks by the arms and given to them by the good faith of a non-Greek people, had been rightly bestowed (34.49.11). This is neither a threat not to contravene Roman interests nor a warning to be obedient to the Senate. Rather, Flamininus' point about the responsible use of *libertas* is that the Greeks themselves should avoid civil strife within their polities, while avoiding wars among their polities (34.49.8–10, explicit); he had developed a good sense of the problems that could exist within Greek states and among the contending Greek polities.[124] Flamininus ends by

[122] Polybian derivation: cf. Briscoe 1981: 124.
[123] The Romans were perfectly familiar with the idea of "unequal but nevertheless real friendship" – as opposed to *clientela*; it had been the relationship between Rome and Syracuse for fifty years (263–214 BC): see Eckstein 1980, and now Burton 2003.
[124] On constant warfare as a major characteristic and problem of the Hellenistic anarchy, see above, Chapter 1.

stressing that it was now the responsibility of the Greeks to keep their freedom by their own efforts: *sua cura custodirent servarentque* (34.49.11). This is the opposite of domination and *clientela*. Yet simultaneously there is an undeniable air of superiority on Flamininus' part, of *de haut en bas*, which Livy (or rather, Polybius) well understood, for he says that Flamininus – then still only 34 years old – addressed the assembled Greek statesmen *velut parentis* (34.50.1).[125]

To sum up. The reason the Romans did not impose upon Greece direct rule by governors, or even indirect rule through a permanent hegemonic alliance (as a victorious Hellenistic monarchy probably would have done, and as a victorious Macedon had indeed done in the 220s), is probably because with the power of Macedon decisively diminished, the majority of the *Patres* in Rome believed (or preferred to believe) that the crisis depicted to them by the Greek ambassadors of 200 was now over. Hence the aftermath of the Second Macedonian War witnessed the usual Roman policy east of the Adriatic of "smash and leave."[126] The Senate was wrong in its assessment of the eastern situation. Flamininus himself was wrong.[127] But the point to stress is that the decision by the *Patres* in 194 to withdraw all Roman troops from east of the Adriatic reflects both a continued lack of intense interest at Rome in Greek affairs and a continued unwillingness to become deeply involved in them. Not every senator felt this way, or that the crisis in the East was over: Scipio Africanus argued in the Senate that it was a great mistake to withdraw the Roman army from Greece with Antiochus the Great still on the advance (Livy 34.43.1–5). But Scipio's advice – even though the Great King had already crossed over into Europe in 196 and again in 195 and had seized a good part of Thrace (see below), and even though Rome's redoubtable enemy Hannibal was now one of Antiochus' advisors – was ignored.[128] Having established a structure of politics in Greece that appeared unthreatening to Rome, and under the assumption that the Greek states understood the implications of the Roman victory against Macedon, i.e., that the Romans would now have their wishes obeyed in European Greece whenever they needed to

---

[125] See Eckstein 1987a: 311–13.

[126] The strain of serious Roman military commitments and fighting elsewhere, both in Spain against Celtiberians and simultaneously against the Celts of northern Italy, probably also played a role in the Roman desire to withdraw from Greece: see Sherwin-White 1980, and Sherwin-White 1984: 9–10.

[127] All this was seen long ago by Mommsen 1903: 721, quoted below, p. 316.

[128] Hannibal, expelled from Carthage, had joined Antiochus in the autumn of 195, after the king's second campaign in Thrace; discussion and sources in Grainger 2002: 121–2.

(though the *Patres* did not expect to have such wishes very often), the majority of the Senate wished to leave the Greeks on their own.[129]

CONCLUSION

The study of state expansion, especially in Mediterranean antiquity, must be seen within the context of *competing* empires.[130] The period 207–188 BC in the ancient Mediterranean witnessed a classic example of hegemonic war among great powers, within the context of a power-transition crisis caused by the faltering and then increasing collapse of the Ptolemaic state. And while it is correct to underline the aggressiveness and militarism of Rome, the Republic was merely one unit within the disturbed and roiling Hellenistic state-system. The Ptolemaic crisis resulted first in a hegemonic war among the great Greek states, in which the dominant powers were Macedon under Philip V and the Seleucid Empire under Antiochus III, a war that in itself would have created a new systemic structure in the East, with new system leaders. The aggressively expansionist actions of Philip V and Antiochus III led, in turn, to embassies to Rome from a series of frightened Greek polities. The arrival of these embassies was the catalyst that convinced the *Patres* that Rome must attempt a powerful intervention in the East, in order to prevent the emergence of a situation which would be profoundly dangerous for Rome itself. Intervention came in the form of war against Philip, and an embassy to Antiochus III attempting to keep him from attacking Egypt proper.[131]

There was nothing new in such crises, for this was how the heavily militarized multipolar anarchy of the ancient Mediterranean had functioned for several hundred years as periodic changes to the distribution of power-capabilities across the system occurred. It was a fiercely competitive environment, unforgiving to weak or inadequate governments. Demosthenes, like Thucydides before him, proclaimed interstate relations a brutal competition that belonged to the strong: "all men have their rights conceded to them in proportion to the power at their disposal" (*Rhod.* 26). A century and a half later, nothing had changed. The ferocious desire of polities for independence coexisted with and helped

---

[129] Discussion of this decision: Eckstein 1987a: 310–13 and 2006: 297–8.

[130] For this political-science maxim see Hyam 1999: 31–2; cf. in detail Abernethy 2000: Ch. 9. On Rome and its environment in this respect, note the comments of Goldsworthy 2000: 70.

[131] In other words, I am arguing that the position on the Roman decision taken by Holleaux 1935 and by McDonald and Walbank 1937 – and by Mommsen 1903 – is fundamentally a correct analysis.

cause constant interstate conflicts of interest; these conflicts of interest were real; they led to constant warfare; and hence – because someone always wins a war – to conquest, or at least to political subordination. Such conditions were as prevalent in the western Mediterranean as in the eastern Mediterranean, as true in the third century BC as in the fifth century. Rome had grown up amid the fierce intercity competition of central Italy, and as the power of the Romans expanded and they entered into or were drawn into successively larger state-systems (central Italy, then Italy as a whole, then the western Mediterranean, then the Mediterranean as a whole), the ferocity of competition and the heavy stakes involved in terms of survival and power did not abate. The only things that changed as Rome entered each successively larger state-system were the scale of warfare, which expanded – and not merely on the Romans' part – and the power of the states involved.[132]

None of this means that the Roman decision of 200, with all the momentous consequences that followed, was "predetermined" by the structure and general functioning of interstate politics in the Hellenistic Mediterranean. No political scientist argues that the individual actions of the governing elites of states are "determined" by the overarching interstate structure. Governing elites always have agency.

This is true even when those governing elites function and make decisions within bellicose, security-minded, and aggressive internal cultures – war-prone cultures that are themselves, so political scientists argue, in good part merely the adaptive responses to the pressures of the harsh interstate environment.[133] The international relations scholars do argue, further, that the overarching structure of interstate politics put constraints and limits upon the actions of states, not determining but certainly pushing governing elites towards certain types of action and deterring them from others. Thus the pressures of an anarchic and militarized multipolar system make it unlikely that in the face of a systemic crisis, passive or peaceful types of state actions will be taken. Those constraints make it more likely, rather, that aggressive and confrontational state actions will be taken. The pressure towards aggressive, security-minded action is only a general trend – which means that any one historical event or decision cannot be predicted. The more cruelly competitive the system in which a state exists, however, the more likely it is that the governing elite will opt for aggressive conduct – and the Hellenistic state-system was cruel. Moreover, aggressive state decisions are most probable in a system-wide power-transition crisis, because the stakes in terms of

---

[132] See now Eckstein 2006: Ch. 5.
[133] See Gourevitch 1978 (fundamental); cf. Downing 1992 and now Jervis 2001: 287; all discussed in Chapter 1, above.

survival and power are so high. Though again no event was theoretically predictable, it is therefore clear that an important factor in the Roman decision to intervene in the Greek East in 200 in the face of the Pact Between the Kings was the pressure from the brutal system in which Rome existed. It was a system that had taught the Romans many harsh lessons – most recently from Hannibal's invasion of Italy.

The intentions of Rome in foreign relations were not different from those of other states. The extraordinary success of Rome was therefore not based on Rome's possessing an extraordinarily predatory character – though Rome, like all other ancient states, was indeed aggressive, even predatory. Fundamentally, that success was based on the fact that from the 330s BC Rome had possessed an extraordinary capability for mobilizing the resources necessary for the inevitable struggles with those other states. This capability arose, in turn, from Roman political skill at reaching workable accommodations with a multitude of Italian states and peoples, an accomplishment that eventually gave Rome access to the military resources of all of Italy.[134] In the long process by which the Romans had succeeded in attaching Italy to themselves, they had learned not merely military skill but skill in effective alliance-management.[135] This experience they naturally put to work as they became more deeply involved in the Hellenic world, creating for the first time in 200–196 a whole series of informal, ad hoc, but politically effective relationships with the most important states in European Greece.

Roman success against Macedon is partly to be explained not only by Roman military, social, and political strengths but also in part by the relative weakness of Rome's ferocious competitor. The Macedonian resource-base turned out to be inadequate to fulfill the world-wide ambitions of Philip V; the Romans could absorb defeats at Philip's hands (as occurred both in 199 and in 198), but Macedon could not recover from the disaster at Cynoscephalae in 197. This is a good example, however, of what the political scientists call "the uncertainty principle" and the "mutual opacity of states," for no one in 200 BC knew that the relative power of Macedon would turn out to be so limited in comparison with that of Rome. The events of the First Macedonian War, which was all the information that the *Patres* had to go on in 200 BC, would have suggested otherwise. As so often, the realities of power as they stood ca. 200 BC only became evident from the grim test of war.[136]

[134]   Capability of mobilization of resources as a central factor in state success: Aron 1973: 51; Rosen 2003: 215–16.
[135]   Alliance-management: see Strauss 1997: 134.
[136]   On the uncertainty principle and the mutual opacity of states, with relevant international-relations scholarship, see above, Chapters 1 and 6.

Nevertheless, the persistent theme in this study is that the interest of the senatorial elite in the regions east of the Adriatic remained limited and sporadic. This lack of interest in the Greek world, and the lack of concrete Roman interests there, helps explain the numerous times the Senate ordered Roman withdrawals from the East once a specific perceived danger had been removed. I have called this the Roman habit of "smash and leave." It was an attitude evident in the decision of the Senate to order the withdrawal of all Roman military forces from Greece and the Adriatic once a satisfactory settlement of Greek affairs in the wake of Philip V's defeat had been achieved.

The Roman habit of "smash and leave" expressed itself as well in the declaration at the Isthmian Games in 196 that henceforth the Greek states were to be "free." In one sense, the Romans came to the idea of "the Freedom of the Greeks" late, and primarily because of the influence of his Greek allies upon the Roman commander T. Quinctius Flamininus. But it has been proposed here that the Roman government really intended that European Greece and the Aegean would henceforth be populated by free friends of Rome – real friends, not submissive *clientes*; they would be friends whose relationship to Rome would, to be sure, create a congenial geopolitical situation in Greece for the Republic – but friends who would not impose responsibilities on the western power. These friendships had originated in a convergence of interest between Rome and the Greek states that had focused on placing constraints on Macedon and the Seleucids. The Roman withdrawal of all military forces from Greece in 194, combined with the continuing advance westward of Antiochus the Great, who was undeterred by Roman warnings, would put those friendships and that convergence of interest between Rome and the Greek states to an immediate test. Macedon had been dealt with, but Seleucid power, under Antiochus' direction, was continuing to expand dramatically. The period of power-transition and hegemonic war did not end with the Isthmian Declaration.

8

Hegemonic War, II: Rome and Antiochus the Great, 200–188 BC

INTRODUCTION

If the *Patres* in Rome believed that the victory over Philip V of Macedon won at Cynoscephalae in summer 197 and the Isthmian Declaration of "the Freedom of the Greeks" in summer 196 had ended the crisis in the eastern Mediterranean – and it is clear that many of them did believe this (see below) – they were wrong. Macedonian military power had been greatly weakened and Philip curbed, but a much greater power still remained in the field, led by an aggressively expansionist monarch with world-conquering ambitions and a world-conquering reputation: the Seleucid Empire under Antiochus III the Great. Senatorial belief that the crisis in the East had been resolved to Roman satisfaction led to the total withdrawal of all Roman troops from European Greece and the Adriatic back to Italy in the early summer of 194. But the result was that in autumn 192 Antiochus III landed at Demetrias on the central Aegean coast of Greece, with the intention of establishing himself in a hegemonic position over the European Greek states.

The first stage of the world-historical struggle for power in the Mediterranean state-system had begun with the faltering of the Ptolemaic Empire, ca. 207 BC. The resulting power-transition crisis within the state-system of the eastern Mediterranean led to the alliance of Philip and Antiochus in winter 203/202 to destroy the Ptolemaic regime, and to the outbreak in 202 of what political scientists call a hegemonic war – a war to establish the new configuration of power in the Greek state-system as it emerged from the power-transition crisis, to establish the new structure of that system, to establish the new leaders and dominant powers of that system. The second stage of the struggle set off by the faltering of the Ptolemaic state began with the Roman intervention against Macedon in 200. The catalyst for the Roman intervention was the decision of no fewer than four of the weaker Greek states to turn to a great power that hitherto had been peripheral to the Greek state-system in order to gain help in rescuing that system from the aggressive expansionism of Philip and/or Antiochus. In the process of appealing to Rome, the envoys of these weaker Greek states widened the traditional diplomatic field in which the struggles of the Greeks among themselves had always occurred; and hence they were crucial actors in bringing about the transformation of what previously had been two separately existing Mediterranean regional subsystems, the eastern and western subsystems, into one large, Mediterranean-wide and interlocking system of states. This, of course, was Polybius' *symplokē* – the growth of Mediterranean-wide interconnectedness of geopolitical events. The energetic Roman diplomatic intervention and then large-scale military intervention across the Adriatic led to the curtailing of Macedonian power in Greece and the Aegean, for the Romans at the head now of a great coalition of Greek states defeated Philip V, and created with the Isthmian Declaration a political arrangement in European Greece and parts of the Aegean that was congenial both to the Senate and its Greek allies.

The third and final stage of this epic struggle, the third and final stage of the massive violence of the power-transition crisis, now becomes our focus. The war that began in 192 with the Seleucid invasion of European Greece was the crucial system-wide war that established Rome as the sole remaining superpower in the Hellenistic Mediterranean. The war was caused by the failure of Rome and Antiochus III to maintain the situation of bipolarity that had emerged by 196, as the establishment of a Roman sphere of influence in European Greece was matched by the advance of Antiochus westward to the Aegean and into Europe itself. Diplomacy was unable to resolve the sharp conflict of interest between the two great powers – and this was not surprising, given the primitive and often public nature of such diplomacy among ancient states. The consequent hegemonic war did indeed restructure the Mediterranean state-system, and reduced the number of great powers from two to one, establishing the Republic of Rome as the sole remaining superpower. As in the war fought against Philip in the early 190s, however, we need to remember that Rome came to its position of preponderance not by its own efforts alone, large though they were, but rather as the leader of a powerful coalition of Greek states. That fact had important consequences for the character of the initial arrangements that emerged in the Peace of Apamea in 188, after the final defeat of Antiochus the Great by the coalition forces led by Rome, as well as important consequences for the character of the initial stage of Roman unipolarity in the two decades that followed.

THE ROMAN DIPLOMATIC CONFRONTATION WITH ANTIOCHUS III[1]

The same Roman embassy that the Senate sent out from Rome in the spring of 200 to attempt to force Philip V to stop his attacks on the Greeks (and which failed) also had a mandate from the Senate to interview Antiochus. As far as we know, this was the first official contact between the king and Rome. This embassy to Antiochus, as we saw in Chapter 6 above, is evidence in itself that in 200 the Senate was concerned simultaneously about both Philip V and Antiochus, and thus it constitutes evidence that Rome intervened in the East because the envoys from the Greek states had warned of the activities of both of the kings, and in particular (I have suggested) about the existence of the Pact Between the Kings (cf. Polyb. 15.20.5–6). In Polybius' version of the Roman mission to Antiochus, the envoys' task was to try to get Antiochus and the Ptolemies to compose their differences and make peace (16.27.5). Other sources say that the Roman message was more blunt – the message was that Antiochus should stop attacking Egypt. Many scholars are dubious that the Roman envoys took that tone, but our sources are unanimous that, however they phrased things, the envoys attempted to protect at least Egypt proper from Antiochus' aggression.[2]

What was the nature of this Roman protection of Egypt? Polybius covered the activities of this Roman embassy to the East in great detail (see Polyb. 16.27 and 16.34), but his narrative on this topic does not survive, and our remaining sources are sparse and late; so reconstruction must be tentative. After the confrontation with Philip at Abydus in summer 200, where Philip rejected the Roman ultimatum to stop attacking the Greeks (see above, Chapter 7), the envoys journeyed on to Antioch, where they met Antiochus that autumn. The Great King had in all probability just won his crushing victory over the Ptolemaic army at Panium, and was now in control of almost all of Phoenicia,

---

[1]   Parts of this chapter recapitulate but also significantly expand on the second half of Eckstein 2006: Ch. 7.
[2]   Justin 30.3.3 and 31.1.2; App. *Mac.* 4. The "orders" to Antiochus as later Roman propaganda: Badian 1964b: 114; Gruen 1984: 616; Gera 1998: 68–9; Grainger 2002: 28–9.

Coele Syria, and Judaea – or he soon would be. Thus Antiochus when he met the Roman envoys stood at a new apogee of Seleucid power, the consequence of his own military talents and energy, and it is reasonable to assume that the conqueror of Asia was ready for more.[3] But Justin reports that in the colloquy with the king, the Romans distinguished between the regions of "Syria" occupied by Antiochus, about which they had no opinion, and Egypt itself: Antiochus should not invade Egypt (31.1.2). The phraseology in Appian is similar: Antiochus should keep his hands off of "Egypt" (*Mac.* 4).[4]

The current scholarly *communis opinio* is that this Roman embassy to Antiochus achieved little or nothing.[5] Yet in the strategic situation in the Levant in the autumn of 200 BC, to make a distinction between Egypt proper as opposed to the outlying Ptolemaic provinces – which were now falling or had already fallen to Antiochus – makes sense. And the fact is that Antiochus did not invade Egypt proper, although after his crushing victory at Panium the way seemingly lay open to him. Moreover, we know that after 200 Antiochus' ambitions for the conquest of Egypt proper did not go away. On the contrary: in 196 he made a large-scale naval descent on Egypt with the purpose of taking over the entire country; he only turned back when he learned that Ptolemy V, despite rumors circulating to the contrary, was still alive.[6] Similarly, Antiochus' son, Antiochus IV, actually did invade Egypt proper in 169 and 168, actually did occupy all of Lower Egypt, and indeed besieged Alexandria itself – an unprecedented Seleucid military achievement.[7]

In other words, there needs to be a reason why in the autumn of 200, when the army of the Ptolemies had been crushed at Panium, and the Seleucid advance south through Coele Syria and Judaea had gone quickly, and the road to Egypt lay open to him, Antiochus thought better of it. Grainger has recently argued that Antiochus believed an invasion of Egypt proper would be too difficult at this point, and that the administration of Egypt (half of which was still in rebellion against

---

[3] On the course of the Fifth Syrian War, and Antiochus' gains, see Grainger 1991: 99–105. The Ptolemies never regained control of Judaea, Phoenicia, and Coele Syria. That the great Seleucid victory at Panium had occurred before the arrival of the Roman embassy at Antioch is demonstrated by the arrangements now made (see below).
[4] See Ager 1996: 166–7 (no. 60).
[5] See Badian 1964b: 113–14; Will 1982: 120; Gruen 1984: 617; Ager 1996: 167; Ma 1999/2002: 81–2; Grainger 2002: 29–30.
[6] Note especially Livy 33.41.3: *suam fore Aegyptum . . . censebat* [*Antiochus*]. Livy 33.41.3–9 derived from Polybian material: see Briscoe 1973: 2 and 322; cf. also App. *Syr.* 2. The incident is discussed in detail in Chapter 4, p. 143, above.
[7] The Ptolemies were only saved once again by Roman diplomatic intervention; see Lampela 1998: Ch. 4, for sources and detailed discussion.

the Ptolemies) was beyond him.[8] But he clearly did not believe this to be the case in 196 – when, indeed, the indigenous rebellion was still unchecked (see above). And the Great King had surmounted many difficulties in his career, was habituated to ruling a restless empire with a strong hand, and his continued ambitions for Egypt are obvious. A reasonable answer to the mystery here is that in 200 BC Antiochus agreed with the Romans to desist – at least for the moment – from advancing beyond southern Judaea. It was no small thing. Indeed, the sudden relaxation of Seleucid military pressure after 200 may have had an important impact on the ability of the government at Alexandria to impose its authority as far south as Upper Egypt – for in 198/197 we find documents from the Thebaid being issued, for the first time in a decade, in the name of the Ptolemaic regime. But the indigenous rebellion soon broke out again with great force – both in Upper Egypt and even in the Nile Delta; and the rebellion would last for another decade or more. But this is simply another indication of just how weak the government at Alexandria actually was in this period – and hence why Antiochus would have been tempted to go to Egypt.[9]

Antiochus certainly did not view his (momentary) decision to forego the conquest of Egypt as placing a limit on his huge ambitions to expand his power elsewhere. He concentrated first on the conquest of the city of Sidon in Phoenicia, which still held out for the Ptolemies (199?). And then he personally led his army and fleet to large gains in Asia Minor, starting with the campaign of 198, including the conquest of Ptolemaic towns all along the southern coast.[10] The Seleucid advance westwards soon began to shift the balance of power in Asia Minor in Antiochus' favor, and the balance shifted even more in his favor with the sudden death of Attalus I of Pergamum in spring 197. This brought Attalus' son Eumenes II, a new and untried monarch, to the Pergamene throne.[11] Meanwhile, the Rhodians – a potentially significant impediment to Seleucid expansion – struck a *modus vivendi* with Antiochus after the news of Cynoscephalae removed the threat of cooperation between Antiochus and Philip V of Macedon.[12] By the spring of 196 Antiochus and his army were encamped in Ionia, on the Aegean, and he was

---

[8] Grainger 2002: 29–30.
[9] The temporary restoration of Ptolemaic authority in the Thebaid in 198 and 197: see Veïsse 2004: 19.
[10] Detailed discussion of this campaign: see Grainger 2002: 31–41.
[11] The possible unsteadiness of Eumenes II: see McShane 1964: 135 and n. 156.
[12] The Rhodian shift in policy towards Antiochus after Cynoscephalae: see above, Chapter 5. Rhodes gained new holdings on the mainland in 197 with Antiochus' help, and in 196 he suggested Rhodes as arbitrator in his conflict with the cities of Lampsacus and Smyrna (Polyb. 19.52.1–4).

ROME AND ANTIOCHUS THE GREAT, 200–188 BC

proclaiming his intention to bring all the cities of Asia Minor under his control (Livy 33.38.1).[13] The Great King soon also crossed the Hellespont into Europe, seizing the towns of the Thracian Chersonese (the Gallipoli Peninsula), including Lysimacheia – claiming them all as ancestral Seleucid holdings. These were enormous advances.

At some point in this period the Roman Senate had declared Antiochus "a friend and ally of the Roman people." He had received this honor by 198 (Livy 32.8.13 and 33.20.8), and since Antiochus was barely known at Rome in 200, I would suggest (with due caution) that the honor came about after his decision in late 200 not to invade Egypt. But as Antiochus came conquering westwards through Asia Minor in 197, Roman concern heightened. The new attitude was revealed in talks with Antiochus at Lysimacheia in summer 196. Members of the senatorial Commission of Ten, sent out to Greece to oversee the peace settlement with Philip, now publicly demanded that Antiochus keep his hands off "independent cities" in Thrace, that he withdraw from the Ptolemaic towns he had conquered in southern and western Asia Minor, that these be turned back over to Ptolemy V, and that Antiochus finally make peace with Ptolemy.[14] Gruen argues that at Lysimacheia the Roman envoys were merely trying to reconcile two warring *amici populi Romani* – that is, Antiochus and the Ptolemaic regime.[15] This is too sunny an interpretation. The Romans at the Lysimacheia conference were attempting to set clear boundaries to Antiochus' behavior – and the attempt failed. Antiochus debated the Romans on every point. Nor did he even feel constrained to keep his hands off Egypt proper, as he had done in 200: when he heard at Lysimacheia a (false) rumor that Ptolemy V had died, he dropped the conference and made a descent upon Alexandria with his large war-fleet instead, confident that he would take over the entire country.[16]

What was definitely emerging by 196, then, was a geopolitical situation in the Mediterranean that political scientists call bipolarity – and it was an unstable bipolarity at that. There were only two remaining

[13]   This was a long-standing Seleucid claim, on which Antiochus had acted as early as 210/209: see Ma 1999/2002: 2–28.
[14]   Polyb. 18.50.1–9; Livy 33.39.2–7; App. *Syr.* 3; Diod. 28.12. The Roman demands in 196 about the Ptolemaic holdings were apparently a senatorial response to a new embassy to Rome from Egypt: App. *Syr.* 2. On the senatorial Commission of Ten and what became of the Isthmian Declaration of "the Freedom of the Greeks," see above, Chapter 7. The Commission included P. Sulpicius Galba (cos. II 200) and P. Villius Tappulus (cos. 199), both of whom had commanded against Philip in Greece.
[15]   Gruen 1984: 622.
[16]   See above, pp. 309–10, and Chapter 4, p. 143.

great powers – the Roman Republic and Antiochus the Great's huge realm. Each possessed exceptional resources; relations between them were unsettled, and indeed were relatively new, because distance had previously prevented significant contact; and because of the on-going process of hegemonic rivalry between the two great states, those relations were never in the 190s put on a stable basis.[17]

The Roman position, reiterated in a series of diplomatic interactions with Antiochus or his envoys starting at Lysimacheia in 196, was that Antiochus should withdraw from Europe; that Rome had the right to "free" all the previous conquests of Philip V, including those in Asia Minor – some of which had already fallen into Antiochus' hands (a demand by which Rome extended "the Freedom of the Greeks" from Europe into Asia); and that Rome had the additional right to protect the three cities of Lampsacus, Smyrna, and Alexandria Troas, which had specifically appealed to the Senate for protection. Antiochus' position, also first adumbrated at Lysimacheia in 196, was that his new possessions in Europe were his both by right of inheritance and by right of (re)conquest; that the same held true for all the polities now under his control in Asia Minor; and that Rome had no right – either by right of inheritance or by right of conquest – to interfere in Asia.[18] The Senate's position seems to have been motivated in part by fear of Antiochus' further ambitions: since he had crossed the Hellespont into Europe with a substantial army, and was eventually operating increasingly deeply into Thrace for three years in a row (196, 195, and 194), who could tell where he would stop?[19] Conversely, one may assume that Antiochus for this part distrusted the ambitions of the Romans. In any case, during the next four years of diplomatic interchange, involving several major embassies sent by one side or the other in attempts to settle the issues between them peaceably, neither side ever budged from the fundamental positions outlined above. Neither Rome nor Antiochus ever made any important concession concerning the issues of contention along what almost immediately became what political scientists call a "contested periphery" – that is, a border zone where two different hegemonies intersect and where their interests conflict. Such contested peripheries, students of international relations say, have historically been very fertile ground for major conflict, and so it was here.[20]

---

[17]   On the characteristics of bipolarity as an interstate structure, see Evans and Newnham 1998: 52; Geller and Singer 1998: 113–17.
[18]   See Polyb. 18.51.3–6; Livy 33.40.4–6.
[19]   See Polyb. 18.50.9 in general; Seleucid operations in Thrace: see Grainger 1996.
[20]   On the political-science concept of "the contested periphery," see Allen 1997: 49–51 and 320–1; cf. Cline 2000: 7.

The differences between the two sides were significant but not enormous. What was missing – on both sides – was a willingness to compromise. That is the central diplomatic phenomenon of these years.[21] To be sure, both Antiochus and the Roman Senate each had in mind the creation of a balance of power which would make it possible to live peaceably at least into the foreseeable future with the other great state. But if each side sought an acceptable balance of power with the other that would allow peaceful coexistence, each side simultaneously engaged also in a firm effort to get "the better of the balance" – that is, to create a situation where its side possessed a more advantageous strategic position than the other side did.[22] For the Romans, getting the better of the balance (we may call this, in political-science terminology, the Romans' established expectation level) meant that Antiochus would be excluded totally from Europe, so that Greece essentially became part of the Romans' perimeter of defense, while Rome would simultaneously retain at least some right to interfere in western Asia Minor. To Antiochus, getting the better of the balance (that is, *his* established expectation level) meant that the Romans would be totally excluded from Asia Minor, while he would retain a substantial province and substantial army in Europe (in Thrace), from where he could exercise influence over what he conceived of as a neutral zone – Greece – between himself and the Romans.[23] And to paraphrase Jeffrey Taliaferro on great power interactions along a contested periphery: an aversion to perceived loss of relative power and international status, an aversion to accepting less than the established expectation level, caused both Antiochus and the Roman leadership in 196–192 to pursue a series of highly risk-acceptant diplomatic strategies.[24]

The attitude where each side is willing to find a peaceful resolution to a conflict of interest but only on condition of a resulting balance of power where the strategic advantage lies with itself and its own diplomatic level of expectations are met: this may strike us as aggressive. But it does not mark out either Rome or Antiochus in 196–192 as *exceptionally* aggressive. This situation is not unusual in great power politics under conditions of structural anarchy. Rather, political scientists stress

---

[21]   Rightly emphasized by Ma 1999/2002: 97, and by Grainger 2002: 135 and 139. Yet Derow 2003: 61–5, follows Harris 1979: 219–23, in depicting Rome in its interactions with Antiochus as the sole aggressor in the dyadic relationship. So too Mandell 1989: 91.

[22]   "Getting the better of the balance": the phrase – and the concept – is that of Lowes Dickenson 1926: 4–7 (pioneering).

[23]   On the often negative impact of competing and stubbornly held levels of expectation in diplomatic interactions between states, i.e., benchmarks of expectation against which diplomatic outcomes are evaluated, see Taliaferro 2004: 14–18.

[24]   For comparisons, see Taliaferro 2004: 94–5 and 144.

that seeking "the better of the balance" is a natural behavior of states under conditions of anarchy and in fact is a common occurrence in inter-state diplomatic interactions.[25] The Romans certainly acted here as if their demands were the only ones that counted. But Antiochus acted in the same fashion – as if his demands were the only ones that counted. And the hard fact is that Antiochus had always operated in this fashion, as one can see as early as the failure of Seleucid talks with Ptolemy IV in the dispute over the Coele Syria region in winter 218/217, which led to war (Polyb. 5.67.11–68.2). Antiochus' spectacular military successes and huge territorial gains since then – his conquests of Iran and Afghanistan, of Lebanon and Judaea, and now of much of Asia Minor, achievements that had led him to adopt the title *Megas*, "The Great" – will hardly have softened his attitude in interstate negotiations.[26]

The resulting deadlock, however, was not only a typical deadlocked diplomatic interaction between two powerful ancient states under the pressures generated by the anarchy – though it certainly was that. Nor was it simply a sincere clash of culture-driven perceptions (especially perceptions of present power combined with past vulnerability) – though it was that as well.[27] In addition, this conflict over the bound-aries of the contested periphery quickly developed into what political scientists call a "contest of resolve" – and it was a contest of resolve conducted almost totally in public.[28] One side's demands only intensified the stubbornness of the other side to "show resolve" by not yielding, by not making major concessions: it was a matter of honor, of saving face before an audience consisting of the governing elites of the secondary states, and of not scaling down one's definition of a favorable diplomatic outcome. Saving face was important because the contest was in public, and signs of weakness or irresolution could lead to the lessening of real-world support from lesser states (in the case of Rome) or one's subjects (in the case of Antiochus). Hence neither side

---

[25] See Lowes Dickenson 1926: Ch. 1, *passim*; Taliaferro 2004, Chs. 1–2.

[26] From ca. 200 BC, Antiochus was not only styling himself "Antiochus the Great" (Μέγας), but had also taken the traditional title of the Achaemenid emperors: "Great King" (βασιλεὺς μέγας): discussion and evidence in Ma 1999/2002: 272–7. Not to be followed is Mandell 1989: 92, that the Romans, by making public demands on Antiochus, were treating him as a "subject" rather than as an independent ruler, and that this shows exceptional Roman aggressiveness; after all, Antiochus was making public demands on the Romans as well: see rightly Rich 2004: 237. Such was the primitive nature of much of ancient diplomacy: see Eckstein 2006: Chs. 3, 4, and 5.

[27] So Ma 1999/2002: 97–102, explicitly discounting political-science paradigms in favor of cultural history and "clashing discourses."

[28] On the prevalence of "contests of resolve" between states in antiquity, see Eckstein 2006: Ch. 3.

was ever willing to scale down its aspirations, but each stubbornly held to its benchmark expectation level.[29] This is probably why, as diplomatic interactions increased, as the "contest of resolve" between Rome and Antiochus intensified, the harsher (not more moderate) the tone of the diplomatic exchanges actually became.[30]

This public contest of resolve had many causes (including the bellicose internal culture of the two states involved), but the prime cause was the uncertain hierarchy of power and status in a system of states that had undergone increasingly severe disruption since 207. That system of states was now undergoing a transformation both in form and simultaneously in scale (a transformation into a new, Mediterranean-wide scale). Interviews between Roman representatives and Antiochus or his envoys down to 193 failed to clarify the boundaries of power between the two states, or to resolve the issue of hierarchy, and so the crisis intensified.[31]

The problem was that Antiochus' territorial claims were rapidly expanding, but the Romans wanted limits set upon his conduct with regard to their own expanded sphere of influence. Antiochus was unwilling to accede to such limits on his conduct, either in European Greece or in Asia Minor, in part because Roman demands hampered his own expanding ambitions, which were based on military and political talents that had led him to huge success, in part because those demands in themselves raised the crucial issue of status. Similarly, despite Antiochus' diplomatic pressure, the Romans were unwilling to forgo their own claims either about European Greece or in western Asia Minor. The resulting situation of tense and unstable bipolarity might have lasted for a significant length of time; Badian draws an explicit parallel with the Cold War between the United States and the Soviet Union.[32] But given the extraordinarily harsh character of interstate relations in the ancient Mediterranean, the odds were against that outcome, and there soon followed another system-wide "hegemonic war" – the final war to

---

[29]   Such deadlocks in public had happened often enough in Mediterranean history. The deadlocked negotiations between Athens and Sparta in winter 432/431 are a famous example (on which, see Eckstein 2006: Ch. 3); so is the diplomatic deadlock at the beginning of the Second Punic War (two years of warnings and negotiations, 220–218: on the "honor" aspect of this contest of resolve, see Hoyos 1998: Ch. 15). The example of the deadlocked negotiations between Antiochus III and Ptolemy IV in winter 218/217 (above) is another case.
[30]   See Livy 35.16.7–17.2, the ugly scene at the negotiations at Ephesus in summer 193 (from Polybian material: Briscoe 1981: 2 and 162).
[31]   For Derow 2003: 64, this complex situation resolves itself into the statement that even before the end of the war against Macedon, "the Romans had had Antiochus in their sights." But for general causation of conflict between major states in terms of uncertain boundaries of status and power, see Gilpin 1988: 592.
[32]   Badian 1964b.

determine the new leadership and the new structure of the disrupted Hellenistic state-system.[33]

Antiochus' conquests in Thrace continued in 195, and the senatorial Commission of Ten returned from Greece to Rome with frightening reports of the scale of his army and navy.[34] Complicating the situation was that although the interests of Rome east of the Adriatic were now more extensive than they had been before 200, including desire for stability in European Greece as well as protection of Pergamum and Rhodes (and Egypt proper), after spring 194 those interests were not backed by any military presence. Mommsen recognized long ago that it was a major strategic error for the Senate to withdraw from Greece in 194 when relations with Antiochus were still unsettled and the king was advancing westward. It sent the wrong message. The temptation presented by a European Greece freed from both Macedonian and Roman military domination, and hence without either direct Macedonian or Roman protection, proved a temptation too much for Antiochus the Great to resist:

> The war with Antiochus would not have occurred at all except for the Roman political mistake of "the Freeing of Greece"; and the war would have remained without major danger to Rome except for the military mistake of the decision to withdraw Roman troops from the great Macedonian fortresses in European Greece – which formed a frontier against him.[35]

There were certainly men within the Senate, led especially by Scipio Africanus, who argued that a strong Roman military presence in European Greece was the best way to deter the threat of Antiochus' advance. The belief that tough diplomacy backed by force was the best way to deter a rival or aggressor was typical of most states in antiquity – and, of course, the same is true in the modern world.[36] Thus what is

---

[33] Emphasizing the complex and difficult nature of the diplomatic standoff: Grainger 2002: Chs. 4–9. In the case of the modern Cold War the presence of nuclear weapons probably militated against the interstate pressures of unstable bipolarity leading to hegemonic war – but we must also give much credit to good diplomacy on both sides. Such diplomacy was missing here.
[34] Seleucid conquests in Thrace: see sources and commentary in Gruen 1984: 624–5 and Grainger 1996. The alarming report on the scale of Seleucid armed forces brought to Rome by the senatorial commission: Livy 33.44.6–9, cf. 33.43.6 and 34.33.12.
[35] Mommsen 1903: 721; cf. also the comments of Raditsa 1972: 564–5, and Grainger 2002: 127.
[36] An obvious example from antiquity is the refusal of the Athenians to give up the siege of Potidaea or to revoke the Megara Decree during the "peace negotiations" with Sparta in winter 432/431: see, e.g., Pericles' tough statement at Thuc. 1.140–1, with Wick 1977. For the modern world, see the statements from various leaders on the value of toughness leading to deterrence in Taliaferro 2004: 109 (Japan in 1940) and 142 (Truman on Korea).

remarkable in spring 194 is not Scipio's military recommendations regarding the threat from Antiochus, but that the Senate did not accept even the *auctoritas* of the conqueror of Hannibal on this issue; Scipio could not convince the *Patres* to maintain Roman troops in Greece. The position taken by T. Quinctius Flamininus and his supporters prevailed instead. They argued that the best buffer against Antiochus' advance westward would be the goodwill of the European Greek states towards Rome, and that Rome could best gain this goodwill by fulfilling completely the promise of "the Freedom of the Greeks" – by withdrawing all Roman military forces back to Italy.

Flamininus had previously warned the Senate about the approach of Antiochus towards the west; if now he urged the Roman military withdrawal from Greece, it was probably both because he believed that Greek goodwill would best maintain the Roman sphere of interest in the face of Antiochus, and because of his desire for the personal *gloria* of bringing the army home from Greece after the victory over Philip. And no doubt Flamininus' prestige as the conqueror of Philip V helped push his proposals forward.[37] But more important than Flamininus' motives, whatever they were, is that his position won the day in the Senate. This indicates that though the number of contacts and the scale of Roman interests in Greece had expanded as a result of the Second Macedonian War, the goals of the Senate in Greece even in the mid-190s remained highly restricted.

The *Patres* evidently thought that an informal sphere of influence in European Greece was sufficient for their purposes – but this was because their purposes were limited, and hence those purposes did not require any Roman presence or direct control. The Roman stance did aim at the exclusion of Antiochus (and any other power) from Greece, and there is no doubt that despite the withdrawal of their military forces, the Senate intended that Roman wishes in Greece would be obeyed – whenever, that is, the Senate had such wishes. This sense of Roman superiority is clearly present in the patronizing tone of Flamininus' farewell address to the Greek governing elites at Corinth, even as the Roman troops were marching away from their garrison on the Acrocorinth citadel (Livy 34.49.1–50.1).[38]

Yet it is striking that the Roman decision to withdraw from European Greece was probably made as Antiochus himself was advancing westward through Thrace, where he had been active in 195 and was probably active

---

[37] See Eckstein 1987a: 308–15; cf. also Walsh 1996.
[38] Discussion of Flamininus' speech in Livy: Eckstein 1987a: 311; cf. above, Chapter 7.

again in summer 194.[39] Moreover, the decision was taken by leaders who had fought the Hannibalic War, men who in the 190s were the senior makers of opinion in the Senate – and they made this decision even though it was known at Rome that the redoubtable Hannibal himself had now joined Antiochus' court.[40] Roman tradition later asserted that Hannibal's influence was decisive in pushing Antiochus towards war with Rome; no doubt this tradition is exaggerated, but it probably reflects contemporary Roman suspicions.[41] The decision to withdraw was also taken at a time when there was a substantial Seleucid army on the European side of the Hellespont, employed by Antiochus to protect and extend his recent Thracian conquests. We know that this large Seleucid military presence in Thrace was of serious concern to prominent figures in the Senate such as P. Villius Tappulus, consul 199 (see Livy 34.33.12) – a man with extensive experience in Greece. And yet the decision still went forward under these conditions.[42] Some scholars, intent on painting the Romans not merely as normally aggressive predators within the Mediterranean interstate system but as exceptionally aggressive predators, assert that the Romans withdrew from Greece precisely in order to provoke Antiochus into an invasion, so that Rome could then go to war with him as the innocent party. Considering the massive damage that Antiochus' arrival even with a moderate force did to the Roman political position in Greece (see below), this is far too baroque a reconstruction.[43] There is no way one can construe the Roman action of withdrawing from Greece as an aggressive act.

The senatorial decision of 194 was in fact a very short-sighted one. It destabilized Greece and the Aegean region because it presented Antiochus the Great with what appeared to be a power vacuum precisely in the region where his own empire was expanding.[44] Moreover, this power vacuum in Greece and the Aegean occurred in a situation which at the system level was, as we have said, a bipolarity: and the great danger in any bipolar structure is that it creates "zero-sum" conditions where

[39] Arguments in Grainger 1996: 340.
[40] Hannibal, fleeing Carthage under Roman pressure, came to the Great King in late summer 195, at Ephesus in Ionia, after Antiochus' second campaign in Thrace: for the chronology, see Grainger 2002: 121–2.
[41] Roman suspicions: Livy 34.33.12. The senatorial decision made even in the face of Hannibal at Antiochus' court: noted by Grainger 2002: 123.
[42] Grainger 2002: 125, suggests that the Seleucid army in Thrace at this time numbered 20,000 men. Villius had commanded against Philip – not very effectively – during the Second Macedonian War, and served on the senatorial Commission of Ten that went out to Greece in 196; he had personally met Antiochus at Lysimacheia. See Broughton 1951: 326, 331, and 338.
[43] See Mandell 1989: 91; cf. Derow 2003: 63–4, and in general Harris 1979: 219–23.
[44] Grainger 2002: 127; cf. Mommsen 1903: 721.

one side's gain in territory, power, or influence tends automatically to be the other side's loss. The situation in 194–192 was additionally complicated by one great power (Rome) appearing to send what the other took to be mixed messages: diplomatic assertiveness and warnings (see below) were combined with the hard fact of complete military withdrawal. Political scientists suggest that such unstable bipolar structural situations, in and of themselves, make system-wide "hegemonic" war likely.[45] Mixed messages also make war more likely.[46] The militaristic internal cultures of both great powers and the long-term "socialization" of their governing elites towards the employment of violence as a natural means of settling objective conflicts of interest with foreign states were additional factors greatly conducive to a war. So was the fact that, as usual in antiquity, much of the diplomacy between them took place in public, increasing the intensity of "the contest of resolve" and the threat to honor for both sides in any diplomatic interaction – or concession.[47] Finally, while the Roman Senate occasionally meddled diplomatically in "the Seleucid space" created by Antiochus on the western coast of Asia Minor (namely, in asserting Roman protection of Lampsacus, Smyrna, and Alexandria Troas), it is the case that Antiochus engaged in actual large-scale military operations in what he knew the Senate claimed as "the Roman space" in European Greece (namely, his expanding conquests in Thrace). Similarly and crucially, it was military action by Antiochus, not Rome – namely, Antiochus' invasion of central Greece in late 192 – that disrupted the delicate political equilibrium. To put it bluntly: though the Roman Republic and the Seleucid Empire were both expansionist geopolitical entities, in the conflict between Rome and the Seleucid king, in the end Antiochus was the aggressor.[48]

Yet it is often the case that a specific catalytic event or influential catalytic lesser actor is required in order to turn the probability under given conditions of system-wide war into an actual system-wide war. And in the Greek Mediterranean in the 190s those catalysts were not lacking.[49] The specific catalysts for the clash of the great powers were provided, as we have seen before in this study, by fearful or discontented second-tier

---

[45] Cf. Gilpin 1998: 593 and 596.

[46] See now Taliaferro 2004: 133, 151, and 153 (on the origins of the Korean War).

[47] On the dangers of public diplomacy among "honor societies" in antiquity, see Eckstein 2006: Ch. 3; on "contests of resolve," see above, this chapter.

[48] Again, those scholars who see Rome as an exceptionally predatory state within a relatively benign Hellenistic state-system find various unconvincing ways to explain away Antiochus' invasion of Greece: see Harris 1979: 219–23; Mandell 1989: 92–3; Derow 2003: 63–4.

[49] Catalytic events or actors as necessary for initiation of system-wide war: Gilpin 1988: 596–7; Lebow 2001: 614.

powers. On one side stood Eumenes II, the new king of Pergamum. He ruled a domain that was suddenly losing influence and power, hard-pressed by new Seleucid conquests both to its north and to its south. In addition, Prusias I of Bithynia, an old enemy of Pergamum, himself was taking advantage of Eumenes' initial weakness in order to seize territory.[50] Eumenes allegedly told the Roman envoys who came out to negotiate with Antiochus in 193 that he would soon be reduced to a subordinated creature of Antiochus (Livy 35.13.9). As Eumenes later told the Senate, he faced a trial by fire such as his father Attalus I had never had to face (Polyb. 21.20.6–7). That was the opinion of Philip V as well: the Romans saved Eumenes and his kingdom from destruction (Livy 39.28.6).[51] To save his kingdom from Antiochus, Eumenes there-fore initiated complaints to Rome about the Great King's aggressions (winter 194/193). And the other side was the Aetolian League. The Aetolians had always made it clear that they were profoundly dis-satisfied with the relatively small territorial gains allowed them under Flamininus' peace settlement of 196. Just as Eumenes worked on the Romans, stressing the threat Antiochus posed to the order in the East that Rome had sought to create, so the Aetolians began to work on Antiochus, fostering his ambitions to come to Greece and establish a new structure of interstate relations from which the Aetolians themselves would be great beneficiaries (see below). Such conduct by secondary states was a natural process of the interstate anarchy, and was one of the reasons that war between the great states was so frequent. The phe-nomenon of the second-tier states as catalysts for war had happened often enough in the Mediterranean past – and had been pointed out as early as Thucydides. So it turned out here.[52]

Envoys from the desperate Pergamene government appeared at Rome in winter 194/193 to complain about Antiochus, and envoys from Antiochus also came to Rome that winter. They were confronted in pri-vate negotiations and then publicly with a demand from T. Quinctius Flamininus and the members of the old senatorial commission of 196, including P. Sulpicius Galba, who had led the political fight for war with Philip in 200, and P. Villius: Antiochus must withdraw from Thrace. The demand was backed by threats to intervene in Asia Minor if

---

[50]   See Polyb. 21.36.10 and Livy 38.39.15 with Habicht 1957: 90–6 and Schmitt 1964: 276–7.
[51]   Eumenes' role in exacerbating conflict between Rome and Antiochus: McShane 1964: 131–43; Grainger 2002: 155 and 164. Seriousness of Antiochus' threat to Pergamum: McShane 1964: 134–5; Grainger 2002: 155. Livy 35.13.9 and 39.28.5 are based on Polybian material: see Briscoe 1981: 165; and Walbank 1940: 232–3.
[52]   On the destructive role of the secondary states in bringing on the crisis of late 192, see Grainger 2002: 163–4. In general: Eckstein 2006: esp. Chs. 3, 4, and 5.

Antiochus did not respond, though Flamininus and his colleagues also offered to leave the king a relatively free hand in the region if he agreed to leave Europe.[53]

The talks at Rome were inconclusive – as had been the previous talks at Lysimacheia in 196. That is: the Roman demands were rejected. A Roman embassy was nevertheless sent out to Asia to negotiate again with King Antiochus the following summer (193). The embassy met first with Eumenes II at Pergamum – who again warned the Romans of Antiochus' ambitions, and urged war (Livy 35.13.6–10). Talks directly with Antiochus followed, and then more talks, this time with the king's representatives – but again none of this led anywhere.[54]

In early 192 Antiochus was back in Thrace with an army – extending his European dominions westward by force again. It was probably now that the king seized the economically and strategically important cities of Aenus and Maronea on the Thracian coast, which the Romans in 196 at the Isthmia had declared free and henceforth to be independent (previously they had belonged to Philip). Maronea in particular was a striking Seleucid westwards advance along the coast, 100 miles west from Gallipoli, and the conquest and absorption of these cities into Antiochus' empire constituted a direct overturning of arrangements made by Rome in the Isthmian Declaration.[55] We should stress that Antiochus campaigned westwards along the Thracian coast in 192 well knowing that his possessions in Europe had become the bitterest area of contention between himself and Rome, and he must have known as well that Aenus and Maronea had been declared free and neutral at the Isthmia. The conduct of Antiochus here completely undermines the thesis of Grainger that the Great King at this time was attempting to be conciliatory.[56] It is not an accident that an alarming report of Antiochus'

---

[53] See Gruen 1984: 626–7. The tougher Roman line on withdrawal of Antiochus from Europe may also have been provoked by the presence of Hannibal as a military advisor at Antiochus' court: cf. Livy 33.49.1–8; App. *Syr.* 4.

[54] Gruen 1984: 629–30, is far too sanguine about the outcome of these conferences; and Grainger 2002: 160–1, cf. 165, wrongly sees Antiochus as very conciliatory. In fact, no important concessions were offered by either side: see rightly Hammond, in Hammond and Walbank 1988: 449. This is true even if one believes in the list of minor concessions found in App. *Syr.* 12, as opposed to the grimmer version of events in Livy (which is based on Polybian material: see Briscoe 1981: 1 and 162). Even Grainger admits (161) that Antiochus at these meetings kept completely off the table the key question of his large army and province across the Hellespont in Thrace.

[55] Livy 35.23.10; cf. 35.35.7 and 37.60.7. On this campaign, see Briscoe 1981: 32–3, 179 and 395, 448; Grainger 1996. Economic importance of Aenus and Maronea, especially in terms of gold mines: see Rostovtzeff 1941: 111.

[56] Conciliatory: so Grainger 2002: 163 (the problem is later indirectly admitted by Grainger, 187).

campaign in Thrace came to Rome; moreover, it came through a Pergamene envoy of extraordinary status – Attalus, a royal brother of Eumenes.[57]

Meanwhile, the leaders of the Aetolian League concluded that the time had come for the League to take revenge for the slights in territorial rewards and respect which they felt Aetolia had suffered at the hands of Rome. They calculated as well that the League would gain great geopolitical advantage if it became the leading ally of Antiochus in a new and Seleucid-imposed restructuring of European Greece.[58] Aetolian envoys went to Antiochus in 193, asking for his help against Rome and proclaiming that he would be welcomed in Greece as a liberator. At first there was no substantive response (Livy 35.13.1). But the Aetolians were persistent, and when the new Aetolian *strategos* Thoas journeyed personally to Antiochus' court in western Asia Minor in winter 193/192 to ask for his support (Livy 35.32.4), the king found it impossible to say no – despite the fact that Rome had persistently warned him away from European Greek affairs.[59] In the spring of 192 Antiochus' minister Minnio accompanied Thoas back to Aetolia and described to the Panaetolian Assembly the king's vast wealth and military power, promising them Antiochus as a true champion of "Greek liberty" (Livy 35.32). The Panaetolian Assembly responded by passing a decree proclaiming Antiochus the liberator of Greece and appointing him the arbitrator of the quarrels between Aetolia and Rome. Antiochus' territorial realm and beyond his formal territories empire his sphere of political influence now extended much farther than that of any other Seleucid king, including even the great Seleucus I, founder of the dynasty: much of Thrace was now Antiochus' province (an advance to the west which Seleucus I had desired but never achieved), and with Aetolia as his new ally Antiochus' power now extended all the way from Afghanistan to the Adriatic.[60]

The Aetolian decree of spring 192 was both a challenge and an insult to Rome – for, like all ancient great powers, the Republic never accepted an outside arbitrator in its quarrels with other states.[61]

---

[57]   See Livy 35.23.10–11, with McShane 1964: 142; Hansen 1971: 77.

[58]   On revenge for material injuries, and for slights to honor and status, as a widespread motive for Greek interstate warfare, see Lendon 2000.

[59]   In terms of the conduct of the second-tier states in exacerbating relations between Rome and Antiochus, the unprecedented personal journey of the Aetolian *strategos* to Antiochus' court is an instructive parallel to the appearance of Eumenes II's brother Attalus before the Senate in Rome to complain about Antiochus (see above).

[60]   On the enormous ambitions of Seleucus I, see Grainger 1992.

[61]   See Eckstein 1988, and now the comments of Grainger 2002: 177–9.

T. Quinctius Flamininus, whom the Senate had already sent back to Greece that spring of 192 at the head of a Roman diplomatic delegation to shore up political support in the face of the growing threat from Antiochus, protested to the Aetolians that as allies of Rome they should bring any grievances directly to the Senate. In other words, the Aetolians had no need for an outside arbitrator, and indeed to propose one was to show a lack of good faith. We are told that the response of the Aetolian leader Damocritus to Flamininus' remonstrations was that the Aetolians would indeed soon come to Rome – where they would dictate terms of peace on the banks of the Tiber.[62]

And the Aetolians did more than make threats – they acted. In the summer of 192 they attempted to seize the fortress-city of Chalcis on Euboea by a coup de main. This city was one of Philip's former "Three Fetters of Greece" (Livy 35.37.4–38.14), a strategic polity that the Isthmian Declaration had explicitly left free of any great power. As it happened, the Aetolian attempt on Chalcis failed – but it was a stunning subversion of the Isthmian arrangements. Somewhat later the Aetolians successfully brought the city of Demetrias into the League. Demetrias was a port city on the central Aegean coast of Greece and a great naval base – another of Philip's former "Three Fetters of Greece." The populace of the city feared that they would be turned over back to Macedon as Philip's price for supporting Rome in any confrontation with Antiochus. The Aetolians' success in incorporating Demetrias into the League was yet another overturning of the Roman arrangements of 196, for, according to the Isthmian Declaration, Demetrias was to be – like Chalcis – an independent state (though a member of the local Magnesian League). And yet the only Roman response to the Aetolian coup at Demetrias was an attempt by the ex-consul P. Villius Tappulus, one of the envoys accompanying Flamininus, to persuade the people of Demetrias to reconsider their decision and abide by the Isthmian Declaration. The result was an angry confrontation between the Magnesians and Villius as he spoke to them from a warship kept anchored offshore (Livy 35.39.3–8: the Magnesians had even refused Villius landing rights). A humiliating scene – and that was the extent of the Roman reaction.[63]

Meanwhile, the government of the Achaean League had decided in the spring of 192 to renew war against King Nabis of Sparta – against the advice of T. Quinctius Flamininus. For those scholars who believe

[62]   Livy 35.33.3–10; App. *Syr.* 21; Zon. 9.19. There is no reason to reject the story of this insult: Briscoe 1981: 194.
[63]   The dramatic scene in Livy 35.39 is based on Polybian material: see Briscoe 1981: 181.

that Roman domination was fastened onto Greece by the Isthmian Declaration, one can only say that to brush aside Flamininus' advice on a matter of war and peace was hardly the action of a subordinated state, let alone a government that knew it was bound to Rome by the stern obligations of *clientela*.[64] Nabis himself had already taken advantage of the Romans' military withdrawal from Greece by attempting in the summer of 193 to seize the towns on the Laconian coast that the peace treaty of 195 had removed from Spartan rule and given over to the Achaeans.[65] The Achaean attack on Nabis in the spring of 192 turned out to be indecisive; but later that summer an Aetolian plot at Sparta led to the assassination of Nabis, as the Aetolians tried to seize the city for themselves. This provoked another military response from the Achaeans: the *strategos* Philopoemen marched an Achaean army into the city, and officially brought Sparta into the Achaean League. The Achaean occupation and annexation of Sparta certainly blocked Aetolian ambitions in the southern Peloponnese. But Philopoemen's annexation of Sparta into the Achaean League overturned the Roman peace settlement with Sparta in 195, which had allowed the city to remain independent – and the Achaean action had been accomplished by straightforward military force. Like Nabis in 193 – and, for that matter, like the Aetolians – the Achaeans in 192 simply ignored the peace settlement. Flamininus in fact opposed the Achaean annexation of Sparta, as he had opposed the Achaean attack on Sparta that spring; but the Achaeans had not listened to him then, and they rejected his attempts to save Sparta from them now (Livy 35.25.5).[66]

The actions not only of Antiochus and the Aetolian League but of Nabis and the Achaean League indicated that the system of interstate relations in Greece which the Romans had created through the Isthmian Declaration in 196 was now cracking apart from several directions at once. The cause of the failure of the Isthmian system, as Justin explicitly says (31.3.2), was the withdrawal of the Roman army from Greece. But the only apparent responses from the Roman side were diplomatic protests which were notably ineffective – ineffective not merely with the Achaeans and Aetolians but even with the populace of Demetrias. Grainger may well be correct, then, that it is not merely the

---

[64] Discussion of this interaction in Gruen 1984: 462–5, with sources. On the previous war between Nabis and Rome and a coalition of Greek allies in 195, see above, Chapter 7.

[65] See Justin 31.3.2, explicit that Nabis acted to reconquer the coast from the Achaeans because the Roman army was now gone. Noted by Gruen 1984: 463.

[66] The Livian narrative here is clearly derived from Polybian material: see Briscoe 1981: 181. On Flamininus' failure to stop the Achaeans by means of diplomatic intervention, see the comments of Gruen 1984: 465–7.

Roman military withdrawal of spring 194 which sent the wrong message to Antiochus. The lack of forceful Roman response to the events of 193 and especially to the events of summer 192 – as several Greek states started to pursue again their traditional expansionist policies, disrupting with impunity the political arrangements the Senate had established and proclaimed satisfactory in 196 – may have reinforced the message that Rome was not prepared to risk much for Greece. Roman actions – the withdrawal from Greece in spring 194, and the lack of response to aggressive Seleucid, Aetolian, Spartan, and Achaean conduct in 193 and 192 – appeared to be speaking louder than Roman words.[67]

In the autumn of 192 envoys from Aetolia came again to Antiochus in northwest Asia Minor, where he was putting some sort of pressure on the cities there that had previously sought Roman protection (Livy 35.42.3). The Aetolians brought the news that Demetrias on the Aegean coast of Greece had now voluntarily joined the Aetolian League. It was a demonstration both of Aetolian popularity and forcefulness, and, conversely, it was a demonstration of the Romans' lack of will. Antiochus' response was immediate and military: he crossed the Aegean at the head of the forces he had with him, and landed at Demetrias.[68]

Antiochus' decision to come to Greece with an army appears spur-of-the-moment, but it should not be seen as a sudden and eccentric act on his part; rather, it fits with the pattern of Antiochus' aggressive advance to the west beyond the Hellespont which had been pursued with large-scale military operations in Thrace almost every year since 196. The decision fits especially with Antiochus' occupation of Aenus and Maronea earlier in 192 – overturning the Roman arrangements at the Isthmia that had left these two cities independent (see above). Antiochus' original army at Demetrias was relatively small – though not as small as some scholars prefer to think.[69] Those forces were large enough, at any rate, to ensure that over the winter of 192/191 most of the Thessalian polities came over to Antiochus' voluntarily, or else resisted his army in vain; the cities of Boeotia also came over to Antiochus' side; and Chalcis on Euboea, which had resisted the Aetolians throughout 192 (see above), now opened its gates. States as far south as Elis in the

---

[67] See Grainger 2002: 186–7 and 191.

[68] Mandell 1989: 92–3, manages to discuss the outbreak of the Syrian War, blaming Roman imperialism for provoking it, without mention of Antiochus' invasion of Greece. Derow 2003: 63, also minimizes the highly aggressive nature of Antiochus' action and what it meant in terms of relations with Rome.

[69] Antiochus' original forces were certainly larger than the figure of 10,000 infantry that is often asserted: see the comments of Bar-Kochva 1977: 15–17, and Briscoe 1981: 207; Grainger 2002: 231. But note the attempt of Derow 2003: 63, to downplay the fact that Antiochus did bring an army with him to Demetrias.

Peloponnese joined in support of the Great King, and, strikingly, so did major cities of the Acarnanian League, far to the west on the Adriatic.[70] The behavior of King Amynander of Athamania is particularly instructive. From 210 BC, he had sided with whichever forces he believed would be dominant in European Greece: first the Aetolian League, then Philip V, then Rome. He had been the most pliable of T. Quinctius Flamininus' Greek friends. But now he went over to Antiochus, in the hopes of gaining Athamanian control over cities in western Thessaly, and in return for the Great King's support to place Amynander's own brother-in-law on the throne of Macedon.[71] Meanwhile, the Aetolian League elected Antiochus its *strategos* for 192/191. By the spring of 191 only Athens, Philip V in the north, and the Achaean League in the south had yet to declare themselves for Antiochus. To be sure, they would eventually side with Rome, because of their own calculations of self-interest; but in the case of Athens, where there were factions impressed with the power of the Great King, this required the insertion of an Achaean garrison in order to ensure loyalty.[72] In sum, Antiochus tore completely to pieces the system established in Greece in 196 by Flamininus and the Isthmian Declaration.[73]

The Aetolians' action in inciting Antiochus to come to Greece was, of course, typical of that process of ancient (and modern) international relations by which a weaker state invites in a stronger state for help and protection.[74] Yet the final decision to invade Greece was the Great King's alone: it was an act of will intended to dominate his environment, and a spectacular demonstration of his refusal to be limited by Roman demands that he stay away from Europe. Antiochus could have refused the Aetolian inducements of 193 and 192 to intervene in European Greece – just as the Roman Senate could have refused the pleas of the Greek embassies of 200 to intervene east of the Adriatic. And if Antiochus had refused the Aetolians, then the possibility of an eventual stable relationship with Rome, and a relatively stable bipolar structure within the

---

[70]   On the behavior of the Thessalians, Boeotians, Chalcis, Elis, and the Acarnanians, see conveniently Gruen 1984: 476–8 (with sources).
[71]   For Amynander's close relationship with Flamininus, see Sacks 1975: 102–3. On Amynander's aims in going over to Antiochus, see conveniently Gruen 1984: 476 (with sources).
[72]   On the situation in Athens, see Gruen 1984: 477 (with sources). Here, as in 200 BC when the Athenians called upon Rome, we see a small state in a difficult situation attempting to find a way to survive amid the clash of great powers.
[73]   On the widespread impact of Antiochus' invasion in destroying the system established by Flamininus in 196, see Deininger 1971: 78–116; Eckstein 1987a: 314–15.
[74]   On the political-science idea of "empire by invitation," see Lundestad 1986 and Lundestad 1990: Ch. 1 (the example is Europe and the United States after 1946).

Mediterranean, cannot be ruled out – with untold social, cultural, economic, and political consequences for the history of the ancient world. Like the Romans' decision of 200, however, Antiochus' decision of 192 was not exceptional in his environment: the pressures of a bellicose internal culture, the constraints and inducements imposed on every Hellenistic regime by a harsh interstate system, the indications of a lack of intense Roman interest in Greece despite what the Senate proclaimed, all pushed Antiochus in 192 to act as he did, and to accept the Aetolians' invitation to Greece.

It appears that almost simultaneously with Antiochus' landing in Greece (ca. November 192), the Senate and People of Rome formally declared war on both the Aetolians and the Great King.[75] The declaration of war was not a response to Antiochus' landing at Demetrias, since this news could not have been known at Rome yet; the declaration refers instead to the actions of the Aetolians at Demetrias and Chalcis, and to the Aetolians' invitation to Antiochus to come to Europe for the purpose of "making war on the Romans" (Livy 36.1.5–6). Rumors of an invasion of Italy by Antiochus had already been rife at Rome in the previous winter of 193/192 (Livy 35.23.2); and the Senate must have been hearing bad reports from Greece throughout the summer of 192. Here, then, was the *Patres'* response.[76] Indeed, already in September or October, before the declaration of war, the Senate had ordered a large force under the praetor M. Baebius Tamphilus across the Adriatic to Apollonia – the first military reaction to the deteriorating situation in Greece. Perhaps if Antiochus had known of the dispatching of Baebius' force he would not have come to Greece at all (though Apollonia was itself still very far from the Aegean) – but of course he did not know. Once more we see the impact of the mutual opacity between ancient states, of poor communications between them, and of decisions made on the basis of out-of-date and poor information.[77]

Thus came the final clash between the two greatest powers still left standing at the climax of the Hellenistic Age, one power emerging from

[75] The solar November date may have coincided with March 15 on the Roman calendar, so out of line was that calendar with the solar year; if so, the Senate had deferred decision until the entry of the new consuls into office. On the calendar, see Derow 1976.
[76] Thus there is little to be said in support of the thesis of Derow 2003: 64, that the timing of the declaration of war shows that the war had nothing to do with aggressive moves on Antiochus' part.
[77] On the opacity of states to one another, and the danger this poses in a competitive and complex international environment, see, e.g., Morgenthau 1973: 208; Blainey 1988: 114; Jervis 2001: 282 and n. 2; and Taliaferro 2004: Ch. 5 *passim* (and esp. 151–3).

the eastern periphery of the Hellenistic world, one from the western periphery.[78] The resources available to each of these antagonists were far greater than those available to most states in antiquity, and the result was, in political-science terminology, a true hegemonic war to establish the new leadership for the new interstate structure that was emerging in the Mediterranean.

Antiochus' landing in Greece led at first to new Roman fears that the Great King was about to invade Italy itself – an invasion backed by Hannibal as one of his generals. Since we know the final outcome of this war was a Roman victory, the fears appear ludicrous to us; and some scholars suspect this is mere Roman propaganda.[79] But good evidence shows this is not propaganda – for the Roman government engaged in serious defensive actions to protect Italy at this time. The praetor A. Atilius Serranus, originally slated for command in Spain, was instead given Bruttium to guard, with two legions; the praetor Baebius, who was also originally scheduled for Spain, was instead sent (as we have seen) with a large force to the west coast of Greece; a naval squadron was sent specially to guard Sicily from invasion, and a special emergency force of two legions was mobilized for service on the island.[80] In the spring of 191 the defensive measures continued: the Senate gave the praetor A. Cornelius Mammula an army with which to guard the Italian coast from Tarentum to Brundisium, and sent a second praetor to Sicily, in order to divide the command of naval and land forces there for the sake of greater military efficiency. These measures were all important and costly state actions.[81] And we must remember (once again) that the Romans lived in the shadow of the memory of Hannibal's devastating invasion – and indeed in the shadow of Hannibal himself, for he was serving with Antiochus. The Romans lived, too, in the shadow of Alexander the Great, who had shown everyone how a single power, if led by a general of genius, could annihilate the independence of all other polities. Antiochus Megas was the greatest Hellenistic king since Alexander, with spectacular conquests to his credit, and he had proclaimed himself Alexander's heir.[82]

The Senate ordered large Roman forces mobilized for this war: 50,000 infantry and seventy-five quinquiremes were sent to Greece, more

---

[78] The overview of Liska 1978: 12–14.
[79] Roman fear of Antiochus discounted, and the tradition on it disbelieved: Harris 1979: 221–3.
[80] Discussion in Siebert 1995: 243 (with sources).
[81] See ibid.: 243–4 (with sources). Earlier: Will 1982: 172; cf. Badian 1964b: 117.
[82] On the claim, see Ma 1999/2002: 275. Why a tradition stressing Roman fear as a justification for military action should have developed in a society which, according to Harris 1979, unashamedly and openly celebrated imperial aggression is in any case never explained. See in general Eckstein 2006.

than twice the size of the army sent against Philip. The war effort in the East in fact necessitated not sending reinforcements out to Spain, as had been planned, and halving the size of the Roman army fighting in northern Italy against the Celts.[83] Once the Romans demonstrated such a real will to fight, thereby erasing the record of 194–192, they were joined, as in the Second Macedonian War, by numerous Greek polities: Pergamum and Rhodes, Macedon and the Achaean League, many others. Some no doubt acted from fear of the Romans; some no doubt feared both great powers; but others (especially Pergamum) acted primarily from fear of Antiochus. Most states in the eastern Mediterranean (and states as far away as Carthage in the western Mediterranean) participated in some fashion in what had now become a true Mediterranean-wide "hegemonic war" – fought on land and sea, in Europe and then in Asia Minor. Both Rhodes and Pergamum in fact made crucial contributions to the eventual victory. The Rhodian navy – the most highly skilled naval force in the Mediterranean in this period – played a key role in the two victories over Antiochus' formidable navy in 190.[84] Pergamene cavalry commanded by Eumenes II personally led the crucial cavalry charge that brought the decisive victory over Antiochus' army at Magnesia-ad-Sipylum in 189, and brought the war to an end.[85]

The pattern taken by the war was a determined Roman counter-offensive against Antiochus. The Great King seemed willing to rest on the gains he had made in Greece in winter 192/191, and in the summer of 191 the consul M'. Acilius Glabrio with the Roman main force attacked Antiochus' fortified position at Thermopylae. Glabrio won an important though fiercely fought victory over Antiochus' army (a battle in which Cato the Elder, consul 195, distinguished himself); and with that, Antiochus suddenly abandoned Greece, sailing back to his base at Ephesus in Ionia. Glabrio did not pursue the Great King, but turned instead to reducing the King's central ally Aetolia. But here operations went slowly, and in 190 Glabrio was replaced by the consul L. Cornelius Scipio – on whose staff served Scipio Africanus himself. The Scipio brothers changed Glabrio's strategy: they concluded a six months' truce with Aetolia (the negotiations took a significant amount of time), so that they could take up the pursuit of Antiochus into Asia

---

[83] See Livy 36.2.6–3.1, rightly emphasized by Grainger 2002: 211.
[84] On this campaign, see Berthold 1984: 157–62 (with sources); on the skills and reputation of the Rhodian navy, see Morrison 1996: 210–12.
[85] See McShane 1964: 145–6 (with sources). The Carthaginians provided supplies to Rome – and offered ships; conversely, tradition held that Hannibal attempted to get Antiochus to back an expedition to establish Barcid rule in Carthage: discussion in Hoyos 2003: 204–5.

Minor. But because in the summer of 190 the combined Pergamene–Rhodian–Roman fleet had not yet won naval supremacy in the eastern Aegean, the Scipios were forced to march to Asia Minor along the coast, up through Macedon and Thrace – which in itself took a significant amount of time. The Roman army – after waiting on the European side of the Hellespont for another month while Scipio Africanus performed his sacred duties as a Salic priest (which among other things forbade him to cross water during the period of the Shield Dance), eventually crossed into Asia Minor at Gallipoli in the late summer of 190. It was the first Roman military crossing into Asia. Shortly before this, the coalition fleet won a decisive naval victory over Antiochus' forces at Myonessus near Samos (sinking forty-two of the Great King's eighty-nine quinquiremes), establishing coalition naval supremacy and forcing Antiochus to abandon even the great new Seleucid fortress of Lysimacheia in Thrace. Once the Roman forces had crossed into Asia, and were encamped near Pergamum, Antiochus attempted a negotiated peace; but the negotiations failed to reach a satisfactory conclusion – primarily because of the opposition of Scipio Africanus. The result was a decisive battle fought at Magnesia-ad-Sipylum, somewhat inland from Smyrna, in December 190 or January 189. It was another fiercely fought battle, and Antiochus came close to winning it (the entire Roman left wing almost collapsed); but in the end – thanks in good part to a decisive charge of Pergamene cavalry (see above) – the Great King was decisively defeated.[86]

Did this war witness the emergence of a new, more domineering Rome, which preferred to fight Antiochus unilaterally instead of with the help of the Greek allies – the latter being the way they had fought their two wars against Macedon previously? Did the war against Antiochus see a qualitatively different and more brutally domineering Roman attitude towards the Greek states than what we saw above with the Isthmian Declaration and "the Freedom of the Greeks"? Both hypotheses have recently been argued.[87]

The fact is, however, that the Romans fought this war with significant help from their Greek friends, and, furthermore, they handled these states as if they were friends, not submissive clients. This is demonstrated, for instance, by Roman relations with the Republic of Rhodes during the war. The naval campaign of 190 "shows the Rhodians strategizing

---

[86] Convenient discussions of the course of the war in Errington 1972: 168–83 and Errington 1989b: 282–7.

[87] See Derow 2003: 65: for Rome, the Antiochene War "had not been fought alongside allies"; and 66: the Peace of 188 BC saw the onset of "Roman rule" in Hellas.

with the Romans, offering advice, and speaking with the candor and openness typical of close friendships," while the Rhodians also pursued their own strategic interests whenever it suited them, even when the Romans wished them to engage differently.[88] Thus when the combined Roman–Rhodian–Pergamene fleet was besieging Samos (which had gone over to Antiochus), the Romans always included the Rhodians in war-councils on how to proceed; and meanwhile, they agreed to allow half the coalition fleet to go off to beseige the town of Patara in Lycia – a polity that clearly would fall into the sphere of interest of Rhodes after the war (Livy 37.15.6–8).[89] Then, as a result of a request to the Rhodian government by Iasian exiles, the Rhodians convinced the Romans to lift the siege of Iasus (Livy 37.17.5–7).[90] When Antiochus began to sue for peace and the Romans held a council of the allies on this matter at Elea, the Rhodian envoys openly advocated a compromise peace with Antiochus even though the Roman commanders at the meeting (the Scipio brothers) favored the opinion of Eumenes II of Pergamum that war be continued until total victory.[91] When the siege of Samos was dragging on and the praetor L. Aemilius Regillus wished to abandon it in order to go to the Hellespont and provide protection for the crossing of L. Scipio's army into Asia, the Rhodian admirals prevailed upon Regillus to continue the siege instead (Livy 37.26.9–13).[92] Then the Rhodian fleet, operating on its own, won a strategically important victory at Side (summer 190), thus blocking the attempt of Hannibal to sail with Seleucid reinforcements into the Aegean. And in late summer the Rhodians formed a key section of the coalition fleet at the battle of Myonessus, where the Rhodian admiral Eudamas, through a daring maneuver, saved Regillus' hard-pressed Roman warships. Berthold concludes that without Eudamas and the Rhodians, Regillus would have been crushed, and thus the Roman invasion of Asia Minor delayed for at least a year; instead, a great victory was won, and the way was opened for the eventual victory at Magnesia.[93]

---

[88] See Berthold 1984: 153; Burton 2003: 359 (the quote).
[89] See Berthold 1984: 155. The Livian passage is from Polybian material: see Briscoe 1981: 303.
[90] Again, this passage in Livy is derived from Polybian material: see Briscoe: 1981: 303.
[91] Polyb. 21.10; Livy 376.18.12. The Rhodian position at Elea probably reflects the fact that Rhodes' diplomatic history with Antiochus had been less fraught with hostility than that of Eumenes and Pergamum.
[92] This Livian passage, again, is derived from Polybian material: see Briscoe 1981: 329.
[93] On the battle of Side (summer 190), see Berthold 1984: 157–8. On the battle of Myonessus (late summer), ibid.: 159–61 (with sources).

These incidents all demonstrate that the Rhodians operated during the Antiochene War on the basis of equality and friendship with Rome: they spoke their minds openly to the Romans and acted as *amici* and equal allies in the anti-Antiochus coalition, to which they made the kind of crucial contributions that in turn allowed them to speak their minds openly. Later, the Rhodian state dedicated the famous statue on Samothrace which has a spectacular winged Victory descending onto the prow of a warship; it was a celebration of the Rhodian military prowess in this war – the Rhodian role in winning the battle of Myonessus.[94]

The same holds true of Eumenes II of Pergamum, Philip V of Macedon, and the Achaean League. Commanded by Eumenes in person, the fleet of Pergamum helped win the battle at Cissus in 191, which temporarily gained the southern Aegean for the allies.[95] Much more importantly, the Pergamene army provided the crucial military maneuver at Magnesia, with an attack led by Eumenes personally that started the crumbling of Antiochus' battle line. Dedications at Pergamum to Athena-Bringer-of-Victory vaunted the exploits of the king and his brother Attalus during the fighting.[96] Meanwhile, the army of Philip V forced into submission many of Antiochus' European Greek allies; Philip operated independently, and expected considerable territorial expansion from his success.[97] The same holds true of the Achaean League. The Achaeans officially sided with Rome against Antiochus at the urgent request of Flamininus in winter 192/191 – one of Flamininus' few diplomatic successes up to that point – and the Achaeans sent troops in 191 to help out the Romans at Athens and to support Eumenes at Pergamum. But they mostly spent the war in conquering the entire Peloponnese for themselves. During 191 and 190 a combination of military action and harsh political pressure led to the inclusion of both Elis and Messene for the first time within the League, as well as the forceful retention of a restless Sparta. Flamininus registered diplomatic objections to all these actions as they occurred, one by one, but in each case thought it wise to go along with the wishes of the Achaean government. Nor did the League suffer for its assertive attitude; the Achaeans were rewarded in this period with a permanent treaty of alliance with Rome, the first such formal treaty of alliance we are certain of east

---

[94]   See Berthold 1984: 153; Burton 2003: 359–60.

[95]   Hansen 1971: 80. The Rhodian fleet arrived late for this battle: see discussion in Berthold 1984: 153–4.

[96]   On the Pergamene contribution to Magnesia, see McShane 1964: 146 and n. 199; Hansen 1971: 86–7. On the great dedications in the temple complex at Pergamum: ibid.: 87.

[97]   On Philip's independent military activities and territorial gains during the Antiochene War, see Walbank 1940: 199–217.

of the Adriatic. Naturally, it was a treaty on equal terms.[98] Diophanes of Megalopolis, the Achaean *strategos* in 191/190 BC, would later personally claim on an inscription that he had been the first man in history to unify the entire Peloponnese (Paus. 8.30.5). Once again, there is nothing here of the humble obedience of a *cliens* to the wishes of Rome; there is only the traditional aggressive pride of an independent and militaristic Greek polity. To be sure, it was a polity which, unlike its neighbors, had made a series of wise choices in foreign relations ever since 198, and as a result had engineered a great enhancement of its power, partly through Roman favor (as in the gaining of Corinth and the Acrocorinth in the peace settlement of 196), but mostly through its own vigorous military efforts unimpeded by Rome.[99]

In the new structure of interstate relations in the East which Rome and its allies established in 188 in the Peace of Apamea with Antiochus, several friends of Rome in fact received huge territorial rewards. Not only was the Achaean League allowed a free hand to conquer the entire Peloponnese, but Pergamum and Rhodes gained enormous swathes of territory in Asia Minor. This was because the Romans at Apamea forced Antiochus to cede away all the huge gains he had won in Asia Minor since 198, and placed the western boundary of his empire along the Taurus Range (between modern Syria and Turkey). Enormous areas in Asia Minor were thus freed from Antiochus – but they were turned over by Roman *Dictat* to Rome's friends.[100] This seems a divergence from the Isthmian policy of 196, but not completely: the areas turned over to Pergamum and Rhodes were not primarily Greek, whereas Apamea did leave numerous Greek cities in Asia Minor – those that had joined the allied cause before the battle of Magnesia – politically free of anyone's control.[101] And in Europe, Philip V was eventually forced to give back most (though not all) of his conquests, after these polities protested to Rome against Macedonian rule. Given his large-scale

---

[98]   On Achaean expansion during the Syrian War, despite Flamininus' objections, see Gruen 1984: 467–75. On the date and conditions of the Roman–Achaean formal treaty of alliance, see Badian 1952.

[99]   Flamininus did deny the Achaeans the acquisition of the large island of Zacynthus, off the northwestern coast of the Peloponnese; perhaps it was too close to Italy. Discussion in Gruen 1984: 470–1.

[100]   Partly this was Roman gratitude (see Polyb. 21.18–24, explicit); partly, perhaps, the idea was a permanent balance and shield against the Seleucids.

[101]   See Errington 1989b: 287–8. Among the non-Greeks, Cappadocia and Pontus, and the Celtic tribal entities of central Anatolia all remained free – despite A. Manlius Vulso's ferocious campaign of 189 against the Celts (which temporarily eased the fears of the cities of the coast concerning the pervasive threat of Celtic raiding). On Vulso's campaign, see Rich 1993: 56–9.

independent efforts against Antiochus in the war, Philip felt betrayed by this Roman action, and his anger was public; and this demonstrates that he, too, was no humble client-king ready to accept any Roman ruling.[102]

The Aetolian League was finally defeated in 189, by a large Roman army under the consul M. Fulvius Nobilior. The peace treaty dictated by the Senate contained the requirement that henceforth the Aetolians would respect τὴν ἀρχὴν καὶ τὴν δυναστείαν τοῦ δήμου τῶν Ῥωμαίων (Polyb. 21.32.2), that is, "the supremacy and power of the Roman people," and that the Aetolians would henceforth take as enemies any people with whom the Romans were at war.[103] The first part of this clause of the peace treaty is an overt promise to obey Roman orders; but Aetolia was the only state from which that promise was extorted. It was a unique situation, and explained by the role of the Aetolians both in betraying (from the Roman point of view) their previous association with Rome and in provoking the war.[104] Yet even in the case of Aetolia, we know of no Roman further contact during the next fifteen years, let alone the issuing of any orders, and during that time the League functioned perfectly well on its own.

Antiochus the Great was himself severely punished: not only did Rome and its allies push the boundaries of the Seleucid Empire back hundreds of miles into eastern Asia Minor, but Antiochus had to pay Rome an enormous war-indemnity, and a large war-indemnity to Pergamum; the Seleucid army was forbidden to cross the Taurus mountains for any reason; and the Seleucid war-fleet was limited to almost nothing.[105] This

---

[102]   On Philip's dissatisfaction, see Colin 1905: 204–12; Walbank 1940: 223–36; Badian 1958a: 92–4; Welwei 1963: 50–4; Errington 1971: 195–201; and now Derow 1989: 294, and 2003: 67. If Philip had sided with Antiochus, the result could have been disastrous for Rome: see Hammond, in Hammond and Walbank 1988: 449–50. But Antiochus made a pact with King Amynander of Athamania to depose Philip and put a relative of Amynander on the Macedonian throne; so Philip had no choice but to back Rome (see above, this chapter). Antiochus' bargain with Amynander shows how far we are now from the politics of the Pact Between the Kings – but then Polybius thought that even during the period of the pact the two monarchs intended to betray each other (cf. Polyb. 15.20.6 init.).

[103]   The verb in the Polybian text of 21.22 is missing. Livy 38.11.2 translates Polybius' Greek as: imperium maiestatemque populi Romani . . . conservato – which sounds very imperial but may be late first-century BC phraseology (see Gruen 1984: 279 and n. 33).

[104]   Note the reproving warning sine dolo malo in Livy 38.11.2 (the parallel passage is lost from the Polybian manuscript).

[105]   On Apamea, see conveniently Errington 1972: 18–27; Sherwin-White 1984: 18–27; Errington 1989b: 286–9. Antiochus' navy hugely reduced: Walbank 1979: 159–60 (with sources). The comment of Gruen 1984: 643, that the peace settlement established Antiochus III as "an associate in the enterprise to maintain Mediterranean concord," goes too far in the opposite direction from the excessive cynicism of Derow 2003: 63–5.

could only have pleased the Ptolemaic regime in Alexandria, which for the past fifteen years had faced the specter of the Seleucid conquest of Egypt. Yet even now Seleucid ambitions were not completely curbed, and within twenty years a Seleucid army would be besieging Alexandria itself. The weakness of the Ptolemaic regime, which had set off the great power-transition crisis in the first place, still remained an important factor in the politics of the Greek Mediterranean.[106]

Peter Derow marks the treaty of Apamea as the moment when Roman empire in the East first came into being, which is why he speaks henceforth of both "Roman dominion" beyond the Adriatic and even of "Roman rule" – though he admits that he is antedating Polybius' own dating of that imperial moment by a full generation.[107] Yet in 188 as in 196–194 we confront the spectacle that while the Romans rewarded their friends, the Senate took no territory for Rome itself: once more, no *provincia* was established east of the Adriatic to be ruled by Roman governors and garrisoned by Roman troops; the victorious Roman armies and fleet were withdrawn completely back to Italy. The state structure in European Greece remained essentially what it had been under the Isthmian Declaration, except that the Achaean League was now much stronger, Macedon somewhat stronger, and Aetolia much weaker. Everywhere else the regional confederations of independent *poleis* remained undisturbed. Nor did Rome now employ the classic tools even of indirect hegemony: no Roman political overseers – not even any Roman diplomats – were left behind when the Roman armies returned to Italy in 188. And although as the result of two wars Rome had now developed a set of traditionally dependable Greek allies for Rome in the East, a group of independent states centered on Achaea, Athens, Rhodes, and Pergamum, the Senate did not attempt to convert these individual friendships into a permanent league of Greek states with Rome at its head. As in 196–194, this rather obvious idea by which to impose and institutionalize Roman hegemony, familiar from the history of the kings of Macedon, seems never to have entered the head of any Roman.

Thus in 188 the Pergamenes, Rhodians, Athenians, Ptolemies, and Achaeans could congratulate themselves on having survived in good fashion the violent and massive power-transition crisis that had begun ca. 207, and the subsequent hegemonic wars that had naturally flowed from that crisis. Indeed, the Pergamenes, Rhodians, and Achaeans had through careful decision-making in their own interest even profited handsomely from the crisis through the expansion of their power, territory, and prestige. It is true that out of the system-wide hegemonic wars of

---

[106]   See Lampela 1998: 124–38.
[107]   Derow 2003: 65.

this period there emerged a new Mediterranean interstate structure, and that the structure came primarily at Roman dictation, and was in good part based on Roman military and political preponderance. Yet one must stress that – as in 228, 219, 205, and 194 – Roman military forces in 188 were again totally withdrawn back to Italy; and no Roman soldier was to appear anywhere in the Greek East for nearly twenty years. Nor were any Roman officials, or political overseers, or administrators of any kind left behind in the East – nor even any Roman diplomats. This is a strange "empire." Indeed, it can be argued that the new interstate structure that had emerged in the eastern Mediterranean was not yet even a stable Roman hegemony, let alone Roman "rule" or empire – for informal arrangements such as the ones Rome left behind in the East in 188 need constant cultivation to remain effective instruments for the assertion of power, and with Antiochus decisively defeated the Senate reverted quickly to its old, habitual stance: disinterest in the affairs of the Greeks.[108]

What had emerged from the power-transition crisis that had begun ca. 207 is best described, then, as what the political scientists call a situation of "unipolarity." That is: Rome was now the sole remaining superpower. To be sure, this was a large step forward on the road towards hegemony and perhaps eventually towards empire: thus in the decade after the Peace of Apamea we see friends and allies of Rome even employing the general authority of Rome as a support for enforcing their own local will.[109] But the achievement of unipolarity was only one step along the spectrum of interstate relations that leads towards empire. And unipolarity, even when once achieved, can nevertheless be reversed; historically this has frequently occurred. Events, as we will see in our final chapter below, would tell.[110]

CONCLUSION

Modern students of international relations hypothesize that a power-transition crisis of major proportions, caused by a severe decline in the relative or absolute power of one of the large states that previously had

---

[108]   On the difficulties in maintaining informal "spheres of interest," see above, Chapter 2, on Illyria, and above, this chapter, on the events in Greece after 196.
[109]   This is the meaning of the inscription recording Eumenes II of Pergamum's letter to the town of Tyriaion on southeast Phrygia, bestowing upon it the status of polis: for the inscription, see Jonnes and Ricl 1997. It is highly doubtful that anyone in the Senate had ever heard of Tyriaion. Contra: Derow 2003: 65.
[110]   On the historical reversibility of unipolarity, see Wilkinson 1999; Ikenberry, ed. 2002 (and in detail below, Chapter 9).

been a pillar of an interstate system, often leads to hegemonic war among the great powers. Such large-scale hegemonic war disrupts the previously existing interstate system, and leads in turn to the redistribution of territory, influence, and prestige within that system so that they come to match the really existing distribution of power and capability. Eventually, this redistribution of systemic rewards through massive violence leads the state-system back to a period of relative stability – though under a new configuration. The years between ca. 207 and 188 BC witnessed in the Hellenistic Mediterranean a classic period of power-transition crisis and hegemonic war among great powers.

Ever since ca. 280 BC the Hellenistic state-system had been a tripolar system, in which an unstable balance of power among Antigonid Macedon, the Seleucid Empire, and Ptolemaic Egypt had more or less regulated interstate life in the eastern Mediterranean. The power-transition crisis caused by the sudden faltering and weakening of the Ptolemaic state after ca. 207 wrecked this long-standing tripolar situation. The first stage in the crisis saw Antigonid Macedon and the Seleucid Empire strive to take advantage of the faltering power of the Ptolemies in order to expand their own power on a huge scale within the system. As the number of great powers was reduced from three to two, the weaker polities in the system came to fear direct domination and rule by one or the other of the two great states – or perhaps even the emergence of a single system hegemon, recreating the authoritarian empire of Alexander. These states, desperate to preserve their independence against Macedon and the Seleucid Empire – an independence that the previous tripolar structure had allowed – appealed to Rome, a power hitherto only on the periphery of the eastern Mediterranean state-system. The second stage of the crisis saw Roman intervention in the East from 200 BC, the catalyst for which was the appeal for help from at least four of the weaker Greek states. The Senate first put diplomatic pressure on Philip V of Macedon and Antiochus III the Seleucid emperor to desist from their aggressive expansion, and when that failed in Philip's case, the result was outright war against Philip (the Second Macedonian War). That war ended with the defeat and significant weakening of Macedon at the hands of Rome at the head of a large military coalition of Greek states (including the Achaean League, the Aetolian League, Athens, Pergamum, and Rhodes). The Isthmian settlement of 196, with its announced principle of "the Freedom of the Greeks," allowed the Romans to set up a security situation more to their own liking, characterized by the absence of any one overarching and dominant Greek power. This outcome pleased most of the Romans' allies as well (though not the government of the Aetolian League, which was dissatisfied with its territorial acquisitions and status).

This very power vacuum, however, exacerbated by the senatorial decision in 194 to withdraw all Roman forces back to Italy, in turn attracted the expansionist aggression of Antiochus III the Great, the monarch who by the 190s had become the most powerful ruler on the planet (except perhaps for the emperor of China). Antiochus' interference in what the Romans now viewed as their informal sphere of influence and buffer zone in European Greece, followed in 192 by Antiochus' outright invasion of European Greece for the purpose of setting himself up as the hegemonic power there, led to the third stage in the crisis: the Syrian or Antiochene War. This was a second round of hegemonic war to determine leadership of the Mediterranean system.

An important catalytic function here was once again played by second-tier states – the Aetolian appeals to Antiochus for intervention in Greece, the Pergamene attempts to frighten Rome about the intentions of Antiochus. But at the level of the great powers, this was also an ineluctable clash between two sternly competing and expansive political entities. The establishment of a Roman sphere of influence in European Greece and the Aegean coincided with the startling advance of Antiochus westwards through Asia Minor. This advance may have been compensation in part for the Great King's decision not to invade Egypt proper after his crushing victory over the Ptolemies at Panium in 200, but to be satisfied with absorbing Coele Syria and Judaea into his empire instead; I have suggested that Antiochus' decision to forgo Egypt (for the moment) was in fact the result of the Roman embassy that came to the Great King at Antioch in autumn 200, and that it was this decision that led the Senate to declare Antiochus an *amicus populi Romani*. But in any case, the Great King's advance across Asia Minor, which began in 198, was so rapid and on such a large scale that by summer 196 he dominated much of the southern and western coasts of Asia Minor and had indeed sent forces across the Hellespont into Europe to seize the Gallipoli Peninsula.

The Seleucid advance in turn provoked a harder Roman stance towards the Great King. At the Lysimacheia conference in 196, representatives of Rome demanded that Antiochus withdraw from European Greece, and that he disgorge the Ptolemaic possessions he had seized in Asia Minor. Antiochus refused, and thus emerged the Aegean and European Greece as a "contested periphery" between Rome and the Seleucid realm – that is, a frontier zone where two different large-scale hegemonies intersected and where their interests clashed. Yet senatorial interest in Greece and the Aegean was still so limited that even in the face of Antiochus' court taking up residence at Ephesus on the Aegean, and even in the face of the continual expansion of Antiochus' province in Thrace by military operations, and despite the presence of Hannibal himself now as one of Antiochus' military advisors, the *Patres* went ahead in spring 194 to order the compete withdrawal of Roman troops back to Italy. Scipio Africanus warned the Senate of what might occur if Roman forces were not maintained in European Greece to ward off the Great King. But Scipio's advice was rejected, and once more the Romans reverted to their traditional habit in the East of "smash and leave" – their habit of dealing with an immediate perceived threat across the Adriatic militarily, but then departing back to Italy as soon as feasible. This stance had already found expression in T. Quinctius Flamininus' declaration at the Isthmian Games in 196 that henceforth the Greek states were to be "free" – untaxed, ungarrisoned, under their own traditional laws, free not merely from Macedon but from Rome itself.

Flamininus, the Roman commander in Greece, believed that the Isthmian Declaration and Roman withdrawal would leave the Aegean and European Greece populated by free Greek friends of Rome – friends whose relationship to Rome would create a geopolitical situation across the Adriatic congenial to Rome's new and larger scope of security concerns, but without continual entanglement in Greek affairs. These friendships were based on a convergence of interest between Rome and the Greek states, focused on placing constraints on Macedon and the Seleucids. To be sure, the Senate intended that no other great power but Rome would now have powerful political influence among the European Greek polities, and thus that European Greece would henceforth be a Roman sphere of interest as modern political scientists define that term. But this did not stop the *Patres* in 194 from ordering the complete Roman military (and even diplomatic) withdrawal from Greece, despite the looming presence of Antiochus. They acted in a mistaken belief that the crisis in the East was over, and absolutely no institutions or proto-institutions of Roman domination were left behind. But the fragility of the resulting political situation was almost immediately shown by the conduct of the Aetolians, the Spartans, the Achaeans, and above all Antiochus, each of whom, within two years of the Roman departure, were pursuing by military force their traditional aggressive expansionism. The conduct of Antiochus and the Aetolians led eventually to a second round of hegemonic war with Rome.

The resource base of Antiochus III was much larger than that of Macedon, but as with any Hellenistic monarchy the stability of Antiochus' regime depended on his military prestige, and hence military misfortunes gravely threatened internal stability.[111] The series of defeats inflicted upon Antiochus by the coalition headed by Rome,

---

[111] On this structural weakness of Hellenistic monarchy see Austin 1986, and Eckstein 2006: Ch. 4.

first in Greece, then in the Aegean, and then in Asia Minor, above all at the battle of Magnesia in 189, thus led the Great King to make peace rather than test the loyalty of his people and army any further. As was the case with Philip and Macedon, we can see that the potential weaknesses and fragility of Rome's fierce rivals were crucial factors affecting the redistribution of power that occurred so dramatically during the Mediterranean system-wide crisis of ca. 207–188.[112] As Kenneth Waltz bluntly puts it: "States are alike in the tasks they face, though not in their ability to perform them."[113]

In one way or another, the power-transition crisis initiated in the East by the faltering of the Ptolemaic state was going to mean the replacement of the old tripolar Hellenistic balance of power with a new geopolitical order – a new order that would benefit those states with the most power. In the first stage of the crisis, it appeared that Antigonid Macedon and the Seleucid Empire would dominate a new bipolar system in the East, or even that either Macedon or the Seleucid Empire would emerge as a true system hegemon or even world ruler. As it happened, the tripolar balance of power was replaced instead by Roman patronage over an artificially restored balance of power in which the Ptolemies were saved from destruction, the power of those states which allied with Rome was increased, the power of those states which opposed Rome was severely curtailed, and Roman influence hugely enhanced. Antiochus' aggressive actions from 198 and 196 onward, culminating in his invasion of Greece in late 192, ended any chance that the Mediterranean world would be a bipolar system. And in the course of the crisis the eastern and western regional subsystems of the Mediterranean had now merged into a single unified state-system east and west (Polybius' *symplokē*). And it was a unified unipolar system under Rome's predominance, stretching from Spain to Syria.

This profound geopolitical transformation was achieved through massive violence. We should not be shocked; such system transformations usually are achieved in that fashion.[114] But just as there had been a lag in the perception among governments concerning the developing Mediterranean *symplokē* (see above, Chapter 3), and just as Philip and Antiochus operated after 204 as if Rome did not exist (see above, Chapters 4–6), so we will see below that there was also a lag in the recognition

---

[112]   On the impact upon international relations of the varied state capacities to mobilize internal resources, both short-term and long-term, see Aron 1973: 46–7, 50–3, and 131. This type of analysis has recently been employed in a series of important historical case studies: see, e.g., Friedberg 2000; Mearsheimer 2001.
[113]   Waltz 1979: 96.
[114]   See Gilpin 1988.

of the situation of unipolarity: to many intelligent and experienced Greek politicians, the situation did not actually become clear until after ca. 168 BC (see Polyb. 1.1–4, and 29.21 and 27).

Though its conduct was assertive and aggressive against the kings, it is unlikely that the Senate itself in 200 BC thought it was now entering a contest for "control of everything" (Polybius' phrase to describe the ambitions of the kings: 5.101.10; 15.24.6) – though that, in the end, was the result. To Polybius, writing forty years later, the events of 200–188 BC sealed the geopolitical unification of the western and eastern halves of the Mediterranean world, and pointed towards the Roman domination of the Mediterranean which was the outstanding political fact of his time. But that was hindsight: in the 190s Rome's victory in the hard-fought war against Philip led merely to an unstable bipolar situation between Rome and Antiochus the Great. Antiochus' invasion of Greece quickly overturned most of the Roman arrangements – arrangements not backed now by force – but this led in turn to a new round of hegemonic war. Out of the new and final round of hegemonic war Rome eventually emerged as the unipolar power. It was, to be sure, a rather surprising ending to the power-transition crisis that began with the faltering of the Ptolemaic regime ca. 207. The question now was, what would Rome do in this new geopolitical situation?

9

Hierarchy and Unipolarity, ca. 188–170 BC

INTRODUCTION

At what point does a state begin to have an empire? Many states in the ancient Mediterranean had contended for power, but no single state had unquestionably and irreversibly eclipsed all others. Rome was eventually the exception. But Rome's secure predominance came rather late in Mediterranean history, only in the mid-second century BC, and it emerged from an unstable, violent, and multipolar interstate system. The great victories won by Rome in 201–188 BC (over Carthage, then Macedon, then the Seleucid Empire, over Hannibal, then Philip V, then Antiochus the Great) established Rome on the path towards secure predominance. By 188 BC Rome had achieved what political scientists call "unipolarity": it was a situation where the Mediterranean world had only one political and military focus, and only one dominant actor; there was a preponderance of power in the hands of a single state; Rome was now the sole remaining superpower.[1] To use the terminology of Kenneth Waltz, hierarchy was now beginning to substitute for anarchy in the Mediterranean world, and states were beginning to become functionally differentiated instead of functionally similar (i.e., militarized); hence from 188 not all polities in European Greece were obsessively

---

[1] For these definitions of unipolarity (admitted to be imprecise): see Mastanduno 1997: 52; cf. Geller and Singer 1998: 114; Evans and Newnham 1998: 500. On the general geopolitics of "unipolarity" – a configuration of power naturally much studied of late – see esp. Kapstein and Mastanduno, eds., 1999 and Ikenberry, ed., 2002.

focused, as they traditionally had been, on the military (see below), while Rome itself was becoming somewhat functionally focused on mediating (from a distance) the conflicts between Greek polities, a process that itself reinforced the evolution of hierarchy.[2]

But one should stress that even predominance and unipolarity do not yet constitute "rule," or an "empire." And one should equally stress that predominance and unipolarity are at their beginnings still unstable and can be reversed – as the United States is now discovering. In this final chapter of our study we will examine the geopolitical situation that existed in the Greek Mediterranean in the two decades following the great victories won over Philip and Antiochus by the coalitions of states headed by Rome, employing for this purpose the theoretical framework of hierarchy, unipolarity, and empire as political scientists have defined these terms. This latter is a procedure rarely pursued among scholars of Mediterranean antiquity. Our conclusion is that this was a period of ambiguity and continued Roman hesitation in the East – though the pressures were clearly beginning to run in one direction.

THE AMBIGUITIES OF UNIPOLARITY

Three phenomena constituted the foundation of the relationship between Rome and the Greek states after 188 BC, and explain why the next twenty years were a period of ambiguity regarding the character of Roman predominance.

First, the Roman Republic emerged from the great wars that had convulsed the Mediterranean at the end of the third century BC by far the strongest single state. Carthage, Macedon, and the Seleucid Empire had all been decisively defeated. The armies of Rome had formed the irreplaceable core of the forces that defeated these powers; that was obviously true in the West, but also true in the East. Without Rome, there would have been little chance of the second-tier Greek states bringing either Philip V or Antiochus III to heel.[3] But now, treaties of peace imposed upon the monarchs had stripped each realm of crucial territory, military resources, military power. At least for the moment, neither monarchy constituted a major competitor for Rome, and the Romans intended that this interstate hierarchy with Rome at the top, established at such a cost in blood and treasure in wars in both the West and the East that had exhausted the Roman state, would be long-lasting.

---

[2]   On functional (militarized) similarity, functional differentiation, and hierarchy, see Waltz 1979: 81 and 114–16; cf. Donnelly 2006: 141.
[3]   See above, Chapter 5.

But second, as in the war against Philip V, so too the victory over Antiochus III had been won by Rome at the head of a large voluntary coalition of Greek states. In this coalition as in the one against Philip V, Rome was politically the indispensable senior partner – organizing, persuading, occasionally restraining; but Rome did act as a partner not a commander, within the alliance and not above it.[4] Indeed, ironic as it may seem to us now, Rome had first appeared in the East as a counter-hegemonic power – the champion of the second-tier major states against the aggression of the great monarchies. And the alliances that Rome formed with the Greeks were not merely for show. Hence at Cynoscephalae in 197, a significant role in the victory over Philip V was played by the Aetolians; similarly at the great sea-battle against the Seleucid fleet at Myonnesus in 190, a decisive role was played by the fleet of the Rhodians, and at Magnesia in 189, the battle that ruined Antiochus III, a decisive role was played by the Pergamene cavalry, whose charge (led personally by Eumenes II) started the collapse of Antiochus' army. Recent assertions that the Romans fought the war against Antiochus essentially alone and without depending on their Greek allies are simply wrong.[5]

That the Romans were able to establish such a successful military coalition with states that were culturally quite different from Rome and with governmental elites that did not even speak the Romans' Latin language was a tremendous diplomatic achievement. There is no doubt that Rome stood at the head of this coalition, both militarily and diplomatically, and that the representatives of the Republic in the East made certain that Rome obtained what it wanted out of the conflicts. But beyond the weight of Roman military power, the other key to this diplomatic success was that the Romans listened to and often accepted the advice of their Greek friends, both with regard to strategy during the wars and in the creation of the geopolitical outcomes after the wars, resulting in outcomes that were relatively congenial to all.[6] To be sure, Polybius says

---

[4] On this sort of diplomatic situation, in contrast with a situation where an imperial power acts from above and outside, see the theoretical discussion of Ingram 2006: 1–2.

[5] Derow 2003: 65. On the significant contributions of Rome's Greek allies to the victory over Philip and then to the victory over Antiochus, see discussion above, Chapter 8.

[6] On Greek influence over both war strategy and geopolitical results against both Philip and then Antiochus, see conveniently Errington 1989a: 267 (on the peace negotiations with Philip in winter 198/197); 270 (the influence of Rhodes and Pergamum on Roman relations with Antiochus); 286 (the influence of Eumenes II on Roman strategy against Antiochus); and 287 (the influence of Rhodes and Pergamum on the peace settlement in Asia Minor in 188). See McShane 1964: 146 and Burton 2003: 359–60 (both emphatic), and cf. above, Chapter 8.

that the final peace settlement at Apamea depended ultimately upon the will of Rome (21.18.2); that was a fact of power. But we also get the extraordinary scene in summer 188, when Eumenes II personally appeared before the Senate (the first reigning Hellenistic king to do so), along with representatives of the Republic of Rhodes, and the *Patres*, having loaded them all with gifts (but especially the king), simply asked Eumenes and the Rhodians what territorial rewards they wished from the victory over Antiochus, promising them anything they desired.[7] Moreover, the speeches of Eumenes and the Rhodian envoys to the Senate, as recorded by Polybius, emphasized to the *Patres* how much the Pergamene and Rhodian military efforts had contributed to the coalition victory. These were proud friends and allies, emphasizing the shared dangers they had all manfully undergone, not submissive *clientes*.[8] The same attitude can be seen from Pergamum three years later in the dispute between Rome and Philip V over the important cities of Aenus and Maronea on the coast of Thrace: the Pergamene envoys claim that either the cities belong to Eumenes II as a rightful reward for his manly actions as an ally of Rome, or, they say, the Romans should be true to their given word at Apamea and let these two cities be totally free; but in no case should they belong to Philip. These, too, are forthright comments, hardly indicative of the submissive attitude of a client.[9]

The major block to the expansion of the power of Pergamum and Rhodes at this point came not so much from the Romans as from the mutual antagonism of these two states. This rivalry, which had been suppressed from 201 BC because of the exigencies of the power-transition crisis in the East, now reemerged to be played out before the Senate, where each ally criticized the other for greed.[10]

---

[7] The scene in the Senate: Polyb. 21.18–24, cf. Livy 37.52.1–56.10, with Walbank 1979: 111–18. The Senate's request to Eumenes and the Rhodians that they state whatever they wished as territorial rewards: Polyb. 21.18.4, 7, and 9.

[8] Shared dangers manfully withstood by Pergamum with the Romans: Polyb. 21.20 *passim*, cf. Livy 37.53.6–19. Eumenes' claim to a moral *right* to large territorial rewards: Polyb. 21.21.4 and 9, cf. Livy 37.53.19–23. The Rhodians' exposition of their services to Rome: Polyb. 21.22.5 and 23.11, cf. Livy 37.54.3 and 54.28.

[9] See Livy 39.27.2–6, based on Polybian material; discussion: Walbank 1940: 233. Neutrality and independence of Aenus and Maronea under the Peace of Apamea: see Livy 39.27.10 with Walbank 1940: 216. Economic importance of these cities: Rostovtzeff 1941: 111. Somewhat different but also interesting here is the sharp tone of Polybius' father Lycortas, as *strategos* of the Achaean League in 184/183, to the Roman envoy Ap. Claudius Pulcher, protesting what he takes to be Roman interference in Achaean internal affairs – namely, Achaean oppression of newly conquered Sparta (Livy 39.36.6–37.17, from Polybian material).

[10] Eumenes' suspicions of the Rhodians, expressed to the *Patres*: Polyb. 21.19, cf. Livy 37.53.1–5; the Rhodians' suspicions of Eumenes: Polyb. 21.22.8–9, cf. Livy 37.54.7 (and *passim*).

The third crucial factor in Roman relations with the Greek states after the Peace of Apamea was the total withdrawal of the Romans back to Italy. In theory, the Senate – as in 196 – could have decided in 188 to turn Greece into a permanent Roman province, a formal and permanent administrative *provincia* ruled by a magistrate sent out periodically from Rome, backed by a garrison of Roman troops. The case for such an arrangement was stronger in 188 than it had been eight years previously, because the Aetolian League had been a primary instigator of Antiochus III's invasion of Greece in 192, and most of central Greece had gone over to the Great King, demonstrating that the system of indirect and loose hegemony established by T. Quinctius Flamininus had utterly failed – had, indeed, shown itself to be a security risk for Rome in the East.[11] But clearly no imposition of direct Roman administration ever crossed the minds of the *Patres* in 188. Nor was the establishment of colonies of Roman or Latin veterans at strategic locations in Greece – a key tool in the Roman structure of control in Italy – ever contemplated.[12] Instead, no Roman generals, no Roman troops, no veterans, no garrisons, no governors, no political overseers, not even any diplomats were left behind in the Greek world when the main Roman armies departed back to Italy in 188.

Again, in theory the Senate could have established Rome at the head of a formal and permanent league of Greek states based on the wartime coalition it had cobbled together against Antiochus in 192/191. The conversion of the ad hoc wartime coalition into a large, permanent, and multifunctional league, where Rome's voice would be the most important voice, would have created a powerful instrument to regulate Greek interstate politics and to exert Roman influence throughout European Greece and the Aegean world. The model for such a league existed, as it had in 196, in the Hellenic Symmachy through which Antigonid Macedon had sought to control Greek politics from the 220s down into the 190s.[13] As in 196, however, the creation of such an institution – and hence Roman involvement on a formal and continuous basis in helping to oversee the interstate politics of European Greece and the Aegean – never seems to have been considered by the *Patres*. Instead,

---

[11] Detailed discussion of the collapse of Flamininus' system in 192/191: see Chapter 8, above.

[12] On the *coloniae* as a key tool to Roman control over Italy, and their absence from Greece, see Sherwin-White 1984: 15. The first Roman *colonia* in Greece is at Corinth in 44 BC – that is, 130 years after the period now under discussion.

[13] Discussion of the Hellenistic tradition of leagues that functioned to exercise the will of the hegemonic state: see above, Chapter 7. And on the quite frequent transformation of wartime coalitions formed to deal with a single catalytic threat into permanent and multifunctional institutions to regulate postwar international life, see Davis 2001: 9–30.

once the threat posed by Antiochus had been defeated, i.e., once the catalytic threat that had led to the formation of the grand coalition in the first place had receded, the coalition was simply allowed to dissolve. Thereafter, individual states that had allied with Rome in the crises of the 190s continued merely as individual states to have good relations with the Republic (though strains soon appeared with Macedon, and to a lesser extent with Achaea).[14] In sum, having disposed of what the *Patres* saw as the major strategic threat posed by Antiochus the Great's invasion of European Greece, and having established what the *Patres* viewed as a congenial international environment in the East in its place, the Romans left the Greeks primarily to themselves.

Indeed, that the Romans in this period were still not all that focused on the world outside of Italy proper is shown by the following remarkable fact: of the seventy consuls between 201 and 166 BC whose assigned spheres of activity (*provinciae*) are known, fifty-seven operated in northern Italy. And this number of fifty-seven includes both consuls in every year between 188 and 172 BC – the very years now under discussion.[15] Moreover, because the Romans after great effort had finally brought the Gallic peoples of the Po Valley under permanent control by 190 BC, the scale of fighting in northern Italy decreased from that point, for only the Ligurians in the far northwest remained a problem. Thus the Italy-centered stance of the Senate in regard to assignments to the consuls could not be more clear.[16] Praetors, men holding the second-highest elected office, did operate outside of Italy as military commanders in the 180s and 170s, and the two assigned to Spain often were involved in heavy fighting. Yet even so, four of the six praetors elected every year did not have assignments in these decades involving significant military activity – and meanwhile *no* praetor (and no consul) was ever assigned to the Greek East.[17]

Now, as J. S. Richardson has remarked, the most regular encounter with foreign and imperial affairs by the men in the Senate was the annual senatorial allocation of *provinciae* in the senatorial debates every spring on that topic. Thus the Roman governing elite most naturally saw imperial power in terms of the presence of a magistrate in a *provincia*.[18]

---

[14] Discussion below.

[15] The Senate termed such assigned spheres of magisterial activity *provinciae*. Hence *provincia* here need not mean a province with a permanent administrative structure and apparatus – though such provinces did exist in the West and were regularly assigned (no such province, of course, existed in the Greek East – see above).

[16] See the comments of Sherwin-White 1984: 11–12.

[17] Praetors with little or no military activity annually: the two praetors who acted as judges in Rome, and the two praetors whose *provinciae* were the permanent provinces of Sicily or Sardinia/Corsica: see Sherwin-White 1984: 13.

[18] Richardson 1979: 6.

And here we face not only the Italy-centered distribution of the *provinciae* of the consuls in the 180s and 170s (see above), but also the fact that *no provincia* – consular or praetorian – was assigned anywhere east of the Adriatic after 187 BC until 171 BC, i.e., for sixteen years. Moreover, after the war against Perseus of Macedon (171–168 BC), no *provincia* was assigned in the East again until 150 BC, i.e., not for *another* seventeen years.

The Romans did leave behind in the East four major states possessing formal treaties with Rome. Three of those treaties, however, were merely peace treaties: with Macedon, with the Seleucid realm, and with Aetolia. In the first two cases, the long-term result of the peace was mere informal *amicitia*.[19] True, the peace treaty with the defeated Aetolian League (189) included explicit statements of Aetolian submission to future senatorial wishes – but this was absolutely unique, at the time and later.[20] And the treaty of alliance between Rome and the Achaean League (probably 192/191) implied that Achaea would in the future follow Rome into war.[21] In fact, however, none of these treaties, not even the Aetolian one, acted as a real restraint upon Greek action. As far as we know, the Romans had no interaction with the Aetolians for a decade and a half after the swearing of the peace treaty. And the lack of postwar Roman interaction with the Seleucid government was similar (see below). Meanwhile, the Achaeans conquered the Peloponnese outright in 191–188 BC, including their great enemy Sparta, though the Romans were uncomfortable with this.[22] Thereafter the Senate sought to moderate Achaean oppression of Sparta, but was only somewhat successful; and when in 183–182 the Messenians in the southwest Peloponnese rebelled against Achaean overlordship as well, the League simply suppressed Messene by war, despite a senatorial refusal to give the Achaeans support.[23]

---

[19]   Despite some scholars, it is clear that Macedon possessed no treaty of alliance with Rome, only a treaty of peace: see Gruen 1973.

[20]   The Aetolian treaty contained a clause requiring the Aetolians henceforth to support "the *dynasteia* and *arché* of the Roman people" (Polyb. 21.32.2). There was also a clause, quite traditional in treaties among Greek states, that the Aetolians would have the same friends and enemies as Rome (Polyb. 21.32.4: see Gruen 1984: 27–8). These strictures in the peace treaty arose from the fact that from the Roman point of view the Aetolian League had not simply been an enemy state but a treacherous ally (see above, Chapter 8).

[21]   Date of the Achaean–Roman treaty of alliance: see Badian 1952.

[22]   See above, Chapter 8.

[23]   For a detailed account of the oppressive Achaean relations both with Sparta and Messene, combined with a nuanced discussion of Roman inability truly to effect a more moderate Achaean policy, see Gruen 1984: 481–96, far preferable to the version of Roman "rule" over Achaea found in Derow 2003: 66–7.

Otherwise, the Romans possessed only informal friendships, no treaties at all, with states east of the Adriatic, and they could not invoke legal obligations – not that legal obligations per se carried great weight among any of these Hellenistic polities.[24] It is the case, of course, that refusal to annex, as in this geopolitical situation, is in itself no proof of reluctance to control.[25] But the desire for intense control then needs to be proven. Here, the facts are that the Senate after 188 not only depended predominantly on informal influence, on "sway," to have its wishes followed in the East, but, most importantly, the *Patres* seem to have had few such wishes. This was the same Roman stance we have seen before, in maritime Illyris from 230 onward and in European Greece after 194. It was an arrangement that only worked when the geopolitical desires of the unipolar power were minimal, and when its goal was primarily negative – that is, simply to prevent the rise of threats – rather than anything more ambitious, let alone the desire to shape in a continuous manner the course of Greek interstate politics.[26]

For these reasons, while one may think of the Romans as having achieved by 188 a position of unipolarity as the sole remaining superpower, they had not yet an empire. The winning of the great wars at the end of the third century and the beginning of the second certainly did not lead to the same results for all the partners in the coalition.[27] The main result was a seismic shift in the distribution of power across the Mediterranean state-system in favor of Rome – a systemic shock that simultaneously affected all actors within the interstate system. Yet that system of states continued truly to exist and to function as an interstate system, although (simultaneously) Rome now dominated the geopolitical terrain, and its superior military capabilities allowed the Senate the possibility of advancing Roman interests strongly almost anywhere in the Mediterranean and on whatever issues the *Patres* wished.[28]

[24] On treaties, though sworn to the gods, as having minimal impact on pragmatic state decision-making in the ancient Mediterranean, see, e.g., Wheeler 1984: esp. 255–6 (with sources); admitted even by Adcock and Mosley 1975: 222, and Bederman 2001: 179; and see above, Chapter 3.

[25] The famous maxim of Robinson and Gallagher 1953: 3.

[26] Writing of this period, Badian – like Robinson and Gallagher – warns that non-annexation does not necessarily mean non-intervention (1968: 4); but the warning is obviated here because in the twenty years under discussion, Roman intervention in the Greek world was minimal. As Kallet-Marx remarks (1995: 5): "Even the power to compel submission does not necessarily imply its use." The nature of the goals of the unipolar state is crucial.

[27] A common enough outcome in coalition wars: see Aron 1973: 44.

[28] For this formulation of the geopolitical impact produced by unipolarity, see Mastanduno and Kapstein 1999: 1.

The new reality was obvious to Greek statesmen, as numerous statements in Polybius and other sources indicate.[29] Recent assertions, however, that already by 188 there was nothing left for the Greeks to do but to obey Rome, or that from 188 onwards Rome was "the controller of the Greek states," are highly exaggerated.[30] Polybius himself places the emergence of such a situation only a generation later, after 168/167.[31]

There are several reasons why we should accept Polybius' judgment here. First, Rome in the 180s and 170s had many direct responsibilities in the West, including in Spain and northern Italy, where we see the consuls and praetors regularly employed; by contrast, Rome still had no direct responsibilities in the East, which is precisely why we see no consuls or praetors employed there. To the Romans, the Greek Mediterranean now constituted a large constellation of friendly but independent states, and this was a situation which the Senate evidently found satisfactory.[32]

Thus in European Greece there was relative peace in the 180s and 170s, except for the war between the Achaean League and Messene, and Philip V's large-scale conquests in inland Thrace.[33] This relative peace stands in striking contrast to the constant interstate warfare that had beset Greece throughout the third century BC, and there is obviously a connection between Roman predominance and the relative peace that prevailed.[34] Though Rome interfered neither with Philip V's

---

[29]   See Polyb. 21.23.4, 22.3.2, 22.24.11–13; cf. Plut. *Flam.* 16.4, with Richardson 1979: 7; Gruen 1984: 329–34.

[30]   Derow 2003: 65–6; cf. Dahlheim 1977: 117 ("ein Verhalten aufzwingen . . . die die Griechen an den politischen Willen Roms gebunden hatten"); Hammond, in Hammond and Walbank 1988: 502–3 (the quote in the text); or Reiter 1987: 118–19 (Roman policy after 188 was an intentional scheme "designed . . . to make Greece subservient to Roman will"). Mandell 1989 puts the establishment of unbreakable Roman rule over the Greeks even earlier: with, paradoxically, Flamininus' proclamation of "the Freedom of the Greeks" in 196 (see above, Chapter 7). Harris 1979: 161 n. 3, asserts that violence and the threat of it were the foundation of Roman policy in Greece – true enough as far as it goes, and true of almost all ancient states, including those with which Rome interacted (see Eckstein 2006: Chs. 4, 5, and 6), but misleading in terms of the complexities and ambiguities of our period.

[31]   Polyb. 3.4.2–3, cf. 1.1.5 and 6.2.3. See discussion below.

[32]   On the consistent Roman avoidance of committment in the East, see Gruen 1984: Chs. 1 and 2; and of course above, Chapters 2, 3, 7, and 8. On the Senate in this period as consistently in favor of almost any status quo local situation in the East, though such situations varied widely, see Sherwin-White 1977: 66.

[33]   Though Philip's conquests in Thrace added much to the potential power of Macedon (see Hammond, in Hammond and Walbank 1988: 468–71), the Senate showed absolutely no interest.

[34]   On the constant wars of the third century, see the bitter comment of Polyb. 5.106.1–5, with Eckstein 2006: Ch. 4. On the beginnings of "the Roman Peace" under the Republic – a characteristic of this period which is crucial but not often noted – see Cornell 1993: 154–60.

large war of expansion in Thrace, nor in the Achaean–Messenian War, it is clear that other conflicts between Greek states were often taken to the Senate now, rather than settled by arms. Polybius is explicit that the Senate preferred this (though, equally, senatorial responses and subsequent actions were not always effectual).[35] Good examples of the phenomenon of consulting Rome are the multiple embassies sent to the Senate in the mid-180s by states threatened by Philip (instead of their attempted creation, say, of a new anti-Macedonian military alliance); or the multiple embassies the Spartans sent to Rome to protest their mistreatment by the Achaean League, which had included the exiling and even judicial execution of many Spartan leaders. Indeed, the Spartans sent so many embassies of complaint that the *Patres* eventually tired of issuing statements to the Achaeans on the matter.[36]

The Roman interventions in the continuing imbroglio between Achaea and Sparta were more than a typical Hellenistic foreign arbitration of a Greek internal dispute.[37] Rather, the Senate – and/or, important senators – sought a Roman right to judge and pressure Achaean actions, i.e., to assert political hierarchy. But Roman conduct here was, simultaneously, less than the oppressive or treacherous assertion of imperial might that some scholars have suggested.[38]

Three aspects stand out. First, the Romans sought to soften Achaean rule at Sparta, e.g., through urging the return of various groups of Spartan exiles, or preventing future judicial execution of Spartans at Achaean hands; but Rome did not seek to end Achaean rule there. Second, insofar as the Senate was not merely responding politely to specific and varied Spartan pleas for help, through the making of a gesture (so Polybius thought: 24.10.11), the *Patres* were in fact offering the Achaean government good advice; the measures Rome advocated might well have led to better relations between the Spartans and their Achaean overlords, and therefore defused the problem. Perhaps it was this same spirit that (in part) led Q. Marcius Philippus to urge the Achaeans in 183 to delay resorting to war against the rebellious Messenians and to refer matters to the Senate instead (Polyb. 24.9.13). Third, whatever their intent, Roman interventions in Peloponnesian affairs in the 180s were for the most part ineffective. The Achaean government throughout the 180s

---

[35] "The Romans were displeased if all matters were not submitted to them": Polyb. 23.17.4; but note that the context is senatorial acquiescence in the Achaean victory in the war with Messene. Ineffectual responses: ibid.; cf. also Polyb. 24.9 *passim* (opinion of Callicrates), cf. 24.8.1–6 (opinion of Lycortas), and 24.10.11–12 (opinion of Polybius himself).

[36] See Polyb. 23.9.11, with Gruen 1984: 491–2.

[37] Despite Gruen 1984: 490. On Hellenistic arbitration, see Ager 1996.

[38] See, e.g., Derow 1989: 295, and 2003: 66.

consistently stood its ground against Roman complaints about Achaea's oppressive behavior towards Sparta and Messene, and there were no repercussions. Q. Marcius Philippus' advice to refer the Messenian issue to Rome was ignored by the Achaean Council – with no ill effects, as Achaea then went on to wage a successful war against Messene, suppressing the rebellion by military force. Polybius' father Lycortas was the most successful Achaean commander in this war, and the brutality of Lycortas' tactics shocked even his son (Polyb. 23.15).[39] The Roman response to the news of the eventual Achaean victory over Messene was not angry but, on the contrary, conciliatory: the status quo was immediately accepted and the Achaeans were assured that Rome had indeed done its part as an ally, by forbidding any war-materials going from Italy to rebels against the League (Polyb. 23.17.3). Only in 180 – and it was not by Roman initiative – did the Senate begin to exercise somewhat more influence in Achaean internal politics, but even in the 170s, Roman interest and interference in Achaean politics did not go far (see below). The Romans here were certainly *not* "exercising their power to decide things."[40]

Nevertheless, all these embassies from Greece seeking Roman mediation or arbitration of local conflicts constituted a new diplomatic phenomenon, a new method for dealing with Greek interstate conflict – by recourse to Rome. To be sure, European Greek states in this period also appealed occasionally to polities other than Rome for mediation or arbitration of disputes.[41] Rome, however, received the majority of such appeals, and the tone of Roman responses to those appeals was strikingly authoritarian – even when those Roman responses were not in fact followed. Such embassies can be traced back to the crucial Greek embassies of winter 201/200, and to those that came to the Senate from Rome's Greek allies several times during the subsequent war with Philip (see, e.g., Polyb. 18.10.8–11.1); they soon became a habit. In European Greece they certainly became a less destructive means than traditional warfare as a way of dealing with interstate conflicts, but these embassies were also increasingly a recognition of the new prevailing

---

[39] See Polyb. 23.15, with Walbank 1979: 247.
[40] Despite Derow 2003: 66.
[41] Thus Megara mediated issues between Boeotia and the Achaean League (187/186): see Ager 1996: 280–1 (no. 105), with sources; Rhodian judges attempted an arbitration of a conflict between Amphissa and Delphi in 179: see Ager 1996: 314–17 (no. 117); Rhodian judges arbitrated a dispute ca. 175 between the Achaean League and Eumenes II of Pergamum concerning the scale of honors to which Eumenes was entitled in Achaea: Polyb. 28.7.8–13 with Ager 1996: 319–20 (no. 119).

hierarchy, of Rome's unique status, and a recognition of a specific function (the amelioration of local warfare) that Rome now fulfilled within that hierarchy. Hence this type of interaction between the European Greek states and Rome in the two decades after Apamea corresponds well to Waltz's description of interstate hierarchy as a situation in which "the actors are functionally differentiated according to their degrees of authority" and there is a "social division of labor among units specializing in different tasks."[42] In other words, Rome in relation to the European Greek states had an increasingly recognized and special function within the new system. This was a function, the amelioration of interstate disputes, which the Greek states still occasionally practiced with each other; but it was a function which they, in turn, did not have with regard to Rome (the amelioration of Rome's interstate disputes).[43]

It is also the case, however, that the farther away from Italy events – including major interstate conflicts – were occurring, the less was the Romans' interest in them; the more peripheral to events the Romans were; and the less effective was any Roman intervention. Roman interactions with the states of Asia Minor and the Levant, farther away from Italy than European Greece, were thus less frequent in this period and had less impact than Roman interactions with the states of Greece.[44]

For a full decade after the Peace of Apamea in 188, Asia Minor was dominated by the wars of Eumenes II of Pergamum with his rivals: first with the Gauls (189–187), then with Prusias I of Bithynia (185–183), and then finally with an anti-Pergamene coalition led by Pharnaces I of Cappadocia (182–179). These wars were large in scale, and Eumenes always emerged victorious from them. He did not depend upon Roman help for his victories. The attitude taken by Eumenes towards Rome was not that of a subject or a client, but that of an independent and powerful friend. We have already noted the frank tone the Pergamene envoys adopted at the conference at Thessalonica in 185 concerning the cities of Aenus and Maronea on the Thracian coast, seized by Philip V in violation of the Peace of Apamea: the Romans should either set the cities free, or give them to Eumenes himself, as a just reward for his

---

[42] Waltz 1979: 81, 114.

[43] On the importance of the action of weaker states in recognizing the special status of the state with unsurpassed power, and thus their role in constituting the new interstate order, see Buzan 2004: 69, and Donnelly 2006: 153.

[44] Cf. the general theoretical statement of Donnelly 2006: 144: "At any given time, different parts of international relations, defined by substance, geography or particular relationships, may lie at very different points" in relation to a unipolar power.

efforts as an ally against Philip and then against Antiochus. These are not the words of emissaries from a submissive client-state.[45]

Similarly, Roman constraints on Eumenes' power in Galatia after he defeated the Gallic tribes were in reality minimal.[46] And while there was an attempt by Rome, at both sides' request, to mediate the war between Prusias and Eumenes in 183, the results of that attempted mediation are unclear. In any case the outcome of the war itself was evidently determined by Pergamene military advantage, and was celebrated at Pergamum as a major military victory. Rome's attempted mediation of the war between Eumenes and the coalition led by Pharnaces of Pontus that immediately followed the Pergamene victory over Bithynia was, in turn, a humiliating failure, with Pharnaces dismissing all Roman suggestions of compromise. The ultimate result occurred on the battlefield – and was another Pergamene victory. As a result of this sequence of victories, the Attalid capital was adorned with new victory-monuments (including the gigantic Altar of Zeus which now stands in the Pergamum Museum in Berlin), and the government instituted a major new festival honoring Athena-Bringer-of-Victory, to whose inauguration the entire Hellenistic world was invited.[47] By the mid-170s, Pergamene armies were marching all the way east to the frontiers of Syria, where they had never appeared before, in order to put a Pergamene candidate (Antiochus IV) on the Seleucid throne at Antioch. The Romans did not interfere – and may not even have been aware of the Pergamene action at the time. One result of this Pergamene success was a formal military alliance between Antiochus and Pergamum (Polyb. 30.30.4 and 7). This was a startling reversal of status between Pergamum and the Seleucids, since, as we have seen (above, Chapter 8), the Seleucid monarchs had traditionally viewed the Attalids as mere rebellious provincial governors. The rise in Pergamene power came about in part because of the Attalid alliance with Rome, but also in part because of the heroic battlefield successes of Attalus I and now Eumenes II – as the Pergamene kings made clear both to their subjects and to the world at large.[48]

---

[45]   Livy 39.27.2–5, derived from Polybian material; see above, this chapter. On the frank tone often taken by Greek friends of Rome, see Burton 2003. Aenus and Maronea were eventually set free – though not before Philip arranged a massacre at Maronea in response to the Roman decision (Polyb. 22.14.6, cf. 23.8.2). Yet the Senate did nothing about it. And by 171 both Aenus and Maronea were somehow back under Macedonian control: see the comments of Hansen 1971: 107.

[46]   Discussion in Mitchell 1993: 210–12.

[47]   On the Nicephoria Festival, see Hansen 1971: 104, with sources. Eumenes' letter to the Aetolian League announcing the Festival (*Syll.*[3].629) is noteworthy for its tone of military triumph.

[48]   Eumenes' march to the Taurus provided crucial help to put Antiochus IV on the Seleucid throne: see App. *Syr.* 45 and *OGIS* 248, with McShane 1964: 163–4.

Similarly again, modern scholars often make much of a senatorial letter sent to the Rhodians ca. 177, scolding them about their oppression of the Lycians, who had come under Rhodian control as a result of the Peace of Apamea. This letter, scholars often allege, is an example of Roman treachery and imperialist ambition against an ally who was now perceived at Rome as being over-powerful.[49] But we should stress that the practical impact of the senatorial letter to Rhodes was nil, and the Rhodians continued to oppress the Lycians, often very violently, for another full decade after receiving it – and without any Roman protest or interference. In fact, the letter of 177 was probably merely a polite gesture by the *Patres* in response to the passionate speech of the Lycian envoy Nicoratus, begging for help – the type of gesture that Polybius thought typical of senatorial action of this period. This explains Cato the Elder's opinion in 167 BC that before the war with Perseus (171–168), the Rhodians had enjoyed *libertas*, a condition which they understandably wished to preserve.[50] Regarding states even farther away from Italy, the Roman lack of interest after 188 is even clearer: the Seleucid court was not sent an embassy from the Senate between 188 and 172 (that is, not for sixteen years) – except for a single courtesy call by Flamininus in 183.[51] And as for Egypt, the Ptolemies were sent not a single embassy by the Senate between 200 and 173 BC – that is, not for fully twenty-seven years (!).[52]

None of this – not Pergamum, not Rhodes, not the Seleucids, not Egypt – can be seen as constituting "Roman control of the East."[53] If the men in the Roman Senate followed any overall policy, it was to maintain the basic status quo and the balance of power among the Greek states which they had been the primary (but not sole) force in establishing in 188. And the reason the Senate wished to do this was because it left Rome free to deal with what the *Patres* saw as more pressing military issues in the West.[54]

---

[49]   The letter: Polyb. 25.4.1–5; Livy 41.6.8–12; and App. *Mithr.* 62. Romans as treacherous: Schmitt 1957: 134–72; Liebmann-Frankfort 1969: 96–8; Deininger 1971: 184–91; Errington 1972: 192–4 and 249–53; Berthold 1984: 177; Derow 1989: 302 and 2003: 67.

[50]   Cato *ORF*, frg. 164. See the convincing analysis of the senatorial letter of 177 in Gruen 1975: 66–7. Polybius' comments on the senatorial habit of making gestures in response to suppliants: 24.10.11–12, cf. 24.8.1–6 and 24.9 *passim*: above, this chapter, and n. 34.

[51]   In discussing the attempted mediation of the Pergamene–Bithynian war by Flamininus in 183, Polybius mentions in passing that he was also scheduled to visit Seleucus (23.5.1). Courtesy call: so Gruen 1984: 646 n. 169 (convincing).

[52]   No Roman diplomatic contact with the Ptolemies: see Lampela 1998: 97–110.

[53]   Despite Hammond, in Hammond and Walbank 1988: 502–3, and the other scholars cited in n. 30, above.

[54]   For a great power that is still essentially peripheral to a system to limit itself to seeking to maintain balances of power within that system is common (and efficient): see Sheehan 1996: 69–70.

And here it is important to understand that while the victory over Antiochus did not lead to the same results for all partners in the anti-Antiochus coalition, since the main result of the victory was a major shift of the Mediterranean balance of power in Rome's favor, the victory had nevertheless also increased the power of the second-tier major states that were Rome's allies. Even Derow admits that many Greek statesmen in the postwar period sought to interact with Rome on a basis of *isologia*: equality.[55] Many were quite successful in doing this – as the examples of Achaea, Pergamum, and Rhodes demonstrate (see above). And not only had the power of these second-tier states increased in absolute terms by 188 (true especially of Achaea, Pergamum, and Rhodes, all of which now enjoyed greatly expanded territory and resources as a result of their success in recent wars), but it is also clear that although Rome had gained greatly in power relative both to Macedon and the Seleucids and to the second-tier states as well, the second-tier states themselves had also grown greatly in power relative to both Macedon and the Seleucids. The latter two monarchies had been the immediate and pressing problem ca. 200. This means that the security problems facing many Greek states in their immediate locales were far less pressing in 188 BC than those problems had been in 200. That is: both their power and their security situation had greatly improved.[56]

In sum, the geopolitical situation in the East was still fluid. Moreover, although Rome had now achieved unipolarity, situations of unipolarity have, historically, often been temporary, in the sense of lasting only fifteen or twenty years: they have tended to revert from unipolarity back into multipolarity far more commonly than they have proceeded forward from unipolarity into hegemony and empire.[57] One of the primary propositions of Kenneth Waltz, the leading theoretician of contemporary Realism, is in fact that unipolarity tends to be brief: for the achieved preponderance of one state tends to provoke balancing behavior on the part of other states.[58]

---

[55] Derow 2003: 66.

[56] As political scientists note, it is only natural that successful war-coalitions lead to improved status, interstate capabilities, and security situations for all members of the coalition: Davis 2001: 6. A parallel is the improved security situations of lesser states in Europe after the Cold War: see Schweller 1999: 37. The defeated Seleucids, however, eventually regained wide power, as is proven by Antiochus IV's massive invasion of Ptolemaic Egypt in 169. Antigonid Macedon, defeated in 197, was by 188 in a similar position of gradually regaining a large capacity for action: see Hammond, in Hammond and Walbank 1988: 453–87.

[57] Discussion in Wilkinson 1999. The proposed time-scale of the alleged "unipolar moment": see now Layne 2006: 264 n. 1, with references to earlier studies.

[58] Waltz 1979 and 1993; cf. Layne 1993 and 2006 (esp. 143), and Posen and Ross 1996: 123–4 and 132.

Political scientists in the late 1990s came to question the idea of inherent balancing against unipolarity, however, for it seemed that balancing against the unipolar position achieved by the United States through its victory over the Soviet Union in the Cold War was not occurring. Contrary to Waltz, these scholars therefore asserted that unipolarity, once achieved, is relatively easy to maintain, and likely to be long-enduring.[59] If that is the case, if unipolarity once achieved is relatively easy to maintain, then the Roman accomplishment after 188 BC – the maintenance of Rome's unipolar position, followed over time by a transition into hegemony and empire – would still be very substantial; but it would also appear in a somewhat lesser light than if the Waltz balancing hypothesis is correct.

But now, at the time of writing, the situation looks quite different. In part because of what seem major policy mistakes made by the administration of George W. Bush (especially the war in Iraq), American power appears to many political scientists (though not all) to be weakening across the global system; meanwhile, balancing behavior against the United States – led by Russia, China, and Iran, but including even Venezuela – is becoming an increasingly important factor in international relations.[60] This interpretation of recent events is still controversial.[61] But if counterbalancing is in fact the more frequent trajectory in situations of unipolarity, or if a position of unipolarity is not relatively easy to maintain but the trend is back towards multipolarity, as Waltz hypothesized and as recent analyses are beginning to suggest, then the Roman achievement after 188 BC appears enormously greater.

The recent American experience that unipolarity can be unstable thus raises the question of why effective balancing did not occur against Rome in the period of still-unstable unipolarity lasting from 188 BC down at least to 168/167 BC. Some Greeks clearly hoped that a Greek state would arise that was powerful enough to be a peer competitor to Rome, or that a coalition of Greek states would emerge to balance Roman power.[62]

---

[59] See Wohlforth 1999 and 2002, the articles in Kapstein and Mastanduno, eds., 1999, and the declarations in Mastanduno and Kapstein 1999: 5 and 9–10.

[60] Mastanduno 1997: 88, had earlier warned that American attempts to exercise power unilaterally and arbitrarily could call forth balancing conduct: the stability of unipolarity depended on the quality of human decision-making by the elite of the unipolar power. Meanwhile, the Waltzian theorist Charles Layne predicted in 1993 that US unipolarity would give way to multipolarity by 2010 at the latest (Layne 1993: 7) – a prediction that appears correct at this point.

[61] For arguments that balancing against American power is still not occurring, see Lieber and Alexander 2005.

[62] This is the prophecy attributed by Phlegon of Tralles (second century AD) to Antisthenes the Peripatetic at the time of the Antiochene War; discussion and sources in Gauger 1980.

But perhaps as early as the destruction of Macedon in 168/167, Rome achieved what Wohlforth has called the "threshold" or "tipping point," where the power of the strongest state becomes so strong that the costs of military counterbalancing seem prohibitive. The consequence of that realization is that political opposition itself also comes to seem increasingly useless.[63] That was Polybius' analysis of the Mediterranean situation after 168/167 BC. Yet for a generation, between 188 and 168, this did not necessarily appear to be the case in the Greek East, and it is this period we are discussing.

The distribution of power across the interstate system helps shape the behavior of states; Thucydides was the first analyst to recognize this.[64] And unipolarity shaped the behavior of the governing elites of the Greek states after 188. Greek governments recognized the reality of Roman preponderance, recognized the high costs of challenging it, and tended to adapt themselves to the situation. But while insecurity in relation to Rome had increased, the security dilemma created by Roman power was balanced by the fact that unipolarity itself made many Greek states within the unipolar structure more secure against local threats and competitors, and that certain Greek states had dramatically increased in power. That is, Rome's unipolarity provided important benefits both to the interstate system and to specific Greek governments – governments whose primary concern had always been threats from their neighbors.[65] Thus it is not an accident that great wars between the more powerful Greek polities were less frequent after 188 BC than they were before. But such wars did not disappear altogether, and it is an interesting fact that the less interest the Senate took in a region of the Greek world, the more frequent and destructive such wars were.[66]

And so the Greek states still maintained significant capacity for independent action. Sometimes this capacity was achieved through the mustering of internal military resources, a process political scientists call "internal balancing." Polybius praises Philip V for following such a

---

[63] Wohlforth 2002: 103–4.
[64] On Thucydides and the founding of international systems theory, see conveniently Eckstein 2003.
[65] See above, this chapter, pp. 350–6.
[66] On the receding of wars between powerful states as a characteristic of unipolarity, see Mastanduno and Kapstein 1999: 22. Greece received more Roman diplomatic attention between 188 and 171 than areas farther east, and it was quite peaceful; as we have noted, Asia Minor after 188, where Roman interest was only very intermittently visible, saw widespread warfare, just as in the third century (and see below); and by 169 Ptolemaic Egypt and Seleucid Syria, which received almost no Roman attention, were involved in a large-scale war (see below).

policy from ca. 196 BC onwards – for it was a policy that significantly strengthened Macedon.[67] Governments could also seek some room for geopolitical maneuver through the cultivation of regional alliances – such as the one between Achaea and Ptolemaic Egypt.[68] Indeed, in 185 Apollonidas of Sicyon could say in the Council of the Achaean League that "most of our deliberations, and the most important of those deliberations, concern our points of difference with the kings" (Polyb. 22.7.6–7). To Greek statesmen, the world after 188 was still not yet completely Rome-dominated.[69]

At Rome the handling of issues involving the Greeks was primarily the work of the Senate. The Senate heard embassies from the Greek states, and occasionally sent out commissions to the East to investigate or to remonstrate; the Roman People were involved only at the point of declaring war, and this occurred with a Greek state only once in our period, at the very end (with Macedon in 171). The *Patres* expected to be deferred to by Greek polities if the Senate had specific wishes – and if deference was not shown, there was resentment. But except in one case (Macedon) such resentment never led to military intervention. In addition, the Senate wanted disputes between Greek states, and eventually even some disputes *within* Greek states, to be referred to Rome (Polyb. 23.17.4: a criticism by Polybius) – but in many cases the *Patres* as a whole then shifted decisions either to a panel of a few senators or to Greek mediators. The issue, then, was recognition of Roman status, recognition of the hierarchy, not the pure exercise of Roman control.[70]

This is because to the Romans, the widespread existence of *libertas* did not eliminate hierarchy, nor did it eliminate the natural deference expected to be shown by the less powerful to the *dignitas* and *auctoritas* of the more powerful. The concepts were not contradictory, and they structured Roman understanding of international relations in this period.[71] But Roman desire for deference was also not the same as the ruthless exercise of superior power in the service of extending empire,

---

[67]   See Polyb. 15.10. Similar information on the recovery of Macedonian power is provided by Livy 39.24.1–4, based on Polybian material but given a negative evaluation from the Roman perspective. On the phenomenon of "internal balancing," see Waltz 1979: 118 and 168; cf. Waltz 2000: 28.

[68]   On the renewal of the Achaean–Ptolemaic treaty of alliance, see Polyb. 22.7–9. On coalition-building as "external balancing," see Waltz 1979: 118, 168; Layne 2006: 143.

[69]   For the date of Apollonidas' statement, see Walbank 1979: 189.

[70]   See Yoshimura 1984: 4 and n. 16; cf. also Linderski 1995, and Rosenstein 2007: 227–9.

[71]   Good discussion in Yoshimura 1984: 1–3.

expanding stern and continuous control.[72] Political scientists have observed that great powers generally seek to rule the interstate system, or (to put it less harshly) seek to enforce order upon the interstate system, either through coercion of the recalcitrant or through the providing of positive incentives; the nature of the positive incentives can vary widely, and coercion, too, covers a wide spectrum of behavior, from mere threats all the way to punitive action.[73] But not only did the Senate never offer inducements to the occasionally recalcitrant Greek governments it faced between 188 and 171, but on the spectrum of possible coercive behavior towards the recalcitrant what we see in European Greece in this period are only (1) the senatorial decisions in the immediate aftermath of Apamea against Philip V's continuing hold over several small Greek states outside the traditional boundaries of Macedon that were unwilling to be under his rule, and (2) some statements to the Achaean League about Sparta that could be taken as threats (though words were all they were). Meanwhile, elsewhere in European Greece as well as east of the Aegean there was nothing on either spectrum.

This complex situation meant that many Greek statesmen walked a tightrope, complying with the Romans when necessary while retaining as much freedom of action as possible – for retention of significant freedom *was* possible. Polybius directly addresses this political problem in his depiction of a debate ca. 184 BC between the Achaean statesmen Philopoemen and Aristaenus on how to retain Achaean honor and independence in the face of Roman power (24.11–13). Aristaenus urges that the Achaeans should quickly give in when confronted by any serious Roman demand, since resistance will ultimately be futile anyway and will serve only to anger the Romans (and to no purpose, since ultimately it will not work). By contrast, Philopoemen is for fighting for one's legal rights as stipulated in the Achaean treaty with Rome, which is a treaty based on legal equality, and only bending to Roman demands at the last moment, when it is clear that the Romans are absolutely serious about something. Modern political scientists describe this as employing a treaty of alliance as a "pact of restraint" – a pact of restraint upon the behavior of the more powerful alliance-partner in an asymmetrical alliance.[74] Polybius prefers Philopoemen's position on how to handle the Romans, but he does not think Aristaenus' position is dishonorable, since

[72] Rosenstein 2007: 227–9, suggests that the Roman concern for status arose in part because Roman military resources, while large, were never sufficient to impose Roman will everywhere by direct force. Hence public acquiescence in Rome's superior status was seen as an acceptable alternative.
[73] Basic here is now Gortzak 2005: 664–8.
[74] See Press-Barnathan 2006: 272 and 282–4.

Aristaenus' purpose, too, is ultimately to retain as much Achaean independence as possible (24.13.8–10). The Achaean historian obviously intended his discussion here to carry a lesson to Greek governing elites: he meant to praise those Greek leaders who can accomplish, in various ways, the difficult task of maintaining their state's independence while also accepting (as exercises in responsible governing) the occasional acts of compliance required by Roman preponderance.[75]

THE FAILURE OF THE GREEK STATES TO BALANCE AGAINST ROME

The Roman government, as the unipolar power, faced a different task: how to pursue its own interests without triggering the creation of a backlash coalition against it. The most important player in the system, its goal was above all to maintain the interstate hierarchy and the relatively unthreatening international environment which the great victories of 201–188 had created for Rome both in the western and eastern Mediterranean. This task was accomplished, and eventually Roman unipolarity became a stable, unchallengeable fact of interstate life.[76] The question, again, is: how did Rome do it? How did Rome avoid Greek counterbalancing at a point when unipolarity was still relatively unstable and counterbalancing might have been effective?[77]

One explanation is that counterbalancing against a unipolar power is inherently difficult. Different states have differing and often conflicting interests; it is hard for them to coordinate an effort against a hegemon or potential hegemon in a timely fashion; it is hard for them even to overcome local quarrels – local quarrels which ordinarily loom larger in people's minds than the actions of a potential hegemon – in order to

---

[75] For the conundrum faced by weaker states in a unipolar structure which nevertheless wish to remain independent, see Mastanduno and Kapstein 1999: 6. For Polybius' praise of Greek statesmen able to walk this tightrope, see Eckstein 1995: Ch. 7. On the date and authenticity of the debate between Philopoemen and Aristaenus in Polyb. 24.11–13, see Walbank 1979: 264–5.

[76] For the goal of maintaining unipolarity as the main goal of the unipolar power in such geopolitical situations, see Joffe 1995: 101; Mastanduno and Kapstein 1999: 6–7.

[77] To repeat: if unipolarity is inherently fragile because it naturally calls forth counterbalancing by the less powerful states (so Waltz), then this was a tremendous Roman political achievement. And even if unipolarity tends to be relatively stable (though the American example can no longer be adduced to show this, as it previously often has been), the Roman achievement was still significant, for the Romans did not throw away their opportunity.

cooperate at all.[78] Thus if Macedon, Pergamum, Rhodes, and Achaea, the dominant local powers in the Aegean in the 180s–170s, had found a way to cooperate, such a coalition might have been a very significant counterweight to Rome. But the recent growth in the power of Pergamum, Rhodes, and Achaea was owed in great part to their having been allies of Rome itself, so the benefits of a pro-Roman stance to these governments were obvious. Only the government of Macedon was dissatisfied with the post-Apamea situation, for Philip V believed that he had been shortchanged in territorial rewards for his part in the victory of the anti-Seleucid coalition.[79] But here the problem was that neither the Achaean League nor Pergamum had good relations with Macedon. The Attalids and the Antigonids were hereditary enemies and remained bitter and mutually suspicious competitors, while many Achaeans (including Polybius) considered Macedon as great a threat to Achaean independence in the 180s and 170s as Rome was. And meanwhile, Pergamum and Rhodes were, themselves, as we have seen, hereditary rivals. Indeed, in the 170s the Attalid regime may have had a hand in stirring up trouble for Rhodes in Lycia on the southern coast of Asia Minor, control of which Rhodes had received at Apamea. Coalition-building among such states was not easy to attain.[80]

Yet despite the inherent difficulties of coalition-building, successful counterbalancing against hegemons and potential hegemons had been a common practice among the Greek states for the previous 250 years: against Athens in the fifth century; against Sparta and then Thebes in the fourth century; against Macedon in the late fourth and then in the third century; and against the coalition of Philip V and Antiochus III after 203/202 BC.[81] In the latter case, the threat had been so obvious that even the hereditary rivals Pergamum and Rhodes had been driven into military alliance against it.[82] Indeed, Rhodes, Pergamum, and

---

[78]   On the difficulties inherent in counterbalancing, see Waltz 1979: 105; Mearsheimer 2001: 341–45; Davis 2001: 7. On the importance of local rivalries as an obstacle to counterbalancing, see Mearsheimer 2001: 155–62; Wohlforth 2002: 107; Walt 2002: 137.

[79]   For the dispute between Philip and the Senate over the extent of his territorial rewards after 188, see conveniently Hammond, in Hammond and Walbank 1988: 455–72 (with sources). Permanent rewards to Macedon included, however, the regaining of the important city of Demetrias (ibid.: 475–6), but Philip wanted more.

[80]   On the bitter dispute between Philip and Eumenes II in 186–183 over Macedonian control of the cities of Aenus and Maronea in Thrace, see above, this chapter. On continued Achaean fear of Macedon in the 180s and 170s, see Walbank 2002c. On Rhodian accusations of Pergamene interference in Lycia, which embittered Attalid–Rhodian relations in the 170s, see McShane 1964: 174 and n. 84, and Hansen 1971: 109–10.

[81]   Discussion in Eckstein 2006: Chs. 3 and 4.

[82]   See above, Chapter 5.

Aetolia did not seek to counterbalance against Rome during the war of 200–196 BC (the Second Macedonian War) precisely because they wanted the coalition headed by Rome to defeat the threat posed by Philip V. And Rhodes, Pergamum, and Philip V did not seek to counterbalance against Rome in the Antiochene War (192–188 BC) precisely because they wanted the coalition headed by Rome to defeat the threat posed by Antiochus III (and Aetolia). Thus serious counterbalancing occurred in the period covered by this study, but the counterbalancing was against Philip and Antiochus.[83] Thus difficulties in creating counterbalancing coalitions are therefore not enough to explain the lack of counterbalancing against Rome. Other explanations must be sought.

Several answers are available. First, unlike Greek hegemons or potential hegemons of the past, Rome was physically distant from the second-tier states, far across the Adriatic Sea to the west. The sheer distance separating Italy from the Aegean world, and the existence of a significant water-barrier between them, perhaps made Rome appear less directly threatening, the unipolar situation more acceptable to the second-tier states – certainly more acceptable than the situation that would have resulted from the victory of Macedon or Antiochus III in the previous hegemonic wars.[84] Moreover, we should remember that because of the primitiveness of ancient transport technology, the distances involved here, and the difficulties for Roman power-projection, seemed far larger to Hellenistic contemporaries than they even do to us.[85] Conversely, the instinctive stance of the Senate towards Greece after 188 was what modern political scientists call "off-shore" or "long-distance" balancing, rather than constant entanglement in Greek affairs.[86] The Romans in fact only dealt with the Greeks when Greek embassies came to Rome to complain about other Greeks; the *Patres* were never proactive in this involvement with Greek issues; and their responses to the Greek complaints about other Greek states were often minimal. It is

---

[83] See above, Chapters 7 and 8. Political scientists argue that because states form coalitions to balance against the *main* perceived threat, they will desire the most powerful state in the coalition to lead them successfully to victory against that main perceived threat: Walt 1987, Chs. 1–2; Lieber and Alexander 2005: 114 and 133; Press-Barnathan 2006: 275–6.

[84] See briefly Lampela 1998: 114. The link between geographical proximity and the rise of counterbalancing: Walt 1987: 22–6. Distance and the barrier of the oceans as an American advantage in maintaining unthreatening unipolarity, both for Europe and Asia: so Mearsheimer 2001; Wohlforth 2002.

[85] Hence Heather 2005: 25, concludes that in terms of practical administration, the size of the established Roman Empire was actually five times larger than what appears on our maps.

[86] On "off-shore balancing" by the unipolar power (and its virtues as opposed to constant entanglement), see Joffe 1995; Layne 2006.

striking that weaker Greek states sometimes complained not about Roman interference but the opposite: that Rome was too far away to help them against local bullies.[87] In any case, the fact of Roman self-restraint (originating, I have suggested, in a lack of intense interest) was a significant factor in guaranteeing the stability of the post-Apamea system in the Greek East, and the absence of anti-Roman coalition-building.[88]

To be sure, the absence of an obvious Greek peer-competitor after 188 BC allowed the Roman governing elite to decide with complete freedom which issues among the Greeks were important to Rome and which were not, which ones might require diplomatic or even military intervention and which did not; and it is significant that military intervention in this period never occurred.[89] Once again, distance itself – as well as Roman commitments in the West – may have acted to reduce the incentives for intervention in the East.[90] Only when the Aegean appeared to be on the verge of producing a peer-competitor again, with the obvious resurgence of the power and prestige of Antigonid Macedon in the 170s, did Rome intervene militarily, and after the war of 171–168 the Romans left Greece again, the Senate once more resorting to dealing with the Greeks at long distance, and did not return for another two decades.

Second, this generally lackadaisical stance taken by the Senate meant that despite the obvious fact of Roman power, Roman diplomatic interventions in Greek affairs in these years were neither very frequent nor very forceful. If one calculated correctly, then, Roman remonstrances and warnings need not be followed; the Senate might issue advice, or declarations, or even scoldings, but its bark was often worse than its bite. Thus the Romans remained far away in Greek thinking, as we see

---

[87] See Livy 39.25.11–12, on the situation ca. 185: *procul enim abesse libertatis auctores Romanos; lateri adhaerere gravem dominum* (25.11); based on Polybian material: see Nissen 1863: 222–3. Note also Livy 39.36.10–11, on the fate of Peloponnesian coastal towns under attack by Sparta in 193, in violation of the peace treaty of 195 between Sparta and the Rome-led coalition (*cum vos [Romanos] procul esstis . . .*). Callicrates of Leontium in 180 made a similar point about Roman lack of interest in Greece, and urged a change: Polyb. 24.9 (see below).

[88] On the impact of a unipolar power's self-restrained conduct (whatever its source) in stabilizing the new unipolar situation, see Ikenberry 2001; Lieber and Alexander 2005: 114.

[89] Such freedom to decide whether to intervene in local issues is typical of a situation of unipolar power: see Waltz 2000. By contrast to Rome and the Greek East in the years after 188 BC, American military interventions since the victory over the Soviet Union in 1990 have, of course, *not* been rare. On the concept of "peer-competitor," see Posen and Ross 1996: 32.

[90] On the impact of distance (especially overseas distance) in lessening the desire of the unipolar power for direct control, see Levy 2004: 42. And see above, n. 84.

in the already-cited remarks of Apollonidas in 185 that the main foreign issues facing Achaea were with the Greek kings.[91]

Third, we have noted that Rome generally supported the existing status quo among the Greek states – not surprising, since it had been the major force behind creating it. Hence Rome was both a disturbing factor in Greek interstate conditions and a guarantor of them, and thus for many Greeks it was the provider of an important public good to the system. This, too, helps explain why Greek resentment at occasional Roman diplomatic interventions did not develop into outright coalition-building.[92]

Of course, this status quo among the Greek states perpetuated the divisions within the Aegean world. And this was as the *Patres* wished: they had rewarded their allies well, but they were not willing to see a huge concentration of power in any one Greek state. Since opposition to the power of any one Greek state had also been the traditional stance of all the Greek second-tier major powers themselves (a spectacular example being their diplomacy at Rome in winter 201/200 BC), the Roman elite could expect at least some Greek support in preventing the rise of a Greek peer-competitor. And one sees this, for instance, in the diplomatic efforts of Eumenes II of Pergamum against a resurgent Macedon in the 170s.[93]

ROMAN PREPONDERANCE
AND GREEK *LIBERTAS*

The Senate was certainly determined not to let a new Greek peer-competitor arise – there the line was drawn. When the *Patres* became convinced at the end of the 170s that such a peer-competitor was emerging (in a resurgent Macedon), there was a vigorous Roman military response – and that, in turn, was a strong reminder of Roman military might, and hence of Roman political authority. But in the almost forty years between 188 and 150 BC there was only one such war, against Macedon (171–168 BC), which was again followed by the withdrawal of all Roman military and diplomatic presence back to Italy. During and

[91] Polyb. 22.8.6 (see above, p. 359).
[92] For the link between the stability of unipolarity and the unipolar power as a bringer of system-wide stability and other public goods, see Gilpin 1981: 144–5; Mandelbaum 2005. Yet awareness of the collective goods brought by the unipolar power does not mean that the elites of less powerful polities are necessarily satisfied with the relative distribution of power in the system: see Grieco 1988: 500.
[93] On the crucial role played by Eumenes of Pergamum in warning the Senate about the rise of Macedon under King Perseus, the son of Philip V, see Polyb. 27.7.5–6; Livy 42.6.3 and 11–14; Diod. 29.34; App. *Mac.* 11.1–3, with the judgment of Walbank 1977, and Gruen 1984: 409–10.

immediately after this Third Macedonian War, Roman commanders supported and aided the creation of overtly pro-Roman governments in Greece. This was a sharp change, and in terms of Greek freedom a negative change, from the previous situation, when there was little Roman interference in the internal politics of the Greek states; Polybius was bitter about it.[94] But this simply underlines the ambiguity of the 180s and 170s. And without minimizing the stern attitude of the Romans in Greece after ca. 170, even these harsh measures were still on a fundamentally less intrusive scale of intervention from the direct and continual interference (garrisons, appointed political overseers, taxes) that in the past had brought on Greek counterbalancing against Greek hegemons.[95] The great Greek monarchies had directly threatened the second-tier states: their independence, and even their existence (as with Pergamum in its confrontation with Antiochus the Great). But the situation with regard to Rome in the two decades after Apamea was one where, in an interstate order led by Rome, the interests of the weaker states appeared relatively protected.[96] Hence the expected value to be gained in these years from attempting a counterbalancing coalition against Roman unipolarity, which was politically difficult to achieve in any case (see above), was for many states significantly reduced by the indirect character of Roman predominance and Rome's physical distance from Greece – while the risks of such attempts at balancing remained obvious.[97]

The Roman governmental elite adopted such a stance of "off-shore" or "long-distance" balancing because, after 188 as before, the interest of the *Patres* in the East, and concrete interests there, remained limited. The result was that after 188, as before, Rome might suddenly use serious violence in a military crisis, seeking to reestablish a Roman political authority that had been challenged, but during periods of equilibrium this gave way to distant relations with the Greeks – neither benevolent nor heavy-handed interaction but rather, little or no interaction.

---

[94]   See Polyb. 30.13; 30.29; 32.4–6. Both Polybius himself and his father Lycortas, among many other Achaean politicians, were taken as deportees to Italy as a result of this policy: discussion and sources in Eckstein 1995: 5–7.

[95]   The pro-Roman regimes of the early 160s were not permanent, and the Senate did not respond when the political situation in Greece shifted in the early 150s and those regimes mostly disappeared; see discussion and sources in Gruen 1984: 514–19.

[96]   On restraint as a method of extending the timespan of unipolarity, see Ikenberry 2001; Walt 2002; Layne 2006: 135–6.

[97]   On this element as an explanation for the non-balancing behavior of weaker states in a unipolar situation, see Lieber and Alexander 2005. Of course, not only was the incentive to counterbalance reduced by Roman restraint, but everyone understood the great risks in attempting to counterbalance Rome militarily.

Yet the Greek politicians who originally cooperated with Rome as the leading state but on a basis of honor and mutual respect – who accepted the ambiguities of unipolarity and indeed wished to preserve them, in lieu of something more controlling – found their position inside their own states undermined even before the Third Macedonian War. From ca. 180 BC, we find Greek politicians who advocated more complete and unquestioning cooperation with Rome. The enormous weight of Roman power, even though far away, led the latter to use the prospect of that power to their own advantage in local politics: one might call them real Quislings, as opposed to honorable collaborators with Rome such as the Achaean Aristaenus (see above). The Quisling-type of politician had a significant impact, in part because now that the Mediterranean was one large unified system (as Polybius emphasized), they could – if they tried hard enough – involve Rome in supporting them in local Greek politics.

The rise of such politicians was inevitable in antiquity in a geopolitical situation where there was one predominant power. Aratus of Sicyon, one of Polybius' political heroes, had worried about just such a phenomenon arising among Achaean politicians – in this case, the rise of pro-Macedonian sycophants – after Macedon became the dominant power in the Peloponnese in the late 220s BC, and Aratus had striven vigorously and fairly successfully to combat the growing influence of such men. This is why, from Polybius' point of view, dealing with the predominance of *any* hegemonic power required men of character in the weaker state.[98] Macedonian power in fact declined in the Peloponnese from ca. 210 BC, and waned after 200 because of Philip V's conflict with Rome and the rise of a new Achaean army created by the Achaean statesman Philopoemen; and the result of the Aratean tradition in Achaean politics was that the Achaeans were ready to break completely free of Macedon in late 198 and to ally themselves with Rome instead, and they possessed both the political will and the military power eventually to become masters of the entire Peloponnese themselves.[99]

To Polybius, conversely, the worst example in the early stages of Roman predominance of the type of politician whom Aratus had feared was Callicrates of Leontium. Callicrates represented an Achaean faction that wished to pursue a more conciliatory policy towards Sparta than did the group once led by Philopoemen, and then – after Philopoemen's heroic death in the Messenian War – headed by Archon and by Polybius' father Lycortas. In 180, Callicrates appeared before the Roman Senate as a

---

[98]   See Polyb. 4.82.2–5, with the comments of Eckstein 1995: 199–200.
[99]   On the Achaean conquest of the Peloponnese between 192 and 188 BC, see Gruen 1984: 462–75.

member of an Achaean embassy once more defending the League from complaints from Sparta. But, Polybius says, Callicrates, out of personal ambition, now betrayed the tradition of Achaean independence by urging the Romans to take a stronger stance concerning their own interests among the Greeks, including Achaea. Callicrates told the *Patres* that Rome had stood by for a decade while Greek states treated communications from the Senate with disdain and flouted Roman recommendations (Achaean oppression of Sparta and Messene were obvious examples of this). The *Patres* would only get their way, Callicrates said, if they began overtly to support those politicians who believed in accommodating Roman desires – that is, if they changed their current stance of non-interference in Greek internal politics (Polyb. 24.9 *passim*). Polybius in his own voice then agrees with Callicrates' analysis of the situation as it stood ca. 180: it was still possible in this period for the Achaeans to deal with Rome on more or less equal terms (κατὰ ποσὸν ἰσολογίαν, especially because they had been allies of Rome in the great eastern wars: 24.10.9). Indeed, the League itself was now stronger and more prosperous than it had ever been before (24.10.9–10). This is a depiction not of oppressive Roman imperialism ca. 180 but – precisely – of the ambiguities inherent in unipolar politics.

But Polybius goes on to argue that Callicrates' speech to the Senate in 180 began to transform the situation. Henceforth the Senate preferred puppets and sycophants in the Greek polities, rather than the "true friends" they had won there by previous policies (24.10.3–7).[100] In response to Callicrates' speech, the *Patres* thus sent a letter to the Achaean League, saying that there ought to be more men – more accommodating men – such as Callicrates among the Greeks; and the Senate also sent versions of this letter to the Aetolians, Epirotes, Athenians, Boeotians, and Acarnanians (24.10.6–7). Some scholars believe that from this point onward, the Romans moved overtly to dictate politics within the Greek polities – an example of sheer imperialism.[101] But this is not

---

[100] Note the phrase φίλοι ἀληθίνοι at 24.10.6. These were, then, the statesmen who predominated in Greek politics in the 180s. Polybius also describes them as "the men who worked for the best policy" regarding Rome (24.10.4: τὸ βέλτιστον) – by which he means independent friendship (see 27.15.10–11, explicit). See Eckstein 1995: 41, and 206–7.

[101] See Badian 1958a: 89–91; Lehmann 1967: 289–96; Errington 1969: 200–5; Deininger 1971: 136–43 and 199–202. Of course, as we have noted, other scholars – such as Dahlheim, Mandell, and Derow – wish to place this development even earlier, either in 188 or even 196 (and we have argued that neither is correct). On direct attempts by a preponderant state to determine the internal affairs of the less powerful states as signifying a stage in interstate inequality beyond unipolarity, see below.

actually what Polybius says in 24.10. True, Callicrates began a shift in Roman–Greek relations towards a worse (i.e., more oppressive) situation (24.10.8). But, according to Polybius, this shift towards a worse (more oppressive) situation after Callicrates' speech in 180 occurred little by little, and was gradual (24.10.5: κατὰ βραχύ, τοῦ χρόνου προβαίνοντος . . .). We can see just how gradual it was when we observe how successful the diplomacy of King Perseus of Macedon was among the governments of the Greek states in the 170s – many of which adopted a friendly stance towards the resurgent Antigonid state.[102]

Moreover, there is reason to believe that even Polybius' depiction of the immediate impact of the Romans' political intervention in Achaea in favor of Callicrates is somewhat exaggerated. Backed by Rome, Callicrates won his immediate point in the Achaean Assembly about moderating the oppressive Achaean policy towards Sparta (as well as towards Messene, which was not even originally an issue as far as the Senate was concerned) – not that either state would be allowed to leave the League.[103] And soon Callicrates was elected League *strategos*, thanks to his use of the senatorial letter that spoke in his favor (24.10.13–15). Here Polybius breaks off, and one is therefore left with the impression that Callicrates had now become the dominant figure in Achaean politics. But this may be an accident of the fragmentary preservation of Polybius' text – for of the elected Achaean *strategoi* in the next ten years whose names we know, all four belong to the fiercely anti-Callicrates faction centered around Archon and Polybius' father Lycortas, heirs of the Philopoemen tradition who followed an independent line towards Rome.[104]

Polybius reveals his own general conception of Roman–Greek relations in this period more clearly in a statement discussing the political stance of Greek statesmen later accused of having pro-Macedonian sentiments. He says that there was a significant group of these leaders who refrained from choosing sides in the Roman war against Perseus

---

[102] Extent of Macedonian influence under Perseus: see Hammond, in Hammond and Walbank 1988: 490–7 ("The Successes of Perseus"). The extent of Macedonian influence was, precisely, the problem that Eumenes brought before the Senate in 172.

[103] A point stressed by Gruen 1984: 498–9.

[104] On possible exaggeration of the impact of Callicrates' speech before the Senate, see the good discussion in Gruen 1984: 499–500. The anti-Callicrates Achaean *strategoi*: Xenarchus, 175/174; Archon, 172/171; Archon again in 170/169 (with Polybius as hipparch); Xenon (before 167); see Gruen 1984: 500 and n. 85. Note that the two elections of the Philopoemenist Archon occurred as the crisis between Rome and Perseus of Macedon worsened, and then war actually broke out. Polybius had good reason to be hostile to Callicrates, who in 168/167 procured his deportation from Achaea (cf. Polyb. 30.13.9–11).

that began in 171 (the Third Macedonian War), for they feared that whoever won, the Greeks would fall under the domination of a single power (ὑπὸ μίαν ἀρχὴν: 30.6.5). Such an analysis takes it as a given that the Greeks before the Third Macedonian War were not yet under the domination of a single power, a situation these statesmen wisely wished to preserve. Similarly, Polybius praises the Epirote statesman Cephalus, who followed "the best policy" as the war appeared imminent ca. 172: he wished to preserve the current status quo, which provided a relatively congenial situation for the smaller states, and though he was prepared to support Rome against Macedon, he was not prepared to be servile (27.15.10–12). Cephalus is depicted as fearing a new war because it would establish a heavy-handed hegemony of either Rome or Macedon (27.15.11), which is why he wanted to avoid it. This passage implies that in the view of both Cephalus and Polybius, in 172/171 BC no heavy-handed hegemony existed as yet in Greece.[105]

Livy (42.30.5–6), drawing on different Polybian material, presents a broader but similar picture of the Greek political leaders in this period. He says that among these leaders, the category deserving praise are those responsible and intelligent men who if forced to make a choice of a master who was superior in power, preferred being under Rome to being under Perseus, but who if given a free choice of destiny, preferred neither Rome nor Perseus to become more powerful through the downfall of the other; they understood that a continuation of peace on terms of equality would be best for the free Greek states, since one power would always be there to protect the weak against wrongdoing by the other.[106] The passage seems somewhat over-theoretical, in that even with a powerful Macedon in existence, one might doubt its ability to balance Rome (though perhaps the thought is ultimately of a Macedon at the head of a Greek coalition). Nevertheless, the passage indicates once again that in Polybius' analysis, the Greek states before the Third Macedonian War had no overpowering master, and hence enjoyed significant freedom; this was because no power was so dominant that it could engage at will in the oppression of weaker states; this was the condition these statesmen wished to preserve; and they received Polybius' praise for it. Given the characteristics of Roman unipolarity as we have described it above,

---

[105]   Discussion: see Eckstein 1995: 41, 206, and 209 n. 58. Cephalus is also praised at Polyb. 30.6.7.

[106]   *tertia pars, optima eadem et prudentissima, si utique optio domini potioris daretur, sub Romanis quam sub rege malebat esse; si liberum in ea re arbitrum fortunae esset, neutram partem volebant potentiorem altera oppressa fieri, sed illibatis potius viribus utriusque partis pacem ex aeque manere; ita inter utrasque optimam condicionem civitatem fore, protegente altera semper inopem ab alterius iniuria.* Based on Polybian material: see Nissen 1862: 276–7; Gruen 1975: 62–3.

one can understand why such statesmen hoped to preserve the current political conditions.[107]

There is evidence even more impressive than Polybius or Polybian-derived material here – for we have the point of view of an important Roman statesman at the time. Cato the Elder (consul 195, censor 184), later a friend of Polybius, is on record as thinking in 167 BC that the situation the Greek states enjoyed before the war against Perseus had been one of *libertas*. In his speech *For the Rhodians*, delivered in 167 and partly preserved, Cato argues against Rome going to war against its old ally Rhodes, despite Roman anger at the Rhodians for allegedly having acted in Perseus' interest during the recent new war with Macedon. Cato says that the Rhodians, like other Greek states that had leaned towards Perseus, had done so not really to betray Rome, but merely "in order to preserve their *libertas*"; and he explains: "for if there was no longer a man whom we feared, they would then come under our sole rule (*sub sole imperio nostro*) and be in servitude to us."[108] The analysis of the negative impact of overwhelming power in the hands of a single state is close to Polybius' own analysis of the situation the Greek statesmen who followed "the best policy" feared might happen if there was a new war between Rome and Macedon, as well as being close to Polybius' analysis of what did happen in Greece after the war. For our purposes, what is important is Cato's belief that before the Third Macedonian War, the Rhodians and other Greek states had enjoyed *libertas*. And this was because Rome, though predominant, was restrained in its conduct by the existence of other large and powerful states within the international system. Thus Cato perceived the situation in the East before 171 as Polybius did: the Greek states had been in a situation of real freedom.[109]

---

[107]   Polybius in these passages was also depicting – and in fact defending – the political stance he himself had taken at the time of the war against Perseus: to work with the Romans but to preserve Achaean independence above all. See Eckstein 1995: 5–6 and 209 n. 58. Note Polybius' praise early in the *Histories* of Hiero II of Syracuse for aiding Carthage during its war with the Mercenaries in 241–238 BC, so that Syracuse would not be faced with only one power – Rome (1.83.3–4). Polybius then makes Hiero's policy a general rule for second-tier states to follow (83.4). Polybius' theme here is consistent. See Eckstein 1985.

[108]   Gellius 6.1.3 = Cato *ORF*, frg. 164 (speech for the Rhodians): *ne sub sole imperio nostro in servitute nostra essent. libertatis causa in ea sententia fuisse arbitror.* On Greek *libertas*, see also above, this chapter, p. 355.

[109]   On the friendship between Cato and Polybius, based on a mutual personal tie to the Aemilii Paulli and on many intellectual agreements, see Eckstein 1997. Note that for Cato as for Polybius, the foundation of Greek freedom actually lies in the realities of the distribution of power across the interstate system.

Our argument is therefore that before 171 BC the gradual emergence of admittedly dangerous Greek "Quislings" to challenge the position of the moderates and "honorable collaborators" with Rome had not yet proceeded very far in the Greek states. That is: a workable *modus vivendi* based on Roman unipolarity and Greek freedom not only existed in the 180s in the immediate aftermath of Apamea, but was still in place in the late 170s.[110]

EMPIRE, HEGEMONY, AND SPHERE OF INFLUENCE

Finally, when scholars ask whether Rome had an "empire" in the Hellenistic East after 188 BC – and especially when they assert that Rome in fact did have such an empire – it is necessary to define what we mean by the term. The modern study of empire began as the study of legal structures, and if one restricts oneself solely to legal structures (for instance, to the existence of formal Roman annexation, and Roman governors exercising *imperium* – legal right to rule – over administered populations), then there are no ambiguities: either you have submitted to this and are therefore in the empire, or you have not submitted to this and therefore you are out of it.[111] The Romans in our period possessed such a formal-legal empire, of course, with permanent provinces directly ruled and administered by Roman governors and garrisoned by Roman troops, but only in the West: the provinces of Sicily, Sardinia-Corsica, Nearer and Further Spain. These provinces were themselves the byproduct of Rome's wars with another great power, Carthage, and were created originally for strategic reasons (and not for profit), primarily as a way to prevent any recovery of geopolitically important territory by a defeated enemy.[112] In the Greek East, however, such direct Roman rule did not exist during our period, and even after our period it was very long in coming. In the legal sense, then, there was simply no Roman empire in the eastern Mediterranean in the period we are discussing.[113]

Nevertheless, many modern scholars now define "empire" more broadly than the existence of formal-legal administrative structures and

---

[110] For the widespread coexistence of real independence (both legal and factual) with "international inequality" in modern interstate systems, see now Donnelly 2006: 145–53.
[111] See Baumgart 1982: 1–9; Doyle 1986: 20.
[112] On the origins of these provinces, see the important comments of Sherwin-White 1977: 66; cf. Dahlheim 1977 and Kallet-Marx 1995: 4.
[113] See Kallet-Marx 1995.

the presence of direct rule, and for a good reason. They emphasize not administrative legalities but power-political realities. Hence they argue that empire is ultimately "*effective* control, whether formal *or* informal, of a subordinated society by an imperial society."[114] Here we enter the realm of "informal empire." Yet "informal empire" is a concept that has itself come under attack in recent years from political scientists, on grounds of being vague and insufficiently rigorous conceptually, and subject to analytical (or propagandistic) abuse. Jack Donnelly makes the theoretical point: "Empires are composite polities, knit together and defined by an imperial core that rules over, rather than simply influences . . . subordinated polities." Anything short of actual rule by the imperial center, its direct control over both the external and internal policies and politics of subordinated polities, is a situation of influence which – although asymmetrical and hierarchical in power – is nevertheless short in essential aspects of being an empire.[115]

The most detailed of the theories concerning "informal empire" is that of Michael Doyle, and it has been widely influential among political scientists. But Doyle differentiates sharply between various levels of informal but effective control, with only the most all-embracing of these situations of control constituting "informal empire." Examination of Doyle's differentiated levels of informal but effective control will help us in conceptualizing the complex situation that existed in the Greek East in the twenty years after the end of system-wide hegemonic warfare in 188.[116] And it is clear that under Doyle's analytical rubrics, Rome did not possess an "informal empire" in the Greek East in this period, any more than it possessed a formal-legal one.

Rome by 188 had shown that it was by far the most powerful of all Mediterranean polities. But empire is not mere inequality of power among states. Power in ancient interstate relations was always very unequally distributed, and large inequalities of rights, obligations, and opportunities were usual; the same is true in the international system today.[117] Because these complex conditions prevail in interstate systems, Doyle argues that empire should be narrowly defined: it is one state's effective control (as we have noted, either by formal *or* by informal means) over both a subordinate state's external policies and its internal politics

---

[114]   Doyle 1986: 30 (emphasis added), cf. the similar definition at 45.
[115]   Donnelly 2006: 140.
[116]   The carefully differentiated spectrum of informal control: Doyle 1986: 12, 40, 55–60, and the chart on p. 44. Doyle's influence among political scientists: see Watson 1992: 15–16, 27–8, and 122–8; Motyl 2001: 20; Rosen 2003: 211; Donnelly 2006: 156.
[117]   On this point , see Donnelly 2006: esp. 157; cf. Doyle 1986: 30–47.

and policies. Anything less than this all-embracing control may be interstate inequality, asymmetrical influence, or hierarchy, or even hegemony, but it is not empire.[118]

When a metropole desires to establish certain constraints on the foreign relations of weaker states, but neither to interfere in weaker states' internal politics nor to control their external relations continuously, such a situation for Doyle is not empire, or even "hegemony," but something much less stringent – mere "sphere of influence."[119] And at the next stage, when a metropole does desire to control the foreign relations of weaker neighbors continuously, but still does not wish to control their internal politics and structures, this for Doyle is not empire, nor even informal empire, but still something less stringent than empire: namely, "hegemony."[120] And as Donnelly stresses, "Hegemonically subordinated 'allies' have little choice about their continued participation in the 'alliance'. But the political life of a hegemonized state that controls its internal policy is very different from that of an imperialized polity that does not. . . . *Influence* is simply not *rule*."[121] Within this broad middle range of inequality and hierarchy distinct from empire, but even farther along towards empire than either "sphere of influence" or even "hegemony," Adam Watson places what he terms "dominion," which he defines as a situation where the metropole controls weaker states' foreign relations and now to some extent determines their internal government as well, "but they nevertheless retain their identity as separate states and some control over their own affairs." This is an uncomfortable situation for the lesser state – but even this is still not empire.[122]

It is analytically important to distinguish each of these geopolitical situations of interstate hierarchy from one another. And it is analytically important to distinguish all of them from empire, even "informal empire," in order to avoid employing the terms "empire" or "rule" too loosely, or even as mere pejorative political or moral slogans, rather than proper analytical categories. The latter sort of usage works to obscure rather than to enhance our understanding of complex political and geopolitical situations and processes.[123] Yet it is precisely such usage that has often occurred in recent accounts of the growth of Roman international

[118]   Cf. now Donnelly 2006: 140.
[119]   Doyle 1986: 30–47, esp. the chart on p. 44. On this stage of seeking informally merely to "set limits" on foreign relations of weaker states, see the groundbreaking discussion of Murphy 1961.
[120]   Doyle 1986, 30–47, esp. p. 44.
[121]   Donnelly 2006: 158 (my emphases).
[122]   Watson 1992: 15–16; accepted by Donnelly 2006: 154 (chart) and 156.
[123]   See Donnelly 2006: 159.

power under the Republic.[124] In fact, however, historical situations of interstate inequality retain so much ambiguity that it is not nearly as easy in practice as it is in theory to separate a situation of "sphere of influence" from one of "hegemony" from one of "dominion" from one of "informal empire"; in the real world this can be difficult because the interstate relationships are so complicated and ambiguous.[125]

Moreover, what is the meaning even of Doyle's term "control"? Modern scholars of antiquity often use the term "control," as they use the term "empire," as if its meaning is immediately clear.[126] But there are different intensities of "control," and this is especially true when dealing with a "control" that is exercised only informally. In addition, the facet(s) of weaker states' policies that are subjected to control, and the intensity of that control, may vary widely both over time and (especially in the Roman case) geographically. Thus not every interstate asymmetry of power, not every external influence, not even every external interference or intimidation, amounts to "control" – or empire.[127] Nor is the power-configuration now termed "unipolarity" by international-systems theorists – in which one state is "the sole remaining superpower" and the political center of an interstate system, as Rome was the center of the Mediterranean system after 188 – necessarily the same as a situation of hegemony, or dominion, let alone empire.[128] And because *some* asymmetry of power is normal in all interstate relationships (see above), and because there is both a spectrum and a continuum of increasing and decreasing asymmetry of power between states, the actual relationship between states of differing or even greatly differing power can be difficult to define at any given moment – nor is it always in states' interest to define them.[129]

Yet another complication here is that the stages along this continuum of asymmetry of power – from true independence through unipolarity/

---

[124] See Harris 1979; Mandell 1989; Derow 1989, 1991, and 2003: all with heavy moralizing and rhetorical bitterness.

[125] But again, *formal* empire is indeed easily distinguished from all these other situations: see above, p. 372.

[126] Assertions of Roman direct or indirect "control" over other states, with no attempt to define what is meant: see, e.g., Badian 1968: 11; Dahlheim 1977: 122; Harris 1979: 162; Will 1982: 421.

[127] See Doyle 1986: 30–47; Donnelly 2006: 158; and for antiquity, see Kallet-Marx 1995: 11 and n. 3, based on Doyle. Robinson and Gallagher 1960: 9, prefer to use the terminology of "sway" or even "informal sway" here, which as terminology is even vaguer, but does mitigate the misimpression to which the term "control" is liable.

[128] Definitions of situations of unipolarity: see above, this chapter, pp. 342–3 and n. 1.

[129] On the difficulties here, see Doyle 1986: 45, and now Donnelly 2006: 144 and 156.

sphere of influence to hegemony and dominion and then on to empire – are not in themselves politically stable situations. Rather, they are quite fluid situations. Depending on internal political conditions and decisions, and external geopolitical circumstances and pressures, "unipolarity" (in Realist terminology) or a "sphere of influence" (in Doyle's terminology) can revert back towards normal interstate "asymmetry of power" (that is, multipolarity), or conversely can proceed forward into "hegemony" (in Doyle's terminology) or "dominion" (Watson). Similarly, depending on internal political conditions and decisions, and external geopolitical circumstances and pressures, an existing situation of hegemony (in Doyle's terminology) can revert back towards mere "sphere of influence," or proceed forward into a situation of "dominion" (Watson) or empire itself. Thus the developmental trajectory even of very powerful states is simply not set in stone – for even these states exist within a complex interstate environment in which internal decisions on both sides of the asymmetrical relationship, as well as contingent interstate events, can effect important shifts in power.[130] The fluidity and instability of the power situation at any given moment is in fact the foundation of the debate between Aristaenus and Philopoemen in Polybius' Book 24, which we discussed above; it is a debate on the best way for the Achaeans by their own decisions to delay an advance along the spectrum of increasing asymmetry of interstate power in favor of Rome, and in that debate it is assumed that the actions of the weaker state, the choices its government makes, have an important impact on such developments.

CONCLUSION

Between 201 and 188 BC, the Republic of Rome achieved stunning victories over Carthage, Macedon, and the Seleucid Empire, and the result was a transformation of the Mediterranean state-system. But even dominant states rarely create new political orders from scratch.[131] In the two decades after the Peace of Apamea, the geopolitical situation in the Hellenistic East did not look greatly different from the situation in the mid-third century, in the sense that it remained a world of independent states – and of states proud and conscious of their independence. Though peace prevailed far more widely in European Greece than previously, and the European Greek states had greater contact with

---

[130]   On this point, see especially Wilkinson 1999.
[131]   See the comments of Gortzak 2005: 677.

Rome than ever before, east of the Aegean there was – as usual – fairly constant warfare among the larger polities (and among some of the smaller ones as well), and none of these latter states had much contact with Rome.[132]

The Roman Republic in this period had emerged as the preponderant power on the Mediterranean stage, and – as political scientists argue is natural for any such powerful state – Rome sought to organize that world according to its own preferences.[133] In such geopolitical situations as that achieved by Rome by 188 BC, the sole remaining superpower certainly comes to exercise extensive and unequal influence over weaker states, and it enjoys special rights and privileges if only because there is now no countervailing power to challenge it.[134] But powerful states (great powers) have always sought and enjoyed unequal influence over the course of interstate relations and the condition of the world order. This is the case whether one is dealing with the behavior of great powers under conditions of multipolarity, or conditions of bipolarity (the Cold War is a good example), or unipolarity (although under unipolarity the situation is the most obvious). And the great powers have always employed both inducements and threats to achieve this aim of ordering the world as much as possible according to their preferences. This condition of great power privilege and unequal influence was as true in the ancient world as it is in the modern world. Nevertheless, such behavior is different from an assertion of an imperial right to rule.[135]

Hence, though in the two decades after Apamea the Romans usually exercised great and asymmetrical influence in the Hellenistic East when they wished to do so, as powerful states had always done in the international world, it is still not true that Rome now possessed an "empire" among the Greek polities.[136] Nor, given the work of Doyle and others, can an assertion of Roman empire and "rule" in the Hellenistic East be made on the sole grounds that in the two decades after Apamea there was no countervailing power, no obvious peer-competitor, to challenge

---

[132] In other words, I find the reconstruction offered by Gruen 1984: Chs. 11–18, fundamentally convincing. Wars between the large states of Asia Minor, 188–179 BC: see above. Wars between smaller states: for instance, between Miletus and Magnesia-on-the-Meander in the 180s, which also drew in several Greek neighbors (but not Rome); see Errington 1989b.

[133] On this axiom concerning the behavior of great powers, see Lieber and Alexander 2005: 134.

[134] See Donnelly 2006: 144.

[135] Prevalence of such behavior by great states: see Davis 2000; Nathan 2002; Donnelly 2006: 152. On the widespread existence of inequality among states even in conditions of multipolarity: ibid.: 155.

[136] The unipolar power as colossus, but not yet an empire: see O'Brien and Clesse, eds., 2002; Ferguson 2004; Donnelly 2006: 157.

Rome – though that seems to be the unexamined premise of some modern scholars of antiquity.[137] On the contrary: I would suggest that employment of emotionally loaded terms such as "Roman empire" or "Roman rule" and "control" to describe the situation in this early period works to obscure rather than to enhance our understanding of the period's actual complexity, as well as our understanding of the interstate hierarchy that in the two decades after Apamea began (but only began) to replace the long-reigning Hellenistic anarchy. Occasional use of asymmetrical influence, persuasion, scolding, and even attempted intimidation against weaker states is hierarchical behavior, but it is also to a significant extent the common and natural behavior of powerful states – and it is a qualitatively different form of interstate inequality than empire. As Donnelly has said, historians and political scientists should learn to accept "the genuine variety of qualitatively different forms of hierarchy."[138]

This chapter has briefly described the situation as it existed in the two decades after 188, and has argued that the geopolitical situation Rome had achieved and which it maintained over the next two decades in the East was a situation best described as unipolarity. Within this unipolar situation the states of European Greece between 188 and 171/168 BC constituted in Doyle's terms merely a Roman "sphere of influence." This was a sphere in which Rome indeed exercised influence, and occasionally strong influence, over sovereign states – but not an overwhelming authority that compelled obedience by terror and force (as one can see from the continued Achaean oppression of Sparta and Messene despite Roman protest, and the continued Rhodian oppression of the region of Lycia, despite Roman protest).[139] The Roman Senate employed persuasion, cajoling, scolding, even indirect threats to get its way – and sometimes it failed to get its way. But *how* one gets one's way (i.e., the form which interstate interaction takes) really does matter on the international stage, and the kind of interaction being

---

[137]   See Dahlheim 1977: 117; Reiter 1987: 118–19; Hammond, in Hammond and Walbank 1988: 502–3; and Derow 2003: 65 and 66, where we find consistent declarations of the beginning of outright Roman rule and total control in the Greek East from 188 BC. (With Mandell 1989, it is from 196 BC.)

[138]   See Donnelly 2006: 159 and 161, with a general warning about misuse of the term "empire," and 162 (the quote). Cf. Davis 2000.

[139]   On Achaean oppression of the states of the southern Peloponnese and the Rhodian oppression of the Lycians, see above. On the distinction between influence but not authority ("imperial right to rule") in situations of unipolarity, see Donnelly 2006: 144.

described here is very different from "control" or "rule."[140] The states of European Greece were a Roman "sphere of interest" in another sense too, because the goal of the Senate in its relations with these states was merely (as Doyle would put it) to limit some of the foreign policy choices these states made. That is: the Senate did not seek to control the foreign relations of these states in general or continuously, nor did it seek (at least not before 180, and only a little in the succeeding decade) to interfere directly in these states' internal politics.

It is not a mere matter of semantics to call this a situation of unipolarity (or sphere of influence), nor is this terminology merely a more tactful name for empire. The situation between Rome and the polities of the eastern Mediterranean in 188–171 was analytically different from empire, and called forth a qualitatively different form of political interaction.[141]

Meanwhile, east of the Aegean the Roman presence was hardly felt at all. Roman attempts even to limit the foreign relations choices of states (including the waging of major wars) were very infrequent, and often not effective. One thinks here, for instance, of the great war waged between Eumenes II of Pergamum and the anti-Eumenes coalition headed by Pharnaces of Pontus, which roiled all of Asia Minor in 182–179 BC, and which several embassies of mediation sent by the Senate failed to stop; or the fact that the government of Rhodes simply ignored the Roman request of 177 to stop oppressing the Lycian polities; or the fact that the Senate sent only one brief embassy to the Seleucid court on any topic over a span of sixteen years during this period; or the fact that the Senate sent no embassies at all to the Ptolemies in Alexandria for an astonishing twenty-seven years. This is not empire.[142]

Polybius did note with distress the beginning of Roman political interference in the internal affairs of the Greek states in Europe ca. 180 – an indication, in Doyle's terms, of an emerging stage of empire, or in Watson's terms the emergence of "dominion." But the Achaean historian said that this interference was still only in its beginning stages before the Third Macedonian War (171–168 BC) – the war fought by Rome against a resurgent Macedon under King Perseus, the son of Philip V.

---

[140] On inequality as not contradictory to sovereignty, see Abernethy 1986: 105–8; Donnelly 2006: 158.

[141] The sharp differences in interstate interaction in situations of empire, unipolarity, and sphere of influence mean that the latter terms are not euphemisms for the former: see Donnelly 2006: 160–1.

[142] On the major wars in Asia Minor, and Roman lack of contact with the Seleucids and Ptolemies, see this chapter, above, pp. 353–5. The Rhodian oppression of Lycia: above, p. 355.

Polybius also stressed that the initiative for such Roman intervention as occurred in the internal affairs of the Greek states came originally from the Greek side (with Callicrates), and was not originally some sort of Roman imperialist plot.[143] Finally, Polybius stressed that the Senate ca. 180 BC certainly wished Greeks to come to Rome with their problems.[144] But this was more to demonstrate the Greeks' acceptance of Roman status, and acceptance of the international hierarchy that Rome had established, than for the Romans to exercise real control – for the *Patres* often allowed subsequent Roman statements, investigative commissions, and even scoldings of Greek states to have no real impact.[145] We have suggested that the *Patres* maintained this stance because – again – most Greek issues were not that important to them. Yet this meant that a real Roman recognition of the independence of these Greek states emerged from – or rather, was maintained by – the actual practice of interstate politics as carried out over these two decades. If this situation strikes the reader as ambiguous and even paradoxical, such is the nature of unipolarity.[146]

But Polybius believed that the Third Macedonian War changed everything. It changed the relatively congenial situation within an acknowledged asymmetry of power that the friends of Rome among the Greek states had accepted as the natural consequence of the victorious hegemonic wars waged at the end of the third century and the beginning of the second century. The crucial event was that the Romans, after being hard-pressed by Perseus, decided after victory was finally achieved to abolish the kingdom of Macedon altogether. On the plane of the general balance of power, the disappearance of the Macedonian monarchy, one of the great potential counterweights to Rome, fundamentally altered even more in Rome's favor the balance of power

---

[143] On the other hand, Polybius may have judged the rise of someone like Callicrates to be inherent in the hegemony of a great power over lesser powers; see 4.82.2–5 on the rise of pro-Macedonian sycophants among politicians in Achaea during the period of Macedonian hegemony over the Peloponnese in 223–200 BC, and Aratus' attempts to prevent such men from controlling Achaea: above, p. 367.
[144] See Polyb. 23.17.4 (discussed above, this chapter, p. 351 and n. 35).
[145] See Polyb. 24.8.2–5 and 10.10.11–12; indeed, the passage where Polybius remarks on the preference of the Senate to have Greek matters referred to it is actually a description of Roman acquiescence in the Achaean military victory over Messene.
[146] For the sovereignty of the weaker states within a hierarchical situation as emerging – or being maintained – via the actual day-to-day practice of interstate politics, see Abernethy 1986: esp. 103–8; Donnelly 2006: 151. Polybius himself emphasizes this aspect of the situation, in his depiction of the debate between the Achaean statesmen Philopoemen and Aristaenus on the different ways one might handle the Romans (24.11–13).

within the Mediterranean. And this was perceived and acknowledged both by Polybius and by his older Roman contemporary Cato the Elder.[147] And beyond the massive violence that accompanied this war – violence on a scale not seen in European Greece for a generation – the war also changed the actual Roman practice of interstate relations with the Greek polities. It became much harsher. The new Roman attitude towards both the enemy and even towards Rome's Greek supporters as Perseus and his coalition continued the fight helped lead to a transformation of politics both between the Greek states and Rome and within the European Greek states themselves. What we see is an increasingly demanding Roman attitude, combined with the emergence of a generation of Greek politicians who employed the tactics of Callicrates (pledges of obedience to Roman wishes) to gain direct Roman support for personal domination of their individual polities. These developments, in sum, constituted a fundamental transformation of the political situation as it had existed before 171. The prewar situation had been one, Polybius said, of *isologia* between Rome and its Greek friends – a situation, Cato said, of *libertas*.

Examination of the worsening situation for the Greek states after 171–168 BC, and its evolution into a true Roman Empire in the Hellenistic Mediterranean over the century that followed, lies beyond our scope. It has been the purpose of our present study to examine the entrance of the Republic of Rome into the Hellenistic multipolar anarchy, to examine it in good part with the help of a theoretical framework provided by modern international systems theory, and we have now concluded with a brief examination of the ambiguous and complex period between 188 and 171/168 BC, again with the help of theoretical models of interstate inequality and hierarchy provided by modern theories of international relations. It is with this reinterpretation of the two decades when the long-prevailing Hellenistic multipolar anarchy first began to be replaced by a Rome-centered hierarchy (but not yet an empire) that we have brought our study of the entrance of Roman power into the Greek East to an end.

[147] The geopolitical transformation caused by the disappearance of the Macedonian counterweight to Rome is stressed not only by Polybius (see 30.6, esp. 30.6.5; cf. Polyb. 27.15, and Livy 42.30.5–6 [based on Polybian material]), but by Cato himself in a speech in 167 (*ORF* frg. 64): passages discussed above, pp. 369–71.

Bibliography

Abernethy, D. B. 1986. "Dominant–Subordinate Relationships: How Shall We Define Them? How Do We Compare Them?" In Triska, ed.: 103–23.

Abernethy, D. B. 2000. *The Dynamics of Global Dominance*. New Haven.

Adams, W. L. 1993. "Philip V, Hannibal and the Origins of the First Macedonian War." *Ancient Macedonia* 5: 41–50.

Adcock, F. E. and D. M. Mosley. 1975. *Diplomacy in Ancient Greece*. London.

Africa, T. 1961. *Phylarchus and the Spartan Revolution*. Berkeley and Los Angeles.

Ager, S. L. 1991. "Rhodes: The Rise and Fall of a Neutral Diplomat." *Historia* 40: 10–41.

Ager, S. 1996. *Interstate Arbitrations in the Greek World, 337–90 BC*. Berkeley and Los Angeles.

Ager, S. L. 2003. "An Uneasy Balance: From the Death of Seleukos to the Battle of Raphia." In Erskine, ed.: 35–50.

Albert, S. 1980. *Bellum Iustum: Die Theorie des "Gerechten Krieges" und ihre praktische Bedeutung für die auswärtigen Auseinandersetzung Roms in republikanischer Zeit*. Kallmünz.

Allen, M. J. 1997. *Contested Peripheries: Philistia in the Neo-Assyrian World-System*. PhD diss., University of California at Los Angeles.

Alonzo, V. 2007. "War, Peace, and International Law in Ancient Greece." In Raaflaub, ed.: 206–25.

Ameling, W. 1993. *Karthago: Militar, Staat und Gesellschaft*. Munich.

Ampela, A. 1998. *Rome and Ptolemaic Egypt: The Development of their Political Relations, 273–80 BC*. Helsinki.

Anderson, E. 1999. *Code of the Street*. New York.

Armstrong, D. and J. J. Walsh. 1986. "*SIG*³ 593: The Letter of Flamininus to Chyretiae." *CP* 81: 32–46.

Aron, R. 1973. *Peace and War: A Theory of International Relations*. New York.

Astin, A. E. 1968. "Politics and Policies in the Roman Republic." Inaugural Lecture, Queen's University. Belfast.

Astin, A. E. 1978. *Cato the Censor*. Oxford.

Austin, M. M. 1981. *The Hellenistic World from Alexander to the Roman Conquest: A Selection of Ancient Sources in Translation*. Cambridge.

Austin, M. M. 1986. "Hellenistic Kings, War, and the Economy," *CQ* 36: 450–66.

Aymard, A. 1938. *Les premiers rapports de Rome et de la confédération achaïenne*. Bordeaux.

Badian, E. 1952. "The Treaty between Rome and the Achaean League." *JRS* 42: 76–80.

Badian, E. 1958a. *Foreign Clientelae (264–70 BC)*. Oxford.

Badian, E. 1958b. "Aetolica." *Latomus* 17: 197–211.

Badian, E. 1964a. "Notes on Roman Policy in Illyria (230–201 BC)." In E. Badian, *Studies in Greek and Roman History*: 1–33. Oxford. [= *PBSR* 20 (1952): 72–93.]

Badian, E. 1964b. "Rome and Antiochus the Great: A Study in Cold War." In E. Badian, *Studies in Greek and Roman History*: 113–39. Oxford. [= *CPh* 54 (1959): 81–99.]

Badian, E. 1966. "The Early Historians." In T. A. Dorey, ed., *Latin Historians: Studies in Latin Literature and its Influence*: 1–38. London.

Badian, E. 1968. *Roman Imperialism in the Late Republic*. Ithaca.

Badian, E. 1970. *T. Quinctius Flamininus: Philhellenism and Realpolitik*. Cincinnati.

Badian, E. 1971. "The Family and Early Career of T. Quinctius Flamininus." *JRS* 61: 102–11.

Badian, E. 1979. "Two Polybian Treaties." In *Miscellanea in onore di E. Manni* I: 161–9. Rome.

Badian, E. 1983. "Hegemony and Independence: Prolegomena to a Study of Rome and the Hellenistic States in the Second Century BC." *Actes du VIIᵉ Congrès de la F.E.I.C.*: 397–414. Budapest.

Bagnall, R. S. 1976. *The Administration of the Ptolemaic Possessions Outside Egypt*. Leiden.

Baker, P. 1991. *Cos et Calymna, 205–200 a. C.: esprits civiques et défense nationale*. Quebec.

Baldwin, D. A., ed. 1993. *Neorealism and Neoliberalism: The Contemporary Debate*. New York.

Balsdon, J. P. V. D. 1954. "Rome and Macedon, 205–200 BC." *JRS* 44: 30–42.

Bar-Kochva, B. 1977. *The Seleucid Army: Organization and Tactics in the Great Campaigns*. Cambridge.

Barré, M. L. 1983. *The God List in the Treaty between Hannibal and Philip V of Macedon*. Baltimore.

Baumgart, W. 1982. *Imperialism: The Idea and the Reality of British and French Colonial Expansion, 1880–1914*. Oxford.

Bayley, C. A. 1988. *Imperial Meridian: The British Empire and the World, 1780–1830*. New York.

Beck, H. and U. Walter. 2001. *Die frühen römischen Historiker*, Bd. I: *Von Fabius Pictor bis Cn. Gellius*. Darmstadt.

Bederman, E. 2001. *International Law in Antiquity*. Oxford.

Bengtson, H. 1944. *Die Strategie in hellenistischer Zeit* II. Munich.

Berthold, R. M. 1976. "The Rhodian Appeal to Rome in 201 BC." *CJ* 71: 97–107.

Berthold, R. M. 1984. *Rhodes in the Hellenistic Age*. Ithaca.

Bickerman, E. J. 1952. "Hannibal's Covenant." *AJPh* 73: 1–23.

Blainey, G. 1988. *The Causes of War*. 3rd ed. New York.

Bleicken, J. 1964. Review of Badian 1958a. *Gnomon* 36: 176–87.

Blümel, W. 2000. "Ein rhodisches Dekret aus Bargylia." *Ep. Anat.* 32: 94–6.

Braunert, H. 1964. "Hegemoniale Bestrebungen der hellenistische Grossmächte in Politik und Wirtschaft." *Historia* 13: 80–104.

Briscoe, J. 1972. "Flamininus and Roman Politics, 200–189 BC." *Latomus* 31: 22–53.

Briscoe, J. 1973. *A Commentary on Livy, Books XXXI–XXXIV*. Oxford.

Briscoe, J. 1981. *A Commentary on Livy, Books XXXIV–XXXVII*. Oxford.

Brooks, S. G. 1997. "Dueling Realisms." *Int. Org.* 51: 445–77.

Broughton, T. R. S. 1951. *The Magistrates of the Roman Republic*. Vol. 1. Cleveland.

Brulé, P. 1978. *La piratie crétoise hellénistique*. Paris.

Buraselis, K. 1996. "*Vix Aerarium Sufficeret*: Roman Finances and the Outbreak of the Second Macedonian War." *GRBS* 37: 149–72.

Burton, P. 1996. "The Coming of the Magna Mater to Rome." *Historia* 47: 312–35.

Burton, P. 2003. "*Clientela* or *Amicitia*? Modeling Roman International Behavior in the Middle Republic (246–146 BC)." *Klio* 85: 333–69.

Buzan, B. 1993. "Beyond Neorealism: Interaction Capacity." In B. Buzan, C. Jones, and R. Little, *The Logic of Anarchy: Neorealism to Structural Realism*: 66–80. New York.

Buzan, B. 2004. *The United States and the Great Powers: World Politics in the Twenty-First Century*. Cambridge.

Cabanes, P. 1976. *L'Épire de la mort de Pyrrhos à la conquête romaine (272–167)*. Paris.

Campbell, B. 2002. "Power Without Limit: 'The Romans Always Win.'" In Chaniotis and Ducrey, eds.: 167–80.

Carr, E. H. 1939. *The Twenty Years' Crisis, 1919–1939*. London.

Carr, E. H. 1952. *What is History?* London.

Cartledge, P., P. Garnsey, and E. Gruen, eds. 1997. *Hellenistic Constructs: Essays in Culture, History, and Historiography*. Berkeley and Los Angeles.

Casaubon, I. 1609. *Polybius*. Amsterdam.

Chambers, M. H. 1966. *Polybius: The Histories*. New York.

Chamoux, F. 2002. *Hellenistic Civilization*. Cambridge.

Champion, C. 1997. "The Nature of Authoritative Evidence in Polybius and Agelaus' Speech at Naupactus." *TAPA* 127: 111–28.

Champion, C. 2000. "Romans as *BAPBAPOI*: Three Polybian Speeches and the Politics of Cultural Indeterminacy." *CPh* 95: 425–44.

Champion, C. 2004. *Cultural Politics in Polybius's Histories*. Berkeley and Los Angeles.

Chaniotis, A. and P. Ducrey, eds. 2002. *Army and Power in the Ancient World*. Stuttgart.

Christensen, T. J. 1993. "System Stability and the Security of the Most Vulnerable Significant Actor." In Snyder and Jervis, eds.: 329–56.

Cimma, M. R. 1976. *Reges socii et amici populi romani*. Milan.

Clarysse, W. 1978. "Notes de prosopographie thébaine, VII: Hugonaphor et Chaonnophris, les derniers pharaons indigènes." *Chron. Eg.* 53: 23–53.

Claude, I. 1962. *Power and International Relations*. New York.

Cline, E. H. 2000. "Contested Peripheries in World Systems Theory: Megiddo and the Jezreel Valley as a Test Case." *JWSR* 61: 7–16.

Coarelli, F. 1977. "Public Building in Rome Between the Second Punic War and Sulla." *PBSR* 45: 1–23.

Colin, G. 1905. *Rome et la Grèce de 200 à 146 avant Jésus Christ*. Paris.

Collatz, C. F., M. Gutzlaf, and H. Helms, eds. 2003. *Polybios-Lexikon*, Vol. 1, Pt. 2. Berlin.

Copeland, D. C. 2000. *The Origins of Major War*. Ithaca, NY.

Coppola, A. 1993. *Demetrio di Faro*. Rome.

Cornell, T. J. 1993. "The End of Roman Imperial Expansion." In Rich and Shipley, eds.: 139–70.

Cornell, T. J. 1995. *The Beginnings of Rome: Italy and Rome from the Bronze Age to the Punic Wars (c.1000–264 BC)*. London.

Cornell, T. J. 1996. "Hannibal's Legacy: The Effects of the Hannibalic War on Italy." In Cornell et al., eds.: 97–117.

Cornell, T. J., B. Rankov, and P. Sabin, eds. 1996. *The Second Punic War: A Reappraisal*. London.

Corsten, T. 1991. "Der Hilferuf des akarnanischen Bundes an Rom: Zum Beginn des römischen Eingreifens in Griechenland." *ZPE* 94: 195–210.

Crane, G. 1992. "Power, Prestige and the Corcyrean Affair in Thucydides 1." *CA* 11: 1–27.

Dahlheim, W. 1968. *Struktur und Entwicklung der römischen Völkerrechts im dritten u. zweiten Jahrhunderts v. Chr.* Munich.

Dahlheim, W. 1977. *Gewalt und Herrschaft: Das provinziale Herrschaftssystem der römischen Republik*. Berlin.

Dany, O. 1999. *Akarnanien im Hellenismus: Geschichte und Völkerrecht in Nordwestgriechenland*. Munich.

Davis, J. W. 2000. *Threats and Promises: The Pursuit of International Influence*. Baltimore.

Davis, J. W. 2001. *Victims of Success? Post-Victory Alliance Politics*. Munich.

Deininger, J. 1971. *Der politische Widerstand gegen Rom in Griechenland, 217–86 v. Chr.* Berlin.

Dell, H. J. 1967a. "The Origin and Nature of Illyrian Piracy." *Historia* 16: 344–58.

Dell, H. J. 1967b. "Antigonus III and Rome." *CPh* 62: 94–103.

Dell, H. J. 1970a. "The Western Frontiers of the Macedonian Monarchy." *Ancient Macedonia* 1: 115–26. Thessalonica.

Dell, H. J. 1970b. "Demetrius of Pharus and the Istrian War." *Historia* 19: 30–8.

Dell, H. J. 1973. "Macedon and Rome: The Illyrian Question in the Early Second Century BC." *Ancient Macedonia* 2: 305–15. Thessalonica.

de Regibus, L. 1951. *La repubblica romana e gli ultimi re di Macedonia*. Genoa.

de Regibus, L. 1952. "Tolemeo V Epifane e l'intervento romano nel Mediterraneo orientale." *Aegyptus* 32: 97–100.

Derow, P. S. 1973. "Kleemporos." *Phoenix* 27: 118–34.

Derow, P. 1976. "The Roman Calendar, 218–191 BC." *Phoenix* 30: 265–81.

Derow, P. S. 1979. "Polybius, Rome, and the East." *JRS* 69: 1–15.

Derow, P. S. 1989. "Rome, the Fall of Macedon, and the Sack of Corinth." In *The Cambridge Ancient History*, 2nd ed., Vol. 8: 290–323. Cambridge.

Derow, P. S. 1991. "Pharos and Rome." *ZPE* 88: 261–70.

Derow, P. S. 1994. "Historical Explanation: Polybius and His Predecessors." In S. Hornblower, ed., *Greek Historiography*: 84–90. Oxford.

Derow, P. S. 2003. "The Arrival of Rome: From the Illyrian Wars to the Fall of Macedon." In A. Erskine, ed., *A Companion to the Hellenistic World*: 51–70. Oxford.

de Sanctis, G. 1916. *Storia dei Romani*. Vol. 3.2. Turin.

de Sanctis, G. 1923. *Storia dei Romani*. Vol. 4.1. Turin.

Desch, M. C. 1998. "Culture Clash: Assessing the Importance of Ideas in Security Studies." *Int. Sec.* 23: 141–70.

de Souza, P. 1999. *Piracy in the Graeco-Roman World*. Cambridge.

Dillery, J. 2002. "Quintus Fabius Pictor and Greco-Roman Historiography at Rome." In J. F. Miller, C. Damon, and K. S. Myers, eds., *Vertis in Unum: Studies in Honor of Edward Courtney*: 1–23. Munich.

Donnelly, J. 2000. *Realism and International Relations*. Cambridge.

Donnelly, J. 2006. "Sovereign Inequalities and Hierarchy in Anarchy: American Power and International Society." *EJIR* 12: 139–70.

Dorey, T. A. 1959. "Contributory Causes of the Second Macedonian War." *AJPh* 80: 288–95.

Dorey, T. A. 1960. "The Alleged Aetolian Embassy to Rome." *CR* 10: 9.

Downing, B. 1992. *The Military Revolution and Political Change: Origins of Democracy and Autocracy in Early Modern Europe*. Princeton.

Doyle, M. 1986. *Empires*. Ithaca, NY.

Doyle, M. 1991. "Thucydides: A Realist?" In Lebow and Strauss, eds.: 169–87.

Dreyer, B. 2003. "Der 'Raubvertrag' des Jahres 203/2 v. Chr.: Das Inschriftenfragment von Bargylia und der Brief von Amyzon." *Ep. Anat.* 34: 119–38.

Dusanic, S. 1983. "The *ΚΤΙΣΙΣ ΜΑΓΝΗΕΙΑΕ*, Philip V, and the Panhellenic Lykophryna." *Epigraphica* 45: 11–48.

Eckstein, A. M. 1976. "T. Quinctius Flamininus and the Campaign against Philip in 198 BC." *Phoenix* 30: 119–42.

Eckstein, A. M. 1980. "*Unicum Subsidium Populi Romani*: Hiero II and Rome, 263–215 BC." *Chiron* 10: 183–203.

Eckstein, A. M. 1982. "Human Sacrifice and Fear of Military Disaster in Republican Rome." *AJAH* 7: 69–95.

Eckstein, A. M. 1984. "Rome, Saguntum, and the Ebro Treaty." *Emerita* 55: 51–68.

Eckstein, A. M. 1985. "Polybius, Syracuse, and the Politics of Accommodation." *GRBS* 26: 265–82.

Eckstein, A. M. 1987a. *Senate and General: Individual Decision Making and Roman Foreign Relations, 264–194 BC.* Berkeley and Los Angeles.

Eckstein, A. M. 1987b. "Nabis and Flamininus on the Argive Revolutions of 198 and 197 BC." *GRBS* 28: 213–33.

Eckstein, A. M. 1988. "Rome, the War with Perseus, and Third-Party Mediation." *Historia* 37: 414–44.

Eckstein, A. M. 1989. "Hannibal at New Carthage: Polybius 3.15 and the Power of Irrationality." *CPh* 84: 1–15.

Eckstein, A. M. 1990. "Polybius, the Achaeans, and the 'Freedom of the Greeks.'" *GRBS* 31: 45–71.

Eckstein, A. M. 1994. "Polybius, Demetrius of Pharus, and the Origins of the Second Illyrian War." *CPh* 89: 46–59.

Eckstein, A. M. 1995. *Moral Vision in the Histories of Polybius.* Berkeley and Los Angeles.

Eckstein, A. M. 1997. "*Physis* and *Nomos*: Polybius, Rome, and Cato the Elder." In Cartledge, Garnsey, and Gruen, eds.: 175–98.

Eckstein, A. M. 1999. "Pharos and the Question of Roman Treaties of Alliance Overseas in the Third Century BC." *CPh* 94: 395–418.

Eckstein, A. M. 2000. "Brigands, Emperors, and Anarchy." *Int. Hist. Rev.* 22: 862–79.

Eckstein, A. M. 2002. "Greek Mediation in the First Macedonian War (209–205 BC)." *Historia* 52: 268–97.

Eckstein, A. M. 2003. "Thucydides, the Outbreak of the Peloponnesian War, and the Foundation of International Systems Theory." *Int. Hist. Rev.* 23: 757–74.

Eckstein, A. M. 2005. "The Pact Between the Kings, Polybius 15.20.6, and Polybius' View of the Outbreak of the Second Macedonian War." *CPh* 100: 228–42.

Eckstein, A. M. 2006. *Mediterranean Anarchy, Interstate War, and the Rise of Rome.* Berkeley and Los Angeles.

Edlund, I. 1977. "Invisible Bonds: Clients and Patrons through the Eyes of Polybius." *Klio* 59: 129–36.

Eisen, K. 1966. *Polybiosinterpretationen.* Heidelberg.

Elman, C. and M. F. Elman. 1997. "Diplomatic History and International Relations Theory: Respecting Differences and Crossing Boundaries." *Int. Sec.* 22: 5–21.

Errington, R. M. 1969. *Philopoemen.* Oxford.

Errington, R. M. 1971. "The Alleged Syro-Macedonian Pact and the Origins of the Second Macedonian War." *Athenaeum* 49: 336–54.

Errington, R. M. 1972. *The Dawn of Empire.* London.

Errington, R. M. 1986. "Antiochos III., Zeuxis und Euromus." *Ep. Anat.* 17: 1–8.

Errington, R. M. 1989a. "Rome and Greece to 205 BC." In *The Cambridge Ancient History*, 2nd ed., Vol. 8: 81–106. Cambridge.

Errington, R. M. 1989b. "The Peace Treaty between Miletus and Magnesia (*I. Milet.* 148)." *Chiron* 19: 279–88.

Errington, R. M. 1990. *A History of Macedonia*. Berkeley and Los Angeles.

Errington, R. M. 1993. "Inschriften von Euromos." *Ep. Anat.* 21: 15–32.

Erskine, A., ed. 2003. *Troy between Greece and Rome: Local Tradition and Imperial Power*. Oxford.

Evans, G. and J. Newnham. 1998. *The Penguin Dictionary of International Relations*. London.

Ferguson, N. 2004. *Colossus: The Price of America's Empire*. New York.

Ferguson, W. S. 1932. *Athenian Tribal Cycles in the Hellenistic Age*. Cambridge.

Ferrar, L. L., Jr. 1981. *Arrogance and Anxiety: The Ambivalence of German Power, 1848–1914*. Iowa City.

Ferrary, J. L. 1988. *Philhellénisme et impérialisme: Aspects idéologiques de la conquête romaine du monde hellénistique*. Rome.

Ferro, B. 1960. *Le origini della seconda guerra macedonica*. Palermo.

Fischer, F. 1964. *Griff nach der Weltmacht: Der Kriegszielpolitik des kaiserlichen Deutschland, 1914–1918*. Düsseldorf.

Fischer, F. 1969. *Krieg der Illusionen: Die deutsche Politik von 1911 bis 1914*. Düsseldorf.

Fontenrose, J. 1978. *The Delphic Oracle, its Responses and Operations, with a Catalogue of Responses*. Berkeley and Los Angeles.

Forde, S. 1986. "Thucydides on the Causes of Athenian Imperialism." *Am. Pol. Sci. Rev.* 80: 443–8.

Foucault, J. A. 1972. *Recherches sur la langue et le style de Polybe*. Paris.

Frank, T. 1914. *Roman Imperialism*. Baltimore.

Friedberg, A. L. 1988. *The Weary Titan: Britain and the Experience of Relative Decline, 1895–1905*. Princeton.

Friedberg, A. L. 2000. *In the Shadow of the Garrison State: America's Anti-Statism and its Cold War Grand Strategy*. Princeton.

Fustel de Coulanges, N. 1893. "Polybe: ou, la Grèce conquise par les Romains" (1858). In C. Jullian, ed., *Questions historiques*. Paris.

Gaddis, J. L. 2005. *Surprise, Security, and the American Experience*. Cambridge, Mass.

Garoufalias, P. 1979. *Pyrrhus: King of Epirus*. London.

Gauger, J.-D. 1980. "Phlegon von Tralleis, mirab. III." *Chiron* 10: 223–61.

Gehrke, H.-J. 2002. "Die Römer im ersten punischen Krieg." In *Res publica reparta: Der Verfassung und Gesellschaft des römischen Republik und des frühen Principats (Festschrift J. Bleicken)*: 153–71. Stuttgart.

Geller, D. S. and J. D. Singer. 1998. *Nations at War: A Scientific Study of International Conflict*. Cambridge.

Gera, D. 1998. *Judaea and Mediterranean Politics, 219 to 161 BC*. Leiden.

Gilpin, R. 1981. *War and Change in World Politics*. Cambridge.

Gilpin, R. 1988. "Theory of Hegemonic War." *Journ. Interdisc. Hist.* 18: 591–613.

Glaser, G. L. 1992. "Political Consequences of Military Strategy: Expanding and Refining the Spiral and Deterrence Models." *World Politics* 44: 497–538.

Glaser, G. L. 1997. "The Security Dilemma Revisited." *World Politics* 50: 171–201.

Golan, D. 1985. "Autumn 200 BC: The Events at Abydus." *Athenaeum* 63: 389–404.

Goldsworthy, A. 2000. *The Punic Wars*. London.

Gortzak, Y. 2005. "How Great Powers Rule: Coercion and Positive Inducements in International Order Enforcement." *Soc. Studies* 14: 663–97.

Gourevitch, P. 1978. "The Second Image Reversed: The International Sources of Domestic Politics." *Int. Org.* 32: 881–911.

Grainger, J. D. 1991. *Hellenistic Phoenicia*. Oxford.

Grainger, J. D. 1992. *Seleukos Nikator: Constructing a Hellenistic Kingdom*. London.

Grainger, J. D. 1996. "Antiochus III in Thrace." *Historia* 45: 329–43.

Grainger, J. D. 2002. *The Roman War of Antiochos the Great*. Leiden.

Grant, J. R. 1965. "A Note on the Tone of Greek Diplomacy," *CQ* n.s. 15: 261–6.

Green, P. 1990. *From Alexander to Actium: The Historical Evolution of the Hellenistic Age*. Berkeley and Los Angeles.

Grieco, J. 1988. "Anarchy and the Limits of Cooperation: A Realist Critique of the Newest Liberal Institutionalism." *Int. Org.* 42: 485–507.

Griffith, G. T. 1935a. *The Mercenaries of the Hellenistic World*. Cambridge.

Griffith, G. T. 1935b. "An Early Motive for Roman Imperialism." *CHJ* 5: 1–14.

Gruen, E. S. 1973. "The Supposed Alliance between Rome and Philip V of Macedon." *CSCA* 6: 123–36.

Gruen, E. S. 1975. "Rome and Rhodes in the Second Century BC: A Historiographical Inquiry." *CQ* 25: 58–81.

Gruen, E. S. 1984. *The Hellenistic World and the Coming of Rome*, 2 vols. Berkeley and Los Angeles.

Gruen, E. S. 1990. *Studies in Greek Culture and Roman Policy*. Leiden.

Gruen, E. S. 1992. *Culture and National Identity in Republican Rome*. Ithaca.

Günther, W. 1971. *Das Orakel von Didyma in hellenistischer Zeit*. Tübingen.

Gulick, E. V. 1967. *Europe's Classical Balance of Power*. New York.

Habicht, C. 1957. "Samische Volksbeschlusse der hellenistischen Zeit." *Ath. Mitt.* 72: 152–274.

Habicht, C. 1982. *Studien zur Geschichte Athens in hellenistischer Zeit*. Göttingen.

Habicht, C. 1992. "Athens and the Ptolemies." *CA* 11: 68–90.

Habicht, C. 1997. *Athens from Alexander to Antony*. Cambridge, Mass.

Hamilton, C. D. 1993. "The Origins of the Second Macedonian War." *Ancient Macedonia* 5: 559–67. Thessalonica.

Hammond, N. G. L. 1966. "The Kingdoms of Illyria, circa 400–167 BC." *ABSA* 61: 239–53.

Hammond, N. G. L. 1967. *Epirus*. Oxford.

Hammond, N. G. L. 1968. "Illyris, Rome and Macedon in 229–205 BC." *JRS* 58: 1–21.

Hammond, N. G. L. 1989. "The Illyrian Atintani, the Epirotic Atintanes, and the Roman Protectorate." *JRS* 79: 11–25.

Hammond, N. G. L. and F. W. Walbank. 1988. *A History of Macedon*, Vol. 3. Oxford.

Hansen, E. V. 1971. *The Attalids of Pergamum*. 2nd ed. Ithaca.

Harris, W. V. 1979. *War and Imperialism in Republican Rome*. Oxford.

Harris, W. V. 1984a. "New Directions in the Study of Roman Imperialism." In Harris, ed. (1984b): 13–31.

Harris, W. V., ed. 1984b. *The Imperialism of Mid-Republican Rome*. Rome.

Harris, W. V. 1990. "Roman Warfare in the Economic and Social Context of the Fourth Century." In W. Eder, ed., *Staat und Staatlichkeit in der frühen römischen Republik*: 494–510. Stuttgart.

Heather, P. 2005. *The Fall of Rome: A New History of Rome and the Barbarians*. London.

Heftner, H. 1997. *Der Aufstieg Roms vom Pyrrhoskrieg bis zum Fall von Karthago*. Regensburg.

Heidemann, M.-L. 1966. *Die Freiheitsparole in der griechisch-römischen Auseinandersetzung (200–188 v. Chr.)*. Bonn.

Heinen, H. 1972. *Untersuchungen zur hellenistische Geschichte des 3. Jahrhunderts v. Chr*. Wiesbaden.

Herrmann, P. 1965. "Antiochos der Grosse und Teos." *Anatolia* 9: 26–139.

Heuss, A. 1933. *Die völkerrechtlichen Grundlagen der römischen Aussenpolitik in republikanischer Zeit*. Leipzig.

Hobson, J. 1902. *Imperialism: A Study*. London.

Hoffmann, W. 1934. *Rom und die griechischen Welt im 4. Jahrhundert*. Leipzig.

Hölbl, G. 2001. *A History of the Ptolemaic Empire*. London.

Holleaux, M. 1928. "Rome and Philip: Philip against the Romans." In *The Cambridge Ancient History*, Vol. 8: 116–37. Cambridge.

Holleaux, M. 1935. *Rome, la Grèce et les monarchies hellénistiques au IIIe siècle avant J.-C. (273–205)*. Paris.

Holleaux, M. 1952a. "Trois decrets de Rhodes." In *Études d'epigraphie et d'histoire grecques*, Vol. IV: *Rome, la Macédoine et l'orient grec*: 146–62. Paris. [= *REG* 1899: 20–37.]

Holleaux, M. 1952b. "L'expédition de Philippe V en Asie." In *Études d'epigraphie et d'histoire grecques*, Vol. IV: 211–335.

Holleaux, M. 1957. "Rome, Philippe de Macédoine et Antiochos." In *Études d'epigraphie et d'histoire grecques*, Vol. V: *Philippe V et Antiochos le Grand*: 295–432. Paris.

Hopkins, W. K. 1978. *Sociological Studies in Roman History*, Vol. 1: *Conquerors and Slaves*. Cambridge.

Hoyos, B. D. 1985. "Treaties True and False: The Error of Philinus of Agrigentum." *CQ* 38: 92–109.

Hoyos, B. D. 1998. *Unplanned Wars: The Origins of the First and Second Punic Wars*. Berlin.

Hoyos, B. D. 2003. *Hannibal's Dynasty: Power and Politics in the Western Mediterranean, 247–183 BC*. London.

Huss, W. 1976. *Untersuchungen zur Aussenpolitik Ptolemaios' IV*. Munich.

Hyam, R. 1999. "The Primacy of Geopolitics: The Dynamics of British Imperial Policy." In R. D. King and R. W. Wilson, eds., *The Statecraft of British Imperialism: Essays in Honour of Wm. Roger Louis*: 27–52. London.

Ikenberry, G. J. 2001. *After Victory: Institutions, Strategic Restraint and the Rebuilding of Order after Major War.* Princeton.

Ikenberry, G. J., ed. 2002. *America Unrivaled: The Future of the Balance of Power.* Ithaca.

Ingram, E. 2006. "Pairing Off Empires: The United States as Great Britain in the Middle East." In T. T. Petersen, ed., *Controlling the Uncontrollable? The Great Powers in the Middle East:* 1–21. Trondheim.

Jervis, R. 1976. *Perception and Misperception in International Politics.* Princeton.

Jervis, R. 1997. *System Effects: Complexity in Political and Social Life.* Princeton.

Jervis, R. 2001. "Variation, Change, and Transitions in International Politics." *Rev. Int. Studies* 27: 281–95.

Joffe, J. 1995. " 'Bismarck' or 'Britain': Toward an American Grand Strategy after Bipolarity." *Int. Sec.* 19: 94–117.

Johnson Bagby, L. M. 1994. "The Use and Abuse of Thucydides in International Relations." *Int. Org.* 48: 131–53.

Jonnes, L. and M. Ricl. 1997. "A New Royal Inscription from Phrygia Paroreiros: Eumenes II Grants Tyriaion the Status of a Polis." *Ep. Anat.* 29: 1–30.

Kallet-Marx, R. 1995. *Hegemony to Empire: The Development of the Roman Imperium in the East from 148 to 62 BC.* Berkeley and Los Angeles.

Kapstein, E. B. and M. Mastanduno, eds. 1999. *Unipolar Politics: Realism and State Strategies after the Cold War.* New York.

Kascéev, V. 1997. "Schiedsgerichte und Vermittlungen in den Beziehungen zwischen den hellenistischen Staaten und Rom." *Historia* 46: 419–33.

Kaufman, R. G. 1992. "To Balance or Bandwagon? Alignment Decisions in 1930s Europe." *Sec. Studies* 1: 417–47.

Kauppi, M. V. 1991. "Contemporary International Relations Theory and the Peloponnesian War." In Lebow and Strauss, eds.: 91–124.

Keal, P. 1986. "On Influence and Spheres of Influence." In Triska, ed.: 124–44.

Kegley, C. W., Jr. 1993. "The Neoidealist Moment in International Studies? Realist Myths and the New International Realities." *Int. Studies Quart.* 37: 131–47.

Kegley, C. W., Jr., ed. 1995. *Controversies in International Relations Theory: Realism and the Neoliberal Challenge.* New York.

Keohane, R. O. and R. S. Nye, Jr. 1987. "Power and Interdependence Revisited." *Int. Org.* 41: 723–53.

Klose, E. 1982. *Die völkerrechtliche Ordnung der hellenistichen Staatenwelt in der Zeit von 289–168 v. Chr.* Munich.

Kokaz, N. 2001. "Between Anarchy and Tyranny: Excellence and the Pursuit of Power and Peace in Ancient Greece." *Rev. Int. Studies* 27: 91–118.

Konstan, D. 2007. "War and Reconciliation in Greek Literature." In Raaflaub, ed.: 191–205.

Konterini, V. 1983. "Rome et Rhodes au tournant de IIIe. S. av. J.C. d'après une inscription inédite de Rhodes." *JRS* 73: 24–32.

Kostial, M. 1995. *Kriegerisches Rom? Zur Frage von Unvermiedbarketi und Normalität militärischer Konflikte in der römischen Politik.* Stuttgart.

Kugler, J. and D. Lemke. 1996. *Parity and War: Evaluations and Extensions of "The War Ledger."* Ann Arbor.

Kuijper, D. 1972. "De Alcaeo Messenio unius carminis bis retractore." In *Studi classici in onore di Q. Cataudella*, Vol. 2: 243–60. Catania.

Labs, E. J. 1992. "Do Weak States Bandwagon?" *Sec. Studies* 1: 383–416.

Labs, E. J. 1997. "Beyond Victory: Offensive Realism and the Expansion of War Aims." *Sec. Studies* 6: 1–49.

Lake, D. A. 2001. "Beyond Anarchy: The Importance of Security Institutions." *Int. Sec.* 26: 129–60.

Lampela, A. 1998. *Rome and the Ptolemies of Egypt: The Development of Their Political Relations, 273–80 BC.* Helsinki.

Larsen, J. A. O. 1935. "Was Greece Free between 196 and 146 BC?" *CPh* 30: 193–214.

Layne, C. 1993. "The Unipolar Illusion: Why New Great Powers Will Rise." *Int. Sec.* 17: 5–51.

Layne, C. 2006. *The Peace of Illusions: American Grand Strategy from 1940 to the Present.* Ithaca.

Lazenby, J. F. 1978. *Hannibal's War.* London.

Lazenby, J. F. 1996. "Was Marharbal Right?" In Cornell et al., eds.: 39–48.

LeBohec, S. 1987. "Demetrius de Pharus, Scerdilaidas, et la ligue hellénique." In AttiConv. *L'Illyrie meridionale et l'Epire dans l'antiquité*: 203–8. Clermont-Ferrand.

Lebow, R. N. 1981. *Between Peace and War: The Nature of International Crisis.* Baltimore.

Lebow, R. N. 1991. "Thucydides, Power Transition Theory, and the Causes of War." In Lebow and Strauss, eds.: 125–65.

Lebow, R. N. 2001. "Contingency, Catalysis and International Systems Change." *Pol. Sci. Quart.* 105: 591–616.

Lebow, R. N. and B. S. Strauss, eds. 1991. *Hegemonic Rivalry: From Thucydides to the Nuclear Age.* Boulder, Colo.

Lehmann, G. A. 1967. *Untersuchungen zur historischen Glaubwürdigkeit des Polybios.* Munster.

Lemke, D. and J. Kugler. 1996. "The Evolution of the Power Transition Perspective." In J. Kugler and D. Lemke, *Parity and War: Evaluations and Extensions of the War Ledger*: 3–33. Ann Arbor.

Lendon, J. E. 2000. "Homeric Vengeance and the Outbreak of Greek Wars." In van Wees, ed.: 1–30.

Lévêque, P. 1968. "La guerre à l'époque hellénistique." In J.-P. Vernant, ed., *Problèmes de la guerre en Grèce ancienne*: 261–87. Paris.

Levy, J. S. 1983. *War in the Modern Great Power System.* Lexington, Ky.

Levy, J. S. 1988. "Domestic Politics and War." *Journ. Interdisc. Hist.* 18: 553–73.

Levy, J. S. 2004. "What Do Great Powers Balance Against and When?" In T. V. Paul, J. J. Wirtz, and M. Fortman, eds., *Balance of Power: Theory and Practice in the 21st Century*: 29–51. Stanford.

Levy, J. S. and W. R. Thompson. 2005. "Hegemonic Threats and Great-Power Balancing in Europe, 1495–1999." *Sec. Studies* 14: 1–33.

Lieber, K. A. and G. Alexander. 2005. "Waiting for Balancing: Why the World is Not Pushing Back." *Int. Sec.* 30: 109–39.

Liebmann-Frankfort, T. 1969. *La frontière orientale dans la politique extérieure de la République romaine.* Brussels.

Lind, L. R. 1972. "Concept, Action, and Character: The Reasons for Rome's Greatness." *TAPA* 102: 235–83.

Linderski, J. 1993. "Roman Religion in Livy." In W. Schuler, ed., *Livius: Aspekte seines Werkes*: 53–70. Constance.

Linderski, J. 1995. "Ambassadors Go to Rome." In E. Frezouls and A. Jacquemine, eds., *Les relations internationales: Actes du Colloque de Strasbourg, 15–17 juin 1999*: 452–78. Paris.

Liska, G. 1978. *Career of Empire: America and Imperial Expansion over Land and Sea.* Baltimore.

Lomas, K. 1993. *Rome and the Western Greeks, 350 BC–200 AD: Conquest and Acculturation in Southern Italy.* London.

Lowes Dickenson, G. 1926. *The International Anarchy, 1904–1914.* New York.

Luce, T. J. 1977. *Livy: The Composition of His History.* Princeton.

Lundestad, G. 1986. "Empire by Invitation? The United States and Western Europe, 1945–1952." *Journ. Peace Research* 23: 263–77.

Lundestad, G. 1990. *The American "Empire" and Other Studies of US Foreign Policy in Comparative Perspective.* Oxford.

Ma, J. T. 1999/2002. *Antiochus III and the Cities of Western Asia Minor.* Oxford.

Ma, J. T. 2000. "Fighting Poleis in the Hellenistic World." In van Wees, ed.: 337–76.

Ma, J. T., P. S. Derow, and A. R. Meadows. 1995. "RC 38 (Amyzon) Reconsidered." *ZPE* 109: 71–80.

Magie, D. 1939. "The 'Agreement' between Philip V and Antiochus III for the Partition of the Egyptian Empire." *JRS* 29: 32–44.

Mandelbaum, M. 2005. *The Case for Goliath: How America Acts as the World's Government in the Twenty-First Century.* New York.

Mandell, S. 1989. "The Isthmian Proclamation and the Early Stages of Roman Imperialism in the Near East." *CB* 65: 89–94.

Mandell, S. 1991. "Roman Dominion: Desire and Reality." *AW* 22: 37–42.

Manni, E. 1949. "L'Egitto tolemaico nei suoi rapporti politici con Roma." *RFIC* 27: 79–106.

Mantel, N. 1995. "Der Bündnisvertrag Hannibals mit Philipp V. von Makedonien: Anmerkungen zur Verknüpfung des zw. Makedonischen Krieges mit dem zw. Punischen Krieg bei Livius." In *Rom und der griechischen Osten (Festschrift H. H. Schmitt)*: 175–85. Stuttgart.

Marasco, G. 1986. "Interessi commerciali e fattori politici nella condotta romana in Illiria (230–219 a. C.)." *SCO* 36: 35–112.

Mari, M. 2003. *Polibio: "Storie," Vol. V. Libri XII–XVIII.* Milan.

Mastanduno, M. 1997. "Preserving the Unipolar Moment: Realist Theories and US Grand Strategy after the Cold War." *Inst. Sec.* 21: 49–88.

Mastanduno, M. and E. B. Kapstein. 1999. "Realism and State Strategies After the Cold War." In Kapstein and Mastanduno, eds.: 1–27.

Mastny, V. 1996. *The Cold War and Soviet Insecurity: The Stalin Years.* Oxford.

Mastrocinque, A. 1979. *La Caria e la Ionia meridionale in epoca ellenistica, 323–188 a. C.* Rome.

Mastrocinque, A. 1983. *Manipulazione della storia in età ellenistica: I Seleucidi e Roma.* Rome.

Mattern, S. 1999. *Rome and the Enemy.* Berkeley and Los Angeles.

Mauersberger, A., ed. 1961. *Polybios-Lexikon,* Vol. 1, Pt. 2. Berlin.

McDonald, A. H. and F. W. Walbank. 1937. "The Origins of the Second Macedonian War." *JRS* 27: 180–207.

McGing, B. C. 1986. *The Foreign Policy of Mithridates VI Eupator, King of Pontus.* Leiden.

McGing, B. C. 1997. "Revolt Egyptian Style: Internal Opposition to Ptolemaic Rule." *AfP* 43: 273–314.

McShane, R. B. 1964. *The Foreign Policy of the Attalids of Pergamum.* Urbana, Ill.

Meadows, A. R. 1995. "Greek and Roman Diplomacy on the Eve of the Second Macedonian War." *Historia* 42: 40–60.

Meadows, A. R. 1996. "Four Rhodian Decrees: Rhodes, Iasus and Philip V." *Chiron* 26: 251–66.

Mearsheimer, J. J. 2001. *The Tragedy of Great Power Politics.* New York.

Meister, K. 1975. *Historische Kritik bei Polybios.* Wiesbaden.

Meloni, P. 1955. *Il valore storico e le fonti del libro macedonico di Appian.* Rome.

Mendels, D. 1984/1986. "Did Polybius Have 'Another' View of the Aetolian League?" *Anc. Soc.* 15/17: 63–73.

Meritt, B. D. 1936. "Greek Inscriptions, no. 15: Decree in Honor of Cephisodorus." *Hesperia* 5: 419–28.

Merton, M. 1965. *Fides Romana bei Livius.* Frankfurt a. M.

Mitchell, S. 1993. *Anatolia: Land, Men, and Gods,* Vol. 1: *The Celts in Anatolia and the Impact of Roman Rule.* Oxford.

Mittag, P. F. 2003. "Unruhen im hellenistischen Alexandreia." *Historia* 52: 161–208.

Momigliano, A. D. 1977. "Athens in the Third Century BC, and the Discovery of Rome in the *Histories* of Timaeus of Tauromenium." In *Essays in Ancient and Modern Historiography*: 37–66. [= *RivStorItal* 71 (1959): 529–56.]

Mommsen, T. 1903. *Römische Geschichte* I. 9th ed. Berlin.

Mommsen, W. J. 1986. "The End of Empire and the Continuity of Imperialism." In W. J. Mommsen and J. Osterhammel, eds., *Imperialism Before and After: Continuities and Discontinuities*: 333–58. London.

Morgan, M. G. 1990. "Politics, Religion and the Games in Rome, 200–150 BC." *Philologus* 134: 14–36.

Morgenthau, H. J. 1973. *Politics Among Nations: The Struggle for Power and Peace.* 5th ed. New York.

Morrison, J. S. 1996. *Greek and Roman Oared Warships.* With contributions by J. F. Coates. Oxford.

Morrow, J. D. 1993. "Arms versus Allies: Trade-Offs in the Search for Security." *Int. Org.* 47: 207–33.

Motyl, A. J. 2001. *Imperial Ends: The Decay, Collapse, and Revival of Empires.* New York.

Murphy, G. 1961. "On Satelliteship." *Journal of Economic History* 21: 641–51.

Nathan, J. 2002. *Soldiers, Statecraft, and History: Coercive Diplomacy and International Order.* Westport, Conn.

Niese, B. 1899. *Geschichte der griechischen und makedonischen Staaten set der Schlacht von Chaeronea.* Vol. 2. Gotha.

Nissen, H. 1863. *Kritische Untersuchungen über den Quellen der vierten und funften Dekade des Livius.* Berlin.

North, J. 1981. "The Development of Roman Imperialism." *JRS* 71: 1–9.

Oakley, S. P. 1993. "The Roman Conquest of Italy." In Rich and Shipley, eds.: 9–37.

O'Brien, P. K. and A. Clesse, eds. 2002. *Two Hegemonies: Britain 1846–1914 and the United States 1941–2001.* Aldershot, UK.

Oost, S. I. 1954. *Roman Policy in Epirus and Acarnania.* Dallas.

Organsky, A. F. K. and J. Kugler. 1980. *The War Ledger.* Chicago.

Passarini, A. 1931. "Le relazioni di Roma con l'oriente negli anni 201–200 a. C." *Athenaeum* 9: 260–90.

Passarini, A. 1936. "Un episodio della battaglia di Zama." *Athenaeum* 14: 1–10.

Paton, W. R. 1925. *Polybius: The "Histories."* Vol. 4. Cambridge, Mass.

Pédech, P. 1954. "Polybiana." *REG* 67: 391–5.

Pédech, P. 1964. *La méthode historique de Polybe.* Paris.

Pédech, P. 1969. *Polybe, Histoires Livre I.* Paris.

Peremans, W. and E. van't Dack. 1972. "Sur les rapports de Rome avec les Lagides." *ANRW* I: 1: 660–7. Berlin.

Pestman, P. W. 1956. "Harmachis et Anchmachis, deux rois indigènes du temps des Ptolemées." *Chron. Eg.* 40: 157–70.

Pestman, P. W. 1995. "Hannophris and Chaonnophris, Two Indigenous Pharaohs in Ptolemaic Egypt (205–186 BC)." In S. P. Veeming, ed., *Hundred-Gated Thebes*: 101–37. Leiden.

Petzold, K.-H. 1940. *Die Eröffnung des zweiten römisch-makedonischen Krieges.* Berlin.

Petzold, K.-H. 1971. "Rom und Illyrien: Ein Beitrag zur römischen Aussenpolitik im 3. Jahrhundert." *Historia* 20: 199–223.

Pohl, H. 1993. *Die römische Politik und die Piraterie im ostlichen Mitelmeer vom 3. bis zum 1. Jahrhundert v. Chr.* Berlin.

Posen, B. and A. Ross. 1996. "Competing Visions of US Grand Strategy." *Int. Sec.* 21: 5–53.

Press-Barnathan, G. 2006. "Managing the Hegemon: NATO under Unipolarity." *Sec. Studies* 15: 271–309.

Pritchett, W. K. 1954. "An Unfinished Inscription, IG II2 2362." *TAPA* 85: 159–67.

Quillin, J. M. 2004. "Information and Empire: Domestic Fear Propaganda in Republican Rome, 200–149 BCE." *Journ. of Institutional and Theoretical Economics* 160: 765–85.

Raaflaub, K. R. 1996. "Born to be Wolves? Origins of Roman Imperialism." In R. W. Wallace and E. M. Harris, eds., *Transitions to Empire: Essays in Greco-Roman History, 360–146 BC in Honor of E. Badian*: 273–314. Norman, Okla.

Raaflaub, K. R., ed. 2007. *War and Peace in the Ancient World.* Oxford.

Raaflaub, K. R. and N. Rosenstein, N., eds. 1999. *War and Society in the Ancient and Medieval Worlds: Asia, the Mediterranean, Europe and Mesoamerica.* Cambridge, Mass.

Raditsa, L. 1972. "Bella Macedonica." *Aufsteig und Neidergang des Antiken Welts,* Vol. 1, Pt. 1: 564–89. Berlin.

Rawlings, H. R. 1976. "Antiochus the Great and Rhodes." *AJAH* 1: 2–28.

Rawson, E. 1986. "The Expansion of Rome." In *The Oxford History of the Graeco-Roman World*: 420–35. Oxford.

Reiter, W. 1987. *Aemilius Paullus: Conqueror of Greece.* London.

Rich, J. W. 1976. *Declaring War in the Roman Republic in the Age of Transmarine Expansion.* Brussels.

Rich, J. W. 1984. "Roman Aims in the First Macedonian War." *PCPhS* 210: 126–80.

Rich, J. W. 1989. "Patronage and International Relations in the Roman Republic." In A. Wallace-Hadrill, ed. (1989b): 117–36.

Rich, J. W. 1993. "Fear, Greed and Glory: The Causes of Roman War-Making in the Middle Republic." In Rich and Shipley, eds.: 38–68.

Rich, J. W. 1996. "The Origins of the Second Punic War." In Cornell et al., eds.: 1–38.

Rich, J. W. 2004. "Review of Grainger, *Roman War of Antiochos III*." *CR* 54: 236–8.

Rich, J. W. and G. Shipley, eds. 1993. *War and Society in the Roman World.* London.

Richardson, J. L. 1994. *Crisis Diplomacy: The Great Powers Since the Mid-Nineteenth Century.* Cambridge.

Richardson, J. S. 1979. "Polybius' View of the Roman Empire." *PBSR* 17: 1–11.

Richardson, J. S. 1986. *Hispaniae: Spain and the Development of Roman Imperialism, 218–82 BC.* Cambridge.

Richter, H. D. 1987. *Untersuchungen zur hellenistischen Historiographie: Die Vorlagen des Pompeius Trogus für der nachalexandrischen hellenistischen Geschichte.* Frankfurt am Main.

Robert, J. and L. Robert. 1983. *Amyzon: Fouilles d'Amyzon en Carie,* Vol. 1: *Explorations, histoire, monnaies et inscriptions.* Paris.

Robert, L. 1960. "Inscriptions hellénistiques de Dalmatie." In L. Robert, ed., *Hellenica: Recueil d'épigraphie, de numismatique, et d'antiquités grecques,* XI–XII: 503–41. Paris.

Robinson, R. and J. Gallagher. 1953. "The Imperialism of Free Trade." *EHR* 6: 1–15.

Robinson, R. and J. Gallagher. 1960. *Africa and the Victorians.* London.

Rosecrance, R. 2003. "Is There a Balance of Power?" In J. A. Vasquez and C. Elman, eds., *Realism and the Balancing of Power: A New Debate*: 154–65. Upper Saddle River, NJ.

Rosen, S. P. 2003. "Imperial Choices." In A. J. Bacevich, ed., *The Imperial Tense: Prospects and Problems of American Empire*: 211–26. Chicago.

Rosenstein, N. 1990. *Imperatores Victi: Military Defeat and Aristocratic Competition in the Middle and Late Republic.* Berkeley and Los Angeles.

Rosenstein, N. 1999. "Republican Rome." In Raaflaub and Rosenstein, eds.: 193–205.

Rosenstein, N. 2004. *Rome at War: Farms, Families and Death in the Middle Republic.* Berkeley and Los Angeles.

Rosenstein, N. 2007. "War and Peace, Fear and Reconciliation at Rome." In Raaflaub, ed.: 226–44.

Rostovtzeff, M. I. 1941. *Social and Economic History of the Roman Empire,* 2 vols. 2nd ed. (1957). Oxford.

Roussel, D. 1970. *Polybe: "Histoires."* Paris.

Rowland, R. J. 1983. "Rome's Earliest Imperialism." *Latomus* 42: 749–62.

Roy, J. 2000. "Review of Dany, *Akarnanien in Hellenismus.*" *BMCR* (2.21).

Sacks, K. S. 1975. "Polybius' Other View of Aetolia." *JHS* 95: 92–106.

Sacks, K. S. 1980. *Polybius on the Writing of History.* Berkeley and Los Angeles.

Sands, P. C. 1908. *The Client Princes of the Roman Empire under the Republic.* Cambridge.

Schmidt, B. 1998. *The Political Discourse of Anarchy: A Disciplinary History of International Relations.* Albany.

Schmitt, H. H. 1957. *Rom und Rhodos.* Munich.

Schmitt, H. H. 1964. *Untersuchungen zur Geschichte Antiochos' des Grossen und seiner Zeit.* Wiesbaden.

Schmitt, H. H. 1969. *Die Staatsverträge des Altertums.* Vol. 3. Munich.

Schmitt, H. H. 1974. "Polybios und die Gleichgewicht der Mächte." *Entretiens Fondation Hardt* 20: 67–102.

Scholten, J. B. 2000. *The Politics of Plunder: The Aetolians and their Koinon in the Early Hellenistic Era, 279–219 BC.* Berkeley and Los Angeles.

Schroeder, P. W. 1997. "History and International Relations Theory." *Int. Sec.* 22: 64–74.

Schumpeter, J. 1952. *The Sociology of Imperialisms.* New York.

Schweighauser, J. 1789–95. *Polybii Megalopolitani "historarium" quidquid superest.* Leipzig.

Schweighauser, J. 1822. *Lexicon Polybianum.* Oxford.

Schweller, R. 1994. "Bandwagoning for Profit: Bringing the Revisionist State Back In." *Int. Sec.* 19: 72–107.

Schweller, R. 1998. *Deadly Imbalances: Tripolarity and Hitler's Strategy of World Conquest.* New York.

Schweller, R. 1999. "Realism and the Present Great Power System: Growth and Positional Conflict over Scarce Resources." In Kapstein and Mastanduno, eds.: 28–68.

Scott-Kilvert, I. 1979. *Polybius: The Rise of the Roman Empire.* Harmondsworth.

Scullard, H. H. 1973. *Roman Politics, 220–150 BC.* 2nd ed. Oxford.

Scullard, H. H. 1980. *A History of Rome, 753–146 BC.* 4th ed. New York.

Seager, R. 1981. "The Freedom of the Greeks of Asia from Alexander to Antiochus." *CQ* n.s. 31: 106–12.

Segre, M. 1944/1945 (1952). "Tituli Calymnii." *ASAA* 22/23: 1–52.

Sheehan, M. 1996. *The Balance of Power: History and Theory.* London and New York.

Sherk, R. K. 1969. *Roman Documents from the Greek East: Senatus Consulta and Epistulae to the Age of Augustus.* Baltimore.

Sherwin-White, A. N. 1977. "Roman Involvement in Anatolia, 167–88 BC." *JRS* 67: 62–75.

Sherwin-White, A. N. 1980. "Rome the Aggressor?" *JRS* 70: 177–81.

Sherwin-White, A. N. 1984. *Roman Foreign Policy in the East, 168 BC to AD 1.* Norman, Okla.

Sherwin-White, S. M. 1978. *Ancient Cos.* Göttingen.

Sherwin-White, S. M. and A. Kuhrt. 1993. *From Samarkhand to Sardis: A New Approach to the Seleucid Empire.* Berkeley and Los Angeles.

Shipley, G. 1987. *A History of Samos.* Oxford.

Shuckburgh, E. S. 1889. *The "Histories" of Polybius.* 2 vols. London.

Siebert, J. 1995. "Invasion aus dem Osten: Trauma, Propaganda, oder Erfindung der Römer?" In C. Schubert, K. Brodersen, and U. Huttner, eds., *Rom und der griechischen Osten: Festschrift für H. H. Schmitt*: 237–48. Stuttgart.

Singer, J. D. 1961. "The Level-of-Analysis Problem." *World Politics* 14: 77–92.

Snyder, J. 1991. *Myths of Empire: Domestic Politics and International Ambition.* Ithaca.

Snyder, J. and Jervis, R. eds. 1993. *Coping With Complexity in the International System.* Boulder, Colo.

Sofka, J. R. 2001. "The Eighteenth-Century International System: Parity or Primacy?" *Rev. Intern. Studies* 27: 147–64.

Spirtas, M. 1996. "A House Divided: Tragedy and Evil in Realist Theory." In B. Frankel, ed., *Realism: Restatements and Renewal*: 385–423. Portland, Oregon.

Starr, C. G. 1938. "Rhodes and Pergamum, 201–200 BC." *CPh* 33: 63–8.

Sterling, R. W. 1974. *Macropolitics: International Security in a Global Society.* New York.

Stevenson, D. 1997a. "Militarization and Diplomacy in Europe before 1914." *Int. Sec.* 22: 125–61.

Stevenson, D. 1997b. *The Outbreak of the First World War: 1914 in Perspective.* New York.

Stewart, R. 1998. *Public Office in Early Rome: Ritual Procedure and Political Practice.* Ann Arbor.

Stier, H. 1952. *Roms Aufstieg zur Weltmacht und die griechische Welt.* Cologne.

Strachan-Davidson, J. L. 1888. *Selections from Polybius.* Oxford.

Strauss, B. S. 1986. *Athens After the Peloponnesian War: Class, Faction and Policy, 403–396 BC.* Ithaca.

Strauss, B. S. 1991. "Of Bandwagons and Ancient Greeks." In Lebow and Strauss, eds.: 189–210.

Strauss, B. S. 1997. "The Art of Alliance and the Peloponnesian War." In C. D. Hamilton and P. Krentz, eds., *Polis and Polemos: Essays on Politics, War, and History in Ancient Greece in Honor of Donald Kagan*: 127–40. Claremont, Calif.

Taliaferro, J. W. 2000. "Security Seeking under Anarchy: Defensive Realism Revisited." *Int. Sec.* 25: 128–61.

Taliaferro, J. W. 2004. *Balancing Risk: Great Power Intervention in the Periphery.* Ithaca.

Tarn, W. W. 1928. "The Greek Leagues and Macedonia." In *The Cambridge Ancient History*, Vol. 8: 732–51. Cambridge.

Taylor, P. J. 1994. "The State as Container: Territoriality in the Modern World System." *Progress in Human Geogr.* 18: 151–62.

Taylor, T., ed. 1978. "Power Politics." In T. Taylor, ed., *Approaches and Theory in International Politics*: 121–39. London.

Thompson, W. R. 1988. *On Global War: Historical-Structural Approaches to World Politics.* Columbia, SC.

Thornton, A. P. 1965. *Doctrines of Imperialism.* New York.

Triska, J. F., ed. 1986. *Dominant Powers and Subordinate States.* Durham, NC.

Tritle, L. A. 2007. " 'Laughing for Joy': War and Peace among the Greeks." In Raaflaub, ed.: 172–90.

Ullmann, R. 1929. *Étude sur le style des discours de Tite Live.* Oslo.

Urban, R. 1979. *Wachstum und Krise der Achaischen Bundes: Quellenstudien zur Entwicklung des Bundes von 280 bis 222 v. Chr.* Wiesbaden.

van Evera, S. 1998. "Offense, Defense, and the Causes of War." *Int. Sec.* 22: 5–43.

van Evera, S. 1999. *Causes of War: Power and the Roots of Conflict.* Ithaca.

van Wees, H., ed. 2000. *War and Violence in Ancient Greece.* London.

Vasquez, A. 1999. *The War Puzzle.* New York.

Veïsse, A.-E. 2004. *Les "révoltes égyptiennes": Recherches sur les troubles intérieurs en Egypte du règne de Ptolémée III à la conquête romaine.* Paris.

Veyne, P. 1975. "Y a-t'il eu un impérialisme romain?" *MEFR* 85: 793–855.

von Ungern-Sternberg, J. 1976. *Capua im zweiten punischen Krieg.* Munich.

Walbank, F. W. 1933. *Aratus of Sicyon.* Cambridge.

Walbank, F. W. 1936. "The Accession of Ptolemy V: A Study in Chronology." *JEA* 22: 20–34.

Walbank, F. W. 1938. "Φίλιππος τραγῳδούμενος: A Polybian Experiment." *JHS* 58: 55–68.

Walbank, F. W. 1940. *Philip V of Macedon.* Cambridge.

Walbank, F. W. 1943. "Alcaeus of Messene, Philip V, and Rome, Part II." *CQ* 37: 1–13.

Walbank, F. W. 1949. "Roman Declarations of War in the Third and Second Centuries." *CPh* 44: 15–19.

Walbank, F. W. 1957. *A Historical Commentary on Polybius.* Vol. 1. Oxford.

Walbank, F. W. 1967. *A Historical Commentary on Polybius.* Vol. 2. Oxford.

Walbank, F. W. 1972. *Polybius.* Berkeley and Los Angeles.

Walbank, F. W. 1977. "Polybius' Last Ten Books." In *Historiographia Antiqua: Commentationes Lovanienses in honorem W. Peremans septuagenarii editae*: 139–62.

Walbank, F. W. 1979. *A Historical Commentary on Polybius.* Vol. 3. Oxford.

Walbank, F. W. 1982. "Sea-Power and the Antigonids." In W. L. Adams and E. N. Borza, eds., *Philip II, Alexander the Great, and the Macedonian Heritage*: 213–36. New York.

Walbank, F. W. 1985. "*Symplokē*: Its Role in Polybius' *Histories*." In *Selected Papers in Greek and Roman History and Historiography*: 313–24. Cambridge. [= *YClS* 24 (1975): 197–212.]

Walbank, F. W. 2002a. "*Η ΤΩΝ ΟΛΩΝ ΕΛΠΙΣ* and the Antigonids." In Walbank, ed. (2002d): 127–36. Cambridge. [= *Ancient Macedonia* 5 (1993): 1721–30. Thessalonica.]

Walbank, F. W. 2002b. "Supernatural Paraphernalia in Polybius' *Histories*." In Walbank, ed. (2002d): 245–57 [= I. Worthington, ed., *Ventures in Greek History* (1994): 25–40. Oxford.]

Walbank, F. W. 2002c. "Polybius and Macedonia." In Walbank, ed. (2002d): 91–106. [= *Ancient Macedonia* 2 (1970): 291–307.]

Walbank, F. W., ed. 2002d. *Polybius, Rome and the Hellenistic World: Essays and Reflections.* Cambridge.

Wallace, R. W. 1990. "Hellenization and Roman Society in the Late Fourth Century BC." In W. Eder, ed., *Staat und Staatlichkeit in der frühen römischen Republik*: 278–91. Stuttgart.

Wallace-Hadrill, A. 1989a. "Patronage in Roman Society: From Republic to Empire." In A. Wallace-Hadrill, ed.: 63–88.

Wallace-Hadrill, A., ed. 1989b. *Patronage in Ancient Society.* London.

Walsh, J. J. 1993. "Bones of Contention: Pharsalus, Phthiotic Thebes, Larisa Cremaste, Echinus." *CPh* 87: 208–33.

Walsh, J. J. 1996. "Flamininus and the Propaganda of Liberation." *Historia* 45: 17–31.

Walsh, P. G. 1963. *Livy: His Historical Aims and Methods.* Cambridge.

Walt, S. 1987. *The Origins of Alliances.* Ithaca.

Walt, S. 2002. "Keeping the World 'Off-Balance': Self-Restraint and US Foreign Policy." In Ikenberry, ed.: 121–54.

Waltz, K. N. 1959. *Man, the State and War: A Theoretical Analysis.* New York.

Waltz, K. N. 1979. *Theory of International Politics.* New York.

Waltz, K. N. 1988. "The Origins of War in Neorealist Theory." *Journ. Interdisc. Hist.* 18: 615–28.

Waltz, K. N. 1993. "The Emerging Structure of International Politics." *Int. Sec.* 18: 44–79.

Waltz, K. N. 2000. "Structural Realism after the Cold War." *Int. Sec.* 25: 5–41.

Warrior, V. 1996. *The Initiation of the Second Macedonian War.* Wiesbaden.

Watson, A. 1992. *The Evolution of International Society: A Comparative Historical Analysis.* London.

Wayman, W. F. and P. F. Diehl. 1994. "Realism Reconsidered: The Realpolitik Framework and its Basic Propositions." In F. W. Wayman and P. F. Diehl, eds., *Reconstructing Realpolitik*: 3–26. Ann Arbor.

Weil, R. 1995. *Polybe: "Histoires," xiii–xvi.* Paris.

Welles, C. B. 1934. *Royal Correspondence in the Hellenistic Period: A Study in Greek Epigraphy.* London.

Welwei, K.-H. 1963. *Könige und Königtum im Urteil des Polybios.* Cologne.

Wendt, A. 1992. "Anarchy Is What States Make It: The Social Construction of Power Politics." *Int. Org.* 46: 391–425.

Wendt, A. 1999. *Social Theory of International Politics.* Cambridge.

Wheeler, E. L. 1984. "Sophistic Interpretations and Greek Treaties." *GRBS* 25: 253–60.

Whittaker, C. R. 1978. "Carthaginian Imperialism in the Fifth and Fourth Centuries." In P. Garnsey and C. R. Whittaker, eds., *Imperialism in the Ancient World*: 59–90. Cambridge.

Wick, T. E. 1977. "Thucydides and the Megara Decree." *Ant. Class.* 46: 74–99.

Wiedemann, T. 1987. "The Fetials: A Reconsideration," *CQ* 36: 478–89.

Wiemer, H.-U. 2001a. "Karien am Vorabend des 2. makedonischen Krieges: Bemerkungen zu einer neuen Inschrift aus Bargylia." *Ep. Anat.* 33: 1–14.

Wiemer, H.-U. 2001b. *Rhodische Traditionen in der hellenistischen Historiographie*. Frankfurt am Main.

Wiemer, H.-U. 2002. *Krieg, Handel und Piratie: Untersuchungen zur Geschichte des hellenistischen Rhodos*. Berlin.

Wight, M. 1977. *Systems of States*. Leicester.

Wight, M. 1978. *Power Politics*. New York.

Wilkes, J. 1992. *The Illyrians*. Oxford.

Wilkinson, D. 1999. "Unipolarity Without Hegemony." *ISR* 1: 142–72.

Will, E. 1982. *Histoire politique du monde hellénistique*. 2nd ed. Vol. 2. Nancy.

Will, E. 1989. "The Successors to Alexander." In *The Cambridge Ancient History*, 2nd ed., Vol. 8: 23–61. Cambridge.

Williams, J. H. C. 2001. *Beyond the Rubicon: Romans and Gauls in Republican Italy*. Oxford.

Williams, W. A. 1962. *The Tragedy of American Diplomacy*. New York.

Wiseman, T. P. 1985. "Competition and Cooperation." In T. P. Wiseman, ed., *Roman Political Life, 90 BC–AD 69*: 3–19. Exeter.

Wohlforth, W. C. 1993. *The Elusive Balance: Power and Perception During the Cold War*. Ithaca.

Wohlforth, W. C. 1994–5. "Realism and the End of the Cold War," *Int. Sec.* 19: 91–129.

Wohlforth, W. C. 1999. "The Stability of a Unipolar World," *Int. Sec.* 24: 5–41.

Wohlforth, W. C. 2000. "A Certain Idea of Science: How International Relations Theory Avoids Reviewing the Cold War." In O. A. Westad, ed., *Reviewing the Cold War: Approaches, Interpretations, Theory*: 126–45. London.

Wohlforth, W. C. 2001. "The Russian-Soviet Empire: A Test of Neorealism." *Rev. Int. Studies* 27: 213–35.

Wohlforth, W. C. 2002. "US Strategy in a Unipolar World." In Ikenberry, ed.: 98–118.

Wolfers, A. 1962. *Discord and Collaboration: Essays on International Politics*. Baltimore.

Wörrle, M. 1988. "Inschriften von Herakleia am Latmos, I: Antiochos III., Zeuxis und Herakleia." *Chiron* 18: 421–76.

Yoshimura, T. 1984. "Zum römischen *Libertas*-Begriff im der Aussenpolitik im zweiten Jahrhundert v. Chr." *AJAH* 9: 1–14.

Index

Pinnes (king of Ardiaei, 229–218
BC), 40, 43 n. 63, 52, 70, 72
(disappears), 73, 82, 83
Placentia (Roman colony in Po
Valley), destroyed by Celts,
200 BC, 234, 262 n. 105
Plautus (Roman playwright), and the
Stichus as evidence of Aetolian
embassy asking Rome for
help vs. Philip V, 215–16; as
evidence of Roman exhaustion
in 200 BC, 215, 234
Pleuratus (king of Ardiaei, ca. 210
BC), 48, 97; son of Scerdilaidas
(s.v.), 61 n. 140, 278; joins
Rome in First Macedonian
War, 89; and Peace of Phoenice,
113; joins Rome in Second
Macedonian War, 278, 279
Polybius (Greek historical writer),
establishes basic issues about
Roman expansion in East, 3, 32;
deported to Italy from Achaea,
167 BC, 366 n. 94; friend of
Cato the Elder, 371 and n. 109;
policy as hipparch of Achaean
League, 169 BC, 371 n. 107;
and the Hellenistic power-
transition crisis (s.v.), 25–6,
129, 227, and Chapter 4,
passim; and the *symplokē* (s.v.),
26, 32, 79–83, 116, 118, 122,
224–5, 268, 270, 275, 307,
340, 367; and Tyche, 26 n. 72,
134–5, 221–4, 270 n. 127;
causation in, 135–7; wide
experience and sophistication
of, 226; on the strong answering
appeals from the weak, 245–6;
on piety of the Roman populace
and aristocracy, 249; shocked
by brutal military tactics of
Lycortas (s.v.), 352; as Realist
analyst, 371 n. 109; on causes
of First Illyrian War, 33–4, 35;
interest in Illyria, 50; and treaty

ending the First Punic War, 54;
and Macedonian-Punic treaty of
alliance, 215 BC, 54; and Peace
of Phoenice (s.v.), 112; sees
Demetrius of Pharos as villain,
59, 61, 74; use of Fabius Pictor
(s.v.), 59 and n. 132, 63 n. 148;
sees Aratus of Sicyon as hero,
59, 367; and speech of Agelaus,
217 BC, 79–83; and Greek
mediation of First Macedonian
War, 93, 104; dislike of Aetolia,
97; inclusion of anti-Roman
speeches, 117; and the Pact
Between the Kings (s.v.), 129,
131, 132–50, 168, 169, 170,
179, 189, 221–6, 250 n. 69,
251, 266–7, and Chapter 4,
passim; moral condemnation of
Philip V and Antiochus III, 132,
134–5, 137, 138, 147–8, 176,
221, 223, 268, 270 n. 127; use
of Rhodian sources for this
period, 174, 185; use of
multiple sources, 175, 226;
criticism of Rhodian writers
Antisthenes and Zeno, 174–6,
cf. 226; use of Macedonian
sources for this period, 176–7;
on Athenians and the Ptolemies,
208 and n. 99; criticizes
Athenian action in 201 BC, 208
and n. 99; and Greek embassies
to Rome, 201/200 BC, 220–6,
231–40, 243–4, 252 n. 73,
266–7; on Roman decision
to intervene in East, 200 BC,
220–6, 238–9; and prediction
of Demetrius of Phalerum (s.v.),
223–4; on expansionist Roman
ambitions, 224, 252; on Punic,
Antigonid, and Seleucid
ambitions, 224, 252; on
ambitions of Philip V, 79, 80,
81, 144–5, 341; sees large
historical patterns, 224–5; and

Polybius (*cont'd*)
    impact of human decision-
    making, 225–6; praise of
    Abydus (s.v.), 278; and Corinth
    given to Achaea by Rome, 284
    n. 37; on Aristaenus and the
    "freedom of the Greeks," 283,
    290–1, 294 and n. 90, cf. 295
    and n. 98; positive view of
    Isthmian Declaration, 295–6; on
    ambitions of Antiochus III, 145,
    306, 341; on Roman embassy
    to Antiochus III, 200 BC, 308;
    criticizes Roman ruthlessness
    and duplicity, 296 and n. 99;
    criticizes increasing Roman
    sternness towards Greeks after
    180 BC, 296, 366, 379; and
    dating of the beginning of
    Roman "rule" in the East, 335;
    on Rome and Greek freedom
    before the Third Macedonian
    War, 344–5, 350, 351 and n.
    35, 358–9, 369–71, 381 n. 147;
    praises Philip V for increasing
    power of Macedon after 196 BC,
    358–9; praises Greek desire to
    maintain independence from
    Rome, 360–1, 367, 370, 371,
    376, 380 n. 146; sees Callicrates
    (s.v.) as villain, 367–9, 380; bias
    against Callicrates, 369 n. 146;
    and Third Macedonian War
    as "tipping point" for Roman
    power in East, 358, 381;
    praises Cephalus (s.v.) for
    independence from Rome, 370
M. Porcius Cato (consul 195 BC),
    speech in defense of Rhodians,
    167 BC, 252 n. 74, 371,
    381 n. 147; and moralizing
    arguments, 252 n. 74, 371,
    381 n. 147; and "defensive
    war" at Rome, 252 n. 74, 371,
    381 n. 147; and speech of
    P. Sulpicius Galba in Livy,

255 and n. 84; at battle of
    Thermopylae, 191 BC, 329; on
    libertas in Greek East before 167
    BC, 355, 371, 381 and n. 147;
    friend of Polybius, 371 and
    n. 109; as Realist analyst, 371
    and n. 109
Potidaea (Greek city), 244, 316
    n. 36
power-maximizing behavior of all
    states under anarchy (political
    science concept), 8–9, 15, 40,
    57 n. 125, 181, 227, 229, 237,
    240, 247–8, 265
power-transition crises (political
    science concept), definition
    of, 20–1, 181–2, 336–7;
    characteristics of, 21–2, 125–6,
    127, 227, 265–8, 303–4; the
    small number of, 23–4; and
    origins of World War I, 21, 128;
    in Illyria, 233–228 BC, 34 n. 21;
    and end of the Cold War, 22,
    126 n. 22, 184, cf. 235 n. 20,
    315, 316 n. 33; and origins
    of World War II, 128; and
    crisis of ca. 207–188 BC in
    Mediterranean, 4, 24–5, 26, 28,
    125–6, 180, 181, 183–4, 206,
    215–16, 227–8, 235, 238–9,
    248, 268–9, 273, 299, 302, 335,
    336, 337, 340, and Chapters 4,
    5, and 6, *passim*; historicity of,
    129–80, 227–8, 243, 260,
    267–9
preemptive war (political science
    concept), 253 n. 78
preventive war (political science
    concept), 253 and n. 78,
    258, 260, cf. 269; the Second
    Macedonian War as, 253
    and n. 78, 258, 260, cf.
    269
Primat der Aussenpolitik (primacy of
    external, systemic pressures in
    foreign relations), 229

Sparta (*cont'd*)
    defeated by Achaeans under
        Philopoemen, 207 BC, 103 and
        n. 100; *amicitia* with Rome, 122,
        123, 236; receives Argos from
        Philip V, 197 BC, 148; war with
        Rome-led coalition, 195 BC,
        286; destroys Megalopolis,
        223 BC, 295 n. 98; forced into
        Achaean League, 192 BC, 324,
        332, 348, 351, 368; Achaean
        oppression at, 345 n. 9; appeals
        to Rome about, 351, 368;
        championed by Callicrates (s.v.)
        at Rome, 367–9
    sphere of influence (political science
        concept), definition of, 54, 57,
        298 n. 112, cf. 374, 376; of
        Rome in Illyria, 54–5, 57, 75,
        121; of Ptolemies in southeast
        Aegean, 162, 167, 179; of
        Seleucids in western Asia Minor,
        167; of Rome in European
        Greece after 196 BC, 297–8,
        307, 317, 338, 339, 378, 379;
        of Rome in Aegean after 188 BC,
        336; not a euphemism for
        empire, 379 and n. 141
    status and reputation for power,
        importance of in Hellenistic
        anarchy, 89, 90, 173, 174, 246,
        313, 314–15, 336 n. 109, 337,
        339–40, 353 n. 41, 353 and
        n. 43, 354, 359–60 and 380
        (Roman concern for)
Strato and Poseidonius (pro-
    Macedonian historical writers),
    possible sources of Polybius,
    177 n. 232
Stratoniceia (city in Caria), seized
    by Philip V, 201 BC, 165–6 and
    n. 191; alleged ties to Seleucids,
    166; controlled by Rhodes, 201
    BC, 166; Rhodians failure to
    recapture it, 197 BC, 166;
    Rhodes regains with help of

Antiochus III, 166, 188 and
    n. 21
P. Sulpicius Galba (consul 211 BC),
    Roman commander in Greece,
    210–207 BC, 101, 102 n. 96;
    sabotages peace talks, 207 BC,
    106, 117; alleged atrocity on
    Aegina, 109 n. 123, cf. 196
    n. 51; delay in leaving for
    Greece as consul, 200 BC: for
    religious reasons, 230, 235,
    249–50; because of difficulties
    in the draft, 230, 235, 250
    n. 65, 261 n. 103; advocates
    Roman intervention in East,
    200 BC, 250, 254–5, 259–60,
    269; for turning over Euboea
    to Pergamum, 250 and n. 68;
    historicity of speech for war in
    Livy, 254–5; and the lottery for
    provinces, 200 BC, 255–6, 280
    n. 25; ambition of, 256; lack
    of great success against Philip
    V, 210–207 BC, 256; lack of
    success against Philip V, 200
    and 199 BC, 256–7, 278–9, 282,
    304; reputation for brutality,
    278, 281; seeks Greek allies,
    278–9; and mutiny of Roman
    army, 279; on senatorial
    commission to formalize peace,
    196 BC, 283 n. 33, 311 n. 14;
    and Roman demands on
    Antiochus III, 193 BC, 320–1
Ser. Sulpicius Galba, envoy to
    obtain the Great Mother, 205
    BC, 250; and Pergamum, 250;
    relative of consul of 200 BC,
    250
symplokē (interconnectedness
    of eastern and western
    Mediterranean), 26, 32, 72,
    79–83, 116, 118, 122, 136,
    180, 224–5, 268, 270, 275,
    299 n. 119, 307, 340; theory of
    Polybius: *see* Polybius; ignored

by Philip V and Antiochus III, 136, and cf. Roman Senate, 299 n. 119

Syracuse (Sicilian polity), friendship with Rome, 57 n. 122, 300 n. 123; defects to Hannibal, 214 BC, 87, 202; allegedly appeals to Philip V for help vs. Rome, 87; captured by Rome, 211 BC, 88; ties to Ptolemies, 202; threatens Mamertines (s.v.), 244; misperception of strategic situation in 214 BC of, 266 n. 119

system-oriented analysis (Realism), examples of, 7, 10, 27, 37, 38, 73, 118, 124, 125–8, 131, 136 n. 63, 180, 184, 198, 200, 219, 225, 227–9, 231, 235, 241–6, 264, 268–9, 303, 349; usefulness of, 267

Syrian War, *see* Antiochene War (192–188 BC)

Taliaferro, J. (political scientist), 313

Tarentum (Greek city in southern Italy), 29, 30, 50, 83, 85, 86; defects to Hannibal, 213 BC, 87, cf. 86; and invasion of Italy by Pyrrhus, 29–30, 121, 244; pillaged by Rome, 209 BC, 280 n. 24; and Flamininus, 280 n. 24

Taurus Mountains (between Syria and Asia Minor), Antiochus advances across, 197 BC, 145; boundary of Seleucid empire after 188 BC, 333; Pergamene troops advance to, 354 n. 48

Teanum Sidicinum (Campanian town), asks Capua for help vs. Samnites, 245

Tempe Conference, 197 BC (Flamininus and Greek allies), 294 n. 92, cf. 291

Teos (Aegean coast city), subordinated to Antiochus III, 145 and n. 106, 160 n. 168

Teuta (ruler of Ardiaei), succeeds Agron (s.v.) 40; regent for Pinnes (s.v.), 40; and Ardiaean piracy, 40; quarrel with Roman envoys, 40; loses war with Rome (First Illyrian War), 229 BC, 41, 236; and peace treaty of 228 BC, 41, 51–2; *amicitia* with Rome, 43; strategic mistakes of, 266 n. 119

Thebes (Greek city), great power in fourth century BC, 362; goes over to Rome from Macedonian alliance, 197 BC, 284, 285

Thasos (island polity), atrocity of Philip V at, 148, 208–9; freed from Macedon by Isthmian Declaration, 288

Theangela (town in Caria), Ptolemaic, and seized by Philip V, 201 BC, 156, 161, 167, 174; given by Philip to forces of Antiochus III, 156, 167, 177, 178

Thessaly (region in central Greece), subordinated to Macedon, 113, 295; and Peace of Phoenice, 113; freed from Macedon by Isthmian Declaration, 288; Flamininus' interference in internal affairs of towns in, 293, 294–5; and worship of Zeus Eleutherios, 206; goes over to Antiochus III, winter 192/191 BC, 325

Thermopylae Pass, 100, 102, 329

Third Macedonian War (171–168 BC), 364, 365, 366, 367, 370, 379; great impact of, 380–1

Thoas (Aetolian statesman), invites Antiochus III to Greece, 193/192 BC, 322 and n. 59

48–9, 88–9 (terms), 90, 91, 236; violated by Aetolians, 98, 111, 112; delay of ratification of, in Rome, 91, 99; termed "shameful" by Thrasycrates (s.v.), 108–9

treaty of alliance between Rome and Maronea (s.v.), 160s BC, 46 n. 75

treaty of friendship between Euromus (s.v.) and Zeuxis, 197 BC, 170

treaty of peace between Antiochus III and Ptolemies, after Raphia (s.v.), 217 BC, 204; Ptolemaic attempts to renew, 204/203 BC, 204

treaty of peace between Philip V and the Aetolian League, 206 BC, 104, 111–12, 116, 123, 198, 211, 212, 236; mediated by Rhodes, 111, 116; violated by Philip, 148, 212 n. 114, 215, cf. 190

treaty of peace between Rome and the Ardiaean kingdom, 228 BC, 41, 51, 52, 58, 61, 68, 72, 75

treaty of peace between Rome and Carthage, 241 BC, 54

treaty of peace ending Antiochene War ("Peace of Apamea"), 188 BC, 3, 26, 28, 49, 275, 308, 333–4, 348, 376, 377, 378; and alleged beginning of Roman "rule" in East, 335; influence of Greek allies on, 344 n. 6

treaty of peace ending the First Macedonian War ("Peace of Phoenice"), 205 BC, 72, 112–15, 117, 121, 236; violated by Philip in Illyria, 113; *adscripti* to, 113–14

treaty of peace ending Second Macedonian War, 196 BC, 283, 287, 348

treaty of peace ending the Social War ("Peace of Naupactus"), 79–83, 90, 91, 116

tripolarity (political science concept), definition of, 21; Hellenistic, 21, 25, 126, 128, 179, 181, 182, 183, 200, 209, 227, 267, 273, 274, 337, 340; artificially restored by Rome, 274–5, 340, 355; instability of, as Hellenistic interstate structure, 275, 337 (and *passim*)

Triteuta, mother of Pinnes (s.v.), 58

Tunis (Punic city), appeal to Rome for aid vs. Carthage rejected, 245

Tyche (Fortune), 26 n. 72; importance in Polybius, 134–7, 221–4, 270 n. 127; as avenger of Justice vs. Philip V and Antiochus III, 134–5, 137, 221, 223; and fall of Macedonian power, 223–4; as patroness of rise of Roman power, 224

"uncertainty principle" (political science concept), 242 and n. 39; and war, 242, 265–6 and n. 118; Hellenistic intensity of, 242–3; and "worst-case scenario" (s.v.), 243 n. 43, 244; and Second Macedonian War (s.v.), 243–4, 282 n. 32, 304; and Antiochene War, 327 and n. 77

unequal friendship (and Roman society), 44, 51, 54, 69, 300, 301–2, 305, 330

unequal influence of great states, 373, 374, 375, 376, 377; vs. empire, 377, 381
see also asymmetry of power; hierarchy of states

unipolarity (political science concept), 8, 23, 26, 27, 128, 182, 275, 307, 308, 340, 341,

unipolarity (*cont'd*)
   342, 357, 375, 376, 377, 378;
   reversibility of, 336 and n. 110,
   343, 356, 357 and nn. 61 and
   62, 361 n. 77, cf. the "unipolar
   moment," 356 n. 57; and
   creation of relative peace, 350
   and n. 34, 358 and n. 66;
   maintenance dependent on
   human decision-making, 357
   n. 60; and goal of stability, 361;
   and avoiding counterbalancing
   (s.v.), 361–5; and "offshore
   balancing," 363–4, 366;
   and unipolar state's freedom
   of action, 364 and n. 89;
   geographical proximity as a
   factor in, 364 and n. 90; self-
   restraint as a factor in, 363–4,
   366 nn. 96 and 97; ambiguities
   of, 367, 368, 380, 381, and
   Chapter 9, *passim*; contrasted
   with hegemony, dominion,
   and/or empire, 349, 375; not
   a euphemism for empire, 379;
   Roman, after 188 BC, 336,
   340–1, 342, 361, 378, and
   Chapter 9, *passim*; Roman
   achievement in maintenance of,
   357, 361 and n. 77; and Greek
   libertas, 370–1; post-Cold War
   American, 357 and n. 60, cf.
   361 n. 77

P. Valerius Flaccus, commander in
   Adriatic, 215 BC, 85
M. Valerius Laevinus (consul 210),
   commander in Adriatic after
   215 BC, 85, 87, 263 n. 107;
   defeats Philip V, 214 BC, 86;
   and treaty of alliance with
   Aetolians, 88, 91, 263 n. 107;
   and limited Roman goals in
   First Macedonian War, 115;
   commander in Adriatic, 201 BC,
   262–3

Veyne, P. (modern scholar), 237,
   247
P. Villius Tappulus (consul 199 BC),
   commander in Greece, late 199
   BC, 279; faces mutiny, 279; on
   commission from Senate to
   formalize peace in Greece, 196
   BC, 283 n. 33, 311 n. 14; fears
   power of Antiochus III, 381 and
   n. 42; and Roman demands on
   Antiochus III, 193 BC, 320–1;
   fails to keep Demetrias (s.v.)
   from the Aetolians, 192 BC, 323

Walbank, F. W. (modern scholar),
   81, 133, 239, 140, 152, 192,
   222
Walt, S. (political scientist), and
   formation of alliances, 218, 220
Waltz, K. (political scientist), 9, 17,
   25, 127, 219, 265, 269, 340,
   342, 352, 356, 357
war as "normal" under anarchy,
   9–10, 19, 20, 127
war-fleets, Hellenistic, of Macedon,
   83, 86, 100 n. 87, 192, 194 and
   n. 44, 239, 251; of Rome, 83,
   87, 88, 99, 187, 239, 262–3,
   278, 328, 330, 332, 361; of
   Rhodes, 187, 188, 192, 194
   n. 44, 329, 330–1; of Antiochus
   III, 187, 291, 311, 316, 330,
   334; of Pergamum, 195, 196
   n. 51, 330, 331, 332; of
   Ptolemies, 190; of Pyrrhus,
   249–50
Warrior, V. (modern scholar), 130
Watson, A. (political scientist), 374,
   376, 379
Wiemer, H.-U. (modern scholar),
   191
Will, E. (modern scholar), 153
Wohlforth, W. (political scientist),
   197, 358
Wörrle, M. (modern scholar),
   161

CPSIA information can be obtained
at www.ICGtesting.com
Printed in the USA
JSHW010830100123
36035JS00007B/40